Entrepreneurial New Venture Skills

As business schools expand their entrepreneurship programs and organizations seek people with entrepreneurial skills, it has become clear that the skills and mindset of an entrepreneur are highly valued in all business contexts. This latest edition of *Entrepreneurial New Venture Skills* continues to focus on helping students develop entrepreneurial skills, whether they seek to become entrepreneurs or employees.

Focusing on the entrepreneurial start-up process, the third edition of *Entrepreneurial New Venture Skills* takes the reader through the steps of selecting, planning, financing, and controlling the new venture. The authors cover multiple forms of new ventures, as well as ways to utilize entrepreneurial skills in other contexts, encouraging students to engage with the material and apply it to their lives in ways that make sense for them. Skill development features include:

- Entrepreneurial profiles of small business owners
- Personal applications for students to apply questions to their new venture or a current business
- Global and domestic cases
- Elevator pitch assignments which put students in the venture capitalist position
- Application exercises and situations covering specific text concepts
- Business plan prompts to help students construct a business plan over the course of a semester

Featuring pedagogical tools like review questions and learning outcomes, and a full companion website which expands upon skill development and offers instructor resources, the third edition of *Entrepreneurial New Venture Skills* is the perfect resource for instructors and students of entrepreneurship.

Entrepreneurial New Venture Skills

3rd edition

Robert N. Lussier, Joel Corman, and David C. Kimball

Routledge
Taylor & Francis Group

NEW YORK AND LONDON

Third edition published 2015
by Routledge
711 Third Avenue, New York, NY 10017

and by Routledge
2 Park Square, Milton Park, Abingdon, Oxon OX14 4RN

Routledge is an imprint of the Taylor & Francis Group, an informa business

© 2015 Taylor & Francis

The right of Robert N. Lussier, Joel Corman, and David C. Kimball to be identified as authors of this work has been asserted by them in accordance with sections 77 and 78 of the Copyright, Designs and Patents Act 1988.

Second edition published in 2005 by Cengage Learning.

Library of Congress Cataloging-in-Publication Data

Lussier, Robert N.
  Entrepreneurial new venture skills / Robert N. Lussier, Joel Corman, David C. Kimball. — 3rd Edition.
     pages cm
  Includes bibliographical references and index.
  1. Entrepreneurship. 2. New business enterprises—Management. 3. Strategic planning. I. Corman, Joel. II. Kimball, David Charles, 1959– III. Title.
  HB615.L877 2014
  658.1'1—dc23
  2013040542

ISBN: 978-0-415-82529-0 (hbk)
ISBN: 978-0-415-82530-6 (pbk)
ISBN: 978-0-203-39501-1 (ebk)

Typeset in Sabon
by Apex CoVantage, LLC

Contents

About the Authors

Robert N. Lussier is a Professor of Management at Springfield College. He is a two-time entrepreneur who has also provided venture capital for a small business and who has consulted with small businesses and nonprofits. He is the author of 400 publications; people from seventy-three countries have contacted him regarding his publications. His empirical research has been published in the *Academy of Entrepreneurship Journal, Entrepreneurship Theory and Practice, Family Business Review, Journal of Management Education, Journal of Small Business Management, Journal of Small Business Strategy,* and several others. He has a management, leadership, business, government and society, and human relations textbook and he turned his workshops into a book, *Publish Don't Perish: 100 Tips That Improve Your Ability to Get Published.* More than one million students globally have used his books. He is a member of the Academy of Management, the United States Association for Small Business and Entrepreneurship (Coleman Best Empirical Paper Award winner), and is Fellow of the Small Business Institute. He earned his MBA from Suffolk University and Doctorate in Management with his dissertation in entrepreneurship from the University of New Haven.

Bob's outside interests include spending time with his wife and their six children and four grandchildren. As a former intercollegiate athlete, he continues to lift weights and do a variety of aerobic exercises 5–6 times per week.

Joel Corman is Professor Emeritus at Suffolk University and a three-time entrepreneur. He has consulted with more than 25 small businesses and has overseen more than 500 Small Business Administration (SBA) student consulting projects. His current consulting focuses on profit and nonprofit businesses and strategic planning and board development through the Executive Service Corps (ESC) and SCORE in Massachusetts and Arizona. Joel has published in the *Academy of Entrepreneurship Journal, Business Horizons, Journal of Small Business and Entrepreneurship, Journal of Private Enterprise, Journal of Small Business Management, Journal of Small Business Strategy, Mid-America Journal of Business,* and others. Corman has served on several boards of directors including Arizona State University Art Museum, Arizona State University Film Studies Institute, and Newton Symphony Orchestra. He is a Small Business Institute (SBI) Fellow and Best Paper Award winner, and his MBA and Ph.D. are from the Wharton School, University of Pennsylvania.

Joel's outside interests include reading, film festivals, leading film discussion courses, opera, sailing, and exercising daily.

David C. Kimball is a Professor and Chair of the Business Division at Elms College and regularly teaches entrepreneurship courses. Based on his entrepreneurship experience, he enjoys helping young people to explore starting their own business ventures. David is also an Elms College faculty representative to the Harold Grinspoon Entrepreneurship Institute (EI). The Harold Grinspoon Charitable Foundation (HGCF) supports the EI to foster entrepreneurship education among participating colleges and universities in the region. The EI informs, supports, and inspires student entrepreneurs. Equally importantly, it recognizes and awards students for their entrepreneurial spirit and exemplary business plans. Some of the activities found in this textbook were derived from his years of work helping students learn from the EI. His MBA is from Western New England University and Doctorate in Management with his dissertation about the role and value of the mission statement from the University of New Haven.

David's outside interests include shopping at new business ventures in his community and exercising.

Preface

Rationale, Goal, and Competitive Advantages of the Book

We wrote the first edition of *Entrepreneurial New Venture Skills* (ENVS) back in 2000 before skill development and entrepreneurship became as popular as they are today. Business schools continue to increase their entrepreneurship programs and courses largely because research supports that entrepreneurial skills can be taught and learned. In addition to the importance of new business ventures to society, today virtually all organizations are seeking people with entrepreneurial skills. There has been an argument that we should teach entrepreneurship not only to entrepreneurs but also to everyone as a necessary and useful skill.[1] This new edition continues our goal of developing entrepreneurial skills, featuring the following competitive advantages.

- **Skill development.** Whether students want to be entrepreneurs or employees, they can develop entrepreneurial skills through a variety of activities created by the authors that relate the concepts to their personal lives. ENVS offers more skill development applications than any of the competitors. We also provide more step-by-step "how to be entrepreneurial" models. See the features for details.
- **Startup entrepreneurial process focus.** Rather than trying to be both small business management and entrepreneurship, and covering advanced topics of growing, changing, exiting, etc., we focus the structure of the book on taking the business through the entrepreneurial process of selecting the new venture (Part I, Chapters 1–4), planning the new venture (Part II, Chapters 5–10), and financing and controlling the new venture (Part III, Chapters 11–12). We use a more focused niche strategy with differentiation based on skill development.
- **Shorter, yet comprehensive.** To help engage students to read the book, we have kept the page count down around 400 and the number of chapters down to twelve, as compared to competitors with 600+ pages and 15–21 chapters covering topics beyond the startup. We cover virtually all of the startup topics of the major competitors.
- **Continuing focus on multiple forms of new ventures.** In addition to starting a new business venture, each chapter includes ideas and variations on the concepts for those buying an existing business, franchise, or license rights, as well as corporate and nonprofit entrepreneurship.

■ **Entrepreneurial behavior.** We realize that not everyone who uses the book will become entrepreneurs. So, at the end of the chapters, along with the other new venture options, we provide ideas on how to use entrepreneurial skills as an employee.

■ **Personal readability for business and nonbusiness majors.** We write on a more personal level to engage the reader in the entrepreneurial process. Based on prior adopter feedback with nurses, auto-tech, engineers, a physical therapist, and teachers, the book is written at a level that students without prior courses in the business functional areas (plus those who took the courses and forgot the material) can successfully complete the course without feeling lost or having to refer to other books.

■ **Balanced academic and entrepreneurship authors and references.** All three authors are professors with entrepreneurial experience. Corman and Lussier have published in top-tier entrepreneurship journals, Corman has extensive small-business consulting experience, and Lussier is a two-time corporate entrepreneur. The text also has a balance of top-tier journal research to support text material and popular press to provide "how to" advice and current entrepreneurship examples.

The latest edition of *Entrepreneurial New Venture Skills* has undergone a thorough review and revision process. Instructors indicated they wanted a book that takes a "real life" approach, with lots of resources and projects. As the overall changes and new features and skills development discussion below supports, the revised and updated 3rd edition meets the need for a great entrepreneurship book.

Overall Changes

■ **Title Change.** The 3rd edition title has been changed by adding the word "skills" to emphasize the heavy focus on developing real-world entrepreneurial skills that can be used in all organizations.

■ **Author change.** Robert Lussier has taken the lead on the new edition and David Kimball was added to increase the quantity and quality of the real-world skills component to the text.

■ **Reorganized and chapter title changes.** The number of chapters went from fifteen down to twelve with some reorganization, and the name of every chapter has been changed to better identify what the chapter is all about in real-life entrepreneurial language.

■ **New chapters.** Chapters 1–4 were not revised; they were written from scratch to better explain what entrepreneurship is, explore various options for becoming an entrepreneur, and provide a much more detailed list of ideas for identifying new venture opportunities. These chapters also explain how to develop a business model, assess the chances of a new venture success through feasibility analysis, and protect the new business model.

- **Global.** The inclusion of global entrepreneurship has increased significantly throughout the chapters and every chapter now has a new global case.
- **New Venture Options.** The 2nd edition discussion of differences between entrepreneurial and intrapreneurial ventures (now called corporate ventures) in every chapter has been expanded to also include buying an existing business, franchising, licensing, and developing nonprofit new ventures. Plus, each chapter now discusses using entrepreneurial skills as an employee, rather than starting a new venture.
- **Updated.** The book is completely updated and virtually all the references are new to this edition.
- **Web site.** This edition comes equipped with a companion Web site, featuring learning and teaching resources for students and instructors. This new material can be accessed at: www.routledge.com/cw/lussier.

Skill Development Features

The 3rd edition offers professors and students a number of updated and new skill development features. All features require active engagement from students, unlike competitors' passive reading of boxed examples. All skills features can be used for class discussion and/or as written assignments.

Features Within Each Chapter

- **Entrepreneurial profile.** Each chapter opens with a short video introduction to an entrepreneur from the PBS Small Business School showing the basic values, vision, and competency of small-business owners throughout the world who are illustrating the very heart of free enterprise.

Entrepreneur Profile—Anne Beiler, Auntie Anne's Pretzels

We begin each chapter with a short biography of an entrepreneur and provide a link so you can learn more about the person and his or her business venture. Short 3–5-minute videos of each entrepreneur can be found at the PBS Small Business School at www.smallbusinessschool. org/. Auntie Anne's video can be found at www. smallbusinessschool.org/video.cfm?clip=1068.

In Gap, Pennsylvania's Amish Country, it is a simpler place. And though it may be an unlikely place to have a fast-growing business, maybe there are lessons here for all of us. Auntie Anne's is not small any more. In this episode of Small Business School, you learn why Anne Beiler stirred up a highly successful product. However, it required vision, cash, and courage to open hundreds of locations.

An angel investor stood by her while bank after bank turned her down because the purpose of this business was to make money then give it away. Her generous spirit is infused throughout this company and it is a secret ingredient. Anne has proven that her franchisees want to run a business built on love. While most franchise companies have to market to find new owners, Anne has to turn away hundreds who want to buy into her concept. Products topped with her love of people make Anne Beiler an entrepreneur to follow.

In 1988 Anne Beiler turned a mistake into a new product. She was preparing food to sell at

Saturday's farmers' market. Like so many of us, she did not have the right ingredients and began to substitute things she had on hand. What came out of her oven was a wonderful soft pretzel. But, she wasn't satisfied there. She and her husband further tweaked that new recipe until she heard, "Wow!" from her hungry customers.

Today, Auntie Anne's Hand-Rolled Soft Pretzels are baked fresh in over 800 locations and are the perfect high-carbohydrate, low-fat, back-to-the-basics snack so many people crave. Customers will part with nearly $500 million a year to enjoy this hot treat.

Anne Beiler is mission-driven. She felt that mission statements are plastic, even transparent; and most are too long. Anne's company's first mission statement was several paragraphs. Later she decided that it should be a useful tool—a mission statement should be easy to remember. A team of people at Auntie Anne's came up with the word LIGHT, which is a working philosophy for Auntie Anne's. "L"—lead by example. "I"—invest in others. "G"—give freely. "H"—honor God. "T"—treat others with respect.[1]

Think it over.

Does Anne Beiler exhibit the characteristics of an entrepreneur?

- **Personal applications.** There are several application questions enabling students to apply the concepts to their proposed new venture or a current business.

Personal Application

1. Identify an entrepre-neur and the new venture he or she created.

The Elevator Pitch

This skill-builder puts you in the venture capitalist position. You will watch an elevator pitch from the Internet and assess the pitch and then discuss if they would or wouldn't invest in the new venture. The link for the elevator pitch can be found at: www.geekwire.com/2012/elevator-pitch-43-seconds-means/.

PetHub CEO **Tom Arnold** describes his online pet tracking startup in 43 seconds. Although the pitch doesn't actually occur in an elevator, the idea is that the entrepreneur has 43 seconds to impress a business person in an elevator (or in this video the top

of the Space Needle in Seattle, WA) to invest in the business idea.[109]

Think about it.

1. What score do you give Tom Arnold's PetHub pitch?

Great product idea and pitch		Terrible product idea and pitch	
4	3	2	1

2. Would you invest in Tom Arnold's PetHub business?

3. How would you improve Tom Arnold's PetHub pitch?

Self-Assessment 1-1

Do I Have the Characteristics of Successful Entrepreneurs?

For each of the following statements, identify your level of agreement with each of the following statements on a scale of 1–3. Place the number on the line before the statement.

   1. No   2. Somewhat   3. Yes

_____ 1. Self-starter.[75] I'm a go-getter that takes on responsibility; I don't need a boss to tell me what to do.

_____ 2. Creativity.[76] I think about new products and services and better ways of doing things.

_____ 3. Passion[77] and Innovation.[78] I get excited about a good idea and I am preoccupied with making sure the idea is implemented.

_____ 4. Optimistic[79] and Confident.[80] I'm a positive person and believe I can achieve the goals I set for myself. But I'm not overconfident.[81]

_____ 5. Energy.[82] I have a high level of energy to work hard and get the job done.

_____ 6. Tenacity[83] and Overcome Barriers.[84] When I get passionate, I overcome obstacles and don't give up until I accomplish the objective.

_____ 7. Opportunities[85] and Risk.[86] I can recognize good opportunities and evaluate them, and I am willing to take moderate risk.

_____ 8. Persuasive.[87] I'm good at convincing people to help me to get what I want done.

_____ 9. Discovery.[88] I have thought about an idea(s) for starting a new venture.

_____ 10. Self-identity.[89] I think about and want to be an entrepreneur.

_____ Add up the ten numbers. Your score will be between 10 and 30; mark it below.

               10   15   20   25   30

I don't have strong entrepreneurial characteristics	I have strong entrepreneurial characteristics

The higher your score, the stronger your entrepreneurial characteristics. However, don't be too concerned if your score is not as high as you would like. Most entrepreneurs don't score 30, and you don't need every characteristic to be successful. Remember that you can develop your entrepreneurship skills. Question 10 is important because, if you want to be an entrepreneur, you will tend to act like an entrepreneur,[90] and will try to develop your skill through this course.

Application Exercises

Each chapter has a series of exercises requiring you to apply the specific text concepts. When doing these exercises, be sure to select a specific business where applicable. You can select a business where you worked or a business you would like to own someday. Answers for each exercise should be approximately one page.

1. Interview a small business owner and determine if he or she considers him or herself an entrepreneur.

2. Select a female entrepreneur and compare her with the characteristics of an entrepreneur covered in the chapter.

3. Search for an article at Entrepreneur.com that discusses the Small Business Administration. Describe the main points in the article.

4. Check to see if your professor has a LinkedIn account. If so, send your professor an invitation to connect.

Application Situations

Each chapter has a brief situation with questions that require students to apply the text concepts.

1. Opportunity Strikes

As you are reading the paper about the latest corporate downsizing, a business broker whom you know calls and in the ensuing conversation you learn that a tremendous opportunity exists to buy a small business. The broker tells you that your purchasing this business will result in you never having to worry about being downsized and that the business will guarantee your success in life.

1. What advantages do you personally see in buying a small business?

2. Address the disadvantages that might appear as a result of you purchasing a small business.

3. Critically examine your personal characteristics and compare them to successful entrepreneurs. What are your strengths and weaker characteristics?

4. Knowing the difference between being an entrepreneur and being an employee using entrepreneurship behavior, do you have what it takes to be a successful entrepreneur?

2. Gayle Stratton

Gayle's father owned and managed a hardware store, and after working for her dad, she decided she didn't want to take over the business or to be an entrepreneur. Gayle decided to work for a large business. So after graduating with a degree in production, she got a job in her field. It wasn't long before Gayle realized she had a faster way of producing the product.

1. Should Gayle become an entrepreneur or engage in entrepreneurial behavior?

2. What conditions in the firm would have to exist before Gayle should consider offering her productivity improvement suggestion?

3. Having decided to go ahead with her innovation, what should Gayle do now?

- **The elevator pitch.** This new application puts the students in the venture capitalist position. One or two pitches from the Internet per chapter will be given for students to assess and discuss if they would or wouldn't invest in the new venture, and how to further develop the pitch. Students will be directed to Web sites to analyze the feasibility and the quality of different pitches.

- **Self-assessments.** Several of the chapters have self-assessment exercises that engage students in understanding more about themselves as entrepreneurs and about new business ventures.

Features at the End of Each Chapter

- **Application exercises.** Each chapter has a series of exercises (including new and updated exercises) requiring students to apply the specific text concepts. Many of these have been updated to emphasize the use of the Internet.

- **Application situations.** Each chapter has two or three new brief situations or mini-cases, with questions that require students to apply the text concepts.

- **Cases.** Each chapter now has two cases with questions written by the authors, one featuring a U.S. small business and the other (the "global case") featuring a non-U.S. small business.

Case

Welcome to Livestream!

Livestream was cofounded in 2007 by Max Haot, Dayananda Nanjundappa, Phil Worthington, and Mark Kornfilt, and has offices in New York, Los Angeles and Bangalore. CEO Max Haot is in the United States on a visa. Max is Belgian—yet he shows the American Dream still lives! Before founding Livestream, Haot founded ICF, a media asset management platform, which was sold to Verizon Business in 2005.[122]

Livestream is all about live events. As a member of the Livestream community the user can watch unlimited live events. The user also gets full access to the world's first ad-free live streaming and live blogging service. Livestream's motto is "Discover and Experience Live Events."[123]

Max launched Mogulus in 2007. It was a free streaming service that also had a paid professional service that produces revenues for the company. In 2008, Gannett Newspapers invested $10 million.[124] In 2009, Mogulus paid $100,000 to acquire the name Livestream. The company signed up about 1,000 accounts that were paying $350 per month for online broadcasting services.[125] In 2012, *Inc.* Magazine included Livestream as one of America's fastest-growing private media companies.[126]

Livestream users can stream live video or broadcast pre-recorded video in the channels they select or create. Users may also chat with other producers anywhere in the world. Livestream has a popular online store

that lets users stream live HD videos without the use of a PC.

Facebook has used Livestream to stream videos. Bands such as the Foo Fighters streamed a live Internet only concert from their studio space.[127] A Livestream app can also be accessed for viewing on cell phones. From its studio space, a Livestream video can also be used as part of a Twitter message.

You can watch an interview with CEO Max Haot at: http://videos.huffingtonpost.com/tech/livestreams-max-haot-on-entry-into-the-us-517200930.

1. Did Max show creativity and/or innovation skills in developing Livestream? What's the difference?

2. Is Max an entrepreneur? Is he using entrepreneurial behavior? What's the difference?

3. Is Max replicative or innovative and is he a serial entrepreneur?

4. How is Max a driver of social change and how does Livestream contribute to society?

5. Which characteristics of entrepreneurs does Max possess?

6. Describe what stage of the entrepreneurial process Livestream is currently in.

7. Use the Internet to find competitors offering the same type of live streaming of events.

Global Case—Global Student Entrepreneur Awards (GSEA—Russia)

Entrepreneurs can be found in every country of the world! For example, there is a Global Student Entrepreneur Awards (GSEA—Russia) competition that rewards young entrepreneurs. Russian serial entrepreneur Sergey Vykhodtsev shares his experiences of being an entrepreneur in Russia. Here are some of the observations from the competition.

1. They move quickly. They use modern technology to communicate and travel around Russia as quickly as possible—they are looking for opportunities.

2. They run multiple companies at the same time. In the U.S. young entrepreneurs try to open one startup at a time. But, in Russia, young entrepreneurs rattle off all sorts of businesses they have open in fields such as technology, media, and restaurants.

3. The internet has played a large part in rebuilding Russia. Popular new industries in Russia mirror the rest of the world—e-commerce, online payments, social networks, and digital media.

4. Young Russian entrepreneurs value relationships and networking. This can include finding key suppliers or getting through customs.

Russian organizations that empower young entrepreneurs include Skolkovo, OPORA—Russia, the Center for Entrepreneurship, and the GSEA. Their goal is to help young entrepreneurs build successful businesses.[128]

Think it over.

1. What stage are the businesses at in the GSEA—Russia competition?

2. Do you think the young entrepreneurs are impacting social change in Russia?

3. Research one of the Russian organizations that empower young entrepreneurs. How does the organization support young entrepreneurs?

- **Business plan.** Students can write a business plan during the semester with updated and detailed questions at the end of each chapter to guide them through the thinking, analyzing, and writing process. The business plan sections in Chapters 1–4 are now called "Preparing for Your Business Plan" and Chapters 5–12 are called "Writing Your Business Plan," as students actually write their business plan chapter by chapter. Appendix B has a new sample business plan from a startup company, 21st Century Computer Training Centers, which students can use as a template for developing their own new venture business plan throughout the course.

Preparing for Your Business Plan

Appendix B has an example business plan for 21st Century Computer Training Centers. The business plan is organized using the chapters of the textbook as an outline. Students can write their own business plans either alone or in teams, as assigned by their instructor.

The first step is to format the business plan. Use Appendix B to copy the layout for the Coverage and the Table of Contents. Your goal at this point is to just format the business plan—not to actually write the plan. You will fill in the different sections of the plan that are pertinent to your business as the semester develops. You should begin to consider a business for which you would like to write a business plan during the semester.

New One-Time or Ongoing Features

These are available on the companion Web site and in the instructor's manuals.

- **Your Ninety-Second New Venture Pitch.** Students can develop their own pitch (similar to the elevator pitch videos) that can be presented to the class and entrepreneurs for their critique.

Your Ninety-Second New Venture Pitch

You will research, develop, and present an elevator pitch in this course, similar to the elevator pitches that are in each chapter for the class to watch and evaluate.

Your own elevator pitch will be refined throughout the semester under the guidance of your instructor.

Your instructor can choose to have an elevator pitch contest with judges that can determine which ideas are most feasible and who did the best job making their actual ninety-second pitch.

- **College Entrepreneurial Spirit Award Winners.** Students recruit fellow college students (from their entire college and university) who have already started an entrepreneurial business. Students and the professor in their entrepreneurship class evaluate the nominees and select a winner.

College Entrepreneurial Spirit Award Winners

Students in class will recruit fellow college students (from their entire college or university) who have already started an entrepreneurial business. Students and the professor in their entrepreneurship class will eventually evaluate the nominees and select a winner.

Your initial task is to develop a method to reach all the students on your campus that have already started a business! Some students in your own class might have businesses that could also be nominated.

Community Entrepreneurial Spirit Award

Students will select and invite their small business community nominee to come to class. The class will then work with the small business to develop an outline of a strategic plan. Students could also write an actual strategic plan for the business.

Your goal at this time is for each student to list three potential community entrepreneurs they might consider to nominate for being an excellent local business leader. This exercise is simply a potential list of community leaders that you think are outstanding entrepreneurs. A short list early in the semester will help start the process!

Paper Clip Entrepreneurship Challenge

You will develop entrepreneurial and negotiation skills with a total investment of fifty paper clips. Students can work in teams to create and develop ideas on how to turn their paper clips into a profitable business opportunity. Student reports must include what entrepreneurial skills were utilized in exchanging their paper clips.

Begin to visualize the act of exchanging paper clips for a product that might be more valuable. You might ask yourself how that is possible. Read the following article from msnbc.com: www.msnbc.msn.com/id/12346469/ns/us_news-weird_news/t/trade-paper-clip-house/ You will see that Kyle MacDonald was able to trade his paper clips quite effectively.[129]

Chapter Review and Summary

As we bring this chapter to a close, you should understand what entrepreneurship is and different types of entrepreneurs, the size classification of businesses, and why small business is important. You should also know the advantages and potential disadvantages of being an entrepreneur, and some of the myths and realities of entrepreneurship. In addition, you should know if you have the characteristics of successful entrepreneurs and how to identify any organization's entrepreneurial behavior as conservative or entrepreneurial. You also learned about the entrepreneurial process, and that it is the framework for this course. Last, you know how you can prepare to be an entrepreneur.

This summary lists the learning outcomes from the chapter and their answers.

1. Compare entrepreneurs and entrepreneurial behavior and replicative and innovative entrepreneurs

An *entrepreneur* is a person who creates a new business venture. *Entrepreneurial behavior* is innovation by creating new productivity techniques. Entrepreneurs start a new venture and usually own it, but they don't have to own it. Whereas employees can engage in entrepreneurial behavior without being entrepreneurs, large businesses value entrepreneurial behavior. *Replicative entrepreneurs* open conventional existing businesses, such as a retail store or restaurant, whereas *innovative entrepreneurs* develop new products and services and new productive techniques. They go from idea to its use in the market.

2. Discuss why entrepreneurship is important globally

Small business entrepreneurs are important globally because they make at least

3. Describe advantages and potential disadvantages of entrepreneurship

Advantages include being your own boss, pursuing your own ideas, financial rewards, and contributing to society. Potential disadvantages include uncertain income—no salary, risk of failure and loss, long hours and hard work, which lead to other issues.

4. Compare and contrast entrepreneurial traits and characteristics and entrepreneurial orientation

They are both used to measure entrepreneurship. Entrepreneurial characteristics are the distinguishing individual qualities that contribute to business success, including opportunity-seeking, passion, innovativeness, and risk-taking. Entrepreneurial orientation measures the top management teams' use of entrepreneurial behavior of being innovative, proactive, and risk-taking. Thus, entrepreneurial characteristics refer to the

---

■ **Community Entrepreneurial Spirit Award.** Students will select and invite their small-business nominee to come to class. The class will then work with the small business to develop an outline of a strategic plan. Students can write an actual strategic plan for the business.

■ **Paper Clip Entrepreneurship Challenge.** Students develop entrepreneurial skills with a total investment of fifty paper clips. Students can work in teams to create and develop ideas on how to turn their paper clips into a profitable business opportunity. Student reports must include what entrepreneurial skills were utilized in exchanging their paper clips.

Other Pedagogical Features

■ **Learning outcomes, key terms, and chapter summary.** (1) Each chapter begins with a list of learning outcomes, the last of which lists the key terms. (2) Learning outcomes are also listed in the text prior to the topic's coverage, and the key terms are defined. (3) The chapter summary gives the answers to the learning outcomes and a list of key terms.

■ **Personalized writing style and use of headings.** We wrote the book in a more personal style, placing students in the entrepreneurial seat and continually asking them about how the concepts relate to them to help keep them engaged in the reading. We also use lots of headings to help chunk the material and keep the reader focused.

■ **Entrepreneur examples.** This edition features additional current business examples of how real entrepreneurs apply the concepts that appear throughout each chapter. **Founder** and **company names** are in bold to stand out. Some of the entrepreneurs in the profiles and examples started the new venture while still in college.

■ **References.** All references are current with a good balance of research from entrepreneurial journals (that is, *Entrepreneurship Theory and Practice, Journal of Business Venturing, Journal of Small Business Management*), general management research (*Academy of Management—Journal, Review, Perspective, Learning and Education*), and popular press for current real-world examples (*BusinessWeek, Entrepreneur, Fast Company, Forbes, Fortune, Inc., The Wall Street Journal*). Most chapters also list sources of additional information.

- **Models.** Outlines of step-by-step procedures have been added within the chapters throughout the book, such as how to make better decisions and write objectives, to help students grasp and apply behaviors crucial to the entrepreneurial process.
- **Review and discussion questions.** Each chapter now contains even more review questions (related to chapter concepts) and discussion questions (designed for critical thinking), which provide a ready means of knowledge retention and enrichment.
- **Web site listings and appendix.** Web sites are listed throughout the text for students seeking additional information, and Appendix A provides a list of sources that provide assistance to entrepreneurs.
- **Web site.** The supporting companion Web site at (www.routledge.com/cw/lussier) offers a number of features and resources, including a test bank, PowerPoint slides, and instructor's manuals and student manuals with expansions of in-text exercises and additional pitches, profiles, quiz questions, and video and Web links.

Instructor's Resources

- **Instructor's manuals—written by the authors.** The instructor's manuals, separated by chapter, contain a lecture chapter outline and answers to all learning outcomes, review and discussion questions, application situation questions, case and global case questions. They also provide guidelines and discussion prompts for using videos, as well as instructions and ideas for conducting the one-time or ongoing assignments: writing a business plan, the Ninety-Second New Venture Elevator Pitch, Paper Clip Entrepreneurship Challenge, College Entrepreneurial Spirit Award Winners, and the Community Entrepreneurial Spirit Award.
- **Test Bank.** Traditional questions with explanations for answers.
- **PowerPoint.** Slides for class lectures.

Changes by Chapter

Part I: Selecting the New Venture

Chapter 1, **What's Entrepreneurship About? Do You Want to Start Your Own Business?** This was titled "Entrepreneurship and Defining the New Venture" in the 2nd edition. Rather than revise this chapter, the authors wrote it from scratch and expanded the coverage to include new major sections: The Importance of Entrepreneurship Worldwide, Why Study Entrepreneurship?, Entrepreneurship Characteristics and Orientation, The Entrepreneurial Process, and Preparing to Become an Entrepreneur.

2. **New Venture Options: Do You Want to Start a New Business, Buy One, be a Franchisee or a Corporate or Nonprofit Entrepreneur?** This was Chapter 3, titled "New Venture Ownership Options." Rather than revise this chapter, the

authors wrote it from scratch and expanded the coverage to provide a more detailed step-by-step approach to starting a new venture, buying a business, buying a franchise and license, and being a corporate entrepreneur. New topics in this edition include social entrepreneurship and starting a nonprofit new venture.

3. **What Business? How do You Find Opportunities and Develop a Business Model?** Rather than revise this chapter, the authors wrote it from scratch because developing a business model was not discussed in the last edition, and finding opportunities to start a new business was only briefly discussed in Chapter 1. In this edition, the business model discussion has been expanded into an entire chapter.

4. **How do You Assess the Chances of Venture Success? Feasibility Analysis and Protecting the Business Model Legally.** Rather than revise this chapter, the authors wrote it from scratch because feasibility analysis was only briefly discussed in Chapter 1, so the coverage has been greatly expanded with details of how to conduct the analysis. The second-edition discussion of the legal environment from Chapter 5 ("The Legal Environment and Social Responsibility") has been rewritten and expanded in this chapter.

Part II: Planning the New Venture

5. **Business Planning: What's Your Legal Form and Strategy?** This chapter combines information from the second-edition Chapters 4 ("Legal Form"), Chapter 5 ("Business Plan Steps"), and Chapter 7 ("The Strategic Plan"). Chapter 5 is likely the most important chapter in the book. Chapter 5 is the first chapter in the book to start the actual process of writing the business plan. As was pointed out by instructors during the review process, this chapter is the building block to all the subsequent chapters. So, we developed an expanded approach to showing students exactly how to write a business plan. The result is the following layout—which is developed in the remaining chapters.

Writing Your Business Plan

You (or in teams) can write a business plan during the semester. There are questions at the end of each chapter to help guide you through the thinking and analyzing process. Appendix B has a sample business plan you can use as a template for developing your own new venture business plan. Students should add the mission, objectives, and external analysis.

Highlighted Sections of the Business Plan (Chapters 1–5)

1. *The Executive Summary is written last—but placed first in the business plan. You have to wait until you are finished with the business plan to properly write the executive summary*

2. *Introduction:*

   A. *Background of the business: Includes a short review of its name, address (or addresses if there is more than one location), telephone number(s), email address, Web site address, hours of operation, and a brief history (if any). You want to state when the business was started or will be started.*

   B. *Management credentials and organization structure: It is common to list all the business's key managers and their duties and responsibilities, with their qualifications.*

   C. *Form of ownership: Will your business be a sole proprietorship, partnership, or corporation and how will any profits be distributed?*

3. *Strategy Formulation:*

   A. *Mission: What is the organization's purpose or reason for being (covered in Chapter 3)? The mission section of the business plan includes your business model (covered in Chapter 4), which can include a broad description of your present and future products and services to be offered. In the strategy section, it is not necessary to list all the products and services; they are listed under the marketing section of the business plan and will be discussed in Chapter 6.*

   B. *Objectives (prioritized): What does your organization want to accomplish?*

   C. *Environmental analysis: It includes an analysis of the internal environment (which includes the mission and objectives) and its external environment resulting in a SWOT analysis.*

6. The Marketing Plan: Who are Your Customers? This was originally Chapter 8 ("The Marketing Plan"). We added a learning outcome ("Discuss the use of social media and e-commerce strategies as part of a marketing plan"), based on reviewer suggestions to add more social media and e-commerce material. Within the chapter, budding entrepreneurs are encouraged to use new media such as Web sites, e-commerce, Facebook, Twitter, and viral marketing to reach customers.

7. The Location and Layout Plan: What Facilities do You Need? This was originally Chapter 9 ("The Location and Layout Plan"). An updated section on the increase of home-based businesses is included at the beginning of the chapter. The role of the Internet is explored and how it has influenced the growth of people using their homes as the location of their business.

8. The Operations Plan: How Will You Make the Product? This was originally Chapter 10 ("The Operations Plan"). With the support of the reviewers, we devoted an entire chapter to operations management. The operations plan is a vital concept for students to understand and is often neglected in other entrepreneurship textbooks.

9. The Human Resource Plan: How do You Develop the New Venture Team and Employees? This was Chapter 11 ("The Human Resource Plan"). The chapter now includes a discussion of how to develop a new venture team and employees. The use of the term "venture team" is the beginning of the use of venture capital and venture capitalists, which are frequently used in later chapters. The role of venture capitalists is an important concept directly related to the field of entrepreneurship.

10. The Finance Plan: How Much Money do You Need? Building on reviewer suggestions, great care has been taken in presenting accounting material that both business and non-business students would be able to understand. In response, we streamlined the material about the income statement, balance sheet, and a pro forma cash flow statement from the previous edition. These same financial tools are listed in the business plan for students to complete, which will successfully integrate the chapter material into the business plan.

Part III: Financing and Controlling the New Venture

11. Sources of Funds: Where do You Get the Money? This is a critical chapter because it teaches students how to raise funds to start their own business. Based on reviewers' comments on the increased use of crowdsourcing, examples of Kickstarter and Indiegogo are discussed within the chapter and at the end in the chapter case.

12. Controls: How do You Keep the New Venture on Track? In accordance with reviewer suggestions, additional material has been included on risk assessment and types of insurance that entrepreneurs should buy to reduce the organizational risk. To preserve the distinction between this chapter and Chapter 10 where the accounting process is presented, this final chapter has been modified to focus on key financial ratios to control and monitor the new business.

Appendix A: Where Can You Get Help? Sources of Domestic and Global Assistance. Appendix B: The Business Plan Example.

Part I

Selecting the New Venture

Chapter 1

What's Entrepreneurship About?
Do You Want to Start Your Own Business?

In the first section, you will learn some basic concepts used throughout the book, followed by reasons for and against your becoming an entrepreneur. In the third section, you will find out if you have the characteristics of successful entrepreneurs and how to identify any organization as conservative or entrepreneurial. The fourth section explains the process that entrepreneurs go through from thinking about to running a new venture. To end, you will learn things you can do to prepare for becoming an entrepreneur.

Learning Outcomes

After completing this chapter you should be able to:

1. Compare entrepreneurs and entrepreneurial behavior and replicative and innovative entrepreneurs;
2. Discuss why entrepreneurship is important globally;
3. Describe advantages and potential disadvantages of entrepreneurship;
4. Compare and contrast entrepreneurial characteristics and entrepreneurial orientation;
5. Explain the entrepreneurial process;
6. Identify how to prepare for entrepreneurship;
7. Define the thirteen key terms identified in this chapter.

Entrepreneur Profile—Anne Beiler, Auntie Anne's Pretzels

We begin each chapter with a short biography of an entrepreneur and provide a link so you can learn more about the person and his or her business venture. Short 3–5-minute videos of each entrepreneur can be found at the PBS Small Business School at www.smallbusinessschool.org/. Auntie Anne's video can be found at www.smallbusinessschool.org/video.cfm?clip=1068.

In Gap, Pennsylvania's Amish Country, it is a simpler place. And though it may be an unlikely place to have a fast-growing business, maybe there are lessons here for all of us. Auntie Anne's is not small any more. In this episode of Small Business School, you learn why Anne Beiler stirred up a highly successful product. However, it required vision, cash, and courage to open hundreds of locations.

An angel investor stood by her while bank after bank turned her down because the purpose of this business was to make money then give it away. Her generous spirit is infused throughout this company and it is a secret ingredient. Anne has proven that her franchisees want to run a business built on love. While most franchise companies have to market to find new owners, Anne has to turn away hundreds who want to buy into her concept. Products topped with her love of people make Anne Beiler an entrepreneur to follow.

In 1988 Anne Beiler turned a mistake into a new product. She was preparing food to sell at Saturday's farmers' market. Like so many of us, she did not have the right ingredients and began to substitute things she had on hand. What came out of her oven was a wonderful soft pretzel. But, she wasn't satisfied there. She and her husband further tweaked that new recipe until she heard, "Wow!" from her hungry customers.

Today, Auntie Anne's Hand-Rolled Soft Pretzels are baked fresh in over 800 locations and are the perfect high-carbohydrate, low-fat, back-to-the-basics snack so many people crave. Customers will part with nearly $500 million a year to enjoy this hot treat.

Anne Beiler is mission-driven. She felt that mission statements are plastic, even transparent; and most are too long. Anne's company's first mission statement was several paragraphs. Later she decided that it should be a useful tool—a mission statement should be easy to remember. A team of people at Auntie Anne's came up with the word LIGHT, which is a working philosophy for Auntie Anne's. "L"—lead by example. "I"—invest in others. "G"—give freely. "H"—honor God. "T"—treat others with respect.[1]

Think it over.

Does Anne Beiler exhibit the characteristics of an entrepreneur?

Entrepreneurs and Small Business

Learning Outcome

1. Compare entrepreneurs and entrepreneurial behavior and replicative and innovative entrepreneurs.

In this section, we will define entrepreneurship and small business, discuss the importance of entrepreneurship worldwide, and explain why you should study entrepreneurship, or "What's in it for you?"

Defining Entrepreneurs and Small Business

Let's begin with some important definitions.

Entrepreneurship, Creativity, and Innovation

The word entrepreneur comes from the French words *entre*, meaning "between," and *prendre*, meaning "to take." So its origin described people who take on the risk between buyers and sellers or who undertake a task like starting a new business venture. Entrepreneurship is about creativity and innovation,[2] and they are not the same. *Creativity* is coming up with new ideas, but *innovation* is the actual implementation of new ideas to create new products and services and improve productivity. Let's face it, lots of people come up with good ideas that are never implemented; this is a distinguishing factor between entrepreneurs and non-entrepreneurs.

Entrepreneur and Entrepreneurial Behavior

Entrepreneurship often refers to the "creation of organizations,"[3] or the recognition and exploitation of new business opportunities by founding new ventures.[4] Today, there is no generally accepted definition of entrepreneur. However, it does tend to have at least two principal meanings.[5] First, entrepreneurship refers to taking the risk of *owning and managing a business*. Those who take the risk are called entrepreneurs, self-employed, and business owners. Second, entrepreneurship refers to *entrepreneurial behavior* in the sense of seeking opportunity and innovating new products and services or methods of doing business. So to be an entrepreneur you do not need to be a business owner. For example, you could start a *nonprofit* or a new venture for an existing company as a *corporate entrepreneur*. We'll discuss six options for starting a new venture in the next chapter.

The creation of new business ventures is considered to be a central element of entrepreneurship.[6] So combining these two meanings, here are our definitions. *An entrepreneur is a person who creates a new business venture. Entrepreneurial behavior is innovation by creating new products or services or productivity techniques.* Entrepreneurial behavior is concrete and observable,[7] for example developing or improving a product, speeding up manufacturing, or delivering existing products to the customer in a new, faster way. So, without being an entrepreneur, you can engage in entrepreneurial behavior by being innovative. But no new venture is started without entrepreneurial

Personal Application

1. Identify an entrepreneur and the new venture he or she created.

2. Describe an entrepreneurial behavior where you work(ed).

behavior, and existing businesses seek employees with entrepreneurial behavior skills.[8]

Replicative and Innovative Entrepreneurs

Entrepreneurs can be classified as replicative or innovative, and most entrepreneurs are replicative.[9] Replicative *entrepreneurs open a conventional existing business,* such as a retail store or restaurant. Think about your home town. It most likely has lots of them. So many entrepreneurs engage in entrepreneurial behavior, but don't have to. They don't have to be innovative because they can copy other business products and services and/or productivity techniques.

The one thing highly successful entrepreneurs tend to have in common is the systematic practice of innovation.[10] Innovative entrepreneurs *develop new products and services and/or new productive techniques.* They go from idea to its use in the market. **Steve Jobs** cofounded **Apple** and innovated the PC market, how we listen to music on the iPod and buy it on iTunes, plus the iPhone and iPad that also bring some of these products together. Jobs also launched NeXT and Pixar Animated Studios. **Jeff Bezos** started **Amazon.com** and changed the way many people buy books, and added other products, and more recently how we read books with the Kindle. **Mark Zuckerberg** cofounded **Facebook** and changed the way many people communicate.

Small, SME, or Large Business?

As with entrepreneurship, there is no generally accepted definition of small business. What constitutes "small" in terms of government support and tax policy varies by country and by industry. The **European Union** generally classifies business by size as follows: Micro has fewer than (<) 10 employees, Small < 50, Medium < 250, and larger ≥ 250 or more employees.[11] A business has to have fewer than 500 employees to qualify for many **U.S. Small Business Administration** (SBA, www.sba.gov) programs.[12] The SBA actually defines a small business concern as one that is independently owned and operated, is organized for profit, and is not dominant in its field. It gives different definitions based on size in six different industries.[13]

For our purposes, let's use the **U.S. Department of Labor**'s commonly used definition:[14] *a small business employs fewer than 100 workers.* Also, small to medium-size enterprises (SME) *employ fewer than 500 workers.* That leaves large businesses *as employing 500 or more workers.*

In the U.S., more than 99 percent of businesses are small, and there are around 28 million small businesses compared to around 18,500 large businesses.[15] Most large businesses started as small businesses. **Michael Dell** founded **Dell Computer**[16] and **Mark Zuckerberg** with others started **Facebook**[17] in their college dorm rooms. **Steve Jobs** and **Steve Wozniak** started **Apple Computer** in Jobs's garage, and Wozniak built the first PC by hand. Apple has grown into the biggest ever U.S. company based on company value, while Walmart has more sales.[18] However, most entrepreneurial new ventures never grow to become large companies, especially replicative entrepreneurs.

Personal Application

3. Is the entrepreneur you selected in PA 1 a replicative or innovative entrepreneur?

Personal Application

4. Briefly describe a business, preferably a small one you work(ed) for, and identify its size by name and number of employees.

The Importance of Entrepreneurship Worldwide

Learning Outcome

2. Discuss why entrepreneurship is important globally.

Business and entrepreneurship today is global, and the Global Entrepreneurship Monitor (GEM) helps us to better understand global entrepreneurship.

Global Entrepreneurship

Entrepreneurs are drivers of social change,[19] and they create a better world.[20] Entrepreneurship and innovation are fundamental drivers of economic growth and wealth creation.[21] Today's entrepreneurs are looking for international opportunities,[22] and international entrepreneurs are fueling global growth.[23] Even though small firms have a risk of failure, the risk doesn't increase with cross-border sales; in fact international sales are associated with better survival prospects.[24] Because of the importance of small business, entrepreneurship education is growing rapidly throughout the world,[25] as entrepreneurship has become an established scholarly discipline.[26] Because global entrepreneurship is so important to the world economy, more research is needed to better understand, explain, and predict entrepreneurship success vs. failure.[27] That is what GEM is all about.

GEM

GEM (www.gemconsortium.org) is the world's largest study of entrepreneurship. The GEM project is an annual assessment of the entrepreneurial activity, aspirations, and attitudes of individuals across a wide range of countries.[28] GEM tracked entrepreneurship in fifty-nine countries in 2010. Some 250 million people are involved in entrepreneurship in these countries. The highest rates of entrepreneurial startups are in low-income countries (people who can't find good jobs tend to turn to self-employment), but high-income countries also have respectable numbers. GEM reports the percentage of the country's population starting a new business. See Exhibit 1-1 for a list of a ten selected countries.[29] The U.S. GEM rating of 7.6 percent means that 1 out of every 13 adults in America is actively engaged in starting a business, or is the owner or manager of a business that is less than three and a half years old. Highlighting their global importance, 97 percent of all U.S. exporters are SMEs.[30]

Exhibit 1-1

GEM Entrepreneurship Rates

Country	Percentage of Population Starting a New Business
Peru	27.2%
Brazil	17.5%
China	14.4%
Argentina	14.2%
Turkey	8.6%
U.S.	7.6%
U.K.	6.4%
France	5.8%
Germany	4.2%
Russia	3.9%

Contributions of Entrepreneurs and Changing Demographics

Small-business entrepreneurs are important globally because they make at least four major contributions. Here we include U.S. data only.

Job Creation and Economic Development

Small business is BIG! Business grows the economy, and over 99 percent of employers are small businesses.[31] The 23 million small businesses in America have accounted for 54 percent of all U.S. sales, provided 55 percent of all jobs, and 66 percent of all net new jobs since the 1970s. While corporate America has been "downsizing," the rate of small business "startups" has grown. Since 1990, as big businesses eliminated 4 million jobs, small businesses added 8 million new jobs.[32] So entrepreneurship plays a strong role in economic development.[33]

Innovation and Society

Many of the new technology innovations that help us as a society come from SMEs.[34] Let's face it, new products and services have made our lives easier, enhanced our productivity, improved our health, and our entertainment. Some of the technology in your cell phone that you depend on for multiple functions comes from SMEs. **Larry Page** and **Sergey Brin** founded **Google** as a small business to improve how we search on the Internet. In addition to jobs and products and services, many entrepreneurs help to solve social problems and volunteer in their communities.

Support Large Business and Government

Many small businesses provide products and services to large businesses as their sole customers. Outsourcing from large to small business is common today, and provides opportunities for SMEs. Many large companies, like **Microsoft**, also acquired small businesses to obtain new technologies. The federal, state, and local governments also buy products from and outsource work to small businesses.

Personal Application

5. Select a business, preferably a small one you work(ed) for, and describe some of its important contributions.

Demographic Changes in U.S. Entrepreneurship

As small business startups continue to increase, there is a slow demographic change away from the stereotypical white male entrepreneur. More women are starting new ventures. More seniors are self-employed, and more so after they retire from employment. More young people are starting businesses, even while they are still in high school and college. Also, as American minorities increase (by the year 2040, less than 50 percent of the U.S. population will be Caucasian) their percentage of business ownership will continue to increase.[35] Entrepreneurs in the U.S. come from all walks of life and from every corner of the country, as well as globally.[36] See Exhibit 1-2 for current entrepreneurship statistics.

Exhibit 1-2

Entrepreneurship
Demographic Data

Average and median age	40 years old
First-born child and number of siblings	43%, 3
First in family to start a business	52%
Married when started business, and had at least one child	70%, 60%
Come from middle-class background, and extremely rich or poor background	72%, 1%
Bachelor's degrees or higher, and advanced degrees	95%, 47%
Highest rates of entrepreneurship, and lowest rates	Arizona, Texas, California, vs. West Virginia, Pennsylvania, Hawaii
Think luck is an important factor in their success	73%

Source: Ewing Marion Kauffman Foundation, Taking the measure of entrepreneurs, *The Wall Street Journal* (November 12, 2012): R6.

Why Study Entrepreneurship: What's in it for Me?

Researchers are studying formal education and entrepreneurship thinking,[37] and find that knowledge[38] and learning[39] are the foundations of entrepreneurship. Knowledge is a main source of competitive advantage.[40] So research supports that entrepreneurship can be taught and learned.[41] Why would your college teach this course if you couldn't learn it?

So "What's in it for me?" Part of the answer depends on your career plans. If you want to be an entrepreneur and start your own business someday, obviously this course is for you. But even if you don't ever want to start a new venture, with the downsizing of large companies and the hiring by small businesses, you may end up working for an entrepreneur. Wouldn't it help to know what entrepreneurship is all about? If you work for a large company, you could become a corporate entrepreneur. Also, large companies (as well as government and nongovernmental organizations (NGOs)) realize that innovation is critical for their survival and success, so they value and hire people with *entrepreneurial behavior skills*.[42]

Personal Application

6. Answer the question, "Why study entrepreneurship: What's in it for me?"

Pros, Cons, and Myths of Entrepreneurship

Learning Outcome

3. Describe advantages and potential disadvantages of entrepreneurship.

In this section, we discuss advantages and potential disadvantages of entrepreneurship, and dispel some of the myths you may have heard about entrepreneurship.

Advantages of Entrepreneurship

Here are just four of the many advantages, or reasons, why people become entrepreneurs.

Be Your Own Boss

The #1 reason entrepreneurs give for starting a business is to be their own boss.[43] Many entrepreneurs want to do what they want to do and what they enjoy doing—to have fun. While at MIT, **Vivek Ranadive** (born and raised in India) started a computer consulting business having students do programming jobs. As a *serial entrepreneur*, he went on to start another consulting company, and today is chairman of the board and CEO of **Tibco Software** (stock sold on NASDAQ: TIBX), with offices in more than 30 countries. **Blake Mycoskie** is a serial entrepreneur starting four businesses. He says entrepreneurial success is more than status and money. It's about fulfillment in making a contribution, and living and working on your own terms.[44]

Pursue Your Own Ideas

This is the #2 reason for starting a new venture. Frustrated with the difficulty of buying comic books, **Kevin Mann** quit his job and started **Graphic.ly** to bring the business online. Sir **Richard Branson** sold **Virgin Records** for a billion dollars. Branson actually cried after the sale because it wasn't about the money, it was the thrill of pursuing his own ideas in building a business and seeing the success of his initial idea.[45]

Personal Application

7. Would you like to be your own boss and/or pursue your own ideas?

Financial Rewards

Many entrepreneurs do start a business seeking the opportunity to make lots of money. **Kelly Flatley** and **Brendan Synnott** became millionaires before age thirty by starting **Bear Naked** all-natural granola products. After getting the products in some major retailers, they sold their company to **Kellogg's Kashi** subsidiary for $122 million.[46]

REPLICATIVE VS. INNOVATIVE ENTREPRENEURS Innovative entrepreneurs have a much better chance of becoming millionaires than replicative entrepreneurs. Some research supports that entrepreneurs are significantly wealthier than people who work in paid employment.[47] In reality, the average replicative entrepreneur doesn't make any more money than people with a comparable-level job.[48]

PURE VS. HYBRID ENTREPRENEURS Hybrid entrepreneurs outnumber pure entrepreneurs in many countries.[49] Pure entrepreneurs *are only self-employed*—no paycheck from any job, whereas hybrid entrepreneurs *maintain a wage paying job while starting and running a new venture.* They often want the security of a paycheck, or simply want to supplement their current income. Some businesses don't provide enough income to support the desired lifestyle. **Justin Arrigo** works days for Herb Chamber Company as an Internet marketing manager and on nights and weekends he provides DJ entertainment and light shows, with his co-owner **Craig Matarazzo**, managing **Spotlight Entertainment**

Personal Application

8. Identify a hybrid entrepreneur, preferably one you know.

Boston (www.spotlightboston.net).[50] Justin also designs and builds sets for haunted attractions in the witch city of Salem, MA and all over New England. He is currently the designer and technical director for Salem's 13 Ghosts in 3D (www.salems13ghosts.com). After building up the business, some hybrids become pure entrepreneurs.

Contribute to Society

Employing people and providing products and services, especially new, innovative ones like the PC and cell phone, contribute to society, and this is a reason some entrepreneurs start a new venture. Social entrepreneurs *start a new venture to help solve societal problems.* They seek to combine their concern for social issues with their desire for financial rewards. With the environmental problems, many new ventures have been created in green management.[51] **Bob Shallenberger** and **John Cavanaugh** launched **Highland Homes** in St. Louis to build environmentally friendly condos and houses.[52]

Blake Mycoskie founded his fourth business **TOMS** shoes at age twenty-nine to make money and help solve a social problem of children in Argentina having no shoes to wear resulting in blisters, sores, and infections. His business model is: "With every pair you purchase, TOMS will give a pair of new shoes to a child in need. One for One." Mycoskie says there are six key factors to his success: (1) Find your story, (2) Face your fears, (3) Be resourceful without resources, (4) Keep it simple, (5) Build trust, and (6) Giving is good business. These six factors are chapters in his book *Start Something That Matters* (Spiegel & Grau, 2012). He wrote the book to help others start something that matters to help society.[53] You will learn more about Mycoskie and TOMS in the coming chapters.

Personal Application

9. Have you given any thought to being a social entrepreneur or starting an NGO?

NONPROFITS Some entrepreneurs start nonprofits to benefit society. Hybrid entrepreneurs **Pat Sears** and **Barry Kingston** cofounded **New Spirit** (http://newspiritinc.org), a youth ministry organization. During the first eighteen years, they've run 1,700 retreats and rallies for 85,000 teenagers.[54] Some people start nonprofits as pure entrepreneurs. We will discuss nonprofit new ventures in the next chapter and throughout the book. In the next chapter, we will also explain differences among a for-profit, a nonprofit, and an NGO.

Potential Disadvantages of Entrepreneurship

Here are three of the disadvantages, or reasons why people don't become entrepreneurs.

Uncertain Income—No Salary

Although implementing the material in this book can help you, the financial rewards and consequences of pure entrepreneurship are unknown.[55] The important thing you need to realize is that, if you become a pure entrepreneur, you don't have a real salary, even though you can draw money out of the business on a regular basis. You earn the profits or losses based on the venture's performance. Even if your business is well established, your profits (or losses) can also fluctuate greatly from year to year.

Becoming an entrepreneur is usually a long process from the idea through the startup.[56] It is also common for a new venture to lose money for the first two to three years, so pure entrepreneurs commonly live on savings. Uncertain income is a major reason why many entrepreneurs start out as hybrids and some never become pure entrepreneurs,[57] and some become corporate entrepreneurs and keep their paychecks and hope for additional compensation.

Risk of Failure and Loss

Many pure entrepreneurs risk giving up a paying job and investing their money in the businesses, but the business fails and they lose their pay, time, and money.[58] So some important questions to answer are: "What is the worst that could happen if I start a business and it fails?" (such as how much money will I lose?), "What are the odds of failure?" (we discuss this in Chapter 4), "What can I do to lower the risk of failure?" (such as being a hybrid entrepreneur).

Long Hours and Hard Work, Which Lead to Other Issues

Starting a new venture commonly takes long hours. Many entrepreneurs work 60–70 hours 6–7 days a week without any paid vacation. The average small business owner with an established business works fifty-two hours a week. Some don't take vacations, saying they are too busy.[59]

Starting a business can be really satisfying, but it can also be stressful, such as continuing to have to overcome obstacles, solve problems, and meet employee payroll. The buck stops with you; if anything goes wrong, such as an employee or customer getting hurt, you are responsible. With long hours and hard work comes stress through the difficulty of maintaining work–life balance. Time with family and friends often has to come second to working the business, causing strains on relationships that can even end. Many entrepreneurs continue to think about the business when they are done for the day, which can also affect relationships.

ENTREPRENEURS VS. PROFESSIONALS AND MANAGERS There are two things you should realize. One is that if you go into professional sales, and other jobs like finance (commissions and bonuses), you most likely will not have a certain income either. Second, if you want to climb the corporate ladder to the executive suite in a large corporation, you too will need to work long, hard hours. Entrepreneurship isn't for everyone. If you want a paycheck and lots of vacation time; don't want to work long, hard hours, risk failure, can't handle stress well, and don't want to be in charge, entrepreneurship may not be for you.

Personal Application

10. How do you feel about living with an uncertain income?

Personal Application

11. How willing are you to work long, hard hours to start a new venture?

Personal Application

12. Why or why don't you want to be an entrepreneur?

Myths and Realities of Entrepreneurship

Have you heard any of these myths about entrepreneurship?

Entrepreneurs are Motivated Primarily by Making Money

We have already stated that research shows that money is a factor, but not the first or second reason why entrepreneurs start a business.

Entrepreneurs are Born, Not Made

Hundreds of studies have shown that entrepreneurs are genetically no different than employees.[60] So you can learn to be an entrepreneur,[61] and research supports that entrepreneurship education can play an important role in developing more and/or better entrepreneurs.[62] So taking courses, including this one, can develop your skills and increase your chances of being a successful entrepreneur.

Entrepreneurs are Gamblers

The reality is that successful entrepreneurs don't gamble. They take moderate risks, like non-entrepreneurs.[63] They also carefully assess the chances of the venture success before they start a new business (you will learn how to do this in Chapter 4), and they try to minimize risk, such as by being hybrid entrepreneurs.

Most Small Businesses Fail

Yes. Many small businesses fail. But there is a great discrepancy in the reporting of business failure rates and the reasons for failure.[64] According to the Small Business Administration, seven out of ten new employer firms survive at least two years, and half at least five years.[65] As the rate of small business startups has grown, the rate for small business failures has actually declined.[66]

Part of the problem is defining failure and putting it into proper perspective. Most never fail by filing for Chapter 7 or 11 (bankruptcy protection and bankruptcy) and many firms close without losing any money. Some owners close the business and take jobs that provide more income, to retire, and for other reasons. So did they really fail?

BUSINESSES FAIL, ENTREPRENEURS DON'T Most entrepreneurs learn from the experience and some go on to launch successful new ventures. Just about every entrepreneur will tell you they experienced some type of failure along the way to success. One of the reasons for failure is the lack of entrepreneurial training and education and experience.[67] So this course can help you to avoid failure.

Advantages of Entrepreneurship	Potential Disadvantages of Entrepreneurship	Myths of Entrepreneurship
• Be your own boss. • Pursue your own ideas. • Financial rewards. • Contribute to society.	• Uncertain income—No salary • Risk of failure and loss. • Long hours and hard work, which lead to other issues.	• Entrepreneurs are motivated primarily by making money. • Entrepreneurs are born, not made. • Entrepreneurs are gamblers. • Most small businesses fail. • Entrepreneurs need a lot of money and a great idea to start a business.

Exhibit 1-3

Pros, Cons, and Myths of Entrepreneurship

Entrepreneurs Need a Lot of Money and a Great Idea to Start a Business

More than 50 percent of small businesses are home-based and more than 75 percent have no employees,[68] and many new ventures have been started with $1,000 or less. In fact, *Inc. Magazine* profiles entrepreneurs who started their businesses on $1,000 or less. **Lori Bonn Gallagher** started with $1,000 worth of jewelry samples and turned **Lori Bonn Design** (www.LoriBonn.com) into a $2.8 million business.[69] Many replicative entrepreneurs don't have great ideas; they copy them successfully.

As a summary of this section, see Exhibit 1-3.

Personal Application

13. What myths have you heard that you were surprised to find out were wrong?

Entrepreneurship Characteristics and Orientation

Research has shown that successful entrepreneurs have certain personality traits and characteristics that help them to succeed.[70] Research also supports that having an entrepreneurial orientation leads to superior performance.[71] So, in this section, we discuss these two important concepts.

Learning Outcome

4. Compare and contrast entrepreneurial characteristics and entrepreneurial orientation.

Characteristics of Entrepreneurs

Entrepreneurial characteristics *are the distinguishing individual qualities that contribute to business success, including opportunity seeking, passion, innovativeness, and risk-taking.* They are sometimes measured through questionnaires. The best way to find out about the traits and characteristics of successful entrepreneurs is to take Self-Assessment 1-1 to find out which ones you have and the ones you may want to improve. However, there is no generally accepted list of distinguishing characteristics between entrepreneurs and non-entrepreneurs. Our self-assessment includes fifteen traits that are commonly identified in research articles supporting their validity. Great entrepreneurs have a passion for their business.[72] Passion brings emotion, enthusiasm, and energy to start a new venture.[73] Some say passion is the number one characteristic shared by successful entrepreneurs, in both startups and existing businesses.[74]

Personal Application

14. What is your entrepreneurial characteristics score, and how do you feel about it? What traits can use strengthening?

Self-Assessment 1-1

Do I Have the Characteristics of Successful Entrepreneurs?

Identify your level of agreement with each of the following statements on a scale of 1–3. Place the number on the line before the statement.

   1. No   2. Somewhat   3. Yes

_____ 1. Self-starter.[75] I'm a go-getter that takes on responsibility; I don't need a boss to tell me what to do.

_____ 2. Creativity.[76] I think about new products and services and better ways of doing things.

_____ 3. Passion[77] and Innovation.[78] I get excited about a good idea and I am preoccupied with making sure the idea is implemented.

_____ 4. Optimistic[79] and Confident.[80] I'm a positive person and believe I can achieve the goals I set for myself. But I'm not overconfident.[81]

_____ 5. Energy.[82] I have a high level of energy to work hard and get the job done.

_____ 6. Tenacity[83] and Overcome Barriers.[84] When I get passionate, I overcome obstacles and don't give up until I accomplish the objective.

_____ 7. Opportunities[85] and Risk.[86] I can recognize good opportunities and evaluate them, and I am willing to take moderate risk.

_____ 8. Persuasive.[87] I'm good at convincing people to help me to get what I want done.

_____ 9. Discovery.[88] I have thought about an idea(s) for starting a new venture.

_____ 10. Self-identity.[89] I think about and want to be an entrepreneur.

_____ Add up the ten numbers. Your score will be between 10 and 30; mark it below.

                10   15   20   25   30

I don't have strong   I have strong
entrepreneurial characteristics   entrepreneurial characteristics

The higher your score, the stronger your entrepreneurial characteristics. However, don't be too concerned if your score is not as high as you would like. Most entrepreneurs don't score 30, and you don't need every characteristic to be successful. Remember that you can develop your entrepreneurship skills. Question 10 is important because, if you want to be an entrepreneur, you will tend to act like an entrepreneur,[90] and will try to develop your skill through this course.

One other characteristic you have no control over is your gender. It is generally accepted that men have stronger entrepreneurial intentions than women.[91] In virtually every country males are more likely to become entrepreneurs.[92] Men are also more likely to start and grow larger firms.[93] This is partly due to cultural views of entrepreneurship and opportunities in different countries.[94] The good news is that more women, and minorities, are starting new ventures.[95]

Entrepreneurship Orientation

Entrepreneurship orientation (EO) is one of the most important and established concepts within the field of entrepreneurship.[96] Danny Miller is credited with introducing the concept of EO,[97] and EO has been a prominent research topic for thirty years.[98] While entrepreneurial characteristics focus on the individual, EO is a firm-level of analysis focusing on a company's top management team.[99] Thus, EO focuses on *entrepreneurial behavior*.[100] So, again, you don't have to be an entrepreneur of a new venture; you can use entrepreneurial behavior as an employee. Several studies have reported a positive relationship between EO and firm performance.[101] Thus, it pays to pursue an EO.[102]

EO has become the most widely used measure of entrepreneurial behavior, and it is generally agreed that it applies cross-culturally.[103] One of the studies tested the EO scale in seven countries and found it to be valid.[104] *Entrepreneurial orientation* measures top management teams' use of entrepreneurial behavior of being innovative, proactive, and risk taking.[105] We have already discussed innovation and calculated risk-taking. Proactive means top managers aggressively take risks in pursuing innovation to beat the competition to market with new products and services and with productivity improvements. Managers recognize and move quickly to take advantage of international opportunities.[106]

There is some overlap between entrepreneurship characteristics and orientation traits of the individual that lead to team orientation. EO focuses on entrepreneurial behavior that can be measured on a continuum ranging from conservative to entrepreneurial.[107] To expand on this EO definition, and to find out if an organization you work(ed) for is conservative or entrepreneurial on an adapted EO scale,[108] complete Self-Assessment 1-2.

Personal Application

15. What is your top team's entrepreneurial orientation score, and how do you feel about it? What areas could be strengthened?

The Elevator Pitch

This skill-builder puts you in the venture capitalist position. You will watch an elevator pitch from the Internet and assess the pitch and then discuss if they would or wouldn't invest in the new venture. The link for the elevator pitch can be found at: www.geekwire.com/2012/elevator-pitch-43-seconds-means/.

PetHub CEO **Tom Arnold** describes his online pet tracking startup in 43 seconds. Although the pitch doesn't actually occur in an elevator, the idea is that the entrepreneur has 43 seconds to impress a business person in an elevator (or in this video the top of the Space Needle in Seattle, WA) to invest in the business idea.[109]

Think about it.

1. What score do you give Tom Arnold's PetHub pitch?

Great product idea and pitch		Terrible product idea and pitch	
4	3	2	1

2. Would you invest in Tom Arnold's PetHub business?

3. How would you improve Tom Arnold's PetHub pitch?

Self-Assessment 1-2

How Entrepreneurial is Your Top-Management Team?

Identify your level of agreement with each of the following statements on a scale of 1–5. Place the number on the line before the statement.

1	2	3	4	5
Disagree				Agree

Risk-taking

_____ 1. Top management tends to engage in higher risk and return projects, rather than conservative normal rates of return.

_____ 2. During times of change in our industry, top management moves quickly with radical change, rather than slowly with incremental wait and see changes.

Innovating

_____ 3. Top management actively seeks and offers new products and services, rather than sticking with established ones.

_____ 4. Top management actively seeks and develops productivity improvement techniques, rather than sticking with established ways of doing things.

Proacting

_____ 5. Top management initiates innovations before competitors, rather than copying them.

_____ 6. Top management actively competes to take business from competitors, such as lower prices, rather than avoiding competitive clashes.

_____ Add up the six numbers. Your score will be between 6 and 30, mark it below.

Conservative				Entrepreneurial
6 10 15		20 25 30		

The higher the score, the stronger is the use of entrepreneurial behavior in the organization. You may not be a top manager, but if you start a new venture, you can focus on using entrepreneurial behavior, rather than be conservative. You will learn more about entrepreneurial behavior throughout this book.

The Entrepreneurial Process

Learning Outcome

5. Explain the entrepreneurial process.

Based on entrepreneurial characteristics and orientation, entrepreneurs follow a process of starting a new venture.[110] Although there is no generally accepted list of steps or stages in the process, opportunity recognition is a key element in the entrepreneurial process.[111] There are at least two components: discovery and exploitation of venture opportunities.[112] For our purposes, here is our definition that includes opportunities within the first step of the process.

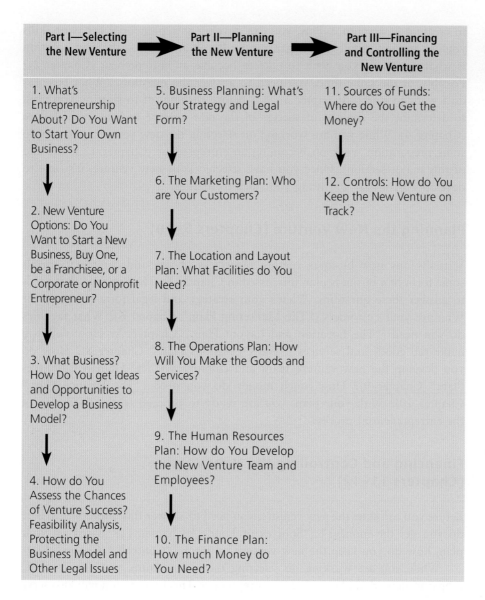

Exhibit 1-4

The Entrepreneurial Process Model

Part I—Selecting the New Venture → **Part II—Planning the New Venture** → **Part III—Financing and Controlling the New Venture**

1. What's Entrepreneurship About? Do You Want to Start Your Own Business?

2. New Venture Options: Do You Want to Start a New Business, Buy One, be a Franchisee, or a Corporate or Nonprofit Entrepreneur?

3. What Business? How Do You get Ideas and Opportunities to Develop a Business Model?

4. How do You Assess the Chances of Venture Success? Feasibility Analysis, Protecting the Business Model and Other Legal Issues

5. Business Planning: What's Your Strategy and Legal Form?

6. The Marketing Plan: Who are Your Customers?

7. The Location and Layout Plan: What Facilities do You Need?

8. The Operations Plan: How Will You Make the Goods and Services?

9. The Human Resources Plan: How do You Develop the New Venture Team and Employees?

10. The Finance Plan: How much Money do You Need?

11. Sources of Funds: Where do You Get the Money?

12. Controls: How do You Keep the New Venture on Track?

The entrepreneurial process includes selecting the new venture, planning the new venture, and funding and controlling the new venture. We actually use the entrepreneurial process as the model or framework for this book, so see Exhibit 1-4 for an illustration.

Selecting the New Venture (Chapters 1–4)

The first step of the entrepreneurial process is to ask yourself, "Do I want to be an entrepreneur?"[113] If you answer no, you can still benefit by knowing the characteristics and orientation of entrepreneurs and the process they go through

Personal Application

16. What type of new business venture appeals to you? Either to start, or to work for with entrepreneurial behavior.

17

to create a new venture. Plus, you can develop entrepreneurial behavior skills you can use in virtually any organization. If you answer yes, the next question is what option do you want to take to become an entrepreneur (Chapter 2)? Possibly, at the same time, you need to answer the question, "What business do I want to start?" (Chapter 3). But before rushing off to startup, you need to determine the chances of success of the new venture to help avoid failure (Chapter 4). While you are working on selecting the new venture, you can do some preparation work on becoming an entrepreneur (Chapter 1, at the end of this major section). Once you have selected your new venture, it's time to develop a plan that will bring your idea to market.

Planning the New Venture (Chapters 5–10)

Virtually any new business venture regardless of size and complexity needs some form of a business plan (discussed in Chapter 5). The business plan needs to answer these questions. What's your strategy and legal form (Chapter 5)? Who are your customers ("The Marketing Plan," Chapter 6)? What facilities do you need ("The Location and Layout Plan," Chapter 7)? How will you make the goods and services ("The Operations Plan," Chapter 8)? How do you develop the new venture team and employees ("The Human Resources Plan," Chapter 9)? How much money do you need ("The Finance Plan," Chapter 10)? With your plan, you are ready to proceed to the third step of the entrepreneurial process.

Financing and Controlling the New Venture (Chapters 11–12)

Before you can start the new venture, you need to answer this question: "Where do you get the money?" ("Sources of Funds," Chapter 11). Based on your plan, how do you keep the new venture on track ("Controls," Chapter 12)?

While you are working on selecting the new venture, you can do some preparation work on becoming an entrepreneur. This preparation will also serve you well while planning and controlling the new venture. It's our next topic.

Preparing to Become an Entrepreneur

In this section we present some of the things you can do in preparation to becoming an entrepreneur.

Get Moral Supporters

Starting a new venture can be frustrating, so having family and friends providing psychological support for your efforts can help keep you motivated and moving forward through the entrepreneurial process. Try to avoid negative people. Research has shown that spousal (and significant others) support can be helpful in many ways, but when not supportive can be a liability.[114] Some entrepreneurs are called *copreneurs*—entrepreneurial couples who work together as co-owners.

Get a Mentor

Having a successful entrepreneur as your role model can help you succeed.[115] Find one that is able and willing to guide you on your way to starting your own venture. Learning though courses helps, but gaining knowledge from entrepreneurs is also important.[116] Good mentors are sounding boards to help you through all the steps of the entrepreneurial process.[117] Mentors should be successful entrepreneurs, but they don't have to be in the same type of business you want to start.

How do you find a mentor? Ask one! A qualified professor can make a great and long-time mentor. Professor **Joel Corman** mentored **Robert Lussier** from his MBA to the present. If you don't know any potential mentors, maybe your family and friends do. **SCORE** (www.score.org) provides mentors across 62 industries and free counseling to help you start a new business venture.[118] The **Executive Service Corps**—United States **(ESC)** (www.escus.org) also provides mentoring with a focus on nonprofit organizations. Your local **Chamber of Commerce** and **Rotary Club** are also good places to find mentors.

Develop a Professional Network

Networking is important to entrepreneurship success,[119] because it helps connect you to people who can help you launch a new venture.[120] It is the exchange of information and resources among people with a common goal with mutual benefits. Yes, you are on **Facebook** and are already social networking with friends and family, but you should also have a professional network. Other Web sites like the general professional network **LinkedIn** and ones that focus on specific professions and industries may be better. Mentors can introduce you to other successful entrepreneurs that can help you build your professional network. The key to expanding your network is to ask each contact who they know that will network with you. Online is a good way to get knowledge, but when it comes to getting advice on your venture, one-on-one, face-to-face is very valuable, especially with your mentor.

Get Professional Assistance

Professional assistance has a significant effect on small business success.[121] Virtually every country has some type of public assistance. Many provide training, grants (free money), and loans (often low rates). For example, in the United States there is the **Small Business Administration** Web site (www.sba.gov) that anyone in the world can access for information that can help them at all stages

Personal Application

17. Which family and friends would be supportive of your being an entrepreneur?

Personal Application

18. Who do you know who has an entrepreneurial lifestyle that you would like to have? Who could be a mentor to you?

Personal Application

19. Who do you know that could be added to a new or current professional network? Are you willing to ask those people for other network contacts?

Personal Application

20. What sources of assistance will you use during the entrepreneurial process?

of the entrepreneurial process. We will be providing resources throughout the book; see "Appendix A: Where Can You Get Help? Sources of Domestic and Global Assistance" for more ideas. Part of your networking should be to get assistance.

Learn About Entrepreneurs and Your New Venture Industry

Work (or Intern) for an Entrepreneur

A great way to learn about entrepreneurship and your proposed new venture industry is to work for a successful entrepreneur who runs a business you would like to start. This can also be accomplished through an internship. Interning can be very helpful, especially if you go away to college, in learning how a similar business in one area operates and taking that knowledge home to start your new venture competing against local businesses.

Talk to Entrepreneurs

You should go and talk to entrepreneurs. You may be surprised at how much they enjoy talking about their success, and if they are really successful, they will usually help you even if you will compete with them. Your college business or entrepreneurship club should provide opportunities to meet entrepreneurs. By going to local **Chamber of Commerce** and **Rotary Club** meetings you can usually find lots of entrepreneurs to network with.

Read About Entrepreneurs and Your New Venture Industry

Personal Application

21. What efforts will you now and in the future make to learn about entrepreneurship and your new venture industry?

You can take more entrepreneurship classes and read entrepreneurship books on your own. Here are a few magazines you can read (hard copy or online): *Entrepreneur*, *FastCompany*, *Fortune Small Business*, and *Inc. Magazine*.

The more you know about the industry your new venture competes in and your competitors, the better. You most likely will never know everything about the industry. But you can read books and magazines on just about any industry in which you can start a new venture. Your future competitors most likely have Web sites. Visit them.

Chapter Review and Summary

As we bring this chapter to a close, you should understand what entrepreneurship is and different types of entrepreneurs, the size classification of businesses, and why small business is important. You should also know the advantages and potential disadvantages of being an entrepreneur, and some of the myths and realities of entrepreneurship. In addition, you should know if you have the characteristics of successful entrepreneurs and how to identify any organization's entrepreneurial behavior as conservative or entrepreneurial. You also learned about the entrepreneurial process, and that it is the framework for this course. Last, you know how you can prepare to be an entrepreneur.

This summary lists the learning outcomes from the chapter and their answers.

1. Compare entrepreneurs and entrepreneurial behavior and replicative and innovative entrepreneurs

An *entrepreneur* is a person who creates a new business venture. *Entrepreneurial behavior* is innovation by creating new productivity techniques. Entrepreneurs start a new venture and usually own it, but they don't have to own it. Whereas employees can engage in entrepreneurial behavior without being entrepreneurs, large businesses value entrepreneurial behavior. *Replicative entrepreneurs* open conventional existing businesses, such as a retail store or restaurant, whereas *innovative entrepreneurs* develop new products and services and new productive techniques. They go from idea to its use in the market.

2. Discuss why entrepreneurship is important globally

Small business entrepreneurs are important globally because they make at least four major contributions. They create jobs and economic growth. They develop new, innovative products and services and productivity that benefit society and help solve social problems. Many small businesses support large businesses and government by providing products and services to them.

3. Describe advantages and potential disadvantages of entrepreneurship

Advantages include being your own boss, pursuing your own ideas, financial rewards, and contributing to society. Potential disadvantages include uncertain income—no salary, risk of failure and loss, long hours and hard work, which lead to other issues.

4. Compare and contrast entrepreneurial traits and characteristics and entrepreneurial orientation

They are both used to measure entrepreneurship. Entrepreneurial characteristics are the distinguishing individual qualities that contribute to business success, including opportunity-seeking, passion, innovativeness, and risk-taking. Entrepreneurial orientation measures the top management teams' use of entrepreneurial behavior of being innovative, proactive, and risk-taking. Thus, entrepreneurial characteristics refer to the individual, whereas entrepreneurial orientation refers to the top-management team use of entrepreneurial behavior.

5. Explain the entrepreneurial process

The entrepreneurial process is a three-step procedure. First, the entrepreneur selects the new venture. Second, the entrepreneur plans the new venture. Last, the entrepreneur finances and controls the new venture.

6. Identify how to prepare for entrepreneurship

To prepare for entrepreneurship, you can get: moral supporters, a mentor, and professional assistance. Developing a professional network helps. You can also learn about entrepreneurship and their new venture industry and competitors by working or interning for an entrepreneur who runs a business you would like to start, by talking to them, and reading about them.

7. Define the thirteen key terms identified in this chapter

entrepreneur

entrepreneurial behavior

entrepreneurial characteristics

entrepreneurial orientation

entrepreneurial process

hybrid entrepreneur

innovative entrepreneur

large business

pure entrepreneur

replicative entrepreneur

small business

small to medium-size enterprises (SME)

social entrepreneur

Review and Discussion Questions

Be sure to explain all your answers.

1. What is the difference between creativity and innovation as they apply to being an entrepreneur?

2. Are most entrepreneurs replicative or innovative?

3. Why are entrepreneurs drivers of social change?

4. What were the results of Global Entrepreneurship Monitor (GEM) study on entrepreneurship?

5. Explain why corporate America has been downsizing while the rate of small business startups has increased.

6. Using demographic results, what type of people are opening new businesses?

7. Can entrepreneurship be taught and learned?

8. Why is Vivek Ranadive considered a serial entrepreneur?

9. What is the difference between pure entrepreneurs and hybrid entrepreneurs?

10. The text states that according to the Small Business Administration, seven out of ten new employer firms survive at least two years and half at least five years. As the rate of small business startups has grown, the rate for small business failures has actually declined. How would you explain this data?

11. What role does gender play in entrepreneurship?

12. Does entrepreneurship orientation (EO) occur only in small entrepreneur-owned businesses?

13. What questions do you need to ask about starting a new venture?

14. What is a copreneur? Do you know any?

15. Who would you select to be your mentor to help you to become an entrepreneur?

16. What magazines tend to have a large number of articles about entrepreneurs?

Application Exercises

Each chapter has a series of exercises requiring you to apply the specific text concepts. When doing these exercises, be sure to select a specific business where applicable. You can select a business where you worked or a business you would like to own someday. Answers for each exercise should be approximately one page.

1. Interview a small business owner and determine if he or she considers him or herself an entrepreneur.

2. Select a female entrepreneur and compare her with the characteristics of an entrepreneur covered in the chapter.

3. Search for an article at Entrepreneur.com that discusses the Small Business Administration. Describe the main points in the article.

4. Check to see if your professor has a LinkedIn account. If so, send your professor an invitation to connect.

Application Situations

Each chapter has a brief situation with questions that require students to apply the text concepts.

1. Opportunity Strikes

As you are reading the paper about the latest corporate downsizing, a business broker whom you know calls and in the ensuring conversation you learn that a tremendous opportunity exists to buy a small business. The broker tells you that your purchasing this business will result in you never having to worry about being downsized and that the business will guarantee your success in life.

1. What advantages do you personally see in buying a small business?

2. Address the disadvantages that might appear as a result of you purchasing a small business.

3. Critically examine your personal characteristics and compare them to successful entrepreneurs. What are your strengths and weaker characteristics?

4. Knowing the difference between being an entrepreneur and being an employee using entrepreneurship behavior, do you have what it takes to be a successful entrepreneur?

2. Gayle Stratton

Gayle's father owned and managed a hardware store, and after working for her dad, she decided she didn't want to take over the business or to be an entrepreneur. Gayle decided to work for a large business. So after graduating with a degree in production, she got a job in her field. It wasn't long before Gayle realized she had a faster way of producing the product.

1. Should Gayle become an entrepreneur or engage in entrepreneurial behavior?

2. What conditions in the firm would have to exist before Gayle should consider offering her productivity improvement suggestion?

3. Having decided to go ahead with her innovation, what should Gayle do now?

Case

Welcome to Livestream!

Livestream was cofounded in 2007 by Max Haot, Dayananda Nanjundappa, Phil Worthington, and Mark Kornfilt, and has offices in New York, Los Angeles and Bangalore. CEO Max Haot is in the United States on a visa. Max is Belgian—yet he shows the American Dream still lives! Before founding Livestream, Haot founded ICF, a media asset management platform, which was sold to Verizon Business in 2005.[122]

Livestream is all about live events. As a member of the Livestream community the user can watch unlimited live events. The user also gets full access to the world's first ad-free live streaming and live blogging service. Livestream's motto is "Discover and Experience Live Events."[123]

Max launched Mogulus in 2007. It was a free streaming service that also had a paid professional service that produces revenues for the company. In 2008, Gannett Newspapers invested $10 million.[124] In 2009, Mogulus paid $100,000 to acquire the name Livestream. The company signed up about 1,000 accounts that were paying $350 per month for online broadcasting services.[125] In 2012, *Inc. Magazine* included Livestream as one of America's fastest-growing private media companies.[126]

Livestream users can stream live video or broadcast pre-recorded video in the channels they select or create. Users may also chat with other producers anywhere in the world. Livestream has a popular online store that lets users stream live HD videos without the use of a PC.

Facebook has used Livestream to stream videos. Bands such as the Foo Fighters streamed a live Internet only concert from their studio space.[127] A Livestream app can also be accessed for viewing on cell phones. From its studio space, a Livestream video can also be used as part of a Twitter message.

You can watch an interview with CEO Max Haot at: http://videos.huffingtonpost.com/tech/livestreams-max-haot-on-entry-into-the-us-517200930.

1. Did Max show creativity and/or innovation skills in developing Livestream? What's the difference?

2. Is Max an entrepreneur? Is he using entrepreneurial behavior? What's the difference?

3. Is Max replicative or innovative and is he a serial entrepreneur?

4. How is Max a driver of social change and how does Livestream contribute to society?

5. Which characteristics of entrepreneurs does Max possess?

6. Describe what stage of the entrepreneurial process Livestream is currently in.

7. Use the Internet to find competitors offering the same type of live streaming of events.

Global Case—Global Student Entrepreneur Awards (GSEA—Russia)

Entrepreneurs can be found in every country of the world! For example, there is a Global Student Entrepreneur Awards (GSEA—Russia) competition that rewards young entrepreneurs. Russian serial entrepreneur Sergey Vykhodtsev shares his experiences of being an entrepreneur in Russia. Here are some of the observations from the competition.

1. They move quickly. They use modern technology to communicate and travel around Russia as quickly as possible—they are looking for opportunities.

2. They run multiple companies at the same time. In the U.S. young entrepreneurs try to open one startup at a time. But, in Russia, young entrepreneurs rattle off all sorts of businesses they have open in fields such as technology, media, and restaurants.

3. The internet has played a large part in rebuilding Russia. Popular new industries in Russia mirror the rest of the world—e-commerce, online payments, social networks, and digital media.

4. Young Russian entrepreneurs value relationships and networking. This can include finding key suppliers or getting through customs.

Russian organizations that empower young entrepreneurs include Skolkovo, OPORA—Russia, the Center for Entrepreneurship, and the GSEA. Their goal is to help young entrepreneurs to build successful businesses.[128]

Think it over.

1. What stage are the businesses at in the GSEA—Russia competition?

2. Do you think the young entrepreneurs are impacting social change in Russia?

3. Research one of the Russian organizations that empower young entrepreneurs. How does the organization support young entrepreneurs?

Preparing for Your Business Plan

Appendix B has an example business plan for 21st Century Computer Training Centers. The business plan is organized using the chapters of the textbook as an outline. Students can write their own business plans either alone or in teams, as assigned by their instructor.

The first step is to format the business plan. Use Appendix B to copy the layout for the Coverage and the Table of Contents. Your goal at this point is to just format the business plan—not to actually write the plan. You will fill in the different sections of the plan that are pertinent to your business as the semester develops. You should begin to consider a business for which you would like to write a business plan during the semester.

Your Ninety-Second New Venture Pitch

You will research, develop, and present an elevator pitch in this course, similar to the elevator pitches that are in each chapter for the class to watch and evaluate.

Your own elevator pitch will be refined throughout the semester under the guidance of your instructor.

Your instructor can choose to have an elevator pitch contest with judges that can determine which ideas are most feasible and who did the best job making their actual ninety-second pitch.

Paper Clip Entrepreneurship Challenge

You will develop entrepreneurial and negotiation skills with a total investment of fifty paper clips. Students can work in teams to create and develop ideas on how to turn their paper clips into a profitable business opportunity. Student reports must include what entrepreneurial skills were utilized in exchanging their paper clips.

Begin to visualize the act of exchanging paper clips for a product that might be more valuable. You might ask yourself how that is possible. Read the following article from msnbc.com: www.msnbc.msn.com/id/12346469/ns/us_news-weird_news/t/trade-paper-clip-house/ You will see that Kyle MacDonald was able to trade his paper clips quite effectively.[129]

College Entrepreneurial Spirit Award Winners

Students in class will recruit fellow college students (from their entire college or university) who have already started an entrepreneurial business. Students and the professor in their entrepreneurship class will eventually evaluate the nominees and select a winner.

Your initial task is to develop a method to reach all the students on your campus that have already started a business! Some students in your own class might have businesses that could also be nominated.

Community Entrepreneurial Spirit Award

Students will select and invite their small business community nominee to come to class. The class will then work with the small business to develop an outline of a strategic plan. Students could also write an actual strategic plan for the business.

Your goal at this time is for each student to list three potential community entrepreneurs they might consider to nominate for being an excellent local business leader. This exercise is simply a potential list of community leaders that you think are outstanding entrepreneurs. A short list early in the semester will help start the process!

Chapter 2

New Venture Options

Do You Want to Start a New Business, Buy One, be a Franchisee, or a Corporate or Nonprofit Entrepreneur?

As indicated in the chapter title, you will learn six options for becoming an entrepreneur. In sequence, you will learn about starting a new business venture, followed by buying an existing business, a franchise or license, and about being a corporate or nonprofit entrepreneur. For each option, you will learn about the advantages and disadvantages and the steps to starting this business venture. We end with a discussion of family business as an entrepreneurial opportunity within the six options.

Learning Outcomes

After completing this chapter you should be able to:

1. Identify six options for starting a new venture;
2. List major advantages and disadvantages of starting a new business, and ways to leverage the risk;
3. Describe the steps in buying a business, including three methods of valuing a private business;
4. Discuss franchising, types of franchises, and the Franchise Disclosure Document (FDD) laws;
5. Compare and contrast the two types of licensing rights;
6. Identify how corporate entrepreneurship is different in risk and structure than the other options for starting a new venture;
7. Discuss reasons for starting a nonprofit organization rather than a for-profit business;
8. Define the fifteen key terms identified in this chapter.

Entrepreneur Profile—Mingo Lee, Wahoo Fish Taco

We begin each chapter with a short bio of an entrepreneur and provide a link so you can learn more about the person and his or her business venture. Short 3–5-minute videos of each entrepreneur can be found at the PBS Small Business School at www.smallbusinessschool.org/. Wahoo Fish Taco video can be found at http://smallbusiness school.org/video.cfm?clip=1798#.

Wahoo Fish Taco was started by the three Lee brothers. The brothers thought they would grow to three locations. They would share the business infrastructure and each brother would run one location. This is the owner-operated model they had learned from their parents. They ended up having over forty restaurants selling their simple but delicious meals such as char-broiled steak, fish, and chicken.

How did that happen? People loved the Wahoo surfboard-themed restaurant experience from the first store they opened. They added locations but then were stuck because they had the one-owner-one-location idea in mind and they had no experience to grow past that stage. Steve Karfaridis magically appeared. He loved the taste of the food and the simplicity of the operation. He saw that the restaurant concept had growth potential and he knew how to grow it because he had restaurant chain experience.

A franchise today costs an initial fee of $35,000. Depending on location, the actual restaurant can cost between $425,000 to $700,000 to build. The franchisee pays 5 percent of monthly sales back to the Wahoo headquarters. Wahoo would like the new franchisee owners to have enough money to own up to three stores. Two percent of sales should be used for producing advertisements.[1]

Franchise restaurants still have the surfer attitude. Everything in the store looks loose and oriented to fun. However, that is only for appearances. Behind the scenes there are many policies that have been put in place to monitor inventories, reduce waste, and improve efficiency.[2]

Think it over.

1. What does it cost to open a typical Subway?
2. Would you rather be a franchise owner of a Wahoo or Subway franchise?

What Type of New Venture do You Want to Start?

Your starting point is determining if you want to be an entrepreneur and actually create a new business venture (which is the focus of this chapter), or do you want to engage in entrepreneurial behavior as an employee by creating new products or services or productivity techniques for an existing organization? If you do want to be an entrepreneur, this chapter will help you select a method of doing so. If you want to be an employee using entrepreneurial behavior, this chapter can help you select for which type of venture you want to work.

Why do You Want to be an Entrepreneur?

Personal Application

1. Why would you want to be an entrepreneur, assuming you do want to be one?

Before you select an option to entrepreneurship, you should state why you want to start a new venture. Answer the often unasked question, "What's in it for me?" In Chapter 1, we identified common reasons why entrepreneurs start new ventures. Do you want to be your own boss? Do you want to pursue your own ideas? Are you seeking financial rewards? Do you want to contribute to society? Your list of reasons should be in priority order. Based on your list, you can write out some objectives, like "To start a new venture while still in college." "To help reduce pollution in (list your city)." "To be a millionaire by age thirty-five."

Selecting an Option to Being an Entrepreneur

Learning Outcome

1. Identify six options for starting a new venture.

Selecting the option to becoming an entrepreneur is a critical decision.[3] So you should analyze your mode of entry into entrepreneurship.[4] So let's start with a self-assessment to help you to better understand which option to entrepreneurship (starting a new business venture, or another option) may be the most appropriate for you. After, see Exhibit 2-1 for an overview of some of the differences between the six options.[5] We will get into the details of each option throughout this chapter.

Self-Assessment 2-1

Should I Start a New Venture?

Identify your level of agreement with each of the following statements on a scale of 1–5. Place the number on the line before the statement.

No   1   2   3   4   5   Yes

_____ 1. Optimistic[6] and Confident.[7] I'm a positive person and believe I can achieve the goals I set for myself.[8]

_____ 2. Risk.[9] I am a risk-taker when I'm confident.

_____ 3. Operations Independence.[10] I like to do things my way; I don't like to follow standard procedures and rules set by others.

_____ 4. Marketing. I'm confident I can develop and sell a product or service on my own.

_____ 5. Management. I'm confident I can manage a business on my own.

_____ 6. Profit. I don't want to pay any fees or royalties on my business to others for their help in establishing and running a business.

_____ 7. Discovery.[11] I have thought about an idea(s) for starting a new venture.

_____ 8. Self-identity.[12] I think about and want to be an entrepreneur.

_____ Add up the eight numbers. Your score will be between 8 and 40; mark it below.

| 8 | 15 | 20 | 25 | 30 | 35 | 40 |

I shouldn't start a new business   I should start a new business

The higher your score, the greater the chances of successfully starting a new business venture. Questions 1 and 2 relate to your confidence and willingness to take risk. Starting a new business is the most risky option of entrepreneurship. For questions 3–6, if you like to follow procedures, want help with marketing and managing your business, and don't mind sharing some of the profits, starting your own business or nonprofit may not be a good option. Consider buying a business, franchising/rights, or being a corporate entrepreneur. For questions 7–8, if you haven't thought about, and don't really want to be an entrepreneur, you are not ready to start any new venture. But you can engage in entrepreneurial behavior.

Characteristic	Start New Business	Buy a Business	Buy a Franchise	Buy Licensee Rights	Start a Corporate Venture	Start a Nonprofit Venture
Risk to entrepreneur	High	Moderate	Moderate	Moderate	Low	Moderate
Independence to do things your way	High	High	Low	Moderate	Moderate	Moderate
Location	None	High	May find	None	High	None
Brand reputation recognition	None	Local	National	Varies	Corporate	None
Marketing support	None	None	High	Varies	High	None
Training to run venture	None	Possible	Usually	Possible	Possible	None
Established procedures	Low	High	High	Possible	Possible	Low
Customers	None	High	Moderate	Possible	Possible	None
Suppliers/ vendors	None	High	High	High	Possible	None
Access to low-cost inputs	Low	Moderate	High	Varies	High	Low
Financing	Needed	Owner often helps	Assistance Possible	Assistance Possible	Provided	Needed
Fees and royalties paid to others	None	Possible	Ongoing	Ongoing	Possible	None

Exhibit 2-1

New Venture Options

Personal Application

2. Do you have the characteristics it takes to start a new venture (Chapter 1)? Are you interested in starting a new venture?

Learning Outcome

2. List major advantages and disadvantages or starting a new business, and ways to leverage the risk.

Starting a New Business

The creation of a new business is what many consider to be the principal building block of entrepreneurship.[13] It is the primary focus of this book, and serves as a basis for all six options to entrepreneurship. So we will keep this section short and discuss advantages and disadvantages of starting a new business and starting a new business with partners.

Advantages and Disadvantages of Starting a New Business

If you want to pursue your passion and do things your way, and you are a risk-taker who doesn't need much assistance in starting and running your new venture, starting a new business may be a good option for you. Starting a new business is the greatest risk,[14] but can lead to the greatest rewards.[15] See Exhibit 2-2 for a list of pros and cons to starting a new business versus the other options to entrepreneurship. Read and think about them, but remember that you can hedge your risk by being a hybrid entrepreneur,[16] having a low-cost home-based business, and by getting a partner.[17]

Partners

Personal Application

3. Which advantages tempt you to want to start a new business, and which disadvantages discourage you the most? Are you interested in starting a new venture?

4. Can you think of anyone you would like to start a new venture with?

A partnership is a legal form of business ownership, and we will discuss it in detail in Chapter 5. But for now, you can be thinking about starting a new business with one or more other people without regard to the legal form of ownership. New businesses are often started by partners with prior shared experience, such as a friend going to school or working together. Partners can exchange and refine business ideas.[18] Integrating their expertise and skills commonly benefits new venture performance.[19] Partners also combine needed resources to start the new venture.[20]

Some of the highly successful innovative entrepreneurs started with partners or at least with the help of others. **Microsoft** was founded by **Bill Gates** and **Paul Allen. Apple** was established by **Steve Jobs, Steve Wozniak,** and **Ronald Wayne. Facebook** was founded by **Mark Zuckerberg** with his college

Exhibit 2-2

Advantages and Disadvantages of Starting a New Business

Advantages	Disadvantages
• You can pursue your passion, not your employers'.	• You will be taking the highest risk of losing your time, effort, and investment—uncertain income.
• You have unlimited potential financial and non-financial rewards (personal satisfaction).	• You have no company reputation and often brand recognition to help get customers.
• You can do things your way.	• You usually have no marketing support, management training, and established procedures for conducting business.
• You don't have to share your profits.	
• You can set your own work schedule.	• You usually have no established suppliers, vendors, or access to low-cost inputs.

roommates and fellow students **Eduardo Saverin, Andrew McCollum, Dustin Moskovitz,** and **Chris Hughes.**[21] Many new businesses are started by a new venture team,[22] and we will discuss how to develop a team in Chapter 9.

The Elevator Pitch

This skill-builder puts you in the venture capitalist position. You will watch an elevator pitch from the Internet and discuss if you would or wouldn't invest in the new venture. The link for this elevator pitch can be found at:

www.cbsnews.com/8301–505183_162-28545966-10391735/top-10-lousy-elevator-pitcheson-video/?pageNum=2

ILovePhotos President Lorenz describes his online photo-sharing business. Do you think he has a unique business idea?

Think about it.

1. What score do you give Lorenz's ILovePhotos pitch?

Great product idea and pitch		Terrible product idea and pitch	
4	3	2	1

2. Would you invest in Lorenz and his ILovePhotos business?

3. How would you improve Lorenz's pitch?

Buying an Existing Business

An acquisition *is the purchase of an existing business.* If you want to be an innovative entrepreneur, you typically have to start a new business venture. However, if you want to be a replicative entrepreneur there are usually existing businesses you can buy.[23] Many successful businesses today were acquisitions by entrepreneurs. **Ray Kroc** was a salesman calling on **McDonald's,** and he ended up acquiring the single-location business and turned it into the highly successful company it is today.[24] In this section, we give the advantages and disadvantages of buying a business, steps in selecting the business, and how to determine how much to pay for a business.

Before buying a business, franchise, or license be certain to do your research to understand what you are and are not buying and what your ongoing obligations are now, and in the future (legally, financially, operationally, and reporting). Also, be sure to get experienced professional advisors.[25] They can help to determine the price to pay and legal assistance in drawing up the contractual agreement.

Advantages and Disadvantages of Buying an Existing Business

If you want to own and manage your own business, but want some help and to skip the startup, and you want to do things your way, buying an existing business may be a good option for you. See Exhibit 2-3 for a list of pros and cons to starting a new business versus the other options to entrepreneurship. Note that buying an existing business has the same advantages as starting one, so we will not relist them all. Also, some of the disadvantages of starting a new business are overcome by acquiring an existing business.

Personal Application

5. Which advantages tempt you to want to buy a business, and which disadvantages discourage you the most? Are you interested in acquiring a business?

Exhibit 2-3

Advantages and Disadvantages of Buying an Existing Business

Advantages	Disadvantages
• You avoid the startup process. • You will know the profitability of past performance, and the odds of your success—reduced risk. You may get a good deal. • You may get some financing from the prior owner, and if not it is easier to finance an existing business than a new one. • You have an established location (it could be the best one), and possibly a company name, reputation, and brand—goodwill. • You have equipment and inventory. • You will have established suppliers and customers with credit terms. • You can pursue your passion and do things your way to improve and grow the business. • You can inherit experienced employees. • You may get the prior owner to train you to run the business.	• You could buy a business that the owner wants to bail out of because it doesn't have a good future. • You may pay a high price and it may take years to get a return on your investment. • You could buy a business that may not fit your passion and lifestyle and you could get bored with it. • Your location may no longer be good, and/or you may need to modernize the facilities, and the inventory may be dated, slow-moving, or obsolete. • You may be inheriting problems and ill will. • Your current accounts receivables may be slow and uncollectable, and it may be difficult to change credit practices to speed up cash flow. • You could get unwanted or unnecessary employees as part of the deal.

Steps in Buying a Business

Learning Outcome

3. Describe the steps in buying a business, including three methods of valuing a private business.

Acquiring a business has risk, so to decrease your risk you can follow the six steps presented below.[26] You can use the services of a business broker to help you through each of the steps of buying a business. If you do, be sure the broker is well qualified. Get details of their experience and ask for and check references. A good place to find a broker in your area is at the **International Business Brokers Association** Web site (www.ibba.org).

1. Self-Analysis and Criteria

Don't be tempted, like many would-be entrepreneurs, to begin immediately searching for a business. Begin with a self-analysis to identify the ideal business for you to buy. Through a self-analysis, you answer these types of questions:

- Why do I want to buy a business? What are my objectives?
- What are my skills, abilities, and interest?
- What industry or market do I want to enter? Does it have potential growth?
- What type of business would I enjoy owning and managing?
- What size company do I want to buy? Usually, the larger the business, the greater the cost.
- Where do I want to buy a business (location)?

Personal Application

6. Assume money is not an issue. If you were to buy a business, what type of business would it be and where would it be?

Based on your self-analysis, write a list of criteria the business has to have to be considered. For example, what industry, size, location, and price range does it have to be in? A women's mid-sized health club in Middlesex County, MA is in the $100,000 range.

2. Generate a List of Potential Acquisitions—Including Businesses Not for Sale

Let's start with what is called the *hidden market*—businesses not advertised as being for sale. If you work for a business, you can ask the owner to sell it to you. **Charles R. Walgreen, Sr.** bought a single pharmacy that he worked for because he didn't like the way it was run. He changed the name to Walgreens and made innovative changes resulting in today's major corporation, **Walgreens Co.**[27]

You can just *walk in* and make an offer to any existing business that is not for sale. After graduating from college, **Art** and **Alan McCraw** went back home to Simpsonville, SC and made an offer to buy **B.W. Burdette and Sons** hardware store. Several months later, they negotiated a deal. They kept the name and expanded to three **Ace** hardware stores.[28]

You can also *network* to find a business. Contact trade associations, bankers, investment bankers, accountants, attorneys, and others. A network contact can introduce you to the owner. There are professionals who can help you find potential businesses to buy. See Exhibit 2-4 for a listing.

Personal Application

7. Identify a small private business you would like to own. Be sure to explain why.

Exhibit 2-4

Sources of Information and Businesses for Sale

Small Business Administration (SBA) (www.sba.gov)	Has articles providing information on buying an existing business; do a search for "buy existing business."[29]
International Business Brokers Association (www.ibba.org)	It is the trade association of business brokers. Visit the Web site for a local listing of brokers who can help you find and buy a business.[30]
BizBuySell (www.bizbuysell.com)	A marketplace for buyers and sellers of businesses and franchises. For $20–$60, you can get a valuation report for a business to gain insight into the business, to determine an asking price, and to get a valuation price of the business.[31]
Business for Sale (www.BusinessesForSale.com)	A marketplace for buyers and sellers of businesses and franchises. Find the help you need in its business advice section, where you can learn about home-based businesses, valuing and financing a business purchase, as well as read buyer and seller tutorials. Recommends and sells the book, *How to Buy a Good Business at a Great Price.*[32]
Business Broker Net (www.businessbroker.net)	Is an online advertising service that helps business owners and franchises sell their businesses by connecting them with prospective buyers.[33]
BizQuest (www.bizquest.com)	Has leveraged the power of the Internet to create an efficient marketplace for buying and selling businesses and franchises online. Has business valuation report.
Craigslist (www.craigslist.org)	Free listing of sellers and buyers. See the For Sale, Business category.[34]
Newspapers and trade journal listings of businesses for sale (e.g., *The Wall Street Journal*, www.startupjournal.com)	Check your local newspaper and trade associations. *The Wall Street Journal* also has articles with information to help entrepreneurs.[35]
Banks	Bankers that deal with business accounts may also know of businesses for sale.

3. Evaluate the Alternative Potential Acquisitions—Due Diligence

Due diligence is the process of evaluating a business for sale. At this stage, you contact the owner stating your interest in buying the business. Be prepared to sign a *nondisclosure document* stating that your evaluation will be held strictly confidential with each alternative potential business. Realize that the owner will also be conducting due diligence on you. After some initial due diligence, you may ask the seller to sign a *letter of intent*—a nonbinding agreement that you are entering negotiations to acquire the business in good faith. The seller is giving you the exclusive right for a set time to step up due diligence as the only potential buyer.[36]

Your investigation should generally include three areas. (1) Personally observe the business and talk to the owners and employees. (2) Talk to outsiders, including suppliers and customers. (3) Talk to experts, like a business broker, accountant, or banker who can help you evaluate the business and appraise the value of the business for sale. Review the disadvantages in Exhibit 2-3 and avoid them. Some of the questions to ask include:

- Why is the business for sale (get the truth)?
- What is its SWOT compared to competitors (strengths, weakness, opportunities, and threats)?
- What is the financial position (review audited income statement, balance sheet, and cash flow—accounts receivable statements and tax returns for the past 3–5 years)?
- What is the physical condition of the business assets and the true value (plant, equipment, and inventory), and the local community (is it up and coming, stable, or a declining area; what are the population and property value trends)?
- What is the trend in this industry and for the specific business (sales/customers growing, stable, or declining)?
- What legal issues should you consider (any hidden debt, liens, or lawsuits)?
- Can you maintain, or better yet improve, current operations and profits? If so, what is your plan and how much will it cost?
- How much should you pay for the business; what is its value? Because this is such an important question, we will discuss it as a separate topic after we cover the other steps to buying a business.
- Is seller financing available?

If the owner doesn't want to give you the information or seems to be hiding something, proceed with caution to find out the answers to your questions. Also, watch out for *skimming*—taking money from sales without reporting it as income. The owner may tell you of skimming and want to add to the profits off the record. Skimming is unethical and illegal and you shouldn't increase the reported profits and pay for illegal activity. If you can't get the answers or the owner has been skimming, it may be a good idea to walk away from the deal.

4. Explore Financing Options—Seller Financing

Based on the valuation of the business, where will you find the money to buy it? This is the major topic of Chapter 11. But for now, you should realize that it is easier to get financing for an existing business than a new venture. Also, you have access to a seller who often is willing to help you finance anywhere from 25 to 80 percent of the acquisition price. In fact, to get a **Small Business Administration** (**SBI**) loan, the seller is required to finance at least 10 percent of the deal.[37] If a seller isn't willing to give you any financing, maybe the owner has no confidence in the future earnings of the business.[38] Expect to come up with a down payment and pay back the loan plus interest over a period of years. The terms of financing are part of the negotiations to close the deal.

With seller financing, **Bill Short** acquired **FiberTech** with a 40 percent down payment, financing 50 percent of the additional funds through an SBA loan. The seller financed the other 10 percent to meet the SBA loan requirements through a three-year fixed-rate note. Short makes principal and interest (5.75%) payments every six-months for the seller financing deal.[39]

Personal Application

8. What are your views of seller financing?

5. Negotiate the Purchase Agreement and Close the Deal

Based on your due diligence of the value of the business, done in step 3, negotiate the *purchase agreement,* specifying the purchase price and terms of the deal. Sellers tend to set a price higher than they are willing to accept. So you should determine what is the most you are willing to pay, and what is your target price that you would like to pay. Terms of the deal include seller financing, what is and is not included in the deal, such as paying off debt, and will the owner continue with the business for a set period of time. You can also include a *noncompete agreement* to insure the seller doesn't start a business competing with yours.

Based on the agreement, both parties sign the documents to make the sale final. You make the payment and receive ownership of the business. Professionals, like a broker, can help in negotiating the purchase agreement and a lawyer is usually used to close the acquisition.

6. Transition

No matter how good and detailed the purchase agreement is, be prepared for surprises that can be frustrating. Again, it can be helpful if the previous owner is actually now working, or consulting, with you to help make the transition go smoothly. If you are keeping employees, be open and honest with them. Reassure them of the security of their jobs. Share your vision and goals of the business for the future. Remember that they have experience in the business, so listen to their ideas on how to run and improve the business. Although entrepreneurs tend to be impatient, you should realize that getting through the steps to acquire a new business typically takes six to twelve months.[40]

The Value of the Business

As part of due diligence, step 3, someone has to determine the value of the business you want to buy so you know how much to pay for it. The seller will often have the business valued in setting the sales price, but that doesn't mean you shouldn't obtain your own valuation, and you may be able to negotiate a lower price than the sales price. Our intent here is not to make you an expert in business valuation. Most entrepreneurs leave it to the professionals. Recall that some of the sources of finding a business in Exhibit 2-4 can sell you a valuation report. You can also find an appraiser at the **International Society of Professional Valuers,** through the **American Society of Appraisers (ASA,** www.appraisers.org). What we want you to be able to do is understand the methods that are used by professionals to value businesses.

Asset Value

Business valuation by asset value *is based on the balance sheet.* A starting place is with (1) *book value* or net worth. You take the total assets minus the total liabilities, which equals book value. It is commonly stated as net worth or owner equity. (2) *Adjusted book value.* The balance sheet figures are often not based on the current market value. The asset may be worth more or less, so they need to be adjusted accordingly. Balance sheets also don't tend to include *goodwill*—the value of an established business with its reputation, which often needs to be added. (3) *Replacement value.* If you were starting a new business, what would it cost for the same assets the business has now? (4) *Liquidation value.* How much would be left if you sold all the assets and paid off the liabilities?

Earnings Value

Rather than focusing on buying assets, you focus on buying future earnings or profit potential. Ask yourself, "How much am I willing to pay to earn a particular profit for a given number of years?" You need to consider *opportunity costs*—other alternatives to buying a business, such as starting a new business, lost income from a job, investments with the money, etc., and the risk factor. Next you determine the *capitalization rate* of return you want to get. A rate of 20–25 percent is common, but tends not to be less than 15 percent.[41]

    Business valuation by capitalized earnings *is the value of the business that would bring stated earnings at a specified capitalization rate of return.* Let's say the net income of a business you want to buy is $100,000 (not including any owner salary or other adjustments to the income statement) and the rate of return you want is 25 percent; the business value would be $400,000 (100,000/25 percent). At a 20 percent rate the value would go up to $500,000. You can make the calculations more accurate, and complex, by getting the *weighted-average* capitalized earnings over the past 3–5 years. You can also use the *discounted future earnings* by using the present value of past income.

Market Value or Price/Earnings (PE) Ratio

The market value of the business is the price of comparable private businesses for sale in the area and those sold in the recent past. The market value can give you an idea of what you can expect to pay. Visit **Business Broker Net** and other sources listed in Exhibit 2-4 so you can get an idea of sales prices for a similar business to one you would like to buy.

The PE is used with public corporations with stock traded on exchanges, which are not commonly bought by inexperienced entrepreneurs. You take the price of one share of common stock divided by its earnings per share (any preferred stock dividends). PE ratios are reported at company Web sites, and through business information sources. For both small private and public companies, you take the average of multiple values/PEs of similar businesses to get the final value.

Personal Application

9. Which method(s) of valuing a business would you want to base your offering price for the purchase of a business?

Buying a Franchise

Franchising requires important decisions.[42] The biggest is, "Do I like to work within a set system and follow the rules set up by others?"[43] If you do and you want to own and manage your own business, but don't want to start one, and you want the benefits of assistance with running a business with a brand name, and you don't mind paying fees and royalties for the help, buying a franchise may be a good option for you.

Franchise systems are a unique entrepreneurial structure because they include several different businesses that are legally independent, while being economically interdependent, but they often operate the same way.[44] Over the past four decades, franchising has grown tremendously.[45] Franchising is now a central part of the U.S. economy,[46] and contributes to global growth.[47] There are more than 828,000 franchise businesses across 300 business lines, which support nearly 18 million jobs and generate $2.1 trillion of economic output to the U.S. economy.[48] In this section, we discuss the types of franchises, the advantages and disadvantages of owning a franchise, the steps to buying a franchise, legal aspects, and international opportunities.

Types of Franchises

Franchising involves a long-term legal contractual agreement.[49] *Franchising is a legal relationship in which the franchisor grants the franchisee the rights to sell its products or services, use its trade-name, or business-format for an initial fee and ongoing royalties.* The *franchisor* sells its rights to *franchisees* in

Learning Outcome

4. Discuss the types of franchises and the FDD laws.

essentially an entrepreneurial partnership,[50] which can benefit both parties.[51] So as a franchisee, you use the franchisor's assets,[52] making you to some degree dependent on the direction and level of success of the franchisor.[53] The **Federal Trade Commission (FTC)** has two main categories of franchises, based heavily on who controls the business model and systems of operations—freedom to conduct business your own way or requirement to follow franchisor methods.

Product and Trade-Name Franchising and Business-Format Franchising

Under **product and trade-name franchising,** *the franchisee buys the right to make the franchisor's products and services and use its trade-name, logo, and other identity while conducting business its own way.* But freedom of conducting business must meet the franchisor's standards and be within the constraints of the agreement. **Ford,** and other auto makers, uses this type of franchising with its franchisee dealerships.

You can also buy the right to use just a trade-name. *With a* **trade-name franchise** *the franchisee uses the franchisor's name but doesn't have to sell any particular products, and can conduct business its own way.* Many hardware stores, such as **Rocky's Ace Hardware** use the name **Ace Hardware,** but sell any products and brands they want to any way they want to.

Under the **business-format franchising,** *the franchisee buys the right to the product and trade-name plus the training and ongoing support and must implement the business model and systems of operation.* **McDonald's,** and other major fast food companies, use this type of franchising.

Individual, Area, or Master-Franchise Agreements

Personal Application

10. Which type of franchise is most appealing to you? Why?

You can buy just one franchise or *multiple franchises* within a specified area. The *master franchise* extends the area to include your ability to sell the franchise rights to others in your area. The people who buy a franchise from the master franchise are commonly called *subfranchisees.*

Advantages and Disadvantages of Buying a Franchise

Personal Application

11. Which advantages tempt you to want to buy a franchise, and which disadvantages discourage you the most? Are you interested in buying a franchise?

See Exhibit 2-5 for a list of pros and cons to buying a business-format franchise versus the other option to entrepreneurship. Note that buying a franchise has the same advantages as buying an existing business, so we will not relist them all. Also, some of the disadvantages of starting a new business and buying an existing business are overcome through buying a franchise.

Steps in Buying a Franchise

Buying a franchise is somewhat similar to buying an existing business, so we will follow the same six steps, but discuss major differences. You can use the services of a business broker who has expertise in franchising to help you

Advantages	Disadvantages	
• You get a proven product or service with an established target market. • You get an established brand trademark and/or a business format system of operating procedures. • You will be trained and supported to manage your business. • You get franchisor marketing. • You often get some financing for your franchise. • You get a proven supplying franchisor, often at a lower cost. • Site selection and area protection.	• You lose control of doing things your way, and you usually can't expand your product line. • You have to pay a fee and ongoing royalties, so the cost can be high. • You are dependent on franchisor and other franchisee success; franchisees do fail or have minimum returns on the investment. • You have risk in the franchisor actually providing the support it claims it will give you, and you may have to overpay for its supplies. • You will have difficulty terminating or transferring ownership of your franchise.	**Exhibit 2-5** Advantages and Disadvantages of Buying a Franchise

through each of the steps. If you do, be sure the broker is well qualified. Get details of his or her experience and ask for and check references. A good place to find a broker in your area is at the **International Franchise Association** (IFA) Web site (www.Franchising.org).

1. Self-Analysis and Criteria

Begin with a self-analysis to identify the ideal franchise for you to buy. Answer the same questions as for buying a business, but add a couple more:

- ■ Recall the need for doing things your way, versus following rules—control,[54] and the advantages and disadvantages. Is buying and managing a franchise the best option to entrepreneurship for you?
- ■ What type of franchise do you want to buy (product and trade-name or business-format)?
- ■ In what industry do you want to start a new venture?

Based on your self-analysis, write a list of criteria the business must have to be considered for a $1 million fast-food restaurant on Long Island, NY.

2. Generate a List of Potential Franchisors

If you know the industry and company you want to franchise with, you can go directly to company Web sites and get information on its franchise opportunities. There are also professionals who can help you find a franchise to buy. There are hundreds of franchises, many of which are at low cost that you may not have heard about and that may be a good fit for you. See Exhibit 2-6 for a list of sources. Notice that the step says potential—this means your search has to be realistic based on the amount of money you have to invest. Some of the

Personal Application

12. Identify a franchise you would like to own. Be sure to explain why.

41

Exhibit 2-6

Sources of Franchises
Information and Sales

Small Business Administration (SBA) (www.sba.gov)	Provides articles to help you select a franchise (do a search for franchise), including a list of approved franchises on the Franchise Registry (listed below).[55]
The Federal Trade Commission (FTC) (www.ftc.gov)	Provides a free copy of *Buying a Franchise: A Consumer Guide* (business.ftc.gov/documents/inv05-buying-franchise-consumer-guide). The FTC also enforces Franchise Disclosure Document (FDD) laws.
International Franchise Association (IFA) (www.Franchise.org)	It is a one-stop nonprofit information source for franchising with detailed information for over 1,100 franchises, a complete list of subject matter experts, and the most comprehensive library of franchising information available ranging from basic "how to's" to advanced regulatory and legal information.[56]
The American Association of Franchisees and Dealers (AAFD) (www.aafd.org)	A nonprofit that acts to ensure ethical practices, and gives accreditation to franchisees that meet its standards. It has information to help you buy a franchise (download a free fourteen-page PDF copy of *AAFD Road Map To Selecting a Franchise*), and it has a link to find an attorney and accountant for professional help.[57]
Franchising.com (www.Franchising.com)	Is the most comprehensive source of franchise information on the Web. It provides extensive resources for franchise buyers including a getting started link with a Net Worth Calculator to help you find out what type of franchise you can afford. You can search for franchise opportunities from A to Z, by industry, and by state. It also has links to top and hot opportunities.[58]
Entrepreneur magazine (www.entrepreneur.com)	Its franchise link includes an annual ranking of America's top franchise opportunities in the following categories: Franchise 500, Home Based, Low Cost, Top New, Fast Growing, Top Global, Biz Opportunities, and a list of Franchises for Sale. Includes detailed franchisor information including total investment cost.[59] The January issue of the magazine focuses on franchising.[60]
Franchise Direct (www.franchisedirect.com)	Guides you to the ideal franchise partner. Includes a directory for a comprehensive list of franchises for sale. Its directory includes a ranking of the top 100 global franchises. Lets you search by investment (amount you want to pay) and U.S. or international.[61]
World Franchising (www.worldfranchising.com).	Helps individuals in their quest by providing the most comprehensive and up-to-date information on the maximum number of legitimate franchise systems and service providers.[62]
Franchise Registry (www.Franchiseregistry.com)	Improves and increases loans to franchisees. Franchisors are provided access to an unprecedented multitude of lenders; lenders are provided with the information they need to underwrite SBA and conventional loans. It lists every franchise in the U.S.[63]

Web sites help you calculate how much you can potentially come up with, and some of the sites let you search by how much you can invest.

3. Evaluate the Alternative Potential Franchises—Due Diligence

A franchise broker can help match you with a franchisor, and the franchisor may pay for the consultant fees. Your investigation should generally include these areas. (1) A good starting point is to visit Web sites in Exhibit 2-6 and the franchisors' Web sites for information. (2) Everything you need to know is not on the Web site, so you will need to talk to franchisors for more information. (3) You really should also visit franchisees and talk to the owners to find out their views of the franchise system. The franchisor must give names of all franchisees who have left the system in the past 3–5 years.[64]

Some of the questions to ask three sources include:

- How successful is the franchisor—financial stability?
- What is the initial fee and ongoing royalties—total investment?
- Is franchisor financing available?
- How successful are the franchisees? How much can you expect to earn from the business? What is the return on your investment? Franchisors are required by law to tell you the answers.[65]
- How large will your territory be and what protection do you have from other franchisees competing against you?
- How much, and what type of, assistance do they offer?
- Do you understand the FDD? The Franchise Disclosure Document (FDD) *contains twenty-three categories of information about the franchisor that must be given to the prospective franchisee before any offer or sale.* They can run to 100–200 pages. The FDD is a very important legal contract, so read it carefully with a franchise lawyer and accountant's help.[66] *Entrepreneur* magazine has a short article in simple language to help you understand each of the twenty-three categories of information at: www.entrepreneur.com/article/222438.
- You will be partners, so do you trust the franchisor?[67]
- If you are buying an existing franchise, why is the owner selling?

4. Explore Cost and Financing Options—Franchisor Financing

How much can you afford to pay for a franchise? You can use the Net Worth Calculator to help you find out what type of franchise you can afford at Franchising.com. The startup cost of a major franchise can be expensive. Here are some examples: **Subway** $84,800–$258,500, **H & R Block** $35,500–$136,200, **Anytime Fitness** $46,300–$321,900, **Supercuts** $103,600–$196.500, **Jiffy Lube** $196,500–$331,500.[68] There are lower-cost franchise opportunities as well. You can do a search by cost at some of the Web sites listed in Exhibit 2-6.

Where will you get the money to buy it? This is the major topic of Chapter 11. But for now, you should realize that it is easier to get financing for a franchise than a new venture. Also, you have access to a franchisor that often is willing to help you finance the venture. The **SBA** also provides loans.[69] Expect to come up with a good-sized down payment and pay back the loan plus interest over a period of years. The terms of financing are part of the negotiations to close the deal, but the franchisor may have a set price.

5. Negotiate the Purchase Agreement and Close the Deal

Based on your due diligence with the cost of the franchise, done in step 3, negotiate the *purchase agreement* specifying the purchase price and terms of the deal specified in the FDD. Major franchisors may have a standard price and FDD package, but you can try to negotiate a lower price and more financing.

Based on the agreement, both parties sign the documents to make the sale final. You make the payment and receive the ownership of the franchise. Professionals (franchise brokers and accountants) can help in negotiating the purchase price and a lawyer is usually used to close the deal.

6. Transition

No matter how confident you are in running the franchise, be sure to take advantage of the training and any other support the franchisor has to offer you. **Gina Frerich** bought a **Cold Stone Creamery** in New Jersey and spent two weeks at Ice Cream University in Scottsdale, AZ. The training included classroom and hands-on experience operating a real store. Most evenings she spent studying for the final exam, and Frerich graduated "Scoopa Cum Laude." She used support in finding a location, hiring and training her employees, and advertising.[70]

International Franchises

Franchising is a global business in both developed and emerging economies.[71] The franchising system can help undereducated and undercapitalized people in countries where there is little infrastructure to help them succeed in business.[72] According to the **International Franchise Association,** 61 percent of its members operate internationally, 16 percent depend on international revenues for 25–30 percent of the total revenue, and 75 percent plan to begin or increase franchising operations overseas.[73]

Top Global Franchises

Failure risk doesn't increase with cross-border business,[74] and franchising is a popular form of foreign-market entry.[75] *Entrepreneur* magazine ranks 200 American franchisors that are seeking franchisees outside the U.S. (go to www.entrepreneur.com, click franchises and then "Top Global Franchises").[76] **Yum! Brands** Inc. franchises **KFC, Pizza Hut,** and **Taco Bell** with nearly 38,000 restaurants in over 120 countries and territories.[77] **Subway** has 37,929 restaurants in ninety-nine countries.[78]

Global Operations

The larger franchisors strategically identify countries or regions to expand and actively recruit franchisees. Most prefer to use master or area franchising in other countries. So if you are not in the U.S., you could buy into an American franchise from a native of your own country. Based on ethnic, cultural, religious, and dietary preference diversity, business formats, operations, and menus do vary to meet the needs of the local community. **McDonald's** has more than 33,400 restaurants in more than 100 countries around the globe, and it doesn't sell beef burgers in India; it substitutes them with lamb burgers.[79]

Personal Application

13. Would you consider moving to another country and starting a new business, buying an existing business or a franchise?

Buying Licensee Rights

If you know of a business that has intellectual property that can be the foundation for a new venture and you want a moderately risky venture with possible brand recognition, buying licensee rights may be a good option for you. Let's begin by defining intellectual property. Intellectual property *includes patents, trademarks, and copyrights.* Patents can include products, processes, and technology. Trademarks include company names and products. Copyright includes printed words (including online) and artistic work (software, music, pictures). Some entrepreneurial firms are based on licensing agreements from larger companies. A license agreement *grants the rights to others to use intellectual property for a royalty and/or fee.* The agreement specifies the terms of the rights given from the *licensor* to the *licensee.*

The license can be *exclusive* (you are the only licensee) or *nonexclusive* (multiple licensees). The right can be for a specific purpose, time, and location. In the usual agreement, the licensee pays the licensor an initial payment plus ongoing royalties (such as a percentage of sales) for the use of the intellectual property.

So it is similar, but with differences, from franchising. There is no generally accepted license agreement or FDD; the terms are based on the negotiation of the rights. So be careful and get legal help when entering a licensing agreement and follow the due diligence steps of franchising. The advantages and disadvantages are similar to those of franchising, so see Exhibit 2-5 for the list. The two common types of licensing rights are technology, and merchandise and character licensing.

Technology License Rights

In a *technology license agreement,* the licensor usually has a patent on the technology. There are two common types of technology rights. Firms develop a technology for their own use, often in a product or the process of producing it, and then license the technology to non-competitors to earn revenues. Most smart phones including the **Apple** iPhone use some licensed technology.

There are also companies that are innovative in developing new technologies, but they don't have the interest or resources to manufacture and/or market

Learning Outcome

5. Compare and contrast the two types of licensing rights.

Personal Application

14. Come up with an idea on how you could create a company based on technology licensing rights.

the products themselves. So they focus on licensing the rights to their technology to other firms. **Chris Herbert** and **Christian Smith,** with the help of some others, developed **Phone Halo** to prevent people from losing their cell phones by tracking them. They didn't have the resources to manufacture and distribute Phone Halo in box stores like **Best Buy.** So they approached **Cobra Electronics** and negotiated a licensing agreement in which Cobra produces the Cobra Phone Tag powered by Phone Halo technology to track all types of item, including keys. Herbert (CEO) and Smith (COO) are still running Phone Halo and licensing the rights to its technologies.[80]

Merchandise and Character License Rights

Personal Application

15. Come up with an idea on how you could create a company based on merchandise and character licensing rights.

In a *merchandise and character agreement*, the licensor usually has a registered trademark or copyright. With a merchandise agreement, the licensor commonly gives others the right to use its trademarked name and logo. **Harley-Davidson** licenses its trademark on all types of merchandise including T-shirts, jackets, gift items, and bike accessories. Though licensing, Harley-Davidson not only makes extra income, but it also promotes the sale of its motorcycles.

Disney Pixar, Looney Tunes, and **Marvel** are known for licensing the rights to their characters. **McDonald's** buys the rights to make toys for its Happy Meals and **Mattel** to sell toys, and others sell clothes and other items. These licensors have a two-pronged approach to making money on the movie and characters.

Ethics

In some countries, there are several individual businesses that don't know or care about following intellectual property laws. As an entrepreneur, you need to be sure to follow intellectual property laws and to be ethical in dealing with licensing partners. Don't sell counterfeit knockoffs as the real brands, don't take content in print or online without permission and payment, and be sure to know the source of your suppliers to avoid the risk of receiving stolen property. These behaviors are not only unethical, but they are also illegal and can get you into trouble with the law.

Starting a New Venture as a Corporate Entrepreneur

To be an entrepreneur, you don't have to start an independent new business.[81] If you are not really interested in starting a business, giving up your pay, or you don't have the resources, being a corporate entrepreneur may be a good option to entrepreneurship for you. If you are really not interested in being an entrepreneur, corporations value entrepreneurial behavior from all employees. In this section, we discuss corporate entrepreneurship, its advantages and disadvantages, and the steps to corporate entrepreneurship.

Corporate Entrepreneurship

Corporate entrepreneurs *start new ventures for existing organizations.* Corporate entrepreneurs are also called *intrapreneurs*[82] and their new ventures are often called *corporate ventures.*[83] New business entrepreneurs tend to start businesses that sell product and services directly to customers, whereas intrapreneurs tend to start corporate ventures that sell products or services to other businesses.[84]

The corporate venture can be a new product, process innovation, or entry into a new market including making the business international.[85] **Robert Lussier** is a two-time corporate entrepreneur at **Springfield College.** His first venture was starting Springfield College Training and Development Services, a consulting firm using faculty from business, psychology, and English. The second venture was as Director of Israel Programs, which offered SC master's degrees in Israel.[86]

Recall that *entrepreneurial orientation* is important because it focuses on using *entrepreneurial behavior* of being innovative, proactive, and risk-taking.[87] Thus, corporate entrepreneurship is a potential means for revitalizing large established companies.[88] **Rod Adkins** started a corporate venture for **IBM** applying wireless technology to extend computing beyond the home and office. The venture had sales of $2.4 billion within three years.[89] Companies spent billions of dollars in entrepreneurial new ventures.[90] **3M** and **Google** have a reputation for proliferation of corporate entrepreneurship as they are constantly coming out with innovative new venture products, processes, and entering new markets.[91]

Advantages and Disadvantages of Corporate Entrepreneurship

See Exhibit 2-7 for a list of the advantages and disadvantages of corporate entrepreneurship. One thing we do want to highlight is that corporate entrepreneurship is the least risky of all the types of entrepreneurs, because the company provides the resources for the new venture. In most cases, if the venture fails, the entrepreneur returns to the prior job, rather than becoming unemployed as in the other options.

Advantages	Disadvantages
• You have the least risk to entrepreneurship; you don't have to quit your job and lose your pay, and you should increase your compensation.	• You have to be careful with the deal you make with the company to ensure you get adequate compensation for your new venture.
• Your company provides the resources, including location and financing.	• You lose some freedom to do things your way.
• You have a company name and support in providing marketing and access to low-cost inputs, and possibly established customers and suppliers.	• You have to deal with organizational politics and bureaucracy that slows you down.
• You may get some training and established procedures.	• There is the risk that the company may stop the venture, even if it is profitable.

Exhibit 2-7

Advantages and Disadvantages of Corporate Entrepreneurship

Steps to Corporate Entrepreneurship

Here we list the steps, but it is not a simple linear process. You may be able to work on more than one step at a time, and come back to prior steps as you go.

1. Self-Analysis—Idea

Let's do a self-assessment to find out if you have the characteristics of successful corporate entrepreneurs.

Next, and very importantly, what is your idea for a new venture? Your company should have a mission statement, a strategy (such as growth), and goals. Do you have any ideas that contribute? Many entrepreneurs see opportunities to do new things, or doing things better than the current competition. Our next chapter focuses on getting new venture ideas. But for now, think about answers to these questions. Is there a new product or service I could add to the current company line? Is there a new and/or better way of conducting business? Is there a market niche not being served well? Is there a new market to expand to, including going international? Corporate entrepreneur **Lussier** added a new service of training and development and expanded the market for **Springfield College** masters degrees overseas to Israel.

Self-Assessment 2-2

Do I have the Characteristics of Successful Corporate Entrepreneurs?

Identify your level of agreement with each of the following statements on a scale of 1–5. Place the number on the line before the statement.

	1	2	3	4	5

NO the statement does not describe me Yes the statement describes me

_____ 1. I'm willing to put in extra hours to start a new venture for my company.

_____ 2. I am willing and capable of playing organizational politics to get the approval to start a new venture.

_____ 3. I can convince top managers to provide the resources to start a new venture.

_____ 4. I have the patience and ability to deal with bureaucracy and overcome obstacles.

_____ 5. I have leadership skills to develop and work with a new venture team.

_____ Add up the five numbers. Your score will be between 5 and 25; mark it below.

	5	10	15	20	25

Weak characteristics   Strong characteristics

The higher your score, the greater the chances of you successfully starting a new corporate venture. However, these characteristics can be developed, and intrapreneurs don't usually start on the job with the intentions of becoming a corporate entrepreneur. After some time on the job, often years, they get an idea and turn it into a corporate venture.

2. Get a Champion

A champion is a manager, the higher the better, who supports your venture idea and helps you to find a sponsor. A good starting place is with your supervisor, who can help move you up the ladder to a top-level manager.

3. Get Top-Management Sponsor Commitment

You need to have the commitment from a top-level manager to provide you with the resources to start and run the new venture. Your sponsor is also important in helping you play organizational politics and break through the bureaucracy and obstacles that can slow you down. At this step, you present your idea without a detailed formal plan. The commitment is the green light to proceed to developing a formal plan.

4. Develop a New Venture Plan

Chapter 5 presents an overview of the parts of a business plan, and Chapters 6–10 the details of the different parts of the plan. For a corporate venture, you may not need a complete formal business plan; however, you need to check with your sponsor to ensure the plan provides the details needed to get the commitment to the resources you will need. You will need to include a list of the resources and budget necessary to start and run the new venture. The lower the startup cost, the better the chances of getting the resources. Your champion(s) may be able to help you plan.

5. Negotiate the Deal with Your Sponsor

Going back to your sponsor, you will negotiate and likely make changes to your plan. Important parts of your negotiation may include "Who will you report to?" and "What will your title be?" The person you report to is important because this manager's job is to get you the resources you need to succeed. Also, he or she needs to help you get the cooperation of other functional areas to cooperate with you by sharing ideas, knowledge, and resources. At the same time, you want a boss who will let you run the venture your way within the constraints of the company; so avoid micromanagers.

What will your compensation be? You should at least get a raise for your efforts and a new position. Better yet, can you negotiate a percentage of the revenues, or some type of bonus based on the performance of your new venture, as part of your compensation?

6. Select and Develop Your Team

Your planned resources should also include the team of people who will work with you on the new venture. Chapter 9 will teach you how to develop a new venture team.

Personal Application

17. Do you believe you have what it takes to be a successful corporate entrepreneur? Why or why not?

Starting a New Venture Nonprofit

The nonprofit sector serves a very important entrepreneurial role in our economy.[92] In this section, we present differences between for-profit, nonprofits and non-governmental organizations (NGOs). Next, we will discuss reasons for starting an NGO; then you can determine if it's a good option for you to become an entrepreneur. Last, we present the steps to starting an NGO.

Differences between For-Profit, Nonprofit and NGO

Let's begin by explaining the difference between a nonprofit and an NGO. While the profit motive drives most entrepreneurial activities, you may feel strongly that you want to provide a service that will provide a benefit for the public good. You may want to help those in need, people who lack skills necessary to survive today's world, or even something as obvious as providing access to clean drinking water in an undeveloped country. The needs are numerous. Creating this type of organization requires the same entrepreneurial skills, creativity, and problem-solving abilities necessary in the profit-making world. However, there are some significant differences you should understand.

Revenues Don't Cover Costs—Need for Additional Funds

By providing for the public good, by definition, you are serving a population that cannot afford to pay a market price for these goods. Some groups you are providing services to may not be able to pay anything. Therefore, your revenues will not cover your costs of running the organization. You must develop other sources of revenues such as government, corporate, and individual grants and donations. These funds are a necessary part of your cash flow. Using these and any other source of funds you can think of are added to your revenues to help cover the operating costs of the organization. But the organization is still subject to the principle that total revenues minus total costs must produce, what is now called *fund balance* (profit).

Volunteers

In addition, numerous organizations that are involved with the arts (music, museums, theater) also operate as nonprofits. Most if not all of these organizations utilize and indeed depend on utilizing *volunteers* to keep the out-of-pocket (direct) costs down. Without volunteers most organizations catering to the public good could not exist.

Tax Exempt

Fortunately, society allows the creation of such organizations that can use the funds they generate for the common good and do not have to pay taxes. There are several types of organizations falling under the heading of those designated under U.S. laws and designated in the IRS code as 501(c) organizations. In general these organizations are exempt from some or all taxes (IRS Publication #557 and T.D. 8818).

NGOs

What we have been describing above are organizations that most people would call nonprofits. However, there are also NGOs. NGOs were defined by the **United Nations (UN,** www.un.org) as nonprofits that are not part of a government, though they may use funds raised by and given to them by the government.[93] 501(c) organizations and NGOs eliminate the need for additional government departments or UN councils. In the U.S., we typically refer to mission-based businesses as nonprofit organizations or not-for-profits (NPO). In the rest of the world, these organizations are referred to as nongovernmental organizations or NGOs.

Nonprofit

For the purpose of this book, we will use the term nonprofit to describe mission-based businesses, which can include NPOs and/or NGOs. Nonprofits provide private mission-based service for the public good.[94] See Exhibit 2-8 for a list of differences between nonprofits and for-profits, which also provides advantages and disadvantages between the two options for starting a new venture.

Mission Driven

Virtually all nonprofits have a social mission to help their stakeholders or society in general in some way. The mission of **Silver Bay YMCA of the**

Function	For-Profit Web site/email usually .com, can use .edu	Nonprofit Web site/email usually .org, can be .edu or .com
Ownership and profits	The primary universal measure of performance is bottom-line profit. Owners are entitled to take profits out of the firm.	In mission-driven organizations, there must be an excess of revenues over expenses called "fund balance." The monies in the fund balance are to be used to further the goals of the organization. These organizations are not owned.
Revenues	Raised primarily through sales.	Raised through donations, grants, memberships, and investments, as well as sales or fees. May allow lower cost or no cost to customer.
Taxes	Pay taxes, reducing net profits.	Tax exemption, gives a cost advantage over for-profits in some cases.
Staffing	Primarily all paid employees.	Both volunteer workers and paid employees, helps keep costs down.

Exhibit 2-8

Differences between For-Profit and Nonprofit Organizations

Source: Dr Kathryn Carlson Heler, Professor Springfield College, 2012. Used with permission.

Adirondacks is to offer all people opportunities to renew, refresh, and nurture their spirit, mind, and body.[95] **Mothers Against Drunk Driving (MADD)** aids the victims of crimes performed by individuals driving under the influence of alcohol or drugs, to aid the families of such victims and to increase public awareness of the problem of drinking and drugged driving.[96] **Boston Children's Hospital** provides the highest-quality health care; is the leading source of research and discovery; educates the next generation of leaders in child health; and enhances the health and well-being of the children and families in its local community.[97]

Similarities Between For-profit and Nonprofits

While we have been focusing on the difference between for-profits and non-profits, let's identify important major similarities.

Profit Objective and Business Operation

A nonprofit is an organization that needs a fund balance to survive. Like a for-profit business, nonprofits must strategically plan for the future, spend their money wisely, market their goods and services, and manage efficiently and effectively.[98] Like for-profits, nonprofits need to hire and pay employees with entrepreneurial behavior skills in order to better solve social problems.[99]

Entrepreneurial Orientation (EO)

Nonprofits, like for-profits, are in need of an entrepreneurial orientation. Nonprofits seek *entrepreneurial behavior* from their paid and volunteer employees, such as *innovating* ways to achieve the mission by increasing efficiencies, serving more clients, or enhancing what is done for clients. *Proactiveness* is needed to find new ways of generating sources of revenue needed for survival and growth of the nonprofit. *Risk-taking* is required to start and operate a nonprofit.[100]

Reasons for Starting a Nonprofit

Recall in Chapter 1 that there are four major reasons for becoming an entrepreneur. If you start a new venture nonprofit, for the most part, you can be your own boss, pursue your own ideas, earn a paycheck, and contribute to society—which is often the most important reason. You may be thinking, "Why start a nonprofit rather than a for-profit business and keep the profits for myself?" There are at least five reasons.

Can't Make a Profit—Earn a Pay Check

A reason for starting a nonprofit is because the organization can't price the product or service high enough to make a profit. Therefore you need government or private grants, to have fundraisers, and/or to raise donations and possibly have investment income to cover the cost of operating the organization. A nonprofit can also help keep costs down by not paying taxes and by using volunteers. The arts (music/symphonies, theatre/plays, museums) are often nonprofits. You can't take fund balances out of the nonprofit, but if there is a fund balance, it must be used to further the mission of the organization.

The **Boys & Girls Clubs** offer a variety of programs. Most of the boys and girls can't afford to pay the full cost of these programs, so the clubs have what they call partners (including Coca-Cola, Comcast, and Microsoft) that provide millions of dollars to help pay the cost of these programs.[101] You could start a nonprofit **YMCA** and potentially earn a good paycheck because it is somewhat similar to a trade-name franchise in that you get to use the YMCA name but can select the programs you want to offer to your members using the methods of your choice. The independent local YMCA would be a voluntary affiliate through the national organization, which in turn would be part of both an Area Alliance and the World Alliance of YMCAs that provide training and other support.[102]

Pure Social Contribution—No Paycheck

You can also start a nonprofit to make a social contribution without a paycheck for the sole purpose of serving some higher purpose. **Pat Sears** and **Barry Kingston** cofounded **New Spirit** as a nonprofit youth ministry organization committed to the mission of proclaiming the good news of God's Real Presence in the world. Revenues come from fees for attending retreats and rallies, it take donations, and funding from the Diocese of Springfield. To keep the price of fees and other costs down, it is an all-volunteer organization, operated as home business, and doesn't pay taxes. Sears and Kingston are hybrid entrepreneurs who have full-time day jobs and do not receive any pay for working nights and weekends for New Spirit. Nor do they charge for the use of their homes.[103]

High school teacher **Charles Best** started **DonorsChoose.org** to fund educational requests of his fellow teachers. He spent $2,000 to get the site up and running and he and his aunt anonymously funded the teachers' requests until one of the first peer-to-peer philanthropic Web sites was self-supporting.[104]

See a Problem, Find the Solution

As members of a community we see the problems around us. They can be pollution or littering, homelessness or student drop out, lack of music or art education. We can then see solutions to those problems. Often these solutions are best accomplished through nonprofit organizations. **Chad Pregracke** grew up playing, fishing, and working on the Mississippi River. He "noticed the accumulation of garbage . . . there were tires, barrels, propane tanks, cars, tractors—you name it." He wanted to do something about that. So he on his own began cleaning up the Mississippi River with a donation of $8,400 from Alcoa. Others became interested. The media began coverage. Chad incorporated as a nonprofit **Living Lands & Waters.** Since then, Chad and the organization have spent up to nine months a year living and traveling on the barge, hosting river cleanups, workshops, tree plantings, and other key conservation efforts.[105]

Value Guardian

Many of us believe in the values of our community, our country, our society. Some entrepreneurs start a nonprofit in order to promote our beliefs, our values. **Margaret McNamara** started a reading revolution when she gave books to the boys she was tutoring. She believed that it was extremely important to get books into the hands of children who are learning to read. Owning a book meant wanting to read. Together with fellow retired teachers, she founded **Reading is Fundamental (RIF).**[106]

Robert S. Brookings worked with other government reformers to create the first private organization devoted to the fact-based study of national public policy issues. Today the **Brookings Institute** seeks to strengthen American democracy; foster the economic and social welfare, security and opportunity of all Americans; and secure a more open, safe, prosperous, and cooperative international system.[107]

Philanthropy—Give it Away

TV, movies, and the news media often portray business people in a negative way. However, many entrepreneurs are donating their fortunes to help solve societal problems.[108] **Duty Free Shoppers** founder **Chuck Feeney** has earned $7.5 billion, and has given all but $2 million to charities.[109] Six billionaires have collectively committed more than $100 billion of personal wealth to give back to benefit society.[110]

Some highly successful entrepreneurs start a nonprofit, often called a foundation, to give away part of their fortune (resources including money and other assets) to benefit society. Microsoft's **Bill Gates** cofounded the **Bill & Melinda Gates Foundation.** He stepped down as CEO of Microsoft and with Melinda currently works for the foundation as co-chair and trustee. They have also encouraged other billionaires to donate to the foundation, including Warren Buffet, who is also a trustee. To date, the foundation has given away more than $26 billion.[111]

Many major corporations start an independent but coordinated nonprofit to give away some of their profits on an ongoing basis. Many of their nonprofits have fundraisers and take donations. McDonald's founded the **Ronald McDonald House Charities (RMHC)** as a nonprofit. **Jimmy Wales,** an Internet entrepreneur best known as a co-founder and promoter of the online nonprofit encyclopedia **Wikipedia** (operated by the Wikipedia Foundation), supports the foundation through his for-profit Wibia web-hosting company.[112] So if you are an employee, you could start a new independent nonprofit in cooperation with your company.

Qualities of Successful Social Entrepreneurs

Before you start a nonprofit, let's discuss the qualities of successful social entrepreneurs. According to David Bornstein, there are six qualities.[113] The first is a willingness to self-correct. What is interesting is that this applies also to other entrepreneurs. To self-correct means being able to realistically look at the organization and say, "This isn't working" or "We need to make changes." It means not being so committed to an idea or way of doing business that you can't make corrections along the way.

The second is to have a willingness to share the credit. Talk with Chad Pregracke, and he will over and over tell you that he couldn't have done what he has done without the help of his family, friends, volunteers, and supporters. The third is a willingness to break free of established structures. Remember that a definition of entrepreneur is someone who breaks out of the box, someone who is willing to be innovative. Bill and Melinda Gates set their goal of eliminating rotavirus. By working with the people of Africa and Central and South America, they and the foundation are on their way to do so through public health means as well as vaccines.

The fourth is a willingness to cross disciplinary boundaries. Social entrepreneurs work with people from different fields, bringing together different kinds of knowledge, skills, and experiences, who can find solutions. The fifth is a willingness to work quietly. Being a social entrepreneur is not for those who are seeking immediate name recognition, immediate awards. Social entrepreneurs work to solve problems, bring people together, and make the world a better place, not promote themselves. Finally, social entrepreneurs must have a strong ethical impetus. They have a passion to make a difference in people's lives.

Steps in Starting a Nonprofit

To start a nonprofit organization, follow these steps:

Step 1. What do you want to accomplish?

You will need to have an idea about what you will accomplish with your nonprofit. What is the possible mission? What are the goals? What are the needs and wants to be met? Perhaps you will be like: **Chad Pregracke** who grew up on the Mississippi River and saw the need to clean it; the women who founded **Jewish Geriatric Services** to provide comprehensive and compassionate healthcare services—based upon Jewish traditions and values—to those facing the challenges of ageing.[114] Or the founder of the **Wounded Warrior Project** to "raise awareness and enlist the public's aid for the needs of injured service members, to help injured service members aid and assist each other, and to provide unique, direct programs and services to meet their needs."[115]

So the important thing here is to think about what the needs or wants are in your community, state, or country. Can a nonprofit organization make a difference? What is it that you want to do?

Step 2. Create a Management Team

The next step is to interest others in your idea. You will need a group of interested individuals to join you as you move forward. First of all, you will need support as you put your ideas from a business model to action. Second, you will need to establish a board of directors in order to incorporate your organization with the state. Together you can write your mission statement, goals, and bylaws. (See http://simplenonprofit.com/sample-nonprofit-bylaws/ for sample bylaws.)

Step 3. Incorporate

You need to research how to incorporate your nonprofit with your state. You will need to research the Secretary of State Web site of your state and follow the guidelines of your particular state. You will choose a name for your organization and, in many states, you must research if that name is available.

Step 4. Startup

You launch the organization. Let's put the steps together here. In order to start a senior center in North Manchester, IN, **Jim Garber** and **Kathryn Heler** gathered together friends who were interested in starting a senior center in the town. Then they contacted town officials, conducted focus groups, sought donations, looked for a location, and organized a board. They hired a part-time director, NeVonna Allen, and opened the senior center. Over the years, the center served the senior citizens of the town and surrounding communities, receiving donations from local foundations and individuals. It served the needs of the people for whom it was created. It was launched.

In later chapters, we will present the next steps in registering a nonprofit organization with the Internal Revenue Service, what it does for the organization, and how to go about doing that.

Personal Application

19. Come up with an idea for starting a new venture nonprofit. What interests you about this venture or what would be your reason for starting it? Write a short mission statement for your new venture.

Executive Service Corps

Executive Service Corps (ESC, www.escus.org/) can provide resources and consulting to help you start and run a nonprofit. ESC is a national nonprofit organization whose mission is to enhance the overall impact of the nonprofit community by enabling organizations to operate more effectively to meet the needs of the constituencies.[116]

Family Business as an Entrepreneurial Option

A family business *has ownership or other involvement by two or more family members.* Family business has a prominent role in entrepreneurship.[117] In almost all countries, *families* are central to the ownership and management of the majority of businesses,[118] and they are proactive in being quick to take advantage of international opportunities.[119] Within the U.S. economy, family businesses comprise an estimated 80 to 90 percent of the businesses, contribute more than 50 percent of the total Gross National Product, employ 50 percent of the work force, and about one-third of all *Fortune 500* firms are family controlled.[120] Thus, family business is an important international entrepreneurship topic.[121] In this last section, we discuss starting a family business and some of their potential problems.

Starting a Family Business

Many small businesses don't start out as a family business, but become one as they grow and bring in family members. Some people are a member of a family who owns a business that provides them with the opportunity to work in, manage, and often to become the owner of the business through intentional succession.[122] Children of entrepreneurs tend to start up their own businesses more frequently than people raised by non-entrepreneurs.[123] But having parents who owned a business is not a predictor of entrepreneurial success in multiple countries.[124] Family members also provide *entrepreneurial behavior* to help the family business exploit opportunities over time.[125]

You can become an entrepreneur through the six options discussed in this chapter as a family business following the same steps presented with the option. Let's briefly review them. One option for starting your own new business is to make it a family business. You can start a business as a partnership with anyone in your family, including being a *copreneur* with your spouse. Spouses are commonly part-owners. Spouses can be a great support for the business, but they can also cause family conflict.[126] Having family partners can provide more capital for your startup. Rather than have family members as part-owners, you can also employ them in your new venture. It is common for children and other family members to work in the business.

As a family, you can also buy an existing business, a franchise or licensing rights, or start a nonprofit. Franchisees are often family businesses.[127] With our last option, to be a corporate entrepreneur, you and your family member would most likely have to be employees of the company. But if you start a new corporate venture, you may be able to hire family members for the corporation to work with you in the new venture as part of your plan.

Some researchers found that family business financial performance is not significantly greater than non-family businesses.[128] However, other researchers found that family businesses with a long-term orientation do tend to be financially stronger and more effective.[129] Also, others reported advantages over non-family firm in identifying opportunities.[130]

Non-family and Family Business Differences and Problems

One of the differences is the goal of the business. Non-family businesses tend to have the goal of making a profit. Family businesses have this same goal, but tend to add the family goal of taking care of family members now and in the future. This difference in goals tends to lead to unique problems within the business and family life outside the business, and the treatment of family and non-family business members. There are also some differences in succession planning of who takes over the business, favoring family members, which also varies across cultures and countries.[131]

Family Problems

Problems of favoritism and equity are much more common and magnified in a family business. Certain family members may be perceived as receiving more than other family members. Conflict at work affects relationships at home. Rewards are perceived as belonging to family members despite (or regardless) of ability. Family members with less skill earning more money and being promoted to higher levels based on family status, rather than competencies, leads to potential problems at work, including losing talented employees.

Family businesses suffer from typical family problems of sibling rivalry, succession, favoritism, in-laws, and spousal problems. While these problems are unique to family firms, they are and can be managed and family-owned business can be very rewarding and enriching.

Family and Friend Rules to Avoid Problems

Personal Application

20. What is your level of interest in working in, or starting, a new family business? Who in your family would make a good partner in ownership or employee?

Some of these family business problems, as well as problems with close friends, can be avoiding by following some rules.

Family and friends should have the competencies the business needs to succeed.

The relationship should be treated as a business relationship at work; treat family and friends the same as you do others in the work place.

- Everyone's responsibilities and duties should be clearly understood by all, as well as how disagreements will be settled.
- As much as possible, business issues should be handled at work, not at home. Or what happens at work stays at work; separate your business and personal lives and relationships.
- Have non-family and friends on your advisory board and/or board of directors (and employees if you can) to provide objective assistance to the business.
- Partners should have the same work ethic as you. If you are committed and work hard, and your family member or friend isn't and doesn't, there will be problems.

Chapter Review and Summary

As we bring this chapter to a close, you should understand the advantages and disadvantages and the steps to starting a business venture for each of the six options for becoming an entrepreneur: (1) starting a new business venture, buying an (2) existing business, a (3) franchise or (4) license, and starting a new venture as a (5) corporate or (6) nonprofit entrepreneur. Go back to Exhibit 2–1 for a good review of the options. You should also understand what a family business is and that you can start a family business venture within the other options.

This summary lists the learning outcomes from the chapter and their answers.

1. Identify six options for starting a new venture

The six options for starting a new venture are: starting a new business, buying an existing business, buying a franchise, buying licensee rights, starting a new venture as a corporate entrepreneurship, and starting a new venture nonprofit.

2. List major advantages and disadvantages or starting a new business, and ways to leverage the risk

Major advantages include pursuing one's passion, while doing things your way, with unlimited potential financial and non-financial rewards, and without having to share the profits. Disadvantages include it being the highest risk option to entrepreneurship; not having a company reputation and often brand recognition, customers, marketing and management support; and without established procedures, suppliers, or access to low-cost inputs. Entrepreneurs can hedge the risk of starting a new business by being a hybrid entrepreneur, having a low-cost home-based business, and by getting partners.

3. Describe the steps in buying a business, including three methods of valuing a private business

The first step is to conduct a self-analysis and set criteria for buying a business. The next step is to generate a list of potential acquisitions, which can include businesses not for sale. Evaluating potential acquisitions using due diligence is the third step. Next is to explore financing options including seller financing. Fifth, negotiate the purchase agreement and close the deal. Last, make a smooth transition of ownership. The three methods of valuing a business include (1) asset value based on the balance sheet, (2) earnings value based on the value of the business that would bring stated earnings at a specified capitalization rate of return, and (3) market value, which is based on the price of other comparable businesses for sale in the area.

4. Discuss franchising, types of franchises, and the FDD laws

Franchising is a legal relationship in which the franchisor grants the franchisee the rights to sell its products or services, use its trade-name, or business-format for an initial fee and ongoing royalties. With *product and trade-name franchising,* the franchisee buys the right to make the franchisor's products and services and use its trade-name, logo, and other identity of the franchisor, with the ability to conduct business its own way. With a *trade-name franchise* the franchisee uses the franchisor's name, but doesn't have to sell any particular products, and can conduct business its own way. Under the *business-format franchising,* the franchisee buys the right to the product and trade-name plus the training and ongoing support and must implement the business model and systems of operation. The *Franchise Disclosure Document (FDD)* contains twenty-three categories of information about the franchisor that must be given to the prospective franchisee before any offer or sale.

5. Compare and contrast the two types of licensing rights

The two types of licensing rights are technology, and merchandise and character rights. A license agreement grants the rights to others to use intellectual property for a royalty and/or fee. Technology agreements are usually the granting of the right to use a patent, whereas merchandise and character rights usually grant the right to use a licensed trademark or copyright.

6. Identify how corporate entrepreneurship is different in risk and structure than the other options for starting a new venture

The riskiest option to entrepreneurship is usually starting a new business from scratch, followed by a new nonprofit venture. Buying an existing business, franchise, or licensee rights is less risky because the entrepreneur gets an established product, trade name, and often a business-format. Corporate entrepreneurship is the least risky because the company provides the resources for the new venture, and in most cases, if the venture fails, the entrepreneur returns to the prior job, rather than becoming unemployed as in the other options. The corporate entrepreneurship structure is starting new ventures for existing organizations. All the other options involve a structure of starting a new independent business.

7. Discuss reasons for starting a nonprofit organization rather than a for-profit business

There are at least five reasons. First, some businesses can't make a profit. To cover the cost of operations, the nonprofit can get some or all of its revenues from grants, fundraisers, donations, and investments. To keep costs down, it doesn't have to pay taxes and it can use volunteers. Second, some entrepreneurs start a nonprofit to make a purely social contribution and do not seem to make any compensation from the venture. Third, some entrepreneurs see a problem and find a solution that is best solved by a nonprofit. Fourth, some entrepreneurs want to be value guardians by promoting societal values. Finally, some nonprofits exist purely to provide for the needs of others through philanthropy.

8. Define the fifteen key terms identified in this chapter

acquisition	franchising
asset value	intellectual property
business-format franchising	license agreement
capitalized earnings	market value
	nonprofit
corporate entrepreneurs	nongovernmental organization (NGO)
due diligence	product and trade-name franchising
family business	
Franchise Disclosure Document (FDD)	trade-name franchise

Review and Discussion Questions

Be sure to explain all your answers.

1. Why would anyone want to start a new business?

2. Do the advantages of owning your own business outweigh the disadvantages?

3. Why does an entrepreneur often start a new business with a partner?

4. Why are experienced professional advisors needed when developing a partnership?

5. Is it an advantage or a disadvantage when you acquire a business that has experienced employees?

6. Why are some of the disadvantages of starting a new business, and buying an existing business, overcome through buying a franchise?

7. Analyze the "Buy a Franchise" column in Exhibit 2-1 New Venture Options.

8. Why are due diligence, a nondisclosure document, and a letter of intent important when looking to acquiring a company?

9. In regards to intellectual property, what is the difference between patents, trademarks, and copyrights?

10. What ethical principles should a company follow when dealing with licensing partners?

11. Why are corporate entrepreneurs called intrapreneurs?

12. What companies have a reputation fostering corporate entrepreneurship as they are constantly coming out with innovative new venture products, processes, and entering new markets?

13. What are the main differences between a for-profit and a not-for profit business?

14. What is the difference between paying taxes between for-profit and nonprofit organizations?

15. What is an NGO?

16. What economic data supports the fact that family businesses play a prominent role in entrepreneurship?

17. Why are non-family and friends on your advisory board and/or board of directors important for a family business?

Application Exercises

Each chapter has a series of exercises requiring you to apply the specific text concepts. When doing these exercises, be sure to select a specific business where applicable. You can select a business where you worked or a business you would like to own someday. Answers for each exercise should be approximately one page.

1. Through a partnership with the Small Business Association, the Franchise Registry (www.franchiseregistry.com/index.php) provides a list of approved franchises. The list allows you to search by name if you have a specific franchise in mind or by program/industry if you are doing research in related franchise opportunities. Search the database using "restaurants" as the keyword. Use the registry to find two franchises that you did not previously know existed.

2. Visit www.craigslist.org/about/sites/ to find two different businesses that are for sale in your state or region. You need to select your *State* and then select "*Business*" under the *For Sale* area.

3. Visit www.aafd.org, which is a nonprofit acting to ensure ethical practices, and which gives accreditation to franchisees that meet its standards. It has information to help you buy a franchise (download a free fourteen-page PDF copy of *AAFD Road Map to Selecting a Franchise*).

Application Situations

1. Gregory Smithson

Gregory is the son of a successful business executive. He received a BS and MBA from Ivy League schools. He worked his way up the corporate later to a VP position in finance. Greg has been conservative and does not make changes until a process has been proven as he doesn't want to make any mistakes that could result in poor performance reviews that would affect his promotions. Owning and operating a small business is now appealing to him.

1. Assess his qualifications and characteristics for starting his own new business venture.

2. If he becomes an entrepreneur, what type would you recommend (innovative or replicative)?

3. Would you recommend he starts his own new venture, or to buy an existing small business or franchise?

4. If Greg asked you to lend him money for a new venture, would you? Why or why not?

2. Leila Santos

Leila Santos, a native of Haiti, immigrated to the U.S. so that her children would have a better life. Because Leila came to America without English language skills, in order to communicate she was forced to become fluent in English rapidly, which caused great difficulty. At the same time, Leila recognized that most of the immigrants in her part of town still spoke only Haitian Creole and were therefore unable to find decent jobs and were limited in their ability to seek work because they could not even manage the subway system.

Once she became established, Leila decided to offer the opportunity to acquire English language skills to her fellow Haitians, at little or no cost. Unfortunately, this seemed to be an impossible task as no one was willing to finance a school that was not able to make money, certainly under a traditional profit-making corporate structure. Leila had just about given up, until her friend Bronte indicated that there might be a better form of organization structure that would allow Leila to establish her school, namely a nonprofit corporation. Bronte further recommended that Leila contact friends of hers, an Executive Service Corps consultant and an outreach manager at the Dorma Corporation to help Leila to set up the school.

1. Explain and define a nonprofit corporation.

2. What is the main advantage that the nonprofit structure allows?

3. What are the steps necessary to start a nonprofit corporation?

Case

Popchips CEO Keith Belling

Keith Belling is a serial entrepreneur! Long before Keith (founder and CEO) and Pat Turbin (co-founder and President) found success with Popchips he was starting new ventures during high school. Keith turned dirty-tag sales items into clean flea market products sold at a profit. Some of his past ventures include one of the first coffee bar chains in San Francisco (Oh-la-la!), which he sold to another coffee company. He was one of the founders of the successful restaurant group Paragon Restaurants. He was also the founding CEO and President of the small business portal (Allbusiness.com). Allbusiness.com was sold to NBC, right before the dot.com bust in 2000. Allbusiness.com was sold for a $250 million dollar profit for Keith and his investors to share.[132]

After taking some time off, Keith was brought in to raise money and turn around Restorative Hardware. He then started to look around for a business in the health food industry. He found a firm that used heat and pressure to pop products such as potatoes. He bought the factory in 2007 and used it to make PopChips.

Did you ever try a Popchip? Since 2007, Popchips has seen its sales increase to nearly 100 million dollars by 2012. Its chips are easily found in large bags at Costco. It is also just as likely to be found in vending machines in smaller bags. In 2010, Popchips expanded to Canada and Great Britain in 2012.[133]

Keith had an interesting comment about what he learned about his different experiences. "You have to have a ton of passion for what you're doing, because being an entrepreneur is probably twice as hard as you think it's going to be," Keith says. "The good news is that it's probably twice as much fun when it's going well."[134]

Think it over.

Which of the following six options for becoming an entrepreneur relate to Keith's experiences? Make sure to explain your answer if Keith has used one of the six options.

1. Did Keith start a new business?

2. Did Keith buy an existing business?

3. Did Keith buy a franchise?

4. Did Keith buy licensee rights?

5. Did Keith start a corporate venture?

6. Did Keith start a nonprofit venture?

Global Case—Libra Group, Greece

My brother, Harry, once told me, "You can pick your friends, but you can't pick your family." We lived in a multi-ethnic community that included many Greek families. We heard many stories about wealthy Greek shipping magnates such as Aristotle Onassis.

Today, there is a young man from Greece, George Logothetis, who built his small family business into a global powerhouse called Libra Group. George first joined the family business in 1993. At that time it was called Lomar Shipping, and it was a small London-based company with just three vessels.[135]

As the eldest of four brothers, George was only twenty when he joined the Libra Group. He had spent his summers as a teenager learning the business. His father said about running the family business, "It was very much part of our blood, part of our culture as a family."[136] George's father must have been right, because under George's guidance the company built a fleet of more than seventy ships.

But, most interestingly, George decided to diversify the family business into many different industries such as planes, hospitality, real estate, and construction to name a few. George decided such growth could only be accomplished by using a family member, friend, or current employee to run each new industry that they entered. He could trust the family members to be loyal and stay with the company while they built up market share in each industry. These trusted family members often entered industries where they didn't have experience working. Even though a few failures occurred, the trusted person was more likely to work hard and was successful.

George is also loyal to helping Greece during its economic crisis. He has built businesses and started internships and entrepreneurship programs for young people to learn about business. Greece needs more entrepreneurs because one study indicated that six in ten Greek family businesses say they have downsized in the last twelve months. Although 75 percent of these Greek family businesses are hopeful of an economic turnaround in the next five years, it is not going to be an easy process.[137] The study also found that family businesses in Greece are very negative about the government's attitudes toward them. The majority (over 70 percent) of family businesses feel that the government doesn't recognize their importance to the growth of the country's economy.[138]

Overall, George is always going to choose family values over growing the business to just make more profits. His goal for the Libra Group is to always feel like it is a family business—no matter how large the company grows in the future.

Think it over.

1. What did George consider some of the positives of managing a family business?

2. What was a negative result of having family members run the different businesses that they owned?

3. Why are other Greek family businesses negative about the business environment in Greece?

Do you believe that family members are better off running a family business or should you hire people that are specifically trained to manage the business?

Preparing for Your Business Plan

You (individually or in teams) can write a business plan during the semester. There are questions at the end of each chapter to help guide you through the thinking and analyzing process. Appendix B has a sample business plan for 21st Century Technology Training Centers that you can use as a template for developing your own new venture business plan.

Since this is Chapter 2, the first step is to format the business plan. Your goal is to brainstorm three different types of businesses that you would like to consider for writing a business plan. You can look for product ideas using the Internet. You need to review three different business plans ideas, but you only have to select one to write a business plan for this course. You should write a brief paragraph on the three potential businesses with the goal of developing a business plan for the one you would most like to develop. Chapter 3 will help you to find new business opportunities and to refine your three selections.

Chapter 3

What Business?

How do You Find Opportunities and Develop a Business Model?

This chapter discusses two major concepts: opportunities and business models. Our first two sections focus on being creative in order to find opportunities for starting a new venture. We show how you can use your own entrepreneurial characteristics to recognize and exploit opportunities. Finally, you will discover how to keep your eyes open to opportunities in new or current trends, as well as in creating a new business to solve problems. You will learn how to develop a business model by answering four questions, which can become an elevator pitch to help you sell your new business. We end by comparing the entrepreneurial opportunity in starting your own new business with making use of the five other options for starting a new business venture.

Learning Outcomes

After completing this chapter you should be able to:

1. Define creativity, innovation, opportunity, problem-solving, and decision-making and explain their interrelationships;

2. Briefly explain the steps in the creative process;

3. Briefly explain three techniques for generating creative ideas for new ventures;

4. Describe characteristics of entrepreneurs that aid them in recognizing and exploiting opportunities;

5. List the steps in the problem-solving and decision-making model;

6. List the parts of the writing objective model;

7. Identify the four questions that are answered by developing a business model;

8. Define the twenty key terms identified in this chapter.

Entrepreneur Profile—Joe Boeddeker, the Enterprise Network

Go to PBS Small Business School at www. smallbusinessschool.org/. The Enterprise Network video can be found at http://smallbusinessschool. org/video.cfm?clip=1867.

There are over 1,000 incubators in the U.S. and most of them belong to the National Business Incubation Association (www.nbia.org). Some incubators focus on specific types of entrepreneurs (such as only women entrepreneurs or businesses that focus on technology products), but most will help anyone who is serious about starting a business. The Enterprise Network (TEN) only works with businesses that are trying to launch technology products.

Joe Boeddeker recruits businesses to be part of TEN. He looks for a person whose idea has a market, who has enthusiasm, and is coachable. Joe's goal is for businesses to grow so that they can leave the incubator.

Think it over.

1. Use www.nbia.org/links_to_member_incubators/ to check to see where the closest business incubator is in your area.

2. Do you think being around other early-stage businesses in the incubator would be inspirational?

Creativity and Opportunity

Without an opportunity there's no need for entrepreneurship.[1] In this section, we begin by defining key terms and the interrelationships among them. Next, in order to improve your creative skills we present two theories of opportunity, and then list the steps in the creative process. We end by explaining three techniques you can use to generate creative ideas for a new venture.

The Interrelationships Among Creativity, Innovation, Opportunity, and Problem-Solving and Decision-Making

Let's begin by making sure we understand these terms and the interrelationships among them as they relate to entrepreneurship.

Creativity and Innovation

Creativity *is the ability to originate new and better ways of doing things.* **Innovation** *is the implementation of creative ideas.* So creativity is *thinking* about new things and innovation is actually *doing* new things, or old things in new ways.[2] As you probably realize, many people come up with creative ideas for starting a new venture, but they never actually follow through and start a business. National culture does influence the rate of innovation.[3] Go back and review Exhibit 1-1 for the Global Entrepreneurship Monitor (GEM) ratings for a ten-country comparison.

Innovation impacts a business's performance,[4] because there is a strong correlation between them.[5] Thus, innovation is a necessary and fundamental function of the entrepreneurial process[6] (Chapter 1). It is fueled by incentive,[7] which is usually financial gain, but unfortunately, the average success rate of innovative efforts tends to be much lower than desirable, mainly due to the high level of risk, complexity, and uncertainty in the innovation process.[8]

Opportunity

It is commonly believed that to have entrepreneurship, you must first have opportunity.[9] **Opportunity** *is a set of circumstances that profitably enables the innovation of creative new products and services, processes, or business ventures.* Entrepreneurs think differently about economic opportunity than non-entrepreneurs: if you can't make a profit, you don't have a business opportunity.[10] If you can't make a profit, you can't stay in business.[11] Therefore, entrepreneurship is the result of applying creativity and innovation in exploiting opportunities in the marketplace for a profit.[12]

Generally, a creative idea has opportunity if it is potentially profitable, and it is a big creative idea if it can also change the way people:

■ do something (**Apple** iPod and iTunes);
■ experience something (**Avatar** 3D movie);
■ buy something (**PayPal** purchases);
■ think about something (***Entrepreneurial New Venture Skills*** textbook).

Problem-solving and decision-making

Problem-solving *is overcoming obstacles and identifying and exploiting opportunities.*[13] **Decision-making** *is the process of selecting a course of action that will overcome an obstacle or exploit an opportunity.* Through *entrepreneurial orientation* (Chapter 1), entrepreneurs solve problems and make decisions to be proactive and to select innovations while accepting the risks involved.[14] Important early decisions that entrepreneurs make, often emotionally, include: "What opportunity can I exploit profitably?" and "Should I start a new venture?"[15] Problem-solving and decision-making go hand-in-hand and are a daily challenge facing entrepreneurs, which makes them critical skills that can lead to success or failure.[16] Therefore, improving these skills can increase your performance.[17]

Personal Application

2. Give an example of a problem you faced at work, and/or in life, and the decision you made to solve it.

Their Interrelationship

Creativity is critical for recognizing opportunities and then innovating new ventures. Thus, creative problem-solving and decision-making to exploit opportunities for profit is central to entrepreneurship.[18] Creativity, therefore, is used for solving problems and recognizing opportunities and from this a decision can be made to innovate new products and services, processes, and to create new ventures.

From Entrepreneurship to Entrepreneurial Behavior

Ideally, an opportunity leads an entrepreneur to launch a new venture, and creative innovation of ongoing entrepreneurial behavior enables the venture to survive and grow[19] and possibly lead to corporate entrepreneurial new ventures. Throughout this chapter, realize that innovating to take advantage of opportunities can be the start of a new venture or as entrepreneurial behavior within an existing business. As an employee of an existing business, you can engage in entrepreneurial behavior of creative problem-solving and taking advantage of opportunities that are innovated.

Personal Application

3. Recall a job you have or had. Think of creative entrepreneurial behavior that would improve its products/services or processes.

Opportunity Theories

Researchers have classified two major theories of entrepreneurial opportunity: discovery theory (based on the inductive process) and creation theory (based on the adductive process).[20]

Discovery Theory

Discovery theory states that opportunities arise from shifts in external factors in the market or industry such as changes in government regulation, technology, and customer preferences; opportunities are out there waiting for someone to discover them. So entrepreneurs are people who are more alert and aware and are actually seeking to discover opportunities and turn them into new ventures, or entrepreneurial behavior innovations for existing businesses.[21] Some people discover opportunities by chance.[22] But most entrepreneurs find discovery opportunities through a systematic practice of finding them.[23] Peter Drucker coined the term "systematic practice of innovation."[24]

Jeff Bezos wanted to start an e-commerce business. He quit his job and searched for opportunities. Back in the early 1990s, Internet technology was in its pioneer stages and a few people started to change the way they shopped by making use of online shopping opportunities. Recognizing this developing trend, Bezos opened an online bookstore **Amazon.com**, and as is well-known later recognized entrepreneurial behavior opportunities in selling all types of products online. Bezos further exploited an opportunity to change the way people buy and read books with e-books and the refinement and sale of the first popular selling e-reader, the *Kindle*.[25]

Creation Theory

Creation theory is actually a number of assumptions about the context and behaviors that don't fall within discovery theory. In creation theory, entrepreneurs actually create the opportunities through their actions, reactions, and experiments around new products and services, processes, or entering new markets. Creation entrepreneurs don't search for opportunities; they create them and then carefully monitor how the new venture succeeds. They generalize from small samples of customers and take more risk with less information, relying on their own abilities to develop opportunities.

Steve Jobs was an outstanding creationist. Jobs's vision was to create products that he and his friends would personally like to use. He co-founded **Apple** with the creation of the PC, and went on to create the iPod and iTunes that changed the way we listen to and buy music. The iPhone and iPad were discovery products as Apple improved the smart phone and e-reader and tablets through *entrepreneurial behavior*, which expanded their functions and made them more stylish.[26] Like Apple, **Google** is on a quest to determine what people want before they know they want it.[27]

Copying is Often Not a Real Opportunity

Finding discovery or creation opportunities that lead to launching a successful new business venture is difficult. Simply copying an existing business whose products or services you like, or are even passionate about and want to sell, sounds reasonable, but is often not a very profitable opportunity. A key difference between a hobby and an opportunity is profitability. The entrepreneurial lesson to be learned is to identify a product or service that people need and for which they are willing to pay a reasonable price. This is the lesson of Bezos and Jobs.

Developing Creative Skills

In this section, we present two ways to help you develop your creative skills. First, you can follow the five steps in the creative process, and, second, you can use three techniques for generating ideas for new ventures with the input of others.

The Creative Process

Creativity is important to opportunity identification.[28] Everyone has creative capability, and people can be trained to think more creatively.[29] Therefore, following these five steps of the creative process can help you develop creative ideas that can exploit opportunities through innovations.

1. Investigation

Start with some preparation to think creatively. Based on your background, experience, and knowledge, what is the problem or opportunity you want to work on? What opportunity do you see in this investigation? Affirmatively free your mind of blocks to creativity; see Exhibit 3-1 for a list.

2. Incubation

After thinking about the opportunity and how to exploit it, take a break from working on it. By allowing your subconscious to work on the problem or

Personal Application

4. Which barrier to creativity tends to hold you back the most? How can you overcome it?

Barriers to Creativity	How to Overcome Them
Searching for the one right logical answer; following the rules.	Realize there can be many alternatives; think outside the box.
Fear of looking foolish and making mistakes.	Realize that entrepreneurship is about taking risks. Often an act that seems foolish leads to success. Everyone makes mistakes, but learn from them and don't repeat them.
Fear of failure	ALL successful people have failures. Realize that failure is a part of the creative process. Be persistent. Remember Winston Churchill's quote: "Success is the ability to go from failure to failure without losing your enthusiasm."
Believing you aren't creative.	Believe that we all have creative ability, and can improve by working on it.
Responses that kill creativity: • It can't be done. • It won't work in our industry. • It's too radical a change. • We/you can't get the money to start up. • It costs too much; it isn't in the budget. • We don't have the time. • Has anyone else ever tried it? • We're doing fine now, so why change? • Don't be ridiculous; let's get back to work/reality.	• Don't use these statements, and try to avoid people who do, or at least try to ignore the comments. • Challenge routine, tradition, and customs. • Keep asking: "Is there a better way to do this?"

Exhibit 3-1

Barriers to Creativity and How to Overcome Them

opportunity during the incubation stage, you may gain an insight into a creative solution while doing something totally unrelated to the investigation—even sleeping.

3. Illumination

This is the point when you get a creative idea that enables you to exploit an opportunity; it can happen during investigation or incubation. It is also called Insight! Eureka! Now I've got it! Illumination can also be the realization that your idea will not work and that you need to repeat your prior steps.

4. Evaluation

Before rushing to implement your innovative idea that exploits a possible opportunity, you need to ensure that the idea is, in fact, a really profitable opportunity and finalize it. You will learn how to do a feasibility analysis in the next chapter.

5. Innovation

If the idea passes evaluation, it is now ready for possible implementation. We say possible because you are still in stage 1 of the entrepreneurial process (Chapter 1) and you still need a significant amount of planning (stage 2) and, more importantly, get the financing (stage 3) to make the idea an actual innovation. In the case of a new venture, a business plan would be written (stage 2—Chapters 5–10).

Football player for and later coach of legendary **Notre Dame, Knute Rockne** used the creative process by investigating ways to improve the game of football. While incubating, he got the illumination idea for the backfield in motion (constantly changing positions) while watching a burlesque chorus routine! After evaluating the idea and training his team, he implemented it. He also perfected the forward pass, which was legal, but was seldom used back in the 1920s. These innovations were unstoppable by most other team defensive squads not using them at this time. Rockne's creativity led to a career record of 105 wins, twelve ties, and only five losses.[30]

Techniques for Generating Creative Ideas

Learning Outcome

3. Briefly explain three techniques for generating creative ideas for new ventures.

The following techniques can be used to help you come up with creative ideas for starting a new business and for enhancing entrepreneurial behavior leading to new products and services, a new process, or new corporate ventures. If financially feasible, it is helpful to have experienced professionals involved when using these methods.

Brainstorming

Brainstorming *is the uncritical process of generating creative ideas to solve problems and exploit opportunities.* The group is presented with a problem or

1. *No criticism*. Members should not be negative in their verbal and nonverbal communications (no laughing, frowning, etc.)
2. *Quantity*. Focus on generating as many ideas as possible with no judgment about their quality.
3. *Freewheel*. Encourage the expression of all ideas that come to mind, especially strange, crazy, or weird ideas.
4. *Extend*. Try to build on others' ideas and take them into new directions.
5. *Equality*. Ignore rank and status; all member contributions are of equal value.

Exhibit 3-2
Brainstorming Rules

opportunity and asked to come up with creative ideas. Brainstorming is commonly used for creating new products, naming new ventures and products, and developing advertising slogans. See Exhibit 3-2 for a list of rules. Entrepreneurs use brainstorming to kick-start creative ideas.[31] Dr **Katie Rodan** conducted multiple brainstorming sessions at her house as part of dinner parties and used a number of ideas that helped shape **Proactiv** acne treatment.[32]

There are two offshoots of brainstorming. With *brainwriting*, members write or type their ideas and circulate them (by passing written notes or projecting ideas on a screen for in-person meetings; or using instant messaging or email for written e-communication), which works well with people from different locations globally. *Mind-mapping*, which works well with visual learners, is designed to extend brainstorming to employ both sides of the brain by using graphical techniques.

Focus Groups

A focus group *is a question and discussion meeting in which participants are included based on their relationship to the problem or opportunity.* It is a good follow-up to brainstorming because it can refine a new idea. You could gather a group of five to ten prospective customers or successful entrepreneurs and business experts in order to ask them questions and discuss ways to improve your new venture idea. Focus groups are commonly used to improve current products and services and to participate in the development of new ones. In order to guide the development of their own books, our publisher, **Routledge**, sometimes conducts focus groups with instructors who are teaching a specific course in order to obtain valuable market feedback on the books they use. It also holds focus groups to determine whether or not it should publish a new book in an up-and-coming research area.[33]

Library and Internet Research

Once you have a basic idea, another technique for refining new venture ideas is to do some research to learn about the product and line of business or industry. A good place to start is in your college library (or a large public library) with the help of a reference librarian. By discussing your idea, the librarian can provide you with resources, including industry-specific magazines, trade journals, industry reports, and help you to use the best databases to find information related to your idea. These databases are excellent and are usually available free through the library, but could cost hundreds or even thousands of dollars to access on your own. A reference librarian can teach you how to access these databases from home or anywhere in the world through the Internet.

Personal Application

5. Which technique do you think would help you the most in generating creative ideas?

If you don't have any new venture ideas as of yet, you can start with an Internet search engine (**Google, Yahoo!, Bing**) by typing in "new business ideas" and get links to sources about the hottest and latest new business ideas. With a new business idea in your search engine you can set up an "email alert" using key words to get regular links to information that can help you refine your new venture idea. You can also visit blogs that deal with your idea and **Twitter** about it. But be careful not to get too carried away with discussing your business idea on social media because someone could turn your idea into a new business before you.

Entrepreneurial Characteristics for Recognizing and Exploiting Opportunities

Learning Outcome

4. Describe characteristics of entrepreneurs that aid them in recognizing and exploiting opportunities.

Opportunity recognition is considered to be a key element in the *entrepreneurial process.*[34] Thus, to become an entrepreneur you need the ability to take action to exploit opportunities when you recognize them.[35] In this section, we focus on the skills of actually recognizing a good opportunity based on entrepreneurial characteristics. As you probably realize, some people are better at recognizing opportunities than others. Here are some of the ways entrepreneurs discover and create opportunities.

Knowledge and Experience

Experience is part of the knowledge you have gained over your lifetime,[36] so use your accumulated knowledge to recognize opportunities.[37] More than 40 percent of individuals who became entrepreneurs recognized an opportunity to start a new venture while working as employees for companies in the same or a related industry.[38] In fact, it is often recommended that a prospective entrepreneur work for a company to gain experience before starting a new business venture. This may be because the lack of domain-specific knowledge has been shown to be a predictor of business failure.[39]

Christopher Malec is a potter, wanting to start his own business. He has developed a creative style and design, but doesn't have the experience of running a business on his own. In order to gain that knowledge, he works for a designer pottery shop, which produces mugs, tankards, and goblets for corporate promotions and festivals. After several years, he now feels that he knows how to start his own business and run it profitably. He started small, with a studio in his basement. With the experience and knowledge he gained, he is ready to go on his own.

Using her computer industry knowledge, **Brenda Cannon** started a Web site for her own family's use, and she was asked by others to create a Web site for their family. Cannon recognized the opportunity and became a hybrid entrepreneur, launching **FamilyLobby.com**. After building up her business, she quit her day job at **Microsoft**.[40] You can also talk directly to potential competitors to learn from them, but be ethical. Don't misrepresent who you are.[41]

Personal Application

6. What knowledge and industry experience do you have, or want to get, in search of creating a new venture?

Networks

Because networks contribute to innovation and firm performance,[42] social networking will expose you to more opportunities. Therefore, by working within and outside your industry, utilizing the benefits of social networking, you can build a network of contacts that can help you through the *entrepreneurial process* (Chapter 1) of selecting the new venture, planning it, financing and then controlling your business successfully. Networks can also provide access to resources necessary for founding a new venture.[43]

Jerry Mix, chairman of **Finis** swimming gear, enjoyed swimming for exercise, but he missed listening to music while in the water. So he came up with the idea of developing an MP3 player that could be used in the water. Having no knowledge or experience in developing the MP3 player, he networked and found an engineer to work with and together they developed the SwiMP3. This *entrepreneurial behavior* led to the SwiMP3 accounting for 20 percent of Finis sales.[44]

Personal Application

7. How can you build on your current network to help you through the entrepreneurial process and to gain the resources to start a new venture?

Alertness and Use of the Creative Process

Successful entrepreneurs are more alert to opportunities, but it is important to remember that alertness is largely a learned skill, or what researchers identify as a cognitive skill.[45] Because experience is a source of being more alert to discovering opportunities, you are more apt to find opportunities if you consciously use the creative process. Do you want to be an entrepreneur? If so, you have to actively search for opportunities.[46] Ideas can just come to you. While playing with a piece of wire, **Walter Hunt** got the idea for the *safety pin.*

But you usually have to be alert, seek the opportunity, and then exploit it through a new venture.[47] Young couple **Braden Perkins** (with a literature degree and cooking experience) and **Laura Adrian** (just out of college with a psychology job that didn't suit her) decided to sell their belongings in the U.S. and go to Paris. They picked Paris first, before having an idea of what venture they wanted to start. They estimated their money would last about three-months.

Personal Application

8. Are you alert—actively seeking entrepreneurial opportunities?

They started an informal supper club out of their leased apartment. It caught on and the networking led to making money by writing recipes for **Williams-Sonoma**, until they opened a wine bar, followed by a restaurant upstairs several months later. Today, **Verjus** is a successful venture.[48]

Improvement

Most new venture ideas don't come through creation of a new product or service, but through improving ones that exist. Going along with your experience and alertness, actively think about how to improve existing products, services, and processes.

How Can I Change it for the Better?

"Can I do more with less?" is a good question that leads to entrepreneurial behavior, process improvements and new ventures. Think of ways to beat the competition on price, location, quality, reliability, and speed, and you can create a successful replicative business.

Think about products or the services you use. What frustrates you the most when buying or using the product? What product, service, or process could take away your frustration, or make your life better? Ask yourself, "How can something be improved to create value for the customer (buyer) or the consumer (user)?" "Can I make or deliver it better, cheaper, faster, more convenient, easier to use, smaller/larger, lighter/heavier?"

Travelocity was the first online travel Web site, and it focused on air fares. **Rich Barton** founded **Expedia**, putting more focus on better hotel prices and was the first to enable customers to simultaneously shop price and schedule. In 2012, Expedia had more than $3 billion in sales.[49] **Michael Dell** recognized the opportunity to improve how people buy computers through building your own PC. He started **Dell Inc.** from his college dorm room. Dell's idea of mass-produced custom products was copied by others as entrepreneurial behavior, such as **M&Ms** putting customers' own messages on the tiny candy.

Benchmarking

Benchmarking *is the process of comparing an organization's products, services, and processes with those of other companies.* In benchmarking, through *competitive intelligence*, you find out about competitors and copy them or improve upon them legally and ethically. However, looking at non-competitors can provide good ideas that create opportunities. The first one to focus on free food delivery was **Tom Monaghan**, founder of **Domino's Pizza, Inc.** Then other pizza businesses and other types of foods and product firms copied the entrepreneurial behavior of free delivery. Fast-food businesses pioneered the drive-through window. Today, drive-through services exist at banks, coffee shops, pharmacies, liquor stores, and even a wedding chapel in Las Vegas.[50] Can you put a product, service, or process to another use?

Personal Application

9. What product or process could be improved as an opportunity to start a new venture or as entrepreneurial behavior for an existing business?

Persistence

Realize that starting a new venture takes time and often rejection. You have to be able to overcome fear and criticism, like being told "You're crazy."[51] Blake Mycoskie was told that his business and social mission business model would not be sustainable in the shoe industry. But like Blake, don't quit on your passion if it is a true opportunity.[52] You need to be persistent and use your problem-solving skills (and we will give you a model to help you in this chapter) to overcome the obstacles you will face in starting a new venture.

British inventor **Sir James Dyson** spent ten years and almost his entire savings failing repeatedly before he created the **Dyson** company's Dual Cyclone bag-free vacuum cleaner that made him rich. **J.K. Rowling's** original *Harry Potter* book was rejected by twelve publishers before the small London publisher **Bloomsbury** agreed to publish 1,000 copies. With the series selling more than 400 million copies in multiple languages worldwide, Rowling has become a billionaire.[53]

Using your knowledge and industry experience, networking, being alert, and seeking to improve existing products, services, and processes, while being persistent, allows you to see trends and problems you can solve by creating a new venture—our next two sections.

Personal Application

10. How would you rate your persistence in becoming an entrepreneur or engaging in entrepreneurial behavior? Give an example of when you were persistent in overcoming obstacles through problem-solving in order to achieve an objective.

Opportunities in Trends

Successful entrepreneurs are always searching for change, responding to it, and exploiting it as an opportunity. Here are some trends that bring about changes you may be able to exploit. But first, there are two things to keep in mind. Don't confuse trends (long-term opportunity) and fads (short-term potential). Most entrepreneurs can't get a new business started fast enough to capitalize on a fad—so they are more appropriate for existing businesses through entrepreneurial behavior. Second, realize that the trends are interrelated, or changes in one area affect other areas.

Industry and Economic Trends

Industry Trends

Conduct a library and/or Internet search and use your network to identify trends in your industry that are potential opportunities for creating a new venture. These trends also include other trends we discuss related to your industry.

Economic Trends

When the economy is in a growth period or recession there are changes in opportunities. During growth, people have more money to spend on more products and services that enhance their lives. But when the economy is weak, people cut back on discretionary purchases and so, during a recession, there are opportunities to help people save money. During the recession in November 2008, **Andrew Mason** created **Groupon** featuring a daily deal on the best things to do, see, eat, and buy.[54] **Dustin Coupal** and **Jason Toews** cofounded **GasBuddy.com**. Thousands of people have been regularly visiting its Web sites, which post gas prices identifying the lowest-priced fuel in their area, helping them save money at the pumps.[55]

Social and Sustainability Trends

Entrepreneurs are drivers of social change and as such they create opportunities for other entrepreneurs.[56]

Social Trends

Social trends change the way we live and conduct business by transforming the way products and services are provided and sold. But trends are not just about the product or services. **McDonald's** and other fast-food restaurants aren't successful just because people like the food; they fulfill a social need for people who do not have time or interest in cooking. However, because people are also looking for more up-scale alternatives, the **Murrell** family, under the guidance of **Jerry** and **Janie**, founded **Five Guys Burgers and Fries**, serving only hand-formed burgers cooked to order on a grill served with fresh-cut fries cooked in pure peanut oil.[57] See Exhibit 3-3 for a list of social trends that could create an opportunity for you.

Exhibit 3-3

Social Trends

Trend	Opportunities
An ageing population.	The need for all kinds of assistance will grow as baby boomers age (born 1946–1964). By 2050, there will be more than 88 million people aged sixty-five or older in the U.S. Home-care in the U.S. is an $85 billion industry. Around 10,000 people retire every year and they are interested in recreation activities.[58]
Health and wellness	People are concerned about eating better foods and participating in diet and exercise programs. Seniors are a target market.
Clean energy	The government is pushing for clean energy and providing some funding to develop alternative sources of energy, including bio-fuels, wind, and solar sources of energy. Government, businesses, and home owners are potential customers.
Green products	Recall our discussions (Chapters 1 and 2) of social and sustainable entrepreneurs starting new ventures to capitalize on products that will improve and maintain our environment.
Security and privacy	The terrorist attracts of 9/11 created a new focus on security in society, business, and the home. The Internet has also created the need for security related to privacy of information to prevent identity theft and simply to keep others out of our personal affairs.

Opportunity in Social and Sustainable Entrepreneurship

Social and sustainable entrepreneurship is on the increase.[59] *Social entrepreneurship* (Chapter 1) helps resolve a wide variety of social problems; sustainable entrepreneurship focuses on clean energy and/or green products. Sustainable development is perhaps the most prominent topic of our time.[60] *Sustainability* is meeting the needs of today without sacrificing future generations' ability to meet their needs.[61] Sustainability is now a business buzzword, and it is an important topic for all countries.[62] Because growth shouldn't occur at the expense of our environment, *sustainable development* balances the need for economic growth and the need to maintain our natural environment.

Society expects business to use resources wisely and responsibly by adhering to the following:

- protecting the environment;
- minimizing the amount of air, water, energy, minerals, and other materials found in the final goods we consume;
- recycling and reusing these goods to the extent possible rather than drawing on nature to replenish them;
- respecting nature's calm, tranquility, and beauty;
- eliminating toxins that harm people in the workplace and communities.[63]

Sustainable entrepreneurship includes two related concepts: *social entrepreneurship* (helping societal community) and *ecopreneurship* (environmental entrepreneurship). Thus, sustainability entrepreneurs *start new ventures that focus on maintaining nature, natural resources, and communities.* Nine out of ten business executives believe sustainability is of significant importance to their business.[64] Sustainable entrepreneurs can help preserve ecosystems, counteract climate change, reduce environmental degradation and deforestation, improve agricultural practices and freshwater supply, and maintain biodiversity. These new ventures can enhance education, productivity, socioeconomic status, physical health, and self-reliance of individuals and societies—especially in developing countries. They provide both economic and noneconomic gain.[65]

Entrepreneurs are drivers of social change.[66] Starting a new venture with an innovative sustainability strategy can be a competitive advantage leading to profits while helping solve social and environmental problems[67] as either a for-profit or nonprofit. Sustainable entrepreneurs focus on the *triple bottom line* by creating profits while helping the local community and the natural environment.

A sustainable entrepreneur, **Julie Corbett**, founded **Ecologic Brands** when she had an idea for green containers when thinking about the paper pulp tray from an iPhone and milk bags she used growing up in Montreal. Her design didn't require any unusual materials or new technologies and the containers are less expensive and more efficient. The outer shell is made from paper pulp (which can be recycled or composted) and her bottles use 70 percent less plastic (which is also recyclable). The containers also save shipping costs because the parts are delivered in compact unassembled stacks that reduce space on trucks.[68]

Technology Trends and Political and Regulatory Changes

Technology Trends

Because technology advances create ongoing opportunities,[69] you don't have to be the one to come up with the creation of a new product and industry. In fact, only 10 percent of new firms say they're looking to create their own technology.[70] Self-directed robotic lawn mowers are Europe's fastest-growing garden tool for people who don't like cutting the lawn, see it as a problem, and would rather be doing something else instead. Swedish company **Husqvarna** has been selling them for more than a decade. In 2012, **Deere, Global Products Italy**, and **Robert Bosch** starting selling them and **Honda** joined the competition in 2013.[71]

You can also enhance new technology products. Apple products have hundreds of compatible devices. **H2Audio, now X-1**, produces waterproof, weatherproof, and sweatproof audio solutions for a wider range of athletes, including housings for **Apple** *iPods* and *iPhones*.[72] As you may know, there are hundreds of thousands of apps developed by thousands of entrepreneurs that are sold on **Apple's App Store** and **Google's App Store**. Mobile-apps are a $10 billion business. Twenty-five-year-old Londoner **James Vaughan**, who developed the 99-cent game *Plaque Inc.*, sold it on the Apple App Store, making more than $500,000.[73]

Political and Regulatory Changes

Personal Application

11. Identify a trend that can lead you to a potential opportunity to start an entrepreneurial new venture or as entrepreneurial behavior.

Changes in laws and regulations lead to entrepreneurial opportunities. The *No Child Left Behind Act* put a focus on outcomes and required giving students standardized tests to measure learning competencies. High school teaching entrepreneurs **Kim** and **Jay Kleeman** started a new business venture, **Shakespeare Squared**, which produces materials to help schools comply with the law. Jay continued to teach while Kim was full-time president and CEO.[74] Changes in laws and regulations are creating natural environmental opportunities[75] including clean energy and green-product industry trends.

Solving Problems Creates Opportunities

When others see problems, entrepreneurs see opportunities, so think in terms of finding opportunities through solving problems, such as those identified in trends. Intentionally pursue entrepreneurial opportunities through problem-solving.[76] What complaints do you hear? What recurring problem do you face? Think about better ways to solve problems.

Julia Erickson would race between *Pittsburg Ballet Theater* rehearsals and business classes, eating energy bars and trail mixes. Her problem was that she wanted a nutrient-packed snack with a mix of protein, fiber, and carbohydrates that would provide the stamina she needed to perform, but with fewer processed ingredients and calories. So she made her own snack bar in her food processor. At rehearsal she offered samples to her fellow dancers, who loved the taste and natural ingredients. Several dancers asked her, "Do you sell these?" Seeing an opportunity, she teamed up with **Aaron Ingley** and cofounded **Barre** as a new business venture.[77]

Problem-Solving and Decision-Making

As previously discussed, problem-solving and decision-making go together. Erickson had to make several decisions in order to solve her problem. So let's start with decision-making. Individuals differ in the way they approach decisions. Complete Self-Assessment 3-1 to determine your decision-making style as reflexive, reflective, or consistent before reading on.

Self-Assessment 3-1

What is My Decision-Making Style?

For each of the following eight statements, identify your level of agreement with your behavior on a scale of 1–5. Place the number on the line before the statement.

This behavior is common for me			This behavior is *not* common for me	
1	2	3	4	5

1. _____ Overall, I make decisions quickly.

2. _____ When making decisions, I go with my first thought or hunch.

3. _____ When making decisions, I don't bother to recheck my work.

4. _____ When making decisions, I gather little or no information.

5. _____ When making decisions, I consider very few alternative options.

6. _____ When making decisions, I usually decide well before any deadline.

7. _____ When making decisions, I don't ask others for advice.

8. _____ After making decisions, I don't look for other alternatives or wish I had waited longer.

_____ Total score

To determine your style, add up the numbers you assigned to the statements; the total will be between 8 and 40. Note where you fall on the decision-style continuum:

Reflexive	Consistent	Reflective	
8	20	30	40

Reflexive style—You make quick, often compulsive decisions. In doing so, you may take advantage of opportunities [at great risk?], but without gathering information and analyzing the feasibility of your decisions, you may not be making a good choice.

Reflective style—You are slow to make decisions. You gather lots of information and analyze feasibility, but you may miss the window of opportunity if you move too slowly and cautiously in order to avoid risk.

Consistent style—You make decisions without rushing or wasting time; therefore you make decisions with moderate risk based on analyses of information.

Consistent decision-makers tend to have the best record for making good decisions. They know when they have enough information and alternatives to make a sound decision.[78] If you are too fast or slow, work at being more consistent, especially when evaluating opportunities. Consistent decision-makers tend to follow the problem-solving and decision-making model steps, our next topic.

The Problem-Solving and Decision-Making Model

We have already discussed making improvements to existing products, services, and processes, which is what solving problems is all about. Here is one more example. **Jim Safka** saw a problem in the high cost of college textbooks, so he took the opportunity to help solved this problem by renting books and started **Chegg.com**.[79] *Chegg is open 24/7*, and will buy books from students with a price quote online.[80] **Alain Coumont** opened a restaurant in Brussels, but had a problem getting good bread at a reasonable price. So he made his own and turned it into a new venture bakery, **Le Pain Quotidien**. He took the business internationally to nineteen countries.[81]

Now let's present the steps to problem-solving and decision-making that you can use to make improvements and/or to exploit opportunities in trends, a skill that can be developed.[82] See Exhibit 3-4 for the list of steps in the model and an explanation of each step below. Notice that the steps do not simply progress from start to finish (1–5). At any step, you may have to return to a prior step to make changes. For example, if you are at step 5 and things are not going as planned, you may have to backtrack to prior steps to take corrective action. If you have not defined the problem accurately at any stage, you may have to go back to the beginning.

Step 1. Define the Problem or Opportunity

Start by clearly and accurately stating the problem (when we say problem, we also include an opportunity). An important part of defining the problem is to distinguish symptoms from cause, or focus on getting to the root of the problem.[83] Begin by listing the observable and describable occurrences (symptoms) that indicate a problem exists. Only after doing this can you determine the cause of the problem. If you eliminate the cause, the symptoms should disappear. If not, you haven't defined the problem correctly.

Nick Bayss worked in his family business café in Australia and thought about the danger and liability of coffee and tea. The drink can be so hot that

Exhibit 3-4

The Problem-Solving and Decision-Making Model

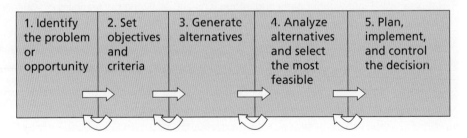

| 1. Identify the problem or opportunity | 2. Set objectives and criteria | 3. Generate alternatives | 4. Analyze alternatives and select the most feasible | 5. Plan, implement, and control the decision |

Model
(1) To + (2) action verb + (3) specific and measurable result + (4) target date
Examples
• (1) To (2) find (3) a new venture opportunity before graduation (4) in May 2015.
• To get an internship in an Italian restaurant during the spring semester 2016.
• To open an Italian restaurant by June 1, 2020.

Exhibit 3-5

The Setting
Objectives Model

it can cause burns. He defined the problem as not knowing when the beverage was too hot to drink rather than selling the drink at a lower temperature.[84]

Step 2. Set an Objective and Criteria

Successful entrepreneurs and managers have a goal orientation,[85] which means they set and achieve goals. Goal orientation can be learned.[86] An objective is an end result. An objective doesn't tell you how it will be achieved—that is the action plan (step 5). You begin to plan with the end result—objective—in mind.[87] Objectives *state what is to be accomplished in specific and measurable terms with a target date.* You can use a model to help you write effective objectives; see Exhibit 3-5 for the model.

Criteria are the standards that an alternative must meet to be selected as the decision that will accomplish the objective. Having multiple criteria helps to optimize the decision. You should distinguish "must" and "want" criteria. "Must" criteria have to be met in order for an alternative to be acceptable, whereas "want" criteria are desirable but not necessary for the alternative to be acceptable.

Nick Bayss came up with two objectives. To develop a method of knowing when a beverage is too hot to drink by December 1998. To open a new business venture that will solve the too hot to drink beverage problem by June 1, 2001. The criterion that must be met was the method must have a price that businesses are willing to pay for, with a profit.

Step 3. Generate Alternatives

Now you come up with several creative ideas on how to solve the problem. It is a good idea to use the creative process and the three techniques for generating creative ideas discussed earlier. Remember the brainstorming rule: no evaluation of alternatives during this step.

Nick Bayss came up with several different ways to know when the beverage is too hot to drink, such as adjusting the temperature in the cup, putting a thermometer on the cup or on the lid, or having the cover change colors to indicate the temperature.

Step 4. Analyze Alternatives and Select the Most Feasible

Now, you go through your alternatives and evaluate each. Be sure to compare alternatives to the objectives and criteria set in Step 2. In addition, compare each alternative to the others. When selecting a particular alternative, you don't always

Personal Application

12. Using the writing objectives model, write three: career objectives, academic objectives, and personal objectives.

select the best one. Why? It may not be feasible because you can't actually do it or it may be too costly. Maybe you can't get the money to buy a **Subway** franchise, but it is feasible to open an independent sub shop, or some other type of franchise. Remember that it's not an opportunity if it isn't profitable.

Nick Bayss analyzed the alternatives and selected the strategy of having the cover change colors to indicate the temperature of the beverage.

Step 5. Plan, Implement, and Control the Decision

This is actually three in one, but they all go together. You need to plan how to solve the problem; then you have to actually make the innovation to solve the problem, such as starting a new venture; and finally you have to control in order to successfully run the business venture.

Nick Bayss didn't have the technical expertise to develop a cup lid that would change color. So his plan was to get the expertise to make the lid. He formed a team of passionate and dedicated entrepreneurs to drive its invention and commercialization. With a little help from research parties in Japan, Switzerland, and the U.S., the Smart Lid was born. If the lid is red, the beverage may be too hot to drink safely. When the lid is a rich-brown it is the perfect drinking temperature. Another safety feature was added to help prevent a possible burn. Your lid is correctly fitted if there is a complete ring around the lid in a darker color and incorrectly fitted if there is a broken ring around the lid. In 2001, **Smart Lid Systems** opened its new venture in Sydney. Today, it continues to be a successful company.[88]

Developing Your Business Model

Based on finding an opportunity to start a new venture, your next step is to develop a business model, which you will test for feasibility in the next chapter. A business model is an unchanging design of business elements and activity characteristics but, as there is no generally accepted definition for business models, definitions vary widely.[89] Trying to keep it relatively easy to understand, we define it as follows: a **business model** *identifies the firm's product and service value, customers, the way it makes a profit, and its operations.* To start with, the business model doesn't have to be overly complex. The first draft of **Herb Kelleher**'s business model that led him to start **Southwest Airlines** was written on the back of a cocktail napkin.[90]

In this section, we have developed a process for answering the four questions for developing a business model for your new venture as an entrepreneur. You can also build a business model for any existing business. You should realize that building a business model is not a linear process. As you answer the four questions, you often need to back track to improve the answers to prior questions. You can also adapt business models from competitors and through benchmarking. **Jim Safka** developed his textbook rental business model for **Chegg.com** from **Netflix**.[91] For an illustration of the process, see Exhibit 3-6, and read on to learn about the parts of each question.

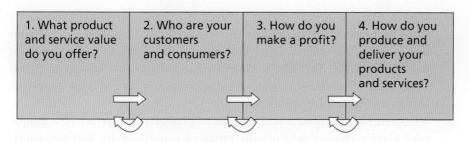

Exhibit 3-6

The Business Model
Questions

What Product and Service Value do You Offer?

Your business model answers this question by stating the products and services you offer, your competitive advantage, your mission statement, and core values and critical success factors.

Products and Services

Without a product and/or service, you don't have a business, or a nonprofit. So product development is critical to entrepreneurial success.[92] Many organizations offer both a product and service. Listing products and services is not always as easy as it sounds. In retailing, you have limited space, especially in a convenience store, so you need to know what your customers want to buy. But within the business model, you can just provide the general list, such as upscale women's apparel. **Barre** uses the slogan "We are the first food product made for dancers, by dancers."[93]

Competitive Advantage—Value

While thinking about opportunities, you need to be developing competitive advantages to exploit the opportunity.[94] A competitive advantage *states why a customer will buy a product or service, rather than from competitors*. It *differentiates* you from the competition in providing *value*—the reason a customer will buy your product or service.[95] Building novelty into products and operations helps develop a competitive advantage.[96] Your advantage identifies your *core competency*, your features and benefits to the customer, your improvement opportunity over competitors, and/or your solution to a customer's problem.

If prospective customers ask you why they should buy your product, rather than XYZ product, what would your answer be? If you don't have a reason, or simply say we are just as good as the competitors, how can you beat the competition and win the sale? Below are six factors that, when combined, are commonly the basis of a competitive advantage.

■ Quality. Is your product or service a higher quality? **John Schnatter** founded **Papa John's** out of the back of his father's tavern at age twenty-two with the motto "Better Ingredients, Better Pizza."[97] Albanian-born **Anthony Athanas** opened his first restaurant, **Anthony's Hawthorne,** and went on to establish five more restaurants with different names, including his world-known **Anthony's Pier 4** restaurant in Boston, which offers upscale food with superior service.[98]

■ **Service.** Do you provide better service? Is it more personal? *Copreneurs* **Doris** and **Don Fisher** started in business with one **Gap** store. Today, Gap Inc. is a leading international specialty retailer with five brands—*Gap, Banana Republic, Old Navy, Piperlime,* and *Athleta.* It has about 3,100 stores with 134,000 employees. Personal customer service is an important part of its competitive advantage.[99]

■ **Selection.** Do you offer a wider range of products or services or a unique one? **Dave's Hockey** sells a wide range of equipment for this one sport. **John Mackey** and **Renee Lawson Hardy** with **Craig Weller** and **Mark Skiles** essentially merged their two natural food stores as founders of **Whole Foods Market** into one store offering natural and organic foods in Texas, which grew as it competed with traditional supermarkets.[100]

■ **Speed or turnaround.** Do you deliver your product or service faster? **Frederick Smith** created the idea for overnight delivery while in college, and started **FedEx** as a small business. Today it delivers to 220 countries and territories with 300,000 employees.[101] Although it dropped its thirty-minute delivery guarantee, **Domino's** still focuses on quick delivery of its pizza.[102]

■ **Time.** Do your products or services save people time? **Zoots** offers home pickup and delivery of dry cleaning, saving customers time going to and from the store.[103] Colonel **Harland Sanders** started **KFC** in one restaurant serving customers delicious, prepared complete family meals at affordable prices, saving customers the time spent cooking and cleaning up. Today there are over 15,000 KFC outlets in 105 countries and territories around the world.[104]

■ **Location.** Is your business more convenient to get to? Most people don't want to travel far to get to services and products. **Andrea Lausier** wanted to be a stay-at-home mom and earn some money. So she started a day care center in her home. Andrea cared for seven children that lived close by, plus her own four kids.[105] Most people shop locally to get their daily and weekly groceries. Online shopping is growing in popularity partly because it saves travel time. You will learn more about location decisions in Chapter 7.

■ **Price.** Is your price less than the competition? **Sam Walton** started **Wal-Mart** as a single store focusing on low prices. Today it employs 2.2 million associates worldwide and serves 200 million customers each week at more than 10,000 stores in twenty-seven countries.[106] However, it is very difficult to compete with Wal-Mart or any large box store on price alone, so most entrepreneurs select other competitive advantages with which to compete. When developing a competitive advantage, you want to try to make it difficult to copy. Why? Because if it is easy to copy, and you become very profitable, the question isn't: "Will competitors come after you?" The question is: "What will you do to keep the competition from stealing your customers?" So most businesses based on competitive advantages have to keep changing to stay one step ahead of the competition.

Personal Application

14. Select a business you want to start, or an existing business, and state its competitive advantage.

A related concept is the *first mover advantage.* If you can be the first to offer a new product or service, you often get name recognition and advantages over time. When you think of a quick oil change, what name comes to mind?

Many people think of **Jiffy Lube**, which started as a small business, because it pioneered the fast oil change industry more than thirty years ago. Today, it is a 100 percent franchise-owned and operated business with more than 250 entrepreneurial individuals and groups serving more than 22 million customers each year in more than 2,000 service centers.[107]

Mission—What Business are You in?

A **mission statement** *reveals an organization's purpose or reason for being*. The statement should be short, concise, and simple with a focus on providing customer value. Here are some mission statements:

- **Google**'s mission is to organize the world's information and make it universally accessible and useful.[108]
- **McDonald's** "brand" mission is to be their customers' favorite place and way to eat.[109]
- **Method**'s mission is to create a better cleaning experience for customers by providing safe, environmentally friendly products in cleverly designed packages, constantly engaging in production innovation, and creating a fun work environment.[110]
- **Toyota**'s mission is to attract and attain customers with high-valued products and services and the most satisfying ownership experience.[111]

A mission statement identifies what business you are in. What business a company is in is not always obvious. What business would you say **Domino's** is in? Many years ago founder **Tom Monaghan** was asked, "What business are you in?" His answer was, "We are in the delivery business, and it just so happens that people want us to deliver pizza."[112] Since then, it has added delivery of wings and then sandwiches. What business would you say **McDonald's** is in? Did you say real estate? We will tell you it is in real estate in the profit part of the business model.

As you may be able to tell, the mission statement integrates parts of the business model. So your mission statement is typically developed after considering the other three questions in developing a business model. In any case, the mission should be written and communicated to all employees repeatedly.[113] Placing the mission statement near major entrances allows everyone who comes to your place of business to know your mission.

Personal Application

15. Without looking at it, write a mission statement for an organization, preferably one for one which you work(ed).

Core Values and Critical Success Factors

What fundamental ethical beliefs and values will drive your new business venture to success? Your values guide you to make *ethical decisions* in all stages of the entrepreneurial process while striving to meet your mission. **Critical success factors** *are the things a firm needs to do well to succeed*. They are often imbedded into the value statement. **McDonald's** value goal is quality, service, cleanliness, and value (QSC&V).[114] **FedEx** values include: people, service, innovation, integrity, responsibility, and loyalty.[115] Both companies believe that, if they live these values, they will be successful.

Personal Application

16. Select a business you want to start, or an existing business, and state its core values and critical success factors.

Who are Your Customers and Consumers?

Your business model answers this question by knowing who your customers and consumers are, by defining your target market, and determining how you will interact with customers to conduct business.

Customers and Consumers are Often Different

It is important to understand the difference between these two terms. Customers *pay for products and services.* Consumers *use the products and services.* So it is important to remember, if someone pays you for your products and services they are your customers. If they use your product or service and don't pay you, they are your consumers. You can have lots of consumers, but without customers you don't have a business. Many dot.com businesses learn this lesson the hard way by going out of business because they can get lots of consumers, but they cannot make a profit because they don't have enough customers.

Who are **Coca-Cola** bottlers' customers and consumers? Coke's customers are primarily the retail stores that buy its soda. Customers buying Coke at retail are the retail store's customers. Coke consumers are anyone who drinks the soda, even though they may not have bought the soda. For example, if you are at your parents' or friend's home and drink a Coke, do you buy it from them? Do you ever get gifts and use products you didn't buy?

Who are **Google**'s customers and consumers? Its customers are primarily the businesses that pay for advertising. If you don't buy anything directly from Google, you are not a customer. If you use its free search engine, you are a consumer. Who are **NBC** TV customers and consumers? The consumers can watch TV for free and its customers are the businesses that advertise.

Who are the customers and consumers of **Jorgan NeuroScience** ER-EER brainwave monitor machines? The hospital administrators who make the purchasing decisions are the customers, and the patients are the consumers. The doctors are neither, but they can help influence the administrators to buy the machine.

Personal Application

17. Select a business you want to start, or an existing business, and state who its customers and consumers are.

Target Market

Who are your potential customers—your target market. *A target market is a segment of the entire customer population that a firm tries to get as customers.* The target is defined by type of customer and common demographics factors such as age, gender, nationality, income, and geography. Here are some questions to answer. Are you selling to other businesses or individuals, or both? What age group is your target? Is your target men, women, and/or children? What nationality are they? Are they of high, medium, or low income, and where do they live?

James Poss founded **Seahorse Power**, a manufacturing company. With the success of its BigBelly solar-powered trash compactors, the name was changed to **BigBelly Solar** with a target market of businesses and cities and municipal governments.[116] **Abercrombie & Fitch** sells higher-priced trendy apparel targeted primarily to males and females in their teens and twenties. *Right Guard* deodorant targets men and *Secret* targets women. Mexican-born copreneurs **Hipolito**

and **Ana Maria Anaya** founded **Mariana's Supermarket** in Las Vegas with a target market of Hispanic (especially Mexican) customers. They now have four stores with 90 percent Hispanic customers.[117]

Customer Interface

How do you deal with customers? Do you sell to them in person in your store, like **Felix Family Restaurant**? Do you sell to them online, like **Amazon.com?** Sales are also made over the phone. **Merrill Lynch** stock transactions and customer service is often conducted through email and phone. Most major retailers like **Wal-Mart** today sell in-store, online, and over the phone. Some businesses will go to your home or business to transact business, like **United Cleaning**.

How Do You Make a Profit?

Again, without profits, you don't have a business. Obviously you want to keep your revenues high and your expenses low to maximize your profits. Here we discuss pricing and revenues, startup cost and expenses, and markups and profit-margins.

Pricing and Revenues

Revenues come primarily from customers; therefore you need to consider the *price* you will charge for your products and services. The price you charge is based on your products and services as well as your target market. Will you sell upscale products at high prices or less expensive goods at lower price points (**Rolex** vs. **Timex** watches)? You will learn the details of pricing in Chapter 6.

Revenues include all the methods of generating income for the business. You must remember that the revenue stream has to be large enough to make a profit. **Facebook** came out with a highly publicized IPO (initial public offering of its stock). However, the price of the stock dropped shortly thereafter. Why? Facebook has grown to more than 1 billion free member consumers,[118] but the customers did not provide adequate revenues to generate profits that satisfied investors. **Google**, on the other hand, has lots of non-paying consumers, and enough paying customers who have provided the company with money to take advantage of multiple opportunities and growth through a variety of new venture revenue streams. Google even has *Startup Lab* to help entrepreneurs launch new ventures including providing venture capital at any stage of development, in return for a share of future revenues, of course.[119]

See Exhibit 3-7 Sources of Revenues, which doesn't include options open to nonprofits that are not available to for-profit businesses. Sources 1–4 are essentially the same, so read them left to right. However, 5–7 are more specific to traditional vs. online sources.

Let's discuss a not-so-obvious stream of revenues. As you likely know, **McDonald's** has revenues from both its company-operated restaurants and from franchisees. Let's, however, look at it being in the real-estate business. Most McDonald's are operated on an independent plot of land. A franchisee, under

Personal Application

18. Select a business you want to start, or an existing business, and state its target market and customer interface.

Exhibit 3-7

Sources of Revenues

Traditional Sources	Online Sources
1. **Sales**. Customer buys product or service in person, can be by phone (**Wal-Mart**).	1. Same but sold online; **e-commerce** (**Amazon.com**).
2. **Subscriptions and memberships**. Customer pays monthly or yearly fee (**Businessweek**, **Gold's Gym**).	2. Same, but online (**eHarmony**, **Angie's List**).
3. **Transaction fees**. Customer pay for services (**Bank of America**, **Visa**).	3. Same, but online (**E-trade**).
4. **Advertising**. Customer pays ad fee to promote products and services (**CNBC TV**).	4. Same, but ad is on the Web or blog (**Google**).
5. **Franchising**. Franchisee (Chapter 3) pays an initial fee and ongoing royalties (**KFC**, **Subway**). There are some online franchisees, but brick and mortar stores are more common.	5. **Pay-per-click**. Web or blog gets paid a small commission every time an ad link is clicked (**Google**).
6. **Licensing**. Licensee (Chapter 3) pays for the use of intellectual property rights. Traditional and online companies are customers (**DuPont**, **DreamWorks**, **Carroll Shelby Licensing**).	6. **Affiliate**, like pay-per-click, but commission is based on actual sales (**1-800-FLOWERS**).
	7. **Freemium**. Web site offers a free basic service and offers customers one or more premium services for a fee[120] (**Dropbox**, **SurveyMonkey**).

the terms of the agreement, is prohibited from owning the land as well as the building, which it must rent from McDonald's. On average, of every dollar that comes into one of its franchisees, 4 cents goes for general franchise fees and 7 cents goes for rent. So McDonald's actually makes more in real estate than franchise fees. Plus, if McDonald's were ever to sell its land that it has owned for ten, twenty, thirty, or more years, the profit would be astronomical.[121]

Peter Clark was on the ground floor working for **Jiffy Lube**, traveling all over the U.S. training franchisees how to run their own business. But Peter decided that he wanted to come home every night to his family and do what he felt he knew he could do well. Peter believed in the business model and liked the idea of being in control of his own destiny. So copreneurs Peter and his wife **Korby Clark** went into partnership with others and eventually became part-owners of nearly fifty Jiffy Lube franchises. Ten years later, **Pennzoil** bought the company and made an offer to buy back franchises. The Clarks and partners sold most of them back and made a nice profit. But the partners also owned some of the real estate and kept ownership of many of the stores and continue to get rent today. Peter and Korby went on to start another new business venture, the upscale **Ranch Golf Club**, with new partners. The Clarks continue to run the business with Peter as the managing partner.[122]

Personal Application

19. Select a business you want to start, or an existing business, and state its pricing and revenue stream.

Startup Costs and Expenses

Most new ventures require some startup costs and, as we discussed earlier, you need to select an opportunity that is feasible so you can get the money to start your business. We will discuss how much startup money you will need in Chapter 10 and where you can find startup money in Chapter 11. Startup costs are commonly one-time costs, whereas expenses are ongoing and commonly paid on a monthly or weekly basis.

Depending on the type of business you start, you will have *key cost drivers*— the higher-level expenses that impact your profits. Here are some examples.

■ Marketing, including advertising. Will the expenses to acquire customers be high (**Nike** spends millions on pro athlete endorsements)? You will learn more about marketing in Chapter 6.

■ Facilities. Will the cost of rent be high (**Italian Hair Salon** located at a shopping mall)? Buying the facility helps keep costs down and builds equity over the years. You will learn more about location and layout in Chapter 7.

■ Inventory. Will products for resale (**Sports Authority**) or raw materials (**Kellogg** cereal) for production be high? You will learn more about inventory in Chapter 8.

■ Operations. Will the cost of producing the products or services be high (**WMECO Power Co.**)? You will learn more about operations in Chapter 8.

■ Employees. Will payroll be high (**Boston Consulting Group**)? You will learn more about human resources in Chapter 9.

Personal Application

20. Select a business you want to start, or an existing business, and state its key cost drivers.

Markups

Your *markup* is how much you charge your customer over your cost. If you make or buy a computer for $300 and sell it for $400, your markup is $100. As a percentage (100/400), you have a 25 percent markup. Markups will vary with the type of products and services and the volume of sales. Most items have different costs, so it is common to just have a general business markup, such as 50 percent. You may be thinking that 50 percent sounds very profitable, but don't forget, your markup needs to be high enough to cover your expenses just to ensure that your company will break even. In early 2012, **McDonald's** was worried about its markup, so it raised prices by an average of 3 percent, and it tried to push its higher markup-priced drinks over lower-priced soda.[123] You will learn more about markups as part of pricing strategies in Chapter 6.

Personal Application

21. Select a business you want to start, or an existing business, and state its markup.

How Do You Produce and Deliver Your Products and Services?

You answer this question by identifying operations and strategic assets, partners that can help you, your distribution method, and the way you will manage the supply chain.

Operations and Strategic Assets

Operations is the term used to describe how you create your products and services, and deliver them, which you will learn more about in Chapter 9. Your strategic assets, what you own, are an important part of operations. They include anything of value that contributes to your competitive advantage, such as employees, facilities (plant and equipment), location, patents, trade-marks, brand recognition, customer data, and partnerships. How you bundle your resources is a source of competitive advantage.[124] Teaming up your competitive advantage with your strategic assets builds a sustainable competitive advantage. *A* sustainable competitive advantage *is unique and not easy to copy.*

Partners and Distribution

Personal Application

22. Select a business you want to start, or an existing business, and state its partners and method of distribution.

Most new ventures don't have the resources to perform all the tasks between making and delivering their products and services, so they have partners. Plus, doing the things that you have a *core competency* for, and letting others do the other tasks (*outsourcing*), makes for a better business model. **Dell** has a core competency in "assembling" computers. It doesn't actually manufacture anything. Dell buys the parts from *suppliers* (also called *vendors*) and assembles the computers and then uses **UPS** or **FedEx** to deliver them. **Nike** also doesn't make anything; it has all of its shoes and other products manufactured by other businesses.

Supply Chain Management

Personal Application

23. Select a business you want to start, or an existing business, and state where it is in the supply chain.

Most services go directly from the business to the customer, but most products are delivered through a channel or chain of intermediaries. *The* supply chain *is the network of all the businesses that participate in the process of producing and delivering a product to the customer.* It is also called the *value chain.* See Exhibit 3-8 for the supply chain. *Supply chain management* is the process of coordinating the flow of information, materials, and products, and the money through the supply chain. **UPS** helps large and small businesses manage their supply chain more sustainably.[125]

Where is the business in the supply chain? **Land O'Lakes** is a farm cooperative with 3,200 direct producer-members who make the butter and other products that it sells to wholesalers and retailers.[126] Chinese **FoxConn Technology Group** makes many of Apple's iProducts, and **Apple** sells some of its products through its Apple Stores. This is a relatively new way for Apple to help manage its supply chain, while exploiting the opportunity of making more profits per item. **Costco** is a wholesaler that sells to retailers and customers,

Exhibit 3-8

The Supply Chain

Raw materials	Manufactures	Wholesalers	Retailers	Customers/consumers
(make or grow—metals, farms) →	(make parts and finished goods) →	(bundle and sell goods) →	(bundle and sell goods) →	(buy and use goods) →

but it also has manufacturers make products for it under its *Kirkland* brand name. **Papa John's** is primarily a retailer. But at the corporate franchise level, it buys tomatoes, cheese, and other ingredients as raw materials and processes them, with the final product being manufactured processed foods, which it has UPS deliver to its retail stores. Papa John's stores make the pizza to order, and employees deliver it to the customer, and the consumers eat it.

Elevator Pitching Your Business Model

The complex business model you just learned about should be condensed down into a clear, concise business pitch commonly called the elevator pitch, and your pitch should tell your story.

The Elevator Pitch

The elevator pitch *is an entrepreneur's one-minute explanation of the business model, and is directed at anyone who might want to provide funding for the startup.* It is called an elevator pitch because it is sometimes heard in an elevator.[127] One of the most important entrepreneurial behaviors is getting funding to start the new venture, and, without a good pitch, you will not get funding.[128]

Research based on the elevator pitches made on TV shows **Dragons' Den** and **Shark Tank** found that the better prepared the pitch, the greater the chances of getting funding.[129] The pitch needs to be a concise presentation of a product, service, or idea covering all critical aspects of your business model. The pitch is delivered within sixty to ninety seconds, which is the approximate duration of an elevator ride. As this chapter explains, having a well-prepared, thought out, and unique business model helps to make the pitch unique and the product more interesting for investors to want to buy into your business model.[130]

What's Your Story?

Founder of **TOMS** shoes **Blake Mycoskie** suggests that you put your business pitch into a story, for the following reasons.[131] Stories used in giving a business pitch are a simple form of communications. Stories capture our ideas, we enjoy them, learn from them, and we pass them on to others. We use stories as roadmaps to understand or make sense of things. Giving facts and figures is important, but they are not as powerful as a well-told story, as stories resonate more than just facts. A well-told story of your pitch can evoke emotions and break down barriers and open doors for you.

Your story tells who you are and why you have a passion for your business model, including its mission and competitive advantage. TOMS is as much a story as it is a product. When asked about their shoes, customers tell the TOMS story. Here is the TOMS story in a sales pitch. Hi, I'm Blake Mycoskie. When visiting Argentina, I saw the poverty of children with no shoes and wanted to help them prevent sores and infections on their feet. So I came up with this business model. With every pair of shoes purchased, TOMS will give a new pair of shoes to a child in need. One for One. To make the story an elevator pitch you would add factual information about the profitability of the new venture, which we don't have for his startup.

Blake suggests telling your pitch as a story to everyone who will listen. He intentionally would wear two different color shoes from two different pairs in public just to get people to ask about his shoes so that he could tell his sales pitch story. He used multiple social media sites to tell his story. He does warn you, however, to manage your online story carefully, as you don't want negative publicity. He also was able to get free publicity in newspapers and magazines and other businesses that told his story.

The Elevator Pitch

This skill-builder puts you in the venture capitalist position. You will watch an elevator pitch from the Internet and assess and discuss if the parties would or wouldn't invest in the new venture. The link for the elevator pitch for Kasper Hulthin, CEO of Podio, can be found at www.youtube.com/watch?NR=1&v=UBNJh2rOOIl&feature=endscreen:

Think about it.

1. What score do you give Kasper's pitch?

Great product idea and pitch		Terrible product idea and pitch
3	2	1

2. Would you invest in Kasper's business?
3. Was the pitch a good story? How would you improve Kasper Hulthin's pitch?

Other Options for Starting a New Venture, and Entrepreneurial Behavior

In Chapters 3–12 we describe some of the differences between starting a new business (the primary focus of this book) and the other five options for creating a new venture. We also discuss engaging in entrepreneurial behavior for those who want to be entrepreneurial without starting a new venture.

Buying an Existing Business, Franchise, or Leasing Rights

Buying an Existing Business

When you become an entrepreneur through an acquisition, the opportunity has already been exploited for you. With your existing business, you can be creative and make major changes to the business model based on your growing knowledge and experience, networks, being alert, making improvements and solving problems, and being persistent. You can also look for industry, social and sustainability, and technology trends, as well as changes in laws and regulations.

Buying a Franchise

When you buy a product and trade-name franchise or trade-name-only franchise, you can be creative in how you develop your business model and run your business. However, with business-format franchising you are not expected to be creative, but simply to implement the franchisor's business model and systems of operation.

Buying Licensing Rights

When you buy intellectual property rights, the license holder has usually exploited an opportunity by developing a technology, merchandise, or character you want to use. But you are typically on your own as to how you develop your business model and run your business. So you are in essence partnering with a company that has an opportunity you want to share with them.

Starting a Corporate or Nonprofit New Venture

Starting a Corporate Venture

A corporate entrepreneur is usually the individual who has been creative and recognized the opportunity for an employer through entrepreneurial characteristics, trends, or by solving problems for the employer's customer. To exploit the opportunity, you need to develop a business model and get management support to let you start the new venture. Networking within and outside your company can help you develop a sound business model, so get out there and refine your elevator pitch.

Starting a Nonprofit

While the profit motive drives most entrepreneurial activities, you may feel strongly that you want to provide a service that will provide a benefit for the public good. You may want to help those in need, people who lack skills necessary to survive in today's world or even something as obvious as providing access to clean drinking water in an undeveloped country. The needs are numerous. Like starting a for-profit business, you have to be creative and recognize an opportunity. You then find support to exploit the opportunity through a new venture. Your business model should be shaped by your entrepreneurial characteristics, trends, and your ability to solve problems creatively.

You may, like an entrepreneur who uses the franchise model, use an existing nonprofit organization as your base. A group of individuals in Wabash, IN wanted to establish a place where families could go to swim, exercise, take classes, and have activities for all age groups. Instead of starting from the beginning, the group decided to establish a YMCA in the city. They contacted the national YMCA and applied for a charter in 2001. By 2009, the Y was built, providing care and support to approximately one-third of the population.[132]

A possible major difference in your business model, versus a for-profit, is your pricing and revenues. Depending on your target market, you may or may not be able to charge your customers a price that will cover your costs and make a profit. Thus, you need to have multiple streams of revenues from other sources to survive. Will you seek government, foundation, and/or corporate funding and/or grants? Will you seek corporate and/or individual donations? Will you have fundraising events? Will you have memberships, sales, or fees? Does your plan include an endowment campaign? Will you have any investment revenues?

Another difference that affects expenses may be the use of volunteers. Your business model may include the ratio or percentage of paid employees to staff if it is relevant to your cost structure. Putting your business model revenues and expenses together, you need to clearly answer the question of how you make a profit if you want to start a new venture.

Entrepreneurial Behavior

Don't forget that if you are not interested in starting a new venture, as an employee you can engage in *entrepreneurial behavior* that can lead to a new venture or the improvement of your current employer's performance. Entrepreneurial behavior is often rewarded. Use and develop your creative skills for entering a new market with your existing products and services, such as going international. Work on recognizing opportunities for offering new products and services that complement your current offerings.

Be creative in coming up with improved processes for doing business. Is there a better way to do your current or past job, or that of others? You can suggest the use of, and volunteer to be part of, brainstorming and focus groups. You can conduct library and Internet research for your firm to generate creative ideas to improve performance through benchmarking best practices of other companies. Your creativity can possibly lead to new business ventures.

Chapter Review and Summary

As we bring this chapter to a close, you should understand what creativity and opportunity are, the five steps in the creative process, and three techniques for generating creative ideas. You should be able to: use your entrepreneurial characteristics for recognizing and exploiting opportunities and recognizing opportunities in trends and solving problems. You should also be able to develop a business model by answering four questions and finally to present the business model in an elevator pitch. Last, you should understand some of the differences in opportunities and business models based on the five other options for becoming an entrepreneur, and how to engage in entrepreneurial behavior.

This summary lists the learning outcomes from the chapter and their answers.

1. **Define creativity, innovation, opportunity, problem-solving, and decision-making and explain their interrelationships**

   Creativity is the ability to originate new and better ways of doing things. *Innovation* is the implementation of creative ideas. An *opportunity* is a set of circumstances that enables the innovation of creative new products and services, processes, or business ventures profitably. *Problem-solving* is overcoming obstacles and identifying and exploiting opportunities. *Decision-making* is the process of selecting a course of action that will overcome an obstacle or exploit an opportunity. Creativity is used for solving problems and recognizing opportunities and a decision can be made whether to innovate new products and services, processes, and new ventures.

2. **Briefly explain the steps in the creative process**

   The steps in the creative process include: (1) Investigation, or exploring the opportunity. (2) Incubation, taking a break and letting the subconscious work on the opportunity. (3) Illumination, recognizing the point when one gets the creative idea to exploit the opportunity. (4) Evaluation, making sure the idea is in fact a profitable opportunity and finalizing it. (5) Innovation, implementing the new venture idea.

3. **Briefly explain three techniques for generating creative ideas for new ventures**

   The three techniques for generating creative ideas include: (1) Brainstorming, the process of generating creative ideas to solve problems and exploit opportunities, without criticism. (2) Focus group, to pose a question and listen to the discussion by people who are selected based on their relationship with the problem or opportunity. (3) Library and Internet research, the activities included in and using sources recommended by a reference librarian, including databases, and using search engines to find ideas online.

4. **Describe characteristics of entrepreneurs that aid them in recognizing and exploiting opportunities**

   The five characteristics of entrepreneurs are as follows. (1) Their knowledge and industry experience provides a basis for recognizing opportunities. (2) Their networking skills provide help going through the entrepreneurial process and gaining access to resources necessary for founding a new venture. (3) Their alertness to actively finding opportunities while use of the creative process leads to opportunity recognition. (4) Their search to improve current products, services, and process leads to new venture opportunities. (5) Their persistence to overcome obstacles using their problem-solving skills leads to exploiting opportunities

5. List the steps in the problem-solving and decision-making model

The five steps of the problem-solving and decision-making model are: (1) Identify the problem or opportunity. (2) Set objectives and criteria. (3) Generate alternatives. (4) Analyze alternatives and select the most feasible. (5) Plan, implement, and control the decision.

6. List the parts of the writing objective model

The parts of the writing objective model are: (1) To + (2) action verb + (3) specific and measurable result + (4) target date.

7. Identify the four questions that are answered through developing a business model

The four questions answered are. (1) What product and service value do you offer?

(2) Who are your customers and consumers? (3) How do you make a profit? (4) How do you produce and deliver your products and services?

8. Define the twenty key terms identified in this chapter

benchmarking	innovation
brainstorming	mission statement
business model	objectives
competitive advantage	opportunity
	problem-solving
consumers	supply chain
creativity	sustainability
critical success factors	entrepreneurs
	sustainable competitive advantage
customers	
decision-making	target market
elevator pitch	
focus group	

Review and Discussion Questions

Be sure to explain all your answers.

1. Why does the average success rate of innovative efforts tend to be much lower than desirable?

2. What did Peter Drucker mean when he coined the term "systematic practice of innovation"?

3. What is the difference between discovery and creation theory?

4. What entrepreneurial lessons did we learn from Jeff Bezos and Steve Jobs?

5. Can people be trained to think more creatively?

6. Why is it important for entrepreneurs to be constantly asking if we can do things better?

7. Why is the illumination moment an important step in creating your own business?

8. Why is brainstorming an important part of the initial stages of developing a new business?

9. How would you organize a focus group to determine which one of two alternatives is a better choice to start a business?

10. Do you have any ideas on how to improve a cell phone?

11. How would a new women's clothing store use benchmarking when trying to enter a shopping mall that has a large number of women's clothing stores?

12. How can an entrepreneur have an increase in business during a recession?

13. What social trends does TOMS shoes focus on to increase their sales while also being a social entrepreneur?

14. Why do problem-solving and decision-making go together?

15. Why is building a business not a linear process?

16. Assume you are starting a new drive-through telephone service. Combine two or more of the six factors that are commonly the basis of developing a competitive advantage to support the new drive-through service.

17. Use the Internet to research if Toyota has lived up to its mission to attract and attain customers with high-valued products and services and the most satisfying ownership experience.

18. Can a company's target market change?

19. What are the key cost drivers for a new local yogurt shop?

20. Why does Apple often have problems with their supply chain manufacturer FoxConn Technology Group?

Application Exercises

Each chapter has a series of exercises requiring you to apply the specific text concepts. When doing these exercises, be sure to select a specific business where applicable. You can select a business where you worked or a business you would like to own someday. Answers for each exercise should be approximately one page.

1. Answer the questions posed in this article from entrepreneurship.com about writing a mission statement: www.entrepreneur.com/article/65230.

2. Select an industry (http://biz.yahoo.com/p/720 conameu.html) of entrepreneurial interest to you and conduct an Internet search to find trends in the industry that could lead to a new venture or entrepreneurial behavior.

3. Use this link (www.forbes.com/sites/meghancasserly/2012/02/06/11-hottest-industries-for-start-ups-food-trucks-wineries-booze/) at *Forbes Magazine* that lists the eleven hottest industries for startup businesses. Explain why three of the industries appeal to you.

Application Situations

1. Jay C. Kuro

While on coffee break, Jay C. Kuro confided to his best friend, Phil Lee, that his present low-level stock clerk job was boring and unsatisfying. After all, he did graduate from college and had several graduate courses under his belt. "All I seem to do is work hard and never get anywhere. Either there aren't any jobs out there or I just don't qualify for those that there are. There must be a way that I can enjoy what I am doing and be rewarded for doing it. What would you think if I went into the ice cream business? Everyone seems to like ice cream." Phil's response was that Jay better have a business model or he could lose a fortune. He continued, "Think and plan ahead before start anything."

1. Was Phil right?

2. What is a business model?

3. What are the questions to be answered by such a model?

4. Give a brief explanation of the above questions.

2. Laura Mullins—Part One

Although she has just graduated from a highly respected university with a graduate degree in social work, Laura Mullins, daughter of an upper middle-class family, has decided that she would like to start and run a small business. An undergraduate major in Women's Studies, during her college years she founded and was the president of the Women's Council and was a driving force in the National Organization of Women. Do you think that Laura has the qualifications to be an entrepreneur? Explain your reasoning.

1. What are the characteristics needed by an individual be an entrepreneur?

2. Which of the above characteristics does Laura have?

3. Considering the state of the economy and any other information in the chapter, list the sectors most likely to grow and state why this is so.

4. Where should Laura concentrate her energy? Why?

3. Laura Mullins—Part Two

As Laura is comfortable with her educational choices and preparation for a career:

1. Should she set up her business as a profit or non-profit organization?

2. List the pros and cons of each of the organizational structures that influenced her decision.

3. Do you think she will be able to succeed in this endeavor?

Case

Pitapal

Pitapal was started because Melissa Navon had a problem. Her husband was downsized from his corporate job and thus her sense of a stable family income was shattered. After considering a few alternatives to start her own business, she decided on purchasing a factory and produced falafel. Falafel is a deep-fried ball or patty made from ground chickpeas, fava beans, or both. However, her love of falafel did not sell well in Houston, Texas. She made enough money to pay her employees—but not to pay herself.

In an effort to save her business, she decided to change her business model. Melissa decided to expand the product line and added hummus. Hummus is a dip or spread whose main ingredient is garbanzo beans.

Melissa then went to Costco in her area and found out the two hummus brands it carried were made by East Coast companies. She felt her Southwest roots would give her a competitive advantage in her local Costco stores. She made a pitch (in an office and not in an elevator) to the local Costco buyers and her idea was accepted. Costco wanted to use her local hummus brand.[133]

Melissa was able to hire a food broker and her food items are delivered in pallets to Costco warehouses around the country. As the business grew, Pitapal (www.pitapal.com) has further expanded its product line to offer items such as salsa and organic products. It has moved into a 93,000 square-foot facility and was named the seventh fastest-growing company in Houston.

Think it over.

1. Did Melissa use the creative process of illumination?

2. Which of the three techniques for generating creative ideas for new ventures do you think Melissa used to start her business?

3. How effectively did Melissa use the five steps of the problem-solving and decision-making model?

4. Analyze Pitapal's business model based upon the criteria presented in the chapter.

Global Case—Paris, France: Clemence Wurtz, CEO SmartRent

The key to success for an early-stage startup business is to develop a business model that is unique enough to attract customers to buy your product or service. It seems like it would be easy to develop a unique business model, but it really isn't as easy as it looks.

At Startup Weekend in Paris, Clemence Wurtz was able to beat the other thirty-three competitors with her business model, which she called SmartRent. Startup Weekend is a competition set up to help startup companies to learn about starting successful ventures.

Clemence has an idea her business model would work—but she decided to try it out in her small home town, Troyes, France, before heading to her real target market of Paris. Like all good business models, she developed her idea because she had a problem with renting furnished apartments at high rates. The other part of the problem was buying and assembling furniture for unfinished apartments. She found it costly and a lot of effort packing and repacking every time a person moved to a new apartment.

So, a 22-year-old female entrepreneur from France developed a business model that would supply different packages of furniture and apartment fixtures for a low monthly price. SmartRent will deliver and pick up the furniture as necessary for the apartment renter.

Clemence and her female business partner continue to develop the business model. They have secured a furniture manufacturer to supply them specific items for each package. They continue to tweak the furniture packages that will fit certain-size apartments. They like to think their female-oriented skills of collaboration will help them to succeed in Paris and other European markets they hope to enter in the next few years.[134]

However, Clemence has found that most people in France, even the younger people, think she is crazy to be an entrepreneur. Most people in France take the more traditional route of going to university and working for large organizations. Clemence Wurtz and her business model of SmartRent might help more young people to want to be entrepreneurs.[135]

Think it over.

1. Did Clemence use the creative process of illumination?

2. Analyze SmartRent's business model based upon the criteria presented in the chapter.

Preparing for Your Business Plan

You (or in teams) can write a business plan during the semester. There are questions at the end of each chapter to help guide you through the thinking and analyzing process. Appendix B has a sample business plan for 21st Century Technology Training Centers that you can use as a template for developing your own new venture business plan.

Since this is Chapter 3, we will help you to find new business opportunities and to refine your three selections. If you don't have a business to start in mind, then you need to brainstorm, hold a focus group, or do some Internet research to uncover some popular new business ideas. You need to answer the four business model questions to help keep yourself organized through the rest of the semester in terms of writing your business plan.

1. What product and service value do you offer?

2. Who are your customers and consumers?

3. How do you make a profit?

4. How do you produce and deliver your products and services?

Chapter 4

How do You Assess the Chances of Venture Success?

Feasibility Analysis and Protecting the Business Model Legally

We begin by defining feasibility analysis and then discuss how to analyze each of the four parts of the business model (products or services, target customers, profits, and operations), followed by a self-assessment of your business model. The second major topic teaches you how to protect your business model legally with contracts, trade secrets, trademarks, copyrights, and patents. We end with a discussion of comparing entrepreneurial opportunity in starting your own new business with using the other five options to starting a new business venture.

Learning Outcomes

After completing this chapter you should be able to:

1. Describe the relationship between feasibility analysis and research, and the types of research;

2. Identify the parts of the feasibility analysis process;

3. Explain the customer purchasing decision process;

4. Discuss two methods for determining the feasibility of the demand for a product or service;

5. Describe what the North American Industry Classification System (NAICS) codes are, how to find them, and how they are used in feasibility analysis;

6. Explain the important parts of a profit feasibility analysis for a new business venture;

7. Discuss legal methods that can be used to protect the ideas in a business model;

8. Define the fifteen key terms identified in this chapter.

Entrepreneur Profile—Steven Weinstein, MovieLabs

Go to PBS Small Business School at www.small businessschool.org/. In this chapter we use two videos from the PBS library to learn more about intellectual property. The following link provides some ideas on how to define intellectual property: www.smallbusinessschool.org/video.cfm?clip= 1239#. This second link provides examples on how to use technology to protect your intellectual property: http://smallbusinessschool.org/video. cfm?clip=1240.

    Most small-business owners don't think about the value of their brand, their logo, their customer list, or even their unique products and services. According to Steve Weinstein, CEO of MovieLabs, intellectual property is either copyrighted material or works of art that people determine that they own and they want to license or permit people to use it under certain conditions.

    Mark Litvack and Michael Novak view intellectual property as the driving force of this country. Businesses and industry are based on patents, on discoveries. That's a source of wealth. Intellectual

property can be shared (such as music and movies) with the world and, as such, needs to be protected. Protection starts by filing your inventions and ideas with the U.S. Patent and Trademark Office. This is easier than it used to be because of the Internet.

    To protect intellectual property, encryption can be used to discourage customers who own a legitimate copy of a DVD. You can post a copyright notice on your Web site and tell customers how to seek permission to make copies of articles. Artwork on a Web site can be shown at a low resolution. This allows customers to select what they want to print, but keeps those same customers from using the artwork for commercial purposes.

Think it over.

1. Why is intellectual property a source of wealth?
2. What other ideas are presented in the videos on how to use technology to defend intellectual property?

Feasibility Analysis

In the last chapter, you learned how to develop a business model by answering four questions. So we hope you have one ready to analyze for a new or existing business in this chapter. However, you should realize that it often takes a year or more to develop and test a business model. In this section, we discuss the role of feasibility analysis within the entrepreneurial process, the importance of feasibility analysis, and the types of research used to test your business model. In the next four sections, you will be answering questions to determine if you do in fact have a plausible feasible opportunity. So we focus on the important question, "How do entrepreneurs evaluate business opportunities?"[1]

The Role of Feasibility Analysis Within the Entrepreneurial Process

Let's get back to the *Entrepreneurial Process Model* (Chapter 1) and see where we are now and where we are going in Exhibit 4-1. Through this process, you search for opportunities and evaluate them.[2] As you test the business model, you revise and improve it,[3] and you often need to continually change the business model over time to keep up with the latest trends.[4] If it fails the test, you either give up becoming an entrepreneur, or go back, develop, and test other business models until you find one that does pass—this is what we called persistence back in Chapter 3. Note that you develop and test a business model, and if it passes the feasibility analysis (Part I of the book) you proceed to developing the business plan (Part II of the book). This entrepreneurial process helps you avoid failing.[5]

Exhibit 4-1

Entrepreneurial Process Model

1 Selecting the New Venture (Chapters 1–4)	2 Planning the New Venture (Chapters 5–10)	3 Financing and Controlling the New Venture (Chapters 11–12)
Decision to be an entrepreneur or engage in entrepreneurial behavior (Chapter 1) ↓ Select an option to become an entrepreneur (Chapter 2) ↓ Develop a business model (Chapter 3) ↓ Test the feasibility of your business model (Chapter 4) ↕ ⎡*Fails—Stop⎤ ↔ Passes—Proceed→	Develop an effective business plan →	Get funding, start the business venture, and run the business successfully

*You can go back to develop and test other business models

The Importance of Feasibility Analysis

Learning Outcome

1. Describe the relationship between feasibility analysis and research, and the types of research.

Let's begin by defining feasibility analysis. Feasibility analysis *is the process of testing a business model to determine the viability of a business opportunity.*[6] It is used to evaluate opportunities before exploiting them.[7] The ability to conduct a feasibility analysis is unquestionably one of the most important entrepreneurial skills you can develop.[8]

Why Should You Conduct a Feasibility Analysis?

Feasibility analysis is a tool that you can use to assess and reduce the risk at startup.[9] One major reason that so many business ventures fail is because entrepreneurs tend to be doers: they rush into starting the new venture without a good feasibility analysis. You should realize that most poor business models can't be fixed after the startup. The purpose of feasibility analysis is to pursue good business models and abandon bad ones.[10] Therefore, it is important for you to conduct a good feasibility analysis in order to perfect your business model, improve your odds of being successful, or realize it is not a profitable opportunity and save yourself a lot of time, effort, and resources following a poor business model. So remember, the better the business model, the greater the odds of having a successful new business venture. The only way to be sure you have a good business model is to test it.

What Happens to a New Venture with a Poor Business Model?

Ever hear of an **eBay** drop-off store? **iSold It** and **QuickDrop** sold franchises to more than 7,000 entrepreneurs with the thought that it would be feasible to get people to drop off their unwanted items and the entrepreneur then to sell them for a 40 percent commission. Is this a good elevator pitch?

Skeptics were right. An after-the-fact feasibility analysis done by talking to prior store owners (testing the four parts of the business model) revealed that products were too diverse for the owner to be a specialist in marketing them, which meant the customer target market was too wide. Thus, few repeat customers. Businesses failed due to several things: the high startup cost of buying a franchise ($100,000–$150,000); the cost of processing an item was the same for a $20 baseball card as a $15,000 boat (people with high-end items didn't want to pay/lose the 40 percent markup, but the low-priced, not-profitable items were popular, creating a low total markup that was not high enough to make a profit); operations costs were high (paying ongoing franchise fees); and shipping items was time consuming and costly. QuickDrop went out of business.[11] i-soldit.com now has fewer than fifty stores, and has expanded the revenue stream to increase profitability.[12]

The Feasibility Analysis Process

Learning Outcome

2. Identify the parts of the feasibility analysis process.

There are four key parts to a feasibility analysis. See Exhibit 4-2 for an illustration. Each of these parts is explained in the following four sections of this chapter. However, it is not clearly a simple "do only one step at a time" process, because you often test the feasibility of more than one part at the same time. In fact, in the sixth section, we put the four parts together in Self-Assessment 4-2 to test the overall feasibility of your business model.

Exhibit 4-2

Feasibility Analysis
Process

Product and Service Feasibility	Industry and Target Market Feasibility	Operations Feasibility	Profit Feasibility
↓↓	↓↓	↓↓	↓↓
*Fails| Passes—	*Fails| Passes—	*Fails| Passes—	*Fails| Passes—
—Stop| Proceed→	—Stop| Proceed→	—Stop| Proceed→	—Stop| Proceed→
			to business plan

*You can revise or go back to develop and test other business models.

Feasibility Analysis is Based on Research

Personal Application

1. Give examples of primary and secondary research you have collected.

There are two major classifications of research: primary and secondary. Primary research *is the process of collecting original data by the entrepreneur.* It is common to talk to industry experts and target market customers, to possibly use a questionnaire, and to use focus groups. Secondary research *is the process of finding data already collected by others.* You use the library and Internet data to test for feasibility. Both types of research are used by entrepreneurs to test the feasibility of a business model in order to decrease the chances of business failure,[13] because conducting research does lead to increased performance.[14]

Primary Research

A common approach to getting data is to use survey research. Get out there and ask people what they think about your products and services. A second approach is through observation, and you can do both with a focus group.

- Survey research *involves developing a questionnaire and collecting answers through interviews or mail.* Interviews can be conducted in person or by telephone, and mail can be through snail mail or email. When you interview a person face-to-face, you can also observe their nonverbal reactions to the questions to give you additional data.
- Observation research *involves determining what to look for and collecting data by watching.* You develop some type of form to record what you see, such as the expression on children's faces and how they play with a new toy you want to sell, or adults as they try your product.
- *Focus groups* (Chapter 3). You can hold a focus group to ask them about your products and services using a combination of survey and observation.

Secondary Research

Recall from Chapter 3 that you can conduct library and Internet research. Researching your target market will give you an understanding of the needs and wants of your consumers or customers. Competitor analysis, which you need to understand your competition, holds a central place in entrepreneurship,[15] and is available online.[16] However, you need to be objective when analyzing data and not emotionally over-optimistic about your business model. Emotions can shape evaluations because they influence how you process information.[17] See Exhibit 4-3 for a list of sources that can help you conduct research.[18] SizeUp (by the **Small Business Administration, SBA**) is highly recommended.[19]

Exhibit 4-3

Feasibility Analysis
Tools

Source	Tools	Cost
SCORE (www.score.org)	Provides mentors, business counseling, workshops, and the Web site provides template and tool links, including a "Feasibility of Your Idea."	Free, but can be a small fee for some workshops.
SizeUp—Small Business Administration (www.sba.gov/sizeup)	Will help you benchmark your business against competitors, mapping your customers, competitors, and suppliers, and locating the best places to advertise. You can create custom demographic reports.	Free.
Market Research (www.marketresearch.com)	Provides thousands of market research reports.	Costs vary based on the report. You can talk to a specialist to help you find the report that best meets your needs.
NextMark (http://lists.nextmark.com)	Gives mailing list providers. You can compare postal mail, email, and telephone lists you can rent from 60,000 firms.	Costs vary with the list; usually the price goes up with the size of the list.
Pick-fu (www.pickfu.com) SurveyMonkey (www.surveymonkey.com) SurveyGizmo (www.gurveygizmo.com)	Will help you develop a survey, collect data, and analyze results.	Varies based on level of service provided (some use freemium model).
Quirky (www.quirky.com) Conceptshare (www.conceptshare.com)	Get feedback data on product ideas and designs.	Free to cost based on level of feedback.
Quora (www.quora.com) Linkedin Answers (www.linkedin.com/answers) Facebook (www.facebook.com) Twitter (www.twitter.com) Yahoo! Answers (www.answers.yahoo.com) Grabstats.com (Grabstats.com)	Allows you to ask questions and get answers. Although you will not get answers from your target customers, www.ask.com and www.wikipedia.org also give answers to questions. Grabstats.com also gives you statistics on most industries.	Most are free.

Source	Tools	Cost
Trade associations Chamber of Commerce (www.chamberofcommerce.com) Rotary International (www.rotary.org)	Do an online search using the industry name and the word "association." Also, your local Chamber and Rotary club will have useful information.	Some of the information will be free. Other sources require membership to get information and costs vary.
Google AdWords (www.google.com/AdWords)	You place ads online and can sell your product or service to gauge the demand for your product.	Cost based on how many people click your ad.
UserTesting (www.usertesting.com) Loop11 (www.loop11.com) OpenHallway (www.openhallway.com)	Get feedback on the usability of your web site or application to improve it.	Costs based on type of testing and feedback provided. You may be able to get feedback from a college or university at low or no cost.
Library	Your reference librarian can help you find useful information.	Usually free.
U.S. Census Bureau/ Statistical Abstract (www.census.gov)	Under data, American Factfinder link allows you to search and collect important demographic data (such as income and education levels to age and home value) for every county and most cities and towns in the U.S.	Free from the Web site.

Ethics

Personal Application

2. Have you ever used any of the tools listed in Exhibit 4-3? If so, which ones? Which feasibility analysis tools will help you to determine if a specific product or service (pick one) is feasible?

So far, we have discussed research as a method of collecting data to determine the feasibility of your business model. As you collect data about and from competitors and potential customers, you need to be honest. Be ethical by telling the truth in stating who you are and why you are collecting data that is not readily available to the general public.[20]

Are Your Products and Services Feasible?

Back in Chapter 3, you developed your business model by identifying the products and services you plan to offer, along with your competitive advantage, mission, core values, and critical success factors. Products and services are the heart of a business venture; it can't survive without them, but keep it simple.[21] Be product and service focused.[22] Now, you need to conduct research to find out if your products and services are desired by customers, and, more importantly, how many people will actually pay for them (demand).

The ways in which you came up with opportunities are also methods of testing feasibility. Let's begin this section with a discussion of how customers make the decision to buy a product or service, and then discover methods to find out if customers will buy your product or service.

Customer Buying Decisions

To test for feasibility, it is important to understand the three-step process customers go through to make the decision to purchase products and services.

Needs, Wants, and Demand

A need is a lack of something. We *need* products and services that will solve a problem we have or make things easier for us in some way. We *want* products and services to meet our need. I'm hungry and I *need* to eat, and I *want* a pizza. We all have a need to eat, but we have competing products and services that will meet a need. We are targeted by our preference of what we want to eat at any given time (Italian, Mexican, Chinese, etc.). Do your product and services really have a *competitive advantage* that solves a problem, improve existing ones, or take advantage of trends?[23]

Demand is the actual purchase of a product or service that will best satisfy our needs and wants within our limited resources. A successful business model fills a need with a product or service that people want that is in demand.[24] So you need to anticipate needs and wants of customers, and answer the question "How does what I plan to sell improve consumers' lives?"[25] It helps to have a product or service in which the demand exceeds the supply.[26]

Market-Oriented

Putting these terms together, what target market customers need your product or service? Do they want your product or service because of your competitive advantage?[27] Will they actually demand your product or service by purchasing it? **Market-oriented** *firms identify needs and wants of target customers and satisfy them better than the competition.* By focusing on researching customers and meeting their needs, and researching the competition to get a competitive advantage to gain customers, market-oriented businesses generally outperform non-market-oriented firms.[28] Many people need to travel somewhere far away and want to fly there. What airline do they demand? Will your new venture be better than the competition?

Do You Need a Prototype or Sample?

Product development is critical to new venture success.[29] If you are coming out with a new differentiated innovative product, target customers need to be able to see it, test it, and actually use it to determine if they will buy it.[30] *A* **prototype** *is a functioning new product that target customers can try.* While building the prototype, you can improve your product before you give it the final feasibility test. If you are going to offer a new or improved product or service, such as food, target customers will want to taste it to determine if they will buy it. **Blake Mycoskie** developed a **TOMS** prototype shoe in Argentina and brought back 250 pairs to the U.S. to use as samples and to start sales.[31]

Customer Demand

It is important to know if you have customers who will actually buy your product or service. So here we discuss how you can find out.

Buying Intentions Survey

You can simply ask people what they think about your products and services, but you should ask them if they will actually buy it. You do so through a buying intention survey that helps determine if there really is a demand that can be profitable. *A buying intention survey asks target market customers questions about the business model, including the likelihood of actually purchasing the product or service.* You survey potential customers with questions like the ones found in Exhibit 4-4. Keep the survey short, and have people review it to make sure the questions are clear, simple, and easy to answer before using it to survey target customers.

As shown in Exhibit 4-4, you can conduct the survey in person, over the phone, or through the mail. But you can do some by email, some in person, and/or on the phone. Whichever way, be sure to select actual target customers who will give you honest, objective answers. So try to avoid friends and family during the feasibility test. Ask potential real customers.[32]

Exhibit 4-4

Buying Intentions Survey

For mailing (email), you start with a written description of the product or service, and the person fills out the answers to the questions.

In person or telephone, you give a verbal description and/or give a demonstration (such as showing the prototype, giving a taste sample, etc.), and you ask the questions and fill out their answers.

1. Do you believe people will buy this product or service?
   ____ Definitely
   ____ Yes
   ____ Maybe
   ____ No

2. Where would you expect to find this product or service?
   _____

3. How much do you believe people will be willing to pay for this product or service?
   $ _____

4. How likely are you personally to buy this product or service?
   _____ Definitely will buy
   _____ Very likely
   _____ Not sure
   _____ Not very likely
   _____ Would not buy

5. How much would you personally pay for this product or service?
   $ _____

6. How many would you buy in a year?
   _____

There are two important questions. First, how many people should I survey? There is no one right answer. As a general guide, the more surveys completed, the more accurate the feasibility. Part of the answer is based on the total population of your target market. A 10 percent sample size is great, but 1 percent or less may be more realistic for your target. Some experts say you need at least 25–30 individuals to run statistical analysis.

Second, where do I find target customers to survey? If you are doing a mailing, as shown in Exhibit 4-3, you can use an online survey and buy mailing lists. For in person, try to go to where the target customers are. Have you ever seen food sampling in a supermarket, or people going around the mall with clipboards asking people questions?

Sales

You should realize that many people who say they like the product and will buy it, don't actually become customers. So even though you get optimistic buying intention results, the product or service may not really be feasible. The best way to find out for sure is to make some actual sales. It is important to start building a customer base to support the feasibility of demand for your product or service before starting the new business venture.[33] **Blake Mycoskie** brought back 250 pairs of **TOMS** shoes as samples and to start sales in L.A. to test their sales feasibility.[34]

If you want to borrow money for a startup from a venture capitalist, one of the common questions he or she will ask you is, "How many sales (dollars and/or or units) have you actually made so far?" Although we are suggesting making sales, you really need to wait as you need a price for the item to be sold to make the sale, which is part of the profit feasibility analysis.

Is the Product or Service Feasible?

After you collect your data, you have to make a final decision as to whether or not your product or service is desirable and if the demand is great enough to warrant moving ahead with your feasibility analysis. Unfortunately, making that decision is not like taking a test in school that is pass or fail. It is a subjective decision. Again, it is common to actually work on more than one part of the feasibility analysis at once. But if there is no enthusiasm for your product or service, you might as well go back and try to find one that has, or give up on becoming an entrepreneur for now. **Blake Mycoskie** essentially sold his 250 pairs of **TOMS** shoes and realized there was a need, want, and demand for his shoes.[35] Let's assume you want to progress to our second question.

Are Your Industry and Target Market Feasible?

The second part of the business model (Chapter 3) includes who your customers are. Very closely related to your product or service is the industry in which they are sold and the target customers to whom you are trying to sell.

Personal Application

5. Based on prior applications, develop a buying intention survey for your product or service.

Personal Application

6. How would you go about making sales for the product or service in prior applications?

Once again, the focus is on the customer. In this section, we discuss the attractiveness of the industry, selecting the target market, and explaining customer buying decisions to help you assess the feasibility of your business model.

Industry Feasibility

Learning Outcome

5. Describe what the NAICS codes are, how to find them, and how they are used in feasibility analysis.

An *industry* is a group of firms competing to sell similar products and/or services, such as the auto and computer industry. The first thing you should do, if you haven't already, is to find out the exact industry in which your products and services will compete. Then you can assess its feasibility. This is the Peter Drucker question, "What business are you in?"[36]

NAICS codes

The **North American Industry Classification System (NAICS)**, formerly called the **Standard Industrial Classification (SIC)** system, is commonly used to identify industries. The same system is used in the U.S., Canada, and Mexico, so it is internationally used in North America.[37] The easiest way to find your NAICS proper industry name and two-six digit code is to go online to the U.S. Census Web site (www.census.gov/epcd/naics) and enter key words to find the best classification for your industry. You can click the number link to get more details of the types of businesses in the industry category. For example, when typing the key words "fast food," the results are:[38]

- 722513 Restaurants, fast food
- 722513 Fast-food restaurants

Personal Application

7. In what NAICS industry would you be most interested in starting a new venture?

NAICS is the standard used by federal statistical agencies in classifying business establishments for the purpose of collecting, analyzing, and publishing statistical data related to the U.S. business economy. A feasibility analysis is based on research, so identifying the industry by its proper name and code aids in finding relevant data to determine if the new business venture is feasible or not. For example, if you do research at the U.S. Census Web site, FactFinder, you can click industry and type in the two-six digit code to get statistics regarding your industry.[39]

Industry Attractiveness Criteria

Below are eight questions to answer that will help you determine if the industry you'd like to enter is attractive or not. The questions are numbered, but the importance of the questions can vary based on the industry and new business venture.

1. What is the size of the industry (units and dollars)? Generally, larger is more attractive.
2. What is the geographic range of the industry in which you want to compete (local, regional, national, or international)?

3. Are industry sales growing, mature and level, or declining?
4. What are the industry trends and sales forecast for the short and long term? Growth industries with positive trends and sales are more attractive.
5. Are the products and services things customers "must have," rather than "want to have"? Must have is more stable, as want to have can be cyclical and vary with the economic stage.
6. What is the industry profit margin?
7. How profitable is the industry? Obviously, higher is more attractive.
8. What is the level of competition? Generally, fewer competitors that are not aggressive is more attractive.

You should realize that the answers to these questions also help you determine the demand for your products and services. Where can you get the answers to these questions? You can refer back to Exhibit 4-3 for sources, especially trade associations for your industry. From the U.S. Census Web site (www. census.gov/eos/www/naics/) put your computer curser on "Business" and a drop-down menu with industry links will appear. Select the link in order to answer the eight questions.

Five-Forces Industry Feasibility Analysis

Michael Porter developed a five-force model for analyzing the attractiveness of an industry. *The* five-forces industry feasibility analysis *assesses the competition, power of customers and suppliers, and the threat of substitute products or services and new entrants.* The level of competition and new entrants are especially important to your analysis.[40] See Self-Assessment 4-1 for an adaptation based on his model that you can use to test the feasibility of your industry.[41] Each of the questions is based on the attractiveness of the industry.

Industry Feasibility Test

To test your industry feasibility, you need to put the two sets of questions from above together. Based on the answers to your eight industry attractiveness criteria questions, overall how feasible is the industry? Now consider your answers to the five-forces self-assessment. Next, combine the two scores, but again don't do a simple average because the criteria questions are often more relevant than the five forces, but may not be for your business venture.

Personal Application

8. Does the industry you selected in question 7 pass the feasibility test?

Target Market Feasibility

If the industry is feasible, are your target market customers also feasible? Recall from Chapter 3 that a *target market* is a segment of the entire customer population that a firm tries to get as customers. It is important to clearly define your target market because you don't want to waste your time trying to sell

Self-Assessment 4-1

Five-Forces Industry Feasibility Analysis

Select a business you would like to start or an existing one.

Start by identifying your industry and listing your major competitors

NAICS industry _____ two-six digit code _____
Major competitors

_____   _____   _____

_____   _____   _____

For each statement, select your answer on a three-point scale:

3   2   1
Describes my business   Does not describe my business

For each of the five-forces categories, place the answer (3, 2, or 1) on the line to the right after each question. Then based on your answers to the group of questions, answer the last question on the line before the question. Note that some questions may be worth more weight than others for your specific business, so don't simply calculate the average of your answers.

Level of Competition

Of the five forces, the degree of rivalry among competing firms is commonly the most important. Some industries have stronger, more aggressive competition than others.

The rivalry among my competitors is not very strong. _____
The competitors vary in size and/or capability. _____
My product or service is in the growth stage of the product life cycle _____
My product or service is different giving me a competitive advantage. _____
_____ My business venture can compete successfully in this industry.

Potential of Substitute Products or Services

Are there possible substitutes to replace your products or services, such as paper print copies of newspapers being substituted by online reading, in-store movie rentals being replaced by mail and now streaming and pay-per-view? Travel by plane, train, bus, or car are substitutes.

There are no substitutes that are lower in price. _____
There are no substitutes that are more convenient to use. _____
It would be difficult or costly for customers to find a substitute for my product or service. _____
_____ There are no good substitutes for my products or services.

Power of Customers

Generally, the fewer customers you have, the more power they have over you to negotiate a favorable sales agreement. If you have a restaurant with hundreds of customers, and you lose one, the loss doesn't have much impact on your business. However, if you have the contract to provide a food service business for one large company and lose it, you are out of business.

There are a large number of potential customers for my product or service. _____

Switching to a competitor would be difficult and/or costly. _____
My product or service has a competitive advantage so that customers will be loyal. _____
_____ Customers have little power to influence my business.

Power of Suppliers

Generally, the more suppliers you have to choose from, the less power they have over you. If you start an auto dealership, you run a franchise and can only buy from the one auto maker, giving it lots of power over you. However, if you start a used-car lot, you have lots of suppliers to choose from.

There are a large number of potential suppliers for my product or service. _____
The supplier provides a commodity, product, or service; no competitive advantage. _____
Switching to a competitor would be easy and/or low-cost. _____
_____ Suppliers have little power to influence my business.

Potential of New Competitors

How easy is it for new companies to enter the industry to compete against you? Generally, the harder it is to enter, the more attractive the industry. However, you have to be able to enter the industry yourself, so this may be more about how to keep competitors from taking your customers.

Startup costs are high. _____
It is difficult to offer large-volume, low-cost products (economies of scale). _____
My product or service has brand loyalty. _____
My product or service's competitive advantage is difficult to copy. _____
_____ It will be difficult for new startup firms to enter the industry and take my customers.

Scoring

To come up with a score to answer the question "Is my industry a good one to enter based on the five forces?" you should not just add up the scores from above and get an average. Some of the forces may not really be relevant, or much less so than others. So give it an overall answer on the new scale of 5–1, going from good to poor.

_____ Based on the five forces, my industry is attractive for starting a new venture.

your product or service to people who are unlikely to buy your product or service. **Blake Mycoskie** originally targeted younger women, which he used as his focus group, as his target market to buy **TOMS** shoes. His first retail store customer, **American Rag,** also has the same target market.[42]

You want to avoid direct competition with large companies by serving a specialized target market, like TOMS. So the target market should be large enough to be profitable, but small enough not to encourage large companies to come after your business. You don't want to go head-to-head against **Wal-Mart,** but it might be feasible to start a **Tom Hockey** sporting goods store with a great variety of gear and services, like sales and sharpening skates. The target could be general sport store sales and sales to hockey teams.

Personal Application

9. What is the target market of the business you selected? Is it feasible?

Here is an important question to think about. Is the target market large enough and will customers continue to buy your product or service? **Anita Roddick** founded the **Body Shop** with a target market of women who want to use natural cosmetic products packaged inexpensively. If there were not enough women interested in natural products, Roddick's target would not be feasible. One option is to change the target market to make it feasible. Note that your target market goes together with buying intentions because it is your target market that completes the survey.

Are Your Operations Feasible?

From your business model (Chapter 3), you also need to determine the feasibility of your ability to produce and deliver your product or service through the supply chain.[43] Here we also expand operations to include management ability and resource capability.

Management Feasibility

Management Credentials

Do you (or you and your management team) have the ability to start and manage a new business venture?[44] From Chapter 3, do you have the knowledge and experience in the market and the network?[45] Do you have the passion to improve products and services, and the persistence to work hard to make the new venture a success? Do you need partners in your management team?[46] Ballet dancer **Julia Erickson** invented a snack for dancers, but recruited Aaron Ingley for his business expertise as cofounder of **Barre.**[47]

Even if you are the sole owner of the business venture, you should have a management team to support you. Who's on the team is important.[48] You can use networking to recruit your management team.[49] These trusted friends and colleagues can help expand your knowledge and experience, and can expand your network of contacts. SCORE (www.score.org) can provide you with a mentor, networking contacts, and free counseling to help you develop and test the feasibility of your business model.[50]

Personal Application

10. Identify the management team for the product or service you selected in prior questions.

If your business model passes the feasibility analysis, and you progress to develop a business plan (Chapters 5–10), the management team should be identified with their qualifications for managing or advising the new business venture. If you need financing (Chapter 11), investors and lenders will require a competent management team because they understand the bond between the entrepreneur and business.[51] To a large extent, the entrepreneur is the new business, because he or she is usually involved in all aspects of the startup.[52] A startup lacks proven profitability; therefore, the decision to invest is more subjective and requires a competent management team to get funding.[53] You will learn more about the management team in Chapter 9.

Elevator Pitch

New business ventures are talked into existence. So an important entrepreneurial behavior is the skill to develop a good elevator pitch. Research has shown that, without a good pitch, you can't start a new business venture.[54] Your pitch needs to get target customers to buy your product or service, because you can convince them you have a competitive advantage that will better meet their needs and wants than the competition. Your pitch also has to be good enough to convince people to provide the resources you need to start your new business venture, which includes your potential profitability. **Blake Mycoskie**'s pitch, including his business story of giving away a free pair of **TOMS** shoes for every pair sold, resulted in free publicity in the *Los Angeles Times, Vogue, Time, People, E,* and *Teen Vogue* that resulted in increased sales.[55] You may be able to get free publicity in your local newspaper if you can develop a good pitch.

The Elevator Pitch

This skill-builder puts you in the venture capitalist position. You will watch an elevator pitch from the Internet and assess if they would or wouldn't invest in the new venture. The link for the elevator pitch for this chapter was delivered at the Collegiate Entrepreneurs' Organization (CEO) National Elevator Pitch Competition. The link to watch Kaeya is at: www.youtube.com/watch?v=YM_lgcw1ol0&feature=g-all-u.

Although the pitch doesn't actually occur in an elevator, the idea is that the entrepreneur has ninety seconds to impress the judges to invest in her business idea. She focuses on her box idea . . . but she also looks for new product ideas in everything that she sees! Kaeya has found that turning an idea into reality takes a lot of hard work. For now, she is focusing on her box idea.

Think about it.

1. What score do you give Kaeya's pitch?

Great product idea and pitch		Terrible product idea and pitch	
4	3	2	1

2. Would you invest in the business?
3. How would you improve the pitch?
4. Does Kaeya have a patent on her product?

Resource Feasibility

You need the resources to establish an entity that will develop and deliver your product or service to exploit your opportunity.[56] However, you might be able to be resourceful without having a lot of resources. Let's discuss both.

What Resources do You Need?

From Chapter 3, can you actually produce and deliver your products and services? Do you have, or can you get, the resources to start the new business venture? Your competitive advantage is largely determined by your competencies related to finding and exploiting opportunities and the resources you control.[57] Your resource bundle is ultimately the source of your competitive advantage.[58] Two common problems with startup resources are the liability of smallness and limited financial resources.[59]

The necessary resources are not just the tangible physical facilities (which you will learn about in Chapters 7–8); they also include intangible assets including competent employees with specialized skills, because people, or human capital, are the most important asset.[60] You may need intellectual property right protection and most likely government licenses and permits (which are covered later in this chapter).

Again, you need to evaluate your opportunity.[61] Keep in mind, given who you are, what you know, and whom you know, can your business model succeed?[62] A good way to test for feasibility is to list your six to twelve most important resources, including your management team, and assess your ability to acquire these resources to start your new business venture. Through your network, if you can't get the resources to start the business, you fail the feasibility test.[63]

Personal Application

11. Identify six to twelve resources needed to produce the product or service you selected in prior applications. Are they feasible?

Being Resourceful with Limited Resources

It takes money and other resources to start a new business, but you might be able to start small with limited resources as a hybrid entrepreneur from home, or start small and grow. **Blake Mycoskie** started **TOMS** shoes part-time and added three interns he got through a free ad on Craigslist. The four of them ran the startup business out of his apartment. As sales increased, he sold his share of another business to his partners and used the money to run TOMS full-time and hired some employees with experience in the shoe industry. Mycoskie had a single mission with a triple bottom line. Within five years, he sold more than 1 million pairs of shoes very *profitably,* and philanthropically gave away the same number being *socially responsible,* while gaining *personal satisfaction.*[64]

Can You Get Any Needed Permits, Licenses, or Certificates?

These are critically important to some businesses, because without them you can't conduct business. If you want to put on a specific event, such as a concert, you may need a *permit.* If you plan to sell food, you will need a city or county health permit.

In most cities and towns, you need a *license* to operate most types of business that deal with the public. Business licenses are usually obtained at the city clerk's office. Certain types of businesses, such as childcare, also require a state license. Others, such as financial advisors, need federal licenses. You can find out the type of licenses and permits you will need for your business from the SBA (www.sba.gov/content/search-business-licenses-and-permits), with links with information on how to obtain a business license in each state or zip code. You can also ask entrepreneurs in your industry.

Some businesses require a *certificate,* an official document that verifies something, to operate. If you are a student who plans to open a sole-proprietor certified public accountant (CPA) firm, you will have to pass the CPA exam and get experience to be certified before you can start your own firm. However, if you can't be certified, you may be able to find a CPA partner or hire CPAs.

Most permits and licenses are relatively easy to get, but not all. If you want to sell alcohol you have to have a liquor license. In some states, the only way to acquire a liquor license is to buy a preexisting license. In some cities, there is a limited number available. So if there is none available, you can't start a bar in that state or city.

Are Your Profits Feasible?

Learning Outcome

6. Explain the important parts of a profit feasibility analysis for a new business venture.

Economic opportunity is a major goal of entrepreneurs.[65] Recall that your business model (Chapter 3) has to be profitable to be feasible; it must make money.[66] Although it is based on the other three feasibility tests we discussed so far (as in accounting, it is the bottom line), profitability is your final test to determine whether or not to pursue a good business model or terminate a bad one.[67] Note profit feasibility is a preliminary analysis: you don't need to prepare detailed projected financial statements until the business plan, which we cover in Chapter 10. However, you do need some profitability information before proceeding to the business plan.[68] In this section, we discuss startup costs and expenses, price and revenues, and markups and profits.

Startup Costs and Expenses

It takes money to make money, or you need capital, often called seed money, to start your new business venture.[69] In multiple countries, having or not having enough money to start a new business is used as a predictor of small-business startup success versus failure.[70] So you need to determine how much money you will need to get your new business started and running. We will discuss how much startup money you will need in Chapter 10 and where you can get startup money in Chapter 11.

Startup Costs

Startup costs are usually one-time costs for capital assets, such as building, machinery, equipment, inventory, and other tangible assets. So, essentially, you need to list the capital assets you need to start your business and find out how much they cost. Startups generally have limited financial resources,[71] so you need to answer the all-important question, "Can you get the startup capital—feasibility?" Lenders and investors will only give you the startup capital if they believe you will repay them or share the profits with them. How will you pay them?

Expenses

Expenses are ongoing and are commonly paid on a weekly or monthly basis, such as rent, utilities, and employee pay. Profits are based on revenues minus expenses, so you need to watch the expenses and keep them under control. It is also helpful to distinguish between fixed (rent, salaries) and variable (utilities, hourly wages) expenses. Through secondary research, you can get data on the expenses of competitors to use as a guide in determining your expenses.

Personal Application

12. Identify some of the major startup costs and expenses to create the product or service you selected in prior applications.

13. Identify the revenues, based on price and sales volume, for the product or service you selected in prior applications.

Price and Revenues

Here you need to set the *price* for your product or service. Your estimated price for testing profit feasibility can be based on competitor prices that you get through your research on industry-comparable data and your buyer intention survey and sales. Next, you need to forecast the volume of sales for a given period of time, such as a week, month, or year. Taking the price and multiplying it by the volume gives you the *revenue* forecast for a set period of time. If you sell pizza for $10 each and forecast sales of a hundred per week, you have revenues of $1,000 per week. You can also get an estimate of revenues based on industry-comparable data. **Blake Mycoskie** started selling **TOMS** shoes for $40 and later added new models for up to $79.[72]

Markups, Profits, and Return on Investment

As the heading suggests, there are three topics to discuss here.

Markups

Recall from Chapter 3 that your *markup* is how much you charge your customer over your cost. If it costs you $5 to make a pizza and you sell it for $10, your markup is $5. As a percentage (5/10), you have a 50 percent markup. Markups do vary with the type of products and services, and the volume of sales. Most items have different costs, so it is common to just have a general business markup, such as 50 percent. You may be thinking that 50 percent sounds very profitable, but don't forget that your markup needs to be high enough to cover your expenses just to break even, and you need to recoup your startup costs as well. You can obtain industry markups to get an idea of what yours should be to enable profitability.

Profits

To obtain your profits, you subtract your expenses from your revenues and you have your profitability projection for a set period of time. Are your projected profits feasible? Profit is the term commonly used before taxes are deducted. *Net profits* are profits after taxes, an additional expense, are deducted. If you have a loss, which is common for new ventures for the first few years, you don't have a profit and don't pay taxes on the business. What you are actually projecting is profit after your turnaround to profitability.

Profit margins are a measure of profitability. **Blake Mycoskie** had to have a profit margin for **TOMS** shoes that would cover the cost of giving away a pair for free.[73] The newer **Microsoft** Surface tablet had the same price of $599 but a higher profit margin than the **Apple** iPad (cost of parts $271 vs. $293; profit $315 vs. $296; profit margin 52 percent [315/599] vs. 49 percent [296/599]) in December 2012.[74]

A word of caution here. Entrepreneurs tend to be optimistic.[75] They tend to underestimate the startup cost and expenses, and overestimate the revenues and profits. Needless to say, this is a contributing factor to business failure. So avoid this mistake. Some advisors suggest coming up with a good estimate of your revenues and expenses, then double or even triple your expected cost and cut your revenues by the same amount.

When setting your price and determining revenues and expenses, be careful with offering freemiums as these were the cause of many of the dot. com failures. **Facebook** is accused of having too many freemiums without enough revenues to offset its high costs and expenses. **Chargify,** provider of billing-management software to small businesses, had hundreds of free users, but only fifty customers paying $49 per month (revenues of $2,450) and was on the path to bankruptcy because its expenses were much greater than its revenues. It dropped the freebees and charges all users a minimum of $65 a month and worked its way up to having 900 paying customers, resulting in more than $58,500 per month in revenues; it is now profitable.[76]

Return on Investment

Return on investment (ROI) is an important measure of profitability.[77] Investors typically take a short cut to the entire feasibility analysis by wanting to know their expected ROI.[78] For a new venture, the return on investment (ROI) *is a profitability percentage calculated by taking the net profit divided by the startup cost.* The investment for an existing business is the startup costs plus all funding added later. As a formula, you take what you made over what you paid multiplied by 100.

Assume you decide to run a one-day business, selling a product you like at a flea market. You worked fifteen hours (five preparing and ten selling), you make a net profit of $300, and you invest $1,750 (cost of goods sold $1,200, sign $50, and booth fee $500). How much is your ROI? Your ROI is 17.14 percent (300/1,750 × 100).

Is this 17.14 percent a good ROI—feasible? What is a good profit and feasible ROI? There is no simple answer. It depends on a number of factors, such as:

- The amount of *capital invested*. You had to come up with $1,750.
- The *risk* involved assessment.[79] Can you accurately predict profits? You could have made less profit than $300, and even lost money. Generally, the greater the risk, the higher the ROI needs to be for it to be feasible.
- The existing *alternative investments*. How much could you have made with a different investment, such as in stocks or another business?
- The existing alternatives for your *time* and *effort*. How much could you have earned if you worked a day for someone else? You made $20 an hour ($300/15 hrs).

You need to create returns from your business venture.[80] But how much ROI do you need to pursue your opportunity? Is the above 17.14 percent a feasible ROI to you? As a student, the answer may be yes. But could you come

Exhibit 4-5

Profitability
Feasibility Analysis
Resources

Source	Tools	Cost
SCORE (www.score.org)	Provides mentors, business counseling, workshops, and Web site template and tool links to help you prepare profit feasibility.	Free, but can have a small fee for some workshops.
SizeUp—Small Business Administration (www.sba.gov/sizeup)	*Benchmark* your new venture by comparing your performance with all other competitors in your industry.	Free.
BizStats (www.bizstats.com)	Will give you a projected custom industry profit and loss, balance sheet, and financial ratio benchmark for your business, based on your sales forecast. You can also determine the net profit-risk for your new venture. Provides business statistics and financial ratios.	Free.
BizMiner (www.bizminer.com) IBISWorld (www.ibisworld.com) Mintel (www.mintel.com)	Produces industry statistical market reports and financial analysis benchmark reports.	Fee based, but might be free if accessed through a college library.

up with the $1,750 investment? With a full-time job, it may or may not be an attractive opportunity for you as a one-time business venture. However, there are *hybrid entrepreneurs* who work during the week and run a business venture like this on weekends or at night.

Profitability Feasibility Analysis Resources

Personal Application

14. Identify the potential profits for the product or service you selected in prior applications. Are the profits feasible?

It is important to compare your potential and actual performance with that of your competition.[81] See Exhibit 4-5 for a list of resources that can help you compare your venture with the competition as you conduct a profit feasibility analysis.[82] The resources also provide information that can be used in the other three areas of product and service, industry and target market, and operations feasibility analysis.

Is Your Business Model Feasible?

Now that you know the four parts of the feasibility analysis of your business model, let's put them together for an overall feasibility test. Do so through Self-Assessment 4-2, "Is Your Business Model Feasible?" Preferably use a business that you would like to start or an existing business.

Self-Assessment 4-2

Is Your Business Model Feasible?

For each of the four parts of the feasibility analysis, rate your business model based on the level of agreement with each statement on a scale of 1–5.

5	4	3	2	1

Describes my business model   Does not describe my business model

When scoring each part, don't use a simple average as some issues may be more important than others. Use a weighted average to give more points to more important issues based on your business venture. If a statement is not relevant to your business, just leave it blank.

Part 1. Are Your Products and/or Services Feasible?

_____ 1. There is a strong need for my product or service.

_____ 2. My product or service has a clear competitive advantage over competitors.

_____ 3. My product or service solves a problem, improves existing ones, or takes advantage of trends.

_____ 4. A buying intention survey supports a demand for my product or service.

_____ 5. My product or service has already been sold to customers.

Weighted average rating _____ (5–1, 5 feasible, 1 not feasible)

Part 2. Are Your Industry and Target Market Feasible?

_____ 1. My industry is relatively large.

_____ 2. My industry is in a growth stage.

_____ 3. My industry doesn't have strong, aggressive competition.

_____ 4. My five-forces industry feasibility analysis is positive.

_____ 5. My target market is large enough to sustain profits without attracting large competitors.

Weighted average rating _____ (5–1, 5 feasible, 1 not feasible)

Part 3. Are Your Operations Feasible?

_____ 1. I have a management team with knowledge and experience in my industry.

_____ 2. We have a passion for the business and persistence to make it a success.

_____ 3. We have the networking contacts to realize the resources needed to start the business.

_____ 4. We have the supply chain contacts to produce and deliver our products.

_____ 5. I can hire employees with the experience and skills needed to succeed.

Weighted average rating _____ (5–1, 5 feasible, 1 not feasible)

Part 4. Are Your Profits Feasible?

_____ 1. My startup cost are reasonable, and I have or can get the funding.

_____ 2. The price of my product provides a markup that will cover my costs and expenses.

_____ 3. My expenses are reasonable compared with industry averages.

_____ 4. My business venture will be profitable.

_____ 5. My return on investment (ROI) makes the risk of starting a new venture feasible.

Weighted average rating _____ (5–1, 5 feasible, 1 not feasible)

Overall Feasibility Analysis Scoring

_____ (5–1, 5 feasible, 1 not feasible) Based on the four parts, again don't calculate a simple average. Use an overall weighted feasibility analysis score giving more points to more important factors, such as profits. Place your score on the continuum below.

5	4	3	2	1

Feasible business model   Not feasible

Business likely to succeed   Business likely to fail

Summary

(Write your justification for you score.)

_____

_____

_____

_____

Score Interpretation

Obviously, the higher your score, the greater is the likelihood of a successful startup. However, there is no major "go/no go" number, and there is no guarantee of success. You should also realize that this is "your" feasibility analysis. To make it more valid, have others complete the feasibility analysis, such as mentors, SCORE counselors, and industry experts. Through their feedback, you can improve each part of your business model. For example, if you can't get the capital to manufacture your product, you might contract to have another business make it for you. They can help you make the decision to proceed to the business planning stage or abandon the new venture.

Personal Application

15. Putting together prior questions, is the entire business model you selected feasible? Explain your answer.

Even if a business model passes the feasibility test, it doesn't guarantee business success and survival. Many people thought **Zipcar** "car sharing" was feasible. The company even went public, selling stock to grow the business. However, it turned out to be just another car-rental company. Zipcar never once turned an annual profit, losing cumulatively about $55 million before the company was sold to **Avis Budget** in 2012.[83] What happened? Most customers only rented on weekends and there weren't enough people who wanted to use a Zipcar. Importantly, it was too small to use economies of scale, and **Hertz** and **Enterprise** started their own car-sharing programs.[84]

Protecting Your Ideas and Intellectual Property Legally

Learning Outcome

7. Discuss legal methods that can be used to protect the ideas in a business model.

If you develop a great business model, the question isn't will copycat knock-offs come to take your customers, the question is how will you keep your customers when they come after you. There are ways to fight the copycats, and they can even lead to opportunities.[85] That's what this section is all about. We discuss contracts, trade secrets, trademarks, copyrights, and patents.

First you should realize that startups should protect their ideas,[86] which you put into your business model. However, almost 85 percent of small firms don't use legal protection in the first four years.[87] Here is what can happen if you don't seek legal protection. Allegedly, **Cameron** and **Tyler Winklevoss** and **Divya Narendra** (The Group) met in a dorm room during their junior year to discuss **Harvard Connection,** later changed to **ConnectU.** They hired **Mark Zuckerberg** to help design their social network. Zuckerberg formed **Facebook** and parted ways with the group. The group brought a lawsuit against him and Facebook over the ownership rights to the social media giant.[88] In addition to discussing how to legally protect your ideas as an *innovative entrepreneur,* we end this section with a discussion of how to ethically and legally copy others' ideas as a *replicative entrepreneur.* See Exhibit 4-6 for an illustration of the ways you can protect your business.

Contracts and Intellectual Property Rights

You can protect yourself and your ideas and business operations through contracts. We also introduce intellectual property rights that you can use to protect your business model.

What is a Contract?

Contracts *are legal oral or written agreements between two or more parties specifying what each party must do, or must not do, for a specified time.* If you have cell phone service, such as with **AT&T** or **Verizon,** you signed a contract specifying how much you agree to pay and the provider states what services they will provide for the specified period of the contract.

Contracts	Intellectual property rights:
	• trade secrets
	• trademarks
	• copyrights
	• patents

Exhibit 4-6

Legal Methods of Protecting a Business

A partnership agreement is an important legal contract that protects all partners. When getting funds from angels and venture capitalist investors (discussed in Chapter 11), the contract specifying your relationship is critically important.[89] You should also realize that a contract is not a substitute for trust. If you don't trust someone to live up to his or her part of the agreement, don't sign a contract.

Breach of Contract

If any party doesn't perform as specified, there is a *breach of contract* and legal action can be taken against the party to require the party to live up to the agreement or pay damages; unless all parties agree to void the contract. Unfortunately, taking legal action can be costly and time consuming. But suing can be well worth it.

Although there was no written contract between **The Group** and **Zuckerberg,** The Group filed a lawsuit against him and **Facebook,** and The Group got at least $65 million by settling out of court.[90] One possible way **The Group** could have prevented **Zuckerberg** from starting **Facebook** would have been to have him sign a non-compete contract specifying that he could not start a social media company that would compete with the group's **ConnectU.**

Small claims courts are commonly used to keep legal costs down. Breach of contracts for less than a specified amount, which varies by state, can be resolved without a lawyer. For example, in Delaware claims of up to $15,000 can be settled through civil action in the justice of the peace courts. This process is similar to what you may have seen on TV court shows. All parties can represent themselves to the court official in small claims court presenting their case. After the official hears all parties' sides, the official makes a legally binding decision on how to resolve the breach of contract.

Legal Help

The safest way to avoid business legal problems is to have important agreements of more than $500 or lasting for more than one year to be in writing and reviewed by a lawyer first. Don't sign any contract without having the lawyer review it first or you reading and understanding it completely, even if the lawyer tells you it is okay, because you are the one held legally responsible. Keep copies of signed contracts in a safe place.

Yes, lawyers are expensive, but hundreds spent on legal fees could save you thousands or even from losing your business. Also, remember that legal fees are a business expense that is tax deductible. Don't select a lawyer based on price. Hire a competent lawyer with experience handling cases like yours.[91]

Personal Application

16. Select a business you would like to start, or an existing one, and identify some of the contracts it should make or have.

Letter of Agreement

You don't always need a full, formal contract involving a lawyer when conducting business when a letter of agreement will do. A *letter of agreement* is a contractual document that puts an oral understanding in writing in the form of a business letter. Some consultants will discuss their services and fees during a business meeting with a client (sales call). After the meeting, the consultant sends a letter specifying his or her services and the cost. If the client responds in writing agreeing to the terms in the consultant's offer, the two parties have a letter of agreement. The downside is that the letter of agreement is not as strong a legal defense as the formal signed contract, and when there is a breach of contract, legal action is often not taken.

Intellectual Property Rights

All businesses have some form of intangible assets and the government helps entrepreneurs protect their rights by giving these assets trademarks, copyrights, and patents under *intellectual property* law. Trade secrets can also be protected under intellectual property law. Your intellectual property can be your sources of competitive advantage, which you should protect. Below we will discuss each of the four types of intellectual property rights that your business may have and how you can protect the ideas in your business model legally.

Trade Secrets

Trade secrets are ideas, processes or other things that give a business a competitive advantage over rivals. They are not common knowledge; therefore, the firm doesn't want competitors to know about them. If competitors find out trade secrets, they can copy the secret and take away the competitor's advantage. **Colonel Sanders'** secret recipe of herbs and spices for **KFC** fried chicken and **Bush's** Baked Beans recipe are trade secrets. In essence, **The Group** accused **Zuckerberg** of taking its trade secret to start **Facebook.** You have two options to protect your idea: confidential and nondisclosure agreement contracts.

Confidentiality Verbal Agreements

When working on developing your business model and testing it for feasibility, you may want to keep it a secret so that others don't steal your idea and launch a new venture before you, which could give them a *first mover advantage.* If you are developing and testing your business model, it can be awkward and even scare people away, if you were to ask them to sign a contract stating that they will not tell anyone about your communication.

However, most people will agree to keep your communication confidential. So you could tell the person, or group, that you are sharing information that you don't want others to know about at this time, and ask them to keep your communications confidential. The downside is that, if you don't have any witnesses, and if the person tells your secrets or uses them, it will be difficult to take legal action against him or her for breach of contract.

Nondisclosure Agreement Contracts

More for existing business with employees, and possibly others like supply chain members that know the secret, you can protect your trade secrets though a formal contract known as the *nondisclosure agreement.* The agreement is

Personal Application

17. Select a business you would like to start or an existing one, and identify some trade secrets it has and how it should or does protect its trade secrets.

129

designed to keep people from telling the secret either while being an employee or after leaving the firm. Being a legally written contract, you can sue any signatory who breaches the contract. As with all formal written contracts, it is wise to have a lawyer draft the agreement. An experienced lawyer will have created contracts for your type of business.

Trademarks

If other entrepreneurs were to use your business name or logo, they could take your customers without them knowing it, but having a trademark makes it illegal for anyone to copy you.

What is a Trademark?

A trademark *is a distinguishing word, name, symbol, or device used to identify a product or service.* Here is an expanded list of items covered under trademark law. Words can be a single word, name, short phrase, and slogan. **Small Business Institute** numbers and letters can be trademarked, for example **3M.** You can trademark your design, logos, or shape, for example the **Nike** swoosh or the **Coca-Cola** curved bottle. With some restrictions, you can also trademark some sounds (**MGM** lion's roar), colors (**Nexium** "the purple pill"), and trade dress (**McDonald's** golden arch building).

There are three offshoot names for trademarks. When a trademark represents a service, it is commonly called a *service* mark, for example **1–800-FLOWERS**^{SM}. When a trademark represents members of a group, it is a *collective mark,* for example **Rotary International.** When a trademark is used by a business other than its owner to certify something, it is called a *certification mark,* for example **UL, ISO 9000.**

Nonregistered Trademarks

To have legal protection, all you have to do is develop and use your trademark; you don't have to register it. You can use the symbol ^{TM} or ^{SM} to indicate you have a trademark, but that it is not registered. "With every pair you purchase, **TOMS** will give a pair of new shoes to a child in need. One for One."^{TM92} However, registration does give you the right to use the registered mark ® and in doing so gives you stronger legal protection. If you decide to start a business without registering your trademark, do follow steps 1 and 2 below.

Getting a Registered Trademark

Here is a three-step process you can follow to get a trademark.

1. *Develop a trademark.* Try to display creativity and strength in a distinctive trademark that creates a favorable impression about your product or service, such as McDonald's golden arches, and made-up names like Google and eBay.

2. *Conduct a trademark search.* To make sure your trademark is not violating another business's rights to it, do a search on the Internet at the **U.S. Patent and Trademark Office** (USPTO or PTO, www.uspto.org). If someone already has the trademark, develop a new one and search again until you find one that you can legally trademark. Neglecting to do a search could result in legal action against you and you would have to remove the trademark from everything (signs, products, letterhead, business cards), which can be very costly.

3. *Register with the USPTO.* Go online to the USPTO Web site (www.uspto.org) and fill out the application for a trademark form as directed. If someone uses your trademark (*trademark violation)*, you can take legal action to stop them and possibly get damages for actions such as for lost sales.

Personal Application

18. Select a business you would like to start, or an existing one, and develop a trademark for it.

Copyrights

If other entrepreneurs were to use your business's copyrighted material, they can take your customers and you would not get paid. Having a copyright makes it illegal for anyone to copy your work. If your business is being a musician, do you want people to download your songs for free illegally, or do you want them to pay for them directly to you or buy them on **Apple iTunes?**

What is a Copyright?

The legal term, copyright, grants authors and artists the exclusive right to make and sell copies of their works, the right to create derivative works, and the right to perform or display their works publicly. From the entrepreneur's protection perspective, *a copyright prevents others from using and distributing original work of authors and artists without permission, which may require a fee for its use.*

What is and isn't Protected Under Copyright Law?

You can't copyright ideas, but you can copyright the specific expression of an idea. You can't receive a copyright for the idea to sing a song about a mountain or to paint one, but you can copyright your specific song or painting. You can't copyright the idea to write a book, song, or movie about a love story, but you can copyright your specific one.

To receive a copyright, your work must be in a tangible form. An oral speech that you give can't have a copyright. However, if you write it down or record it, the speech can have copyright protection. Another person can give a speech and use your ideas, but can't legally use your exact words or PowerPoint slides without your permission. In giving permission, you can charge a fee to use your copyright material.

Copyright Content and Infringement

If people use or distribute your copyright material, as illustrated here, they are illegally infringing on your copyrights. People can't legally engage in (1) printing your literary work (making copies of your book, poem, PowerPoint slides, or brochure), (2) copying it (downloading your musical song, dramatic work movie, app, or computer software), (3) reproducing it (making copies of your painting, photographs, prints, art, cartoon, sculpture, jewelry), (4) publicly performing or displaying it (putting on a play you wrote or dance you choreographed), or (5) publishing it (putting a copy of your work in their book or their album).

In most cases, if people simply use your copyright for personal use without any financial gain, it may not be worth suing them for copyright violation. However, the **Recording Industry Association of America (RIAA)** that represents the music industry filed lawsuits against hundreds of college students from several different colleges and continues to try to prevent illegal downloading of songs.[93]

Electronic Rights

In our Internet digital world, the *Digital Millennium Copyright Act* of 1998 was passed to extend copyright to electronic form to help prevent *Internet piracy* (copyright infringement), primarily through downloading copyright materials illegally. It outlaws the technology used to break copyright-protected devices. Be sure to keep trade secrets from public view and use passwords and other devices to prevent access to your private information. If you put anything private online, such as on your Web site, be sure to make it clear that you hold the copyright and it may not be used without your written permission; include your contact information.

Nonregistered Copyrights

As with a trademark, you don't have to register it. From the moment your work is in a tangible form, you have copyright protection. However, to provide protection, attach a copyright notice (copyright bug), such as the following.

- Copyright © 2013 John Smith.
- Copyright © 2013 John's Pizza (Johnsmith@aol.com). All rights reserved. This material cannot be used in any form without written permission.

On a word-processed document, you can place the copyright notice in the footer so that it appears on all pages, just in case the pages get separated.

Getting a Registered Copyright

Registered copyright comes from the **U.S. Copyright Office.** The process is simple by following the directions at its Web site (www.copyright.gov). All copyright material created after January 1, 1978 last for the life of the author plus seventy years.

Patents

Our last form of legal protection is to get a patent, which is primarily to protect an invention or process related to a product rather than a service, unless your service has some unique process you want to protect that is not obvious.

What is a Patent and Should You Get One?

A patent protects others from making, using, or selling an invention or process for a specified time. To get a patent, it must meet three criteria: (1) it has to have utility (be useful), (2) be novel (new and different), and (3) is not obvious (to a person of ordinary skill in the field).

Should you get a patent? Here are a few questions to consider. Do you plan to invent a product that you intend to market yourself or sell to a manufacturer? Do you plan to license your invention to others to use? Do you believe that another business can copy and sell your invention or process to your target customers? Do you have the time and money to get one? It takes at least two years, on average, to obtain a patent, and it can be very expensive.[94] Legal fees can range from $5,000 for a very simple patent to $15,000 and more for very complex patents.[95] But it could cost you much less if you are capable of doing the design and legal work yourself. But most entrepreneurs who have patents say they needed to pay for some help. More than 85 percent of small businesses don't get a patent in their first four years.[96]

One Year After First Use Deadline and Patent Infringement

One quick word of caution if you do decide to get a patent in the future. You must apply for the patent within the first year it is offered for sale, put into public use, or is described in any printed publication. **Dipin'Dots** learned this lesson the hard way, as it went through the time and expense of getting a patent on its small beads of ice cream and tried to sue **Frosty Bites** for selling its patented ice cream, only to lose the lawsuit for missing the *one year after first use deadline.*[97]

A second thing you should realize is that if someone uses your patent, it can be very costly, and take years, to win a lawsuit. One exception is "if" you can find a lawyer who will take your case and only charge you a percentage of any money you get for settling the case or winning your case in court. You may also be able to make an agreement to give the violator a license to use your patent for royalty fees (see Chapter 2).

Scott White patented and trademarked the "**CondiCup**" and went to **Heinz** to try to sell them licensing rights to use his ketchup packet. Heinz declined the offer and four years later came out with its own "Dip & Squeeze" packet. White is suing Heinz, and Heinz says it is innocent of illegally infringing on the CondiCup. The courts will decide if Heinz is innocent or guilty, unless it settles before going to trial.[98]

Types and Duration of Patents?

There are four major types of patents, but more than 90 percent are utility patents:

- *Utility.* What we generally consider an invention comes under utility patents. It must be a new or useful process, machine, manufacture, or composition of materials, or any new and useful improvement of one of them. **Scott White**'s patent of the "**CondiCup**" was a utility patent. Major drug companies, such as **Pfizer,** have patents on their medications to prevent the sale of generic drugs. The patents last for twenty years from the date of the original application.

■ *Business method.* This is actually a form of utility patent that came from Internet firms. As the name implies, it is a process for doing business. Founder of **Amazon.com, Jeff Bezos,** patented his "one-click" ordering system of charging the customer, getting the item from inventory, and shipping it to the customer. **Priceline.com** patented the "name-your-price" method. Being a utility patent, the duration is twenty years.

■ *Design.* It must be an invention of new, original, and ornamental designs for manufactured products. It doesn't cover the functioning parts (utility): only the appearance. **Nike** and **Apple** have some design patents. The patent lasts for fourteen years from the date of the original application. But be cautious about getting a design pattern because it is very easy to legally modify the design appearance, which knockoffs do.[99]

■ *Plant.* It must be a new variety of plants that can be reproduced asexually. **Monsanto** has lots of patents on seeds that it primarily sells to farmers. The patent lasts for twenty years from the date of the original application.

Getting a Patent

Personal Application

20. Select a business you would like to start, or an existing one, and identify an item for which it should seek copyright protection.

Unlike a trademark and copyright with which you can help protect yourself, to get legal protection for a patent you need to get it from the **U.S. Patent and Trademark Office (USPTO or PTO).** The process is complex. You can get a U.S. or international patent. For more information, and to apply for a patent, visit www.uspto.org. As a general guide (1) make sure your product or process can be patented by meeting the three criteria discussed above, (2) document when your product or process was made, (3) get a patent lawyer, (4) conduct a patent search to make sure no one else has the patent, and (5) file an application with the USPTO. You can also get a patent by buying it from its owner. **Kodak** sold $525 million worth of patents to around a dozen companies including **Apple** and **Google.**[100]

Multiple Protections and Ethical and Legal Use of Others' Ideas

There is a good chance that your business will need several forms of protection, and you want to be ethical and not break the law in using others' ideas.

Multiple Protections

There are some businesses that should combine the various methods of protecting their business model ideas. Let's say you want to develop a video game. You should *trademark* the name of your game. You should *copyright* the printed material on the game disk and online. You could get a *utility patent* for the game itself and a *design patent* on any game console and attachments. You will also likely have some *trade secret* you want to keep with confidentiality agreements. You may also want to sign *contracts* with any supply chain members to ensure you can produce and deliver your game.

Ethical and Legal Use of Others' Ideas

If you are an *innovative entrepreneur,* you will most likely not use others' ideas directly. However, if you are a *replicative entrepreneur,* you are using others' ideas, so you have to do so legally and be ethical and compete fairly. It may or may not be illegal depending on your methods, but it is unethical to steal trade secrets. It is unethical and illegal to use a trademark, copyright, or patent without permission. So, as discussed above, you can do a search to make sure you are being ethical and legal in the methods you use to protect your business.

Piracy

Piracy is the use of legally protected intellectual property, such as downloading songs and movies without paying for them or getting permission to use them. It is generally agreed that piracy is unethical and the courts have ruled that piracy is illegal. So we don't recommend starting a pirate business, or helping others pirate business intellectual property.

As you may know, piracy of songs and movies has been a problem for many years. But did you know that the latest piracy problem is with the mobile app? A lot of small businesses are being hurt as hackers have cut into paid app sales by 20–50 percent. Within days of 25-year-old Londoner **James Vaughan** coming out with his 99 cent game **Plague Inc., Apple App Store** hackers made it available online for free. Up to 35 percent of downloads have been pirated illegally, at an estimate loss to Vaughan of more than $500,000.[101]

Personal Application

21. As you know, piracy is illegal, but do you consider it ethical or unethical?

Patent Trolls

A *patent troll* is a company that is solely in business to attempt to make money by threatening to sue companies who are using intellectual property that the business (troll) has ownership of.[102] Companies obtain patents only to license them, often using the threat of an injunction to extract a high price from infringers.[103] The patent holder has often never used or has no intention of using the patent. Even though it can be very expensive, it is often easier to just pay the patent holding company the licensing fee. Some entrepreneurs pay the licensing fee even if the accusation of using a particular process seems quite frivolous.

On the other hand, some entrepreneurs fight the patent troll companies because they strongly believe they do not use the patented technology. **Steve Vicinanza** of **BlueWave Computing** fought back against Project Paperless. Project Paperless owns a patent on scanning documents into an email attachment. Project Paperless wanted BlueWave to pay a one-time licensing fee of $1,000 per employee. However, BlueWave doesn't make office equipment—it only installs it. Vicinanza ended up paying $50,000 dollars in legal fees instead of $200,000 for a license fee or much more money if it went to court. Vicinanza felt it was worth the legal fees to protect his own business.[104]

Other Options for Starting a New Venture, and Entrepreneurial Behavior

As in all chapters, in this last section we discuss some of the major differences in starting a new venture with the other five options to becoming an entrepreneur, and how to engage in entrepreneurial behavior as an employee.

Buying an Existing Business, Franchise, or Leasing Rights

Buying an Existing Business

When you become an entrepreneur through an acquisition, the prior owner has financial records to verify that the business is viable. However, you may want to make some changes to the business model, and in doing so test the feasibility of your changes. It is also recommended that you do a profit analysis including an ROI based on past performance. If you need to raise money to buy the business, you will most likely need a business plan. Being able to come up with the money to buy the business is a key feasibility analysis for you.

The prior owner may have some contracts that you will want to honor, but you will have to obtain new contracts to sign. If the prior owner has any trade secrets, you will want to know them and keep them secret. As a new owner, you may have to acquire new trademarks and copyrights. If the prior owner has a patent, you will have to buy it or pay a licensing fee to use it.

Buying a Franchise

If you buy a franchise, the franchisor will help you do a feasibility analysis to ensure that you can succeed at your location. Being able to come up with the money to buy the franchise is a key feasibility analysis for you. Based on profit data from other franchisees, you should be able to determine your profitability and ROI.

The franchisor will have a contract that you have to sign. If the franchisor has any trade secrets, you will be told and need to keep them secret. The franchisor will have trademarks and copyrights, and possibly a patent. You will be paying a royalty fee for the use of this intellectual property.

Buying Licensing Rights

You are typically on your own as to how you develop your business model and run your business. Therefore, you should conduct a feasibility analysis similar to starting a new business. If you need to come up with a onetime fee for the licensing rights, can you get the money? You will need to sign a contract regarding your use and fees for buying the rights to use the firm's intellectual property rights.

Starting a Corporate or Nonprofit New Venture

Starting a Corporate Venture

You will more than likely have to conduct a feasibility analysis to convince your employer to let you start a new venture, just like for a new business. Your employer will need to know your startup costs and your projected profitability. You may need contracts within the supply chain, and your employer may already have trademarks, copyrights, and/or patents. But you may need others to suit the new venture.

Starting a Nonprofit

Starting a new venture nonprofit is starting a new business and will require a feasibility analysis to convince the government, foundations, businesses, and donors to give you the startup capital you need. Will you need the ongoing support of each group? To help you conduct a feasibility analysis, SCORE (www.score.org) has feasibility analysis material within its "Templates & Tools—Business Planning for Nonprofit Organizations" section that you can use. Also, the Executive Service Corps—United States (ESC, www.escus.org) specializes in helping nonprofits, and there may be a Small Business Development Center (www.sba.gov, search SBDC) in your area that can help you. You will most likely engage in contracts and need intellectual property protection.

Entrepreneurial Behavior

If you are not interested in starting a new venture, as an employee you can engage in *entrepreneurial behavior* that can lead to a new venture or new or improvement of your current employer's products and services or processes. Over the years **McDonald's** has increased its menu options to include more healthy choices and added additional drink items. Employees are the ones who come up with the new products and processes. **Fred Turner** is called the "Father of Chicken McNuggets."[105]

Personal Application

22. Select an existing business and give ideas for new products or services the firm could offer, or how it can improve the ones they already have. Or give ideas for improving any processes within the firm, or along the supply chain.

Chapter Review and Summary

As we bring this chapter to a close, you should be able to conduct a feasibility analysis by conducting research to determine if your products and services, industry and target market, operations, and profits are feasible to determine if your business model should be taken to the next level of developing a business plan. You should also understand how to protect your business model ideas legally by using contracts, keeping trade secrets, and using trademarks, copyrights, and patents to protect your intellectual property rights. You should also know some of the major differences in starting a new business venture with the five other options for becoming an entrepreneur, and how to engage in entrepreneurial behavior.

This summary lists the learning outcomes from the chapter and their answers.

1. Describe the relationship between feasibility analysis and research, and the types of research

Feasibility analysis is the process of testing a business model to determine the viability of a business opportunity. The business model is tested by collecting data through research. There are two types of research. *Primary research* is the process of collecting original data by the entrepreneur, commonly through survey (in person, phone, or mail), observation, and focus groups. *Secondary research* is the process of finding data already collected by others, commonly through library and Internet searches.

2. Identify the parts of the feasibility analysis process

Feasibility analysis is the four-part process of testing a business model's (1) products and services, (2) industry and target market, (3) operations, and (4) potential profitability through research. If the business model fails the feasibility analysis, it is not a real opportunity and the new business venture is not started. If it passes, the entrepreneur proceeds to develop a business plan.

3. Explain the customer purchasing decision process

The purchasing decision process begins with a *need* for a product or service to solve a problem or to make things easier in some way. Thus, we *want* a product or service to fulfill a need. There are usually competing products and services to choose from to meet a need. *Demand* is the actual purchase of a product or service that best satisfies the need and want within the customer's limited resources.

4. Discuss two methods for determining the feasibility of the demand for a product or service

The two methods for determining the feasibility of the demand for a product or service are the buying intention survey and sales. A *buying intention survey* asks target market customers questions about the business model, including the likelihood of actually purchasing the product or service. Through *sales*, the entrepreneur begins to build a starting customer base to support the feasibility of demand for the product or service before starting the new business venture.

5. **Describe what the NAICS codes are, how to find them, and how they are used in feasibility analysis**

NAICS codes refer to the North American Industry Classification System that is commonly used to identify industries in the U.S., Canada, and Mexico. The NAICS proper-industry name and two-six digit code can be found online at the U.S. Census Web site (www.census.gov/epcd/naics) by entering key words to find the most accurate classification. NAICS is used by the U.S. federal statistical agencies to classify businesses for the purpose of collecting, analyzing, and publishing statistical data. A feasibility analysis is based on research, so identifying the industry by its proper name and code aids in finding relevant data to determine if the new business venture is feasible or not.

6. **Explain the important parts of a profit feasibility analysis for a new business venture**

Profit feasibility begins with determining the *startup costs* for the new venture. Profits are estimated by the *price* of the product or service multiplied by the forecasted *sales volume* to determine *revenues,* then by subtracting the *expenses* for a given period of time. The *return on investment (ROI)* is a profitability percentage calculated by taking the net profit divided by the startup cost.

7. **Discuss legal methods that can be used to protect the ideas in a business model**

There are five methods. *Contracts* are legal oral or written agreements between two or more parties specifying what each party must do, or must not do, for a specified time. *Trade secrets* are ideas, processes, or other things that give a business a competitive advantage over rivals that is not common knowledge and that the firm doesn't want competitors to know about. The government helps entrepreneurs protect trade secrets and other rights by giving these assets trademarks, copyrights, and patents under *intellectual property* law. *Trademarks* are distinguishing words, names, symbols, or devices used to identify a product or service. *Copyrights* prevent others from using and distributing original work of authors and artists without permission, which may require a fee for its use. Patents protect others from making, using, or selling an invention or process for a specified time.

8. **Define the fifteen key terms identified in this chapter**

buying intention survey	patent
contracts	primary research
copyright	prototype
feasibility analysis	return on investment (ROI)
five-forces industry feasibility analysis	secondary research
market-oriented	survey research
observation research	trade secrets
	trademark

Review and Discussion Questions

Be sure to explain all your answers.

1. What is the risk of not conducting a feasibility analysis?

2. Distinguish between the four key parts to a feasibility analysis.

3. What is the difference between primary and secondary data?

4. Why would NextMark (http://lists.next mark.com) be important if you were trying to reach potential customers in your community?

5. How are needs, wants, demand, and competitive advantage all intertwined?

6. Is a company market-oriented or product-oriented if it builds a prototype? Explain your answer.

7. What is the goal of conducting a buying intention survey?

8. What makes Blake Mycoskie a unique and successful entrepreneur?

9. It is often difficult to answer Peter Drucker's question, "What business are you in?" Why is this?

10. How can you determine if the industry you'd like to enter is attractive or not?

11. Which of the five-forces industry feasibility analysis is considered the most important? Why?

12. How do you determine if your operations are feasible?

13. What is the difference between a tangible and intangible asset?

14. What is the problem with entrepreneurs being optimistic?

15. Using Self-Assessment 4-2, did you score high or low on the feasibility of your business model?

16. What is a contract?

17. What is the difference between a trademark, patent, and copyright?

18. What is the difference between a contract and a letter of agreement?

19. What should you consider when deciding if you need a patent for your product?

20. Why does a nonprofit still need to conduct a feasibility analysis even if the organization has a mission to help people?

Application Exercises

Each chapter has a series of exercises requiring you to apply the specific text concepts. When doing these exercises, be sure to select a specific business where applicable. You can select a business where you worked or a business you would like to own someday. Answers for each exercise should be approximately one page.

1. The goal of this application is to practice doing research at the North American Industry Classification System (NAICS), which is part of the U.S. Census Bureau (www.census.gov/eos/www/naics/). Your research has four parts.

   a. Enter an industry, such as "computers" in the keyword search box. Summarize the results of that search.

   b. Enter the industry for one of the companies you used during this course. Summarize the results.

   c. Click the "Business" link and follow the Business Topic of E-Commerce. Summarize the latest report on the performance of e-commerce.

   d. Click the "Business" link for a topic that relates to a project you have used in this course so far. What topic did you pick and what did you learn?

2. Use the following link (www.forbes.com/sites/markgibbs/2013/01/05/a-patent-troll-wants-to-charge-you-for-emailing-your-scans/) from *Forbes Magazine* to learn about "patent trolls." You should also search for additional articles on patent trolls to help answer the following questions.

   a. What is a patent troll?

   b. How do these companies actually make money on patents?

   c. What does it take for a small-business entrepreneur to stop patent trolls?

Application Situations

1. Ed Kramer

Ed Kramer was talking to his close friend Jerry Small about his new idea for a business venture. Ed wanted to raise money to finance his "sure fire venture". He was certain it would be a success and make him millions. Jerry listens to the idea and at the end of Ed's presentation said "Okay, sounds good, of course you've done a feasibility study?" Ed's reply was in the negative. He had no idea that such a study was necessary and, besides that, he didn't even know what a feasibility study was.

1. Was Jerry right in asking for such a study and why was he right or wrong?

2. What is a feasibility study?

3. What should be included in such a study?

2. Judy and Melisa

Judy and her friend Melisa own a bakery. In an effort to attract customers, Judy was able to obtain a recipe from a competitor who had the most delicious pastry tart. Their competitor would not release the recipe for this tart and forbade a New York employee from doing so. Further employees had to sign a statement affirming that they would never reveal the recipe. Melisa, however, was able to somehow obtain a copy of the recipe. They were now ready to start making the product.

1. Can they go ahead and make the product without any problems?

2. Does this recipe come under the definition of intellectual property?

3. What is the definition of intellectual property?

4. Identify the various types of intellectual property.

5. How can you best protect yourself in this situation?

Case

Mexico: Grupo Bimbo Breads

Have you ever heard of Bimbo Breads? You most likely will recognize its brands: Freihofer's, Thomas, Arnold, Entenmenn's, Sara Lee, and many more bakery goods. Where did this 13 billion dollar company with 124,000 employees start? Mexico in 1945. It entered the U.S. market in 1996. It also has large brand names in Asia and Europe.

How did Bimbo know its business model would work around the globe? How do you know when your business model is feasible? Feasibility analysis is the four-part process of testing a business model's (1) products and services, (2) industry and target market, (3) operations, and (4) potential profitability through research. If the business model fails the feasibility analysis, it is not a real opportunity and the new business venture is not started. If it passes, the entrepreneur proceeds to develop a business plan.

Bimbo had a marketing problem when it initially developed its business plan for the U.S. market. The name "Bimbo" means baby in Italian. But, the pronunciation is given on packaging as "Beembo" to distinguish it from the U.S. slang term "bimbo". At an Enactus leadership conference, which Bimbo is a large sponsor of because Enactus is a global youth leadership organization, there was an executive from BIMBO leading a chant of "Beem-Bo, Beem-Bo" in an attempt to teach the conference attendees about the U.S. presence of Bimbo.

When Bimbo was a small bakery business, could it ever have had expected to grow so large? Bimbo Bakeries operates thirty-three bakeries and employs more than 15,000 associates in the U.S. It distributes products through over 7,000 sales routes throughout the U.S.

It would seem impossible for the original owners to know why they would need a large number of lawyers to handle the contracts to acquire so many brand names. Did the owners know that their lawyers would need to protect the trademarks and brand names so that copycat companies could not use their hard-earned brand names and trademarks?

Think it over.

1. How do you think the original owners (Lorenzo Servitje, Jose T. Mata, Jaime Sendra, and Jaime Jorba) in 1945 would have answered the four-part process of testing the business model?

2. Using the different Bimbo Web sites, what are three other brand names that Bimbo owns that you recognize?

Global Case—Single Patent System in the European Union

After thirty years of hard work and many rounds of negotiation, the European Union (EU) has finally removed a major hurdle to innovation and economic growth. On December 11, 2012, the European Parliament approved the Unitary Patent Regulation, a language proposal and a plan for a Unified European Patent Court. Following ratification by each member state, it is likely that the new system will be operational starting on January 1, 2014 and that the first unitary patents will issue later that year.[106]

Hopefully, the new patent system will give innovative entrepreneurs the opportunity to become major contributors to the economic recovery of Europe. The patent application will be in English, French, or German, which are the three official languages of the European Patent Office (EPO).[107]

The objective is to create a level playing field for entrepreneurs. The benefits of a single patent system are numerous:

1. The single patent system will offer SMEs (small to medium enterprises) more exposure to national markets.

2. SMEs will have a simpler system to register their innovations at significantly lower costs. This will stimulate innovation across Europe as SMEs are able to protect their intellectual property through a coordinated system.

3. A unified patent court is to be created through an international agreement among EU member states to handle the implementation of the single patent system.[108] Once implemented, the costs of a patent will be reduced by 80 percent. This will help Europe to compete against the U.S. and Japan, where patents have been cheaper. Currently, due to the lack of a unified patent litigation system, there can be about 300 parallel lawsuits in different countries, sometimes with different outcomes.

4. The decisions of the new patent court will apply in all participating EU member states.

Currently, a European patent issued by the EPO providing protection in the twenty-seven EU Member States can cost up to €36,000, including up to €23,000 in translation fees alone. According to the European Commission, the new unitary patent will cost a minimum of €4,725, when the new rules are fully implemented, up to a maximum of €6,425. The costs for translation will drop significantly and will now range from €680 to €2,380. The renewal fees will be set at a level that takes account of the special needs of small firms, so that they too benefit from reduced costs. It is going to be important for EU nations to encourage adoption of the single patent system and provide on-going support for the new system. Without proper implementation and control it is still possible that European patent law will be a messy situation for many years.[109]

Think it over.

1. Do you agree that a single patent system will encourage entrepreneurship in the EU?

2. What are the benefits of a single patent system in the EU?

Preparing for Your Business Plan

You (or in teams) can write a business plan during the semester. There are questions at the end of each chapter to help guide you through the thinking and analyzing process. Appendix B has a sample business plan you can use as a template for developing your own new venture business plan.

Since this is Chapter 4, we will help you to determine if there are any legal issues you might have with your product. Are you using any copyrighted material by mistake? Is your product infringing on a competitor's patent?

Part II

Planning the New Venture

Chapter 5

Business Planning
What's Your Legal Form and Strategy?

In this chapter, we begin by tying the business model with the business plan. We will learn about the elements of a business plan and how to put them together systematically so that you can predict how your business will react both internally and externally to changes in the environment. We will then learn how to develop the introduction and strategy sections of this business plan. The introduction has three parts: background, management and organization, and legal form (sole proprietorship, partnership, and corporation). Strategy formulation is an analysis of the internal environment (management, mission and objectives, resources, the transformation process, and structure) and the external environment (customers, competitors, suppliers, labor force, stockholders, society, technology, governments, and the economy). Through the environmental analysis you determine the strengths, weaknesses, opportunities, and threats of the firm.

Learning Outcomes

After completing this chapter you should be able to:

1. Explain what a business plan is and who will read it;

2. Describe the "5 Cs of Credit";

3. List the main sections of a business plan;

4. Explain why the executive summary is written last but placed first in the business plan;

5. Describe what the introduction section of the business plan includes;

6. Discuss the differences among the legal structure of the sole proprietorship, partnership, corporation, and limited liability company (LLC);

7. Describe the strategy formulation section of the business plan process;

8. Identify the five internal environmental components and the two primary external environmental factors that affect organizational performance, and the difference between these two environments and their interrelationship;

9. Define the nineteen key terms identified in this chapter.

Entrepreneur Profile—John Hawkins, Cloud 9 Shuttle

Go to PBS Small Business School at www.small businessschool.org/. You can access the video for Cloud 9 Shuttle at www.smallbusinessschool.org/video.cfm?clip=1642#.

Books use the word "model" with many of the functions of business—for example, you can have a financing model, an organization model, a manufacturing model, etc. What we mean by business model in this chapter is that we identify the firm's product and service value, customers, the way it makes a profit, and its operations. The business model is the way you develop your product or service and how you deliver it to customers. Are you retail, wholesale, manufacturing, distribution, or a sales organization? Who are your customers and how do you reach them?

Much like a taxi service, Cloud 9 is a shared-ride transportation company. Cloud 9 is completely unlike any other shuttle company. What John Hawkins envisioned when he created the name was to do something bold and radically different than his competition.

John Hawkins took a failing shared-ride company and turned it around because he could see that growth would not come from catering to tourists, but to residents. John changed the strategy from a visitor only-based focus to a resident-based focus. The airport was only a short $5 ride to downtown. But the residential market lives in the suburbs around the city and the average fare for residents is $15. Cloud 9 now has repeat business from its suburb market customers.

Cloud 9 actually makes money at both the retail and wholesale level. It collects money from end-user customers who make their own reservation and pay when they use the service. It also sells its services to meeting planners who buy the transportation then provide it to people attending meetings and conventions in San Diego. The second revenue stream is a result of expansion and Hawkins's investment in limos and buses.[1]

Think it over.

1. What is the business model for Cloud 9?
2. How will Cloud 9's business model incorporate the Internet into its business model?

From Business Model to Business Plan

Let's get back to following the *Entrepreneurial Process Model* (Chapters 1 and 4), which helps you avoid failing.[2] See Exhibit 5-1 to see where we are now and where we are going. Part I of the book (Chapters 1–4) essentially focuses on developing a business model. Part II assumes that you have a feasible business model and are progressing to developing a business plan with a strategy, as they are essential dimensions of entrepreneurial orientation.[3]

In this chapter, we discuss the business plan and its introduction and strategy that are based on the business model, so let's be clear on the differences between these terms. Recall that a *business model* identifies the firm's product and service value, customers, the way it makes a profit, and its operations. It is relatively short and commonly condensed down into an elevator pitch. The *business plan* gives the details of the business model in a formal written document. The business model focuses on opportunity, whereas strategy focuses on the competitive environment and how the new venture will compete. Strategy *is the process of optimizing the effectiveness of the business model configuration against the external environment, including the potential to change the configuration, alter the underlying opportunity, or seek out new opportunities.*[4] The business plan combines and explains the business model and strategy.

Exhibit 5-1

Entrepreneurial Process Model

1. Selecting the New Venture (Chapters 1–4)	2. Planning the New Venture (Chapters 5–10)	3. Financing and Controlling the New Venture (Chapters 11–12)
Decision to be an entrepreneur or engage in entrepreneurial behavior (Chapter 1) ↓ Select an option to become an entrepreneur (Chapter 2) ↓ Develop a business model (Chapter 3) ↓ Test the feasibility of your business model (Chapter 4) ↕ **STOP** ↔ Passes—Proceed→ *You can go back to develop and test other business models	Develop an effective business plan →	Get funding, start the business venture, and run the business successfully

The Business Plan, Why it is Important, and Resources

Learning Outcome

1. Explain what a business plan is and who will read it.

In this section, we will discuss the need for business planning and strategy. We will also present the major sections of the business plan that will then be covered throughout the remaining chapters in this book.

The Business Plan

Here we discuss what a business plan is, why it is important, and resources to help you develop your business plan.

What is a Business Plan?

Like a good book, your business plan tells your story. The business plan *is a written description of the new venture.* It tends to state the objectives of the firm and the steps necessary to achieve them. It is a document that describes all relevant internal and external elements for starting a new venture. The business plan generally projects 3–5 years ahead and outlines the route a company intends to take to reach its yearly milestones including revenue projections. A well-thought out plan also helps you to step back and think objectively about the key elements of your business venture and informs your decision-making on a regular basis.[5] The business plan answers three questions, "Where am I now?" "Where am I going?" "How will I get there?"

A business plan is a key element for all types of small businesses, whether it is a startup venture or an on-going concern. For the startup venture, a plan may be likened to developing a blueprint for a new building because it is the first activity that should be undertaken before work on the structure itself begins. For an on-going concern, a business plan can be used as a forecasting tool for future expansion and development.

Is the Business Plan Important?

You should realize that not all the research on business planning concludes that you need a business plan to succeed.[6] But a business plan does state how the business will be successful,[7] and quality planning has been shown to increase performance.[8] Here is what the Small Business Administration (SBA) says about it: "Creating a business plan is one of the most important steps you will take because the plan serves as your road map for the early years of your business."[9] The business plan forces you to sit down and articulate the details of how you will start and run your business, and research supports that the better prepared you are to start a new venture, the greater are the odds that you will succeed.[10] Most new entrepreneurs start with limited financial resources,[11] and, if you want to raise money to start a new venture, most investors and lenders will require a business plan.[12] You may have a good business model, but don't be overconfident and make the mistake of not planning.[13]

Global business plans are similar to a one-country market plan. However, a global business plan does require a focus on customers in other countries, global pricing and currency issues, and legal issues that pertain to each country. The global business plan helps to communicate the goals of the new company to the employees located in different countries.[14]

Resources to Help You Develop Your Business Plan

You can buy software or get free help to develop your business plan:

- **Business Plan Pro** (www.businessplanpro.com) is the bestselling software you can buy. It also lets you read more than 500 existing business plans.[15]
- **The Small Business Administration (SBA)** offers a free "Build Your Business Plan" at www.sba.gov/business-plan/1. You can complete each section of the SBA's Business Plan Tool online and save it as a PDF for up to six months. It also provides some business plans you can read.[16]
- **SCORE** has a free template to use to develop your new or existing business plan (www.score.org, templates & tools link).[17]
- SBA resource partner SCORE, a **Small Business Development Center,** or a **Women's Business Center** also provide free counseling to help you develop and refine your business plan (information on all three can be found at www.sba.gov).

Who Reads a Business Plan? and the 5 Cs of Credit

A business plan is also written for the stakeholders of the organization to read. Stakeholders *are those groups of people who can either affect or are affected by the organization.* The key stakeholders who will read your business plan are investors and lenders. Why? Because they want evidence that they will get a return on their investment (ROI) and their money back with interest. Your business plan supports your ability to succeed.[18]

Stakeholders such as management and employees need to understand the mission and strategies expected to be achieved. Family members are often key stakeholders for small businesses. Motivated employees are key stakeholders because a happy employee does a better job helping customers.[19] Suppliers, investors, and banks all want to make sure they are supporting a new venture that will succeed.

Creditworthiness is important to you as an entrepreneur.[20] Banks usually want to read a business plan that includes the 5 Cs of Credit to determine if they want to give your small business a loan. The 5 Cs (Character, Capacity, Capital, Conditions, and Collateral) are as follows:

Character

Bankers and lenders have to believe that the key managers are honest and trustworthy and will be successful. Lenders have to make a decision based on the quality of the business plan, the owners' credit histories, and the skills and experiences in the industry of the owners and managers.[21]

Capacity

Capacity is often considered the most critical of the 5 Cs. What is the company's borrowing history and success in repaying past loan obligations? How much debt (loans) can a company add to its financial structure? Will a company be able to repay its debt? Do the borrowers have a secondary source of income in case the business is unable to pay off the loan?[22]

Capital

How much money has the entrepreneur invested in the business? Investors and lenders want entrepreneurs to have a financial commitment to help motivate them to be successful.

Conditions

The current economic conditions affect the success of the business. The owners cannot control what happens in the current economic conditions. However, investors and lenders will still want a ROI and loan payments during a downturn in the economy.

Collateral

Cash flow will usually be the primary source of repayment of a loan. However, lenders also look for collateral assets (usually in the form of real estate and office or manufacturing equipment) that the company pledges as an alternate repayment source for the loan if the business fails to repay the loan. Accounts receivable and inventory can also be pledged as collateral. Unless you're a business with a proven payments track record, you will almost always be required to pledge collateral.[23]

The ultimate success or failure of your business is based upon your decisions.[24] If you have a business plan, you will have a road map that allows you to look at the alternatives and the consequences of your management decisions.

Personal Application

1. Rate yourself on the 5 Cs of credit.

The Elevator Pitch

This skill-builder puts you in the venture capitalist position. You will watch an elevator pitch from the Internet and discuss if investors would or wouldn't invest in the new venture. The link for the elevator pitch for this chapter can be found at: www.youtube.com/watch?v=i6O98o2FRHw&feature=related.

Cup Ad CEO Josh Light describes his paper cup advertising business at the Utah State University Pitch Contest. Although the pitch doesn't actually occur in an elevator, the idea is that the entrepreneur has ninety seconds to impress the judges to invest in his or her business idea.

Think about it.

1. What score do you give Josh Light's pitch?

Great product idea and pitch		Terrible product idea and pitch	
4	3	2	1

2. Would you invest in Josh Light's business?

3. How would you improve Josh Light's pitch?

Major Sections of the Business Plan

We begin this section with a list of the ten major sections in a typical business plan. See Exhibit 5-2 for a listing. However, there is no generally accepted number of sections. Some sources will list fewer than these ten, but they tend to combine some of the content into one section. Next, we discuss the executive summary and introduction sections. Later in this chapter, we discuss the third section—strategy formation.

The Executive Summary

The executive summary is written last because you have to write a business plan before you can summarize the main points of the plan. Even though you have to wait for the end of the process to write the executive summary, it is still a critically important part of the process. Stakeholders will read the executive summary and then decide if they want to read the entire business plan. The executive summary is often one to two pages that summarize the entire plan. The executive summary primarily answers the question, "Why will this business be successful?" It should provide the following information:

- A brief explanation of the product or service that the business will provide. Why this product or service will satisfy customer needs (competitive advantage).
- A brief summary of the key people (management team) starting the business.
- The potential profitability.
- The possible expansion of the business in the future.

The Introduction Section of the Business Plan

The introduction section of the business plan includes three parts: background of the business, management and organization, and form of ownership. Let's review the three parts of the introduction section of the business plan.

Exhibit 5-2

Sections of the Business Plan

1. The executive summary (written last, placed first).
2. Introduction.
3. Strategy formulation.
4. The marketing function.
5. Location and layout.
6. The production/operation function.
7. The human resources function.
8. The financing function.
9. Controls.
10. Appendix.

Background of the Business

The background of the business includes its name, address (or addresses if there is more than one location), telephone number(s), email address, Web site address, hours of operation, and a brief history (if any). You want to state when the business was started or will be started.

The introduction should begin with a description of the type of business that you intend to conduct—your industry. Is your business primarily service or manufacturing, retailing or wholesaling? What products or services are provided to consumers? Your plan should indicate whether the business is a startup firm or an expansion of an ongoing concern.

The background of the business can include the hours of operation as well as any seasonal factors (e.g. annual period of high sales or services demanded) that may affect your business. If, for example, your business is affected by seasonal swings, you may want to incorporate another product or service to offset the negative profit swings. An example of this would be a lawn-care company that covers its profit swings in the winter by providing snow removal. If adequate profits can be earned in the spring, summer, and fall to sustain the business through the winter, then the owners may not need to consider methods of surviving through the winter. A complementary type of service or product, however, can enhance the resources of the firm.

Management and Organization

Some venture capitalists say that there are three important things in a business plan: management, management, and management. All other things being equal, venture capitalists would rather fund a project that has an average product, but excellent management, than a company with an excellent product, but only average management.

It is common to list all the business's key managers and their duties and responsibilities, with their qualifications. Include personal information about management such as your formal education, your business background, and any skills and experience you have that could be brought to bear on your firm. Any information about you that will help your company be successful should be included within this section. Managers with global experience and/or education should be highlighted if the new company expects to do business in different countries.[25] Résumés of the management team also should be included in this section. If the résumés are extensive, put them as exhibits in the back of the plan in the appendix.

The management section should contain an organization chart that details the primary operations such as production, accounting/finance, and sales/marketing (see Exhibit 5-3).

Many small businesses are not big enough to have a dedicated person for each position or job function. In many small businesses, one person can, and

Exhibit 5-3

Sample
Organizational Chart

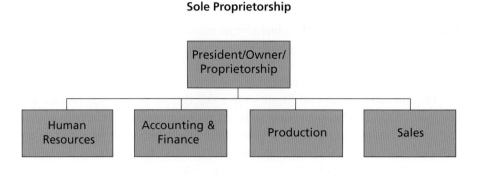

Sole Proprietorship

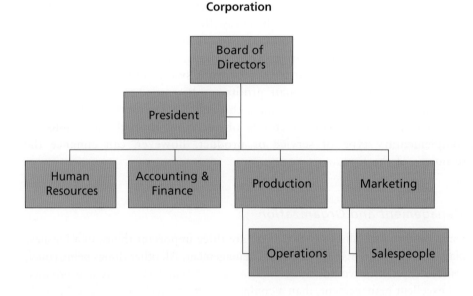

Corporation

frequently does, perform more than one function. For example, the president may also be the person in charge of sales. Production may also involve personnel, while the accounting function may be performed by an outside accountant on a weekly or monthly basis.

If you are writing a business plan for a smaller business with limited employees, you can describe the responsibilities included within each job in the firm. Each position on the organization chart should be explained in detail showing the chain of command. You should also include the outside resources that will be available to you such as accountants, lawyers, or consultants.

Form of Ownership

Include the form of ownership (proprietorship, partnership, or corporation) and distribution of business profits (if partnership or corporation) and any

Personal Application

2. Select a business you would like to start, or an existing business, and briefly describe the introduction section of its business plan.

salaries of key managers. We discuss form of ownership in detail in the next section.

Legal Form of Ownership

While the decision to own or operate a small business represents a major step in your life, it is important not to jump into the myriad operating details of such a venture before carefully considering what form of ownership your business will take. Your choice will determine the amount of taxes you will pay, whether you can be sued for unpaid business debts, and whether or not the organization will survive your death or absence. Our discussion in this section will examine the common forms of ownership. Because there is no single correct form for an organization, you must examine the pros and cons of each form and decide which is best for you.

Number of Owners, Taxation, and Liability

Before we begin, there are three important differences in the forms of ownership to consider when selecting one of them. First, there are the number of owners; you can have from one to thousands. Second, there is single or double taxation; we will explain the difference with corporations. Third, there is limited or unlimited liability. **Unlimited liability** *means that, if the business fails, the business owners not only lose the assets put into the business, but the owners will also have to use personal assets to pay the obligations of the business.* Some entrepreneurs put up their life savings to start a business, only to have it fail. But they didn't only lose their life savings; some lost personal assets including boats, cars, and even houses. We will define each of the forms of ownership based on these three considerations.

Learning Outcome

6. Discuss the differences among the legal structure of the sole proprietorship, partnership, corporation, and LLC.

Sole Proprietorship

The sole proprietorship is a business owned and operated by one person. The name of the business can be the entrepreneur's name, or another name to identify the business. This is the most common form of ownership. In this form of ownership, as a single proprietorship you will receive all the profits of the business, but you will bear all the costs and have unlimited liability springing from the firm's operations. The **sole proprietorship** *is a business owned by one person that has unlimited liability and pays personal income taxes on profits.* When starting out, this form of business ownership is the easiest and least expensive to set up.

Advantages and Disadvantages of Sole Proprietorship

See Exhibit 5-4 for a list of pros and cons to the sole proprietorship form of ownership.

Personal Application

3. Identify a sole proprietor and state the entrepreneur's name and the name of the business.

Exhibit 5-4

Advantages and
Disadvantages of Sole
Proprietorships

Advantages	Disadvantages
• Ease of startup. It is not difficult to start your own business.	• Unlimited liability. Because you own and operate the business, there is no legal distinction between you and the business and therefore you are liable for all its debts. Difficulty in raising capital. Because only you can raise money, the amount of funds available is strictly dependent upon your assets.
• Free to take profits. As you are the sole owner of the firm, you are free to take all the profits and use them for whatever purpose you desire.	
• Freedom to manage as you choose. Because you are the sole owner of the business, you have total authority to take any action you see fit.	• Maintaining the overall direction of your business. As the business expands, it becomes more complex and therefore quite difficult for one person to retain control in order to provide the necessary direction.
• Few legal restrictions. You have the freedom to operate (subject to the appropriate licensing and regulations) anywhere in the country and to add or remove products or services as you desire. Easy to dissolve. The firm only exists as long as you want it to.	• Demise of the firm. The death of an owner terminates the firm. Should someone else acquire the business, it will then be considered a new company.
• Taxes. Because you own and operate the firm, as the owner, you, rather than the business, are taxed.	

Partnerships

A partnership *is an association of two or more co-owners of a business.* Many CPA and law firms are partnerships, and the business name is often a listing of the partners' names, such as **Ryan & Downey, P.C.** There are two basic kinds of partnerships: general and limited, and other classifications that we discuss below. But let's start with the advantages and disadvantages of partnerships.

Advantages and Disadvantages of Partnerships

For a list of pros and cons, see Exhibit 5-5.

General Partnership

General partners *participate actively in the operation of the business, pay personal income taxes on profits, and have unlimited liability.* Perhaps the most significant responsibility from the individual's viewpoint is unlimited liability. As the business expands, liability increases correspondingly. Additionally, management of the partnership becomes increasingly more complex; however, too many equal partners slow down decision-making and make it difficult to reach a consensus.

Advantages	Disadvantages
• Ease of startup. Partnerships, as proprietorships, are not difficult to form.	• Unlimited liability of general partners. Limited partners only to the amount of investment.
• As one of the owners, you receive all the profits and have the right and freedom to manage.	• Each partner is liable for the debts of the organization.
• There are few legal restrictions and the organization is easy to dissolve.	• Because the partnership is nothing more than an agreement to be in business together, it can be difficult to raise capital.
• You, rather than the business, will be taxed as in a proprietorship.	• While two or more people can usually raise more money than one person can, there are limits to startup capital of partners.
	• As the business grows, it becomes more and more difficult for the original partners to manage.
	• Most agreements do, and all agreements should, contain a provision with respect to the transfer of a partner's interest in the partnership.
	• As with a sole proprietorship, death, imprisonment, or insanity automatically terminate the firm unless the partnership agreement states otherwise and a contractual clause is negotiated.

Exhibit 5-5

Advantages and Disadvantages of Partnerships

Limited Partnership

Limited partnerships are created in order to limit liability of partners as well as to facilitate the contribution of capital without incurring unlimited liability. A limited partner *does not take an active part in the management of the company, does pay personal income taxes on profits, and has limited liability.* A limited partner's liability extends only to the amount of money invested, not to personal assets. As a limited partner you must be careful, because if it can be determined that you took an active part in the management of the business, your liability becomes unlimited. This type of partnership should be clearly stated in the partnership agreement.

Unlimited Liability

A business may have any number of limited partners but there must be at least one general partner with unlimited liability. So if you need money to start your business and are willing to shoulder unlimited liability, as the general partner you can obtain money from limited partners and share some of the profits, while being able to run the business without their involvement in managing your business.

Personal Application

4. Identify a partnership and state the entrepreneur's name and the name of the business.

The Partnership Agreement

A **partnership agreement** *is a written document that sets forth all of the terms under which the partnership is to operate.* A partnership can be created with only an oral agreement, but this is rarely a good idea. As a matter of prudence, all partnerships should have a written document of agreement (in legal terminology called "articles of partnership"). Writing down the terms of a partnership may eliminate many future disputes. The process of documenting the partnership raises and answers many questions that you might not have considered.

Although there is no legal requirement for a written partnership agreement, common sense dictates that you should not go into business without one. The agreement should spell out all the status, responsibilities, and authority of each partner. Even if you go into business with your best friend, a family member, or relative, do not do it without a written agreement.

People often think they know what they are agreeing to only to discover later, and too late, that they never really understood the nature of their agreement. A written partnership agreement sets forth the details and terms of the partnership for the protection of each of the partners. Having a written agreement forces everyone to be specific and detailed. Also, these details do not fade with the passage of time and remain as permanent and legal reminders of what had been approved. The document will undoubtedly be referred to repeatedly in order to clarify misunderstandings.

It is useful to spell out every detail in order to avoid future misunderstandings and problems.[26] The typical partnership agreement should cover the following situations as delineated in Exhibit 5-6. The terms covered are not intended to be an exhaustive listing of possible provisions. Each partnership agreement will contain clauses that are specific to the organization and its principals. In the absence of a written agreement, the terms of the Uniform Partnership Act apply.

The Uniform Partnership Act

Lacking a written partnership agreement, the **Uniform Partnership Act (UPA)** *stipulates the rights and obligations of each of the partners engaged in the operation of an organization.* The UPA established a partnership as a separate legal entity, and not merely as an aggregate of partners.[27]

The UPA defines a partnership as "an association of two or more persons to carry on as co-owners of a business for profit." A partnership has three common elements:[28]

1. Common ownership;
2. Equal sharing of profits and losses;
3. The right to participate in managing the operations of the partnership.

In the initial startup of the organization, or at various times during the operation of the business, the partners may be called upon to augment the cash flow of the business (discussed in Chapter 10). This money becomes an obligation

Exhibit 5-6

Model Partnership
Agreement

Name of the partnership.

Purpose of the business. Why did you create this business and what will the business do?

Location. Where will the business be located physically?

Duration of the partnership. How long do you think the firm will operate? It is possible to have a partnership that lasts on a continuing basis (at least as long as everyone is alive) or one that is of short duration or established for a specific purpose and/or time.

Name and legal address of all partners.

Contribution of each partner to the business. This spells out who contributed specific assets to the organization. Contributions may consist of cash, real estate, skills, contacts or any other form of assets.

Terms specifying the distribution of profits and losses. Because the income and expenses of the partnership are treated as ordinary income and expenses as far as federal and state taxes are concerned, it is best to specify each partner's appropriate percentage of ownership and distribution. All partners need this protection. Shares of profits and/or losses may not be equal. Spell it out!

Terms specifying the compensation of the partners. Some partners may be paid a salary or commission because of their activity in the business. This compensation can be in addition to their share of the profits. Generally if one partner is more active or makes a bigger contribution to the organization, that partner is entitled to additional compensation.

Definition of profits. Because each partner is entitled to a specific percentage of the profits, it is best to know how profits are determined; which expenses are costs of doing business and which are personal. Obviously the higher the business expenses, the less profit there is to be divided.

Provisions for answering questions. How may a new partner be added or a current partner deleted? How will the partnership be dissolved or sold and how will the assets be distributed? These are all important questions that should be resolved before you begin operating your business.

Provisions governing the absence or disability of a partner will be handled. For example, will the partnership continue? Will the salary or asset-distribution remain the same? Is a disabled partner still responsible for the debts of the firm?

Provisions for altering the partnership agreement. Nothing lasts forever. With changing times and circumstances, partnership agreements should contain provisions to accommodate change.

of the business on which it must pay interest because the owners also function as lenders to the partnership.

Obligations of the partners are:

1. Share in partnership losses;
2. Work, if necessary, without salary;
3. Abide by the majority vote of the partners' decisions regarding operation of the organization;
4. Make available to all partners all information regarding business affairs;
5. Give formal accounting of all business affairs.

Keep in mind that a partnership requires mutual trust, respect, and loyalty.[29] Lacking these qualities, the partnership will be unlikely to succeed.[30]

Corporations

The corporate form of ownership was established to alleviate the major problems inherent in proprietorships and partnerships. Neither proprietorships nor partnerships provide for the continuation of the business when an individual owner or a partner dies or becomes incapacitated. Access to capital, beyond what may be provided by a limited circle of friends, relatives, and others is limited. Perhaps one of the most important problems in both forms of ownership is the individual's unlimited liability for the debts of either the proprietorship or the partnership. Therefore, a form of ownership was needed that had longevity beyond that of any individual, could raise capital, and had limited liability. Thus was born the corporate form of ownership. A corporation *is a legal entity owned by an unlimited number of shareholders that have limited liability under a common name that pays either single or double taxes.* When we use the term corporation, we mean a for-profit corporation. There are also nonprofit corporations that have no individual owners and pay no taxes.

The corporation, which carries on a business in its own name, exists as a separate entity in the eyes of the law. It can raise capital by either selling ownership (stock) or by borrowing (issuing bonds). Ownership of the corporation is established with the issuance of shares of stock; therefore individual owners, as stockholders, have no liability for corporate debt. As an owner, you may run your business without worry that your money and possessions are in danger of being taken to satisfy a business debt. You should keep in mind that if you work for the corporation, even though you may own all or a portion of the stock, you are an employee. As an employee, you are paid, receive benefits, and are taxed in the same manner as every other employee.

If you choose the corporate form of organization, you must form a separate organization that then sells portions of itself (shares) to you and possibly to other individuals (investors). If, for example, the corporation has 100 shares of stock and sells ten of these shares to you, you own 10 percent of the corporation. Your liability is equivalent to the value of the shares you held in the corporation. Note that you can be the sole owner of a corporation by keeping 100 percent of the stock in the company you start.

When a corporation is founded, it accepts all the laws, rules, and regulations of the state in which it is incorporated and in which it does business. As required by law, the corporation must report its financial operations to the attorney general of this state. Although it is logical and sensible for you to incorporate in the state in which you do business, as states have different rules, regulations, and taxes, it might be beneficial to be a foreign corporation. A *foreign corporation* is a company incorporated in a state other than where you do business. Because of its favorable laws, Delaware is the home of many of the largest U.S. corporations, and some have moved overseas to reduce taxes. Where you incorporate will be determined by such considerations as corporate taxes, fees, and restrictions on corporate activities. It pays to study carefully all the costs and regulations associated with incorporation and take steps to minimize them. However, most small business just incorporate in the state in which the founders live and work.

The first step in organizing a corporation is to comply with state regulations that require a certificate of incorporation or a charter, commonly called the articles of incorporation, to be filed with the state's attorney general. A corporate charter is a legal document that sets forth information about how the corporate entity intends to operate. A corporate charter would contain the information shown in Exhibit 5-7.

Exhibit 5-7
Model Corporate Charter

1. **Name of the corporation.** As the corporation is a separate legal entity, it must have an identity. In order to eliminate confusion or to prevent deception, the corporate name cannot be identical or even similar to that of another firm within the state's jurisdiction.

2. **Statement of purpose.** You must clearly state the purpose of the corporation. This is best done in general terms in order to have flexibility as the business develops. You might want to state the purpose of the business as "the sale and servicing of automobiles" rather than "selling Fords."

3. **Duration of the corporation.** In general, corporations are formed for perpetuity. It is possible, however, to incorporate for a specific time period.

4. **Names and addresses of the incorporators.** The incorporators must be identified in the articles of incorporation. These incorporators are legally obligated to attest that all information given in the corporate papers is correct.

5. **Name of business.** The legal address of the principal corporate office must be supplied. All official correspondence will be sent to this address.

6. **Corporate stock authorization.** A corporation is not obligated to issue all the stock authorized in the corporate papers. The corporation must, however, identify the different classes of stock and any special rights or privileges each classification may carry with it. For example, a corporation might want to issue special preferred stock with voting rights and common stock without such rights. In this section, the incorporators also must identify whether the stock has a par or no par value. Par value means that a single stock certificate would be denoted as one share value. No par means that no monetary value was assigned. In some instances, the state may require that a percentage of the stock value be deposited as escrow in a bank before incorporation. There may also be other restrictions.

7. **Preemptive rights or restrictions.** The corporate charter must provide specific details about preemptive rights or restrictions on the transfer of shares. In many cases, because corporate shares are owned by a few people, there may be limitations on how and at what value your shares may be sold and who may sell them.

8. **Name and address of the founding officers and directors of the corporation.**

9. **Rules and regulations under which the corporation will operate.** These are the bylaws of the corporation. Remember that once these are filed with the state's attorney general, you have created the corporate charter. The corporate entity is henceforth required to abide by its own rules and regulations. Once this process is complete, you then hold an organizational meeting of the stockholders to formally elect the directors who, in turn, appoint the corporate officers.

Advantages and Disadvantages of Corporations

If you choose to organize your business as a C corporation (commonly just called a corporation), you will be able to seize certain advantages that would not be open to you under other forms of organization. See Exhibit 5-8 for a list of pros and cons to corporations.

Taxation of the C, S, and Nonprofit Corporations

Personal Application

5. Identify a C and S corporation.

As a legal entity, the C corporation is entitled to the same rights, privileges, and obligations as an individual. One of the obligations a corporation incurs is that of paying taxes. Like individual income, the income of the corporation is similarly taxed by federal, state, and local governments. Taxes must be paid before any owners of the corporation receive dividends and when the owners receive dividends, because they are individuals, they pay individual income taxes as well.[31]

There are three major types of corporations, based on their being subchapter C or S and nonprofit. So far we have been discussing the C corporation, but

Exhibit 5-8

Advantages and Disadvantages of C Corporations

Advantages	Disadvantages
• Limited liability. Owners of corporate shares are only liable for the dollar value of their original or any subsequent investment.	• Cost, Time, and Paperwork. Creation of a corporation, an artificial entity, is not easy because it requires considerable paperwork required by the state. The state also levies a charge for participating in the process. Once corporate papers are filed by an attorney, the organizational process becomes time consuming.
• As the company becomes larger and accumulates more assets, fewer personal guarantees will be necessary.	
• Perpetuity. While the sole proprietorship and the partnership dissolve with the death or disability of the individuals involved, the corporate entity does not; as a legal entity it can exist in perpetuity.	• Limited liability, however, does not apply in matters involving taxes. Nonpayment of withholding taxes pierces the corporate status and becomes the individual owner's liability.
• Funding sources. The capital that can be raised is limited only by the number of shares authorized by the corporate charter that are available.	• Perils of increasing capitalization. When the corporation sells stock, each share usually has voting rights; if enough shares are sold to meet the need for capital, the owners may lose control of the organization.
• Transfer of ownership. Ownership of a corporation is transferable and is determined by the shares owned.	
• The corporate form of organization allows the company to draw on an expanded pool of talent.	• Federal and state control. As legal entities, corporations are subject to federal and state controls.
• Expansion and contraction. Because the corporation has a life of its own and can raise needed capital, it can expand or contract as the marketplace dictates.	• Double taxation. Income is taxed at the corporate and shareholder levels.

let's define it to separate it from the other two based on taxation. *The C corporation pays business taxes on profits and its unlimited number of shareholders with limited liability pay individual taxes on any share of the distribution of profits: double taxation.* While the double taxation of C corporations is a drawback, the ability to reinvest profits in the company at a lower corporate tax rate is an advantage. Most corporations are C corporations.[32]

In a move to equalize the tax burden for all forms of organizations, while limiting liability, particularly for small businesses, in 1954 the Internal Revenue Service (IRS) created a new tax entity, the Subchapter (S) Corporation now called simply the S corporation. So the S combines the advantages of the partnership and C corporation. *The S corporation does not pay business taxes; its unlimited number of shareholders with limited liability have their profit distributions taxed as individual income taxes.* This is single taxation. However, the IRS does place restriction on businesses in order to qualify to be formed as an S corporation:

- Shareholders must be U.S. citizens.
- The S corporation can't be a subsidiary of another corporation, and partnerships and C corporations can't own shares, but certain types of trusts and estates can own shares.
- The S can only have one class of stock, common or preferred.
- It can't have more than one hundred members, and all members must agree to be formed as an S corporation.

Nonprofit corporations don't pay any taxes on profits, and because there are no owners, profits are not distributed. All employees, including the founder, pay individual income taxes on their compensation. We include the nonprofit (NGO) when we compare the different types of ownership form.

Limited Liability Company (LLC)

The LLC is similar to the S corporation, but with fewer restrictions. The major advantage of the LLC is that it combines the benefits of the single-tax advantage of partnerships and S corporations with the limited liability of the C and S corporations. The major disadvantages are that setting up and maintaining the LLC is more difficult and expensive, and that LLC regulations vary by state making taxes and interstate business more complex.

The LLC differs from the C and S corporate form of organization in the following ways:

- Corporations have stockholders; LLCs have members.
- Shares of stock are not issued; ownership is designated in the articles of incorporation.
- Unlike the S corporation, and like the C, the number of members is unlimited.
- An LLC can select to be taxed as any of the other forms of ownership.
- Ownership interests can only be transferred with the unanimous written consent of the other members.

Personal Application

6. Identify an LLC.

Understanding the differences among the forms of business ownership, let's define LLC. *The limited liability company (LLC) provides limited liability for all members that pay personal income tax on profits.* This is single taxation. It is usually easy to spot an LLC because they use the letters LLC in the legal name of the company.

Comparing Legal Forms of Ownership

See Exhibit 5-9 for a comparison of the legal forms of ownership. When starting out, often as a hybrid entrepreneur out of your home, as did **Blake Mycoskie** who founded **TOMS** shoes, the sole proprietorship form of business ownership is the easiest and least expensive to set up.[33] A sole proprietorship is usually a small business, but with employees it can be a small to medium-enterprise (SME) or even a large business. However, if the business grows, the form of ownership often changes to a partnership, corporation, or LLC.

The overriding choice between a C or an S corporation or LLC should be based upon the impact on one's tax situation. The S corporation and LLC permits you to escape double taxation in that all income, expenses, profits, and losses pass through to your individual personal tax base. Thus you can deduct all expenses and perhaps reduce your total tax bill. If a business shows losses, this too can work to the taxpayer's short-term advantage; but it is *unethical* to state that running a losing operation results in larger corporate losses and is a situation to be avoided in the long run. Thus the S or LLC is useful in those situations concerning startup operations or in those situations where the business is highly profitable and would thus have substantial dividends to pay out. Many businesses don't benefit from an S company where the owners receive most of the profits as salaries and benefits. When selecting your form of ownership, it is a good idea to get advice from a lawyer with knowledge of taxes who is experienced in forming legal ownership.

Strategy Formulation of the Business Plan

Entrepreneurial orientation and the entrepreneurial process result in a business model,[34] and you exploit opportunities through implementing strategy.[35] Based on the value of planning,[36] the third section of the business plan requires new ventures to formulate their strategy. The strategy formulation section of the business plan has three sections:

1. **Mission:** It is an organization's purpose or reason for being (Chapter 3).
2. **Objectives (prioritized):** What the organization wants to accomplish.
3. **Environmental analysis:** It includes an analysis of the internal environment (which includes the mission and objectives) and its external environment resulting in a strengths, weaknesses, opportunities, and threats (SWOT) analysis.

Exhibit 5-9
Comparing Legal Forms of Ownership

	Sole Proprietor	General Partnership	Limited Partnership	C Corporation	S Corporation	Nonprofit Corporation	LLC
Number and type of owners	One proprietor	Two or more partners	Two or more, but at least one general partner	Unlimited stockholders	One hundred maximum stockholders	No owners	Unlimited members
Liability	Unlimited	Unlimited for all general partners	Limited for limited partners	Limited	Limited	Limited	Limited
Taxation	Individual	Individual	Individual	Business and individual (double tax)	Individual	Not taxed	Individual
Profit distribution	Proprietor gets all	Shared based on partnership agreement	Shared based on partnership agreement	Dividends paid based on number of stockholders' shares	Dividends paid based on number of stockholders' shares	Surplus can't be distributed	Shared based on members' agreement
Life of firm/ transferable	Ends with death of proprietor	Ends with death or withdrawal of partner	Ends with death or withdrawal of partner	Perpetual	Perpetual	Perpetual	Varies with agreement, most states thirty years
Management control	Only proprietor	Shared by general partners	Limited partners no control	Board of directors elected by stockholders	Board of directors elected by stockholders	Board of directors/ trustees	Based on members' agreement
Ease and cost of legal form	Low	Moderate	Moderate	High	High	High	High
Raising capital	Difficult	Moderate	Moderate	Easiest	Easiest	Difficult	Moderate
Formation procedure	Just get any required licenses or permits. Use social security number. Can get a business number to identify business (ID)	No partnership agreement needed, but highly recommended. Need to get employer ID number	Comply with state laws and file a Certificate of Limited Partnership. Must have a partnership agreement and keep required records	Comply with state laws and file articles of incorporation and other required reports, prepare bylaws and follow corporate formalities	Must meet all criteria to file as an S. Same procedure as C, but then elect S status with the IRS	Meet requirements of state law	Meet requirements of state law

The mission and objectives state what you are doing and where you want the business to go, and the strategy states how you will get there. *A strategy is a plan for achieving the organization's mission and objectives.* Strategy formation assesses the internal environment, the external environment, environmental analysis, and selecting the overall strategy of beating the competition. This section progresses through this process.

The Internal Environment Analysis

The organization's internal environment *includes the management, mission and objectives, resources, the transformation process, and structure that affect the firm's performance from within its boundaries.* See Exhibit 5-10 for an illustration. Let's discuss each factor separately then put them together.

Management

Managers are an important part of strategy formation because they are responsible for the performance of the business.[37] Managers perform the functions of planning, organizing, staffing, leading, and controlling. The leadership style and the decisions made by managers affect the performance of the business. Because managers have such an impact on the success of the business, they need to be selected carefully. We will discuss this in detail in Chapter 9, "The Human Resource Plan."

Exhibit 5-10

Internal Environment Factors

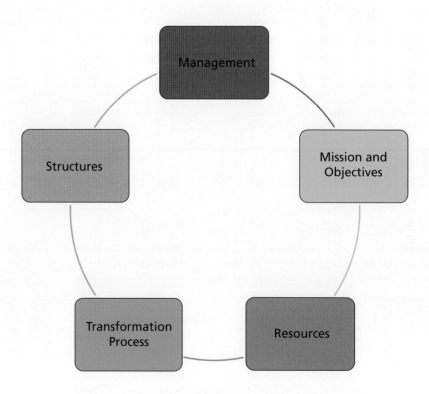

Mission

A mission statement reveals an organization's purpose or reason for being. The mission was included in the business model, what product and service value you offer, and is included in the business plan. **Artsicle** was started by two young entrepreneurs with a mission to change the art world. Their mission is to create a Web site where people can buy or rent art from 150 hand-picked artists. Their service costs $25 a month. They have received over $400,000 from angel investors to help them create a Netflix for art.[38] The mission in the business plan is expanded to include the nature of the business in the areas of product, target customer, competitive advantage, and philosophy. Let's look at each separately.

Personal Application

7. Write a mission statement for a business you would like to start or a small entrepreneurial business in your community.

- ■ **Products and services:** The mission section of the business plan includes your business model plus your present and future products and services to be offered. In the strategy section it is not necessary to list all the products and services; they are listed under the marketing section of the business plan and will be discussed in Chapter 6.
- ■ **Target market:** Your industry and target market were part of the business model and are included in the business plan strategy section.

ESPN magazine targets a large segment of people. To compete head on with them would be very difficult for the small business. However, a small business could pick a niche and offer a sports magazine to people interested in a specific sport. If you want to start a surfing magazine, you will be targeting a different customer than a customer who likes a broader range of sports found in the *ESPN* magazine.

The Internet has allowed small businesses to reach the masses, yet at the same time focus on a small target segment. By selling though the Internet, a small business can grow quickly into a global business. For example, 20-year-old British entrepreneur Calum Bush started Media Devil (http://mediadevil.com/us/), which is a mobile accessories company. He has 300,000 customers in the U.K. He has since expanded his business to Italy and the U.S. His company sells their products on the company Web-site—but they also have many 5-star products that are sold on Amazon.[39]

Personal Application

8. Who are the target customers for a business you would like to start or a local community entrepreneurial business?

- ■ **Competitive advantage:** As developed in the business model, the competitive advantage is an important part of the business plan mission statement. What can your business do better or different than the competition? If you don't have an answer, it may not be a good idea to start your new venture. The competitive advantage is determined based on the environmental analysis. **Red Box** took business from the video store **Blockbuster** because target customers want to pay less money to watch a movie.
- ■ **Philosophy of the business:** The business philosophy essentially puts the business model core values and critical success factors together in the business plan. It answers the questions, "What are the basic beliefs, values, aspirations, and priorities of the firm?" "What is the firm's view of itself and the way it conducts business?" "Will you be ethical and socially responsible?" "What is the image the firm wants its target customers and the general public to have of it?"

The mission statement plan should be communicated to employees and target customers.[40] You should not lose sight of your mission because it should influence how day-to-day business is conducted. Therefore, it should be concise enough to commit its tenets to memory. On the other hand, a mission statement should also be broad enough for the business to be able to move into new markets and products as the external environment changes. Two small business example mission statements are included in Exhibit 5-11:

According to the late W. Edwards Deming, the major reason businesses fail is because management does not look ahead.[42] Under management's directives, the firm produces the wrong product: one with no market, or too small a market. Managers with vision develop and change the mission by offering products and services in demand by customers. You need to know your target market and give them the products they want, at a profit. You also need to stay ahead of your competition by continually being innovative.[43] At different points in time, Holstee's and Vita Coco will have to modify their business to keep up with changing competitive trends in their industries.

Exhibit 5-11

Mission Statement Section of the Business Plan

Holstee sells eco-friendly clothing and accessories. The Brooklyn, NY-based company rose from obscurity after its mission statement, known as the Holstee manifesto, went viral. The document has been viewed online more than 50 million times and translated into twelve languages. Holstee turned the message into a $25 poster—printed on recycled paper. The poster quickly became one of the company's top selling products. You can access Holstee's Facebook page at http://shop.holstee.com/pages/about. The company mission statement is presented below.

- Product: Eco-friendly clothing and accessories.
- Target customer: Cool urban shoppers that relate to their eco-friendly vision.
- Competitive advantage and philosophy: Holstee co-founders **Fabian Pfortmüller** and brothers **Mike** and **Dave Radparvar** felt that mission statements of large organizations sound meaningless. They felt that if a mission is going to work it has to be genuine. Holstee's mission statement was written because the owners wanted to build their eco-friendly company by telling everyone about their desire to create a company that breathes life into the world every day. The unique Holstee mission statement design helped the company to grow from selling about 200 T-shirts to an overnight Internet sensation.[41]

Vita Coco was created while **Ira Liran** was visiting Brazil. Ira realized Brazilians loved drinking coconut water. He started researching the prospect of branding coconut water for the American market. After spending several months working with coconut plantations and producers, making connections, and learning the politics of production in Brazil, Vita Coco was born. Vita Coco has created a new market in the non-carbonated beverage business and redefined the alternative sports beverage category.

- Product: Vita Coco is coconut water that comes from inside younger coconuts filled with a clear, electrolyte-rich juice that contains zero fat and zero cholesterol. It is an all-natural, super-hydrating, fat-free, cholesterol-free, nutrient-packed, potassium-stacked, mega-electrolyte coconut water.
- Target customer: Health-conscious consumers looking for a healthy drink alternative.
- Competitive advantage and philosophy: Vita Coco's competitive advantage is derived from the healthy nutrients associated with its all-natural coconut drink.

Objectives

You need objectives to make it clear what your new venture will accomplish.[44] Recall in Chapter 3 that setting objectives is part of problem-solving and decision-making. As shown in Exhibit 3-5, the setting objectives model is: (1) To + (2) action verb + (3) specific and measurable result + (4) target date. **Tony Petrucciani** and his management team at **Single Source Systems** believe that you should not set too many objectives so that you can focus on a few priorities.[45] Using this model, it is common to write 1–3 long-term objectives and 3–5 short-term objectives in the business plan. When you write objectives, they should be difficult but achievable: specific, observable, measureable results; with a target date, for example, "To make a profit of $75,000 in our 3rd year in business October 31, 2017." They should also be participatively set when possible and accepted by your management team and employees at all levels.[46]

Personal Application

9. Write three objectives using the objectives model for your entrepreneurial business.

Resources

As discussed in Chapter 4, to make sure your operations are feasible, you need the resources to establish an entity that will develop and deliver your product or service to exploit your opportunity.[47] Your resources are a source of competitive advantage because they are needed to compete and achieve your objectives.[48] Your list of needed resources should be included in your business plan, especially if you need money to finance their purchase.[49] Resources are discussed in more detail in Chapter 7.

The Transformation Process

The transformation process *is the system for converting inputs into outputs.* The transformation process has a direct effect on the productivity and substitutability of the firm. The transformation process has four components:

1. *Inputs*: Inputs include the firm's resources that are converted into outputs.
2. *Outputs*: Outputs are the goods and/or services offered to customers.
3. *Process*: The transformation of the inputs into outputs.
4. *Feedback, influence, and control*: Feedback provides a means of control to ensure that the inputs and process are producing the desired results.

A small manufacturing firm like **Myers Motors** produces the Duo electric car. Myers will use raw materials and components such as steel, plastic and metal parts, rubber tires, and so on (inputs) as it makes electric cars (outputs) on the assembly line (process). A service organization such as a **TD Bank** will use loan application forms (inputs) to make a loan (output). The loan officer will process the application and issue the funds.

You will learn more about the transformation process, which is commonly called the operations function, in Chapter 8, "The Operations Plan." See Exhibit 5-12 for an illustration of the transformation process. Note that the transformation process has a feedback loop with influence and control. If electric cars roll off the assembly line, are test-driven, and meet standards, the

Personal Application

10. Explain how a business you would like to start or a small entrepreneurial business in your local community transforms inputs into outputs.

Exhibit 5-12

The Transformation
Process

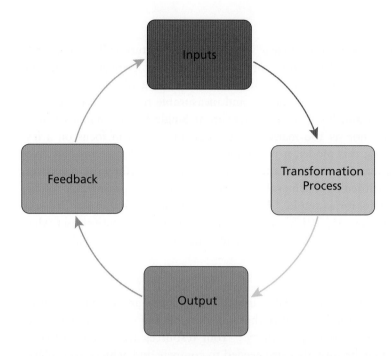

feedback is positive and you should keep up the good work. However, if they don't run according to standard, the feedback is negative and the inputs and/or processes must be changed to meet the standards.

Structure

An organization is a system. A system *is a set of two or more interacting elements in which each part affects the whole, and each part is affected by at least one other part.* An organization, being a system, is structured into departments such as finance, marketing, production, personnel, and so on. Each of these departments affects the organization as a whole, and each department is affected by the other departments. Companies structure resources to transform inputs into outputs. How you structure your resources is ultimately the source of your competitive advantage.[50]

All of the business's resources must be structured effectively to achieve its objectives. And entrepreneurs need to continually review their structure and change with the environment. If the business has many managers and distinct departments, you may want to include an organization chart with the business plan introduction section as an exhibit. Place the department name and the manager of the department in the boxes. Review Exhibit 5-13 for an illustration of the interrelationship between the internal environment components.

The External Environment Analysis

The organization's external environment *includes the factors that affect the business's performance from outside its boundaries.* Unlike the internal environment, managers have little or no control over what happens outside the business,

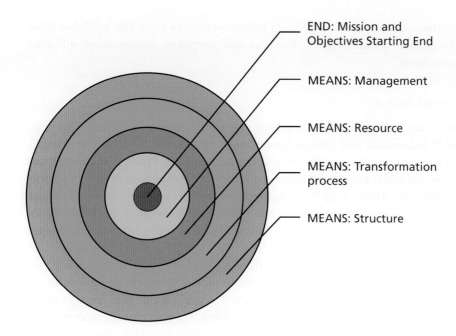

Exhibit 5-13
Means and Ends

END: Mission and Objectives Starting End

MEANS: Management

MEANS: Resource

MEANS: Transformation process

MEANS: Structure

yet these factors can mean the difference between the firm's success and failure. Thus, entrepreneurs need to monitor what takes place in the external environment through research.[51] Consequently, the internal environmental factors should be based on the external factors.

There are nine major external factors. Five are known as *task factors* and the other four are known as *general factors.* Here, we briefly discuss each factor in the two categories.

Task Factors

To be market-oriented, you need to focus on your customers and competitors.[52] These are generally the two most important external environmental factors. Without *customers,* you don't have a business, so you need to understand your customers to create value for them.[53] **McDonald's** listened to its customers wanting more choice and variety, so it offers salads and now sells just about as much chicken as beef.[54] To compete and gain customers, you need a competitive advantage, which is based on a competitor analysis.[55] Therefore, a business is not simply a function of its own actions but must be understood relative to the actions of its rival *competitors.*[56] **Wal-Mart** continues to drop its prices to take customers away from competitors.[57] If **Southwest** lowers its price, rivals generally have to match the lower price, and it can counterattack.[58]

Partnerships with *suppliers* also affect firm performance.[59] **Dell, Lenovo, Toshiba,** and **Fujitsu** all had to recall dangerous laptop-computer batteries made by **Sony.** The employees of an organization have a direct effect on its

Personal application

11. Give an example of how one firm's competitors have affected that business.

performance. Management recruits human resources from the available *labor force* outside its boundaries. Partners and corporate *shareholders* influence management.

General Factors

Personal application

12. Give an example of how technology would be used in a business you would like to start, or how technology has affected an existing business.

Our *society,* to a great extent, determines what are acceptable business practices.[60] Individuals and groups have formed to pressure business for changes, such as the green movement to protect the environment. **Mothers Against Drunk Drivers (MADD)** pressures alcohol companies to promote responsible alcohol consumption. *Technology* has changed the speed and the manner in which organizations conduct and transact business, and technology is often a major part of a firm's systems process, including **Frito-Lay** using handheld computers to track real-time inventory.

The *economy* (growth rate, inflation, interest rates, foreign exchange rates, and so on) affects business performance. During the recession, many businesses lost money. The *government* (federal, state, and local) creates laws and regulations that business must obey. So government matters as it affects how business is conducted.[61] Due to the financial crisis, Congress worked to create new financial regulations to help prevent another crisis and recession. To learn more about the U.S. federal government, visit www. usa.gov.

SWOT Analysis

The third and final part of the environmental analysis is the SWOT, which is based on the internal and external environments. Through a SWOT analysis the firm identifies its strengths, weaknesses, opportunities, and threats. At this point, we are going to change from theory to practice. You are going to learn "how to" perform a SWOT analysis.

Strengths and Weaknesses

Personal Application

13. What are the strengths and weaknesses of a business you would like to start, or a local small entrepreneurial business?

Based on the internal and external factors, how does your business compare with the competition? The way to approach this analysis is to identify the critical success factors (Chapter 3) in your industry. What does it take to be successful? As you are identifying the critical success factors, write them down using a form such as the one in Exhibit 5-14. For each factor, rate your firm and each major competitor on a scale from 1—weak, to 10—strong. If you are not sure what the success factors are, talk to people in both the internal and external environment. The important thing about the analysis is to develop a strategy based on your strengths while you work to minimize your weaknesses. In Exhibit 5-14 , **Minit Car Wash** is not as strong as **Clean Car** or **Keep Clean.** Minit needs to improve where it has its retail locations and the marketing of its company.

Exhibit 5-14
Environmental
Analysis

Strength & Weakness Analysis: Minit Car Wash vs. Competitors

Rating scale 1=weak, 10=strong.

Key Success Factors	Minit	Clean Car	Keep Clean
Strengths			
1. Quality of car wash process	8	10	9
2. Low car wash price	8	9	9
Overall Strength Rating	16	19	18

(Clean Car and Keep Clean both have a better car wash process and a lower price than Minit)

Key Success Factors	Minit	Clean Car	Keep Clean
Weaknesses			
1. Location	4	8	9
2. Marketing	5	10	8
Overall Weakness Rating	9	18	17

(Minit has poor retail locations and weak marketing compared with Clean Car and Keep Clean)

List of Opportunities (in rank order of most likely to implement)
Increase use of coupons and customer loyalty cards.
Increase car wash price.
Improve car wash process.
Open new car wash locations in higher traffic areas.

List of Threats (in order of importance of threat to our success)
Competitors could copy Minit's new coupons and new customer loyalty cards.
Increase car wash price might decrease sales due to the poor economy. Customers could choose to wash their own cars.
It would cost money to improve the car wash process.
Opening a new car wash location would require market research, take a long time to implement, and be a high cost.

Opportunities and Threats

Based on the internal and external environments, what opportunities and threats do you foresee? Possible areas include: market growth/decline, increasing/decreasing competition, price and cost changes, economic expansion/contraction, government changes in regulations, availability of supplies, increasing/decreasing substitute products, changing taste/needs of customers, etc. On a form, such as Exhibit 5-14, write down the major opportunities you can take advantage of to increase size/profits, and areas you need to watch to make sure you remain successful. For example, **Wal-Mart** has so many superstores that it is getting to the point of saturation: no room for more superstores. Thus, it is going to build smaller stores. In Exhibit 5-14, **Minit Car Wash** could decide to use

Personal Application

14. What are the opportunities and threats to a business you would like to start, or a local small entrepreneurial business?

coupons, start a new customer loyalty card, increase its car wash price, or open a new retail location.

Today, entrepreneurs need to gain control over their environment. According to Russell Ackoff, *interactive managers* design a desirable strategy and invent ways of bringing it about. He believes we are capable of creating a significant part of the future and controlling its effects on us. Experience is no longer the best teacher; it's too slow, ambiguous, and imprecise. Experimentation replaces experience. You need to be innovative to remain competitive.[62]

Interactive managers try to prevent, not merely prepare for, threats, and to create, not merely exploit, opportunities. Rather than react or respond, interactive managers make things happen for their benefit and that of their stakeholders. They plan strategies to do better in the future than the best that is presently deemed possible. See Exhibit 5-15 for a review of both the internal and external environments.

Exhibit 5-15

The Organizational Environment

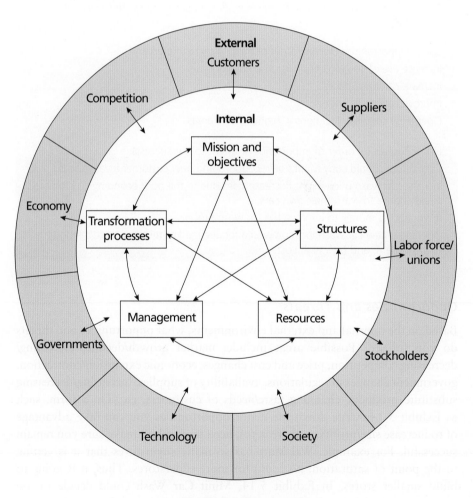

←—→ Feedback, influence, control

The Entrepreneurial Strategy Matrix

Another part of strategy formation is the selection of specific overall strategies.[63] The Entrepreneurial Strategy Matrix (ESM) is used by small-business owners to suggest strategies for new and ongoing entrepreneurial ventures that will lead to optional performance in response to the identification of different combinations of innovation and risk. The matrix answers: What venture situation are you in? What are the best strategic alternatives for a given venture?[64]

Innovation is defined as the creation of something new and different. The newer and more different the product or service is, the higher the innovation. Risk is defined as the probability of a major financial loss. The entrepreneur determines the chances of the entrepreneurial venture failing and how serious the financial loss would be. The same dollar amount of possible loss might be more serious to one entrepreneur than to another. Combining innovation and risk, a four-cell matrix was created as shown in Exhibit 5-16a.

The ESM also suggests appropriate strategies for each cell. Suggested strategies are presented in Exhibit 5-16b. You should notice that most of the strategies complement the mission (competitive advantage, philosophy). Thus, entrepreneurs use the first part of the figure to identify which cell their firms are in. Then, based on their cell, they utilize the appropriate suggested strategies for their matching cell in Exhibit 5-16b.

Personal Application

15. Using the Entrepreneurial Strategy Matrix, select a business you would like to start or an existing small business and select its independent variable innovation and risk cell combination and its business strategy(ies).

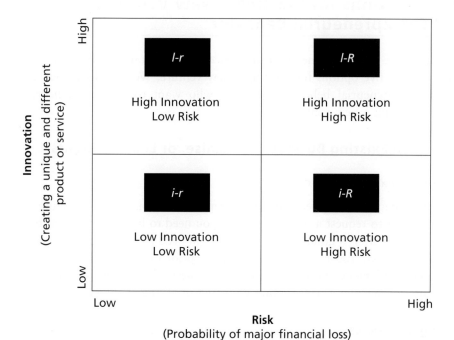

Exhibit 5-16a

The Entrepreneurial Strategy Matrix: Independent Variables

Source: M.C. Sonfield and R.N. Lussier, "The entrepreneurial strategy matrix: A model for new and ongoing ventures. *Business Horizons* 40 (3 1997): 73–77. Used with the authors' permission.

Exhibit 5-16b

The Entrepreneurial
Strategy Matrix:
Appropriate
Strategies

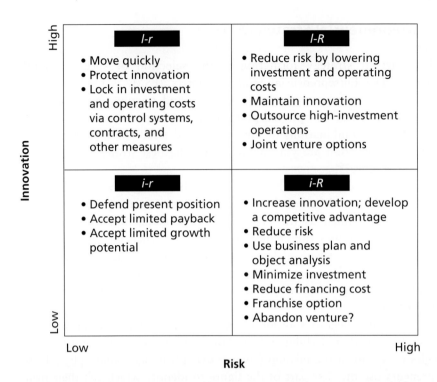

Source: M. C. Sonfield and R. N. Lussier, "The entrepreneurial strategy matrix: A model for new and ongoing ventures. *Business Horizons* 40 (3 1997): 73–77. Used with the authors' permission.

Other Options for Starting a New Venture, and Entrepreneurial Behavior

Once again we describe some of the differences between starting a new business and the other five options for creating a new venture. We also discuss engaging in entrepreneurial behavior for those who want to be entrepreneurial without starting a new venture.

Buying an Existing Business, Franchise, or Leasing Rights

Buying an Existing Business

As part of the process of becoming an entrepreneur through an acquisition, it is a good idea to request a business plan. If you need to borrow money to buy the business, there is a good chance that you will need to write a business plan for your business. You may be able to use the prior owner's business plan as a template and make the changes to the business plan following the same procedures as starting a new venture discussed in all the chapters.

Buying a Franchise

When you buy a franchise you may not need a business plan, but if you need one to raise money to buy the franchise, the franchisor may provide you with important information, such as the startup cost and projected profitability of the business based on the results of other franchisors.

Buying Licensing Rights

When you buy intellectual property rights, you will likely be starting a new venture. If so, it is recommended that you write a business plan, especially if you need to get funding, following the business planning process.

Starting a Corporate or Nonprofit New Venture

Starting a Corporate Venture

If you start a new venture for an existing business, you will need to convince management that you have a feasible business model. A good way to convince management is to develop and present to them a business plan following the same business planning process as for a new business, which you will be starting. Management will especially want to know the startup cost and the potential profitability.

Starting a Nonprofit

If you want to be the founder of a nonprofit, you are starting a new venture and you will more than likely need to get funding. A good way to convince people to provide funding is with your business model elevator pitch backed up with a business plan. However, the nonprofit business plan is somewhat different than a for-profit business plan. We have pointed out some of the differences in prior chapters and in this chapter Exhibit 5-9 compares the forms of legal ownership. The SCORE Web site (www.score.org) provides "Business Planning Tools for Non-Profit Organizations" that you can use to develop your business plan; at the end of this PDF is a list of other resources you can use. The nonprofit **Executive Service Corps**—United States (ESC) (www.escus.org) also provides affordable counseling to help you develop a business plan for a nonprofit. Don't forget that college SBIs and SBDCs provide help as well.

Entrepreneurial Behavior

Don't forget that if you are not interested in starting a new venture, as an employee you can engage in *entrepreneurial behavior* that can lead to a new venture or the improvement of your current employer's performance. The ability to develop a business plan is a valuable entrepreneurial skill.[65] If you do develop a business plan and are seeking a job with an entrepreneurial business, you can make the firm aware of your business plan and possibly bring it to a job interview. If your employer doesn't have a business plan, you could volunteer to develop a business plan for the owner and/or managers.

Take it to the Net

Visit www.routledge.com/cw/Lussier for the book's companion Web site, where you can:

- use learning aids, including taking a quiz
- find links to resources in this chapter, as well as other links including videos
- learn about and start the following activities: Continuing Integrated Case, Your Ninety-Second New Venture Pitch, the Paper Clip Entrepreneurship Challenge, College Entrepreneurial Spirit Award, and the Community Entrepreneurial Spirit Award.

Chapter Review and Summary

As we bring this chapter to a close, you should understand going from the business model to the business plan and the purpose of the business plan and who will read the plan that you develop. You should be able to explain the importance of character, capacity, capital, conditions, and collateral when presenting a business plan to potential financial sources. You should know the ten sections of a business plan. You should also know the differences among the legal forms of ownership: sole proprietorship, partnerships, corporations, and LLCs. You should be able to identify the internal and external environmental factors, conduct a SWOT analysis, and know how to use the ESM.

This summary lists the learning outcomes from the chapter and their answers.

1. **Explain what a business plan is and who will read it**

   The business plan is a written description of the new venture. The business plan generally projects 3–5 years ahead and outlines the route a company intends to take to reach its yearly milestones including revenue projections. A business plan is written for the stakeholders of the organization. The key stakeholders who will read the business plan are investors and lenders because they want evidence that they will get a ROI and their money back with interest.

2. **Describe the "5 Cs of Credit"**

   Potential sources of funding often review the entrepreneur for five important criteria: character, capacity, capital, conditions, and collateral. Investors and lenders do business with people who can be trusted, have a history of paying back debt, have some financial resources of their own invested in the company, can continue doing business if the environment changes, and have assets they can claim if the business fails.

3. **List the main sections of a business plan**

   A business plan consists of the following 10 major sections: (1) the executive summary (written last, placed first), (2) introduction, (3) strategy formulation, (4) the marketing function, (5) location and layout, (6) the production/operation function, (7) the human resources function, (8) the financing function, (9) controls, and (10) appendix.

4. **Explain why the executive summary is written last but placed first in the business plan**

   The executive summary of the business plan has to be written last because it can't be summarized until after the plan is written. The executive summary is a critically important part of the process because stakeholders who read the business plan will read the executive summary first to determine if they are interested in reading the other sections of the business plan.

5. **Describe what the introduction section of the business plan includes**

   The introduction section of the business plan needs to provide the reader with a review of the type of business and the key people starting the business. The introduction section includes the background of the business, a short review of the management credentials and organization structure, and the form of ownership as a sole proprietorship,

CHAPTER 5: BUSINESS PLANNING

partnership, or corporation and how any profits will be distributed.

6. **Discuss the differences among the legal structure of the sole proprietorship, partnership, corporation, and LLC**

The *sole proprietorship* is a business owned by one person who has unlimited liability and pays personal income taxes on profits. A *partnership* is an association of two or more people who carry on as co-owners of a business. There are two types of partnerships. *General partners* participate actively in the operation of the business, sharing all the responsibility and profits, pay personal income taxes on profits, and have unlimited liabilities. A *limited partner* does not take an active part in the management of the company, pays personal income taxes on profits, and has limited liability. A *corporation* is a legal entity owned by an unlimited number of shareholders who have limited liability under a common name and pay either single or double taxes. There are three types of corporations. Under the *C corporation, the unlimited number of shareholders pay* business taxes on profits, and with limited liability pay individual taxes on any share of the distribution of profits: double taxation. Under the *S corporation, the unlimited number of shareholders do* not pay business taxes, and with limited liability have their profit distributions taxed as individual income taxes.

Nonprofit corporations don't pay any business taxes, except for FICA, unemployment insurance and disability. Because there are no owners, profits are not distributed. The *limited liability company (LLC)* provides limited liability for all members who pay personal income tax on profits.

7. **Describe the strategy formulation section of the business plan process**

The strategy formation begins with the mission statement followed by the organization's objectives. Next is the environmental analysis that has three parts. First is the internal environment analysis, second is the external environmental analysis, and third is the SWOT analysis of the strengths and weaknesses of the internal environment and the opportunities and threats of the external environment that affect a business.

8. **Identify the five internal environmental components and the two primary external environmental factors that affect organizational performance, and the difference between these two environments and their interrelationship**

The organization's internal environment includes the factors that affect the firm's performance from within its boundaries. The five internal environmental factors include: management, mission and objectives, resources, the transformation process, and structure. The external environment affects the firm's performance from outside its boundaries. The two primary external factors are customers and competitors. The major difference is that the entrepreneur can control the internal environment, but has little or no control over the external environment. The entrepreneur needs to manage the environmental interrelationship by organizing the internal environmental factors to take advantage of the changing external environment to maximize performance.

9. **Define the nineteen key terms identified in this chapter**

business plan	Limited Liability Company (LLC)	sole proprietorship	Uniform Partnership Act (UPA)
C corporation	limited partner	stakeholders	unlimited liability
corporation	partnership	strategy	unlimited partnership
external environment	partnership agreement	system transformation process	
general partners	S corporation		
internal environment			

Review and Discussion Questions

1. Why is the business plan a key element for all small businesses?

2. List three stakeholders that will affect and/or be affected by a computer recycling plant being built in your own neighborhood.

3. Which of the 5 Cs of Credit do you think bankers consider the most important when deciding to give a small-business loan?

4. If you were consulting with an entrepreneur, how would you describe to him or her the major sections of the business plan that he or she should write?

5. Why does the introduction section of the business plan have three parts?

6. What are the pros and cons of forming your new business as a sole proprietorship?

7. What is a disadvantage of having a partner in your new business?

8. Select and explain what you think are the two most important reasons for forming your new business as a corporation.

9. Why is strategy formulation important to an existing and new venture?

10. What is a strategy? Why is it the starting point of the business plan?

11. Define mission. Why is it important for the existing and new venture to develop a mission statement?

12. List the factors in the internal environment. Explain how they interrelate.

13. Describe the competitive advantage of a local small hardware store versus Home Depot.

14. What purpose do objectives provide to the existing and new venture?

15. Describe the transformation process. Do all businesses have a transformation process? Is it important?

16. Identify any three of the external factors and state how each affects the performance of a business.

17. Is it necessary to conduct the environmental analysis? Why or why not?

18. Give an example of a strength, weakness, opportunity, and threat for a new social media company.

19. Why is the business model similar to a strategy?

20. In your own words, how would you describe the business model?

Application Exercises

These exercises can be completed as individual or group projects. When doing these exercises, be sure to select a specific business where applicable. You can select a business where you worked or a business you would like to own someday.

1. Interview an entrepreneur and ask if he or she ever wrote a business plan for his or her business. Make sure to ask specific questions on how the entrepreneur did or did not write a business plan. If the entrepreneur did write a plan, how long did it take? Did he or she use specific computer software, such as Business Plan Pro to write the business plan? Did the entrepreneur show the plan to the bank to help obtain a loan for the business? If not, was there a reason why he or she didn't write a plan? Does he or she write a business plan now? Does he or she regret not writing a business plan? Why? Write a one-page report of your findings.

2. Use the Internet to find an example of a business plan online. Write a one-page report on whether this business plan includes the ten sections of a business plan as outlined in this chapter.

3. Search for an article at Entrepreneur.com that discusses business plans. Describe the main points of the article. Summarize what you learned from the article in a one-page report.

Application Situations

1. Al Benjamin—Legal Forms

To help pay his college tuition, Al Benjamin took a job as a waiter in a local restaurant. He reasoned that the pay plus tips would be enough to support him through his college years. Besides that, the hours were sufficiently flexible so that he could fit them around his class schedule. After earning his degree in Sociology, he found that jobs in the Sociology field were few and far between. As Al was making enough to satisfy his needs, he kept on being a waiter, figuring that things would turn around and positions in Sociology would become available. Eight years later, the field of Sociology has still not opened up. While looking at the restaurant operation where he works, Al is certain that he will never become wealthy and he is certain that the owner is and will soon be able to retire. Now would be the time to open his own restaurant. Until now Al's savings made this a dream, but he has recently inherited some money from his grandfather, and his close friend, Sam Jackson, has expressed an interest in joining him. Sam also has savings that he is willing to invest. Neither Al nor Sam has any idea what legal form the business should take. Preferably, neither of them wants to lose their investment or expose themselves to needless risks.

1. What are the legal forms of ownership available to Al and Sam?

2. What are the pros and cons of the various forms of ownership available to them?

3. Which should they choose? Why?

2. Vincent Dimato—External Environment

For many years Vincent Dimato had been a carpenter working for a general contractor. The general contractor's main business specialized mainly on new home building, mainly in the Las Vegas suburbs. When the housing boom was in full swing, houses were sold as fast as they were completed, many even before completion. This boom enabled people in the building trades to make an exceedingly good income. However, it all came to an abrupt halt beginning when the market for housing collapsed. Vincent saw both the rise and fall of the housing boom. He was impressed with the money to be made and vowed that, when the rebound came (after all people will continue to need housing), he would, with a few of his skilled and reliable friends, go into home building for himself. He wanted to cut out the middleman, the general contractor, and have all of the profits accrue to him and his friends, now his crew. For several months the media has been saying that the recession is over and that this is reflected in the upswing of housing prices in the Las Vegas area. Conflicting reports have also indicated that this might not be true.

1. Should Vincent immediately start his home building company? Why or why not?

2. In order to confirm his decision, what external factors might he consider?

3. Explain how each of the external factors might impact his decision.

4. Would his analysis confirm or deny his decision (see question 1)?

Case

Dream Studios

Dream Studios is currently based in Springfield, MA. Dream (Dramatically Reaching Everyone's Artistic Mentality) Studios was created by Ben Smith as a nonprofit agency to introduce community youth to the performing arts and to strengthen them academically.[66] Dream Studios gets donations from individuals and businesses. Dream Studios is managed by Ben with the oversight of interested community members serving on the board of directors. He has been the charismatic leader of Dream Inc. since 2003. In 2006, the Boston Celtics honored him with a Hero Among Us Award for his amazing dedication to youth in his community.[67]

Like many new entrepreneurs, Ben currently controls the internal environment functions of Dream Studios, with board approval. For example, he handles payroll, ordering costume materials, designing costumes, fabricating costumes, developing marketing posters, and recruiting new children to the studio. He constantly looks for good deals on material to design costume clothing. It is more likely you will find him sewing outfits instead of collecting unpaid bills.

Also, like many newer entrepreneurs, Ben feels like he needs to do everything himself. Ben is a great person to teach young children how to perform in a theatrical show. However, he typically hires creative people related to producing a new show. If Ben plans on growing the studio, he is going to need more help with business functions, such as marketing and accounting.

Ben's love is spending time producing local theatrical shows. He often writes his own shows, which

is a great accomplishment. Ben has to pay a licensing fee to the owners of a show if he chooses a show that is copyrighted as Music Theatre International (MTI). He then has the rights to be able to put on the show for a limited amount of time.

Ben doesn't have an established salary. With board approval, he gets the minimum amount of money that he needs to pay his personal expenses. Ben created Dream to help kids, not to get rich—Dream Studios is mission driven.

Besides producing theatrical shows, Dream Studios also has afternoon programs designed to help students to complete their homework. Ben also offers summer and winter camps. His goal is to provide a safe environment for kids after school and while on vacation.

Ben does have a unique place for Dream Studios: a space on the first floor of the largest building in Springfield, MA, an eastern city that had a 10.1% unemployment rate in November 2012.[68] Ben chose to stay visible to the entire community by being in the downtown district.[69] He should benefit from being in a part of a downtown area that will soon be voting on building a casino on either end of Main St. His unique Dream Studios could become a key supplier of talented youth for any new casino shows that need children.

Ben is considering expanding his business model to other cities on the east coast. He would like to create a chain of Dream Studios to help children develop their self-esteem through the world of theatrics. However, he knows the challenge will be to hire managers who will have the same type of enthusiasm that he exhibits at each Dream Studio. He would like to find a person in each big city to take on his dream and create more studios for more children. He wants to help children to find a place they can call home after school, on the weekends, and vacations.

You can follow Ben Smith and Dream Studios on Twitter at http://twitter.com/Dreamstudios. You can also follow Dream Studios on Facebook at www.facebook.com/DREAMStudiosInc, or visit its Web site at www.dreamstudios.org

1. Use Twitter and Facebook to help research more about Dream Studios. After conducting your online research, analyze Dream Studios' mission statement.

2. Assess Ben's internal environment for strengths and weaknesses.

3. Assess the external environment for opportunities and threats and how they affect the future of Dream Studios Inc.

4. What type of ownership structure does Dream Studios appear to have selected?

Global Case—Formulating a Global Business Plan, Google China

A globally oriented company needs to evaluate the business conditions in the country in which they will be doing business. Google, for example, had to develop and then reevaluate their business plan to enter different countries. Even though they are an Internet-based company, they still had to be very careful with censorship in China. Google had trouble adjusting to China's privacy laws compared with the laws in the U.S. "The company decided it will no longer censor search results on Google.cn, which it had been doing as a concession to the Chinese government since 2006 in order to be able to operate in China."[70] Google understood their site might be shut down by not complying with the Chinese government.

The following are global issues that need to be included in the business plan, In regards to censorship, Google ended up having trouble with issue #3, evaluating the local customs, political climate, and culture in China.

1. Prepare a budget and establish financial requirements by region (America, Asia, Europe, and Africa) or by country.

2. Find an affordable location (including access to the Internet, utilities, and availability of skilled employees) to run the business in each location.

3. Evaluate the local customs, political climate, and culture for each country.

4. List the details about product variations in different countries.

5. Identify feasible customer target markets in each country or region.

6. Establish a distribution network to bring in supplies and then ship out the final product.

7. List any specific international experiences your employees can contribute to the business operations.

8. List all the legal requirements for each country.[71]

Questions

1. How does an international business plan differ compared with a one-country plan?

2. If a country, such as China, has a very large population, then why is identifying feasible target markets so important?

3. Select a country that you have visited (or studied) and write a short response on the different financial, marketing, and management-related issues for the country you selected.

Writing Your Business Plan

You (or in teams) can write a business plan during the semester. There are questions at the end of each chapter to help guide you through the thinking and analyzing process. Appendix B has a sample business plan you can use as a template for developing your own new venture business plan.

Since this is Chapter 5, the goal is to add the mission, objectives, and external analysis.

Highlighted Sections of the Business Plan (Chapters 1–5)

1. **The executive summary** is written last—but placed first in the business plan. You have to wait until you are finished with the business plan to properly write the executive summary.

2. **Introduction:**
   A. **Background of the business:** Includes a short review of its name, address (or addresses if there is more than one location), telephone number(s), email address, Web site address, hours of operation, and a brief history (if any). You want to state when the business was started or will be started.
   B. **Management credentials and organization structure:** It is common to list all the business's key managers and their duties and responsibilities, with their qualifications.
   C. **Form of ownership:** Will your business be a sole proprietorship, partnership, or corporation and how will any profits be distributed?

3. **Strategy Formulation**
   A. **Mission:** What is the organization's purpose or reason for being? (This is covered in Chapter 3.) The mission section of the business plan includes your business model (covered in Chapter 4), which can include a broad description of your present and future products and services to be offered. In the strategy section, it is not necessary to list all the products and services; they are listed under the marketing section of the business plan and will be discussed in Chapter 6.
   B. **Objectives (prioritized):** What does your organization want to accomplish?
   C. **Environmental analysis:** It includes an analysis of the internal environment (which includes the mission and objectives) and its external environment resulting in a SWOT analysis.

4. **The Marketing Function**

5. **Location and Layout**

6. **The Production/Operations Function**

7. **The Human Resources Function**

8. **The Financing Function**

9. **Controls**

10. **Appendix**

Chapter 6

The Marketing Plan
Who are Your Customers?

In this chapter, you will learn about the marketing plan. The marketing plan is part of the larger business plan. Developing the marketing plan begins by conducting research to segment the market in order to identify the target customer. Through marketing research the new firm and/or product is tested for feasibility before opening the business or offering the new product. If the product will be profitable, the marketing mix (4 Ps—product, price, place, and promotion) is developed and the sales forecast is predicted. Modern entrepreneurs have learned to use social media strategies to complement the traditional use of the 4 Ps.

Learning Outcomes

After completing this chapter you should be able to:

1. Explain the interrelationship between the marketing plan and the other business plan components;
2. Describe the importance of marketing research and its four-step process;
3. Explain the importance of selecting a target market;
4. Identify the four Ps of the marketing mix and how they work together;
5. Describe how a sales forecast is different for the new venture versus the existing business;
6. Explain the difference between express and implied warranties;
7. Differentiate between price skimming and price penetration;
8. Describe the different type of promotional methods;
9. Discuss the use of social media and e-commerce strategies as part of a marketing plan;
10. Define the twenty-four key terms identified in this chapter.

Entrepreneur Profile—Build your Brand: Adams Street Grill

We begin each chapter with a short bio of an entrepreneur and provide a link so you can learn more about the person and his or her business venture. A short 3–5-minute-video of each entrepreneur can be found at the PBS Small Business School at www.smallbusinessschool.org/. The Adams Street Grill video can be found at http://smallbusinessschool.org/video.cfm?clip=1875.

You won't find many small restaurants using the Internet to build their customer base. However, the Adams Street Grill uses monthly emails to stay in touch with existing customers, and find new ones too. It found that customers who receive emails will send them to their friends if you encourage them to do so by offering some type of reward. Monthly emails do not have to irritate customers. If you say something or offer something interesting, customers will like to receive your emails.

Entrepreneurs need to use the Internet to build their brand. Entrepreneurs can start by building a Web site that provides the basic answers to questions any person might have about your product or service. Adams Street Grill's site has easily accessible contact information, the physical address, and phone and fax numbers. Keeping the logo on the page is common-sense branding.

A key point to consider when using the Web is to use concise descriptions of products and services. Be sure there is easy navigation. Make sure to have Frequently Asked Questions (FAQs). If you are selling, be sure to have a clear statement of your competitive advantage and testimonials.

As the Internet becomes more a part of our everyday life, try to avoid too much animation, blinking images or text, and extraneous sounds. Use pictures. Show your personality. If your business is small, chances are you built it by building personal relationships. If you look at a Web site you should find a picture of the founder of the business to help build a relationship with your customers. Doing business on the Internet means your customers could live anywhere in the world. So, you want to give them a picture of who you are so you can build a solid business connection.

Think it over.

1. What are three ideas for finding customers on the Internet?
2. Find a small restaurant in your neighborhood that uses the Internet to build its business.

Think about it.

What do strangers tell you about your Web site? Have you ever asked people to give you their honest impression of your Web site?

The Interrelationship Between the Marketing Plan and the Other Business Plan Components

In Chapters 3 and 4 we already discussed developing and testing a business model (your products and services, customers and consumer, profitability, and operations). In this chapter, we expand on the first two parts of the business model as you formalize who your customers are and what products and services you will offer. The marketing plan *identifies the target customers and product feasibility through marketing research, which leads to the development of the marketing mix (product, price, place, and promotion) and the sales forecast*. Recall that market-oriented firms identify needs and wants of target customers and satisfy them as a competitive advantage.[1] Market-oriented businesses generally outperform non-market-oriented firms.[2] Therefore, developing an effective marketing plan is an important entrepreneurial skill.[3]

All organizations perform the four key functions of accounting and finance, marketing, operations, and human resources. It is critical for the entrepreneur to make decisions based on the firm as a system. The organization is a system because it is comprised of these interacting functions; each of which affects the other functions and the organization as a whole. The production and accounting functions are internally focused, marketing is externally focused, and human resources and financing focus on balancing both environments. Many firms have had strong separate functional areas that have failed because of the lack of coordination between these functions as a system.

Raising money and marketing a new business are inseparable. In order to receive operating capital, you must have a sound marketing plan. The interrelationship between operations and marketing is complex and critical. To say that marketing sells what production produces is simplistic. The marketing function employs the capital resources acquired through the finance function. The firm's funds are spent on marketing research, product development, distribution of the products, and promoting the products and services. The marketing function interrelates with the production function because marketing information leads to selecting new products and changes in present products. A marketing forecast of sales potential must be integrated with a production forecast of capacity to provide a realistic production schedule.

The selection of a distribution system of the products to the customers and promotional methods used affect the human resource function of selection of employees and their compensation. The pricing and credit policies affect the accounting function. Accounting data is needed to record the production and sales of the firm's products. The web of interrelationships between the functional areas is endless. The marketing plan has to coordinate the product, price, place, and promotion with the rest of the business plan.

Identify the Target Customer and Forecast Sales Through Marketing Research

In this section, we present an overview of the new venture's marketing plan. We discuss marketing research, the target market, the marketing mix, and the sales forecast.

Marketing Research

In Chapter 4 we described how the feasibility analysis is based on research. Research is essentially the same in the functional areas of business, and the entire business plan should be based on research rather than opinion. Here we expand our discussion of research focusing on marketing.

Have you ever been walking around a mall and had a person with a clipboard ask you some questions? Have you ever answered questions about the food and service in a restaurant? Have you ever bought a product and filled out and mailed in the post card to register your product for warranty? Did you ever fill out a survey online that was designed using SurveyMonkey.com software? If you answered yes to any of these questions, you have been a part of marketing research. Quantitative research is important because it affects the firm's performance.

You need timely and accurate data.[4] The role of research is to reduce uncertainty in decision-making. Marketing research *is the process of gathering and analyzing data for decision-making.* The steps in the marketing research process are: (1) define the decision, (2) gather data, (3) analyze data, and (4) make the decision.

Step 1. Define the Decision

The major decision the would-be entrepreneur has to make is whether or not to start a business. The development of the business plan aids in making this decision. When defining the decision, it is important to develop questions, which need to be answered. Research questions are often stated as hypotheses. A hypothesis *is a tentative answer to a research question.* Elsie Rodriguez thought (hypothesized) there was a potential market for a computer software package that can help adjust the optical lens acuity so that users do not have to wear their eyeglasses or contact lens to see a computer screen. So she decided to conduct research to test her product before opening a full-time business.

Step 2. Gather Data

Before you actually collect data, you must decide what data you will collect, how you will collect it, and how much data you need. As discussed in Chapter 4,

Learning Outcome

2. Describe the importance of marketing research and its four-step process.

Personal Application

2. Describe the last survey that you filled out.

Personal Application

3. Develop a hypothesis for a potential product and market.

research is commonly classified into secondary and primary research and both types are commonly used to gather marketing data. Refer back to Chapter 4 for details on data collection, especially through survey research and Exhibit 4-3 for a list of sources you can use to help gather marketing data. Also, see Exhibit 4-4 for a buying intentions survey questionnaire.

The data you collect can also be *qualitative* or *quantitative*. *Focus groups* (Chapter 3) tend to use a small sample with minimal use of math in making decisions. *Survey research* (Chapter 4) tends to use a larger sample size (twenty-five or more) and survey research with statistical analysis in decision-making. You can start with a focus group and develop a questionnaire and survey potential customers so that you gather both qualitative and quantitative data as discussed in Chapter 4.

Step 3. Analyze the Data

Based on the type of data you collected, qualitative, quantitative, or both, you need to analyze it. With a focus group, or just asking a few people their opinion, this qualitative data analysis may be very subjective. With quantitative survey data, you can do statistical analysis. On a simple level, you can run the statistic in Excel of the count and percentage of how many respondents answered each question. You can also calculate the mean/average and median/mid-point of the data. You can also make comparisons between the answers of groups, such as males and females.

Step 4. Make the Decision

Personal Application

4. If you were in Elsie Rodriguez's position, would you start a new venture for the computer eyewear software?

There are usually no "hard-and-fast" rules for interpreting marketing research data. Judgment is needed in interpreting the results, but your decision should be based on research. Let's assume that Elsie Rodriguez conducted the above research and has the responses of 200 people from five different stores. Elsie preselected people who either wear eyeglasses and/or contact lens. Results reveal that 45 percent say they would buy the computer eyewear software, and 23 percent say they would pay a premium price for it. If Elsie Rodriguez asked you if she should start a new venture for the computer eyewear software or not, what would you tell her?

See Exhibit 6-1 for a review of the four steps in the research process.

Learning Outcome

3. Explain the importance of selecting a target market.

The Target Market and Marketing Mix—4Ps

You need to determine your target market and marketing mix.

Exhibit 6-1

The Four Steps in the Research Process

Step 1. Define the Decision →	Step 2. Gather Data →	Step 3. Analyze Data →	Step 4. Make the Decision

Target Market

Recall from Chapters 3 and 4 that determining your target market is part of the feasibility study. In the business plan marketing section, you need to clearly state your industry and your target market potential customers, because customers are essential to small-business success.[5] Thus, you need to find a favorable market niche.[6] You can acquire knowledge from customers that will help you start and operate your new venture.[7]

Marketing Mix—4Ps

You use your target market to develop the marketing mix. The marketing mix *is the blend of product, price, place, and promotion that best meets the needs of the target market.* The marketing mix is often referred to as *the 4 Ps.* The selection of the marketing mix is a combination of marketing decisions in which each of the four Ps must be carefully considered and addressed fully. After we discuss sales forecasting, we describe the details of each "P" in the marketing mix in separate sections. However, due to the systems effect they must all be carefully coordinated.

Learning Outcome

4. Identify the four Ps of the marketing mix and how they work together.

Personal Application

5. Identify the target market that you want to select for the business you want to start in this course, or an existing business.

Sales Forecast

The sales forecast is predicted based on the target customer and marketing mix. It is the predicted dollars and/or units of the product that will be sold to the target market during a given period of time. The sales forecast is one of the most critical parts of the business plan because of the systems effect. To be more specific, the expenditure budget, quotas for salespeople, advertising expenditures, asset purchases of plant and equipment, hiring employees, purchasing of raw material and parts, production scheduling, making cash flow statements, developing pro forma income statements and balance sheets, and determining the break-even point are all based on the sales forecast. In other words, the feasibility of a new venture, and the future of an existing business, is based on its sales forecast. The sales forecast is developed differently for the new venture versus the existing small business.

Learning Outcome

5. Describe how a sales forecast is different for the new venture versus the existing business.

Sales Forecasting for the Established Small Business

The existing business can use past sales to aid in predicting future sales. The common sales forecast is used in an established small-business pizza shop, such as **Nino's Pizzeria** (www.facebook.com/pages/Ninos-Pizzeria/418662584838171). Assume that on a typical Saturday night we sell 100 pizzas. This figure may be adjusted for changes in the weather, seasons, special events, etc. Then we prepare accordingly for that night's business. This approach can be improved by looking for trends. The owner, Nino, can keep a record of how many pizzas are sold each day, week, month, and year and plot it on a simple graph. There are more complex quantitative forecasting techniques, but they are not commonly used by small retail and service businesses. (See Exhibit 6-2 for an

Number of Pizzas Sold per Month, January–December 2013

```
4,000
3,800                              X     X
3,600                        X              X
3,400                   X
3,200              X                              X     X
3,000  X                                                        X
2,800      X
2,600
       Jan  Feb  Mar  Apr  May  June  July  Aug  Sept  Oct  Nov  Dec
```

Pizza Sales Revenue Per Year 2007–2014

```
$400,000                                    X
$380,000                               X
$360,000                          X
$340,000            X     X
$320,000   X     X
$300,000                     X
          2007  2008  2009  2010  2011  2012  2013  2014ᶠ
```

ᶠ= Forecasted sales for 2014

example.) Looking at Exhibit 6-2, and the number of pizzas sold per month for the year 2013, Nino can see that sales are greater in the warmer months and can plan accordingly. Nino's sales dropped in 2011 because a new Domino's Pizza opened in the town. Domino's delivered pizza and Nino didn't. Nino didn't want to deliver pizza. After watching sales drop for several months, he added free delivery.

By offering a better-tasting, larger pizza for less money than Domino's (even though delivery is slower), customers came back and sales went up again. Assume it is time for Nino to forecast pizza sales for 2014. Pizza sales revenue per year shows an upward trend in sales from 2007 through 2014. Past sales can help predict future sales, but more information is needed to set the figures. Nino knows that there is a new construction development under way, which could increase his business. About four new houses have been built so far. Nino conducted some research and discovered that there will be about fifty new houses built.

The economic forecast by the local business association predicts the economy to stay about the same in 2014; this has been discussed at the meeting. The trade association Nino belongs to predicts more people will be buying take-out food during the year, and pizza sales should rise about 5 percent; Nino read this in the trade magazine he subscribes to. Based on past sales and these trends, he sets the sales forecast for 2014 at $400,000. The $400,000 in sales becomes a challenging objective for the business to achieve. Nino is also making special plans to increase advertising as a means of increasing sales revenue.

Sales Forecasting for a New Venture

A new venture that will be opening a business or an existing business that will be offering a different new product cannot use past sales to predict future sales. It can be challenging for a new venture to forecast sales without any prior sales history. Marketing research helps you forecast sales, especially if you have some sales and customers before you launch the new venture. Here are three sales forecasting methods you can use.

- *Market share.* Market share *is the percentage of the total sales held by each competitor.* Many industry and trade associations publish market share information. If total sales per year for your products are 100,000, and you estimate that you can get a 2 percent market share, what is your projected sales forecast? The answer is 2,000 units.
- *Comparable businesses.* If you can find a business that is similar to your own, you can ask the entrepreneur for help to forecast sales based on his or her startup experience.
- *Industry and trade associations.* Contact the premier association and ask for help. It may track sales for businesses similar to yours, or it may have statistics such as average sales per square foot or average sales per employee.

Many new ventures are started with an overly optimistic sales forecast. The owner of the business plans to pay the bills based on this money coming in, only to find that the bills cannot be paid and creditors end up taking the owner to court for liquidation of the business. To avoid this scenario, it is often helpful to develop two sets of sales forecast. Start with the best reasonable sales forecast you expect. Then take this number and cut it in half. Strive for the reasonable sales forecast, but only count on half to pay your bills. This type of cushion has saved many businesses from going under. If the original forecast is accurate or underestimated it may cause some problems, but it is easier to spend money you actually have than to pay bills with money you don't have.

It is common for the sales forecast to be wrong, especially for the new venture. However, this does not mean that the sales forecast is not useful. In fact, few creditors will lend you money without seeing a business plan that includes a sales forecast. As the firm conducts business over time, the forecast can be changed. If you develop your forecast on a computer software spreadsheet, changing it is very simple and quick. In later chapters, you will learn more about financial projections and business planning software that makes the job fairly easy.

Product

The company's product is usually the starting place for a new venture. As discussed in Chapters 3 and 4, your product or service should improve customer's lives,[8] it should be differentiated from the competitors,[9] and there must be a demand for your product or service.[10] Within the business plan, each major product and service should be clearly described with the competitive advantage explained.[11] In this section, we will discuss having a product line, timing, brand names and trademarks, warranties, and packaging and labeling.

Product Line

Personal Application

6. Select a business you would like to start, or an existing business, and identify its product line.

Will you offer a single product/service or a line of products/services? The common approach for the small business is to start with a single product or limited variety and add related products to develop a line of products. **McDonald's** started with hamburgers and fries, and over the years added fish, chicken, and salads. McDonald's, also known as MacDo in France, extends its product line in France to include menu items such as an Alpine grass-fed-beef burger with three kinds of cheese and the very popular McBaguette's.[12]

Apple started with PC computers and went on to music with the iPod and iTunes, cell phones with the iPhone and apps, and tablets with the iPad. Your business plan should describe your planned startup products and services and any planned future expansions.

Product Timing

Timing is important.[13] *Product timing* refers to when the product is introduced. A product can be offered too early before people are willing to purchase it. Pen-based computers were expected to do well. However, sales were disappointing in the 1990s and 2000s. However, **Samsung** included a pen in its Galaxy Note 10.1 tablet in 2012. The pen became a popular alternative for market segments that wanted to do creative design work instead of using **Apple**'s iPad touch screen process.[14] On the other hand, if a product is offered too late it will not sell enough units to be profitable. **Microsoft**'s Zune MP3 player was a quality product, but it was also on the market well after the Apple iPod was already the dominant market share leader.[15] Microsoft has also been criticized for being too slow getting into the Internet business, such as with the Bing search engine and mobile devices.

Brand Names and Trademarks

Your marketing plan should include your brand name and any trademarks including logos. A *brand name* distinguishes one product from another and your brand name can be trademarked. Recall that we already discussed *trademarks* as legal protection in Chapter 4. You should develop your own branding.[16] A good name brand can help develop sales of the product or service, and it can be your most valuable asset.[17] Some brand leaders fifty years ago are still leaders today. **Tesco** from the U.K., **Heineken** from the Netherlands, **Tata** from India, and **LVMH** from France are all famous global brand name examples.[18] Recall the importance of repeat customers, thus brand loyalty is important.

Here are a few tips on selecting a successful brand name:[19]

- *Web-friendly.* The name should be easy to find and access when a person wants to learn about your company. It is wise to search Facebook and Twitter to make sure someone else doesn't already use your planned brand name, or have the web address.
- *Short and easy to pronounce.* The fewer the number of words in a brand name, the more likely it will be remembered. The easier a name is to pronounce, the more likely the customers will pass it along to their friends.
- *Memorable.* The brand name needs to be memorable in order to create a buzz. A unique name makes the customer interested in learning more about the product. A unique name can help your business to stand out in a crowd of similar products.

Logos are usually a symbol of some type used to attract recognition and serve primarily as a marketing and promotional tool. They can indirectly imply the mission of the organization. **Apple** uses the logo of an Apple with a bite taken out of it. **Starbucks** uses a green label with the Starbucks Siren.[20]

Warranties

A warranty *guarantees the integrity of the product.* All your products legally offer a warranty that essentially says that your products must perform to reasonable expectation of use. Your business plan should identify if you will offer an express or implied, and a full or limited, product warranty.

Learning Outcome

6. Explain the difference between express and implied warranties.

Express or Implied Warranties

An *express warranty* is an explicit claim made by the producer to the consumer. The expressed claim may be given orally through advertising or through claims made by salespeople. An express warranty is commonly a formal certificate that comes with the product, which the consumer returns to the manufacturer to validate the warranty. An *implied warranty* is an unwritten guarantee that the product is adequate to meet reasonable expectations for intended purposes. What are the "reasonable, prudent person's" expectations of product performance? If you are taken to court, the judge decides what "reasonable" is.

Full vs. Limited Warranty

A *full warranty* must express unconditional assurance that the product will be replaced or repaired within a reasonable time and without charge. A *limited warranty* conditionally excludes certain parts of the product or particular types of defects from coverage. A statement such as "complete satisfaction" without any fine print would be considered to be a full warranty. Most businesses offer a limited warranty. The express warranty certificate should state whether it is limited and what the conditions are.

Personal Application

7. Select a business you would like to start, or an existing business, and identify its product warranty.

Packaging and Labeling

Packaging *involves protecting and promoting products.* When packaging a product, there is a trade-off balance between the costs of under-protection, which leads to damaged goods, and the cost to package the product. Generally, the higher the price of the product, the higher the quality and cost of packaging. Low-cost jewelry often comes without a box or with a thin cardboard or plastic box, whereas expensive jewelry usually comes in a nice, expensive, fabric-covered box. Some firms change the packaging to imply new and improved, while keeping the product the same.

The size of the package is also important. Will your product come in one size only? If not, how many sizes will you have? Check competitor brands and copy them, or differentiate your product size as a competitive advantage to meet your target customer's needs. But remember the systems effect: the more size packages, the greater the cost of production, inventory, packaging, etc.

Labeling is used to both identify and promote the product. The label can include information on product care, contents, directions, disposal, etc. If you sell food in the U.S., the federal government Food and Drug Administration (FDA) and Federal Trade Commission (FTC) have developed guidelines for contents and nutritional information. Today, barcodes that use EAN/UPC symbology (including the UPC-A, UPC-E, EAN-13, and EAN-8 barcodes) are the only barcodes allowed for products scanned at retail point of sale.[21] A universal product code (UPC) *identifies each product with barcode marks that can be read by electronic scanners.* So if you plan to sell retail products, you will have to obtain a barcode for each product you sell. For more information and to obtain a barcode visit **GS1** (www.gs1us.org).[22]

Many companies put the brand name or trademark label on the outside of the product to enhance sales. Many people, especially teens, are willing to pay a lot more for a product because of its brand name, trademark or logo on the product. The **Nike** swoosh logo is always prominently displayed on the footwear and other products. If you have any unique packaging ideas, include them in the marketing plan.

Price

Recall from Chapter 4 that pricing is an important part of the business model's profitability analysis. Pricing the product is important because it is a key factor in the decision to buy. The price must be coordinated with the target market, product, place, and promotion. Your marketing plan should include your price, and the rationale for such a price. In this section, we discuss pricing consideration, and producer, wholesale, retail, and service pricing and credit.

Pricing Considerations

Here are some major considerations to consider when setting your prices.

Competition

What price do the other businesses sell products for that are identical, similar, or substitutes for your product? Generally, the more your product is unique with a competitive advantage, the higher the price you can charge. Also, the more competition for identical products, the more important it is to meet competitive prices. In many industries the small business cannot compete on price with the large businesses due to their having higher volume and greater economies of scale.

Based on her marketing research, Elsie Rodriguez decided to set the price of her eyewear software higher than the competition. This *lower-volume/higher-price strategy is called* price skimming. However, Nino offers a larger, better-tasting pizza for less than **Domino**'s Pizza. Nino can compete on price because he does not have to pay the franchise fee. This higher-volume/lower-price strategy is called **price penetration**.

Customers

Unfortunately, there is no magical way to determine the exact price customers are willing to pay, but research helps. **McDonald's** raised its prices on average by 3 percent in 2012 and had a decrease in sales.[23] Talk to customers and watch their reactions to your prices. If they are perceived as too low, raise them. If they are perceived as high, work to be sure the customers realize that the full benefits are worth the investment. Elsie Rodriguez asked people if they were willing to pay more for her software than their present eyewear. If there are many people who want to buy the product, especially if it's unique or new, the higher the price you can charge.

Other External Factors

In addition to competition and customers discussed above, the other external environmental factors of suppliers, the labor force, stockholders, society, technology, governments, and the economy also affect the price you can charge.

Internal Factors

Regardless of the other three pricing considerations, you must cover all your costs plus adding a margin for profit. If you cannot, don't start the business or close it. This may sound simplistic, but there are many small businesses that underestimate their cost and end up going out of business because they cannot pay their bills.

Taking these four considerations into account, different types of businesses use different pricing methods, and some offer credit. Let's discuss these differences.

Producer Pricing

The common pricing method of producers of goods is the cost-plus method. It is common to determine the cost to produce the good (labor, material, and overhead for the equipment, building, etc.), the cost of selling and administrative costs (salespeople, salary/commission, advertising, delivery, record keeping, etc.), and a profit margin. The totals of these three components are added together to get the price. However, the above considerations must be studied before setting the cost plus price. To be competitive you may have to cut your profit margin, or with a unique product like Elsie Rodriguez's software, you may set a higher margin than competitors'. Every time you can cut your cost and maintain the price, your profit margin increases. Accurate records are needed to determine costs.

Wholesale and Retail Pricing

Wholesalers and retailers buy the goods from the producers and sell them to their customers. While the producer must calculate the cost of the good, the wholesaler and retailer know the cost they pay to the producer. To the cost of merchandise you must add operating expenses (rent, utilities, depreciation, salaries/commissions, delivery, etc.) and a profit margin. The difference between the cost of the good and the selling price is your markup. The markup is commonly used by wholesalers and retailers to set prices. For example, if you buy software for $15 and price it at $25 the markup is $10. As a percentage of the retail price it is 40 percent (10/25), but as a percentage of cost it is 66.67 percent (10/15).

Most retailers compute markup as a percentage of the retail price because operating records are expressed as a percentage of sales, operating expenses, cost of goods sold, and profits are expressed as a percentage of total sales, not the cost of the merchandise being sold. You simply take the cost of goods and divide it by the reciprocal of the markup (100% − markup %). For example, if you pay $6 to make a pizza and use a markup of 35 percent, you price the pizza at $9.23 ($6/100 − 35 = 65% or 6/.65 = 9.23).

The math of marking up prices is easy, but setting the markup percentage is not always easy. The price has to be high enough to allow a profit, while being competitive. Through research, you can find out, or estimate, what your competitors use as markups. Many producers suggest a specific markup or the actual selling price.

Small retailers typically cannot compete on price with the large chain stores. They typically price their products higher, but offer a competitive advantage (service, location, ambiance, etc.) of value to the customer for the extra cost. With a very limited product line, one markup may be all that is needed, but with a variety of goods the markup should change. Generally, highly speculative and slow-moving goods (jewelry) have a higher markup than the fast-moving goods with low carrying cost (grocery items).

Service Pricing

The service firm must also base prices on its cost (labor, materials, travel, etc.), operating cost (rent, utilities, etc.), and a profit margin. Services are commonly set by the job or by the hour. A laundry service has a set rate to clean each item whereas your accountant typically charges by the hour. Repair service business generally charge for parts and labor, but the parts are based on a retail markup and the labor is more than the pay of the mechanic to cover operating expenses and a profit. Find out what your competitors charge, but don't simply match them. Trying to compete by offering a lower price may work, but if you have a competitive advantage you may be able to sell your services to your customers for a higher price. Be careful not to price your services too low because people may get the impression that your quality is also low, and give their business to your competitors.

Credit

Will you sell your product for cash only, or will you let your customers charge? There are four major factors in the credit decision: (1) the type of business (durable goods and large chain retailers tend to offer credit; small grocers don't), (2) credit policy of competitors (can you meet or beat them), (3) income level of customers (higher income tends to get credit), and (4) working capital (can you wait to get your money?). If you do elect to offer credit, it can be a competitive advantage. You must decide to offer your own charge account or accept national credit cards like Visa, MasterCard, American Express, and Discover. They keep the records for you, but for a fee.

Personal Application

8. Select a business you would like to start, or an existing business, and identify its pricing policy and if it offers credit.

Place

Having a good product or service at a price customers are willing to pay is important, but the right place to sell it is also needed. Based on your target customers' needs, you want your product available in the right quantities and locations. Place is clearly important to business success.[24] If you sell a product, your marketing plan should include place—how you will distribute, transport, and store your products. The location of the business is very important, and is closely related to place, which is covered in the next chapter.

Distribution and Transportation

Distribution—Supply Chain Management

Determining how you will produce and deliver your products and services is part of the business model. Without developing and delivering a product or service, you don't have a business.[25] Important questions are, do you need a distributor, and, if so, how do you find one?[26] Refer back to Chapter 3 for a discussion of delivering your products and services, especially supply chain management and Exhibit 3-8, the supply chain. It is common to have problems in delivery systems, so solve them quickly.[27]

Transportation

If you make products, you must get them to their customers, and someone has to pay the transportation cost. There is no such thing as free delivery; the cost is either included in the price of the product or the profit margin is cut. The three major means of transportation, in order by cost, are air (plane), land (truck and railroad), and sea (ships/barges). Pipelines are also used primarily by the petroleum industry. Each means of transportation has its advantages and disadvantages. But cost is not the major consideration, customer satisfaction is. Some products and customers require quick delivery to make the sale, while others can wait.

Producers of services often have transportation cost based on supplies used and/or *travel*. Services that go to the customer either add the average cost of delivery as a set or minimum fee, or bill the customer directly for the charges.

Storage

Personal Application

9. Select a business you would like to start, or an existing business, and identify its delivery, transportation, and storage of its products and services.

Storage involves holding supplies, materials, component parts, and finished products. Storage is necessary because production does not always match sales; it is used to balance supply and demand. Storage is especially important for seasonal products. Producers hold products until they sell them to middle people or consumers. One advantage of using middle people is that they store products until they are sold to consumers. Storage related to products for sale or resale is commonly called inventory. Inventory will be discussed in Chapter 9. Service firms don't usually have products to store for sale as inventory, but they do store various types of supplies. Goods can be stored on the businesses premises or a rented space in a warehouse.

The Elevator Pitch

This skill-builder puts you in the venture capitalist position. You will watch an elevator pitch from the Internet and assess and discuss if he or she would or wouldn't invest in the new venture. You should realize that an elevator pitch often needs to be updated, refreshed, and practiced. Students often think the same pitch can work for every audience. In reality, you should adjust your pitch depending on who is listening and as your business grows. Customers have problems that require products to solve their dilemma. Ask yourself what problem your product is going to solve.[28]

The link for this elevator pitch can be found at: http://video.msnbc.msn.com/your-business/27265816#27265816.

CEO of Hands2Go, Francine Glick, describes her hand sanitizer. Do you think she has a unique business idea?

Think about it.

1. What score do you give Francine Glick?

Great product idea and pitch		Terrible product idea and pitch	
4	3	2	1

2. Would you invest in Francine's business?
3. How would you improve Francine's pitch?
4. Did Francine adjust her elevator pitch for her audience?

Promotion

Learning Outcome

8. Describe the different type of promotional methods.

Having the right product with the right price at the right place will not sell if no one knows about it. Thus, a promotion focus is important to new venture success.[29] Promotion is the process of communicating the other three Ps to target customers to inform, persuade, or remind them to buy the product. "What" is communicated depends on the target customers' needs. "How" the messages are communicated depends on the promotional method chosen. Promotion includes personal selling, sales promotion, publicity, and advertising. We will discuss the first three in this section, and advertising in the next major section.

Personal Selling

Personal selling involves direct one-on-one communication between you and the potential customer. Most personal sales are conducted face-to-face, but telephone sales (telemarketing) is also common. Close relationships with customers are recognized as important for young firms.[30] Personal selling is an important part of customer orientation that leads to success.[31] As part of the marketing plan, you must decide: (1) How many salespeople you need. (2) What kind of salespeople you need. (3) What kind of sales presentation should be used (develop sales scripts). (4) How salespeople should be selected and trained. (5) How they should be motivated.

Personal Application

10. Select a business you would like to start, or an existing business, and identify how important personal selling is to the success of the firm.

Target customers and the other three Ps in the marketing mix influence these five decisions. To many target customers, the salesperson is the company. So get out there and sell.[32] The effective small-business salesperson can give the target customer that personal attention often not available through big business; it can be a competitive advantage. Don't be afraid to get the customer to buy a higher-value product,[33] or to sell more to each customer by creating a bundle of products.[34] The sales approach should be based on the marketing mix. Below is an eight-step approach to personal sales that can be adapted to the situation.

1. **Prospecting:** Define your target customer clearly and go after them because they are most likely to buy your product. The telephone is a good tool for prospecting. The best source of new customers is to get referrals from present customers. You can also ask suppliers for prospects. Ask satisfied customers if they know anyone who may be interested in your product. Ask satisfied customers if you can use them as references with new prospects. Request the use of their names. With creative products, take pictures and show them to prospects and ask the reference if prospects can come to their house or business and see your product as well. Get a short letter of recommendation (often called testimonials) that simply says the customer recommends the product for xyz reasons.

2. **Open:** Start by establishing rapport with the target customer. The first thing you have to do is sell yourself because people seldom buy from anyone they dislike or distrust. Remember that long-term sales success is based on

respect, not hard-sell tactics. Start the sales pitch by saying what you can do for the customer, not "I'd like to tell you about our product."

3. **Listen and ask questions:** Get prospects to tell you about their needs, preferences, and problems so that you can understand their situation and satisfy them.

4. **Presentation:** Explain the benefits of the product by telling prospects how the product will meet their specific needs or wants or solve their problem. You need to be well prepared; know your product and its competitive advantages and be able to answer questions.

5. **Demonstration:** Show prospects how the product works; let them try it out. Be sure to point out your product's competitive advantage.

6. **Objections:** Ask prospects how they like the product. For different reasons, people don't always tell you why they object to buying your product. Be careful not to misunderstand objectives. Listen carefully and try to understand their real objections to the product and overcome them. Point out how your product will meet their needs, or do a better job of meeting their needs than competitor products.

7. **Close: Ask for the order.** The most common reason for losing a sale is that the seller never asks for the order. Get some type of commitment as to what the prospects are going to do next. Once the buyer agrees to buy the product, stop selling it. The salesperson should be ready to close at any time during the process.

8. **Follow-up:** After the sale, be sure to say thank you. Be sure the customer is satisfied. This step is critical for repeat business and an excellent way to get referrals to new prospects. Sending a written thank-you note and, for good repeat customers, a small gift like a fruit basket or taking them out to lunch, are very effective at keeping repeat business.

As an additional follow-up step, the entrepreneur should create a **customer relationship management system (CRM)**. *CRM brings together information from all data sources within an organization to help organize all the records for each customer.* Future sales opportunities to a customer can be determined by the data.[35] Software such as **Salesforce.com** can be purchased to help coordinate the collection and analysis of the data for customers. The CRM can also help entrepreneurs plan their time, track deals and revenues, access old and new revenues, gather leads from the company Web site, and tell them how well they have met goals for each of their customers.[36] Collecting and analyzing the data can take some time—but a good CRM can provide entrepreneurs with a great deal of data for future sales calls.

The eight steps to sales presentations should be developed and tested for their ability to attract attention, interest, desire, and action (AIDA). When preparing the presentation, determine how much standardized script you and your salespeople should repeat and test it with the AIDA model. Does the presentation quickly attract the buyer's attention? Does it hold their interest? Does it create a desire to buy the product? Does it result in the action of a sales transaction? Keep working at it until it's perfected.

Sales Promotion

Sales promotion refers to promotional activities other than personal and mass selling. Sales promotion activities are used to stimulate interest, trial, or purchase. Promotions can be aimed at the target consumer, middle people, or the firm's own sales force.

Consumers

Some of the commonly used sales promotion activities aimed at final consumers include: sales literature, brochures, banners, streamers, free samples, calendars/key chains/magnets, point-of-purchase materials, aisle displays, contests, coupons, and trading stamps. These activities usually try to increase demand or speed up the time of purchase. The store location and trade show are commonly used places of promotions. A few ideas are as follows:

- The trial size and free sample (as well as sale) can be very effective because, if you can get someone to try your product or service, he or she may become a regular customer. If appropriate, pass out free samples in front of your business. Remember that giving a little can result in sales. Give away some free appetizers, coupons, or material (with company info on it).
- Bounce-back coupon. After a customer buys your product, you give him or her a discount coupon, say 10 percent, off the customer's next purchase by a set date, say one week. The coupons can be made up weekly. An off-shoot of this is the free goods or services after buying a set amount—like frequent mileage plans. This gets a person in the habit of doing his or her business with you. The **Big Y Supermarkets** encouraged consumers to buy a loyalty membership card for $20 that allows them to receive lower prices on certain items.
- The Big Y also partnered with the online coupon company **Groupon** to bring discounts to its shoppers.[37] Benefits of using Groupon have been mixed.
- The flier or brochure is also effective. For pennies apiece you may get long-term customers. Keep them to one page, folded or not. Again, the key is to sell your benefit. They can be distributed in a variety of locations: posted on community bulletin boards, handed out on street corners or in front of your business, placed under car windshields, made part of your billings or other regular mailings, placed on the counters and windows of other organizations.
- Your fax cover sheet can also be a form of flier. Make your business card a mini-flier or brochure by using both sides; on the back state the benefits of your product.

Middle People

Personal Application

11. Select a business you would like to start, or an existing business, and identify ways that it can use promotion with customers and/or middle people.

Some of the commonly used sales promotion (sometimes called trade promotion) activities aimed at middle people include: price deals, promotional allowances, sales contests, calendars, gifts, trade shows, meetings, catalogs, and merchandising aids. The objectives of promotions are commonly to encourage stocking new items, buying in larger quantity, or buying early.

Publicity

Publicity is any unpaid form of mass selling. Getting the media to tell the small-business story is not only free, but it also can be more effective than advertising. A target customer may not pay attention to an ad, but might carefully read an article with the same information. The small-business owner can send regular one-page news releases to mass media with the objective of being mentioned with other news or as a full story. Publicity is usually not cost-free, it does take time to "sell" your story to the media to get it publicized. Here are some tips to help you:

- Think like a journalist. How do the issues your business deals with relate to front-page news such as pollution and how might it affect your company or industry? Pitch your story that way.
- Pass the "no kidding!" and "who cares" test. The journalist's job is to communicate to readers, listeners, or viewers something they don't know and about which they are interested in learning.
- Research the media. Read the newspapers and magazines or watch the broadcasts to which you are pitching, to learn what kinds of stories they use.
- Ask for referrals. If one media source turns you down, ask who might be interested.

Personal Application

12. Select a business you would like to start, or an existing business, and identify ways that it can get free publicity.

Recall that sales really took off after **Blake Mycoskie** had his story, "With every pair you purchase, **TOMS** will give a pair of new shoes to a child in need. One for One," told in the *Los Angeles Times, Vogue, Time, People, E,* and *Teen Vogue*.[38] Cofounders of **Verjus** restaurant, **Braden Perkins** and **Laura Adrian**, also increased sales in Paris thanks to glowing articles in food magazines.[39] **Julia Erickson** and **Aaron Ingley**, cofounders of **Barre** company, also had free publicity in *Entrepreneur* magazine with their story, "we are the first food product made for dancers, by dancers."[40] Most local papers will run an article on the grand opening of a new venture, so have your story ready to tell.

Advertising and the Media

Advertising

Although advertising is part of promotion, due to its differences from the other promotional methods, we cover advertising and the media in this section. While personal selling is a flexible one-on-one approach, advertising is less flexible and communicates with a large number of target customers at one time through mass media. Advertising can be cheaper than personal selling. **Daniel Birnbaum** used advertising to grow **SodaStream**.[41] It can be used to promote your brand benefits. Though it is difficult to provide concrete results from advertising, there are audited research studies that show mass selling (advertising and publicity) does work. Advertising works across media for consumer as well as industrial products, and for new and established products. It works in the short term and continues to work years later. Advertising works for small and large business even though the amount spent and media selected do vary by size. Even the smallest ad can get attention and results.

Advertising Objectives and Plans

There are four primary objectives of advertising: to inform target customers about your business and its products, to persuade customers to buy your product, to remind customers about your product, to influence perception of your business and products. The four objectives are interrelated, and virtually every advertisement uses all these elements, but each ad should have a specific objective. Some ads announce sales and seek immediate actions whereas others try to build company image.

Advertising begins with the target customer. The two major planning decisions are what message to send and what medium is best to reach the target customer in the most cost-effective manner to meet the objective.[42] Most large businesses and many small businesses employ the expertise of advertising agencies to develop the message and/or select the media for them.

The Message

The message must be appealing to target customers if it is going to persuade them to buy the product. It is common for advertisements to emphasize the products' competitive advantage. When developing and testing the message use the AIDA model. The key to the message is not to push your company name, it is to get the prospects' attention and sell the benefit of your product, as is illustrated below.

Not too effective:

Charter Consulting—
Call us about your local area network, Internet, or telephone plans.

More effective:

Pick Charter over Comcast-
FREE REPORT
"Ten Insider Tips on How to Make Your LAN Behave Like a Lamb."

Note that the second example gets the reader's attention with a familiar link to childhood and the free report provides a motivation to respond. In the report, you would have promotional material explaining your services asking the prospect to contact you for more information. If you don't hear from the prospect, you can call to see if he or she got the report and if he or she has any questions or would like you to visit them to further explain your services. You may not be a creative ad writer, but you should realize that simply pushing your name and asking for a call is not as effective as promoting your benefit and getting a response from the prospect. Generally, shorter is better. Provide large headings and details in small letters.

Traditional Media

Personal Application

13. Select a business you would like to start, or an existing business, and develop an ad that could be used in traditional media.

The most common traditional media used to advertise are:

- **Newspapers.** They allow specific geographic coverage to a broad audience at a relatively low cost for immediate responses.
- **Television.** It is expensive to go national, but local and cable can be a reasonable cost for visual effect. Home shopping via cable TV is increasing in popularity. An offshoot of the TV ad is the movie ad that flashes on the movie screen before the previews start. It's local, targeted, relatively inexpensive, and projects your business as a part of the community.
- **Direct mail.** It allows you to selectively reach and widen your target market. You can develop a mailing list from directories (city, telephone, membership, etc.). There are firms that will sell you a mailing list and/or conduct the mailing for you.
- **Radio.** It can be used to reach a narrower target market with a friendly message at the time selected.
- **Magazines.** There are local magazines and trade publications that can be very effective at getting your message to your target customers.
- **Outdoor.** Billboards can get a quick message across at a specified place, and your company sign is also a means of advertising.

The Internet and Social Media

Learning Outcome

9. Discuss the use of social media and e-commerce strategies as part of a marketing plan.

Technology has created many opportunities for new business ventures.[43] An offshoot of direct mail is the Internet. Use technology to connect with customers.[44] The latest evolution of using the Internet to promote brands is to develop a social media presence online.[45]

Guerrilla Marketing

Guerrilla marketing is all about small businesses with limited marketing resources coming up with techniques for competing with large businesses with million-dollar marketing budgets. **Guerrilla marketing** *includes creative, unconventional,* *and inexpensive small-business strategies.*[46] Although guerrilla marketing includes traditional offline strategies, the Internet and social media provide unlimited opportunities for marketing at little or no cost. Some might think that social media is a new fad, but social media can find its origin in the 1980s as part of guerrilla marketing.[47]

Social Media

Social media *are online Web sites that engage users to participate in, comment on, and create content as a means of communicating with other users and the public.* Today, companies should be communicating with all of their global customers via the Internet.[48] Companies such as **Zynga** (maker of online games) have consumers around the world "Like" their company on social media sites such as **Facebook** and **Twitter** with links to their ads to Facebook and Twitter where consumers can learn more about their company. Incorporating live content from Facebook and Twitter allows online ads "to feel less static."[49]

Before you launch your new venture, you can dialogue with potential customers using Facebook or Twitter to exchange ideas that can provide valuable information. After you launch your new venture, no matter how small it is, like Holstee Inc., you can get customers to "Like" your business for free. Blogs are also a great way to showcase and grow your entrepreneurial new ventures for free.[50]

Viral Marketing

Social media has increased the frequency of the use of the term viral marketing. Viral marketing *is the marketing phenomenon that facilitates and encourages people to pass along a marketing message.*[51] You hope your customers will quickly pass along positive stories about your products and services. However, viral marketing can also allow Internet users to quickly send around a negative advertisement or product usage. So, a company should be careful when something related to its company "goes viral." A positive example of a viral marketing advertisement is **Coca Cola**'s Happiness Machine. The video link (www.brandchannel.com/home/post/2011/03/28/How-Coca-Colas-Happiness-Machine-Became-a-Viral-Smash-Success.aspx) has been watched by over 3 million people. The link also shows the advertisement was tweaked and also became a success in Brazil.[52]

Web Sites and E-commerce

You should set up your own business Web site. If you sell any products, they can be sold over the Internet. But setting up your site is only the first step. One of the major goals of a Web site is to facilitate e-commerce. E-commerce (electric commerce) *refers to the buying and selling of products and services via electronic channels, primarily the Internet.* Online retail is convenient due to its 24-hour availability every day, its global reach, and generally efficient customer service.[53] E-commerce includes business such as consumer retail stores (**Carrefour.fr**), auction sites (**Ebay.com**), and business exchanges trading goods

Personal Application

14. Find the Facebook page for a company that has a product or service that you buy and recommend to others, and enter a "Like" for the business.

Personal Application

15. Select a business you would like to start, or an existing small business, and develop some inexpensive strategies for marketing the business.

between corporations (**TradeFirst.com**). Carrefour, headquartered in France, created a portal Carrefour.fr to organize all of the Web sites the company offers its 5.5 million unique customers each month. For example, **Ooshop.com** is their online food store offering over 8,000 products. In Spain, Carrefour's e-commerce site sells 14,000 food and non-food products.[54]

Successful e-commerce Web sites include **Amazon** in the U.S. and **Alibaba** in China. Jack Ma has built a massive e-commerce site in China that is similar to Amazon. According to the China Internet Network Information Center, China has the world's largest population of Internet users with 564 million people online as of the end of 2012. Both companies continue to tweak their Web site to improve customer satisfaction.[55] China has more Internet users than the entire population of the U.S. with around 314 million people.[56]

Exhibit 6-3 provides some tips to be successful in the e-commerce environment. E-commerce can be exciting. But you also have to plan, organize, lead, and control your business—just like a business at your local mall.

Choosing the "Best" Promotion, Media, and Budget

Other Sources of Promotion

They include: the Yellow Pages and other directories, transit advertising (appeal to travelers while in town), special events (sponsor a road race, parade), and point-of-purchase ads (Bud sign in a bar). The small business can also use cooperative advertising in which the manufacturer shares the cost of advertising. Many manufacturers also supply free advertising packages to retailers. Another way to save money is to share advertising costs with a group of similar businesses. Many

Exhibit 6-3

Tips to Design an E-Commerce Business and Web site

1. Consider selling a special product online that is not easily found at your local mall or department store.
2. Be aware of shipping costs. It is easier to be profitable shipping a product that isn't heavy.[57]
3. Make sure each page of your Web site provides useful information.
4. Put some thought into how you want to organize your Web site.
5. Include a menu on the top or on the left-hand side of the screen to improve navigation.[58]
6. Provide supplemental information about your company on your Web site. Include information such as product manuals, warranty information, and sizing charts. Customers visit your Web site to order products—but they also like to read about your company.
7. Make sure to include a Frequently Asked Question (FAQ) link so that customers can easily find answers to their questions. The Web site should clearly state, on every page, the company telephone number and email address to allow a customer to contact the company.[59]
8. Consider using shopping cart software from a supplier such as Network Solutions (www.networksolutions.com). Network Solutions can provide a Web site for a monthly fee based on the number of products sold. You can also set up a merchant account to accept electronic payments.

creative entrepreneurs have used bartering with advertisers to exchange products for advertising.

Selecting Media

Not all media are equally effective for all businesses and products and services. The "best" medium depends on how well it fits with the rest of the marketing plan that gets to your market niche.[60] You need the target market to actually understand your product or service and its advantages to get them to buy from you. Also, the best medium depends on the: (1) objective of the ad, (2) target market and their geographic locations, (3) funds available, and (4) nature of the media, which includes who they reach, with what frequency, with what impact, at what cost. Determine if your competitors have found the best medium, and if so use it.

Advertising Budget

A major decision in the planning process is how much money to spend on advertising. Advertising should be part of the overall budget, which is discussed in Chapter 12. Four common approaches to developing the amount to be spent on advertising include:

Personal Application

16. Which advertising budget approach would you use to determine the amount of money to spend on a business you would like to start, or an existing business?

1. *Affordability.* You can't spend money you don't have, so you have to be realistic and be reasonable. Use guerrilla marketing. It is common to start with a small budget and increase over time using your sales income to pay for the ads. **SodaStream,** with company headquarters in Israel, worked its way up to placing an ad during the 2013 Super Bowl football game, and it also got free publicity in *BusinessWeek* magazine after the ad.[61]
2. *Percentage of sales:* One general rule of thumb is to spend 10 percent of projected sales the first year, 7 percent the second year, and at least 5 percent a year thereafter. Advertising costs should be paid for out of the sales and profits that they generate. If it does, advertising is an investment because it more than pays for itself, rather than being an expense. Steps should be taken to measure if the advertising budget is meeting the objectives of increasing sales as an investment.
3. *The objective-and-task method.* You begin by determining the objective then what it will cost to achieve the objective. This takes the most planning.
4. *Competition.* If you can afford it, spend as much as the competition.

Where to Promote your Business

The **Small Business Administration (SBA)** has the SizeUp tool (www.sba.gov/sizeup).[62] SizeUp helps you to find the best places to promote your business by letting you choose from preset reports to find areas with the highest industry revenue and the most underserved markets. You can also create custom demographic reports to help in your selection.[63]

The Promotional Blend

Dividing the marketing promotion budget is a problem, particularly in the competitive world of fast-moving consumer preferences. Today, most promotion blends contain both personal and mass selling as well as sales promotions. The ratio of time, effort, and money spent of each type of promotion depends on the target customer and the other three Ps in the marketing mix. You want to aim at target customers for whom the product meets their needs, not all possible customers. Generally, for products that have high prices and/or are technical, personal selling is usually needed whereas advertising can be used for low-priced nontechnical products. Sales promotion is usually more effective with impulse products than with products that customers shop around for. A wide geographic area tends to favor mass selling and promotion while personal selling is effective in a local market with a relatively small number of customers.

The type of business also has an impact on the promotion blend. Large producers of branded consumer products spend about equally on mass selling to consumers, personal selling to middle people, and sales promotion to middle people and consumers. Small producers and firms that offer relatively undifferentiated consumer products or industrial products put more emphasis on personal selling, with the rest of the budget going mainly to sales promotions. Wholesalers rely heavily on personal selling.

Denise Smith promotes her photography primarily through personal selling and email. Her primary target is the family and she can recruit new families using email and then visit them personally for a consultation. Denise has a Facebook presence to reach more of her target market. Nino from **Nino's** puts more emphasis on advertising than personal selling. He plans to increase advertising to reach his sales objective for food sales at Nino.

For a review of the marketing functions see Exhibit 6-4, but remember that you may need to develop a different marketing mix for each product that is substantially different.

Exhibit 6-4

The Marketing Functions

1. Conduct research to segment the target market and select target customers.
2. Conduct research to determine product feasibility.
3. Develop the marketing mix.
4. Forecast sales.

Product	Price	Place	Promotion
Brand names	Producer	Distribution	Personal selling
Trademarks	Wholesaler	Transportation	Sales promotion
Logos	Retailer	Storage	Publicity
Warranties	Service		Advertising
			• Traditional
			• Social Media
Packaging and labeling	Offering credit		Web sites and E-commerce

Other Options for Starting a New Venture, and Entrepreneurial Behavior

As in all chapters, in this last section we discuss some of the major differences in starting a new venture with the other five options to becoming an entrepreneur, and how to engage in entrepreneurial behavior as an employee.

Buying an Existing Business, Franchise, or Leasing Rights

Buying an Existing Business

When you become an entrepreneur through an acquisition, the prior owner has financial records that should include marketing expenses or budget and can explain the marketing plan for each of the 4Ps. You can keep the same marketing plan, but if you want to increase your sales and profits, you should consider using other ideas—especially guerrilla marketing with the Internet and social media because it is has a very low cost and has helped many small businesses compete with larger businesses. Online, target customers don't know the size of your business, so you can give the impression of being professional and larger than you are.

Buying a Franchise

If you buy a franchise, a major advantage is that the franchisor most likely already has a marketing plan that you will be required to follow—but it will cost you. However, you may also be able to use guerrilla marketing.

Buying Licensing Rights

You are typically on your own as to how you market your own business. If so, all the ideas in this chapter can be used in your marketing plan.

Starting a Corporate or Nonprofit New Venture

Starting a Corporate Venture

You will more than likely have to come up with your own marketing plan to get the firm to start the new business. If you work for a large business with a marketing department, they should be able to help you with the marketing plan and, importantly, the money to pay for the 4 Ps of marketing.

Starting a Nonprofit

Starting a new nonprofit is starting a new business and will require a marketing plan just like a new business venture, so the marketing techniques in this chapter can help you develop your marketing plan. However, many nonprofits have little or no advertising budgets, so you may need to rely more on guerrilla marketing. When selecting board members, try to recruit some people with expertise in marketing to help you. Be sure all potential board members believe in the mission and will be out in the community promoting the nonprofit. Also, as discussed in prior chapters, SCORE, ESC, SBIs, and SBDCs can help you with marketing. You may also be able to get a qualified volunteer college student to design a Web site for your nonprofit and help with social media through an internship or other arrangement; check with the head of the business and computer department for an intern.

Entrepreneurial Behavior

If you are not interested in starting a new venture, as an employee you can engage in *entrepreneurial behavior* that can lead to new ways to market the business. For example, if you work for a business that doesn't use social media, you could talk to management about doing so and volunteer to set it up and be responsible for an ongoing social media marketing plan.

Take it to the Net

Visit www.routledge.com/cw/Lussier for the book's companion Web site, where you can:

- use learning aids, including taking a quiz;
- find links to resources in this chapter, as well as other links including videos;
- learn about and start the following activities: Continuing Integrated Case, Your Ninety-Second New Venture Pitch, the Paper Clip Entrepreneurship Challenge, College Entrepreneurial Spirit Award, and the Community Entrepreneurial Spirit Award.

Chapter Review and Summary

As we bring this chapter to a close, you should understand the importance of the marketing plan as part of the larger strategic plan. The marketing plan requires a company to research how to sell its product or service to a target market. The company uses the 4 Ps (product, price, place, promotion) to reach the target market. The increased use of the Internet as a marketing tool has led to the development of social media marketing.

This summary lists the learning outcomes from the chapter and their answers.

1. **Explain the interrelationship between the marketing plan and the other business plan components**

   The marketing plan includes identifying the target customers and product feasibility through marketing research, which leads to the development of the marketing mix—product, price, place, and promotion plans and the sales forecast. Because the firm is a system, the marketing function affects the production/operations function, the accounting and finance function, and the personnel function. Without marketing, the business will not have customers to sell its products to, the money coming in to run a business, and will not need employees.

2. **Describe the importance of marketing research and its four-step process**

   Marketing research is the process of gathering data for decision-making. The steps in the marketing research process are: (1) define the decision, (2) gather data, (3) analyze data, and (4) make the decision. The decision is often stated as a hypothesis, a tentative answer to a research problem.

3. **Explain the importance of selecting a target market**

   Through the use of marketing research, you want to identify your target customers and target market. The target customers are the segmented group of potential buyers of the firm's products.

4. **Identify the 4 Ps of the marketing mix and how they work together**

   The 4 Ps include product, price, place, promotion. A product is a good and/or service. Pricing is the determination of how much the firm will charge for its products. Place includes the distribution, transportation, and storage of the product. Promotion includes personal selling, advertising, sales promotion, and publicity. The 4 Ps of marketing need to be used together to help build a well-known and respected brand name.

5. **Describe how a sales forecast is different for the new venture versus the existing business**

   The feasibility of a new venture, and the future of an existing business, are based on its sales forecast. The existing business can use past sales to aid in predicting future sales, while the new business venture has no sales history. Marketing research can help forecast sales, especially if there are some sales and customers before the new venture is launched. There are three sales forecasting methods new ventures can use: market share, comparable businesses, and using industry and trade associations.

6. **Explain the difference between express and implied warranties**

An express warranty is an explicit claim made by the producer to the consumer. The expressed claim may be given orally through advertising or through claims made by salespeople. An express warranty is commonly a formal certificate that comes with the product, and that the consumer returns to the manufacturer to validate the warranty. An implied warranty is an unwritten guarantee that the product is adequate to meet reasonable expectations for intended purposes.

7. **Differentiate between price skimming and price penetration**

The difference is based on volume of sales and pricing. Selling a product at a lower-volume and higher-price strategy is called price skimming. Choosing to sell a product at a higher-volume and lower-price strategy is called price penetration.

8. **Describe the different type of promotional methods**

Promotion methods include personal selling, advertising, sales promotion, and publicity. Personal selling involves direct one-on-one communication between you and the potential customer. Advertising is communicating with a large number of target customers at one time through mass media. Sales promotion refers to promotional activities other than personal and mass selling. Sales promotion activities are used to stimulate interest, trial, or purchase. Publicity is any unpaid form of mass selling. Getting the media to tell the small business story is not only free, but it can also be more effective than advertising. Although each promotional method is important separately, they have even more impact on customers if they are blended together.

9. **Discuss the use of social media and e-commerce strategies as part of a marketing plan**

Social media allow consumers to interact with the company by using Web and cell phone-based technologies. New entrepreneurs can have an honest dialogue with potential customers using social media sites such as Facebook or Twitter to exchange their ideas and feelings. Social media include designing customer-friendly Web sites to create higher levels of e-commerce sales.

10. **Define the twenty-four key terms identified in this chapter**

brand name	price penetration
channel of distribution	price skimming
	product
customer relationship management	promotion
	publicity
e-commerce	sales forecast
guerrilla marketing	sales promotion
hypothesis	social media
marketing mix	storage
marketing plan	UPC
marketing research	viral marketing
market share	warranty
packaging	
place	

Review and Discussion Questions

1. In your own words, how does a marketing plan interact with the strategic plan?

2. What is the purpose of marketing research, and what is it used for?

3. What are the two classifications of data? Explain each.

4. Why is a survey questionnaire used to collect data online?

5. Explain when qualitative and quantitative data analyses are commonly used.

6. What is a feasibility study and why should the new firm use a feasibility study?

7. What is the difference between sales forecasting for the established versus the new small business or product?

8. Why does the entrepreneur have to select the target market before the marketing mix and why is the marketing mix so important?

9. List and explain the three important features of a product.

10. List and explain the four considerations when pricing.

11. How does the difference in the way producers, wholesalers and retailers, and services price their products affect the entrepreneur?

12. List and explain the two major channels of distribution.

13. Describe the difference between personal selling, advertising, sales promotion, and publicity.

14. Do the advantages of a customer relationship management system outweigh the disadvantages?

15. Describe how a new video game entrepreneur can use social media to better understand his or her customers.

16. Research online for three viral marketing examples that helped a company to promote its product.

17. Instead of using expensive television ads, develop a guerrilla marketing idea that Pets.com could have used to sell more pet food online.

18. Use Exhibit 6-3 to analyze how many tips are used on the Zappos.com e-commerce site.

Application Exercises

These exercises can be completed as individual or group projects. When doing these exercises, be sure to select a specific business where applicable. You can select a business where you worked or a business you would like to own someday.

1. Develop a logo for a small pizza shop in your community.

2. Develop an outline of a viral marketing advertisement for your most recent employer.

3. In the role of an employee engaging in entrepreneurial behavior, create a social media marketing campaign for a major at your college that you would like to help grow.

4. Describe the target customers and target markets for a specific product for a specific small business.

5. Use The Small Business Administration (SBA) SizeUp tool (www.sba.gov/sizeup) to locate how many baseball card and memorabilia shops are in a large city near your college or university.

Application Situations

1. Alex White: Marketing Research

Alex White and his college roommate were very excited to utilize the newest and best electronic technology. With the development of the computer, Internet, and smart phones, communication between people became easy and ubiquitous. Rather than write letters and mail them it was easier to get online and communicate, if desired, in real time. Recently Alex's grandmother was diagnosed with a mild form of dementia and had to stay in a nursing home until other arrangements could be made for her home care. Every time Alex would visit, his grandmother would become animated and communicative. Alex noticed that the same thing happened with other patients who heretofore were withdrawn and silent. On questioning the medical staff, he was told that studies have shown that the more interaction the patients have with family and friends, the more responsive they become. Inversely, lack of human contact will cause increasing withdrawal. Knowing that with some inexpensive cameras and TV monitors you could talk to anyone anywhere, Alex reasoned there might be a good business opportunity for creating communication access for hospital patients and their families. "Not so fast," his roommate Angelo cautioned. "You had better do some marketing research before we lose a lot of money."

1. Was Angelo correct? Why and why not?

2. Define marketing research.

3. What are the steps in the marketing research process? Explain briefly each of the steps.

2. Raul Sanceza: Sales Forecasting

Raul Sanceza, who graduated from a community college with an associate degree last spring and has with his friend Juan been working for a gardener over the summer, now finds that as winter approaches they both will be without work. As a consequence, they are debating whether or not they should start their own business. They want the business to have a year-round demand that would assure predictability of income. Neither had any idea of what would be a good business until they noticed there were many types of service trucks in the neighborhoods in which they were working. Because the housing stock in their town was fairly old, it seemed that there could be a demand for floor sanding and refinishing in both older houses and any new construction.

1. Before starting the business, what should be the first step they take?

Answer: Before committing to any type of business venture they should determine the demand for their service. The sales forecast is the necessary first step in the business plan.

2. How would they go about forecasting the sales for their new venture? Describe three possible sales forecasting methods.

Answer: **Market share**. Market share is the percentage of the total market they could expect. If there are three competitors each manufacturing the same product and they share a demand for 100,000 units, an entrepreneur estimates that he or she could achieve a market penetration of 2 percent of the sales forecast, which would be 2,000 units. This assumes that the total demand for your product remains constant. If the market expands or contracts, your share of the market will still be 2 percent of whatever the total sales, or units, will be. Many industry and trade associations publish market share information.

Comparable businesses. If you can find a business that is similar to your own, the entrepreneur may be able to help you forecast based on his or her own experience.

Industry and trade associations track sales and statistics for many small businesses, aggregate them and make the aggregated information available for public or association members. Using this information will enable a business owner to forecast sales.

Case

Twitter Founder Jack Dorsey

Back in 2006, Twitter was just a funny word. But that is also when Jack Dorsey and his cofounders started Twitter, which is a micro-blogging social network. Twitter started out as an idea that Dorsey had with his cofounders, Biz Stone, Evan Williams, and Noah Glass, while working at a popular startup company called Odeo. Twitter ended up becoming more popular than Odeo, so Twitter was spun off as its own company. By 2008 Dorsey was forced out as CEO of Twitter, keeping the chairman's job but no longer involved in day-to-day management. In response to the change in management, Dorsey started Square Inc., which allows small merchants to accept plastic, with a smart phone, that can swipe cards, for a 2.75 percent transaction fee.[64] Dorsey is a serial entrepreneur looking for his third big idea!

Since 2006, the words tweet, retweet, and many other versions of the word have become part of the social media world. Sixteen percent of CEOs say they already use social media. However, 57 percent more CEOs expect to use social media in the next five years to engage customers.[65]

Users are able to send and read messages—also known as tweets—that are up to 140 characters long. User names are generally a series of letters and numbers preceded by the @ sign. Users often follow friends—but they can also follow their favorite companies and their brands. For example, Richard Branson from Virgin Airlines has 2.4 million followers on Twitter, 250,000 on Facebook, and 2.9 million on Google+; each month, 500,000 people check out his blog.[66]

With 100 million active users worldwide, businesses need to make sure they are using Twitter to build closer relationships with their customers. A new business can highlight the unique aspects of a company founder to help build a following. A company can announce a new contest or promotion to attract online users. You can link articles related to your business for followers to learn more about your business.

A new entrepreneur would also benefit from a Facebook presence. However, new social media sites are also being created. Pinterest is a very popular site for people to exchange product ideas on hobbies. Google+ is a site with which Google has been able to compete quite successfully against Facebook and Twitter—even though Google was late to enter the social media market. [67]

Think it over.

1. Search "Twitter entrepreneurship" to visit the Twitter link devoted to entrepreneurship (https://twitter.com/search?q=entrepreneurship). What are four of the most recent tweets entrepreneurs have made at the site?

2. Briefly describe a video attached to the Twitter link devoted to entrepreneurship. You can also use the Twitter search box and search for "entrepreneurship video."

3. Briefly explain an article (cite the source) attached to the Twitter link devoted to entrepreneurship.

4. Use the following link to tweet Jack Dorsey on Twitter (https://twitter.com/jack). Did Dorsey tweet about Square Inc., marketing, or entrepreneurship lately?

5. Use the following link to tweet Biz Stone on Twitter (https://twitter.com/biz). Did Biz discuss Twitter, Square Inc., marketing or entrepreneurship lately?

Global Case—Bedriye Hulya, B-fit in Turkey

Bedriye Hulya is giving women a chance to exercise in Turkey. For women, Turkey offers more opportunities to start a business than other countries in the Middle East. Turkey bans gender discrimination and women have had the freedom to vote for the past eighty-two years. Although a lower percentage than in Europe, women are still 24 percent of the labor force. Unfortunately, only 9 percent of entrepreneurs are women in Turkey.[68]

However, women like Bedriye Hulya are starting to own their own businesses. Bedriye studied management science in Dokuz Eylil University in Turkey. She then went to Istanbul University and studied International Relations. After graduation, Bedriye set out to be a serial entrepreneur. She started a fusion restaurant, two hotels, and an importing company. Her latest idea is B-fit, which is a gym only for women. She selected a specific target market—women. She selected specific locations to place her fitness stores—middle-income neighborhoods. Thus, the first store was placed in Izmir in 2006. She used a franchising model to grow to over 200 gyms in different middle-class neighborhoods throughout Turkey.[69]

Bedriye sells her franchises only to women. She calls this "positive discrimination." Her gyms offer more than just physical exercise. It is a social center for 130,000 members. B-fit holds book clubs and breakfasts for women to meet each other professionally. The members act as mentors for each other.[70] Joe Biden, the Vice-President of the United States, noted Bedriye as one of Turkey's great entrepreneurs in a speech at the Global Entrepreneurship Summit held in Istanbul.

1. How did Bedriye use market segmentation and target marketing?

2. Based upon the material in the case, did Bedriye use marketing research?

3. Why do you think Bedriye was able to overcome the challenges of starting a women-only gym in Turkey?

4. Do you think it is a good strategic idea to only sell franchises to women?

5. B-fit is a member of Endeavor Turkey. Endeavor is the leading high-impact entrepreneurship movement in the world. Research Endeavor online to better understand why B-fit relies on Endeavor for mentoring.

Writing Your Business Plan

You (or in teams) can write a business plan during the semester. There are questions at the end of each chapter to help guide you through the thinking and analyzing process. Appendix B has a sample business plan you can use as a template for developing your own new venture business plan.

Since this is Chapter 6, the goal is to add the marketing plan as part of your business plan.

Highlighted Sections of the Business Plan (Chapters 1–6)

1. **The Executive Summary** is written last—but placed first in the business plan. You have to wait until you are finished with the business plan to properly write the executive summary.

2. **Introduction:**
   A. **Background of the business:** Includes a short review of its name, address (or addresses if there is more than one location), telephone number(s), email address, Web site address, hours of operation, and a brief history (if any). You want to state when the business was started or will be started.
   B. **Management credentials and organization structure:** It is common to list all the business's key managers and their duties and responsibilities, with their qualifications.
   C. **Form of ownership:** Will your business be a sole proprietorship, partnership, or corporation and how will any profits be distributed?

3. **Strategy Formulation**
   A. **Mission:** What is the organization's purpose or reason for being (covered in Chapter 3)? The mission section of the business plan includes your business model (covered in Chapter 4), which can include a broad description of your present and future products and services to be offered. In the strategy section, it is not necessary to list all the products and services; they are listed under the marketing section of the business plan and will be discussed in Chapter 6.
   B. **Objectives (prioritized):** What does your organization want to accomplish?
   C. **Environmental analysis:** It includes an analysis of the internal environment (which includes the mission and objectives) and its external environment resulting in a SWOT analysis.

4. **The Marketing Function**
   A. **The marketing plan:** Your marketing plan must identify your target customers and product feasibility (Chapter 4) by using marketing research to better understand your industry and marketplace.
   B. **The marketing mix:** You need to include the 4 Ps of marketing in your marketing plan. What is your product? At what price point will you sell your product? Where (place) will you sell your product? And, how will you promote your product?

5. **Location and Layout**

6. **The Production/Operations Function**

7. **The Human Resources Function**

8. **The Financing Function**

9. **Controls**

10. **Appendix**

Chapter 7

The Location and Layout Plan
What Facilities do You Need?

Location and layout affect the profitability of your firm. In this chapter you will learn about the importance of the geographic location of your business and how the physical facilities of the company should be designed. You will learn some of the important factors you will need to consider in making these decisions. The final decision will balance the many different considerations allowing you to operate profitably. The increase in home-based businesses due to the growth in the Internet is highlighted.

Learning Outcomes

After completing this chapter you should be able to:

1. Describe the important factors to consider in making a location decision;
2. Examine the growth of home-based companies due to the popularity of the Internet;
3. List the important location decisions that manufacturing, retailing, wholesaling, and service firms must consider;
4. Identify the factors affecting whether you build, buy, or lease your facilities;
5. Examine the layout parameters for retail, wholesale, and service firms;
6. Utilize the Small Business Administration (SBA) and other sources for finding information on location and layout of a new entrepreneurial organization;
7. Define the ten key terms identified in this chapter.

Entrepreneur Profile—Brian Grano, CEO Mickey Finn's Brewery

We begin each chapter with a short bio of an entrepreneur and provide a link so you can learn more about the person and his or her business venture. Short 3–5-minute videos of each entrepreneur can be found at the PBS Small Business School at www.smallbusinessschool.org/. Mickey Finn's Brewery video can be found at: http://smallbusinessschool.org/video.cfm?clip=1115#.

Many of us live in a city where downtown is virtually abandoned and no longer the hub of business activity. Pat Elmsquest and Bill Sugars decided this was the perfect location for Mickey Finn's Brewery in Libertyville, IL. The old downtown in Libertyville was over 60 percent vacant. Pat bought a little pub with a $2 million loan. He expanded it to make a brewery and restaurant and the old downtown transformation was underway. Elmsquest and Sugars were true pioneers and visionaries. Today, Libertyville is an award-winning historic business district.

Think it over.

1. Is the downtown district in your hometown a good location to start a new business?
2. Would opening a casino in your downtown district help turn around the area?

The Interrelationships Between Location and Layout and Other Business Plan Components

Throughout this book we have seen that the organization is a system composed of interacting and interrelated components. The location and layout of your business provide its structure, and your structure affects your firm's performance.[1] Let's see how the location and layout decisions affect and are affected by these components. Developing the organization strategies—the products and services you wish to sell and the market you wish to serve—requires making decisions about where you must locate your business. It would be inappropriate to locate a supermarket other than in the midst of its intended customer area. Marketing information helps formulate business strategy that affects location and layout decisions.

In specific organizations, common internal designs may be used to maximize profitability. These internal designs dictate specific layout patterns. Both the location and layout decisions require use of the capital resources acquired through the financial function. The accounting function must receive all information associated with these decisions in order to determine the firm's profitability. How these costs are treated—as current cash or depreciable assets—directly affect the profitability of the firm.

In certain circumstances the production function can affect location. If you are going to market high-fashion clothing, you may plan on locating in Paris and/or New York. Layout is determined by the type of production process used. Assembly lines dictate one form of layout, retailing another. Human resource considerations also play a part in the location decision. You would not locate your organization in an area where you could not hire the right kind and number of people to employ. Labor supply is often an important location consideration.

Selecting the Location

Because of its long-term and lasting effects on profitability, a firm's location deserves thoughtful analysis. Location is so important that the most famous quote in the retail industry is "location, location, location." While it seems to be true that a location decision is made only when the business is first established or purchased, there are times when a business will want to expand or relocate. The firm's growth might force expansion requiring the business owner to make a decision about expanding at the same location, if possible, or moving to another area. The economy or demographics may dictate a change in location. Regardless of the reason, the location decision may involve a significant expenditure and you will most likely have to live with your decision for a relatively long period of time. You should know the various factors that are important in making your location decision. Knowing the criteria to use will explain why some companies choose to locate in a particular area and why other companies are forced to do so.

Selecting a location to operate your business in different countries adds even more complexity to the decision. **Global Location Strategies** (www.global locationstrategies.com/) helps companies find the best locations in different countries. It also assists companies that want to relocate businesses within or to a different country. For example, Global Location Strategies received a request for proposal from Kuwait Petroleum Corporation (KPC)/Sinopec to assist with the evaluation of four sites in Guangdong Province in China to locate an $8 billion to $10 billion refinery. After conducting an evaluation of all the sites, it chose Zhanjiang, because it offered the best combination of factors KPC needed to build its refinery.[2]

Preferences, Home-Based and Online Businesses

Learning Outcome

2. Examine the growth of home-based companies due to the popularity of the Internet.

Important considerations in starting any new business venture are your personal preferences as to where you want to live and work. Today, with technology and the Internet, a preference for many is a home-based and/or online business.

Personal Preferences

From a strictly logical point of view, if no other consideration were allowed to influence your decision-making, location selection should be made in sequence. After extensive research, you would:

1. Determine the geographic region of the country best suited for your type of enterprise.
2. Pick a city within the region that would yield maximum profitability.
3. Narrow down the city location to a specific area within a city.
4. Pick the specific site in the area.

Most entrepreneurs do not have the freedom to pick up and move. Nor do they have the resources to conduct an extensive study in order to relocate. Most entrepreneurs decide to start their new business ventures in their home community. Here they have friends, family, relatives, and contacts they have made. They know the banks, insurance agents, and other people who would be able to extend credit or expertise. In short, the local community often has an infrastructure that is both necessary and familiar to support the small business. It would take a great deal of effort to duplicate this infrastructure even if you desired to do so, in a new location. Staying in your home community is not a poor decision as long as location weaknesses do not overpower the choice. For example, opening a garden and lawn care store in the middle of a city might not be practical. You might not want to open an upscale food store in a declining neighborhood.

The reason you might choose your home community, however, may not preclude choosing to move elsewhere. If, for example, you've always wanted to live in the Southwest, now is the time to make the move before you start the company. The choice of where to move is yours; there are many good business locations no matter where you choose to settle.

Because location affects profitability, careful investigation is needed to reveal the good and bad aspects of any location. If you select to start your business in your local community, you still have to decide exactly what address will be your place of business, and many hybrid entrepreneurs start their businesses at home.

Home-Based and Online Businesses

Personal Application

1. Do you believe you could be more productive working from home or from a place of business?

A home-based business *is an organization based in the owner's home.* Generally, the owner uses some spare space for operations—a basement, garage, or spare room. It is common to start a business at home; **Steve Jobs** and **Steve Wozniak** started **Apple** in the Jobs family garage. **Michael Dell** started **Dell Computers** in his college dorm room. **J.K. Rowling** wrote at least four of her seven **Harry Potter** books from her nineteenth-century home in Edinburgh, UK.[3] Entrepreneurs operate millions of businesses from their homes. Many of those home-operated businesses are full-time businesses.

Here are a few general comments about home-based businesses:

Personal Application

2. Describe the strengths and weaknesses of a place in your home (including your dorm room) that can be used for operating your own business.

1. Make sure that you have a defined work space for your business. This is necessary otherwise the home and business activities may interfere with each other to the detriment of both. Moreover, the IRS requires it if you are going to deduct business expenses on your federal taxes.
2. You can set up a home-based business easily if it complies with all the necessary zoning requirements. For example, you cannot have a business in a purely residential area unless you get a variance. Operating in violation of a zoning ordinance will cause problems. IRS law requires that you separate all your business from your personal expenses.
3. Home-based businesses became more popular with the development of the Internet. As the Internet became more popular in the 1990s, people started developing their own online businesses. The initial dot.com era led to the end of many businesses, such as pets.com and toys.com, soon after the dot.com bubble burst in 2000.[4] However, some online businesses such as Alibaba in China, eBay, and Amazon grew quickly and offered people an opportunity to develop their own online business. Many people now sell their products directly to consumers on eBay.[5] Products sold on eBay include perfume, electronic equipment, clothing, baseball cards, and antique prints.[6]

Although it is hard to tell online, **RJ Printseller,** Robert Hirshhaut, is an 85-year-old serial entrepreneur who continues to own, manage, and market his own business. Earlier in his career, he managed the family furniture business. When that business was sold, he started an antique art shop with a storefront near a busy Rotary. As he neared the age of retirement, he moved his entire business online using eBay as his primary method to reach local and global customers. He runs his antique print shop from home and takes great pride in being able to list fifty prints per month for free and then pays a commission to eBay on whichever prints sell. After selling an antique print on eBay, RJ Printseller takes great pride in professionally packaging his prints to ensure the product is delivered as advertised. RJ Printseller has a 100% positive feedback and purple star for a feedback rating of 781. The rating score increases as the number of successful transactions increases. The purple star means he has between 500 and 999 evaluations from former customers. The higher number of positive evaluations means the seller has been in business a long time and is a reputable seller. RJ Printseller has also sold many antique prints to customers in the UK and Israel. In particular, his antique collection of maps of different parts of the world has been one of his bestselling products to sell globally.[7]

RJ Printseller could have started a business as a merchant at **Amazon.com.** Amazon has a webpage devoted to Seller Success Stories. Amazon reports that **Netfitco (Netfitco.com)** is an exercise-equipment seller that, instead of waiting for people to come through its door in Vermont, can now reach customers from coast to coast. It can now reach customers 365 days a year.[8] Amazon offers a Fulfillment by Amazon (FBA) program where it can provide storage for your product, pick it, pack it, and sell it with free delivery for the customer. FBA is a pay-as-you-go process. Companies are charged for the storage space and the orders Amazon fills. The cost of shipping is included in the fees.[9]

If you elect to start a new business from home/online, your location decision is made for now. However, many hybrid and full-time entrepreneurs become successful and find that they outgrow their home space, such as Apple moving out of the Jobs garage. So it is helpful to understand factors to consider in selecting a location, and you will most likely need some type of a layout for your home business. So read on.

General Location Factors

Aside from personal choice, which can vary from individual to individual, there are specific factors to consider when identifying where to locate your business. There is no specific formula that allows you to weigh each criterion and come up with the ideal site. Each factor must be considered with specific reference to your business. Examine each of the criteria and pick the location that best meets the needs of your business model. Some of the important factors to examine are discussed here.

Shipping Costs

The importance of freight costs increases as the value of the goods decreases in proportion to their bulk. Diamonds, for example, are expensive in proportion to their weight. Thus diamond cutters can be located anywhere in the world. Transportation costs to ship cut diamonds to various markets are insignificant factors in the retail value of the product. Cement, on the other hand, is bulky and intrinsically of low value. It is possible to ship it long distances, but the cost of transporting it beyond a radius of twenty-five to thirty miles

Personal Application

3. Identify any home businesses you know of and describe some businesses that you could start from home/online.

Personal Application

4. What are the shipping costs for a product you buy from a local small business?

from the plant would soon make the price prohibitive. Transportation costs would increase and finally represent the bulk of the final price, reducing profit considerably. **Pets.com** went out of business because it was too expensive to ship pet food, kitty litter, and other heavy products to customers. Customers could buy these heavy products at retail stores for less.[10] However, **Wags.com** and **Amazon.com** later succeeded in overcoming the cost of shipping.

Proximity to Market

Designing high-style garments can be done anywhere in the world because low labor costs play a pivotal role in generating profits. However, a garment designer at the very least must have a sales office and showroom, and New York City is the place to be, in order to service major garment buyers (the customers) who travel there to see the latest styles and to place their orders. In this case, proximity to the market also facilitates faster and better customer service, not unimportant location aspects in themselves. And because many garment firms are located in New York, it is advantageous to maintain visibility along with your competition, particularly in the high-fashion, rapidly changing garment industry. Any other location is apt to leave the firm "out of touch" with current demand conditions.

Retail establishments sell different products in different locations. The products sold cater to the economic, religious, and ethnic composition of the surrounding population. Expensive art galleries may be found in "upscale" areas; discount stores are not. Retail food markets will also carry products catering to the surrounding populations' economic, religious, and ethnic composition.

Transportation Facilities

It is important for most businesses to be near to or on good transportation facilities such as highways, railroads, trucking and airline terminals. Parts and raw materials are shipped to the company and finished goods are shipped out. Customers may come to the premises to view or buy the product. No less important, employees have to be able to get to work either by automobile or public transportation.

Labor Supply

An extremely important consideration for any firm is the availability of workers. Availability here refers not only to the number obtainable but also the quality and type. Because each firm needs employees trained to perform its specific tasks, it is not wise for a firm to hire just any individual.

A great source of labor for the electronic industry was the availability of industrially trained and skilled workers in and around Boston, MA. Many of these workers were available because garment, textile, and leather manufacturing firms had moved out of the area leaving an employment vacuum with an ample supply of skilled workers. In America, nearly all of the labor force is industrially trained, that is, the workers are accustomed to, and expected to, put in an eight-hour day every day at their place of employment. A significant problem in less developed countries is that workers are not industrially trained. Firms must think twice about locating in an area where workers must be trained. In some instances, where there is a need for semi- or unskilled labor, it might be advantageous to locate in a surplus labor area.

Community Attitude

A precondition for a successful location is a community's attitude towards a particular firm. Many communities will not allow a business they deem undesirable, such as pornography-related businesses, to locate in their areas. Although a location may be perfect in all other respects, if the community does not welcome a particular business, it is usually not a good idea to locate there. Hostility towards industry can be shown in many different ways. It is never easy to fight community ill-will and therefore it is easier, and perhaps economically more advantageous, to locate elsewhere. **Wal-Mart** has been blocked from opening stores in some locations that don't want them. It has learned to seek out communities that want to have the benefit of having Wal-Mart stores.[11]

Communities, or states, that truly desire industry will do all they can to make conducting business easier. There are some communities that offer incentives such as financial aid or tax breaks.

Cost of Facilities

In deciding where to locate, the cost of land and other facilities, by itself, is often a relatively less important factor compared with the other factors. Because location is a long-term consideration, the purchase price of land and facilities will be spread over many years, each year representing only a small part of the initial cost and only minimally affecting the business's total cost picture per year. If the cost of facilities is high, you often have the option of leasing. We will discuss building, buying, or leasing facilities after we finish the location decision.

Taxes

Closely tied to land and building costs, but much more important, is the local tax structure. Taxes are a continual expenditure; the higher they are, the less desirable the location. This is true because the entire tax cost represents, in accountants' terms, a burden cost.

Climatic Conditions

For some businesses, climate can be a deciding factor; you can't sell air conditioners where it never gets very hot. Ski shops are generally found close to ski areas. If running a sailing school is your dream, you need access to water and seasons of warm weather.

Coordination

Grouping integral components together may provide advantages such as close communication and coordination; the presence of congenial business neighbors who are able and willing to supply the firm with financing, supplies, power, and transportation facilities might make certain locations more desirable than others.

Suburban or Rural

Once the choice of the general area has been made, you must decide whether to settle in an urban, suburban, or rural location. Each locale has had its proponents. Years ago the "proper" location for any firm was in a large city. The next trend was to locate plants in rural areas which lack city congestion, unwelcome political interference, or taxes. But because there were also no city facilities and amenities (public transportation for employees, for example), firms started moving closer to, but not into, the cities. Today, a suburban location outside of a large city is often desirable. This location tends to provide the benefits and facilities of large cities and some freedom from congestion and politics.

Site Selection

Critical factors to be considered in site selection are costs, including taxes, development, parking, customer accessibility, traffic, and neighborhood conditions. Manufacturing firms, wholesalers, and service companies need not locate in high-rent districts. Small manufacturing firms need adequate parking for employees. Retailers need adequate parking for customers and must locate where their customers can reach them.

In locating your business, you should assess the importance of the location factor and determine the combination of location factors that best meets the needs of your business model. The following are examples of factors affecting the location of manufacturing, retailing, wholesaling, and service types of businesses.

Personal Application

5. Select a business you would like to start, or an existing business, and identify which of the general factors are more important to the location of the business.

Learning Outcome

3. List the important location decisions that manufacturing, retailing, wholesaling, and service firms must consider.

Manufacturing Location

Recall that in Chapter 4 we discussed the **North American Industry Classification System (NAICS)**, formerly called the **Standard Industrial Classification (SIC)** system, commonly used to identify industries. Manufacturing is numbered in the 31–33 range.[12] In addition to the general location factors to consider, when locating a small manufacturing plant, there are other important factors to consider, as discussed here.

Transportation

Transportation has been discussed, but it is especially important for manufacturing. Your receipt of goods and/or raw materials coming into the factory as well as finished products being shipped out depend heavily on the availability of airports, highways, waterways, and railroads. You should have easy access to the transportation alternatives you generally use.

Weight Loss

Because freight shipping costs money, firms tend to locate, if possible, at the source of a large process weight loss. A large process weight loss *is the loss of raw materials that occurs naturally as an outcome of the manufacturing process.* An example of this can be seen in the typical location of steel firms. In Pennsylvania there are large supplies of coal and no significant deposits of iron ore. Although both ores are necessary, the process consumes the entire weight of the coal, which is used as fuel in the refining process. Thus, the transportation of coal, beyond any distance which is absolutely necessary, is a needless expenditure. It was cheaper to ship the iron ore from the Mesabi region of the Great Lakes to Pittsburgh for refining because much more coal than iron ore is needed to produce a ton of steel. Because the coal is completely consumed in the process (five tons of coal to one ton of iron ore), you ship as little coal as possible.

Raw Materials

Some location decisions are preordained by the need to be close to the source of raw materials. It is obvious that the only location possible for a diamond or gold mine is at the source where the ore is found. You can only grow wheat where proper growing conditions are available. These facts supersede the availability of cheap transportation and market considerations. Boat yards that cater to recreational boating have to be situated in a place that boaters can reach easily.

Water Power

In addition to using water for transportation, it may be advantageous to locate on or near water if it is a source of power in the manufacturing process. The supply and price of water is important to many small businesses. Some types of small manufacturing plants need water to produce their products. The cost of water as well as the importance of keeping it clean in accordance with environmental laws is increasing. A business location could be determined by the availability of clean, inexpensive water. The **Massachusetts Green High Performance Computing Center** in Holyoke, MA starts at the Holyoke dam on the Connecticut River. The dam generates hydroelectricity that is sold to industrial users for about 8 cents a kilowatt hour, compared with a state average of 12.59 cents. Hydropower isn't only cheap; it's also considered clean because it doesn't rely on fossil fuels.[13]

Site Selection

Even though the site may be ideal in terms of size, transportation, topography, and construction, it is no longer easy to obtain the appropriate zoning variances, licenses, and required permits. There are so many conflicting interests and desires that permitting and licensing delays have become longer and longer. The opening of a **McDonald**'s franchise in Freeport, ME, was delayed several years while the community tried to prevent it. In order to secure the town's approval, McDonald's had to install the store within an existing white wood-frame structure and eliminate the golden arch structure outside the building. A similar situation occurred at a McDonald's in Long Island, NY, where there is now a McDonald's inside the exterior of a *circa* 1795 farmhouse.[14] On the other hand, it is also possible that the required zoning changes may never come through. So, it might not be worth it to consider a site where there are real or potential problems.

Retail Locations

Under the prior SIC code, retail and food and beverage (bars) businesses were classified together under retail. However, under the new NAICS codes, retail is numbered 44–45 and food and beverage is now coded 72 under the accommodations and food service classification.[15] Because retail and food and beverages are similar in location decisions, when we refer to retailing here we include food and beverage businesses.

Marc Andressen, a technology entrepreneur who started and sold **Netscape,** predicts that "retail is dead."[16] However, Andressen might be slightly biased towards the success of the Internet. Consumers still like to get out of the house, try out products at different stores, and have enjoyable retail experiences at different stores. It is more likely that the result will be an annual increase in the amount of online shopping—while customers will still visit physical stores to browse products, compare prices, socialize with their friends and families, and to actually buy products. Also, people will continue to want prepared meals rather than cook for two major reasons. People don't have the time or interest in cooking and want a quick meal, either take-out or eat in. They also like to go out for a family meal or for a more upscale dining experience.

Retail locations are particularly sensitive to specific characteristics of the surrounding area. As there are different kinds of retail stores catering to different clienteles, it is important that the local criteria match your needs. Here let's consider the city, type of location and business, some other considerations, and four primary options for locating your business.

City

You will need marketing research information on:

- size of the city's trading area;
- population and population trends in the trading area;
- total purchasing power and the distribution of purchasing power;
- total retail trade potential for different lines of trade;
- number, size, and quality of competition;
- progressiveness of competition.

Type of Location

Once you have determined which city you are going to open in, you must then evaluate a number of factors concerning the area or the type of location you want. These factors include:

- customer attraction power of the particular store and the shopping district;
- quantitative and qualitative nature of competitive stores;
- availability of access routes to the stores;
- nature of zoning regulations;
- direction of the area expansion;
- general appearance of the area.

Type of Business

One final set of criteria should be examined concerning the specific site—or property—in which you wish to open your business. If you plan to open a large discount store, for example, you will want a site that is visible to and accessible by a high volume of drive-by traffic. A smaller store, however, may be appropriately located in a neighborhood where it attracts local residents. While not specifically a location factor, small retailers can survive by finding a specialized niche and providing service to the customer. In either case, the following criteria should be kept in mind:

- adequacy and potential of traffic passing the site;
- ability of the site to intercept traffic *en route* from one place to another;
- complementary nature of adjacent stores;
- parking facilities or space;
- vulnerability of the site to competition;
- cost of the site.

Other Considerations

Although you have evaluated what you earnestly believe to be all-inclusive criteria, you might want to consider the following:

- How much retail, office, storage or workroom space to do you need?
- Is parking space available and adequate?
- Do you require special lighting, heating, cooling or other installations?
- Will your advertising expenses be much higher if you choose a relatively remote location?
- Is the area served by public transportation? Is it necessary for your business that it is?
- Can the area serve as a source of supply of employees?
- Is there adequate fire and police protection?
- Will sanitation or utility supply be a problem?
- Is exterior lighting adequate to attract evening shoppers and make them feel safe?

- Are customer restroom facilities available? Is the store easily accessible?
- Does the store have awnings or decks to provide shelter during bad weather? Will crime insurance be prohibitively expensive?
- Do you plan to provide pick-up or delivery?
- Is the trade area heavily dependent on seasonal business? Is the location convenient to where you live?
- Do the people you want for customers live nearby? Is the population density of the area sufficient?

Four Retail Choices

You will want to weigh all the criteria with respect to the type of retail operation you plan to operate. For example, if your new business will be a discount store, you will be targeting an entirely different customer than a store selling exclusive, high-price merchandise. An important question is where do your target customers like to shop? Realizing that retail stores are not home-based or online, there are four major choices:

1. **Downtown.** Think about your home town. What types of businesses are doing well downtown? Is there a need for eating and drinking establishments? Depending upon the city, downtown can range from high to low costs.
2. **Stand-alone structure.** Many convenience stores operate out of a single building. If you can buy your own building, in the long-run you can save on rent and even make a profit. However, can you come up with a down payment and get a mortgage?
3. **Small block of stores.** Some independent shoe and sporting goods stores are located in what is sometimes called a strip mall. The rent is usually less than a mall and your business is visible to auto traffic, but you don't get as much foot traffic as a mall.
4. **Mall.** Many specialty retailers locate in a large mall with walking traffic. It can be the most expensive, but walk-in traffic can offset the cost. In 2012, Converse Inc. opened its first mall-based location at the Westfield Garden State Plaza. Customers can design one-of-a-kind footwear, apparel, and accessories.[17]

Personal Application

7. Using your home town area, or a city you are familiar with, identify businesses that are located downtown, in stand-alone structures, a small block of stores, and malls.

For each option, we have given general cost comparisons, but you will obviously need to visit possible locations for your business and compare cost and potential profitability with one location selection over another. Again, where do your target customers like to shop? This is a critical consideration in your location decision.

Wholesale Locations

NAICS organizes wholesalers in the 42s.[18] Wholesalers are similar to retailers in that they must locate where there is ease of access to an identified target market. The wholesalers' market is, however, the retailer, which is a derived demand—*a market that springs up not from people wanting goods for their personal use but for the use those goods have in completing a demanded product or process.*

Traditional Wholesalers

Wholesalers generally sell only to retail businesses for resale and thus they must be available in a centralized location. This gives rise to "wholesale" districts within a city. Retailers know where to go and, when buying, can visit a number of their suppliers. Wholesale locations generally are in less expensive areas as they are not dependent upon end-user consumers. Generally you will find wholesalers tend to congregate in older, less expensive areas of the city in older, multistoried buildings. Rental costs are substantially less when you don't have to project an "image."

Wholesalers tend to group together as they need to be accessible to the same retailers. Inability to secure such a location may give rise to wholesale centers outside the city. These areas can be advantageous in that they allow truck access to both the city and to suburban markets. Wholesale locations are greatly influenced by: (1) the availability of large, inexpensive buildings in less costly areas within the city or beyond; and (2) proximity to other wholesalers.

Wholesale Clubs

Wholesalers also have to stay abreast of changes that are taking place at the manufacturing, retail, and service levels. As large manufacturers and retailers continue to get larger, they are also likely to perform the tasks normally performed by the wholesaler. For example, *wholesale clubs* **Costco, BJ's, and Sam's Club** allow entrepreneurs to buy supplies in bulk at a cheaper price. They also sell to non-business customers, but they usually must pay a membership fee.

Technology allows wholesalers to become more efficient in regards to services they provide, such as inventory management. However, online retailers such as **Amazon** also have huge warehouses and provide many services often delivered by a traditional warehouse. Wholesalers can improve their situation by offering online catalogs of the services and products they do have for resale. Distributors can also offer logistical help to manufacturers and retailers to improve their inventory management.[19]

Personal Application

8. Research where the wholesale district and the warehouse clubs are located in your community.

Manufacturing, Retailing, and Wholesaling Coordination

Overall, the manufacturer, wholesaler, and retail distribution network will continue to evolve into new configurations as it has done for decades. At times, the services that each offers will shift from one to another. Manufacturer **Dell** started the trend for selling directly to the customer, eliminating some of the wholesale and retail sales, and **Apple** has opened its own stores to sell directly to retail customers. But, in the end, tasks such as inventory management, product storage and transportation, and the actual sale to the final customer will have to be completed by a manufacturer, wholesaler, retailer, or some combination to allow the product to be used by consumers.

The Elevator Pitch

This skill-builder puts you in the venture capitalist position. You will watch an elevator pitch from the Internet and assess and discuss if he or she would or wouldn't invest in the new venture. The success of a good elevator pitch is dependent on getting the venture capitalist hooked on the product. The link for the elevator pitch is from Jacqueline Haberfeld, designer of the patent pending Popover easy snowwear for babies. The Popover video can be found at: www. youtube.com/watch?v=fG7-wHfPUUl.

Think about it.

What score do you give the pitch?

Great product idea and pitch	Terrible product idea and pitch	
3	2	1

1. Would you invest in the Popover business?
2. How would you improve the pitch?
3. What is the hook in the presentation?

Service Locations

NAICS classifies Professional and Business Service supersectors 54–56.[20] We classify service location decisions in two ways. Does the customer come to your place of business or do you go to the customer to conduct business?

Customer Comes to Business

These service businesses are similar to retail stores in that they may locate near their markets. The business must be both accessible and visible. The factors that drive a good retail location will apply.

Business Goes to Customer

Operating a service where you make visits to the customers provides more flexibility in choosing a location. For example, if you are a plumber or a piano tuner, you can have your office wherever you choose because customers or suppliers seldom visit your premises. Locate where you want as long as your costs are kept at a minimum.

Personal Application

9. Identify some service businesses in your community in which the customer comes to the business and the business goes to the customer.

To assist you in making a decision, you should use a site rating sheet such as the one based on information provided by the Small Business Administration (SBA). It will help you evaluate the factors and come up with the highest rated location. Exhibit 7-1 is an example.

Factor	Grade	Weight
Grade each factor: 1 (lowest) to 10 (highest)		
Weigh each factor: 1 (least important) to 5 (most important)		
1. Centrally located to reach my market.	____	____
2. Raw materials readily available.	____	____
3. Quantity of available labor.	____	____
4. Transportation availability and rates.	____	____
5. Labor rates of pay/estimated productivity.	____	____
6. Adequacy of utilities (sewer, water, power, gas).	____	
7. Local business climate.	____	____
8. Provision for future expansion.	____	____
9. Tax burden.	____	____
10. Topography of the site (slope and foundation).	____	____
11. Quality of police and fire protection.	____	____
12. Housing availability for workers and managers.		____
13. Environmental factors (schools, cultural, community atmosphere).	____	____
14. Estimate of quality of this site in years.	____	____
15. Estimate of this site in relation to my major competitor.	____	____

Exhibit 7-1
Rating Sheet on Sites

Source: C. Beesley, How to choose the best location for your business. U.S. Small Business Administration (January 9, 2013).

Lease, Buy, or Build Facilities

Based on your location decision, another important consideration is whether to lease, buy, or build the facilities needed to run your business. In this section, we discuss these three options.

Learning Outcome

4. Identify the factors affecting whether you buy, build, or lease your facilities.

Leasing

Being in a small business almost guarantees that capital will be in short supply. Most small businesses have difficulty raising capital so any method of operation that requires less capital outlay is usually considered attractive. In an effort to minimize capital outlay, many firms have turned to, or at least considered, leasing. A *lease is an agreement to rent an asset, which will be used as if it were owned.*

For example, many firms lease vehicles, other equipment, and buildings from third parties. In any case, the lessee, *who is the party leasing the equipment, makes periodic payments* to the lessor, *the party who owns the equipment being leased,* for the use of the asset. Because the lessor holds title to the asset being leased, the lease payment covers both the purchase price of the equipment as well as a profit for the owner. Who are lessors? As the popularity of leasing increases, the number of companies in the leasing business has grown. Leasing is now a billion-dollar industry. In addition to independent leasing, you can lease from companies, banks, insurance companies, and finance companies. In many instances, you can lease equipment directly from the manufacturers. As a matter of fact, you can lease almost everything you need in any business.

Advantages and Disadvantages of Leasing

Advantages

In general, the primary advantage to leasing rather than buying or building is that you get to use the asset—the building, the truck, or other asset—without making a large capital payment required for ownership. Your regular lease payments are generally less than you will pay to own the asset in question because a lease usually requires a smaller down payment than a purchase, and sometimes does not require a down payment because: (1) it can allow a longer term than a loan for repayment; and (2) it does not have to cover the entire cost of the asset during the term of the lease. This allows you to use as operating capital the money that you would have paid to own the asset.

Also, because of the opportunity to walk away at the end of the lease, either by prior negotiation or industry standard, your equipment may be better maintained and automatically upgraded as new technology arrives.

Equipment such as motor vehicles can be easily replaced at the end of the lease, which roughly corresponds to the time when they begin breaking down more frequently. Technology increases at such a rapid rate that some assets quickly become obsolete while leased assets can be exchanged at minimal costs to acquire state-of-the-art technology as it becomes available. Because the lease payments are deductible as operating expenses, there may be some tax advantage as well. Operating expenses reduce the profits upon which taxes are based. Owned assets also have advantages in that you can treat both depreciation and investment tax credits as deductions.

Disadvantages

When the lease period is over, you return the asset to the lessor. Whatever value it has at that time is lost to you and reverts to the owner. However, the lessor can, at additional cost, extend your lease or sell you the asset. If you owned the asset, you could continue using it at no added costs. To take a current example, the monthly costs to own a new car whose original price was $22,000 dollars, with a 3-year note at 3.35 percent, would be approximately $645 a month. To lease the same automobile for the same term, you might only have to pay $216 per month resulting in a $429-per-month cash saving. By itself, this is attractive. However, at the end of the 36-month period you don't own the vehicle. Its value reverts to the lessor. In effect, you have paid $7,776 and, because you own nothing, you must then replace it. Of course, if you owned it, you could continue using it. Over the long run, leasing costs more than owning because included in the lease payment is a profit to the lessor, which you could avoid paying by buying. The same argument can be made for buying an office building or factory.

A lease is a legal obligation and as such generally cannot be canceled. If there is a cancellation clause, it will be fairly expensive. You will continue to pay off the lease whether or not you actually use the equipment. On the other hand, owning an asset gives you the ability to sell it and recover some of your investment.

Types of Leases

While all leases have the same general advantages and disadvantages, leases can be classified into two categories: operating leases or sale and leaseback.

Operating Leases

An **operating lease** *will permit you to use equipment in your business, while the title remains with the lessor.* The lessor agrees to maintain the asset and may allow cancellation. Electronic equipment, furniture, buildings, and motor vehicles, which can be leased in this manner, are written for a specific time period that is usually shorter than the life of the equipment. During this generally non-cancelable term, the lessee makes payment to the lessor. Maintenance is the lessee's responsibility. When the lease period is over, the lessor recovers the property. Office space is a typical example of such a lease. Short-term leases allow a firm to have time to evaluate if they like the product before they actually have to spend large amounts of money to buy the item.[21]

Leaseback

Leaseback, short for *sale-and-leaseback*, is a financial transaction. In a leaseback, *you buy an asset and sell it to another party and lease it back.* Therefore, you continue to be able to use the asset, but no longer own it. The transaction is generally done for long-term fixed assets notably real estate and expensive equipment, but also for planes, trains, and trucks. The purposes for a leaseback are varied, including financing, accounting, and taxing. Capital that is not tied up in assets can then be used for operating expenses. At the expiration of the long-term lease period, you may renew the lease or repurchase the asset.

Buying or Building Facilities

As discussed, with advantages and disadvantages, you do have the option of buying existing facilities, such as a stand-alone building, or building one. Also, there are businesses that will build the facility to your specifications and lease it to you. It was not long ago that firms rented or bought an existing building or space and fit their operation into it. As the concept of efficiency assumes more importance, the building is considered to be facilitating equipment in the productive process. As such you should make sure that the facilities are appropriate to the type of business you are in. Two major considerations are important.

Construction and Design

Buildings today are designed with primary consideration given to the function of the building. If the business you are in does not require heavy equipment, such as that which might be needed for manufacturing, the building can be light in structure and design. If there is need for heavy equipment and machinery, make sure that the floors and walls can support the required loads. If you foresee the need for a library, make sure the building can support the weight of the books, which are heavier than you think.

Function

Personal Application

10. Select a business you would like to start, or an existing one, and identify major assets and if they will be or are leased or owned, and if they will be or were built for the business or not.

If you are a manufacturer, the manufacturing facilities should be on one level to facilitate material handling. Office space can be accommodated on multiple levels. Other factors to consider are the age and condition of the building. An old building will require extensive renovation of most of its systems: heat, plumbing, air conditioning and electrical. Further, restrooms may have to be added and/or rebuilt to conform to newer building codes and the Americans with Disabilities Act (ADA) laws. There must be an adequate number of entrances and exits. For example, retail business might need more entrances and exits than a factory. The importance of these factors varies with respect to the different kinds of businesses. Each factor should be analyzed so that the facilities chosen are those best suited to the organization.

Facility Layout

Learning Outcome

5. Examine the layout parameters for retail, wholesale, and service firms.

Layout *is the spatial arrangement of the physical facilities in the most efficient manner for the specific business.* Layout must be given careful consideration because the principles of layout vary depending upon the nature of the business. You should choose a layout that fits your business.[22] To illustrate the different approaches to layout, we begin with Exhibit 7-2, then examine facility layouts for manufacturing, retailing, wholesaling, and service firms.

Manufacturing Layout

As important as the location decision is, your decision regarding the type of production layout it needs is even more critical. Layout is a long-term matter. As it concerns itself with the design of the production process and the placement of the equipment and machinery, layout involves heavy expenditures. Once decided, the firm must depreciate the particular type of layout decision over a long period of time; it is now locked into its decision and these costs must be correct, for change can be effected only at great costs.

In the past, buildings were designed from the ground up to fulfill a general function at the least possible cost and manufacturing firms configured their production layout to fit them. Unless they are developed for speculation, buildings today are custom designed, and they are built specifically for the business that will occupy them. The most popular type of building today is the sprawling single-story structure, located on a large tract of land in the suburbs. The single-floor concept permits easy and economical transportation patterns within the

1. **Product Layout**—commonly used in manufacturing with a set sequence of assembly line flow of high-volume and low-variety products, but it is also used with services.[23]

   Start → assembly → assembly → assembly → assembly → Finish product/car

2. **Process or Function Layout**—commonly used in retail stores and healthcare in which the customer or patient only uses some processes/functions and can go to only where the product is located (department or aisle) or the service is performed. Most offices are set up functionally, with assigned areas/departments such as human resources and finance.

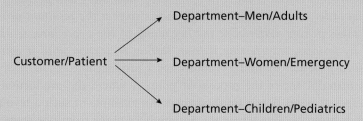

3. **Cellular Layout**—commonly used in retail restaurant food preparation and repair services. Activities and equipment involved in creation or repair of a product are located near one another to improve productivity.[24] Your kitchen layout at home is a cellular layout.

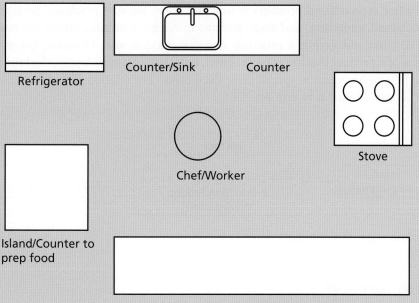

4. **Fixed-Position Layout**—commonly used in construction (build a house or remodeling) and services (cleaning rugs and mowing lawn) in which the job is done at the customers' place of business or home, or the product doesn't move during manufacturing (Boeing making passenger planes).

Exhibit 7-2
Facility Layouts

building itself. The land area provides shipping, parking, and expansion potential. The layout used in a building may be of the process (functional) or the product (line) type. These are the two extreme methods used and, as with extremes, most firms probably use a combination of the two. Because the type of layout depends upon the characteristics of the production process, it is then necessary to define the two layout types so that it can be seen where each is best utilized.

Product Line Layout

The **product line layout** *is the arrangement of machinery and personnel in the sequential order of the manufacturing process so that the resultant production process takes in raw material at the beginning of the procedure, works on it process by process, transferring it from station to station until it emerges as the finished product.* Exhibit 7-3 illustrates a product line.

The material enters the process at point A where the production begins and emerges at point B as a finished good. An example of such a layout is the automobile assembly line where the automobiles move from one stage of production to another, emerging in finished form at the end of the line. The use of a line layout will depend upon the balance between the advantages (profit) to be gained and the disadvantages (losses) to be sustained.

Use of product layout enables a business to produce large volumes of one or a few standardized products at low unit costs. Because machines are highly specialized, expensive, and single purpose in design, a product layout has heavy fixed costs and is thus a relatively costly method to use. However, the more units of a product that are manufactured, using product-type layout, the broader the base upon which to spread these fixed costs. The relationship of fixed costs to volume is shown in Exhibit 7-4.

Exhibit 7-3

Product-Type Layout

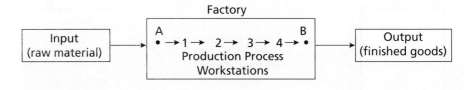

Exhibit 7-4

Fixed Cost to Volume Ratio

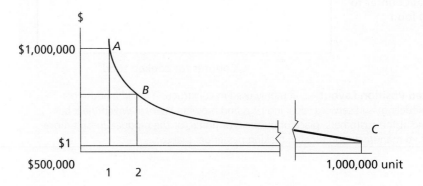

Fixed cost of product layout diminishes per unit as the number of units increases.

At point 1, the cost to manufacture one automobile is $1,000,000. At point 2, because we are spreading the fixed costs over two units, the cost to manufacture two automobiles is $500,000. Finally, if we plan to produce 1,000,000 automobiles, the fixed cost each vehicle must bear is $1.00 per unit.

Process or Functional Layout

In a process layout, all machines are grouped according to function. There is no predetermined route that products follow in the production process; the route is determined by the nature of the product. All products are involved in some of the same processes; however, because the products differ, they may be routed through these processes in different sequences. Exhibit 7-5 illustrates a functional layout.

Both manufacturing layouts have their applicability. The use of either depends upon the product. Both have their strengths and weaknesses. It is up to you to weigh their relative costs, and use either the product or process layouts or some combination.

If you are growing grapes and producing wine, each type of wine you are producing uses some, but not necessarily all, of your equipment. For example, after all grapes are initially picked, the white wines must have skins removed but the red wines require the grape skins to remain. Some wines are bottled immediately with screw caps; others are placed in casks for ageing and are then placed in corked bottles.

Flexibility, however, has a high cost; although there is considerable latitude in the production process, more inspection is needed to make certain that what is produced is what is desired. Close control is not possible and economies of scale are not applicable in this process. In comparison to a product line setup, goods produced in a process layout have a higher unit cost.

Cellular Layout

The cellular layout can also be used when assembling component parts of the product or the entire product. Some high-tech companies, like **IBM**, that make

Personal Application

11. Select a manufacturing business you would like to start, or an existing one, and make a simple drawing of its layout.

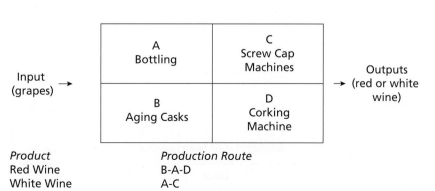

A Bottling	C Screw Cap Machines
B Aging Casks	D Corking Machine

Input (grapes) → □ → Outputs (red or white wine)

Product   *Production Route*
Red Wine   B-A-D
White Wine   A-C

Exhibit 7-5

Process or Functional Layout

computer chips and circuit boards place the parts, materials, and tools in an easy-to-reach, often circular layout.

Retail Layout

The function of a retail store is to maximize sales by providing customer convenience and service. Layout can facilitate this goal by directing the customer to those goods that provide maximum profitability. Recall that retailers tend to use the *process layout*. The store has to make it easy for the customer to access these goods. Researchers have found that shoppers may leave a store if the aisles are too narrow, causing people to brush up against each other when they pass.[25] A recent study conducted by the University of Washington found that combining music in the store with an appropriate smell can improve store sales. Scentair.com can help find the right combination of the type and speed of music combined with the right smell. During the holiday season you might combine Christmas music with a cinnamon smell to encourage shoppers to stay longer in your store.[26]

Studies have also shown that because people entering a store are more likely to turn right rather than left, the best place to display high-profit items would be on the right side of the store as the customer enters. Generally, those goods are not demand items, *which are specific items that a customer needs to purchase*. They are *impulse items* that people want or that people buy on the spur of the moment; they are relatively expensive and, where customers can choose among products with significant differences, they encourage weighing one item against another before purchasing.

Low-margin items are generally on the left of the store. In order to buy the low-margin-profit items, a customer would have to walk through the store, past all of the attractive high-profit impulse items. Thus, in a drug store, prescription items are on the back wall, greeting cards on the left, and cosmetics on the right. The middle of the store displays goods that fall between these categories such as books and candy. Exhibit 7-6 illustrates this process layout.

In designing the layout of the retail store, you would make a scale drawing of the floor space, recognizing each area and utilizing it for goods yielding the appropriate profit margin. This approach would produce a typical grocery store layout as shown in Exhibit 7-7.

Exhibit 7-6

Typical Drug Convenience Store Process Layout

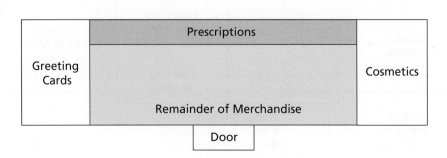

Exhibit 7-7
Typical Grocery Store
Process Layout

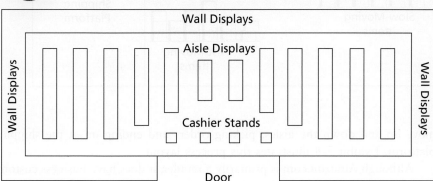

Other layout patterns can be developed but because the objective for any retail store is to maximize profits, low-traffic areas get low-margin goods and high-traffic areas receive high-profit items. **Walgreens** opened its 8,000th location in Los Angeles. However, this store is not your typical drugstore layout. The new store features a fresh sushi bar, expensive wines, a smoothie bar, and a coffee bar.[27]

In 2013, **Apple**'s retail store design was granted a trademark from the U.S. Patent and Trademark Office. Apple's store design includes the clear glass storefront, the special Italian floors, lighting, unique shelves, the rectangular tables arranged in a line, and the layout of the Genius Bar at the back of the store.[28] The layout, as designed by Steven Jobs, has been a huge success considering that Apple stores are always full with customers receiving personal attention.

Personal Application

12. Select a retail business you would like to start, or an existing one, and make a simple drawing of its layout.

Wholesale Warehouse Layout

A major difference between retailers and wholesalers is their total layout. A retail store has most of its total space displaying its products for shoppers to select, with a much smaller area to store (or warehouse) the products until they are placed on the sales floor. Traditional wholesalers, however, have very limited sales floor space, and a very large warehouse. But wholesaler membership clubs have combined the two models.

Maximizing customer satisfaction in a wholesale operation is paramount. In most traditional wholesale operations, because customers usually phone, mail, or fax their orders, the wholesaler's job is to fill these orders as quickly and efficiently as possible. Today they often deliver the order as well. To do this, the wholesaler locates the faster-moving items closest to the shipping and receiving platform or deck. Slower-moving items are farther away. In filling orders, then, employees minimize the distance traveled in putting the order together. This would necessitate having wide aisles, to maximize the use of material-handling equipment. Using this equipment an employee could quickly

Exhibit 7-8
Typical Wholesale
Warehouse Process
Layout

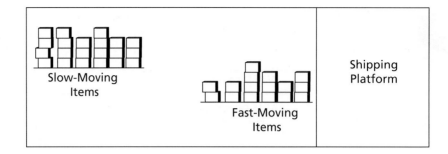

move up and down the aisles, picking orders and ending up at the shipping platform. Exhibit 7-8 illustrates this process layout.

Although **Amazon.com** is primarily a retailer, it does have business customers. Because it is an online shopping experience, Amazon doesn't have a sales floor. It has to deliver the products from its warehouses. Therefore, it consistently tries to speed up the time from taking the order to delivering the products from its warehouses. The back storage rooms of retail stores are also similar to the warehouse process layout.

Costco Wholesale is an interesting combination in that it is a wholesale club where retailers can buy food items in large quantities and yet it also is a retailer that sells to final customers. Costco's mission is to keep its costs and prices to its members down.[29] Costco looks like a large warehouse with wide aisles to allow forklifts to store items on high shelves. From all appearances, Costco looks like a cold warehouse with cement floors. The interesting twist is that customers psychologically consider Costco to be a small place where employees look like regular people because there are no uniforms, where it is easy to hear employees having work conversations, and the stores have simple grey cement floors. Even though the store is physically large, customers (known as members because they buy an annual membership) easily find their way around the simple grid layout.[30]

Personal Application

13. Select a wholesale business you would like to start, or an existing one, and make a simple drawing of its layout.

Service Layout

Because service establishments are so diverse, it is virtually impossible to describe a typical layout. However, there are two major considerations: (1) Does the customer comes to your place of business? If so, it is common to use a *process layout*. (2) Do you go to the customer to do the service? If so, it is common to use the *fixed-position layout*.

Service businesses need to examine customer traffic and traffic flow before making layout decisions. Keep in mind that the needs of the business dictate the layout. A special layout will be designed to meet the needs of the business. Service businesses provide direct services that customers must come to the premises to acquire, such as restaurants and hotels, which have as their cornerstones customer convenience and a pleasant appearance or atmosphere.

Personal Application

14. Select a service business you would like to start, or an existing one, and make a simple drawing of its layout.

An automobile repair shop, on the other hand, may be set up much like a manufacturing company. The customer won't see and most likely is not interested in what goes on when the automobile is brought in for repairs. All the customer desires is that the vehicle is fixed and aside from the reception or waiting area, really doesn't care how the repair shop is arranged. Similarly, if you go to the customer to provide the service, they don't care what your business location looks like.

Sources of Information

There are many publications to aid entrepreneurs in searching for the best location. One of the most popular sites is the **Small Business Administration** (www.sba.gov). The Community page (www.sba.gov/community/) can be used to network with other small business owners and get advice on starting, growing, and managing your business. Small businesses can post comments and participate in blogs and other social media activities to gather location and layout information.

The U.S. **Census Bureau** (www.census.gov/) also publishes information about the U.S., dividing it into Standard Metropolitan Statistical Areas (SMSAs). Factors about each area's population such as age, income, home value, and education are analyzed. The Census Bureau also publishes an Introduction to Census Data.

You can also try the U.S. **Department of Labor Bureau Statistics** (www.bls.gov/bdm/entrepreneurship/entrepreneurship.htm), which has a specific page about entrepreneurship and the economy.

> **Learning Outcome**
>
> 6. Utilize the SBA and other sources for finding information on location and layout of a new entrepreneurial organization.

Other Options for Starting a New Venture, and Entrepreneurial Behavior

In this last section we discuss some of the major facility differences in starting a new venture compared with the other options to becoming an entrepreneur. We also discuss how to engage in entrepreneurial behavior as an employee.

Buying an Existing Business, Franchise, or Leasing Rights

Buying an Existing Business

The existing business will already be at a certain location and the business will have an existing layout. However, you have the ability to move the new business to a different location where you believe, based on research, that the business can do better. You can also remain in the same location, but decide to rearrange the layout to appear to have a more modern appearance. The SBA suggests that you be careful about zoning laws at a potential new site to make sure your new business and the location you select are following all of the correct laws.[31]

245

Buying a Franchise

In comparison, the location and layout for a franchise opportunity require the new franchisee to follow the guidelines set forth by the franchisor. The franchisor already has established guidelines on issues such as site location.[32] The strength of this situation is that you invested your money into the franchise chain to benefit from the location, layout, and design knowledge offered by the franchisor—so you have to do as most franchisors request. Overall, when investing in a franchise, the strength of the standard design normally outweighs the negative of not being able to express your own creativity in designing your storefront. If you want to be creative, it might be better to start your own business, and not invest in a franchise.

Buying Licensing Rights

If you buy a license, you are starting a new business and will have to select the location and design the layout as discussed throughout this chapter.[33]

Starting a Corporate or Nonprofit New Venture

Starting a Corporate Venture

If you become a corporate entrepreneur, you will more than likely run the business from the existing location. However, if the business grows, you may have to select a new location and design the layout. Depending on the corporate structure, the company may select the location and layout for you, or at least help you to do so. **Apple** set up a separate location where a group of employees worked alone to build the Macintosh. Employees considered themselves pirates and liked being separated from the main group of Apple employees that were designing the Lisa computer. The Macintosh computers built by the separated group were ultimately a much greater marketing success than the Lisa computer.[34]

Starting a Nonprofit

When selecting a location for your new nonprofit, you want to work closely with your board because they may have knowledge and access to a location for little or lower cost than the going commercial real-estate rates.

Starting a new nonprofit organization also requires careful thought on where your customers will most likely get your products and services. For example, a nonprofit organization with a vision to help seniors over 65 years old should review the demographic data for the area which they are considering. It would be logical to locate the new business where there is the highest percentage of senior citizens. Additionally, it would make sense to make sure the layout is designed to allow easy access to the building because the seniors will often have reduced mobility.

Your nonprofit should have a website location and layout that is simple to navigate with useful information, and be donor friendly. Viewers should find it easy to access information about your nonprofit. Donors should find the process of donating money as easy as possible. Journalists should be able to locate information about your organization so they hopefully can help spread the news about your nonprofit. Plus, the site should also have multiple places where volunteers can sign up to help your organization.[35]

Entrepreneurial Behavior

If you are not interested in starting a new venture, as an employee you can engage in *entrepreneurial behavior* that can lead to new ways to organize the existing business.

Take it to the Net

Visit www.routledge.com/cw/Lussier for the book's companion Web site, where you can:

- use learning aids, including taking a quiz;
- find links to resources in this chapter, as well as other links including videos;
- learn about and start the following activities: Continuing Integrated Case, Your Ninety-Second New Venture Pitch, the Paper Clip Entrepreneurship Challenge, College Entrepreneurial Spirit Award, and the Community Entrepreneurial Spirit Award.

Chapter Review and Summary

As we bring this chapter to a close, you should understand the interrelationship between location and layout and other business plan components. The organization is a system of interacting and interrelated components. While location and layout are not considered to be functional areas of the firm such as accounting, finance, marketing, production/ operations and personnel, they affect and are affected by all organization components. Location is often determined by labor supply and market consideration. Layout is affected by decisions regarding production/operations. Both location and layout decisions require resources supplied by the finance function.

This summary lists the learning outcomes from the chapter and their answers.

1. **Describe the important factors to consider in making a location decision**

   Other than being in a home-based business, you must consider where to locate your business. If you buy an established business, you should know if its location is advantageous or you should consider changing its location, perhaps expanding to another site.

   After your own personal preferences are examined, you want to consider such general location factors as: (1) process weight loss, which is the loss of raw materials that occurs normally as an outcome of the manufacturing process; (2) proximity to the market; (3) transportation facilities; (4) availability of raw materials; (5) labor supply; (6) community attitude; (7) water power; (8) land costs; (9) taxes; (10) specialized communities; (11) climatic conditions; (12) sister plants or warehouse; (13) the question of urban, suburban, or rural sites; and (14) how these factors affect specific site selection.

2. **Examine the growth of home-based companies due to the popularity of the Internet**

   As the Internet became more popular in the 1990s, people started developing their own online businesses. The initial dot.com era led to the end of many businesses, such as pets.com and toys.com, soon after the dot.com bubble burst in 2000. However, some online businesses such as eBay and Amazon grew quickly and offered people an opportunity to develop their own online business. Many businesses now sell their products directly to consumers (thus bypassing the wholesaler) on their own websites through eBay or Amazon.

3. **List the important location decisions that retailers, wholesalers, service, and manufacturing firms must consider**

   After examining the general location factors, you will be able to apply them to specific location requirements of retail, wholesale, service, and manufacturing firms. Retail decisions are often influenced by personal preferences on where the entrepreneur wants to start his or her business. Wholesalers are located in areas that offer more warehouse space and a lower rent per square foot than retailers. Service firms are normally located near the customers that need the service provided.

4. **Identify the factors affecting whether you build, buy, or lease your facilities**

   Another aspect of the location decision is whether you want to buy, build, or lease your facilities. A lease is an agreement to rent an asset that will be used as if it were owned, requires a contract between the lessee (the party leasing the equipment) and the lessor (the party that owns the equipment that is being leased). An operating lease will permit you to use the equipment in your business, while title remains with the lessor, who agrees to maintain the asset and may allow cancellation. Leaseback leases are used where you already own the equipment or building and wish to generate cash to be used in other parts of the business by leasing the asset back to a third party. There are arguments both for and against leasing, but your decision should be based on what is most profitable for your company.

5. **Determine the layout parameters for retail, wholesale, service, and manufacturing firms**

Having committed to a building, you must develop a layout, the arrangement of the physical facilities in the most efficient manner for the specific business, for the interior in order to maximize profitability. The differences in layout of the retail, wholesale, service, and manufacturing firms depend upon the demand of customers or clients. A manufacturing firm wants to minimize production costs while a retail store wants to ensure that customers, upon entering the facility, have the opportunity to select high-profit impulse items. A manufacturing firm might utilize a product layout, which refers to the arrangement of the machinery and personnel in the sequential order of the manufacturing process or in a process layout where machinery is grouped according to machine function. A retail store, which makes a low profit on demand items, specific items that a customer needs to purchase,

wants to assure that these are accessible only after the customer passes by the high-profit impulse items. A wholesale firm's layout is dependent upon minimizing the cost of filling the derived demand order of the retailers. The location of service companies depends upon whether the customer goes to the location for service or the service people go to the customer. In the former case, service firms have to consider most of the location considerations affecting the retail store. In the latter case, it might not matter where the source company had its location, except that it should be located where cost is at a minimum.

6. **Utilize the SBA and other sources for finding information on location and layout of a new entrepreneurial organization**

There are many publications to aid entrepreneurs in searching for the best location. One of the most popular sites is the SBA (www.sba.gov). The Community page (www.sba.gov/community/) can be used to network with other small business owners and get advice on starting, growing, and managing your business. You can also use the U.S. Census Bureau (www.census.gov/), which publishes information about the U.S., dividing it into SMSAs. Factors about each area's population such as age, income, home value, and education are analyzed.

7. **Define the ten key terms in the chapter**

demand items	lessee
derived demand	lessor
home-based business	operating lease
	process weight
layout	loss
leaseback leases	product line layout

Review and Discussion Questions

Be sure to explain all your answers.

1. Location may be a significant factor for some types of firms and not for others. Why? Give several examples.

2. Is personal preference important in locating a company? Explain and justify.

3. How do most small business owners choose their location?

4. Using a specific type of business, if you were to locate a new venture, how would you select

   a. the geographic area; and
   b. the site within the area?

5. What factors would you consider when you evaluate a region in which to locate? Where would you find appropriate information?

6. Are there circumstances that would persuade you to locate in a declining area? What are they and how would you make your decision?

7. In locating a manufacturing plant, what factors would you consider?

8. In locating an upscale clothing store, what factors would you consider?

9. What factors should a computer sales and service operation and an asphalt manufacturing plant consider in their selection of a location? Compare the location factors you would utilize in each decision.

10. Would it be wise to locate your firm near others of the same kind? Why or why not?

11. What part would census information play in your location decision? Where would you get it and how would you use such information?

12. What are the advantages of buying rather than leasing your equipment or building?

13. You have been given the opportunity to plan the layout of a brand new food store. What are the general rules you would use to enable maximum profitability?

14. Manufacturing plants need to minimize cost. How would you lay out a plant in order to minimize costs?

15. What types of businesses need to be concerned with customer accessibility? Why?

16. While keeping costs down is appropriate, a cheap location might not be the best idea. Why would this be true? Show an example where this would not be true.

17. Why is the location decision for a manufacturing plant, retail store, or service operation important?

18. When does a manufacturing firm use process layout and when would it use product layout?

19. When would a manufacturing firm use general purpose equipment and when would it use special purpose equipment? Explain.

Application Exercises

Each chapter has a series of exercises requiring you to apply the specific text concepts. When doing these exercises, be sure to select a specific business where applicable. You can select a business where you worked or a business you would like to own someday. Answers for each exercise should be approximately one page.

1. Visit a local retail store and draw a diagram of the layout of the store. Draw a line through the aisle in the store that was most frequently visited by customers.

2. Visit a local retail store and see if the windows "tell a story" that would entice you to enter the store.[36]

3. Visit http://smallbusiness.chron.com/retail-layout-strategies-11464.html for some more ideas on how to improve retail-level strategy.

4. Visit a local service business, such as a doctor's office, and develop a diagram of the traffic pattern in the business. Is there a place where the customer or patient is waiting unnecessarily long?

5. Visit the SBA.gov site and find three issues related to location and layout connected to starting your own business. Briefly describe the three issues you found.

Application Situations

1. Two Colleges

In order to determine future location facilities it would be helpful to use a rating sheet showing the grades and weights for each alternative. When using such a sheet remember that there could be many non-quantifiable factors that outweigh all other considerations.

Grade each factor (0 being the lowest) and weigh each factor (0 being the least important).

College A should stay at its present location in the city due to its close as well as historic connection, the desire to use internal funding, and the strong desire of its board to remain where it is presently located, to build no dormitories nor attempt

Factors	College A		College B	
	Grade	Weight	Grade	Weight
Close connection with present location	10	5	2	3
Desire to expand programs	3	5	9	5
Desire to build large campus	0	4	10	5
Desire to build dormitories	0	5	10	5
Desire to provide parking	0	5	10	5
Desire to use government funding	0	5	10	5
Desire to use internal funding	10	1	10	5
Desire to enlarge student body	8	5	10	5
Desire of Board				
To stay at present location	10	1	0	0
To move to suburban location	0	5	10	5
Create national reputation	0	5	10	5

to attract a residential student body. Any expansion will be done with internally generated funds, will be modest in scope and in line with the ability of the neighborhood to accommodate such expansion.

College B should start looking for a large tract of suburban land to develop into a campus. It will require significant government funding, (loans or grants) to finance its expansion.

College A will have to expend considerable effort to get along with its neighbors. It will have to raise internal funds, donations from board, friends, graduates and interested parties. It will have to have approval of the city and will have limited land available for expansion.

College B will have to look for a large tract of land within commuting distance in order to maintain access by present and future students and additionally to build dormitories to house students requiring on-campus housing. It will also need as much funding as it can obtain from the federal, state and local governments where possible.

2. Quantity Shopper

The supermarket chain looking for a location for a new location to sell in bulk at low prices must be willing to accept lower profit margins as it hopes that volume will be sufficient to be profitable. The chain can pick one of several alternatives.

First it can, as Costco does, look for cities or suburbs with large concentrations of population looking to save money on groceries, plus a wide variety of other items. There should be a tract of land available large enough to accommodate a large box store and gas station, if desired. There should also be room for store expansion as well as ancillary facilities if desired. The site should also have utilities already available or able to be brought in. As the store will draw from a large area there should be adequate parking facilities and good roads. The political climate must be favorable a business cannot locate in a hostile environment. There are other factors to consider but these will be common to all location decisions.

Second, Quantity Shopper can take look at the model created by a former Trader Joe's executive (*Arizona RepublicTalk Magazine*, November 10. 2013, p. 16) Doug Rauch to sell outdated products in bulk to lower socioeconomic levels. His belief was that this population who also deserve to benefit from lower prices would be willing to buy lower priced food. A population that meets these criteria can be located by analyzing the census tracts for those areas in or around cities having lower incomes and lower per capita income than the average for the area. Most of the above characteristics will apply. However, as selling in a low-income neighborhood will require even lower prices, Doug decided that a good way to lower the costs would be to sell outdated products which would still be top quality. It is too early to tell if this approach will be successful. His initial approach will be to use a different name and to make the market a nonprofit entity.

Case

Max Restaurant Group Founder Richard Rosenthal

Many chefs and people who love to cook food dream of opening their own restaurant. Their passion in life is to cook delicious food that customers enjoy. However, cooking food is only about 20 percent of the real work involved in owning a restaurant. You have to decide on a concept such as a country or seafood theme, do some market research on your target market, conduct a fantasy location search to see what you could do with a large amount of financing, do some telemarketing to find local food and utility service suppliers, build your model restaurant using Excel spreadsheets to calculate expected annual costs, and calculate food and labor costs.[37] Building a model of your ideal restaurant will prepare you for the realities of opening your own restaurant.

The good news is that many entrepreneurs are able to open up all sorts of restaurants. These entrepreneurs often stamp their restaurants with a theme that reflects their personality and the culture of the local community. For example, Max Burger is the latest restaurant creation by Rich Rosenthal of the Max Restaurant Group (maxrestaurantgroup.com). With the latest Max Burger, Rich has developed a successful, distinct, and independent group of restaurants. All of the restaurants are currently based in the Greater Hartford, CT/Springfield, MA region. The restaurants include Max A Mia Ristorante in Avon, CT. Max Amore Ristorante and Max Fish are both in Glastonbury, CT. Max Downtown and Trumbull Kitchen are in Hartford, CT. Max Oyster Bar and the original Max Burger are in West Hartford, CT. Max's Tavern is at the Basketball Hall of Fame in Springfield, MA.

Max Burger, the latest restaurant, was built in an old Blockbuster Video store at the Longmeadow Shoppes in Longmeadow, MA. Max Burger was developed in response to the sluggish economy in the last few years.

Max Burger offers an American-style comfort food such as all-natural gourmet burgers and sandwiches, and craft beers. Max was built to complement the other stores in the Shoppes. These stores include five women's upscale clothing stores, a locally based Japanese restaurant, a Bertucci's Italian restaurant, a men's suit store, a CVS, a small-town sandwich shop, and a Gap store.

How does Rich select the locations for his distinctive restaurants? Does he rely on his instinct? Did Rich know to use PRIZM (search PRIZM and Claritas and then enter the Zip Code Look up) to research the demographics in the communities where he placed a restaurant? PRIZM allows the user to enter a zip code and find all sorts of data about a community: their salaries, their lifestyles, what types of cars they buy, the age distribution of the people that live in the community, etc.

It is your job to help Rich learn to use PRIZM and answer the following questions.

Think it over.

1. Which of the communities listed in the case has the highest median income?

2. What are the population and average age in Longmeadow, MA?

3. Select one of the communities where a Max is located and compare it to your own zip code where you live.

4. Interpret the data in the case to select the next location to place a Max Burger in a community that already has a different Max Group Restaurant.

5. Does Max Burger have a good location in the Longmeadow Shoppes?

Global Case—Junior Achievement in Africa Helps to Start Home-Based Businesses

Mfonobong Nsehe went looking for the Top 30 young entrepreneurs in Africa. He found thirty great young entrepreneurs in a variety of industries such as real estate, financial services, manufacturing, media, technology, green technology, healthcare, agriculture and fashion. He feels the entrepreneurs that he found are ready to change Africa. As one would expect, many of these businesses are startup operations that the entrepreneurs operate as home-based businesses. However, they also have been able to grow beyond the startup stage and are now developing new locations and operations throughout Africa.[38]

Andrew Mupuya is a 20-year-old African entrepreneur who started his paper bag-making business as part of his Junior Achievement (JA) in school. In 2008, as part of his JA Entrepreneurship course, he organized over 200 people to collect plastic bottles and sell beads to companies in Norway and Uganda.

Andrew was encouraged by his JA teacher to write a business plan. In 2011, he won an International Labour Organization business plan competition. He won for writing a business plan for his own company, Youth Entrepreneurial Link Investments (Yeli). He won for writing a business plan for the extension of his paper bag business into new locations throughout Africa.

Initially, Andrew conducted marketing research on the viability of his paper bag idea. He found that the government was considering a ban on plastic bags for environmental reasons. Andrew was allowed to use his school as a location to produce his paper bags.

Andrew found local Ugandan suppliers had less quality paper than what he could source in Kenya. Using the Kenyan paper supply, he was able to train the other students in school on how to make the paper bags. He eventually employed fourteen people and had customers such as local hospitals, retail shops, supermarkets, restaurants, local flour manufacturers such as Maganjo and Akamai Foods, and even some roadside sellers.[39]

Overall, Andrew has trained over 500 students to make paper bags. His vision is to build a paper bag-making plant that will help create a cleaner Africa. He wants to build a paper recycling center in Namanve Industrial Park. He has researched the expensive machines to recycle paper and expects to acquire them gradually. Andrew credits his entrepreneurial spirit, started with JA, for his motivation to build his business operations and help create a cleaner Africa.

Think it over.

1. Research online at www.forbes.com/sites/mfono bongnsehe/2013/02/23/30-under-30-africas-best-young-entrepreneurs/ for an example of a different African entrepreneur and how he or she started his or her own business. Focus on an entrepreneur who discusses the location of his or her business or the layout of his or her store.

2. Research online for the international operations of JA in a different country than your own country. Where are some of the entrepreneurial companies located that are highlighted on the JA site?

Writing Your Business Plan

You (or in teams) can write a business plan during the semester. There are questions at the end of each chapter to help guide you through the thinking and analyzing process. Appendix B has a sample business plan you can use as a template for developing your own new venture business plan.

Highlighted Sections of the Business Plan (Chapters 1–7)

1. **The Executive Summary** is written last—but placed first in the business plan. You have to wait until you are finished with the business plan to properly write the executive summary.

2. **Introduction:**
   A. **Background of the business:** Includes a short review of its name, address (or addresses if there is more than one location), telephone number(s), email address, Web site address, hours of operation, and a brief history (if any). You want to state when the business was started or will be started.
   B. **Management credentials and organization structure:** It is common to list all the business's key managers and their duties and responsibilities, with their qualifications.
   C. **Form of ownership:** Will your business be a sole proprietorship, partnership, or corporation and how will any profits be distributed?

3. **Strategy Formulation**
   A. **Mission:** What is the organization's purpose or reason for being (covered in Chapter 3)? The mission section of the business plan includes your business model (covered in Chapter 4), which can include a broad description of your present and future products and services to be offered. In the strategy section, it is not necessary to list all the products and services; they are listed under the marketing section of the business plan and were discussed in Chapter 6.
   B. **Objectives (prioritized):** What does your organization want to accomplish?
   C. **Environmental analysis:** It includes an analysis of the internal environment (which includes the mission and objectives) and its external environment resulting in a SWOT analysis.

4. **The Marketing Function**
   A. **The marketing plan:** Your marketing plan must identify your target customers and product feasibility (Chapter 4) by using marketing research to better understand your industry and marketplace.
   B. **The marketing mix:** You need to include the 4 Ps of marketing in your marketing plan. What is your product? At what price point will you sell your product? Where (place) will you sell your product? And, how will you promote your product?

5. **Location and Layout**
   A. **Location:** You want to consider such general location factors such as: (1) proximity to the market; (2) transportation facilities; (3) availability of raw materials; (4) labor supply; (5) community attitude; (6) water power; (7) land costs; (8) taxes; (9) specialized communities; (10) climatic conditions; (11) potential sister plants or warehouse; (12) the question of urban, suburban, or rural sites; and (13) how these factors affect specific site selection as either a home-based, Internet, or traditional manufacturing or retail location.
   B. **Layout:** Having committed to a location, you must then develop a layout. The layout is an arrangement of the physical facilities in the most efficient manner for a specific business, for the interior in order to maximize profitability. You should draw a diagram of the layout you expect to utilize in your business.

6. **The Production/Operations Function**

7. **The Human Resources Function**

8. **The Financing Function**

9. **Controls**

10. **Appendix**

Chapter 8

The Operations Plan
How Will You Make The Product?

In this chapter, you will learn the importance of the production/operations function of a small business. Producing quality tangible goods or services in the most efficient manner will enable firms to survive and prosper. Accordingly, we will look at the definition of the product/operations function and the way firms determine how to make products in the most efficient manner. Attention must also be given to the question of supply chain management and how to manage inventory and the production function so that inventory costs are at a minimum and the flow of goods or services is properly monitored. As the production of goods and services are intertwined with quality considerations, we will also examine this topic.

Learning Outcomes

After completing this chapter you should be able to:

1. Identify the components of the transformation process;

2. Describe why a time and motion study is conducted to determine how to make the product in the most efficient time;

3. Describe Material Requirements Planning (MRP) and Just-In-Time Inventory System (JIT) as two tools used to control the production process;

4. Discuss economic order quantity (EOQ) and determine how to arrive at the lowest cost inventory;

5. Identify the two approaches to production control, loading and scheduling;

6. Discuss the importance of quality considerations in the production process and how to integrate Total Quality Management (TQM) in the production process;

7. Define the twenty-eight key terms identified in this chapter.

Entrepreneur Profile—Dale Crownover, Texas Nameplate

Go to PBS Small Business School at www.small businessschool.org/. Texas Nameplate can be found at: http://smallbusinessschool.org/video. cfm?clip=937.

Texas Nameplate faced a decision—improve its structured quality program with the purpose of decreasing defects or risk losing Lockheed, its biggest customer. Texas Nameplates can be found on virtually everything. It prints specialized labels that often outlast the item to which they are attached. Although Dale Crownover felt his product quality was already high, he was convinced by Lockheed that a statistical process control program would significantly decrease the number of defects.

Dale became obsessed with tracking all the statistical aspects of his manufacturing business.

After five years he ended up taking Texas Nameplate from being just another print shop to become the first small business to be given the Malcolm Baldrige Quality Award. The Baldrige award is a very prestigious award and is normally won by large businesses such as General Electric. Texas Nameplate, at the end of the 5-year period, experienced 30 percent more output with 30 percent fewer employees.

Think it over.

1. Do you think having a quality control program would always increase profits?

2. Would employee morale be affected by a Total Quality Management (TQM) program?

The Interrelationship Between the Production/Operations Function and Other Business Plan Components

The relationship between the production/operations function and the other functional areas of accounting, finance, marketing, and human resources is critical. Defining the product or service you will provide and identifying the market and its size determines the production process you will use. To satisfy mass markets, you will need large-scale production facilities. Operating a small repair shop might require state-of-the-art test facilities or just small hand tools.

The production process must be able to meet sales forecasts provided by the marketing function. Defining the production process enables you to determine the equipment you need and how much it will cost. Defining the production process also will lead you to discover what resources must be supplied by the finance function. All equipment acquired for the production/operations function must be identified by the accounting function. The accounting function also determines whether to expense or depreciate equipment expenditures—a decision that will affect the firm's profitability. Frequently decisions about equipment acquisitions are driven by tax considerations. Once the decisions are made, you are then able to project your need for personnel to operate the machinery and to supervise the overall operation. This information is needed by the personnel function so that it can identify the appropriate people to hire.

Operations and the Transformation Process

Operations Management

Learning Outcome

1. Identify the components of the transformation process.

Without a product or service, you don't have a business. The old definition of "production management" concerned itself only with the manufacturing process, but time and technology have forced us to enlarge the scope of "production management" to include any business whose function is the creation of utility, tangible products, or intangible services. Also, today many small businesses that sell a product also provide services. In this case, *utility* is a good or service, which is of some value to the purchaser or final consumer. Thus, the creation of utility is called operations management. Corresponding to this change in emphasis, production management is now called "operations management."

Simply stated, if we view any organization as the creator of utility from specific resources, whatever they may be, we are able to include in the definition of production-oriented firms not only typical manufacturing firms, but also any type of organization as dissimilar as hospitals, insurance companies, or educational institutions. Instead of calling the techniques used to operate and control these firms "production management," a newer term, "operations management," was devised to denote the applicability of these management techniques to industries other than manufacturing because the U.S. is more of a service economy today. Viewed in this manner, every business owner is also an operations manager. Therefore a production/operations process can be described as transforming inputs into outputs to optimize the firm's resources.[1]

Transformational Process

The transformational process consists of three elements: input, process, and output as Exhibit 8-1 illustrates. The chief difference in managing these various production processes stems from the fact that the emphasis given to each element is determined by the nature of the individual entity in which the process occurs. Obviously, the problem of inventory maintenance in a hospital is far more critical than for an inn. But managing this process efficiently in order to produce goods or services in a timely manner is the task of any organization.

Input

Although all firms do not use identical input, every business must utilize three general elements: people, capital, and material. The combination of input differs between firms and is, of course, determined by the product or output, but all are used in some form or another as the initial step in managing operations.

People, often referred to as human resources, are required in every business. However, education, skill, expertise, and other desirable attributes are dependent upon the demands of the firm. Bigger and more complex firms generally require higher levels of expertise and the demands of a professional organization may by its nature expect high levels of expertise. Legal, educational, and medical institutions are examples of organizations requiring high skill levels. Relatively low levels of education and skill may be required in other types of service occupations. In general, as the technology or educational needs of the organization increase, the skill and knowledge level demanded of the employees must keep pace. Correspondingly, the work itself tends to become less physically demanding.

Capital can be viewed in several ways. First, capital refers to the physical assets of the company, such as machinery, equipment or plant, and other assets used to produce a utility. These assets are accumulated over long periods of time and are invaluable to that specific business. If the business ceases operations, the liquidation value of these assets is often only a fraction of their value to a going concern. Second, a firm must have capital—in this case, cash—to pay operating expenses. There must always be enough cash to pay all expenses, even if the firm has to borrow to pay its debts. You, the entrepreneur, cannot delay paying bills indefinitely.

Personal Application

1. Analyze a transformation process for a product or service where you have worked.

Exhibit 8-1

Typical Transformation Process

Inputs ←——— Conversion ———→ Outputs

Materials **refer to the material or physical goods** that any operation must consume. These goods are either used or are a part of the final product itself. In manufacturing clothing, the plant needs yarn, thread, zippers, buttons, and many other associated items if it is to produce a completed garment. In a service industry, where the good produced is often intangible, the demand for material is not quite so obvious. In an accounting firm, the primary material would be the knowledge and skills of the professional staff. In a hospital, pharmaceutical drugs, beds, and X-ray film are properly considered to be material, which contribute towards producing a healed person.

The Conversion Process

We have now identified the input that will be transformed into products or services. This procedure is known as the production/operations process, which converts one form of material to another. It can be as simple as that of a store where the actual product is not manufactured but derives its value from being available where and when the customer wants it. In this case the conversion process would involve changing the location and time of availability. Or the process can be complicated and technologically impressive such as that involved in the production of computers or electronic components. It should be noted that production can consist of either breaking raw material down into component parts, such as in the refining of bauxite, or combining material to create the final products, such as a garment or components.

Output

The end result of the production/operations process is the conversion of materials into the final product. It should be recognized that the production process is not pure. That is, while we are producing the goods and services we want, there are other products being created that may have unintended consequences. These products may be extremely costly to society. For example, the generation of electric power from coal has indirectly caused black lung disease among coal miners and air pollution in areas surrounding generating plants. Although we cannot completely avoid producing unwelcome by-products, a great deal of time, energy, and money is going into determining either alternative production methods or ways to cope with these outcomes. The elements of a production process are shown in Exhibit 8-2. In order to ensure that the process produces goods or services in the most efficient manner, the process must be controlled. Some of the control mechanisms are also shown in Exhibit 8-2.

Exhibit 8-2

Production Processes and Controls

Components of Production Process	Control of Production Process
1. Material	1. Quality
2. Make–buy	2. Scheduling
3. Capacity	3. Work Measurement

Outsourcing

Many companies have chosen to outsource the conversion of inputs into outputs. Outsourcing *means that a company would rather transfer the assembly of its products to outside suppliers instead of doing the work itself.*[2] For example, **Apple** uses **FoxConn** in China where the labor cost is significantly less to assemble iPads.[3] Outsourcing often creates tension for the company because it is moving jobs out of the home country and into less developed countries. FoxConn recently cut work hours to a maximum of sixty per week, making "significant progress" in meeting Apple's standards. However, the Fair Labor Association (FLA) assessed three of FoxConn's factories in China in late 2013. They found that, although FoxConn is largely complying with the FLA sixty-hour/week code standard, it did not meet its target of full compliance with the Chinese legal limit of thirty-six hours of overtime per month. FoxConn has asked for more time to lower the overall number of overtime hours. They have tried to educate employees that they don't have to work excessive hours to earn more money. Plus, FoxConn has started an expensive and lengthy process of using more automated technology to build computer products.[4] **Huawei Technologies Co.**, China's largest maker of telecommunications equipment, said Apple's experience in China shows the importance of supply chain management.[5]

Companies such as **Nike** have recently realized that complying with agreed-upon work standards in its global supply chain can be beneficial to Nike and the employees in countries such as China, Indonesia, Vietnam, and Taiwan. "Factory conditions and human rights issues have been widely criticized by different pressure groups. Even though company responded to these issues with the Andrew Young report, the Dartmouth Study, and Ernst & Young's continual monitoring, Nike still needs a couple of years to eradicate mentioned problems."[6]

Make vs. Buy

The small business must decide whether to make its own materials, inventory items, or component parts or to buy them from a supplier. If a firm can make everything it needs, the usual determinant of the make-or-buy decision is price. If the price of purchasing the goods is cheaper than manufacturing them, the firm will probably purchase the material in question. To make an adequate analysis of the comparative advantages of making or buying, there are quantitative and nonquantitative elements that must be taken into consideration. The measurable aspects of the decision can be listed in Exhibit 8-3.

Make	Buy
Setup	Purchase price
Labor	Receiving cost
Material	Freight
Overhead	Inspection
Inspection	Requisition cost
Machine cost	

Exhibit 8-3

Cost Aspects of Make vs. Buy

Comparison of costs alone may not give a definitive answer, for other nonquantitative factors may outweigh pure price considerations. However, price becomes the significant factor if other reasons either do not exist or are unimportant. Some of the factors that may affect the firm's decision are the following:

1. At times, a firm wants to keep a particular vendor in business. The firm may desire to do this because of a fear that future supplies of the product will be uncertain if the vendor is forced out. For example, a repair service firm may buy parts and be dependent upon one supplier; loss of that supplier could be serious.
2. Under different circumstances, the firm makes rather than buys, even though the purchase price is cheaper. If the firm has idle capacity to utilize, this would be true. In this instance, the contribution rate would be the determining factor.
3. The question of certainty of supply and/or production delays could cut either way depending upon the individual situation. If the firm is busy producing its major line, it might not have the time available to produce smaller parts on schedule. Or, perhaps a supplier firm might not supply the needed quantity because of other commitments.
4. Time considerations may be a deciding factor. Regardless of price considerations, the firm might be forced to either make or buy if it, or the vendor, could not meet required delivery deadlines.
5. If the firm desires to keep a process secret, it would knowingly pay high manufacturing costs.

The Elevator Pitch

This skill-builder puts you in the venture capitalist position. You will watch an elevator pitch from the Internet and assess and discuss if he or she would or wouldn't invest in the new venture. The success of a good elevator pitch is dependent on getting the venture capitalist hooked on the product. The Alabama Institute for Manufacturing Excellence held an "Elevator Pitch Competition" for University of Alabama students as part of the university's Year of the Entrepreneur. The event consisted of a ninety-second pitch to a group of judges and a five-minute question-and-answer period. The link for the car seat safety pitch can be found at: www.youtube.com/watch?v=xphv363k60.

Think about it.

What score do you give the pitch?

Great product idea and pitch	Terrible product idea and pitch	
3	2	1

1. Would you invest in the business?
2. How would you improve the pitch?
3. What is the hook in the presentation?

Time and Motion Study

Learning Outcome

2. Describe why a time and motion study is conducted to determine how to make the product in the most efficient way.

Several of the techniques management use to establish performance standards against which to measure work fall under the heading of motion and time study. These techniques focus primarily on direct labor. The objectives of motion study are to establish the best way to accomplish a task; those of a time study are to establish how much time it should take to accomplish the task. In general, management's goal is to simplify work and arrive at a standard by which progress can be measured.

To differentiate further, motion study is done to eliminate ineffective and wasteful motions. Its objective is to find easier and simpler ways of performing a task. The general term, motion study, includes not only the motions employed by workers in performing their job, but also other facets of the job such as the methods, tools, and materials used. Time study is the process of systematically recording, analyzing, and synthesizing the times required to perform a task.

Direct Time Study

A direct (watch) time study is a procedure using a stopwatch to time a task. It is an accurate systematic and scientific method to determine the time it should take an employee to accomplish a task. The time study engineer uses a stopwatch to time the employee on the production floor. With the information derived, a norm then can be established for the job.

Predetermined Time Standards

Predetermined time standards are determined by using known times for all tasks in a job in order to determine how long it should take to complete it. They are based upon the idea that there are only so many basic motion patterns. Thus, any activity or job would be the result of particular combinations of these motions. After observing many different activities an analyst can segregate such basic motions as:

Personal Application

2. Time how long it takes to complete your own job at work. How long does it take and how can you shorten the time and still complete the job?

- Grasp, the motion that takes place when a hand or body part touches an object and takes control of it;
- or assemble, the action that takes place when parts are put together, or caused to be put together by the operator.

There are seventeen basic motion patterns, and any job is a combination of these. Essentially, this means that, if basic times for these motions are known, a job can be timed by the relatively simple task of analyzing the motions necessary for completion without using a stopwatch or even going on the production floor to observe the process. Predetermined standards are useful because the time necessary for a particular job can be discovered in advance. The firm can then make estimates and bids for new work as it is now able to predict material, labor, machinery, and capital costs in advance.

Product Warranties

A **product warranty** *is a type of guarantee that a manufacturer or similar party makes regarding the condition of its product.* It also refers to the terms and situations in which repairs or exchanges will be made in the event that the product does not function as originally described or intended.[7] Low product quality and poor warranty coverage and repair can significantly tarnish a brand.

A recent study revealed that, while most product companies recognize the critical importance of effective warranty management practices, very few companies are addressing the problem effectively. Joe Barkai, practice director at IDC Manufacturing Insights, says, "The use of benchmarking to assess performance and implement continuous improvement is disappointingly low and the application of IT tools to manage warranty transactions, perform warranty and quality analysis, and improve financial management is very inconsistent. The industry does not have a set of best practices to rely upon."[8]

Supply Chain Management

The **supply chain** *is the network of all the businesses that participate in the process of producing and delivering a product to the customer.* It is also called the *value chain.* **Supply chain management (SCM)** is the process of coordinating the flow of information, materials, and products, and the money through the supply chain. Having a good relationship, especially with suppliers, throughout the supply chain is essential to the success of your small business.[9]

Personal Application

3. Apply one area of a supply chain to a product or service where either you, a friend, or a family member has worked.

IBM further SCM as the process that enables companies to anticipate, control, and react to demand and supply volatility within the supply chain. Managing how and where you fulfill orders, how much inventory you should store, and the planning and execution of your shipments to meet customer commitments are all part of SCM. The goal is to optimize your strategic supply chain planning decisions for the fulfillment of orders, shipments, and inventory.[10] The skills needed to coordinate the supply chain job keep evolving.[11] An entrepreneur has to actively develop, implement, and monitor his or her SCM.

Materials

Because foreign competition is driving American business towards increased efficiency and economy, it is not surprising that the material used in the process of creating utility has come under increasing scrutiny. The more dependent a business is on raw material in its final product, the more significant is controlling material costs. For example, a retail store may have 85 percent of its product costs dependent upon its purchase of goods for resale. If the percent return on sales is 5 percent, a 5 percent reduction in the material cost flows right to the bottom line. This additional savings would technically translate immediately to the profit side of the balance sheet. That is, a 5 percent savings in material costs is all profit. In order to make an additional 5 percent profit, the firm would have to double its sales. Thus, a small savings in the cost of material can pay big dividends. Two important topics deserve special attention. First, the firm is concerned with obtaining needed material at the right time and at the lowest price predicated upon the ability to physically control the material it receives. Second, it must know how much to buy at any one time and when to place the order. Just as a manufacturing firm must make decisions about raw materials, a hospital must make the same decisions about such items as medicine, bandages, and surgical swabs.

Material Requirements Planning

Material requirements planning (MRP) *is the tool used to control the process of ordering and delivering the needed material at the right time, in the right place, and at the lowest cost.* MRP's objectives encompass saving the firm money by reducing inventory levels, controlling the material needed in production, and, by doing so, yielding faster delivery times that, in turn, improve customer satisfaction. A further improvement in the production process has been the introduction of the Just-In-Time Inventory System (JIT).

> **Learning Outcome**
>
> **3.** Describe Material Requirements Planning (MRP) and Just-In-Time Inventory System (JIT) as two tools used to control the production process.

Logistics

The mission of logistics *is to produce the appropriate goods or services in the right quality and quantity, and to distribute them to the right place at the right time.* Logistics encompasses the design, implementation, and management of systems for efficient deployment of personnel, physical facilities, raw materials, in-process inventories, finished goods, and related information or services. Logistics covers the whole supply chain, from the acquisition of raw materials, through production, to the point of consumption.[12]

A current logistics example is currently a long-term project for the Alibaba Group launched by the China Smart Logistics Network. This network will become the backbone of China's $190 billion e-commerce market. The network, which will be able to deliver shipments to any city in China within twenty-four hours, is backed by 100 billion yuan (about $16.3 billion) in funding and slated for completion in eight to ten years. "A stronger logistics network is crucial for China's e-commerce economy because 70% of its current logistics warehouse infrastructure was built before the 1990s and cannot keep up with the speed and volume of current online transactions. The China Smart Logistics Network will provide third-party couriers, warehouses, shipping and other services, as well as analytics to help vendors improve shipment speed and reduce costs."[13]

Inventory

Tracking inventory on a regular basis helps you zero in on the ideal number of goods, parts, and supplies to maintain.[14] Once the material arrives, there must be an adequate system to keep track of it. Arrangements must be made for adequate, secure storage facilities and effective requisition procedures. Inventory records must be kept up-to-date. The information in Exhibit 8-4 should be recorded

Exhibit 8-4

Inventory Control
Card

Inventory Control Card					
Style Name					
Style Number			Storage Location		
Unit Price			Reorder Point Order		
Supplier			Quantity (EOQ)		
Date Date	Units on Hand	P. O. Date Number	Units Rec'd	Balance Due	Issued Issued

and be easily accessible. In the case of a retail clothing store, careful records must be maintained so that the styles, size, and colors of garments are available.

Personal Application

4. Describe how you would improve the inventory system where someone you know works.

Hospitals must keep track of pharmaceuticals, not only for cost purposes, but also in some cases to comply with state or federal regulations. However, you should not depend upon paper or computer records. Mistakes can happen; parts can get mislaid. Thus, you should physically count your inventory at least once a year—more often dependent upon the dollar value of the inventory involved. The more the inventory is worth, the more frequently you want to check it.

Just-In-Time Inventory System

Just-In-Time Inventory System *delivers inventory in the production process when it is needed.* JIT techniques are the result of the demand-pull efforts of a firm to schedule production. Using this system, the actual demand triggers the production process so that inventory is delivered when needed. The advantage to this management technique is that the cost of maintaining inventory will be reduced. Only those materials or goods needed in the process will be delivered at the precise time they are needed. Now the company will not have capital tied up in storing and carrying inventory. A manufacturing firm would have raw material delivered when needed: bandages and medical supplies for a hospital; supplies such as copy paper and textbooks for a college. The more dependent a firm is on materials and supplies, the more important are the savings to be realized.

Inventory Control and EOQ

Learning Outcome

4. Discuss economic order quantity (EOQ) and determine how to arrive at the lowest cost inventory.

The primary questions of inventory control are (1) how much to order at any one time (economic order quantity) and (2) when to reorder (reorder point). If you can answer these questions with any degree of certainty, you can keep your inventory costs at a minimum. In graphic terms, you can see the relationship between time and inventory quantity. Over time, the operations process draws down the inventory. Given enough time, without any additional supply coming in or being made, you would soon run out of inventory and consequently be forced to stop production. Ideally, you'd like to have a new delivery of product parts just as you are using the last product part from your inventory. The amount delivered should be the economic order quantity (EOQ). The EOQ is the amount of goods whose total procurement and carrying costs are at a minimum. Exhibit 8-5 shows the relation between time and quantity of inventory.

Time Relationship to Inventory Quantity

If you order more inventory at point R, CD represents the time lapse between requisition and delivery. Point A is the amount of goods ordered and received. You should order at point R if you don't want to run out of inventory. The costs of maintaining inventory fall into two categories: carrying cost and procurement cost. The ideal inventory (EOQ) quantity will minimize total costs.

Carrying Costs

Carrying costs are those costs associated with ordering materials from the ordering cost through receiving, inspection, and storage. They vary directly with the size of the inventory. The greater the amount of inventory, the greater the costs. The average carrying cost can be as much as 21 percent. This cost component consists of:

1. Storage costs;
2. Maintenance;
3. Clerical tasks such as preparing and filing the requisition;
4. Insurance;
5. Obsolescence (the product becomes outdated);
6. Taxes.

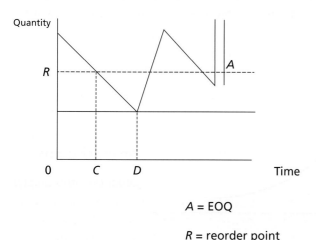

A = EOQ

R = reorder point

Exhibit 8-5

Relationship Between Time and Quantity of Inventory

Exhibit 8-6

Relationship Between
Storage Cost and
Quantity

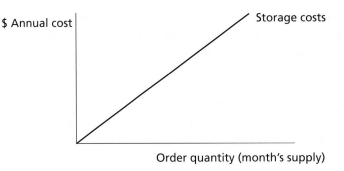

The relationship between carrying costs in annual dollars and inventory quantity (in terms of months of supply) is illustrated in Exhibit 8-6.

Procurement Costs

Procurement costs *are composed of requisition costs, follow up tasks and payment of invoices and they vary inversely with the inventory you have. The more units of inventory you procure, the cheaper the procurement costs per unit.* Each time an order is placed, it is subject to the same procurement costs, which are fixed and do not vary with the size of the order. Total procurement costs vary, however, with the number of times the item is purchased. The greater the supply purchased at any one time, the less the yearly procurement costs. This is shown in Exhibit 8-7. The two cost components vary in opposite directions. Large lots minimize procurement costs while maximizing storage costs. The opposite is true for small lots. Storage costs a minimum; procurement costs a maximum.

EOQ Determination

The object of determining the EOQ is to minimize total variable costs. Because the axes of Exhibits 8-6 and 8-7 are identical, we can superimpose one upon the other as we have done in Exhibit 8-8. Doing so enables us to add the variable costs and show a total variable cost relationship to the quantity ordered.

Exhibit 8-7

Relationship Between
Procurement Costs
and Quantity

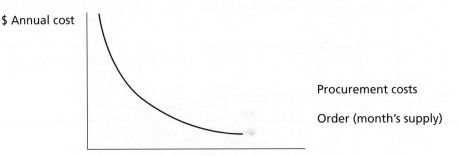

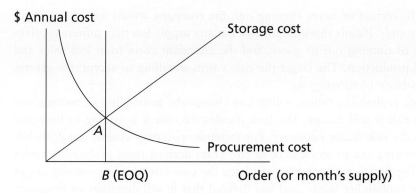

Exhibit 8-8

Relationship Between
Total Variable Costs
and Quantity

The minimum variable total cost occurs at the intersection of the annual storage cost and annual procurement cost. At point *A,* both are equal. Dropping a perpendicular to point B will determine the EOQ. The solution to this problem is handled in the same manner as a breakeven analysis (see Chapter 10). As there is only one point common to both relationships, the formula determining these relationships can be set to equal at this point. To accomplish this, let *E* equal EOQ in terms of the number of months' supply to be ordered at any one time, *U* equal monthly dollar usage of items, *P* equal procurement costs in dollars, and *I* equal inventory carrying costs per year, expressed as a decimal of the total inventory costs per year. This gives us Exhibit 8-9.

Reorder Point

To properly manage inventory, you also need to know at what point to order the EOQ. That is, what quantity of inventory remaining signals the need to reorder? Two elements are important in this decision: (1) usage during lead time, and (2) safety stock desired. The combination of the two will determine the reorder point.

The definition of **lead time** *is the time elapsed between the ordering of the goods and the physical delivery to the company.* During this time, the company continues to use and draw down its inventory. Ideally, the moment that the last unit is drawn out of storage, the new supply should be delivered. However, reality is not coincident with the ideal, and operating as though it were would cause a firm to incur added costs when goods run out and production ceases. It is necessary to carry a safety stock for use if the delivery of the new units of inventory is delayed or the production process and subsequent monthly usage vary.

$$E = \sqrt{\frac{24P}{UI}}$$

Exhibit 8-9

Formula Used to
Determine EOQ

To be certain of never running out, the company would have to carry an infinite supply. Plainly this is impossible but any supply less than infinite involves the risk of running out of goods and the attendant costs from lost sales and stopped production. The larger the risk a firm is willing to accept, the greater the possibility of running out.

From probability tables, a firm can choose the probability of running out and the risk it will accept. The firm decides the cost it is willing to bear and chooses the risk factor necessary. For example, you may assume the probability of running out of stock once in five years derived from probability tables is 1.8. The firm has previously calculated the cost attendant to running out at different probability levels, and has decided that it will maintain an inventory large enough to accomplish the goal of potentially running out of inventory only once in five years. Therefore, the P factor (the probability) will be used to modify the firm's safety stock. Running out less often will involve larger inventory and greater storage costs that the firm is unwilling to bear. The firm has decided that the losses from cancellation of orders and delayed production are too great and that more frequent shortages are unacceptable. The equilibrium position is where the last dollar spent on maintaining the safety stock is equivalent to the last dollar saved. That is, on the marginal dollar, the cost of maintaining safety stock equals the cost of stock outs.

Practical experience has shown that the lead time usually varies by no more than the square root of the length of delivery time. The P factor is a modification of the variance accepted in accordance with the firm's desired goal; thus, if for item A usage during lead time equals 100 units, P equals 1.8 (expected frequency of stock outs once in five years), and R equals reorder point, the generalized expression for reorder point is: $R = U + P \sqrt{L}$. The solution to utilizing the information given above is: The firm reorders when 118 items remain in stock. Exhibit 8-10 illustrates this. Line AB shows what would occur if there were no safety stock. CD allows for delays and other unanticipated problems. Utilizing this safety stock allows production or sales to continue until new products or parts are delivered. The reorder point is constant, regardless of safety stock utilization.

Exhibit 8-10

EOQ Reorder Point

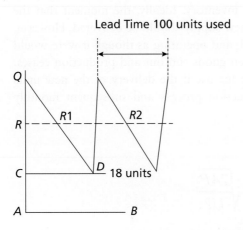

Lead Time 100 units used

Scheduling

There are two approaches to production control: loading and scheduling. Production/ operations control can be very general in approach or it can get very specific. The general approach called loading *is simply defined as assigning work to a facility.* In contrast, scheduling *specifies the time and sequence in which the work is to be done and develops a schedule for it.* Both methods of production control require complete knowledge of the productive process. Before you are able to load or schedule, you must also know the capacity of each production process, how long it will take to get the specific job done, material requirements, the current work load, and the operation sequence for each item. You must know how long it takes to make or buy each unit from the beginning of the process until its completion. With this knowledge you can then balance work to be performed with the machinery, material, equipment, and people. An efficient organization will have everyone working in productive operations all the time. This plan is also important because it provides a yardstick against which progress can be measured. You are able to determine if the schedule is being met and then take corrective action if necessary.

Master Scheduling

There are two general techniques used to control the production process. Master scheduling establishes a production schedule for the facility on a first come/ first served basis. For example, if you own a small job shop printing business and you want to control production by establishing a schedule so that you can plan your time better, it might look like Exhibit 8-11. With this schedule, you will be able to plan personnel assignments and machinery time and determine delivery dates for customers.

In order to establish this schedule, you would need to know:

1. Maximum hours available for work that equals eighty (assume two or three shifts of an eight hour day for five days);
2. Minimum number of job hours needed before you will even open for the week;
3. Once you open, you must be able to cover your fixed costs.

SUPERB PRINTING CO.						
Capacity-weekly 75hrs			Minimum-weekly 16 hrs			
Job	Week					
	1	2	3	4	5	6
1	18	14	9	12	24	8
2	9	16	15	6		
3	10	20	10	16		
4	30	12	18			
5	8					
Total	75	62	52	34	24	8

Exhibit 8-11

Master Schedule for Production Planning

To set up such a schedule you must take each job as it is called in and schedule it in whatever week the customer requires as long as you have available production capacity. You know how long each job takes from start to finish. You do not split jobs, that is, jobs begun in one week must be finished in the same week. Once you reach capacity for a specific week, the week is considered to be fully loaded and you would then schedule work for the next week of production that has the required availability. Generally, each week is considered fully loaded at 80 to 85 percent capacity. You would always leave a little slack for things like rush orders or machinery breakdowns. If everything works well and your slack time is not utilized, you can always do a job scheduled for the following week during the current week. You have to continually update the schedule anyway. In Exhibit 8-11, the first week, which is using seventy-five hours of work, is no longer available for scheduling work. Additional work can be accommodated only where there is a time slot. If a job requiring thirty hours of work had to be scheduled, delivery could not be promised before the end of Week 4.

A number of PC-based computer programs can make this type of scheduling easier. This approach is useful in a wide variety of firms such as copy shops or automobile repair facilities.

Master scheduling is simple and easily understood. Its simplicity makes it easy to keep current. It can be manipulated to reschedule fairly easily. While providing an overall schedule, it doesn't give you any detailed information. The company knows that certain jobs will be accomplished in certain weeks, but not the sequence in which they will be completed nor the specific machinery and personnel needs for each job.

Perpetual Loading

Perpetual loading *tabulates the time necessary to finish unfilled orders and determine how long it will take to finish this work.* If an entrepreneurial accountant starting his own accounting practice specializing in tax returns has forty hours per week available and 200 hours of tax returns to file, it will take him 6.25 weeks of work to complete the tax returns. Any tax returns desired by new clients could not be completed before the end of the sixth week. In tax season this would present a problem and the accountant might want to hire some people so that all tax returns can be filed by the April 15 deadline. The procedure for perpetual loading is shown in Exhibit 8-12.

Exhibit 8-12

Perpetual Loading

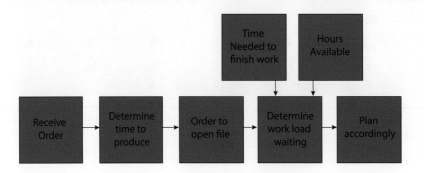

Gantt Charts, PERT, and Job Categories Scheduling

Gantt Chart

It might be very helpful to know how this year's work load compares with last year for the same time period. If last year's demand showed more than 6.25 weeks of work, it might mean that demand had decreased. (One week, however, is not indicative of a trend.) This can be shown easily on a tool named after Henry Gantt. The Gantt chart shows work and how long it should take to be completed. Exhibit 8-13 presents a typical Gantt chart. Plotting the actual work against the forecasts would let you know whether your expectations were being met so that you could take appropriate actions. Perpetual loading is also easy to understand and maintain. It does not, however, provide enough detail to specify the time and sequence in which the work is to be accomplished. A manufacturing plant could require more detail.

Performance Evaluation and Review Technique

Another management production control device used is PERT, an acronym for Performance Evaluation and Review Technique. PERT was developed by the Booz, Allen, and Hamilton Company, a firm of management consultants in connection with the Polaris Missile Program. It is used not only in government, but is also required of all government contractors. Rather than being an entirely new technique, PERT actually represents a refinement of the flow chart analysis first developed by Henry Gantt.

PERT *uses a sequential list of operations and the times required for each operation to establish an operations chart.* This chart allows you to both plan and control. Once the plan is established, you can use it as a yardstick against which to measure actual accomplishments. This method can also be called the critical path method (CPM).

To construct a PERT network, let us use the example of a student who wants to plan his time to study for and take an examination. The first function of the PERT technique would be to develop a step by step plan to accomplish his purpose as shown in Exhibit 8-14. Exhibit 8-14 illustrates several facets of

Weeks of tax returns to file, 2015 vs. 2014

Date 1	Week									
	1	2	3	4	5	6	7	8	9	10
3/4/15										
3/5/14										

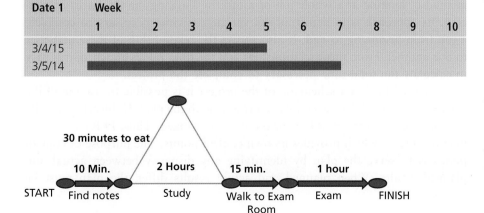

Personal Application

5. Choose a topic in your life that could be analyzed using a PERT diagram.

the PERT presentation: (1) necessary activities are identified; (2) relationships are shown; and (3) the required time to accomplish all facets is identified.

The circles on the diagram signify events. An event takes no time itself. Events signify the completion of an activity. The activities are illustrated by arrows that show the direction in which the work is flowing. Attached to these activities is the time necessary to complete each activity. Thus, an activity represents a specific task over a period of time and is bound by two events. The completion of the job or the final event in the chain is called the objective event.

The analysis of our example consists of three steps:

1. The building of the network to cover all the aspects of our problem's activities. This enables us to draw the diagram.
2. The evaluation of the plan, once it is drawn, to be sure that the steps included are reasonable and that the probability of their completion in the required time is high. In this step, any flaws in the plan should become evident. For instance, we may question the assumption that lecture notes can be found in ten minutes.
3. The use of the plan to control the work as it proceeds. For example, eating should be finished forty minutes after the start of the search for the lecture notes.

Thus, by checking the schematic it can be seen whether or not the student is on schedule. Adjustments can be made accordingly. The diagram reveals the complete picture of what must be achieved and the interrelationship of the various facets of the task. Additional information is acquired because the time necessary for completion of each activity is also given. In this form of presentation it is easy to see problems that may develop and where the project design has been theoretical rather than practical. PERT contributes to good management by forcing the development of a clear, well thought-out plan in advance. If the plan is not developed in advance, it cannot be diagramed. Obviously, a diagram is much clearer and easier to understand than a written description.

Because PERT is universally applicable, you can use it to plan and diagram any job. Networks of this type may look extremely complicated; however, the theory behind any presentation is the same. Essentially, PERT is a schematic method of looking at a whole job or a task by showing the total area of concern. Its approach is to depict all the various activities necessary to complete a job from beginning to end. It also shows the relationship of these activities to one another. From these relationships and the time values attached, it is easy to calculate the total time necessary to complete the project.

Because PERT is a schematic of the project it is possible to use the PERT system as a control device, comparing results with the plan. If the actual results do not agree with the PERT plan, the plan is changed. Thus, PERT is a planning technique, which provides its own control points. The purpose of control points is to serve the plan by identifying any disparity between actual and planned results. When planned and actual results differ, the plan must be changed.

Job Categories and Techniques

There are specific techniques that may be used in controlling and measuring the operations process. For ease of discussion we will break the job situation into two categories and discuss the techniques used in each. The categories are:

1. Interjob. This concerns itself with movements or operations between work stations. The following techniques can be used in this situation:
   a. Process chart
   b. Flow process chart

2. Intrajob. This concerns itself with movements or operations at a specific work station. The following techniques can be used in this situation:
   a. Simo-chart (operator or left-hand/right-hand chart);
   b. Man–machine chart;
   c. Multiple activity chart.

Process Flow Chart

When you are focusing on a complete operation, the best approach to use is process analysis. Here the entire process is studied in an effort to determine if it is being performed in the most efficient manner. This overall analysis is done before segments of the process are analyzed. If the overall analysis were not done first, time might be spent in changing segments of the process that may be eliminated. The tool used to analyze the overall operation, called a process chart, is useful in banks, insurance companies, and financial firms in addition to manufacturing firms. It can be used efficiently to identify and control paper and information flows. Retail firms find it useful, particularly when dealing with perishable foods, to prevent spoilage.

Using standardized symbols, the process chart simulates on paper the operation under analysis. A flow process chart is a process chart superimposed on a floor plan of your manufacturing business. The symbols used are recommended by the American Society of Mechanical Engineers:

● equals Operation

This signifies that something is being done to a part or a product. An activity is being performed.

➔ equals Transportation

This signifies movement of something from one location to another. It may be either the material that is being moved or it may be the worker who is moving.

■ equals Inspection

This signifies a check being made on the product to determine if it meets a previously determined standard.

◗ equals delay

This signifies that the process has been stopped or delayed.

▲ equals Storage

This signifies that the product has been stored either to wait for another step in the process to be completed, or to prevent unauthorized use. It is a relatively simple matter using the above symbols to describe any production process. Exhibit 8-15 is a process chart that describes an existing situation in a garment factory.

Exhibit 8-15 provides an accurate and succinct record of the process. Note that there are totals given for each symbol. Thus the way to improve the production process would be to minimize all activities not adding to the product value. This means that all activities other than "operations" should be decreased. Doing so would decrease the time spent on the entire operation. Additional information such as how long it takes to perform each operation or the distance traveled to and from storage may be added if required. Any improvements in the process would make it more efficient. After studying the process, a new procedure was developed as shown in Exhibit 8-16. Notice that the new procedure has three operations, five transportations, four storages, one inspection, and zero delays. The old procedures had four operations, six transportations, five storages, one inspection and one delay.

Exhibit 8-15

Flow Chart—Old Method

	•	→	▲	■	)	
(1)	•					RECEIVE ON ELEVATOR FROM WASHING
(2)		→				TO TEMPORARY STORAGE AREA
(3)			▲			STORE
(4)		→				TO SEPARATORS
(5)	•					SEPARATE
(6)		→				TRIM COMPLETED—SENT TO CUTTING ROOM
(7)			▲			STORED IN CUTTING
(8)		→				BODIES AND SLEEVES SENT TO STEAMING
(9)			▲			TEMPORARY STORAGE
(10)	•					STEAM
(11)		→				TO CUTTING
(12)			▲			STORE
(13)				■		TO SEE IF ALL PIECES ARE READY FOR PROCESSING
(14)					)	CUTTING DISCOVERIES INCORRECT TRIM
(15)	•					SEPARATE RIGHT TRIM
(16)		→				TO CUTTING
(17)			▲			TO CUTTING TEMPORARY STORAGE UNTIL WORKED AGAIN
TOTAL	4	6	5	1	1	

Exhibit 8-16
Flow Chart—
Proposed Method

	•	→	▲	■	)	
(1)	•					RECEIVE ON ELEVATOR FROM WASHING
(2)		→				TO TEMPORARY STORAGE AREA
(3)			▲			STORE
(4)		→				TO SEPARATORS
(5)	•					SEPARATE
(6)		→				TRIM COMPLETED—SENT TO CUTTING ROOM
(7)			▲			TRIM STORED IN CUTTING ROOM
(8)		→				BODIES AND SLEEVES SENT TO STEAMING
(9)			▲			TEMPORARY STORAGE
(10)	•					STEAM
(11)		→				TO CUTTING ROOM
(12)			▲			STORE IN CUTTING
(13)				■		TO SEE IF ALL PIECES ARE READY FOR PROCESSING
TOTAL	3	5	4	1	0	

Note that a comparison between the present and the proposed procedures shows:

	Present	Proposed
Operation	4	3
Transportation	6	5
Storage	5	4
Inspection	1	1
Delay	1	0

The total savings are two operations, one transportation, one storage, and one delay. The new procedure accomplishes the same task as the old, but in fewer steps. It is more efficient and economical than the old method. Knowledge of how to change the procedure stems from the use of a general questioning approach and the knowledge of the process. You must study the process itself before you can suggest any improvements.

Quality

Quality is that combination of attributes commensurate with the price of a product or service that the customer expects. It may be defined by engineering specifications or consumer expectations.

As automobile manufacturers in the U.S. discovered, it is not enough to create a product; the product must be a quality product offered at a competitive price. The watchword of today's firms must be quality because

Personal Application

6. Overall, how would you rate the overall quality of the product or service you help to manufacture on your job at your workplace?

unacceptable quality reduces sales and profits. The absence of quality may also be responsible for a firm's failure because customers will not buy inferior products. Much of today's emphasis on quality and quality controls stems from the work of Dr W. Edwards Deming, a leading figure in the development of quality controls, whose theories were adopted by Japanese industry following World War II and have now been enthusiastically embraced in the U.S.[15]

While much of Deming's initial work was concerned with manufacturing operations, today's markets demand a constant adherence to quality at all times by all firms. It is just as important for a hotel, dry cleaner, summer camp for children, automobile repair shop, or accounting firm to maintain quality as it is for the traditional manufacturing firms.

Total Quality Management (TQM)

TQM requires a continual commitment from everyone in the organization to continue to improve the process involved in creating the product or service sold. Done properly, TQM involves giving people responsibility for performing their job in the best way. Small business must allow employees to contribute to the quality process. Employees must be true participants in the business. According to Deming, the people best suited to improving the job are the people doing it.[16]

While it is more difficult to measure a service organization's quality than a manufacturing firm's, measures have been defined and the process in true TQM fashion is continuing to refine service measurements. For example, how many complaints does a dry cleaner get? How many check-points does a motel use to measure room cleanliness? These and measures like them make it possible to define quality for all firms. The quest for quality cannot and should not stop. It is a continuous job. Without this commitment, firms will fall behind in today's market.

Necessity for Inspection

Once the basic decisions have been made about the product and how to go about making or providing it, quality standards are expressed. These include engineering drawings and specifications in the case of a manufacturing enterprise or by measures of quality such as number of call backs in an automobile service firm or returns to a dry cleaner. These "specs" are the yardstick against which the product or service is measured to insure that the production/operations process is producing the desired output.

The variation in the attributes of products and services due to chance occurrences causes the firm to produce products where attributes are not identical to specifications. Inspection shows whether the performance measures up to standards. Ideally, the firm would inspect up to the point where cost of inspection equals the savings from inspection.

Benchmarking

As explained by the consultant firm Bain and Company, "benchmarking improves performance by identifying and applying best demonstrated practices to operations and sales. Managers compare the performance of their products or processes externally with those of competitors and best-in-class companies and internally with other operations within their own firms that perform similar activities. The objective of benchmarking is to find examples of superior performance and to understand the processes and practices driving that performance. Companies then improve their performance by tailoring and incorporating these best practices into their own operations—not by imitating, but by innovating."[17] The goal is to find a company in your own industry against which to compare your own performance. You need to identify the key numbers (metrics) that you want to compare. After collecting data on performance and practice, you can then analyze the data and identify opportunities for improvement in your own company. The company can then implement the best programs and goals it learned about from comparing its company versus key competitors.

Statistical Quality Control

Statistical quality control involves using control charts. These charts show expected and actual performance. Statistical quality control is at the heart of Deming's philosophy and the TQM concept. Statistical quality control analyses reveal the quality of the operation process. The primary purpose of inspection is to identify whether the quality of the product falls within certain specifications. Otherwise, the product will not be acceptable. It is necessary to specify limits, because it is impossible to produce each and every unit to exact specifications. Any operation varies because of chance occurrences. Tools wear, raw materials vary, employees become fatigued, and machines slip.

Using statistical reasoning too complex for this text we can derive a traditional control chart. This chart will show whether the production/operation process is producing goods or services within an acceptable range of production/operations variability and whether the variation in the attributes of products is due to chance occurrences. Variations within acceptable limits generally fall in an area around a specified or accepted level of performance, bounded by upper and lower control limits. For example, if a service business were willing to accept an average of two complaints per hour, our control chart could be illustrated as shown in Exhibit 8-17.

The control chart would be used to analyze operations of the business. As long as the number of complaints falls into the area bounded by the upper and lower control limits, no corrective action would be required. When the operation/production process shows complaints falling outside the control limits, corrective action would be needed.

Exhibit 8-17

Control Chart

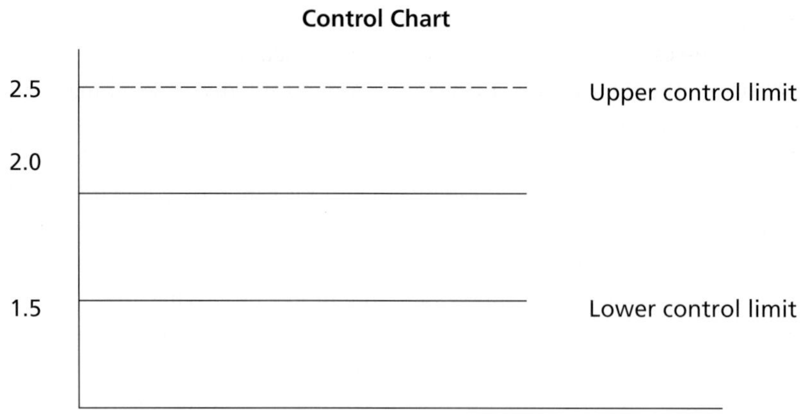

Control Chart

Control chart using two customer complaints per hour as sample average

ISO 9000

Founded in 1947, ISO (International Organization for Standardization) is the world's largest developer of voluntary International Standards. International Standards give state-of-the-art specifications for products, services, and good practice. ISO helps to make an industry more efficient and effective by having standards that cover almost all aspects of technology and business. ISO standards are developed through global consensus.

ISO 9000 specifically addresses various aspects of quality management standards. The standards provide guidance and tools for companies and organizations that want to ensure that their products and services consistently meet customers' requirements, and that quality is consistently improved.

There are many different levels of standards in the ISO 9000 family. For example, ISO 9001:2008 sets out the criteria for a quality management systems. ISO 9001:2008 is implemented by over one million large and small companies in over 170 countries.[18] Companies that have ISO 9000 approval often have banners on the outside of their businesses for the pride they feel in having accomplished the ISO 9000 process. The banners also provide publicity to visitors to the plant and the local community that the company is ISO 9000 certified.

Six Sigma

Six Sigma is a term, originally developed by General Electric (GE), that is a measure of quality that strives for near perfection. Six Sigma is a disciplined, data-driven approach and methodology for eliminating defects (driving toward six standard deviations between the mean and the nearest specification limit) in any process—from manufacturing to transactional and from product to service.[19]

Six Sigma is defined by GE as a program "to achieve Six Sigma Quality, a process must produce no more than 3.4 defects per million opportunities. An 'opportunity' is defined as a chance for nonconformance, or not meeting the required specifications. This means we need to be nearly flawless in executing our key processes."[20] A key concept for entrepreneurs to follow is that Six Sigma, for large or small companies, consistently delivers a flawless product to the customer.

Using Technology

You need to keep up with the changes in technology if you want to be competitive. A technology audit will uncover areas where your business is strong (has the necessary technology) or weak (technology that you need to acquire). Depending on the type of business that you own, you will often need different technology. For instance, a small retailer will need point-of-sale technology. A manufacturer of a new electric automobile engine will need auto supplies and an assembly area to design and build its new engine.

Manufacturing technology provides the tools to produce manufactured goods. Software tools such as computer-aided design (CAD) and computer-aided manufacturing (CAM) use computer software to assist to create a final product.[21] JIT, EOQ, TQM, ISO 9000, and other operations techniques all use computers to minimize defects during production, analyze quality data, calculate when to reorder inventory, and keep track of shipments.

More business continues to be conducted online through Internet e-commerce. See Exhibit 8-18 for a list.[22]

Manufacturing Tips

The following is some guidelines for manufacturing startups to consider when deciding to produce their own product:

- **Purpose.** Small-scale manufacturing can be a cost-effective option for startups. As compared to outsourcing the manufacturing (and cost) to a factory in Asia, making small batches of your own product means you can monitor your costs of manufacturing.
- **Leverage.** Small-scale manufacturing allows the entrepreneur to modify his or her product as necessary. There is built-in flexibility because you can make improvements in the process instead of having to deal with third-party manufacturers in Asia.

Country with Population	Percentage of Population Online
China 1.3 billion	36%
India 1.2 billion	10%
U.S. 314 million	81%
Russia 142 million	43%
South Korea 50 million	83%
Sweden 9.5 million	90%

Exhibit 8-18

Who Has Internet?

- **Process.** The best way to engage customers is to involve them in building and designing the product. Tell your customers a good story, be transparent, and make your development process the focus of your public appearance. Because you are a small business, bringing your customers in to help design your product will lead to more loyal customers.
- **Personality.** Don't get distracted by what everyone else is doing. The best way to differentiate yourself is to be yourself.[23]

Other Options for Starting a New Venture, and Entrepreneurial Behavior

In this last section we discuss some of the major operations differences in starting a new venture compared with the other options to becoming an entrepreneur. We also discuss how to engage in entrepreneurial behavior as an employee.

Buying an Existing Business, Franchise, or Leasing Rights

Buying an Existing Business

The existing business will already have an operation in place that you can decide to keep using, or you can decide to change the operations process to improve efficiency. For example, you might purchase new technology to improve areas such as the computer information processes or the manufacturing operations.

Buying a Franchise

If you buy a franchise, the franchisor will have an operational plan that you are required to follow. One of the reasons to buy a franchise is to use its knowledge in regards to areas such as product warranties and inventory control.

Buying Licensing Rights

If you buy a license, you are starting a new business and will have to develop an operational plan to figure out how to use the licensing rights to make a profit. If the product or service rights have already been given to others, you can copy and benchmark against them and other companies for operations ideas.

Starting a Corporate or Nonprofit New Venture

Starting a Corporate Venture

Starting a new corporate venture may allow you to use an existing facility and operations process if the product is very similar. If it is very different, you may need to set up a new operations procedure to produce a new line of products as discussed in this chapter.

Starting a Nonprofit

When starting a nonprofit, you will have to develop the operations plan as discussed in this chapter. However, most nonprofits offer a service, so the operations are not as complicated as manufacturing. A nonprofit operational plan will often include the recruitment of financial donors and volunteers to help manage and market different fundraising and public relations events.

Entrepreneurial Behavior

If you are not interested in starting a new venture, as an employee you can engage in *entrepreneurial behavior* that can lead to new ways to modify the current operations to improve efficiency and increase employee satisfaction. Some organizations have formal groups, sometimes referred to as quality circles or simply continuous improvement groups, which you can join to contribute to the creativity and innovation of your organization.

Take it to the Net

Visit www.routledge.com/cw/Lussier for the book's companion Web site, where you can:

- use learning aids, including taking a quiz;
- find links to resources in this chapter, as well as other links including videos;
- learn about and start the following activities: Continuing Integrated Case, Your Ninety-Second New Venture Pitch, the Paper Clip Entrepreneurship Challenge, College Entrepreneurial Spirit Award, and the Community Entrepreneurial Spirit Award.

Chapter Review and Summary

As we bring this chapter to a close, you should understand that a firm must produce quality tangible goods or services, in the most efficient manner, to enable the firm to survive and prosper. Using programs such as Just-In-Time Inventory is critical because inventory costs need to be matched with production schedules. TQM programs have to be part of the process of producing quality goods and services.

This summary lists the learning outcomes from the chapter and their answers.

1. Identify the components of the transformation process

To support the production/operation process, all firms need capital, the physical assets of the company, such as machinery, equipment, or plant to support the production/operation process that transforms inputs into outputs.

2. Describe why a time and motion study is conducted to determine how to make the product in the most efficient time

Inseparable from the questions of the production process are the questions of how to produce the product in the best way and in the least time. A motion study establishes the best way to accomplish a task. A time study establishes how much time it should take to accomplish a task. The methodology of time study requires us to understand the difference between a direct watch study, a procedure using a stopwatch to time a task, and predetermined time standards, which are determined by using known times for all tasks in a job to determine how long it should take to complete the job.

3. Describe MRP and JIT as two tools used to control the production process

Inherent in the question of utility creation is the concept of how to manage the necessary raw materials and parts needed to create the final product. In order to be profitable, the costs of this inventory must be minimized. MRP, the tool used to control the process and ensure its efficiency, is useful in this process. The JIT approach delivers inventory in the production process when it is needed.

4. Discuss EOQ, and determine how to arrive at the lowest-cost inventory

While looking at the question of inventory control, it is necessary to understand the concept of EOQ, the amount of goods whose total costs, procurement, and carrying costs are at a minimum. You arrive at this quantity by balancing carrying cost, those costs associated with ordering material from the ordering cost through receiving, inspection, and storage, and procurement costs, which are made up of requisition costs, follow-up tasks, and payment of invoices.

5. Identify the two approaches to production control, loading and scheduling

Once the decision is made to produce the goods or services, it is important to keep track of and control the production/operations process itself. Loading assigns work to a facility. Scheduling specifies the time and sequence in which the work is to be done and develops a schedule for it. Master scheduling establishes a production schedule for the facility on a first come/first served basis. Perpetual loading tabulates the time necessary to finish unfilled orders and determines how long it will take to finish this work.

6. **Discuss the importance of quality considerations in the production process and how to integrate TQM in the production process**

The operations process requires close attention to quality—that combination of attributes commensurate with the price of a product or service that the customer expects. Today, TQM is a process for continuous change and improvement in everything an organization does—including the production process.

7. **Define the twenty-eight key terms found in this chapter**

assemble

capital

carrying costs

direct watch time study

economic order quantity (EOQ)

flow process chart

Gantt chart

grasp

ISO9000

Just-In-Time Inventory System (JIT)

loading

logistics

master scheduling

material requirements planning (MRP)

motion study

outsourcing

perpetual loading

PERT

predetermined time standards

process chart

procurement costs

product warranties

production/operations process

production/operations variability

quality

scheduling

statistical quality control

TQM

Review and Discussion Questions

1. Define the production process.

2. Discuss the difference, if any, between operations management and production management.

3. Describe the operations/production process for the following:

   a) a university; b) a hospital; c) an insurance company; d) a razor blade manufacturer; e) a children's day camp.

4. What is the difference in the operations process between a manufacturing firm and a service firm?

5. It has often been said that a purchasing department is a burden cost and thus cannot contribute to the bottom line or profitability of the firm. Is this a true statement? Support your answer with examples.

6. The timing of purchase decisions is important. Why?

7. Describe the components of total inventory costs.

8. Define economic order quantity. How does it minimize total inventory costs?

9. Define reorder point. Why is it important?

10. What is lead time?

11. How do you determine the reorder points?

12. Compare inventory policies required by a) a manufacturer; b) a retail store; c) a service firm; d) a wholesale firm.

13. Define production/operations control. Why is this concept important?

14. Define: a) scheduling; b) loads. Comment on the similarities and differences between the two approaches.

15. Define the terms: a) master scheduling; b) perpetual loading.

16. PERT is both a planning and a control technique. Defend or refute this statement.

17. Define "statistical quality control." Is this a better control mechanism than 100 percent inspection?

18. Two techniques used to establish performance standards are time and motion study. Define these terms.

Application Exercises

Each chapter has a series of exercises requiring you to apply the specific text concepts. When doing these exercises, be sure to select a specific business where applicable. You can select a business where you worked or a business you would like to own someday. Answers for each exercise should be approximately one page.

1. Interview a local real-estate broker. Using the information gathered from the broker:

   a. Define the production/operations process.

   b. Define "quality control" as used in the operations process.

   c. What is the importance of inventory? Does the broker have any control over the inventory?

   d. Can you set time standards for the broker's operation? Develop a chart showing the various steps in the brokerage process and the time required to complete each step.

2. Visit a local manufacturing firm and define its production/operations process. Using the information gathered from the manufacturer:

   a. Define the production/operations process.

   b. Define "quality control" as used in the operations process.

   c. What is the importance of inventory? Does the manufacturer have any control over the inventory?

3. Using the information from statements a), b), and c), of Situations 1 and 2, identify the input process and output.

Application Situations

1. Paula Cromwell

Having owned a dog all her life, Paula Cromwell was attracted by an article in *The Wall Street Journal,* which stated, "The care and feeding of animals is a big business." Liking animals, Paula decided to start a retail pet supply store. She found a good location in a local strip mall and for the past several years has seen her gross revenues rise by 40 percent per year. However, in reviewing her financials, she found that she can't make a reasonable profit. Despite rising sales and her policy of buying inventory when she needs it, there always seems to be too much inventory remaining of products not wanted by customers.

Recently Paula requested that a student consulting team from a local university review her operation and make recommendations that would lead to profitability. The student team thought her problem was caused by her lack of attention to purchasing and inventory control.

1. Why is purchasing important and how can it contribute to profitability?

2. What suggestions do you think the team made concerning economic order quantities and reorder points?

3. How could Paula implement the suggestions?

2. Steiner Boat Works

Whenever possible, Saul Steiner would take a break from his prestigious job as a vice-president of a large advertising firm and go sailing. While sailing, he felt that he could relax and think. One day he decided to change his career in order to become a builder of small wooden sailboats.

Saul started building his boats only on the basis of firm orders. Each boat was hand-crafted. All wood was carefully cut and fitted with care and precision. It was sanded, varnished, polished, and waxed. As demand increased, Saul hired other workers who shared his desire for, and dedication to, quality.

Seven years after the business began, increased demand forced him to start manufacturing the boats using assembly line techniques and production-type workers. Saul was hesitant about using production workers because he was afraid that his quality would suffer.

1. Does the firm's growth make quality control easier or harder? Explain.

2. How can Saul build quality control practices into the production line?

3. Will Saul's approach to quality increase, decrease, or not have any effect on profits?

3. Owens Sweaters

Owens Sweaters, a local garment manufacturer, is having trouble making timely deliveries to customers. While all sweaters go through the same production process—knit, cut, sew, finish, pack, and ship—Betty Owens cannot seem to keep track of the production process.

1. What production control methods would you recommend to Betty? Name and define the four types of production control techniques.

2. Prepare a production control plan for the Owens Company.

4. Corkum Realty

Corkum Realty owns and operates six large apartment houses. Vinny Green, the maintenance supervisor, is responsible for all maintenance of the 196 apartments. He and his staff of eight maintenance workers do the best they can but are continually behind because, as they say, "Maintenance jobs are totally different from other jobs. Anything that can go wrong will and who knows when it will happen or how long it will take to fix it."

1. Is the above statement true? Why or why not?

2. Can the principles of time and motion study be helpful? How would you recommend that Vinny implement these techniques?

Case

Small-Scale Manufacturing at Industry City Distillery

Home-crafted vodka has been growing in popularity. Consumers like the term "crafted" because it gives small operations feel and taste.[24] Industry City Distillery (ICD), started in 2011 by five 20-or-so-year-olds, operates out of a 12,000-square-foot Brooklyn warehouse. Not content with simply creating a better vodka, the team has built its own distillery to better control the entire operation.

Entrepreneurs are helping small-scale manufacturing to become popular in other alcoholic drinks such as whiskey and especially beer. Entrepreneurs are even inventing their own manufacturing equipment to manufacture small batches of unique products. ICD is the first commercial venture out of the City Foundry Research and Design Group, which is dedicated to improving small-scale manufacturing processes by acting like an agile software startup. Building the machinery from scratch and fermenting and distilling in-house means lower initial capital investment.

The company produces one batch of vodka at a time while looking for the final recipe for a sugar-beet vodka. Rather than going to waste, bottles from the experimental batches are available for purchase for about $21 through the ICD Web site and at New York-area liquor stores.

The company engages its customers with a Web site that includes a video on how its vodka is produced. The bottle design is also meant to be engaging. In addition to the required listing of alcohol content and volume, the clean letterpress labels highlight nothing more than the batch number (currently No. 3) and bottle number (batch No. 2 had a production run of about 2,000). The five young entrepreneurs are having fun making and selling their own vodka.[25]

Think it over.

1. Explain how ICD would use a Just-in-Time Inventory System?

2. Use the following article to learn more about the supply chain management of owning your own vodka manufacturing process: www.forbes.com/sites/larryolmsted/2013/05/10/a-craft-distillery-worthy-of-the-word-craft/.

3. How would ICD use a TQM system?

Global Case—Just-in-Time Inventory Systems: Japan

The goal of JIT is to help manage inventory so a small business doesn't have too much money tied up in inventory. The Japanese perfected the process in the 1980s and it has been widely used by companies such as Toyota and Dell. Learning to manage your inventory means you won't get stuck with outdated product. So, as a car or computer loses favor with customers, you have a limited number of those models on hand.

However, what happens if your customers suddenly have a big interest in your product? What if you have a small inventory and you can't meet demand?

Unfortunately, current environmental issues, such as tornadoes, earthquakes, and a tsunami in Japan, have seriously disrupted traditional supply chains. Toyota and General Motors both had major disruptions in their supply chain after the Japanese tsunami.[26]

Even still, it is better to have a mentality of keeping your inventory at the right level to run your own business. Although unexpected problems can happen in your supply chain, it is still better to learn the lesson the Japanese taught in the 1980s—build your product just-in-time to serve your customers. If you work closely with your production department, you should be able to match your production output with the level of inventory that you want to carry.

Think it over.

1. Review the following Internet link and research why the Italians copied the Japanese concept of the Just-in-Time Inventory System: www.theepochtimes.com/n2/business/the-practical-entrepreneur-purchasing-and-negotiations-part-viii-38346.html.[27]

2. Why does TQM relate to a good JIT program?

3. Read the following article (http://hbswk.hbs.edu/item/6684.html) and determine the effect of the Japanese tsunami in 2011 that weakened the argument to use the Just-in-Time Inventory System.[28]

Writing Your Business Plan

You (or in teams) can write a business plan during the semester. There are questions at the end of each chapter to help guide you through the thinking and analyzing process. Appendix B has a sample business plan you can use as a template for developing your own new venture business plan.

Since this is Chapter 8, the goal is to add information about the actual operations of your new business.

Highlighted Sections of the Business Plan (Chapters 1–8)

1. **The Executive Summary** (Chapter 5) is written last—but placed first in the business plan. You have to wait until you are finished with the business plan to properly write the executive summary.

2. **Introduction (Chapter 5):**

   A. **Background of the business:** Includes a short review of its name, address (or addresses if there is more than one location), telephone number(s), email address, Web site address, hours of operation, and a brief history (if any). You want to state when the business was started or will be started.

   B. **Management credentials and organization structure:** It is common to list all the business's key managers and their duties and responsibilities, with their qualifications.

   C. **Form of ownership:** Will your business be a sole proprietorship, partnership, or corporation and how will any profits be distributed?

3. **Strategy Formulation (Chapters 3, 4, and 5)**

   A. **Mission:** What is the organization's purpose or reason for being (covered in Chapter 3)? The mission section of the business plan includes your business model (covered in Chapter 4), which can include a broad description of your present and future products and services to be offered. In the strategy section, it is not necessary to list all the products and services; they are listed under the marketing section of the business plan and were discussed in Chapter 6.

B. **Objectives (prioritized):** What does your organization want to accomplish?

C. **Environmental analysis:** It includes an analysis of the internal environment (which includes the mission and objectives) and its external environment resulting in a SWOT analysis.

4. **The Marketing Function (Chapter 6):**

A. **The marketing plan:** Your marketing plan must identify your target customers and product feasibility (Chapter 4) by using marketing research to better understand your industry and marketplace.

B. **The marketing mix:** You need to include the 4 Ps of marketing in your marketing plan. What is your product? At what price point will you sell your product? Where (place) will you sell your product? And, how will you promote your product?

5. **Location and Layout (Chapter 7):**

A. **Location:** You want to consider such general location factors such as: (1) proximity to the market; (2) transportation facilities; (3) availability of raw materials; (4) labor supply; (5) community attitude; (6) water power; (7) land costs; (8) taxes; (9) specialized communities; (10) climatic conditions; (11) potential sister plants or warehouse; (12) the question of urban, suburban, or rural sites; and (13) how these factors affect specific site selection as either a home-based, Internet, or traditional manufacturing or retail location.

B. **Layout:** Having committed to a location, you must then develop a layout. The layout is an arrangement of the physical facilities in the most efficient manner for specific business, for the interior in order to maximize profitability. You should draw a diagram of the layout you expect to utilize in your business.

6. **The Production/Operations Function (Chapter 8):**

A. **Production process:** What is your operational plan to transform inputs into outputs?

B. **Quality:** What level of quality will you expect from your finished product?

7. **The Human Resources Function (Chapter 9)**

8. **The Financing Function (Chapters 10–11)**

9. **Controls (Chapters 11–12)**

10. **Appendix**

Chapter 9

The Human Resource Plan

How do You Develop the New Venture Team and Employees?

Staffing is one of the most important aspects of any business, particularly for small firms, which, by their nature, tend to be labor intensive and cannot exist without the appropriate people. The entrepreneur running a small business with fewer than twenty workers is often personally responsible for all aspects of human resources.

The human resources function in your organization involves all aspects of managing the people who work in your business. These tasks include personnel planning, job analysis, job evaluation, compensation, recruiting and selecting (hiring), orienting and training, legal aspects, and benefits.

Staffing also includes filling the strategic-level personnel such as the board of directors, board of advisors, investors, lenders, mentors, and professional advisors (lawyers, accountants, bankers, insurance agents, and consultants). Management succession and exit strategies are also covered as part of the strategic-level staffing.

Learning Outcomes

After completing this chapter you should be able to:

1. Identify the different types of professionals that should be part of the new venture team;
2. Differentiate between a job analysis, job description, and job specifications within the human resource process;
3. Describe the difference between internal consistency and external consistency as they relate to job evaluation;
4. Explain the role of recruitment of employees within the human resource management process;
5. Discuss the role of selection of employees within the human resource management process;
6. Explain the role of the orientation of employees within the human resource management process;
7. Describe the role of compensation of employees within the human resource management process;
8. Define the twelve key terms identified in this chapter.

Entrepreneur Profile—Don Wilkes, CEO AZ Technology

We begin each chapter with a short bio of an entrepreneur and provide a link so you can learn more about the person and his or her business venture. Short 3–5-minute videos of each entrepreneur can be found at the PBS Small Business School at www.smallbusinessschool.org/. You can find Build Beyond Yourself CEO Don Wilkes at: www.smallbusinessschool.org/video.cfm?clip=1905#.

Don has been a space scientist for over thirty years, working with space materials and instruments. However, Don said that that doesn't teach a person about business. Business has its own interest. Surprisingly, Don has enjoyed the business side of owning and managing AZ Technology (www.aztechnology.com/) much more than he thought he would.

Don knew he could only do so much, and therefore he needed good employees. He needed good people to work with him. He tries to keep in mind that, yes, they work for him, but he tries to play that down. They work with him. He hires people of all capabilities from other scientists to engineers, technicians, and clerical people. But they all work together as a team. Don has fun watching the teams grow.

Don likes to enable anybody who works for him to grow something of his or her own, within the confines of the definition of his business. He wants the employees to be able to envision something of their own, like he did, and to grow that into something that they can be proud of, that they can grow something that might be in their dreams. For instance, the software (and the credit) for the education/public outreach and the space station voice system were grown out of Jim Chamberlain's work. Jim's the leader of the software group. His success is good for the company, good for the team, and it's fun to see that happen. Jim has done a great job at growing his business, and we want to reward that.

Think it over.

1. How does Don attract and keep good people at AZ Technology?
2. What benefits can you expect from establishing a team environment in a small business?

The Interrelationship Between the Human Resources Function and the Other Business Plan Components

Viewing business as a system, it is evident that the functional areas that include marketing, production, personnel, finance, and accounting are interrelated. Changes in any one area impact and exert change on the others. Once you decide what you want your business to be and who your customers are, you must then determine the size of your market. Market size, in turn, dictates the machinery and equipment you need to produce the product or services you are selling. Once you know what you are producing and how it is produced, you can determine personnel needs. People, human capital, are your most valuable resource.[1]

Actually, you are really making this determination while you are making decisions about production and organizational structure. In an ideal situation, the personnel function will be able to recruit enough of the appropriate talent to operate your organization. Conversely, personnel can influence other functional areas. For example, if you wanted to locate a high-technology firm, you would probably choose an area such as Boston or San Jose because of the concentration of suitable employees. Lack of workers could also impact your location, or, in some cases, the production technology you might use. Compensating your employees requires the finance function to supply the required resources. Accounting keeps track of all payroll and benefits and the size and complexity of its task are directly related to the number of employees. You cannot produce anything without people and the need for people stems from your production requirements. These requirements are determined externally. Internally, you keep track of, and pay people, through the accounting function.

There are also a number of federal laws requiring specific record-keeping such as having the Immigration and Naturalization Service's I-9 forms on file for every employee or records of required benefits such as Social Security, workers' compensation, and unemployment.

The New Venture Team

There is no clear list of characteristics of the venture team you should have to start your new venture,[2] but you do need to integrate their expertise and skills,[3] as they help you acquire the resources to start the new venture.[4] In this section, we identify some of the people and advisors you should consider having on your new venture team.

Team Members

Founders

Most new ventures are created by entrepreneurial teams,[5] some of whom are copreneurs,[6] as well as spouses who can be a great support.[7] Friends also co-found businesses, For example, Google was founded by Larry Page and Sergey Brin while they were Ph.D. students at Stanford University.[8]

Board of Directors

The entrepreneur can also receive support by forming a board of directors. *The* **board of directors** *is a group of individuals who are elected as, or elected to act as, representatives of the stockholders to establish corporate management-related policies and to make decisions on major company issues.* Such issues include the hiring or firing of executives, dividend policies, options policies, and executive compensation. Every public company must have a board of directors.[9] The board should offer a diversity of experience in different industries to help you in your own industry. Board members can use their own experience to offer advice to help you to stay ahead of the changes in your industry.

Board of Advisors

A **board of advisors** *is a small group of people who meet periodically to offer advice and direction to a company.* Members of the board of advisors do not usually have a share in the company, and therefore do not bear legal responsibilities for the company's actions.[10] Startup and small businesses often use a board of advisors to help them to grow their new business. Advisors can be found by recruiting other small business owners to share their knowledge, by joining an advisory board organization such as **Entrepreneurs' Organization** who will assign you some qualified advisors, or you can hire experts that you trust.[11]

Personal Application

1. Identify three people that you would like to have on your board of advisors.

Friends and Family

You can also look to your friends and family members to provide some financial and social support.[12] Family and friends are often proud their relative has started a business and are often eager to support the new business idea.

Mentors

The new entrepreneur should form alliances with mentors. Mentors provide support to the entrepreneur by sharing their own business ideas. Mentors should be treated with care because they are a critical member of the support team. So, when you find one, it is good to keep him or her forever.

The Small Business Association (SBA) offers many different options for finding mentors. For example, SCORE Mentors provides free and confidential counseling, mentoring, and advice to small-business owners nationwide via a network of business executives, leaders, and volunteers through in-person and/or online counseling. Steve Allen, from **RAD Cab** states, "When I go in to talk to my SCORE Mentor, he really helps me sort it all out and we just get organized and when I go home, I feel confident about what's going on."[13]

Entrepreneurs can also visit the Small Business Development Centers (SBDCs) in their area. SBDCs provide management assistance to current and

Personal Application

2. Identify two people who would be your best mentors in helping you to manage your own business.

prospective small-business owners. SBDC services include financial counseling, marketing advice, and management guidance. The SBDC has over 900 locations. Forty-eight locations are hosted by universities. There are also eight locations hosted on community colleges.[14]

The SBA also offers Women's Business Centers (WBCs), which provide business training and counseling with the unique needs of women entrepreneurs in mind. WBCs are a national network of nearly 100 educational centers designed to support women who want to start and grow small businesses.[15]

Professional Advisors

Professional advisors can include lawyers, accountants, bankers, insurance agents, and consultants. Professional advisors can offer their expertise in areas such as banking and issuance of stocks. Some entrepreneurs want to be fully in control and do not use a board of advisors or consult with enough professional advisors. However, regular meetings with the board of advisors can be part of a new venture team and provide the support and expertise to properly organize and prepare the business for future growth. The small entrepreneur should consider his or her new organization as a team effort where everyone is working to help achieve their vision.

Lawyers

Personal Application

3. What lawyer would you select to advise you about your organization?

The original founder will soon realize he needs a lawyer to help provide legal advice. A good business attorney will provide vital assistance in almost every aspect of your business, from basic zoning compliance and copyright and trademark advice to formal business incorporation and lawsuits and liability.[16] A patent lawyer will help protect the entrepreneur from copycat products made by unethical competitors.

Accountants

Selecting an accountant to review and audit the accounting systems will help manage costs and prepare required financial statements. A professional relationship with an accountant will help manage many financial issues that arise in the growing company. The selected accountant should understand the four basic areas of expertise in a general accounting practice:

1. **Business advisory services.** As an accountant should be knowledgeable about your business environment, your tax situation, and your financial statements, it makes sense to ask him or her to pull all the pieces together and help you come up with a business plan and personal financial plan.
2. **Accounting and record-keeping.** An accountant can help set up bookkeeping and accounting systems and show you how to use them. A good system allows you to evaluate profitability and modify prices. It also lets you

monitor expenses, track a budget, spot trends, and reduce accounting fees required to produce financial statements and tax returns.

3. **Tax advice.** Accountants who provide assistance with tax-related issues usually can do so in two areas: tax compliance and tax planning. Planning refers to reducing your overall tax burden. Compliance refers to obeying the tax laws.

4. **Auditing.** There are many levels of auditing, ranging from simply preparing financial statements to an actual audit, where the accountant or other third party provides assurance that a company's financial information is accurate.[17]

Bankers

Forming alliances with bankers will help the growing business to acquire loans that are normally required to provide funds to pay for items such as building your own business, buying new equipment, and managing the payroll process.

Personal Application

4. Select a bank to handle your daily banking needs.

An entrepreneur can impress a bank (or any other investor) by being armed with excellent data about his or her competitive position within a market. The entrepreneur should be able to show the bank his or her financial statements and expected revenue into the future. The entrepreneur should have all of this financial information in his or her business plan.[18]

Insurance Agents

The basic business insurance package (not including health insurance) consists of four fundamental coverages:

1. Workers' compensation—Covers medical and rehabilitation costs and lost wages for employees injured on the job and is required by law in all fifty states.

2. General liability—Comprehensive general liability coverage insures a business against accidents and injury that might happen on its premises as well as exposures related to its products.

3. Auto—If your business provides employees with company cars, or if you have a delivery van, you need to think about auto insurance.

4. Property/casualty—Most property insurance is written on an all-risks basis, as opposed to a named-peril basis. The latter offers coverage for specific perils spelled out in the policy. If your loss comes from a peril not named, then it isn't covered. Make sure you get all-risks coverage.[19]

Consultants

The entrepreneurial founder hires a consultant to help him or her with something of which the entrepreneur is not personally an expert. A consultant normally has very few costs besides maintaining an office. However, a consultant is only as good as the advice he or she offers to the entrepreneur.[20]

The Human Resource Management Process

Because entrepreneurs play a crucial role in job creation, they need to be proficient at managing people,[21] as there is a relationship between human capital and success.[22] The right employees are often a critical resource to the new venture.[23] The human resource management (HRM) process has four parts. See Exhibit 9-1 for an illustration. If you can set up a consistent set of HRM practices, it can increase your survival chances.[24] In this section, we discuss the first part of the HRM process. The other three parts are presented in other major sections.

Human Resource Management Planning

As an entrepreneur or small-business owner, you expect your business to grow and prosper by selling more goods and services and, at the same time, see it become relatively more complex to manage. A growing firm will require not only more people to meet increasing demands, but also more skilled, knowledgeable, and trained personnel to handle new tasks. If your business is to be efficient and profitable, people must be recruited, trained, compensated, and managed, but too few business owners carry out adequate or timely planning. Entrepreneurs behave differently than managers in large companies, as they have to perform most of the HRM process without the assistance of a professionally staffed HRM department.[25]

Therefore, as a business owner, you should plan ahead so that you know the number of employees you will need, when you will need them, and the skills you will demand of them. Because it is highly unusual for a new employee to have exactly the skills and background you need in your business, you should establish a human resource staffing plan.

If you are operating a retail store, a staffing plan could be based upon the dollar value of sales per employee. For example, last year your sales were $250,000 and you employed five people. Your average sales per person was $50,000 and the sales volume had all employees working at full capacity. Thus, when sales increase to $300,000, you should anticipate adding another employee. Thus, each employee would still equal $50,000 in sales. If your sales increase to $350,000, you will need two more people. Once you create a pro forma (see Chapter 10), you can predict how many employees you will need in the future. In recession periods, projected demand also tells you how many employees you may have to lay off in order to remain profitable. Sales dollars need not be the only criteria; you might use units sold or any other measure

Exhibit 9-1

The Human Resource Management Process

1. HRM planning. How many employees do you need, what jobs do they do, and what are the laws and regulations?	**2. Attracting Employees.** How do you recruit and select good job candidates?
3. Developing employees. How do you orient, train, and evaluate employees?	**4. Retaining employees.** How do you keep good employees from leaving?

Sales Personnel Needed		
Sales Volume	Year	New Hires
$250,000	2000	5
300,000	2001	6
350,000	2002	7
450,000	2003	10

Exhibit 9-2
Sales/Personnel Chart

that enables you to determine employment levels. A personnel planning chart might look like the following in Exhibit 9-2.

Before you hire new people, however, make certain that the organization is operating efficiently. It may be that you can schedule the workload more efficiently with the same number of people. You don't always hire new people as sales increase.

Job Analysis

Each job to be filled must be analyzed and its requirements specified so that, when you hire, you know what has to be done and the requirements (training, skills, etc.) for the people who will fill the job. Job analysis *describes both the worker and the job so that there are no questions about who is doing what within your firm.* A job description *specifies the duties and requirements of the job.* Job specifications *set forth the specific skills and training of the people hired to perform the job functions.* A job description is what the worker does; a job specification is who the worker is. Both terms fall under the overall heading of **job analysis.**

Once the job is so defined, it becomes easy to evaluate whether the worker is performing the exact job required and has the appropriate qualifications. People who are carrying out the annual reviews for every employee need this information as a yardstick for performance evaluation. It is also much easier to know what to pay an employee once you know what job he or she is performing. These topics will be covered later on in this chapter.

Job Description

The description typically begins with a careful analysis of the important facts about a job, such as individual tasks involved, the methods used to complete the tasks, the purpose and responsibilities of the job, the relationship of the job to other jobs, and the qualifications needed for the job.[26]

Job Specifications

The other facet of job analysis involves describing the personal characteristics necessary to fill the job. Important parts of the specifications are the specific educational and experience requirements needed to do the job.[27] Job descriptions and specifications are not confined to any one sector of the economy. Exhibit 9-3 illustrates a job description and specifications for a Senior Database Administrator.

Learning Outcome

2. Differentiate between a job analysis, job description, and job specifications within the human resource process.

Personal Application

5. Practice writing a job description for the job where you currently work, a person that you know, or for the professor you have in class.

Exhibit 9-3

Sample Job
Description and
Classification

Sr. Database Administrator

Job ID 12345R

Position Type: Full-Time Employee

Company Name

Location: San Jose, CA

Salary: Unspecified

Date Posted: July 15, 2015

Experience: Mid to Senior Level

Desired Education Level: Bachelor of Science

Primary Job Responsibilities

Sr. Database Administrator assisting with database architecture, troubleshooting, and resolving escalated database and site issues.

Database design, performance, and monitoring of Oracle databases in a 24 x 7 production environment. Planning, delegating, communicating, and executing database requests from internal customers. Participate in monitoring of Oracle databases in a 24 x 7 production environment. Participate in on-call schedules and NOC shift work.

Working with engineering team to manage project schedules, priorities-related database development, production and application implementation. Manage performance, availability, database maintenance, backup, restore and recovery. Troubleshooting any issues related to production and QA databases. Setup and configuring databases according to internally documented standards. Provide expert direction and advice in Database Administration and technology which includes database design, database development for transactional reporting, and data warehouse system solutions.

Job Requirements and Skills

Strong understanding and experience using Oracle technologies. Strong working experience in troubleshooting and tuning Oracle/UNIX environments. Strong negotiation skills and ability to effectively resolve conflicting priorities from multiple internal customers. Strong decision-making skills, take-charge personality, and the ability to drive a plan to completion. Able to work flexible hours as required by business priorities. Excellent written and oral communication skills.

Education and/or Relevant Experience

Bachelor's degree in Computer Science or equivalent work experience 8+ years DBA experience and 7+ years of application and information systems support with at least 7 years directing database projects or organizations in a diverse computing environment. 5+ years supporting in a 24 x 7 HA environment. Working experience with scripting tools such as Perl, shell, and PL/SQL. Understanding of high-availability architectures

Job Evaluation

Learning Outcome

3. Describe the role of a job evaluation as part of the human resource plan.

Once the job analysis has been performed, the job evaluation performs two necessary functions. Job evaluation *is the process of determining the relative value of each job to the company.* It must ensure that wages are internally and externally consistent. Internal consistency *means that high-worth jobs (to the company) get paid more than low-worth jobs, and that there are clear relationships between jobs.* External consistency *means that the pay structure corresponds to the community wage structure.* Although collective bargaining and other subjective issues can enter into the setting of wages, it should not disturb the internal job structure.

Keeping it simple, you have to pay at least the federal or state minimum wage. In 2013, President Barack Obama called for increasing the minimum wage to $9 an hour, up from the current rate of $7.25.[28] You should not pay anyone more than the job is worth; nor should you pay more if you will fail to make a profit. You should pay people more for work of greater value (internal consistency). You generally should not pay people much less than other companies in your community do for equal work and you likely should not pay much more than the going rate for a job as a startup venture (external consistency). Some entrepreneurs give stock options to attract good talent instead of paying the going rate. Many people who worked for Microsoft as a startup are millionaires today because of the value of the stock. You can find out the going pay for jobs in your area by looking at want ads and asking HRM people.

Here are two other more complex methods, more commonly used by large businesses, of determining how much you should pay your employees for internal consistency:

1. **Ranking system.** All jobs are placed in rank order and the higher-ranking jobs are paid more.
2. **Point system.** Jobs are broken down into those attributes that the company is paying for, such as skill, responsibility, working conditions, effort, and education. The more points, the higher the pay.

In addition to determining how much pay you will give employees, you also have to consider benefits. (Health and life insurance, and pension plans are common. Additionally you will need to think about sick leave, vacation days, and personal time off.) Many startups offer little to no benefits. Because health insurance is so important today, let's discuss the Patient Protection and the Affordable Care Act, otherwise known as Obamacare, and how it might affect your benefits.

Personal Application

6. Analyze the impact of "Obamacare" as part of the healthcare benefit that you use for your own health services.

In March of 2010, "Obamacare" became law. The official name for "Obamacare" is **the Patient Protection and the Affordable Care Act,** a bill signed into law to reform the healthcare industry. Obamacare's goal is to provide affordable health insurance for all U.S. citizens and to reduce the growth in healthcare spending. [29]

A total of 3.1 million younger people, who would otherwise be uninsured, will be able to stay on their parents' health insurance plans until age twenty-six. This will help younger people to continue to have access to healthcare as they start their careers. The Act will also make sure that those with pre-existing conditions don't lose their coverage. Insurance companies can no longer deny coverage to any person under nineteen due to a pre-existing condition.[30]

Your company may qualify for employer healthcare tax credits if you have fewer than twenty-five full-time equivalent employees making an average of about $50,000 a year or less. To qualify for the Small Business Health Care Tax Credit, you must pay at least 50 per cent of your full-time employees' premium costs. You don't need to offer coverage to your part-time employees or to dependents. Starting in 2014, the tax credit is worth up to 50 percent of the company contribution toward employees' premium costs (up to 35 percent for tax-exempt employers).

The following example from Healthcare.gov shows how the tax credit will work. This example is for an employer who qualifies for the maximum credit, which is worth 50 percent of their premium contribution starting in 2014.

Personal Application

7. Develop a package of benefits you would offer to your employees.

- Number of employees: 10.
- Wages: $250,000 total or $25,000 per employee.
- Employer contribution to employee premiums: $70,000.
- Tax credit amount: $35,000 (50 percent of employer's contribution).[31]

Government Laws and Regulations

Government laws and regulations impact entrepreneurs in many different ways. Each employer must contribute and pay taxes based on its employees' wages. They are responsible for withholding from employees' income tax payments including: federal and any state income taxes, social security tax, Medicare tax, and any other state or local taxes. As an entrepreneur, you will, like all businesses, have to pay both employer and employee contributions. You will also pay worker's compensation insurance as well as federal and state unemployment taxes. If you do hire employees, there are software packages that can do your payroll, including withholding taxes, or you can outsource the job to an accountant or HRM consulting firm.

Personal Application

8. Research online the minimum wage for your state. Compare that rate with another state near your own state.

You will also be required to follow the rules and regulations set up by federal, state, and local governments. Homeland Security requires all employees to complete the I-9 Form, which declares them legally eligible to work in the U.S. The Equal Employment Opportunity Commission (EEOC) governs hiring, promoting, and firing employees, including wage and hour laws. The Occupational Safety and Health Administration (OSHA) regulates working conditions in the workplace.

The Elevator Pitch

This skill-builder puts you in the role of job seeker. You need to work on your own elevator pitch to win a job. You can read the attached article (www. forbes.com/sites/nextavenue/2013/02/04/the-perfect-elevator-pitch-to-land-a-job/) and learn more about the nine steps to follow, which are listed below, to help you to develop your own pitch to present in class.

1. Clarify your job target.
2. Put it on paper.
3. Format it—Who are you? What do you do? What are you looking for?
4. Tailor the pitch to them and not you.
5. Eliminate industry jargon.
6. Read your pitch out loud.
7. Practice, practice, practice (then solicit feedback).
8. Prepare a few variations.

Nail it with confidence.[32]

Think about it.

What score do you give your own pitch?

Great pitch		Terrible pitch
3	2	1

1. Would you hire yourself?
2. How would you improve your own pitch?
3. What is the hook in your presentation for the company to hire you?

Attracting Employees and Independent Contractors

Staffing *means placing the right people in their respective jobs.* In step 1 of the HRM process, you determine your staffing needs, and have created specific jobs to fill with job descriptions and specifications. You are now ready to attract people to apply for the jobs and select the best feasible candidate (step 2 of the HRM process). These are the two topics of this section. But first, although you recruit and select employees and independent contractors in the same way, they are different.[33]

An *independent contractor* is not an employee, so you don't have to keep employee payroll records, pay any taxes for them, and they usually don't get any benefits. You essentially pay them a flat rate as a business expense and at the end of the year, if you pay them more than $600, you are required to give them a 1099-MISC tax form and they pay their own taxes.

Recruiting

Recruiting *refers to the first step in staffing, which is finding people.* Each company tends to rely upon only a few of the many possible ways that exist for finding and recruiting employees. Common sense tells us that the greater the pool of applicants, the more likely you can find the best candidate for the position.

Techniques for recruiting employees vary from business to business and among various types of businesses. Many small retail stores tend to rely primarily on a "Help Wanted" poster in the window. Classified newspaper advertising can also be a source for locating potential candidates. Other sources of applicant

> **Learning Outcome**
>
> **4.** Explain the role of recruitment of employees within the HRM process.

supply could include walk-in candidates, recommendations by current employees, public and private employment agencies, schools, and advertisements in trade magazines and online sources, such as for free on Craig's List or for a fee at Monster.com and Career-Builder.com.

The Selection Process

Business success all comes down to the people you choose.[34] So you should only hire and retain people you trust.[35] The process of selecting an employee for a particular position is analogous to being able to survive a series of obstacles. The potential employee can be eliminated by failing to meet a challenge or, as each hurdle test is successfully passed, he or she becomes eligible to progress to the next level. Selection is important because bad hiring decisions can haunt you for quite a while. Here we discuss the numerous parts of the selection process. Note that all parts of the selection process are not used for some jobs and that there is no absolute set sequence of steps to be followed in the selection process, but the one below is commonly used.

Application Form

As part of the selection process, the recruited candidates are typically asked to complete an application. Organizations may use different application forms for different jobs. For professional jobs, a résumé may replace the application form.

Screening Interviews

You may conduct screening interviews to select the top candidates who will continue on in the selection process.

Testing

Tests can be used to predict job success, as long as the tests meet EEOC guidelines for validity (people who score high on the test do well on the job) and reliability (if people take the same test on different days, they will get approximately the same score each time).[36] Although not too common today, you can also have job candidates take a physical exam including a drug test.

Background and Reference Checks

You should verify the information on a candidate's application form and/or résumé. Many applications contain false or erroneous material. For example, people have stated that they have earned college degrees when they have never even attended college.

Interviewing

The interview is usually the most heavily weighted and the last of the steps in the selection process. The interview gives the candidate a chance to learn about the job and organization. You get a chance to assess things about a candidate that can't be obtained from an application, test, or references, such as the candidate's ability to communicate and his or her personality, appearance, and motivation.[37]

Hiring

You compare the candidates and decide who is the best suited for the job. The candidate is contacted and offered the job. If the candidate does not accept the job, or accepts but leaves after a short period of time, the next-best candidate is offered the job.

Developing, Retaining, and Terminating Employees

We will keep this section short. Once you hire an employee, you need to orient him or her to the company and job, train the employee to do the job, and evaluate his or her performance. This is step 3 of the HRM process, and the topics of this section. After good employees or independent contractors are hired, you want to retain them, but if they aren't working up to standard, you should terminate them; this is step 4 of the HRM process.

Developing Employees Through Orientation and Training

The new employee's first day on the job is usually getting oriented with you as the boss, your company, and the job he or she will be doing. Depending on the job, training the employee for the job make take more than one day. Providing good training tends to result in better retention of employees and less engagement of neglectful behavior.[38] One training technique that really works well is job instructional training. *Job Instructional Training* has four steps:

Step 1. Preparation of the Trainee

Put the trainee at ease as you create interest in the job and encourage questions. Explain the task objectives and quantity and quality requirements, and discuss their importance.

Step 2. Presentation of the Task by the Trainer

Perform the task yourself slowly, explaining each step several times. Once the trainee seems to have the steps memorized, have him or her explain each step as you perform the task. Prepare a written list of the steps in complex tasks and give a copy to the trainee.

Step 3. Performance of the Task by the Trainee

Have the trainee perform the task slowly while explaining each step. Correct any errors and be willing to help the trainee perform any difficult steps. Continue until the employee can perform the task proficiently.

Personal Application

9. Either write, or update, a copy of your own résumé.

10. Make a list of three potential job references.

Learning Outcome

6. Explain the role of the orientation of employees within the HRM process.

Personal Application

11. What type of training have you received in the jobs that you have held?

Step 4. Follow-up

Inform the trainee of those who are available to provide help with any questions or problems. Gradually leave the trainee alone. Begin by checking quality and quantity frequently, then decrease the amount of checking based on the trainee's skill level. Watch the trainee perform the task and be sure to correct any errors or faulty work procedures before they become habits. Be patient and encouraging.

Developing Employees Through Performance Appraisal

After you hire and train employees, you need to know how well they are performing. The performance appraisal has two major goals. First, as you assess the employee's performance, you can improve it through coaching and additional training, so it is developmental. Second, your assessment should be used to make administrative decisions regarding whether the employee should be terminated for poor performance or possibly be given a promotion if you grow your business. Of course, the major decision is regarding pay raises. You certainly don't want to give an employee who is not performing up to your standards a raise.

By far the best type of performance appraisal, as in sports, is continuous coaching. You don't want to wait six months or a year to let employees know how well they are performing. However, a formal six-month or yearly evaluation and pay raise decision is appropriate. But during the formal appraisal there shouldn't be any surprises to employees regarding your assessment of their performance. There are standard forms you can use during the formal session. You can get samples online or from your new venture team and advisors. But it is usually a good idea to customize the form for your company-specific jobs.

Retaining and Terminating Employees

Our last step in the HRM process is to retain and possibly terminate employees. In order to keep your good employees, or independent contractors, compensation is important. If you are not paying a comparable salary and benefits with other businesses for the same or similar job, there is a chance that they will leave for a better job. You want to give a respectable compensation, but not at the expense of your own profitability. Also, if you don't treat employees correctly, they may quit and start their own business competing with you.[39]

Compensation is important not just for financial reasons but for the employees' psychological health as well. In addition to financial incentives, employees should also be rewarded by being given deserved promotions and the opportunity to assume increasing levels of responsibility and authority. If an employee performs well on the job, a promotion, a change in position with a change in status and/or pay, may be given.

After hiring new people, you want to make a quick assessment of their performance, as part of step 3 in the HRM process, and if they are not working

Learning Outcome

7. Describe the role of compensation of employees within the HRM process.

out you want to terminate them quickly. The longer you retain a poor employee, the more damage they can do to the productivity of your new venture, and the harder it is to get rid of them.

Hopefully, your business will grow and you will need to add employees. However, with a downturn in the economy, in your industry, or your product or service, you may have to terminate employees through layoffs. It is difficult to let good employees go, but you need to continue to make a profit to stay in business.

Management Succession and Exit Strategies

You may be thinking that you haven't even opened your business and we are discussing hiring and training employees and exiting the business. A typical entrepreneur doesn't usually think about how he or she is going to exit or leave his or her business. A typical entrepreneur usually focuses on how he or she is going to take his or her business idea and turn it into a business. However, it is wise to always consider different options to exit the business from the very beginning when the appropriate time arrives. An *exit strategy is the method by which a venture capitalist or business owner intends to get out of an investment that he or she has made in the past.* The exit strategy is a way of "cashing out" an investment. Examples include an initial public offering (IPO), such as Facebook did, or being bought out by a larger player in the industry.[40] You might find the right time to exit might be if and when you are offered a fair amount of money to sell your company to a larger company in your industry. Facebook and Google have bought lots of small new ventures to get new technology, and they often want the entrepreneurs to be employees. You may also want to move on to building a different business.

You also want a management succession plan on who takes over the business if you unfortunately have a major accident or become seriously ill. Some day you will reach retirement and should have a plan for your succession.

One exit strategy is to build an organization with employees who can lead the organization. The employees might become part-owners of the business over a series of years. As you leave the business, the employees can buy out the remaining shares of the organization from you.

Another avenue to pursue is to leave the business to a family member.[41] Many family members might be very excited to own the family business. However, some family members might already have their own jobs and careers and might not be interested in running the family business. So you need a succession plan to know who will take over the business, which is commonly sold to one or more family members.

You can also sell the business to a new owner. A successful business will attract people who would like to own their own business. So, you should be able to choose from some qualified buyers to find a new owner for your business.

Other Options for Starting a New Venture, and Entrepreneurial Behavior

In this last section we discuss some of the major human resource differences in starting a new venture compared with the other options to becoming an entrepreneur. We also discuss how to engage in entrepreneurial behavior as an employee.

Buying an Existing Business, Franchise, or Leasing Rights

Buying an Existing Business

The existing business will already have people in place in different areas of the company. You can choose to either retain or terminate the employees. You also might decide to hire new employees to bring in some new ideas.

Buying a Franchise

If you buy a retail franchise, the franchisor will provide a policy book on what specific jobs need to be filled in each retail location. Many will also train you on staffing so that you can effectively attract, develop, and retain good employees.

Buying Licensing Rights

If you buy a license, you are starting a new business and will have to develop a staff to complete the production and sale of the licensed product. So, in most cases, you are starting your own business and everything in this chapter relates to your venture.

Starting a Corporate or Nonprofit New Venture

Starting a Corporate Venture

Starting a new corporate venture will most likely require hiring new employees to staff the new venture. However, it is possible for employees from the original part of the company to be transferred to the new venture. The larger company will most likely have a professional HRM staff that will assist you in performing the HRM process.

Starting a Nonprofit

When starting a nonprofit, you will have to develop a staff to complete the charitable work of your organization. Like all organizations, the charitable organization will be trying to attract the most qualified individuals to help achieve the mission of the organization. A key difference is that you will most likely be attracting volunteer workers, which may be more difficult than a paid staff. You also want to make sure you have a good board of directors who can help you with writing the corporate bylaws, preparing the incorporation documents, making policy decisions, and raising funds and other assets to start and keep the nonprofit running.

Entrepreneurial Behavior

If you are not interested in starting a new venture, as an employee you can engage in *entrepreneurial behavior* that can lead to either helping to develop current employees or helping to hire new employees. If you are a manager in the company, you will most likely be responsible for at least part of the HRM process with the help of the HRM department. If the company is going to hire new employees, you can recruit good people from your network. You can volunteer to interview job candidates to give your input on how you believe the person will fit in with the other employees and assess his or her ability to do the job. You can also orient and train new employees.

Take it to the Net

Visit www.routledge.com/cw/Lussier for the book's companion Web site, where you can:

- use learning aids, including taking a quiz;
- find links to resources in this chapter, as well as other links including videos;
- learn about and start the following activities: Continuing Integrated Case, Your Ninety-Second New Venture Pitch, the Paper Clip Entrepreneurship Challenge, College Entrepreneurial Spirit Award, and the Community Entrepreneurial Spirit Award.

Chapter Review and Summary

As we bring this chapter to a close, you should realize that the profitability of your company will be directly affected by the employees you are able to attract and retain. You should understand the HRM process: (1) you need to plan how many employees you will need, (2) how to attract them, (3) how to develop them, and (4) how to retain and terminate them. Your organization is consistently balancing its need for people with the desire to operate with as few costs as possible. You should be thinking about a succession plan and exit strategy while you are writing your business plan

This summary lists the learning outcomes from the chapter and their answers.

1. **Identify the different types of professionals that should be part of the new venture team**

   The new venture team can consist of any of the following different professionals: the founder(s), the board of directors, the board of advisors, investors, lenders, mentors, professional advisors, lawyers, accountants, bankers, insurance agents, and consultants.

2. **Differentiate between a job analysis, job description, and job specifications within the human resource process**

   Each job to be filled should be carefully analyzed so that job descriptions and job specifications can be written. Job descriptions, which are the duties and requirements of the job that define the job, while job specifications setting forth the specific skills and training of the people hired to perform the job functions, define the characteristics or attributes necessary to do the job. Make certain that your company's jobs are both internally and externally consistent.

3. **Describe the difference between internal consistency and external consistency as they relate to job evaluation**

   Job evaluation is the process of determining the relative value of each job to the company and is necessary to ensure that each job is fairly compensated. Internal consistency, which means that high-worth jobs (to the company) get paid more than low-worth jobs, involves making certain that your firm's job and pay relate their worth to the organization while external consistency, where the pay structure corresponds to the community wage structure, assures that your workers are rewarded at a rate of pay that is comparable to the market. Using either the point or the factor comparison method, job evaluation ensures that wages are internally and externally consistent.

4. **Explain the role of recruitment of employees within the HRM process**

   Recruiting refers to the first step in staffing, which is finding people. Staffing, placing the right people in their respective jobs, includes all activities affecting employees, such as recruiting, the hiring of people, and training them. There are many sources that can be used to recruit employees such as newspaper advertising, referrals, and encouraging those who may walk in.

5. **Discuss the role of selection of employees within the HRM process**

   Choosing the best employee is expedited through the use of application forms in order to elicit relevant information. In addition to completing the application forms, prospective employees should submit résumés, which are prepared by the applicant. Interviews, an important part of the hiring process, are helpful in gaining insight into a prospective employee's qualifications.

6. Explain the role of the orientation of employees within the HRM process

Once an employee is hired, it is necessary to familiarize and train him or her so that the employee can fit into your company's environment smoothly and efficiently. Training on the job is the method most frequently used. Other techniques, such as attending seminars or taking courses in college, can also be used.

7. Describe the role of compensation of employees within the HRM process

Compensation is important not just for financial reasons but for the employee's psychological health as well. In addition to financial incentives, an employee should also be rewarded by being given deserved promotions and the opportunity to assume increasing levels of responsibility and authority. If an employee performs well on the job, a promotion, a change in position with a change in status and/or pay, may be given.

8. Define the twelve key terms found in this chapter

exit strategy

external consistency

internal consistency

job analysis

job description

job evaluation

job specification

new venture team

Patient Affordable Care Act

promotion

recruiting

staffing

Review and Discussion Questions

1. What is the role of the new venture team in starting a new business?

2. What is the difference between a board of directors and a board of advisors?

3. Define job descriptions and job specifications. What is the difference between them? Why are they important?

4. If you had to recruit new employees for a small business, what sources would you use?

5. How would you select a good employee? List some of the methods available.

6. How would you train a new employee? List several methods and explain each.

7. If you were to recruit a friend or class-mate to work in your company, what persuasive arguments would you use?

8. Are acquaintances or relatives a good source of employees? Why or why not?

9. Define "internal consistency of wages." Why is this an important concept?

10. Define "external consistency of wages." Why is this an important concept?

11. What methods would you prefer for a training and orientation program for a small electronic company employing ninety-five people?

12. Why is a performance appraisal system necessary? How do you institute such a system?

13. Assuming that you like a prospective employee in the initial interview, do you think it is necessary to check references? Why or why not? How reliable are the references likely to be?

14. Evaluate the pros and cons of increasing the minimum wage in your home state or country.

15. What is the impact of Obamacare on the role that small-business people play in offering healthcare benefits to their employees?

Application Exercises

Each chapter has a series of exercises requiring you to apply the specific text concepts. When doing these exercises, be sure to select a specific business where applicable. You can select a business where you worked or a business you would like to own someday. Answers for each exercise should be approximately one page.

1. Interview four small-business owners. Have any preparations been made for management succession development? If so, outline these plans. Does the presence or lack of a management succession plan indicate any general "laws" you might say apply to small business?

2. Interview an established small-business owner. Determine if the owner has job descriptions and specifications. If such descriptions and specifications are not present, ask the owner how he or she knows what everyone is supposed to do. Prepare a report on your findings.

3. Using the same business as in question 2, take several of the job descriptions and job specifications and see if the jobs and people match the written specifications. If not, prepare realistic specifications. Report on your findings and include as exhibits the job descriptions and specifications. If there are no specifications, prepare the job descriptions and job specifications for two jobs in the company.

4. Interview a small-business owner and find out how candidates are recruited. What sources for candidates are used? How would candidates be evaluated and on what basis would the final choice be made?

5. Using the same business as in question 4, determine how the owner trains and orients new employees so that they will acquire competency on the job as well as being comfortable in the company.

6. Determine how, using the same company as in question 3, employee compensation is determined, how employees are evaluated, and how raises are determined. Report on your findings.

7. Prepare a report for the business in question 4 discussing your recommendations for improving the personnel policies of the company.

8. Go to your college or university placement office and ask him or her to help you prepare a résumé you can use in your job search.

9. Examine your local and regional newspapers to see the job vacancies listed for small businesses. Be sure to have some criterion for judging which advertisements are for small business. Report on your findings about the kinds of jobs available.

10. Ask the owner of a business whether or not he or she is subject to federal, state, or local regulations concerning his or her workers. Include in your report items such as tax and workplace requirements.

Application Situations

1. Julius Sanchez

Julius Sanchez was hired as an administrative assistant in a local manufacturing company. Julius had been a business major in college and he reported to work yesterday morning. Having been recruited and hired last week, he was given a job offer and a brief outline of employee benefits. Based on the letter and his conversations with the recruiter, he decided to join the firm. Upon arrival, the recruiter assigned him to a desk and told him that he would be assisting Joe Samuels. The recruiter then left Julius sitting at his desk. After sitting there for twenty minutes, Julius asked the first person he saw where Joe Samuels was and was told that he was out for the morning but would be back in several hours.

In fact, several hours later Joe returned, greeted Julius, and said, "Well, I guess I'll have to train you, although I don't know how I'll fit it into my schedule. Don't worry though. Follow me around for several weeks and you'll be able to handle yourself."

1. Given the above, how would you rate the company's orientation and training efforts? What are the positive and negative aspects of this approach?

2. How would you orient Julius in his new job? Develop a standard orientation program for this company.

3. From the company's approach, it seems that its total orientation relied on older, experienced workers mentoring the new workers. To what extent should a company rely on the worker to introduce and orient new employees? Is this a good approach? Will newcomers really learn how the firm works? If this approach has validity, how important should it be in the company's overall orientation program?

2. Tony Moore

Tony Moore worked for the Downside Market as produce manager for sixteen months before he finally asked the market manager if he could speak with him. In the manager's office, Tony explained that, while he enjoyed the work and felt he was doing a good job, he hadn't had an evaluation of his performance. Keelson, the manager replied, "Don't worry, Tony. You're doing a good job. Keep it up and you'll have my job someday." Keelson then shook Tony's hand and returned to work.

1. If you were Tony, how would you feel? Would you be justified and what are you really looking for?

2. Design a formal evaluation procedure for this market.

3. Do you think that Keelson should have been better able to handle an evaluation? Design a procedure Keelson could follow in performing employee evaluations.

Case

Buzz Marketing Group: Hiring a Professional to Handle Your Human Resources

Buzz Marketing Group (BuzzMG) has been growing its research and viral marketing firm for the past sixteen years. BuzzMG is a full-service marketing and marketing research provider whose mission is helping companies and organizations build prosperous connections with consumers.[42] To handle this increase of work, the team had grown to include more individual contractors and more full-time employees.

However, founder Tina Wells was frustrated with how much time she spent on human resources, rather than developing new business. Wells estimates that she spent nearly eight hours a week handling human resource-related tasks such as tracking vacation time, updating the employee handbook, and creating job descriptions. Tina also hired several of her five younger siblings, which created tension with non-family members about future job growth at the company.

Tina developed an idea to outsource her HRM process so she can focus on developing new business. She expanded her contract with **Paychex,** a third-party payroll and human resources firm. "Buzz initially started working with Paychex in 2011 to manage its payroll. In 2012, Paychex began managing the firm's human resources, overhauling the company's handbook from 20 pages to 130 pages, codifying the firm's policies, crafting job descriptions and tracking employee performance. With an online HR system, employees could easily access company manuals and forms as well as track paid time-off themselves. After expanding its services, roughly 1 percent of Buzz's budget goes to Paychex, according to Wells."[43]

Paychex also helped ease the transition for two key hires to the company in 2012, a vice-president of marketing and a chief operating officer, creating job descriptions, offer letters, and working with new hires in their first weeks. Hiring an outside expert such as Paychex has improved the overall company culture and everyone feels they have an opportunity to be promoted.

Think it over.

1. Do you think it is ethical to hire an outside human resource consultant to handle personal information?

2. Based on information in the chapter and the case, what retirement pension programs could Tina Wells offer?

Global Case—Richard Branson: The People Behind Virgin Airlines

It seems obvious that an entrepreneur should like the people he or she hires. But, the reality is it is not as easy as it looks. An entrepreneur is a single person with an idea that he or she has developed into a large enough operation to hire people into the growing organization. It can be quite difficult to expand from a small entrepreneurial idea to an organization of twenty or more people. When a small business reaches about twenty people, it starts to need an actual human resource office to handle the needs of the employees.

Richard Branson is a very popular entrepreneur in Britain.[44] He has built the Virgin brand into a global business, but he didn't do it alone. "Good people are crucial to business success. Finding them, managing them, inspiring them and then holding onto them are among the most important challenges a good business leader faces. How you deal with these matters often determines the long-term success and growth of your business."[45]

Branson believes in attracting talented people, developing them, retaining them, and even helping employees that might deserve to be terminated. Here are a few of the amazingly insightful ideas he has for supporting his employees.

- Branson believes his Virgin airline crews should be cheerful, smiling, and pleased to help.
- People on the frontline are your key assets. Those are the people that customers see.
- A good leader, one that listens to his people, is needed if he expects to retain his people.
- A bad leader (such as one who is dishonest or steals) can ruin a business quickly. On Branson's island of Necker in the Caribbean, he had a general manager who tried to change the way things were done. The general manager discouraged the staff from drinking with the guests on the island. This ruined the atmosphere. Virgin's management team replaced the manager and helped to rebuild trust and morale with their employees.

- Give people a second chance. Branson had an employee who was stealing record merchandise. Instead of terminating him, he gave him a second chance because the employee was honest about his lack of ethical judgment. Branson feels that everyone messes up sometimes—including himself. So it is okay to give a second chance when appropriate.
- Listen to your people when they have an elevator pitch for a totally new business. Your people have good ideas. Some of Virgin's most successful businesses came from a pitch from one of its people. Virgin Blue, its Australian airline, was the brainchild of Brett Godfrey, who had been working for Virgin in Brussels. He came up with his business plan on a beer mat—outlining the startup of a low-cost carrier in Australia to take on Qantas and Ansett in their domestic market. In the last ten years Brett has expanded Blue and its sister airlines to the U.S., New Zealand, Thailand, and, soon, South Africa.
- Develop your employees so they can run your businesses. Matthew Bucknall and Frank Reed came up with the idea of a family-friendly health and fitness club in 1999. They had set up and sold a chain in the U.K. in the 1990s and wanted to do it again with the Virgin brand on the door. Branson liked the idea and the management team. He backed the rollout in the U.K., and within two years they were offered the opportunity to buy a chain in South Africa. The Virgin Active team has more than ninety clubs in South Africa and another hundred in the U.K., Italy, Spain. and Portugal.

1. What professional advisors do you think are most important for Branson to rely upon?
2. Which of the bulleted items in the case relate to attracting, developing, rewarding, retaining, and/or terminating employees?

Writing Your Business Plan

You (or in teams) can write a business plan during the semester. There are questions at the end of each chapter to help guide you through the thinking and analyzing process. Appendix B has a sample business plan you can use as a template for developing your own new venture business plan.

Since this is Chapter 9, the goal is to add information about the human resources of your new business.

Highlighted Sections of the Business Plan (Chapters 1–9)

1. **The Executive Summary** (Chapter 5) is written last—but placed first in the business plan. You have to wait until you are finished with the business plan to properly write the executive summary.

2. **Introduction:**
   A. **Background of the business:** Includes a short review of its name, address (or addresses if there is more than one location), telephone number(s), email address, Web site address, hours of operation, and a brief history (if any). You want to state when the business was started or will be started.
   B. **Management credentials and organization structure:** It is common to list all the business's key managers and their duties and responsibilities, with their qualifications.
   C. **Form of ownership:** Will your business be a sole proprietorship, partnership, or corporation and how will any profits be distributed?

3. **Strategy Formulation:**
   A. **Mission:** What is the organization's purpose or reason for being (covered in Chapter 3)? The mission section of the business plan includes your business model (covered in Chapter 4), which can include a broad description of your present and future products and services to be offered. In the strategy section, it is not necessary to list all the products and services; they are listed under the marketing section of the business plan and were discussed in Chapter 6.
   B. **Objectives (prioritized):** What does your organization want to accomplish?
   C. **Environmental analysis:** It includes an analysis of the internal environment (which includes the mission and objectives) and its external environment resulting in a SWOT analysis.

4. **The Marketing Function:**
   A. **The marketing plan:** Your marketing plan must identify your target customers and product feasibility (Chapter 4) by using marketing research to better understand your industry and marketplace.
   B. **The marketing mix:** You need to include the 4 Ps of marketing in your marketing plan. What is your product? At what price point will you sell your product? Where (place) will you sell your product? And, how will you promote your product?

5. **Location and Layout:**
   A. **Location:** You want to consider such general location factors such as: (1) proximity to the market; (2) transportation facilities; (3) availability of raw materials; (4) labor supply; (5) community attitude; (6) water power; (7) land costs; (8) taxes; (9) specialized communities; (10) climatic conditions; (11) potential sister plants or warehouse; (12) the question of urban, suburban, or rural sites; and (13) how these factors affect specific site selection as either a home-based, Internet, or traditional manufacturing or retail location.
   B. **Layout:** Having committed to a location, you must then develop a layout. The layout is an arrangement of the physical facilities in the most efficient manner for specific business, for the interior in order to maximize profitability. You should draw a diagram of the layout you expect to utilize in your business.

6. **The Production/Operations Function:**

   A. **Production process:** What is your operational plan to transform inputs into outputs?

   B. **Quality:** What level of quality will you expect from your finished product?

7. **The Human Resources Function**

   A. Who are the members of your new venture team (founder, investors, lenders, mentors, lawyer, accountant, banker, insurance agent, and any consultants)?

   B. How do you plan on using the HRM process to attract, develop, and retain employees?

   C. What is your plan for management succession and an exit strategy?

8. **The Financing Function**

9. **Controls**

10. **Appendix**

Chapter 10

The Finance Plan

How Much Money do You Need?

It is important to consider government a partner in your business and taxes a cost of being in business. All business decisions should be made with these liabilities and their consequences in mind. For example, in Chapter 5, you saw that there was a tax advantage in being a sub-chapter S corporation rather than the traditional C corporation. Some of the important tax issues will be noted.

In this chapter you will also learn about the importance of financial information in running your business. You will learn about the different types of financial statements that can be prepared from the records you maintain of your business transactions. You will learn about the fundamental accounting concepts of assets, liabilities, and owner's equity.

Financial statements commonly used in most businesses are the chart of accounts, the balance sheet, the income statement, and the profit and loss statement. You will learn how to develop a pro forma cash flow statement. You will also learn about the tax liability that arises from the operation of your business.

Learning Outcomes

After completing this chapter you should be able to:

1. Explain the importance and purpose of an accounting system;

2. Identify the importance of a balance sheet and an income statement and their three parts;

3. State the importance of a pro forma cash flow statement and its two parts;

4. Describe the role of a breakeven analysis in determining when the business actually makes a profit;

5. Identify the most common forms of taxation;

6. Explain the effect of taxes on the form of ownership;

7. Define the thirty-six key terms identified in this chapter.

Entrepreneur Profile—Financial Statements University

We begin each chapter with a short bio of an entrepreneur and provide a link so you can learn more about the person and his or her business venture. Short 3–5-minute videos of each entrepreneur can be found at the PBS Small Business School at www.smallbusinessschool.org/. You can find the Financial Statements University video at: http://smallbusinessschool.org/video.cfm?clip=1136.

Jim Schell was amazed by what he discovered when he started as a volunteer to help small business owners work through problems. He learned that most business owners don't understand how to read a financial statement.

In response, Jim created FSU, which stands for Financial Statement University. This is an imaginary place you can create for yourself by reading, talking to your CPA or banker, or by taking a class in accounting.

Jim explains the financial discussion as simply as possible. "The balance sheet gives you the financial status of your business today. The left side basically shows you what you have, all of your assets; and the right side shows who owns those assets. Part of them are liability; part of them are net worth. The liability part means somebody else owns them, the net worth means you own them. If you have a million dollars in assets and your liabilities, maybe a bank loan or your vendor's payables, are $400,000, then the vendor and the bank own $400,000 of your million bucks and you own the other $600,000."[1]

Think it over.

1. How often should an entrepreneur create financial statements?

2. How should an entrepreneur use the information?

The Interrelationship Between the Accounting Function, Taxation, and the Other Business Plan Components

The accounting function links all other functional areas such as production/operations, marketing, and finance. Each functional area of the company must express its needs and desires for resources in monetary terms. The accounting function records functional requirements and produces a total company demand for funds using the cash flow budget as its primary vehicle. Accounting also keeps track of sales made, bills paid by customers, and bills that need to be paid. Equipment and operations budgets are prepared using inputs from production/operations, marketing, finance, and personnel. The reports generated by the accounting function and the information they contain are needed in each functional area if it is to operate efficiently. Lack of a good accounting function could seriously impact on functional efficiency and company profitability.

Although you may operate your business as you desire, federal, state, and/or local government take a portion of each dollar you generate in the form of taxes. These taxes may, in turn, influence the manner in which you organize your company, what equipment you buy, how long you keep the equipment, and, ultimately, your profitability. Because profits depend upon expenses, your profits will be lower if you are allowed to deduct significantly for depreciation. Organizationally, the choice of organization form, the C or the S corporation, depends in large part upon comparative tax rates.[2]

Additionally, any time you hire personnel, taxes such as Social Security and unemployment taxes increase the cost of doing business and will therefore have to be factored into your strategic plans.

Financial Statement Basics

What are the financial risk and potential returns of your new venture?[3] Having limited knowledge of finance may cause you to make suboptimal financial decisions,[4] as your financial management competencies play a key role in your new venture success.[5] The financial rewards to you the entrepreneur are unknown, but you need to be able to determine if you are going to make a profit,[6] and how much financial support you will need.[7] You should keep in mind that the balance sheet and income statement are compilations of the firm's activity. In order to produce these statements you need records of the business activity from which you can construct the various statements that will make use of ratios and various analytic tools, which will be explained in another chapter. You must keep records:

1. To construct the necessary statements;
2. To be able to compare budget figures (projected versus actual results) to see if you are on target; this will be discussed in Chapter 12;

3. To satisfy the requirements of the Internal Revenue Service (IRS), which requires record-keeping.

Records should be maintained in the following areas (where applicable):

a.	Sales	three years
b.	Inventory	seven years
c.	Accounts receivable	three years
d.	Accounts payable	three years
e.	Cash	seven years
f.	Payroll	ten years
g.	Depreciation	life of assets
h.	Equipment	life of assets
i.	Purchases	three years.

Accounting System

The importance of the accounting function cannot be overemphasized. You, as an entrepreneur, must be able to understand and use the accounting information to:

1. Know if your business is making a profit;
2. Compare your firm's current performance with past performance;
3. Project future performance;
4. Compare your firm's results with the results of other firms in your industry;
5. Make informed decisions about what future actions your firm should take.

The primary purpose of the accounting function is its use as a management tool that enables you to understand your company's performance and to serve as an aid in decision-making.

Ultimately, your goal as an entrepreneur is to know if your firm is profitable; financial statements will tell you this. This chapter covers the necessary information you need to know to do this: the balance sheet, the income statement, and the cash flow statement.

While this material will enable you to understand your firm's operations, it should be clear that every firm needs an accountant or accounting advice in order to set up the books and maintain records that produce the statements you need in order to run the company.

The first task that you or your accountant will do is to review or create the chart of accounts for your business. A chart of accounts is a *list of all of the accounts to which charges are made.* These accounts, which you name, translate your vision of how to financially measure the company into various accounts. All financial reports are generated from the chart of accounts so a well thought-out plan is important at the outset. All the accounts of your business are tracked in the general ledger, a book or computer listing in which entries are made concerning all of a firm's financial transactions.

Personal Application

1. Apply two of the five areas of a good accounting system to a small business in your community.

Personal Application

2. Use Hoovers.com or Yahoo Finance (or a similar source) to look at a balance sheet for a business of your choice. What are the total liabilities of the company you selected?

The Balance Sheet

A balance sheet *is a snapshot view of the financial value of the firm's assets, liabilities, and net worth at a particular point in time.* It is divided into two major sections: the value of the firm's resources and the claims against it. There are two types of claims against assets: (1) the claims of creditors and (2) the claims of owners, also known as equity. All financial statements are structured so that the assets of the firm are equal to the firm's liabilities, plus the firm's net worth (sometimes referred to as owner's equity). All balance sheets are structured so that:

assets = liabilities + net worth (or owner's equity)

Let us look at this equation more closely. If a firm's assets equal $5,000 and its liabilities equal $2,500, the net worth must equal $2,500. An asset is a tangible item or intangible rights owned by the firm. Liabilities are the obligations or debts that the firm owes. Net worth or owner's equity is what remains and is the number that brings the equation into balance. Further, in Exhibit 10-1 we will see that this means: total assets ($77,800) = liabilities ($65,800) + net worth ($12,000).

Assets: What You Own

An asset *is a tangible item or intangible rights owned by the firm.* Tangible assets *are those things (items) that can be seen such as land, cash, equipment, and buildings.* Intangible assets *are items, also owned, that cannot be seen such as patents or copyrights.* It is important to determine the assets you will need to start your business,[8] and how you will acquire these resources.[9] Most new businesses have limited financial resources.[10]

To fully understand the balance sheet, it is necessary to define each entry (or the terms used).

Current assets *consist of cash and any other asset that will be (or can be) converted to cash within a reasonable period of time (generally less than one year).* Cash *refers to bills, currency, coins, and checks on hand or in a checking or savings account.* Accounts receivable *represents the money owed to the company for the sale of goods or services to customers. Any time a sale is made and the customer is given a period of time in which to pay, a* receivable *is created.* Thirty days is a reasonable expectation for payment. **Net receivables** *mean that extending credit bears the risk of the customer not paying for a number of reasons.* Thus an allowance for non-payment (this is determined by the industry you are in) such as 2 percent is made.

Merchandise inventory *is the amount of goods the company holds for sale to customers at a particular moment.*

Supplies *are those items the company holds that are used in supporting the production process. Examples include paper, pencils, lubricating oil, light bulbs, or other similar items.*

Prepaid expenses *are expenses that a company has incurred and paid for, but which have not yet been consumed.* For example, most insurance policy

Exhibit 10-1

Balance Sheet

Brown Corporation
Balance Sheet
December 31, 2015

ASSETS

Current Assets

Cash	$ 7,000
Accounts receivable (net)	3,000
Merchandise inventory	4,000
Supplies	3,000
Prepaid expenses	3,000
Total Current Assets	**$20,000**

Fixed Assets

Fixtures	800
Vehicles	3,000
Equipment	10,000
Leasehold improvements	2,000
Buildings	30,000
Land	14,000
Less depreciation	(2,000)
Net Fixed Assets	**$57,800**
TOTAL ASSETS	**$77,800**

LIABILITIES & NET WORTH

Current Liabilities

Accounts payable	$ 7,000
Current portion LTD	8,000
Notes payable	7,800
Other	10,000
Total Current Liabilities	**$32,800**

Long-Term Liabilities

Notes payable	$ 12,000
Bank loan payable	10,000
Other loans payable	11,000
Total Long-Term Liabilities	**$33,000**
Total Liabilities	**$65,800**
Net Worth: Owner's Equity	**$12,000**
TOTAL LIABILITIES AND NET WORTH	**$77,800**

premiums are payable in advance. The company will pay for one year's coverage and its books will then show the amount of insurance credit still due the company. For example, if the premium is $1,200 due on January 1, this will be the credit for the company. At the end of January, the company will have used up 1/12th or $100, so on February 1 the prepaid insurance will be $1,100; on March 1 it will be $1,000 until December 31 when there is no premium left.

Fixed assets consist of land, buildings, equipment, and assets that are not consumed in the production of the firm's goods and services and will usually last longer than one year.

Land *is the property used by the firm in its operations.* It is generally listed on the balance sheet at cost and rarely changed. In times of rapid and/or large economic change, this value may be under- or overstated. At present, the longer the land is held, the less relation to reality is its price. Generally, it shows on the balance sheet as far less than its present value.

Buildings include the structures the firm uses; all buildings and structures are counted. Generally these are listed at their cost at the time of purchase. However, unlike land, buildings wear out over time and are thus consumed in the production process. *Use of a fixed asset* is called depreciation and accumulated depreciation *is the amount of a fixed asset's value that has been written off over time due to wear and tear.* How much a firm charges to depreciation every year is subject to IRS regulations. Yearly depreciation is tax deductible. That is, it shows up on the income statement as a deduction or expense and this reduces the firm's taxable income and its tax liability. Depreciation is a noncash item; that is, depreciation does not represent a "cash" expenditure. It will not affect the cash flow. However, if the firm is to recover its investment and be able to buy a new plant and new equipment when the need arises, the effects of depreciation must be covered.

Leasehold improvements *are changes made to the building or property to facilitate doing business.* These improvements generally last longer than one year and may be subject to depreciation on an annual basis. Equipment, vehicles, and fixtures are also fixed assets and are also subject to depreciation.

Liabilities: What You Owe

You need to know your liabilities.[11] Current liabilities *are those obligations that are due and payable in less than one year.* These include the following:

1. Accounts payable, *which are payments due to suppliers for inventory and/or services, generally due thirty days from the date of purchase*;
2. Current portion of long-term debt (LTD) and any portion of notes or loans due within the next twelve-month period;
3. Other current liabilities including expenses incurred but not paid such as taxes or wages.

Long-term liabilities *are those obligations due after one year.* These include all notes for loans or other obligations due in the future. Notes payable *are those loans due to lenders other than banks.* **Bank notes** *payable are obligations due to a bank.* Other loans may include loans on equipment or inventory.

Owner's Equity: What You are Worth

Net worth *may have a section called retained earnings, which represents accumulated net income of the company from its inception to the present.* This amount changes every year as it reflects a firm's net income (or net loss). The

December 31, 2015 Income Statement	January 1, 2016 Balance Sheet	Exhibit 10-2
		How Net Worth Changes

December 31, 2015
Income Statement

January 1, 2016
Balance Sheet

Sales

Expenses

Profits —————————————————————→

Assets = Liabilities

+

Net Worth

Difference in Profits = Difference in Net Worth

profit resulting from operation as of December 31, 2015 changes net worth as of January 1, 2016 by the amount of the profit. Corporations may have a separate section in their balance sheet called retained earnings, which may, or may not, show owner's equity as a separate category. Retained earnings may also reflect the value of any new investment in the company by its owners. Exhibit 10-2 shows how net worth changes within a one-year period.

The **balance sheet,** *by definition, always balances*:

assets = liabilities + net worth

Net worth is not cash, does not represent a liquidation value, and cannot be spent. In fact, it may even be a negative value if the amount a company owes is greater than its assets. It is possible for a company to continue to operate for quite some time with a negative net worth as long as its cash flow is positive. Fulfilling the equation is not just a matter of changing the net worth. Net worth reflects profits or losses.

The balance sheet balances because of double-entry bookkeeping. Every transaction the company undertakes is entered twice: once as a debit, once as a credit. That is, if an event is recorded on one side of the balance sheet, it must be offset by something happening on the other side in order for the balance sheet to continue balancing. Exhibit 10-3 illustrates some typical transactions.

The balance sheet always balances because its right-hand side (liabilities plus equity) tells you how the company has been financed while the left (asset) side tells you how the funds have been invested.

The Income Statement

Investors are going to want to see your potential for making a profit,[12] and you will not get credit or favorable terms either.[13] The income statement (profit and loss statement) *shows all the revenues and expenses that result in the profit or loss from operations during a given time period.* Exhibit 10-4 provides an example.

Revenues

Every time your company sells a product or a service, it receives revenue. Remember this amount has not been adjusted for any bad debts or discounts the company offers for paying bills early. The example shown is net of these items.

Personal Application

3. Use Hoovers.com or Yahoo Finance (or a similar source) to look at an income statement for a business of your choice. What is the net income of the company you selected?

Exhibit 10-3

Typical Transactions

A. Purchase and Delivery of Materials

Materials in the amount of $20,000 have been purchased and delivered. The invoices result in two entries:

Merchandise inventory increases $20,000

Accounts payable increases $20,000

Assets	Liabilities
Merchandise inventory + $20,000	Accounts payable + $20,000

B. Bill for Inventory Paid

The invoices for the new merchandise have been presented and now are paid. This results in two entries:

Cash decreases by $20,000

Accounts payable decreases $20,000

Assets	Liabilities
Cash – $20,000	Accounts Payable – $20,000

C. Sale of Stock

The company sells $10,000 worth of stock. The two entries are:

Cash increases by $10,000

Net worth increases by $10,000

Assets	Liabilities
Cash + $10,000	Net worth + $10,000

Cost of Goods Sold

Cost of goods sold (COGS) *represents the cost of the merchandise sold.* It represents the cost to you of your purchases from all sources for resale either in the same form as you bought it (a retail store, which resells merchandise) or in a modified form (a manufacturer who buys raw materials and sells finished products made from the raw materials). The COGS specifically represents the beginning inventory plus any purchases, which increased it, minus the inventory on hand at the end of the period. Gross profits are the difference between sales and the COGS.

Expenses

You need to understand and analyze your expenses.[14] The Federal Accounting Standards Advisory Board (FASAB) defined expenses in its glossary as "outflows or other uses of assets or incurrence of liabilities (or both) during a period as a result of delivering or producing goods, rendering services, or carrying out other activities that constitute the entity's ongoing major or central operations. Examples are cost of goods sold, salaries expense, and interest expense."[15]

Profits (or Loss)

Profits (or loss) *are sales minus COGS and minus operating expenses.* This is shown pretax. Taxes are what you pay to federal, state, and local government for the privilege of doing business; the amount is determined by a tax table and the provisions as shown in Exhibit 10-4.

ABC Trucking Profit and Loss Statement January 1, 2016 through December 31, 2016	
Sales (Revenues)	190,400
(Minus)	
Cost of Goods Sold	
Beginning inventory	$45,000
Plus purchases	$20,000
Total cost of goods sold	$65,000
Gross Profit	125,400
(minus)	
Operating Expenses	
Utilities	8,000
Telephone	5,000
Advertising	8,500
Rent	36,000
Office suppliers	2,000
Office labor	6,500
Depreciation	4,000
Total Operating Expenses	70,000
Net Profit Before Taxes	55,400
Provision for taxes	27,700
Net Profit	$27,700

Exhibit 10-4

Profit and Loss Statement

Net profit (loss) is what is left over. This amount is added to or subtracted from owner's equity (retained earnings) as shown on the balance sheet. If this is the first balance sheet drawn up for your business, this amount becomes the first retained earnings. It is helpful to analyze your income statement and make comparisons with competitors in your industry.[16]

The Elevator Pitch

This skill-builder puts you in the venture capitalist position. You will watch an elevator pitch from the Internet and discuss if investors would or wouldn't invest in the new venture. The link for the elevator pitch for this chapter can be found at: www.youtube.com/watch?v=dqIEE-g_-Uc.

Although the pitch doesn't actually occur in an elevator, the idea is that the entrepreneur has ninety seconds to impress the judges to invest in her female-oriented iPhone applications.

Think about it.

1. What score do you give Katie Sunday's pitch?

Great product idea and pitch		Terrible product idea and pitch	
4	3	2	1

2. Would you invest $100,000 for a 25 percent ownership of Katie's business?

3. How would you improve Katie's pitch?

Pro Forma Cash Flow Statement

As the material in Chapter 5 explained and emphasized, you must have a business plan that forces you to think logically and systematically about what has to be done. Using a systematic approach will result in creating pro forma statements. These statements are key to determining the financial needs of the organization. However, pro forma statements are only an estimate of what might happen given a certain defined set of circumstances and the validity of your assumptions. *Pro forma statements are guidelines against which you can measure how your assumptions relate to reality.* The future is uncertain and, while you may be asked to predict with a fair degree of confidence and certainty about the immediate future, the further you extend your predictions, the less accurate and reliable they tend to be.

As the future unfolds, events are not held constant and you realize that conditions change in unpredictable ways. In the face of uncertainty, consider that the figures you developed are "best guesses" and treat them accordingly. Comparing your plan with what actually does happen tests the validity of your assumptions and enables you to make better, and more accurate, plans as you gain knowledge and become experienced in running the business. While the actual numbers in the future will differ from the pro forma, together both sets help formulate a good initial estimate of your financial needs. Keep in mind that everything generally costs more than you think it will. Thus, make sure you have a safety margin (a little extra money) because you will probably need it.

Pro forma income statements and balance sheets may be determined in the same manner as the following pro forma cash flow statement.

Methods for Calculating Pro Forma Cash Flow Statements

Cash flow problems cause trouble with creditors and can even result in liquidating assets that can stop operations.[17] There are two methods you can use to determine the pro forma cash flow of your company. The first mandates using your present knowledge of the business operation and its operating history to define all the necessary expense categories and any relationships that exist between them. The second, to be discussed later, requires the use of standard industry ratios.

Each expense category has a rationale or assumption upon which it is based. For example, the assumptions for a pro forma cash flow statement for Scrap Metal Recycler are shown in Exhibit 10-5. Based upon these assumptions, Exhibit 10-6, a pro forma cash flow statement for Scrap Metal Recycler, was developed.

The pro forma cash flow statement for Scrap Metal Recycler gives a projected cash flow for one-year of $41,517, as shown in Exhibit 10-6. However, Scrap Metal Recycler will want to plan for extra financing for February when

A. Beginning cash for the present period is the ending cash from the previous period.

B. Sales receipts are the total amount of sales each month.

C. Paper supplies are calculated by taking 10.4 percent of sales each month.

D. Outside vendors for products are calculated by taking 6.2 percent of sales for each month.

E. Print supplies.

F. Freight is calculated at 1 percent of sales.

G. Salaries are based upon total amounts for all employees' base weekly pay multiplied by four weeks.

H. Payroll taxes are 9.82 percent of total salaries and paid quarterly.

I. Auto expense is calculated at 28 cents per mile and varies up to $1,000 per month.

J. Although bank charges will fluctuate, a fixed rate of $25 is used for planning purposes.

K. Commissions are based upon 10 percent of sales brought in by the manufacturer's representative who is responsible for an estimated 30 percent of sales.

L. When dues and subscriptions are paid or renewed for magazines and printing publications and organizations.

M. Workers' compensation is based upon a yearly figure of $2,675. That number is divided by twelve to derive $222 and is prepaid in the first month.

N. Insurance on the building is $5193; the figure fluctuates yearly. The first month consists of prepaid insurance for three months.

O. Interest expense is based upon a line of credit for an estimated annual cost of $1,517.

P. Health benefits are based upon a yearly amount of $24,175. One third of the total is paid in the first month.

Q. Office supplies expense is calculated by using a fixed amount.

R. The monthly lease payment on a printing press is $900 per month.

S. The monthly lease payment on a copier is $300 per month.

T. Postage is estimated at a fixed monthly cost of 1 percent of sales per month.

U. Professional fees for accounting and legal fees fluctuate depending upon how often they are incurred. These costs are broken down as follows: accounting $2,000; legal $2,000. Both are shown calculated on a monthly basis.

V. Rent is a fixed amount of $2,000 each month.

W. Repairs and maintenance are based upon 1.1 percent of sales.

X. Machinery repairs are based upon 1.3 percent of sales.

Y. Sales Tax is 6.5 percent.

Z. Telephone expense is 1 percent of monthly sales.

AA. Utilities are 2.4 percent of monthly sales.

BB. Advertising and promotion is based upon $3,720 annually for online advertising. Advertising for the *Reminder* is $136 and direct mail is $1,065.60; these are paid monthly.

CC. Income tax is paid quarterly at 8.00%.

Exhibit 10-5

Assumptions for Pro Forma Cash Flow Statements

Exhibit 10-6

Scrap Metal Recycler, Pro Forma Cash Flow Statement 2015 (Monthly)

Cash Receipts	January	February	March	April	May	June	July	August	September	October	November	December	Total
Beginning cash (A)	$7,000	−3,283	1,007	5,946	160	11,513	33,182	48,685	44,594	53,493	59,675	57,058	
Sales receipt (B)	28,000	36,300	40,000	43,000	47,000	58,200	59,000	60,000	47,300	39,300	35,700	35,400	
Total cash on hand	35,000	33,017	41,007	48,946	47,160	69,713	92,182	108,685	91,894	92,793	95,375	92,458	
Cash disbursements:													
Paper supplies (C)	3,640	3,434	4,265	5,090	4,905	7,250	9,587	11,303	9,557	9,650	9,919	9,616	88,216
Outside vendors (D)	1,736	2,251	2,480	2,666	2,914	3,608	3,658	3,720	2,933	2,437	2,213	2,195	32,810
Print supplies (E)	2,530	2,251	3,701	4,011	2,003	3,608	2,350	3,007	2,933	2,437	2,213	2,195	33,239
Freight (F)	280	363	400	430	470	582	590	600	473	393	357	354	5,292
Salaries (G)	9,000	9,000	9,000	9,000	9,000	3,000	9,000	9,000	6,000	3,000	9,000	9,000	93,000
Payroll taxes (H)	2,283	2,283	2,283	2,283	2,283	2,283	2,283	2,283	2,283	2,283	2,283	2,283	27,398
Auto expenses (I)	300	300	200	300	200	300	200	250	300	300	300	200	3,150
Bank charges (J)	25	25	25	25	25	25	25	25	25	25	25	25	300
Commissions (K)	840	1,089	1,200	1,290	1,410	1,746	1,770	1,800	1,419	1,179	1,071	1,062	15,876
Dues and subscriptions (L)	200	0	0	0	0	200	0	0	0	0	0	0	400
Workers' comp. ins. (M)	223	223	223	223	223	223	223	223	223	223	223	223	2,675
Insurance (N)	1,298	354	354	354	354	354	354	354	354	354	354	354	5,193
Interest expense (O)	126	126	126	126	126	126	126	126	126	126	126	126	1,517
Health benefits (P)	8,058	1,465	1,465	1,465	1,465	1,465	1,465	1,465	1,465	1,465	1,465	1,465	24,175
Office expense (Q)	75	75	75	75	75	75	75	75	75	75	75	75	900
Printing machine lease (R)	900	900	900	900	900	900	900	900	900	900	900	900	10,800
Copier lease (S)	300	300	300	300	300	300	300	300	300	300	300	300	3,600

Postage (T)	280	363	400	430	470	582	590	600	473	393	357	354	5,292
Professional fees (U)	333	333	333	333	333	333	333	333	333	333	333	333	4,000
Rent (V)	2,000	2,000	2,000	2,000	2,000	2,000	2,000	2,000	2,000	2,000	2,000	2,000	24,000
Repairs and maintenance (W)	308	399	440	473	517	640	649	660	520	432	393	389	5,821
Machinery repairs (X)	364	472	520	559	611	757	767	780	615	511	464	460	6,880
Sales tax (Y)	1,820	2,359.5	2,600	2,795	3,055	3,783	3,835	3,900	3,074.5	2,554.5	2,320.5	2,301	34,398
Taxes (other)	0	0	0	0	0	0	0	0	0	0	0	500	500
Telephone (Z)	280	363	400	430	470	582	590	600	473	393	357	354	5,292
Utility (AA)	672	871	960	1,032	1,128	1,397	1,416	1,440	1,135	943	857	850	12,701
Advertising and promotion (BB)	410	410	410	410	410	410	410	410	410	410	410	410	4,922
Income taxes (CC)	0	0	11,784	0	0	0	17,936	0	0	0	12,616	0	42,336
Total cash disbursement	38,283	32,011	35,061	48,786	35,648	36,530	43,497	64,091	38,401	33,118	38,317	50,941	494,683
Ending balance	($3,283)	$1,007	$5,946	$160	$11,513	$33,182	$48,685	$44,594	$53,493	$59,675	$57,058	$41,517	$41,517

its total disbursements are $3,283 greater than its total cash on hand. A provision might be for Scrap Metal Recycler to consider lowering some of its disbursements, such as paper and print supplies, in February. Another provision to consider is a loan of $3,611, which is the expected deficit of $3,283 plus 10 percent ($328) as a safety margin.

Based upon knowledge and experience acquired over time, the projections have a solid base as defined by the company's operating history. If you do not have an operating history or are dealing with a startup operation, you may arrive at the cash flow by using standard industry ratios, which are developed from data reported to trade associations or governmental units. The resulting "average" firm's financials are then used to develop ratios, which can be used as a benchmark against which to measure your firm's results or to predict operating results for a new firm. How to use ratios is covered in Chapter 12. Industry ratios for all North American Industry Classification System (NAICS) industries are available from trade associations, federal or state government agencies, and such commercial services as www.yahoo.com/finance and the **Risk Management Association (rma.org)**. Utilizing either method, you can develop a projected cash flow.

As long as income exceeds expenditures, you can feel fairly comfortable. However, there are times, even in an established business, when this would not be true. Highly seasonal businesses need to accumulate a great deal of inventory at a time when sales are traditionally slow in preparation for a very short, but hectic, selling season later in the year. To take an extreme example, you have to spend eleven months of the year growing and accumulating Christmas trees for sales that primarily are made in the first three weeks of December. From January through December, it is all expenses, no income; you either make enough money in December to more than cover your expenses in the next eleven months or have a shortfall (deficit).

Breakeven Analysis

Learning Outcome

4. Describe the role of a breakeven analysis in determining when the business actually makes a profit.

While the pro forma cash flow and pro forma statements may show your business to be profitable, it is helpful to know the point at which you actually began to make a profit. A useful tool to determine this point is breakeven analysis. Breakeven occurs when the volume of sales is sufficient to cover all fixed and variable costs; it is the point at which revenues equal costs. The breakeven point is that point at which the company neither makes a profit nor sustains a loss. At this point sales revenues equal the costs (expenses) necessary to generate them. This is useful information because the breakeven point also tells you the minimum level of sales you need to start or continue to operate. In addition, it illustrates the relationship between costs and revenue volume. As long as your forecasted sales are greater than the breakeven point, you may stay in business. If projected, or actual, sales drop below this point, you might decide against starting or continuing the business.

Determining the Breakeven Point

As the breakeven point shows the relationship between cost and volume, let's begin the analysis by identifying the components of breakeven analysis.

1. **Revenue** *is determined by multiplying the unit sales by the unit price.*
2. **Fixed costs** *are those expenses such as rent, loan payments, or insurance premiums that do not vary with the level of production or sales.*
3. **Variable costs** *are costs such as direct labor and raw materials that vary directly with the level of production or sales.*

While you recognize that some costs are semi-variable; that is, they change but not directly with the production level, for the purposes of this technique these costs must be divided into the appropriate fixed and variable components. Electricity, water, and those other cost components that are fixed for certain minimum amounts and then vary with usage are such examples.

Assume that:

Units sold = 10,000
Sales Price = $20.00
Sales Revenue = $200,000 (10,000 units × $20 each)
Variable cost = $40,000
Variable cost per unit = $40,000/10,000 units = $4.00
Fixed costs = $20,000

Using the BEP formula:

BEP (breakeven point) = fixed cost/(1−variable cost/sales revenue)
BEP = 20,000/1−(40,000/200,000) = $25,000 or 1,250 units

Taxation

Everyone recognizes that living in an organized society imposes a financial cost. A government must pay for roads, defense, Social Security, and unemployment benefits. The government, which is not an inherent producer of wealth, can only pay for societal benefits by taking (taxing) money from the wealth created by producers (business organizations) and redistributing it elsewhere. Although few people question the need for taxes, volumes have been published on the proper size of the "benefit" package; that is, how much should be taken from the economy in taxes and who should benefit from these taxes? Ultimately there are two sources of tax revenue, individuals and business.

As April 15 comes close, entrepreneurs, as taxpayers, see the full impact of taxes on their business and individual incomes. The imposition of taxation means reduced business and individual spending. While it is true that the money the government takes out of the economy it returns in the form of benefits, often those paying taxes do not receive an equal share of benefits. The more money paid in taxes, the less they have to spend on machinery, equipment, research, personnel, or just plain consumption. The higher the tax, the less investment, savings, or spending the business can do. Taxes are a vital consideration in business planning and therefore it is important to know what taxes must be paid. These taxes can and will affect the survival, growth, success, and viability of the organization.

Income taxes are only one form of tax. Taxes come in a variety of "shapes and sizes" and are payable on three levels: federal, state, and local. Not all forms of taxes are required at all levels, but you should be familiar with some of the various tax categories. For additional information, refer to the **IRS Publication 535, Deducting Business Expenses** for a complete review of deductible expenses (www.irs.gov/publications/p535/index.html).

Remember, the taxes you pay are based on the records you maintain. If government deems that you have paid insufficient taxes or has some question about your taxes, it can, and will, examine your company's financial records. For your own protection, and to make certain that you don't overpay, you should keep adequate and detailed records. Any time you cannot document your numbers, the IRS can disallow deductions and increase your tax bill. Accurate record-keeping also provides advantages for you as a manager. Additionally, should you need credit, it is a rare bank or venture capital company that will lend you money without examining your records quite carefully.

While some taxes seem quite straightforward, taxes, by their very existence, impact upon your business decisions. A complete explanation of how taxes influence your decisions is far beyond the scope of this book and certainly subject to the fact that, as tax laws change, their impact on decision-making shifts.[18]

Common Business Taxes

Learning Outcome

5. Identify the most common forms of taxation.

- **Income taxes.** Income taxes are those taxes levied on the net income of the business. Generally these are derived by applying a percentage determined by the taxing agency to net income.
- **Social Security taxes.** Social Security taxes are taxes levied on employers and employees to provide for individual retirement. As a self-employed person, you would pay twice as much as an employee. For 2013, the Social Security tax rate is 15.3 percent on net income up to $113,700. This includes a 12.4 percent Social Security tax plus a 2.9 percent Medicare tax. Although you do not pay Social Security taxes on net earnings of more than $113,700, you must continue to pay the Medicare portion.[19]
- **Unemployment taxes.** Unemployment taxes are collected in order to insure those individuals who have lost their job. The employer pays a percentage of the payroll into a fund that the state then distributes to the temporarily

jobless as a weekly stipend. The amount a person receives and the duration of the payments varies from state to state.

■ **Sales taxes.** Sales taxes are determined by a percentage of the sales price of goods and perhaps services purchased. These are general taxes and are remitted to the state or city levying the tax.

■ **Property and excise taxes.** Property and excise taxes are those taxes based on ownership and are generally a percentage of the assessed value of the item. These taxes are levied on personal or real property (such as land), automobiles, boats, inventories, gasoline, to name a few of the taxable categories.

Tax Deductions and Profitability

Because taxes are based on the profits of your operations, you should be well acquainted with the class of expenditures allowed for deduction. The more legal expenses you can deduct, the lower will be your profit and the fewer taxes you will pay. Many entrepreneurs are unfamiliar with allowable deductions and thus may pay more taxes than necessary. The IRS accepts as deductible expenses those that are ordinary and necessary to the operation of your business. Knowing what deductions you are legally entitled to, plus understanding the contents of your business records, should enable you to identify all the expenses allowed in order to minimize your tax bill.[20]

Cost of Goods Sold

As indicated, COGS includes all costs in making or buying the goods or services you sell. Typically, this represents costs associated with the production process such as material, supplies, labor, freight, and overhead. The first four costs are direct costs; that is, they vary directly with the volume produced. Other indirect costs such as overhead and general administrative costs cannot be attributed directly to the production process except by allocation. The more accurately you recognize all production costs, the more likely your taxes will be minimized.

Salaries and Wages

Salaries are the compensation you pay your employees for the service they perform. All compensation must be ordinary, necessary, and reasonable. Further, you cannot pay for work not performed. You can deduct all compensation paid and incurred in the current taxable year.

Rent or Lease

Rent is the cost to you for the use of property. There have been, and still are, qualifications to meet if you deduct the part of your home that is used as an office. It is best to consult a tax attorney or accountant to make certain you are in compliance.

Depreciation

Depreciation is the yearly cost of the use of an asset with a life longer than one year. Any asset with a life of one year or less may be deducted as a business expense in the year of its use. Assets with a life of longer than one year may only have a portion of their total costs deducted. Here the government has permitted you to choose between several methods of depreciation. The more you depreciate an asset in any time period by shortening its depreciable life, the higher your expenses and the lower your taxes. Again, this question is complex and you should seek expert advice.

Automobile Expenses

The IRS permits you to deduct the costs of an automobile, other vehicles, or vessels used in carrying on normal business activities. In the case of an automobile, only business-related expenses may be deducted. You can generally deduct either the actual auto expense or the standard mileage deduction.[21]

Bad Debts

The IRS permits you to deduct as a business expense any uncollectible receivables you may incur. The amount you lost is a bad debt. This loss must have been real and you must be able to demonstrate that you have taken steps to collect the debt. If you have bad debts and can document them as expenses, your profit will be affected.[22]

Travel and Entertainment

The IRS.gov Web site has detailed descriptions of what travel and entertainment expenses can be deducted. In summary, a part of the cost of conducting your business may involve being away from the main office either buying or selling. The costs of being away from home for more than a day qualify for deductions. Be aware that these travel costs must be reasonable and ordinary or they will not be allowed. Unlike meals and entertainment that are limited by 50 percent, travel expenses are 100 percent deductible. These include airfare, hotel, rental cars, valet, taxis, trains, and tolls. Consider all of your travels last year that may have involved a meeting with a client, vendor, or shareholder; a training session; a visit to a competitor's facility or store—the list goes on. Keep good records so that you do not lose anything to which you are entitled.[23]

Personal Application

4. What type of tax deductions will you expect to take for the small-business plan you are writing for this course?

Interest

While you may not deduct interest, the charge for borrowed money, your company may deduct the interest it pays on loans and any borrowed funds necessary to operate the business. There are some exclusions to this general rule. Check the IRS regulations frequently.

Taxes

You are allowed to deduct taxes you pay to state, local, and foreign governments as business expenses. Taxes include sales taxes, property taxes, which are taxes based on the assessed value of property, and employment taxes such as Social Security, Federal Unemployment Taxes (FUTA), and state unemployment taxes. All of these taxes must be calculated and paid or you are violating the law.

Miscellaneous Expenses

These are expenses incurred in operating your company, some of which may be specific to your organization. You should identify all such expenses and deduct them. The questions of which miscellaneous expenses are allowable and which are not, and to what extent you may deduct these expenses are complex, and should be discussed with your tax advisor.

Effects of Taxes on the Form of Ownership

Chapter 5 discussed the differences among forms of ownership. The owners of sole proprietorships, partnerships, S corporations, and limited liability companies (LLCs) pay personal income taxes, no business taxation. Under the C corporation form of ownership, the company pays business taxes. If the company then declares dividends, these are also taxed but at personal income tax rates—double taxation.

So the S corporation and LLC possess limited liability and tax benefits worth examining because they permit you to pass through the corporate structure all revenues and expenses accruing to the corporation so that they can be taxed on your individual income tax return. This allows you to bypass double taxation and thereby to minimize your tax bill. For example, if you choose the C corporation form of organization, its profits are taxed at corporate tax rates. If the company then declares dividends, these are taxed at personal tax rates. If your corporate profit is $10,000 and corporate tax rates are 40 percent, you pay $4,000 in taxes. Of the $6,000 remaining, if you declare dividends of $6,000 you pay personal taxes of $1,680 dollars (28 percent of $6,000). Your total tax bill is $5,680. Using the S or LLC, all income is treated as personal income and, using the 28 percent tax bracket, you are liable for only $2,800 dollars in taxes, a savings of $2,880. Exhibit 10-7 highlights this difference. Tax savings alone is a powerful reason to use the S or LLC form of organization because it limits your liability and taxes. However, as the tax laws change, the organization form you choose can make a big difference in your tax liability.

The previous discussions should serve to acquaint you with some of the tax issues to consider in your decision-making. It is best to seek expert advice because mistakes can be costly.

Exhibit 10-7

Comparison of Tax
Liability from $10,000
Profit

C Corporation	S Corporation/Limited Liability
$10,000 profit	$10,000 profit
.40, corporate tax rate	.28, personal tax rate
4,000, tax paid	2,800, tax paid
6,000, dividend paid	6,000, dividend paid
.28, tax at personal rate (included above)	.00, percent n/a:
1,680, tax paid on dividend	0, tax paid on dividend
$5,680, total taxes paid	$2,800, total taxes paid

Other Options for Starting a New Venture, and Entrepreneurial Behavior

In this last section we discuss some of the major differences in starting a new venture compared with the other options to becoming an entrepreneur in regards to the development of an accounting system. We also discuss how to engage in entrepreneurial behavior as an employee.

Buying an Existing Business, Franchise, or Leasing Rights

Buying an Existing Business

The existing business should already have an existing accounting system in place. However, has the accounting system been updated annually and computerized whenever possible? Does it have an accountant that audits their books?

Buying a Franchise

If you buy a franchise the franchisor will have a prototype financial system in place at all their other stores. The new franchisee owner will find it easier to track all their financial costs using the system provided by the franchisor.

Buying Licensing Rights

If you buy a license, you are starting a new business and will have to report the sale and profitability of adding the licensed product line of products.

Starting a Corporate Venture

If you operate out of headquarters, you may not be charged expenses for rent, telephone, mail, utilities, and other services. However, depending on the size and sophistication of your parent, if you are not given a direct expense, you will most likely be charged an overhead rate to cover these and other such costs.

If you are charged direct or overhead costs, be sure you clearly understand these costs and make sure they are reasonable. For example, if the parent production department is making the product for you, how much is it charging you per unit? To know if the cost is reasonable, you can check with outside manufacturers to find out how much they would charge you to make the product for you. If the cost is significantly lower, you may be able to negotiate a lower overhead cost from the manufacturing department, or you could request to outsource the production to save money. The same case can be made if the parent company is selling the product for you and charging you an unreasonable fee. Also, if you are being charged rent, is the expense reasonable? Again, check with outside sources to see if you can get a lower rate.

Starting a Nonprofit

Nonprofit organizations exist to pursue missions that address the needs of society—instead of trying to make a profit. Nonprofits have several distinctive terms that reflect the manner in which they receive and disburse funds. Remember that they cannot price their services high enough to cover all of their costs and so, while they take in money from fees they charge, they make up the deficit by fundraising (see Chapter 2 for more details of fundraising). While both profit and nonprofit organizations have to show an excess of income versus expenses on their income statements in order to continue functioning, a profit-making firm uses the equation: revenues minus costs or expenses equal profits. The bottom line in the financials is called *profits*. A nonprofit also shows a bottom line but it is called *fund balance*. Nonprofits need and make great use of volunteers and most nonprofits cannot exist without them; therefore, it is a number that is important to potential givers. Although they are not used in the financials, volunteer hours are displayed somewhere in the financial report, such as in a footnote.

Entrepreneurial Behavior

If you are not interested in starting a new venture, as an employee you can engage in entrepreneurial behavior by designing a more efficient or computerized accounting system. Entrepreneurial employees can use a computerized software program, such as **Peachtree Accounting** produced by **Sage Software**, to upgrade the accounting system at their current employer.

Take it to the Net

Visit www.routledge.com/cw/Lussier for the book's companion Web site, where you can:

- use learning aids, including taking a quiz;
- find links to resources in this chapter, as well as other links including videos;
- learn about and start the following activities: Continuing Integrated Case, Your Ninety-Second New Venture Pitch, the Paper Clip Entrepreneurship Challenge, College Entrepreneurial Spirit Award, and the Community Entrepreneurial Spirit Award.

Chapter Review and Summary

This summary lists the learning outcomes from the chapter and their answers.

1. **Explain the importance and purpose of an accounting system**

   Operating a business means that it is important for you to know how to keep accurate and detailed business records so that you can prepare financial statements from your records. Only by using this information in the proper way, and presenting it in a commonly accepted manner, will you be able to truly understand your company's performance. The primary purpose of the accounting function is its use as a management tool that enables you to understand your company's performance and to serve as an aid in decision-making. The first task you or your accountant will perform is to establish a chart of accounts, which is a list of all of the accounts to which charges are made that is tailored to your business. The final service the accountant should perform is to recommend a system of internal control to prevent fraud. All the accounts of your business are tracked in the general ledger, which is a book or computerized listing in which entries are made concerning all of a firm's financial transactions.

2. **Identify the importance of a balance sheet and an income statement and their three parts**

   The balance sheet is important because it is a snapshot view of the financial value of the firm. The three parts of the balance sheet are (1) assets, which are a tangible item or intangible rights owned by the firm, equal (=) (2) liabilities, which are the obligations or debts that the firm owes and (3) net worth or owner's equity (assets minus liabilities), which is what remains and is the number that brings the equation into balance. The income statement is important because it presents the financial performance as a profit or loss from operations during a given time period. The three parts of the income statement are (1) revenues minus (–) (2) expenses equals (=) (3) profit or loss.

3. **State the importance of a pro forma cash flow statement and its two parts**

   Cash flow is important because a company without cash, even though it appears to be a good company, cannot survive because it cannot pay its bills when they are due. The two parts of a cash flow statement are (1) the actual dollars coming into the business as revenues and (2) the money going out of the business to pay its bills. Depreciation or any noncash items (accounts receivable) are not included in the cash flow statement. This statement is also important because we use a cash flow pro forma statement to translate the business plan into future or projected dollars of income and expenses. It forces you to move systematically and logically through your plan, attaching a monetary value to every step. The act of preparing the pro forma cash flow will help determine your financial needs.

4. **Describe the role of a breakeven analysis in determining when the business actually makes a profit**

   Breakeven occurs when the volume of sales is sufficient to cover all fixed and variable costs; it is the point at which revenues equal costs. A useful tool to determine this point is breakeven analysis. The breakeven point tells you the point at which the business actually can begin to make a profit.

5. Identify the most common forms of taxation

Income taxes are those taxes levied on the net income of the business. You are also responsible for paying your share of an employee's Social Security taxes, which are taxes levied on employers and employees to provide for individual retirement, and unemployment taxes, which are collected in order to insure those individuals who have lost their job. Sales taxes are determined by a percentage of the sales price of goods and perhaps services purchased. Taxes are determined on property and any excise taxes, which are taxes based on the assessed value of property.

6. Explain the effect of taxes on the form of ownership

Under the C corporation form of ownership, the company pays business taxes. If the company then declares dividends, these are also taxed but at personal income tax rates—double taxation. The owners of sole proprietorships, partnerships, S corporations, and LLCs pay personal income taxes, no business taxation.

7. Define the thirty-six key terms found in this chapter

accounts payable

accounts receivable

accumulative depreciation

asset

balance sheet

breakeven analysis

buildings

cash

chart of accounts

cost of goods sold (COGS)

current assets

current liabilities

depreciation

fixed-asset list

fixed assets

general ledger

gross profits

income statement (profit and loss statement)

income taxes

intangible assets

leasehold improvements

liabilities

long-term liabilities

merchandise inventory

net worth/owner's equity

notes payable

prepaid expenses

pro forma statements

profits (loss)

property and excise taxes

retained earnings

sales taxes

social security taxes

supplies

tangible assets

unemployment taxes

Review and Discussion Questions

Be sure to explain all your answers.

1. Why is it necessary to keep good financial records? List and explain some of the reasons.

2. Do you feel that every entrepreneur or business owner needs an accountant? Justify your answer.

3. Assuming that you have an accountant, do your year-end statements tell you how to run your business? How much can your accountant help you in making business decisions? Explain your reasoning.

4. What records are required in a good accounting system?

5. Define the following: balance sheet, income statement, and cash flow statement.

6. What is the relationship between the balance sheet and the income statement?

7. How would the accounting system record a materials purchase of $40,000? Which accounts would be affected and why? Illustrate with an example.

8. How would the accounting system record a sale of stock? Which accounts would be affected and why? Illustrate with an example.

9. It is not unusual for a firm to show losses for the year, but still have cash in the bank. Explain this apparent contradiction.

10. Your accountant has just filed your company's tax return, which shows a profit for the past year, yet you don't have any cash to pay your bills. Is this possible? Why is this possible and what does this mean for your future?

11. Define "pro forma statements." Why would you want these statements? How can they be used?

12. Assume you are a bank loan officer and you realize that future projections can be nothing more than best guesses. If you had to choose between a business with a well-developed set of financials and another great sure-fire opportunity that lacks financial data, which firm would you choose to fund and why?

13. As taxes increase, what effect would this have on the health of the business?

14. How important are taxes in business planning? Explain your position.

15. Identify the different taxes that a small business would have to pay.

Application Exercises

When doing these exercises, be sure to select a specific business where applicable, preferably one where you presently or previously work(ed) or a business you would like to own someday. If this is not possible, pick a specific organization to which you will refer. Be sure to identify the organization by name. Limit your answers to one or two pages per exercise.

1. Interview several small businesses. Report on their accounting systems.

2. Would you say that these businesses exhibit a high or low level of sophistication with respect to their accounting systems? Explain the meaning of your findings in a report.

3. Are these, or other businesses like them, profitable without regard to their accounting systems? Explain your position.

4. Interview a local small business and ask if there is a cash flow pro forma for the next year. If so, present this and its assumptions to the class. If this is impossible, choose a well-defined type of business and prepare, using Standard Industrial Classification (SIC) codes and Risk Management Association (RMA) figures, a cash flow pro forma for the business.

5. Interview a local bank loan officer to ascertain the degree of familiarity with small-business accounting systems. What conclusions can you draw from your discussion?

6. Explain whether this information agrees with your inquiries in questions 1 and 2. Does this describe small business in general?

7. Interview a CPA who specializes in or consults with small businesses and, considering the information you acquired from questions 1, 2, and 6, ask how he or she compiles the year-end statements. How accurate are these statements likely to be? Report on your conclusions.

8. Prepare you own pro forma cash flow for the next two years on a monthly basis. Indicate the assumptions upon which you based your projections.

Application Situations

1. Harbor City Chemical Company

The Harbor City Chemical Company has manufactured chemical cleaning agents for fifty years. These chemicals have traditionally been manufactured using relatively the same equipment. The packaging of the products, however, requires three sizes of containers. Each container size is handled by a different product line. Small-size containers are filled with highly automated and mechanized equipment while the large (drum) size containers are filled by equipment that dates back to the founding of the company.

Traditionally, all the company's equipment has been carried on the books as "equipment" and depreciation taken as the total amount of equipment on hand. Recently, the Grand Chemical Company has considered buying Harbor City.

1. What information does the Grand Chemical Company need to know with respect to the equipment before it can make a purchase decision?

2. How would Grand Chemical Company go about establishing a capital equipment list?

3. What would be the significance of the capital equipment list in determining the profitability of each of the filling lines? Of the company as a whole?

2. Dan Espinosa

On a recent trip to Spain, Dan Espinosa happened to visit a series of small towns and villages where they manufactured silk print fabrics the likes of which could not be found in the U.S. Upon returning, Dan convinced a close friend, Matt Ross, to found a business whose objective was to import the silk fabric. Dan was certain of profits from this venture. Both of the men agreed that the corporate form of organization was best and the Madan Company was founded. Neither Dan nor Matt realized that they were subject to many different taxes and hadn't given this aspect of the business much thought. Dan seemed vaguely to recall something about an S corporation and taxation, but he wasn't certain. Matt thought that the best way to mitigate the tax problem was not to keep any records and therefore they would not owe taxes.

1. Explain to Dan what he should have known about an S corporation and how tax structures should affect his decision using the S corporate form.

2. Is Matt's thinking correct? Could this approach lead to trouble? How would you advise Matt to set up, keep, and maintain corporate records? Which records would be important in determining Madan's corporate tax liability?

Case

Accounting Paperwork

Entrepreneurs normally forget a key component when writing their business plan—accounting and tax issues. It certainly is more exciting to think of a great idea for a product or service. It is most likely fairly exciting to build a small business out of the initial idea. But, it probably feels like the process of accounting and figuring out taxes should take place after the first year of being in business. However, a new business should prepare by hiring an accountant to help with developing a solid accounting system. Starting your own business means there will be many complex forms to fill out because you will need to meet federal and state tax codes. Tax codes become more complicated every year—not easier. For example, entrepreneurs underestimate how much time and work is involved in processing payroll taxes.

Many small-business people, in retrospect, wish they had hired a good accountant as early as possible. The tax issues and forms require a large amount of time and knowledge to complete. Computer software can be helpful—but the software might also be too big for your small business. Eventually, the computer software might also be too small if your business grows quickly. Finding either a good accountant, or the proper accounting software, can take time and money. It might be wise to keep an accountant on a retainer of about $150 a month to be able to access the accountant's expertise as quickly as possible.[24]

A well-organized record-keeping process is the first step to properly completing accounting paperwork. A computerized system is necessary to make the entire process more efficient. However, a paper trail should also exist that uses the same accounting system, forms, accounts, and categories. That will make sure your paper and computerized accounting systems are working together to better organize the accounting process.

A separate file should be created to collect all tax-related documents. You should have an active tax file to collect your current tax-related documents. You should also have an archived file from previous tax years that should be separate from your current tax file. Creating a tax folder will allow you to be better prepared to file taxes well before April 15 every year.[25]

Think it over.

1. Why do entrepreneurs often fail to hire an accountant when they start their new business?

2. What financial area in the case appears to take the most time for entrepreneurs to properly follow?

Global Case—Taxes in the Middle East

Taxes in the Middle East tend to be lower than in other areas in the world. Why are taxes so low and how does it impact the small entrepreneur?

Tehran's grand bazaar (a marketplace where trade is conducted) went on strike in protest at government plans to increase taxes there. But it's not just about money. The small-business merchants don't fully accept the idea of letting inspectors pry into their accounts.

In Yemen there is a long-term economic crisis. The government is battling to enforce a sales tax increase against great resistance. Currently, Yemeni businesses pay only about 20 percent of what they are supposed to pay.

The Arab oil producers' taxes account for only about 5 percent of gross domestic product. Taxes rise to 17 percent in the non-oil Middle Eastern countries. Both sets of percentages are very low compared with Germany (39 percent), Italy (41 percent), and Britain (37 percent). The average Total Tax Rate for the Middle East region is 23.6 percent, well below the world average of 44.7 percent and the lowest of any region.[26]

The main reason taxes are lower is because many of the Middle Eastern countries have sources of income other than taxes—such as the oil-producing countries. For example, Egypt benefits from business related to the Suez Canal. The Suez Canal Authority grants Egypt a great deal of authority over global oil supply and transport. Egypt's military had to make safeguarding the Suez Canal a priority—even in the midst of serious political unrest in Cairo.[27]

Taxes are never popular, and the higher the taxes are, the more likely it is that people will demand a say in how the money is spent. It was the cry of "no taxation without representation" that spurred the American revolution in the 18th century, and a quarrel between King Charles I and his parliament over tax that helped to trigger the English revolution in the 17th century.[28] Higher taxes normally act as a force towards democracy. However, where taxes are low the pressure for democracy is less.

But taxes are not just about raising money. The kind of tax system a country has tells us a lot about the relationship between the people and the state. Raising taxes efficiently requires political effort to secure taxpayer consent. The ability of a government to properly collect taxes is a sign that the country has a competent bureaucracy. As Oliver Wendell Holmes, Jr., U.S. Supreme Court Justice, stated, "Taxes are what we pay for civilized society."[29]

Think it over.

1. Do you think small businesses would rather pay direct taxes (such as income tax) or indirect taxes (such as import and export taxes)?

2. As a small-business person, do you think paying taxes will help to build a democratic society?

Writing Your Business Plan

You (or in teams) can write a business plan during the semester. There are questions at the end of each chapter to help guide you through the thinking and analyzing process. Appendix B has a sample business plan you can use as a template for developing your own new venture business plan.

Since this is Chapter 10, the goal is to add information about the accounting practices used by your new business.

Highlighted Sections of the Business Plan (Chapters 1–10)

1. **The Executive Summary** is written last—but placed first in the business plan. You have to wait until you are finished with the business plan to properly write the executive summary.

2. **Introduction:**
   A. **Background of the business:** Includes a short review of its name, address (or addresses if there is more than one location), telephone number(s), email address, Web site address, hours of operation, and a brief history (if any). You want to state when the business was started or will be started.
   B. **Management credentials and organization structure:** It is common to list all the business's key managers and their duties and responsibilities, with their qualifications.
   C. **Form of ownership:** Will your business be a sole proprietorship, partnership, or corporation and how will any profits be distributed?

3. **Strategy Formulation:**
   A. **Mission:** What is the organization's purpose or reason for being (covered in Chapter 3)? The mission section of the business plan includes your business model (covered in Chapter 4), which can include a broad description of your present and future products and services to be offered. In the strategy section, it is not necessary to list all the products and services; they are listed under the marketing section of the business plan and were discussed in Chapter 6.

   B. **Objectives (prioritized):** What does your organization want to accomplish?
   C. **Environmental analysis:** It includes an analysis of the internal environment (which includes the mission and objectives) and its external environment resulting in a SWOT analysis.

4. **The Marketing Function:**
   A. **The marketing plan:** Your marketing plan must identify your target customers and product feasibility (Chapter 4) by using marketing research to better understand your industry and marketplace.
   B. **The marketing mix:** You need to include the 4 Ps of marketing in your marketing plan. What is your product? At what price point will you sell your product? Where (place) will you sell your product? And, how will you promote your product?

5. **Location and Layout:**
   A. **Location:** You want to consider such general location factors such as: (1) proximity to the market; (2) transportation facilities; (3) availability of raw materials; (4) labor supply; (5) community attitude; (6) water power; (7) land costs; (8) taxes; (9) specialized communities; (10) climatic conditions; (11) potential sister plants or warehouse; (12) the question of urban, suburban, or rural sites; and (13) how these factors affect specific site selection as either a home-based, Internet, or traditional manufacturing or retail location.
   B. **Layout:** Having committed to a location, you must then develop a layout. The layout is an arrangement of the physical facilities in the most efficient manner for specific business, for the interior in order to maximize profitability. You should draw a diagram of the layout you expect to utilize in your business.

6. **The Production/Operations Function:**
   A. **Production process:** What is your operational plan to transform inputs into outputs?
   B. **Quality:** What level of quality will you expect from your finished product?

7. **The Human Resources Function:**
   A. Who are the members of your new venture team (founder, investors, lenders, mentors, lawyer, accountant, banker, insurance agent, and any consultants)?
   B. How do you plan on using the human resources management process to attract, develop, and retain employees.
   C. What is your plan for management succession and an exit strategy?

8. **The Financing Function:**
   A. A necessary step before starting your venture requires that you develop all the records, chart of accounts, and accounting processes. You must be able to track the results of your business in real time as it operates. Only if you are able to do so can you determine its profitability. If you have appropriately developed your record-keeping system, it will provide the framework for your financial statements and tax reports. Review the record-keeping process you will develop for your business.
   B. Develop a pro forma income statement, balance sheet, and cash flow statement.

9. **Controls**

10. **Appendix**

Part III

Financing and Controlling the New Venture

Chapter 11

Sources of Funds
Where do You Get the Money?

In this chapter you will learn the answers to two questions vital to business survival and prosperity. You need to know: (1) how to estimate the amount of capital you need to fund an entrepreneurial startup venture or cover the operating costs of an established company and (2) the sources you can use to raise the necessary funds. Remember, the financial plan is only as good as the strategy and marketing plans.

Learning Outcomes

After completing this chapter you should be able to:

1. Describe the three capital needs questions and types of capital to fund a new business venture;
2. Identify sources of equity financing;
3. Identify sources of debt financing;
4. List bootstrap financing opportunities;
5. Discuss sources of government funding;
6. Define the twelve key terms identified in this chapter.

Entrepreneur Profile—Vince Occhipinti, General Partner with Woodside Fund

We begin each chapter with a short bio of an entrepreneur and provide a link so you can learn more about the person and their business venture. Short 3–5-minute videos of each entrepreneur can be found at the PBS Small Business School at: www.smallbusinessschool.org/. You can read about Vince Occhipinti at: http://smallbusiness school.org/page1988.html?epid=211. You can learn more about the Woodside Fund at: www. woodsidefund.com/.

Funding for your new business can be from your own money, the money you could borrow from friends and family, an angel investor, a bank loan, cash flow from an existing business, suppliers, or, you could go after venture capital. So, what is venture capital and how does an entrepreneur attract it?

Venture capital is money invested in a new idea by a group of professional investors who are probably handling other people's money and not their own. So, a venture capitalist is much like a stock broker who is looking for the right investment for his or her customers.

Vince Occhipinti is a general partner of the Woodside Fund. A venture capitalist looks for companies in large demand-driven markets that have a talented management team, a differentiating technology that is truly special, and willingness to work as a partnership. Vince pointed out that they will invest in less than 1 percent of the deals they see.

No one wants to be a passive investor. The entrepreneur has to be willing to take suggestions and be a team player. Also, there must be an exit strategy. An exit strategy is important to the venture capitalist because it is the way the entrepreneur repays the venture capitalist. If the venture capitalists invest 1 million dollars in a company, they want to know when they can get their investment back plus return on investment (ROI). In fact, often venture capitalists will seek as much as 49 percent ownership of the company in the first round of funding. You can be sure that if a venture capitalist is willing to risk losing his or her money, the venture capitalist would only be happy if he or she is able to make more money than the stock market. To keep the venture capital community happy, the entrepreneur must be meeting and surpassing all their projections for development, deployment, sales, and growth. Some founders will go through two or three rounds of funding before explosive sales.

Think it over.

1. Do you have a business idea that would be interesting to a venture capitalist?
2. Why will some entrepreneurs go through two or three rounds of funding?

The Interrelationship Between the Financial Function and the Other Business Plan Components

The interrelationship between all the functional areas of the firm (accounting, financial, marketing, production/operations, and personnel) is rarely more evident than when you consider the finance function.[1] All areas have demands. Production requires material, equipment, and personnel; marketing needs to advertise and promote new and old products. The demands of all functional areas are predicated upon the availability of money and it is the finance function that must determine the organization's financial needs.[2]

Once financial needs are known, it is the job of finance to find and tap sources for these funds.[3] How well finance is able to do its job affects every functional area. Too little cash flow or errors in determining financial needs can force cutbacks in any or all other functional areas.[4] Your company cannot maximize profitability without the appropriate resources.[5]

Determining Capital Needs

Small business provides access to a lifestyle, independence, and monetary return that cannot be achieved elsewhere.[6] Led on by these thoughts, many people start their own business; they open a store, repair shop, or small manufacturing facility. At the outset, most people have limited financial resources to start the business.[7] Some don't consider that such an enterprise needs financial backing, but finance is one of the necessary resources required for new ventures to start.[8] The statement "It takes money to make money" is true. In order to start and to survive in a business, you must have the resources.[9]

You need to know: (1) how to estimate the amount of capital you need to fund an entrepreneurial startup venture or cover the operating costs of an established company and (2) the sources you can use to raise the necessary funds. The second question of determining sources to raise necessary funds is now addressed. There are three major classifications of capital from which you can choose. The three major types of financing are discussed in this section.

Short-Term Capital

Why would you need short-term capital? **Short-term capital** *is funds that are borrowed for less than one year.* It is used when companies have expended their initial capital. Many business owners often overlook the need for this type of capital, which develops because the owner has neglected the task of completing a projected cash flow budget statement (see Chapter 10). For example, every business has certain expenses that arise in one month and not in another such as an insurance payment or an excessively high heating bill. If this expense is not factored into the monthly budget, you will fall short of funds.

A popular type of debt financing used by small business is trade credit, *which is obtained from creditors.* Trade credit is paid within thirty to sixty days depending upon the type of business. Trade credit may also be obtained from a commercial bank, *which may be a good source for a short-term loan source.*

Early-Stage Capital

Early-stage capital, often referred to as **intermediate capital,** *is funds to be paid back within a period of five years.* The need for early-stage financing usually arises as the need for working capital increases, or if accounts receivable rises and sales volume is heading upward. In any case, the business must be at the breakeven point. For example, a business owner may decide to construct an addition on an existing structure. Projects such as these require a large amount of money, the repayment of which has to be stretched out over a longer period of time. A short-term loan to finance these needs would pinch cash flow, thereby hurting the business. Equipment loans represent a form of intermediate capital financing. These loans are paid within five years on an installment basis.

Long-Term Capital

Long-term capital *covers long-term projects lasting longer than five years and includes fixed assets and real-estate purchases, expensive machinery, and franchise financing.* Expensive machinery such as numerically controlled milling machines can take as long as ten to fifteen years to be paid off. Long-term capital is capital that is borrowed for more than five years and is mostly used for major expansions or the acquisition of very expensive equipment.

Capital Requirements

A well-prepared assessment of capital needs and sources is an essential step. The relationships between working capital, fixed-asset needs, and cash flows are sometimes confusing to the novice business person. Often, the entrepreneur overlooks the need to translate plans into dollars. As a result, the business owner grossly underestimates the current and future requirements for capital. Financial hardships and strained relationships among all parties involved are the consequence of failing to formulate a capital requirement plan, which is the cornerstone for estimating money needs.

The entrepreneur should ask these basic questions before initiating a search for capital: (1) How much capital will I need? (2) What type of capital is required? (3) Where can I get the funds? The rest of this chapter focuses on this last and very important question because, without the resources, you can't start the business.[10] Two major types of financing are equity and debt financing.[11] With equity financing you use your own resources and/or give away part of your ownership and profits to get them. With debt financing, you borrow resources and pay them back, usually with interest. We will discuss equity financing in the next section, followed by debt financing.

Sources of Equity Financing

Learning Outcome

2. Identify sources of equity financing.

Many firms fail because of the lack of adequate startup capital.[12] When you seek equity capital for a venture, the traditional paths of financing are usually followed. The path starts out with your personal stake of money and other assets. Because initial capital is typically inadequate,[13] the path may branch out to a number of traditional sources of external investor equity capital,[14] such as friends, relatives, partnerships, or the sale of capital stock. Below, we will explain these traditional paths. Private equity financing has become an increasingly international phenomenon.[15] To raise funds, you need to have a good business or elevator pitch[16] (see Chapter 3).

The Elevator Pitch

This skill-builder puts you in the venture capitalist position. You will watch an elevator pitch from the Internet and discuss if investors would or wouldn't invest in the new venture. The link for Emily McHugh's designer laptop bags, the elevator pitch for this chapter, can be found at: www.nbcnews.com/video/your-business/31875791#31875791.

Think about it.

1. What score do you give the pitch?

Great product idea and pitch		Terrible product idea and pitch	
4	3	2	1

2. Would you fund the 10 million dollars Emily asked for?
3. How would you improve the pitch?

Seed Financing

Personal Application

1. Name three people you know with deep pockets who could invest in your business opportunity.

Typically, *the small business owner has saved a small amount of personal funds that is often referred to as ownership capital, or seed financing.* Such a venture is generally at a pre-revenue stage and seed capital is needed for research and development, to cover initial operating expenses until a product or service can start generating revenue, and to attract the attention of venture capitalists.[17] Seventy percent of entrepreneurs use their own savings as the main source of funding.[18] Usually, this amount of capital is too small to start a successful venture so external seed money is a good option.[19] However, if initial profits are high enough, the venture may be able to thrive on a small initial amount of seed money.

Investors will be more willing to finance the venture if you assume the same amount of risk. A relative or friend is the most typical source for a stake of money. However, this first choice for equity capital may not be the best source. The "right" investor should be one who is fully aware of the supply of funds needed to boost the business into a fairly stable operating state. The right individual will be aware of risks, and have additional funds to provide if needed. Also, the "right" investor will have goals that are compatible with yours. Ideally, the investor should have experience with the nature of the business, and be able to offer guidance. As you see, a person who you may know may not be the best choice.

Savings

What percentage of your personal savings should you put into your business? One alternative is to decide to take a big bet on your business by using all your personal savings and borrowing from your house and/or retirement account. However, this alternative is very risky.

The less risky option is to use considerably less of your savings and find a way to make up the difference. For example, the entrepreneur should keep money in the bank. This money could be your backup money just in case something unexpected arises. You might need the money to pay for a surprise bill or repairs that you did not anticipate.[20]

Friends and Relatives

As in the U.S., entrepreneurs in many countries, including China, have difficulty getting a bank loan and rely mainly on personal savings and family.[21] Though this source of capital continues to be the most frequently sought by most entrepreneurs, troubles frequently arise. Relationships may become strained and it is not uncommon for relatives or friends to interfere with business decisions because they feel their stake in the business allows them to take an active role. Another difficulty develops when a friend or relative demands early repayment of his or her investment or loan, often leading to the frantic search for capital to cover the gap left by the lender. To avoid awkward situations, the terms of the loan, which should be made on a businesslike basis, should specify the role of the lenders in the operational policies of the business.

Personal Application

2. Which two friends or family members would you approach to invest money in your business model?

Partnerships

In order to meet capital requirements more easily, many business ventures are started with one or more partners in order to meet capital requirements more easily. As discussed in Chapter 5, a written agreement listing the duties, responsibilities, and authority must be accepted by all partners. Some partners can be listed as being a limited partner whose main interest lies with the investment, not with the daily activities of the business. However, the limited partner should have some voice in the decisions that affect the business's viability.

Personal Applications

3. Who would you pick for your partner(s) in your business idea? Why?

Angels

Small businesses looking for funding often look for help from an "angel."[22] An **angel** is an individual *willing to invest in promising startup opportunities.* Angel investors can be a good funding source to consider after you've tapped your friends and relatives.[23] Angel investors are deep-pocketed individuals looking for the high returns that risky, early-stage investing can (sometimes) bring.[24] As angels are part-owners of your company, your relationship is important.[25] Venture capitalists often can provide more funds than angels, but angels tend to provide a more empathic and trusting relationship.[26]

Venture Capital

Venture capital *refers to money provided by investors to startup firms and small businesses with perceived long-term growth potential.*[27] Venture capital firms tend to target industries,[28] and they are a good source of capital for businesses demonstrating potential for rapid growth, such as high-tech and Internet ventures.[29] However, they are picky. A study of venture capital firms reported that a venture capitalist managed two funds and reviewed 3,631 deals, but only invested in thirty-five companies.[30] Venture capitalists like to play an active role in the company via being board members, offering strategic marketing advice, governance, and helping to organize the financial structure of the company.[31] Plus, venture capitalists help increase profits, but at the same time take a share of your profits.[32]

Corporate Venture Capital

Corporate venture capital is a form of venture capital provided by large firms. By investing in small advanced technology businesses, larger companies can keep up with fast-paced developments. Corporate venture funds include **Citi Ventures** and **Comcast Ventures,** which is a unit of the largest U.S. cable operator **Comcast Corporation.** These two corporate venture firms have invested millions in startups such as mobile-payment startup **Square Inc.,** social media startup **Flipboard Inc.,** and online video startup **Fullscreen Inc.** Entrepreneurs that receive funding from corporate venture funds have instant credibility and access to partners with international reach.[33] For example, **Starbucks** also invested in the mobile payment startup Square Inc. **Starbucks** felt it was worth the investment to modernize collecting payments in its own coffee shops. In return, **Square Inc.** was able to gain retail-level knowledge about collecting payments from customers from all around the world.

Venture capital firms may appear to be an excellent source of readily available capital. However, the pros and cons, as shown in Exhibit 11-1, of this type of venture capital must be considered before entering into such an arrangement:

Exhibit 11-1

Pros and Cons of Using Venture Capital

Pros	Cons
• Heightened credibility with customers and bankers. • Expert managerial assistance. • Continuing source of financing. • Smaller burden of risk.	• Loss of substantial equity. • Investor makes most of the decisions. • Risk of takeover.

The choice of which venture capital source to approach must be carefully thought out because the financial goals of a venture capital firm can differ from the entrepreneur's plans for the business.

Sale of Capital Stock (IPO)

The sale of stock is not limited to large businesses as a device for raising capital. This type of financing offers an alternative source of funds after the effort to raise capital in less complicated ways has been exhausted. The sale of stock to individual investors involves the dilution of ownership, however, and should be seriously weighed as an option for raising capital.

Capital stock is stock, or ownership shares, issued in exchange for funds needed to operate your business. Stock, which can be sold to investors by private sale, is bought by selected individuals who may be employees and acquaintances. The advantage of a private sale of stock is gained by not having to comply with the laws of the **Securities and Exchange Commission (SEC)**. Equity holders, however, are able to have a voice in running the business, relative to their ownership equity position (that is, the number of shares held relative to the total number of shares issued by the corporation). As owners, equity holders usually share in the earnings of the company.

Stock is sold to the general public at a public sale. This type of sale requires the firm to be operating as a corporation. A public sale of stock is usually carried out by a larger firm that needs additional working capital and whose owner has to keep in mind that the price of the stock is influenced by market conditions. As an example, **Facebook**'s IPO of stock on May 18, 2012 was one of the biggest business media events in many years. The initial price was set at $38 with high expectations of stock price increases due to the popularity of millions of people who were using Facebook at the time of the IPO. However, the stock only increased a few cents above $38 that day and dropped to approximately $29 during the weeks following the IPO. A little after one year, the stock tell to $25. However, after nearly three years (April 2014), Facebook stock was up to $60 a share.

The disadvantage of issuing public stock is that it makes the firm subject to greater regulation by the state in which the firm operates, as well as by the SEC. Another disadvantage occurs because the small-business owner lacks sufficient knowledge of the securities market and the naïve small-business person may enter into contracts with brokers that may not be in the best interest of the business.

Private Placement

To facilitate a small business's access to the equity (stock market), the **Small Business Administration (SBA)** accepted regulations "A" and "D," which permit smaller businesses to make private accounts to interested groups or individuals without having to register them with the SEC.[34] Private placements are direct sales of stock (equity) positions to private investors without SEC registration and with minimal restrictions. For example, a firm may price the stock at $13 per share, but investors will only offer the highest price of $10 per share on a particular market date.

Crowdfunding

Crowdfunding is the recruitment (usually online) and collection of funds through small contributions from many parties in order to finance a particular project or venture. At this time, investors do not receive an actual piece of ownership in the company. The investors receive the perks—a product, a T-shirt, or some other promotional item related to the product in which they chose to invest their small amount of money. If you are going to try crowdfunding, here are some tips that work: use a video business or elevator pitch, provide multiple links to your Web site, offer perks, and send frequent updates on your progress.[35]

There are some 200 Web sites set up by entrepreneurs to profit from the Jumpstart Our Business Startups (JOBS) Act of 2102, but be careful as regulators are scrutinizing some of them for possible threats to investors.[36] **Kickstarter** and **Indiegogo** are two of the best-known crowdsourcing companies, and they have raised hundreds of millions for creative projects and business ventures;[37] an estimated $2.8 billion was raised by the entire industry in 2012.[38] Kickstarter is a funding platform for creative projects. Everything on Kickstarter must be a project. A project is something with a clear end, like making an album, a film, or a new game. A project will eventually be completed, and something will be produced as a result. Every project on Kickstarter must fit into one of its categories. Its categories are Art, Comics, Dance, Design, Fashion, Film, Food, Games, Music, Photography, Publishing, Technology, and Theater.[39] Investors often receive the album, piece of art, video game, etc. in return for their support of the company. **Indiegogo** will raise needed funds. **Mission Cheese** was short $12,000 in capital equipment funding; in desperation after exhausting other options Sarah Dvorak turned to Indiegogo, which raised the money within a month, allowing her to open her café.[40]

One unique aspect of crowdsourcing is that the entrepreneur decides on a project to complete, then he or she sets a financial goal amount, sets a specific deadline to reach that goal, and determines any rewards offered to donors. The key is, the entrepreneur must raise 100 percent of his or her goal before the deadline, or all the donations are returned to the donors. Deadlines are typically less than sixty days.[41]

As of July 2013, regulators are reviewing the process of funding for crowdsourcing through the JOBS Act. Overall, the Act will support more entrepreneurial activity, allow more people to be aware of funding opportunities, and have investors become an actual owner of a percentage of the company. Although the process looks like it will be approved, the final process is still being discussed.[42]

Personal Application

4. What other crowdfunding companies have you heard about? Look online for examples if necessary.

Sources of Debt Financing

There are many feasible ways you can finance your operations once the business is ready to serve its customers. Trade credit has been a long-time source of debt capital and remains one of the small-business person's most valuable financing resources. Imagine if an owner had to pay for inventory with cash in hand! The very existence of small business would be unimaginable.

Let's explore some of the debt-financing resources that are readily available when the new venture is ready to operate.

Commercial Banks

Commercial banks are banks that receive funds from depositors and then lend these funds to businesses. Contrary to what many entrepreneurs believe about commercial bank financing, banks do offer a limited source when initial capital is needed. However, banks require a personal guarantee in the form of personal property such as mortgages—and most startup ventures lack the hard assets banks seek as collateral. But the better your credit rating is, the better are your chances of getting funding, and you can get it at a lower cost.[43]

Commercial banks may offer short-term loans to small businesses rather than lending on a long-term basis. In recent years, many types of financing are available to qualified applicants. Seeking new income after federal rules limited fees from overdrafts and debit cards, **Wells Fargo, U.S. Bancorp**, and other large banks are giving short-term, high-cost loans that resemble payday loans more commonly offered by strip-mall storefront operations.[44] The selection of the bank should be based on the various services offered that best suit your needs. It is to your benefit to establish a good working relationship with a commercial bank in the early stages of establishment.

Community Banks

Community banks have played a large part of the Small Business Lending Fund program, which is part of the Small Business Jobs Act of 2010. Community banks have increased their lending (over $3.5 billion) to small businesses across the country. You should look to community banks and credit unions for loans from local banks.[45] **Ben & Jerry** each put up $4,000 and they got a bank loan for $4,000 and opened their first Scoop Shop in 1978; in 2000 they sold the company for $326 million.[46]

Commercial Finance Companies

If denied a bank loan, you can try to get a loan from over one hundred commercial finance companies, such as GE Capital Business Finance. The downside is the higher rate of fees and interest you will have to pay, and they usually require collateral, often called asset-based lending.

Line of Credit

Entrepreneurs can also arrange a line of credit with a commercial bank. A **line of credit** is an arrangement between a financial institution, usually a bank, and a customer that establishes a maximum loan balance that the bank will permit the borrower to maintain. The advantage of a line of credit over a regular loan is that interest is not usually charged on the part of the line of credit that is unused, and you can borrow money on the line of credit at any time you need to.[47]

It is similar to having a credit card, but the interest charges are usually lower. You can also get a line of credit online through a microlender, such as **Kabbage.** Credit lines tend to range from $500 to $50,000 with fees running 2 to 7 percent over thirty days and 10 to 18 percent over six months. **Gear Geek,** an eBay store, quadrupled revenues with the help of a credit line to buy more inventory.[48]

Matchmaking for Businesses and Banks

Entrepreneurs (**Biz2Credit, BoeFly, CNF Exchange, Lendio**) frustrated with trying to get bank loans decided to help small businesses get bank loans. Matchmakers analyze would-be-borrowers' financial data to assess risk, then send their assessments to banks, credit unions, and alternative lenders. Loans range from a few thousand to a few million dollars. They don't make guarantees a deal will close, but they claim a success rate of 70–80 percent (if they elect to send your loan request to a bank), and get a decision in weeks, rather than months from some banks. They have helped get more than $1.5 billion in lending in 2012.[49]

Vendor Trade Credit

Trade credit is credit extended by a supplier. Inventory is one of the largest investments that most small businesses have to make. An excellent source of capital comes from vendors with whom the business has dealings. This type of credit usually involves an unsecured open-book account. If credit references of the small-business owner are in good standing, the supplier ships inventory to the firm and opens up an accounts receivable record in its books. The dollar volume of trade depends upon the type of buyers and suppliers.

Terms of credit are usually thirty days, although some suppliers offer a discount when the bill is paid early. A common credit term such as 2/10, net 30, means that you can take advantage of a 2 percent discount if you pay the total amount of the bill in ten days. After the ten-day period passes by, you have the responsibility to pay the total amount of the bill within the thirty-day limit. Trade discounts can save the firm money, but failure to use credit properly will not only cost you money, but also the loss of a credit source as well.

A supplier is someone that the entrepreneur will have to rely on for prompt deliveries, undamaged goods, and extended credit in times of emergency. Therefore, you should not just pick the first supplier. Select suppliers carefully, taking note of their reputations. One indicator of good suppliers is to determine if they have qualified for the Organization for International Standards (ISO) 9000 Series Standards.[50]

Equipment Loans and Leasing

Acquiring the equipment a business needs in order to function can be a difficult task. Because vendors routinely offer attractive installment plans, equipment can be bought on an installment basis: a 25–35 percent down payment is usually required with an intermediate loan period of 3–5 years. However, an entrepreneur should exercise caution. Just because it seems so easy to buy on installments, a new entrepreneur may easily forget that lots of small installment payments can add up. Do not buy more equipment than you can afford or lease more space than you need,[51] and a bank or other type of loan may be less costly than an equipment loan.

Leasing is an increasingly popular option. Companies such as **IBM, Honeywell,** and **Xerox** have been offering equipment leasing options for many years. The advantages of leasing equipment are as follows:

1. Flexibility with equipment needs and payment schedules;
2. Smaller capital requirements;
3. Leasing company offers maintenance service for equipment;
4. Leasing offers a way to beat the obsolescence problem.

Disadvantages with leasing options are the absence of depreciation as a noncash outlay and the higher total cost the firm will have to pay out compared with purchasing the equipment outright.

Sources of Bootstrap Financing

> **Learning Outcome**
>
> 4. Explore bootstrap financing opportunities.

Facing the facts, it can be difficult to get outside credit, with the tight lending restrictions and lower interest rates making the financial rewards less appealing for giving loans or credit. Also, venture capital funding is down. So bootstrapping is about starting and growing a business with little or no outside funding.[52] Bootstrap financing means your startup company and growth are accomplished with the assistance of or input from others.[53] Most bootstrappers have similar strategies: spend as little as possible, focus on bringing in revenues from day one to pay expenses, and reinvest revenues for developing and growing the business. They realize that cash flow is king—without cash you can't stay in business long enough to get revenues.[54]

Don't be like many students coming out of college thinking you can't start a successful company without giving away equity or getting outside debt financing. **BuildASign.com** used bootstrapping and grew to $30 million in annual revenues with more than 240 employees. Lady Fortunes grew to $4.5 million in revenue and forty-two employees and has no debt.[55] You should consider the following list as possible bootstrapping strategies. But you need to be creative and come up with your own ideas as well.

■ You can save costs by choosing to be a **home-based business. Apple** started in the Jobs family garage. **eDimensional** started as a home-based business until it was absolutely necessary to get an office; it saved $18,000 a year for four years.[56]

- **Credit cards.** The use of credit cards to finance a startup business is enticing because it is money that is easily available. However, you are personally responsible for money owed on a credit card. Plus, interest rates can be 15 percent or more, which is an extremely high expense of conducting business.[57]

- **Sell personal belongings.** You can decide to sell personal belongings, such as artwork, vehicles, or stock to raise cash. Cofounders Steve Jobs and Steve Wozniak sold a VW van and HP calculator to raise $1,350 seed money to start **Apple.** Dan Smith sold his own motorcycle to raise money for tools and equipment to repair motorcycles, starting as a hybrid entrepreneur in his home garage and eventually opening a shop as a full-time entrepreneur.

- You can also **borrow** and **share equipment.** Many summer yard cleaning businesses are started by borrowing the family lawnmower, and some grow into full-time landscaping businesses. A small frame shop could share its saw with another local shop. The shops could split the cost of a high-quality saw instead of each shop buying its own expensive saw.

- There are private and state-sponsored **incubators** that provide low-cost shared facilities to help new business ventures get off to a profitable start. The incubator business has its own space and shares common support functions, such as receptionist, copy machine, conference room, etc. The members also provide support to each other. The goal is to move the business to its own facility within three to five years.

- **College interns** provide quality work in areas such as accounting and marketing. Internships are often setup as either a paid or unpaid internship. Entrepreneurs Nataly Kogan and Avi Spivack cofounded **Natavi Guides** to publish guidebooks for students. Natavi hires virtual interns to write stories and locates people by posting openings with career offices at more than thirty universities nationwide. Kogan estimates that Natavi saved $100,000 in overhead during the first year in business by not having to pay or furnish office space, computers, and other equipment to interns.

- **Bartering.** Some companies use the traditional method of exchanging items or services instead of using cash. Try giving products or services in exchange for advertising. Corey Blake, president of **Round Table Companies,** said: "Last year, we bartered the creation of a full color graphic novel in exchange for a new website design from one of the top companies. The value of the trade was $50,000. We provided three months of writing services to create the graphic novel storyline (as a marketing vehicle for this company) and then five months of illustration. In exchange, they helped us to define, design, and then program our new website in Expression Engine over the course of six to seven months."[58]

- **Refinance your home.** *Home equity loans* are a popular financing device for new business owners because there's often substantial equity tied up in a home, and the loans are easier to come by.[59] However, the biggest disadvantage to a home equity loan is that it puts ownership of your home at risk.

- **Borrow from or against your retirement account.** This is sometimes used to raise money as some entrepreneurs sell all or part of their retirement accounts or use them as collateral to get a loan. However, the biggest disadvantage is that you risk losing your retirement funds if the business fails.
- **Customer financing and referrals** involves getting paid as much as possible before starting a job and/or as it is in progress and asking customers for leads on new customers.
- **Factoring. Factoring** *involves selling your receivables to a buyer, such as a commercial finance company, to raise capital and is very common in industries where long receivables are part of the business cycle, such as the clothing industry.* You can still make money on your receivables—even though you will share the money with the commercial finance company.

Government-Sponsored Agencies

The government has developed sources that sponsor the small business owner. Two government agencies that help to fund the entrepreneur are the SBA (SBA.gov) and the Minority Business Development Agency (MBDA).

Learning Outcome

5. List sources of government funding.

Small Business Administration Loan Guarantee Programs

The SBA does not lend business owners money directly; it provides a guarantee to banks and lenders for money they lend to small businesses. SBA backing mitigates the risk for banks and lenders and makes them more inclined to provide loans to small businesses who don't qualify for traditional loans, often because of lack of collateral.[60]

Small Business Investment Company

Congress created the Small Business Investment Company (SBIC) program to facilitate the flow of long-term capital to America's small businesses.[61] SBIC loans evolved out of the Small Business Equity Act, which was passed by Congress in 1958. This legislation was aimed at encouraging the private business sector to finance small businesses. SBICs are regulated and must be licensed to operate by the SBA.[62]

Today, only companies defined by SBA as "small" are eligible for SBIC financing. Generally, the SBIC program defines a company as "small" when its net worth is $18.0 million or less and its average after tax net income for the prior two years does not exceed $6.0 million.[63]

Examples of SBIC ventures are shopping center developments, fast-food franchises, cinemas, and grocery or convenience stores. Many SBICs invest a large portion of funds in successful small businesses that are ready to expand.

Another consulting service offered by the SBA is **SCORE** (Service Corps of Retired Executives), an organization of people who donate their time assisting small businesses affiliated with the SBA, and who can assist the entrepreneur in setting up a business plan that will facilitate obtaining a loan.

Minority Business Development Agency

For the last forty years, the United States Chamber of Commerce has overseen the functions of the MBDA (www.mbda.gov). In 2012, the MBDA Business Centers helped minority-owned businesses obtain over $3.6 billion in contracts and capital and create or retain 16,730 jobs, the highest level in the agency's forty-four-year history.[64] For example, the U.S. Department of Commerce offers a grant competition to spur job creation and economic development in states with large American Indian and Alaska Native populations. Approximately $6.6 million in MBDA funds is being invested with local entities to operate new MBDA Business Centers.[65] Minority-owned businesses should find their local MBDA Center for fundraising assistance. Located in areas with the largest concentration of minority populations, MBDA Centers offer a range of business services to minority entrepreneurs. You can locate the center closest to you at www.mbda.gov/businesscenters.[66]

State and Regional Development Companies

Many states offer incentives for entrepreneurs to put roots down and create jobs. Grants, loans, equity capital: it's all out there if you know where to look. In Massachusetts, **the Massachusetts Technology Collaborative (MTC)** has a focus on technology and energy-related companies. It has handed out more than $500 million in grants. The collaborative was launched twenty-five years ago. The MTC runs the John Adams Innovation Institute and the Renewable Energy Trust.

In South Carolina, **SC Launch** focuses on defraying the costs of business services for small businesses. It has offered equity capital, loans, and matching grants to thirty-five companies since its inception in 2005. SC Launch helps startups cover costs related to legal, financial, marketing, and intellectual property protection.[67]

Other Options for Starting a New Venture, and Entrepreneurial Behavior

One of the most difficult challenges facing startup entrepreneurs is getting financing to start the business, and depending on your entry into entrepreneurship, you can get help funding your business.

Buying an Existing Business, Franchise, or Leasing Rights

Buying an Existing Business

Buying an existing business means you will have to find the financing to buy the operation. Don't forget, as discussed in Chapter 2, the business owner often will provide you with a loan for some of the purchase financing, but you will most likely need a down payment. Based on the chapter, where will you get the financing to acquire your business?

Another option, not too commonly used, is to gradually buy the business you work for. This is especially appealing to older business owners looking to retire but who don't have many options for selling the business; or are looking for a special person to take over their business/baby. You would make a purchase agreement in say three to five years and part of your salary would go as a down payment on the business. After you take over, you continue to pay off the debt you owe the prior owner. If you have a business you would like to own, and don't work for, you can approach the owner with an offer to work for and buy the company.

Buying a Franchise

If you buy a franchise the franchisor might offer some type of financing plan and/or help you find a source of funding. But, as with buying an existing business, you will need a down payment to get started.

Buying Licensing Rights

If you buy a license, you are starting a new business and will have to agree with the licensor on how you will pay any upfront fees and repay him or her for use of the licensed product or service You can try to negotiate a low down payment, and possibly pay the down payment along with licensor fees.

Starting a Nonprofit

If you start a nonprofit, you can get financing as discussed in this chapter. However, you have some options not open to for-profit companies. You can generate funding by asking members or followers to donate money to support the organization. You can also write grants to receive money from the government and/or private organizations, often foundations.

When selecting board members, try to recruit some people who will give you funds, or who have expertise in fundraising to help you get financing. Be sure all potential board members believe in the mission and will be out in the community promoting the nonprofit. Also, as discussed in prior chapters, SCORE, ESC, SBIs, and SBDCs can help you with financing advice.

Starting a Corporate Venture

Getting funds is much less of a problem for the entrepreneurial manager because some large companies have funds budgeted for new ventures, or they have profits they can invest or access to equity or debt financing for your new venture. Thus, you may not have to leave a corporation to develop and run your own new venture. Many companies have plenty of money; however, it's not easy selling management on your idea and getting them to fund your new venture through the bureaucracy. So you need a good business or elevator pitch and business plan.

One exception to the entrepreneurial manager not having to come up with his or her own funding to start a new venture is the **spin-off**, which must generally be bought from the parent company. However, some of the parent companies are willing to accept a down payment and payments over a period of time, thus, giving the entrepreneurial manager a bit of an edge over many entrepreneurs. If spinning off the business is part of the growth strategy, you may negotiate to receive an equity state at that time.

Entrepreneurial Behavior

If you have money, you can offer financing to your small-business employer or someone you know who wants to start a business by investing in the company or providing it with a loan. If you have financial contacts, you can introduce management to them to discuss financing. Many startups attract talented employees who are willing to work for lower pay by offering them stock. Many of the early employees at **Microsoft** and **Apple** became millionaires as the value of their stock skyrocketed. If you can't get stock as part of your compensation, many large companies have stock purchase plans so you can buy ownership at below-market value. Thus, financing is provided for your company as you become an equity owner.

Take it to the Net

Visit www.routledge.com/cw/Lussier for the book's companion Web site, where you can:

- use learning aids, including taking a quiz;
- find links to resources in this chapter, as well as other links including videos;
- learn about and start the following activities: Continuing Integrated Case, Your Ninety-Second New Venture Pitch, the Paper Clip Entrepreneurship Challenge, College Entrepreneurial Spirit Award, and the Community Entrepreneurial Spirit Award.

Chapter Review and Summary

This summary lists the learning outcomes from the chapter and their answers.

1. **Describe the three capital needs questions and types of capital to support a new business venture**

   The entrepreneur should answer these basic questions before initiating a search for capital: How much capital will I need? What type of capital is required? Where can I get the funds? The three major types of financing are short-term capital, early-stage capital, and long-term capital. Short-term capital is funds that are borrowed for less than one year. Early-stage capital, often referred to as intermediate capital, is funds to be paid back within a period of five years. Long-term capital covers long-term projects lasting longer than five years and includes fixed assets and real-estate purchases, expensive machinery, and franchise financing.

2. **Identify sources of equity financing**

   Potential sources of equity financing include seed capital, personal savings, friends and family, partners, angels, venture capital, corporate venture capital, sale of public stock offering (IPO), a private placement, or crowdfunding.

3. **Identifying sources of debt financing**

   A potential source of debt financing includes loans (bank loans, a line of credit, installment billing, and insurance or retirement loans). Vendors also offer a source of debt funding. Local community banks provide loans to help spur local business.

4. **List bootstrap financing opportunities**

   Bootstrapping includes using a home-based business, credit cards, selling personal belongings, borrowing and sharing equipment, joining an incubator, using college interns, bartering, refinancing your home, borrowing from or against your retirement account, customer financing and referrals, and factoring.

5. **Discuss sources of government funding**

   The government has developed sources that sponsor the small-business owner. One government agency that helps to fund the entrepreneur is the SBA. The SBA is an agency of the government founded to help small businesses that offers the most assistance with financial help and professional advice. The SBA oversees the functions of Small Business Investment Companies, and a variety of smaller programs such as the Economic Opportunity Loan Program. Other indirect government-sponsored agencies include the Small Business Investment Company, commonly referred to as SBICs. The U.S. Chamber of Commerce monitors the MBDA Program, which stands for the Minority Business Development Agency.

6. **Define the twelve key terms in this chapter**

capital stock	SBA
commercial banks	SCORE
early-stage capital	seed financing
line of credit	short-term capital
long-term capital	trade credit
private placement	venture capital

Review and Discussion Questions

1. Why is a business plan so important in estimating the money needed for a new venture?

2. Why would any source of venture capital consider the business plan as an important document?

3. What basic questions should an entrepreneur ask before seeking sources of capital?

4. What is the difference between equity capital and debt capital? Which would you prefer and why?

5. What problems would you foresee in obtaining loans from friends and relatives? Under what conditions would these be a good source for funds?

6. How can your suppliers of inventory and machinery help provide initial capital for the new business?

7. Are commercial banks a good source of funds? When would you go to a commercial bank and what business ratios would you need to present?

8. Name and discuss several governmental sources of funds. When might you go to these sources and what documentation would you need to provide?

9. "Venture capital companies are a good source of funds." Discuss this statement giving advantages and disadvantages of using venture capital.

10. Does the SBA directly hand out loans?

Application Exercises

When doing these exercises, be sure to select a specific business where applicable, preferably one where you presently or previously work(ed) or a business you would like to own someday. If this is not possible, pick a specific organization to which you will refer. Be sure to identify the organization by name. Limit your answers to one or two pages per exercise.

1. Assume you want to start a small retail store. Prepare a cash flow statement for three years using Standard Industrial Classification (SIC) codes and Risk Management Association (RMA) guidelines. Estimate the first year's sales to be between $250,000 and $1,000,000.

2. Interview a person who has just started or is about to start a business and determine if a cash flow projection was or is being developed. Prepare a report on this person's view of cash flow statements.

3. Interview three local small business owners. Find out how they obtained the funds necessary to start their businesses. Keep your questions general and non-threatening because these people may be reluctant to provide you with actual figures.

4. Assume you have a can't-fail, profit-assured idea for a business but you need $10,000 in initial capital.

   a. Ask your friends and relatives if they would lend you money and what assurances they would want.

   b. Ask the small-business loan officer at your local bank what would be required before lending you money and what the repayment requirements would be.

   c. Ask a venture capitalist if your business would be appropriate for investment and what would be demanded in return?

   d. Visit your local SBA office and ask what they would need before they would discuss a loan with you. They may have a standard loan package including forms and instructions. Report on your findings and include the SBA package.

Application Situations

1. Al Kurrow

Al Kurrow has always loved sailing and was happiest when on the ocean in a good wind. After fifteen years working in a large corporation in the shipping department, he took a chance to realize his life's dream. He borrowed money to buy a sailboat so that he could set up a charter business in the Caribbean. He knew he could be successful and had already found a marina where he could operate his charter service. Until now, finances were not an important question as Al had neither the time nor the desire to do any financial planning. His belief is that he has most of the essential ingredients for success and that success was inevitable.

1. Based on the information provided, do you think Al needs a financial plan? Estimate his needs and draw up such a plan for the next three years.

2. Assuming you find that Al needs money. Where should he get it? What would be good sources of funds for him and what would not? Explain your choices.

3. Is his venture too small to justify financial planning? Is any venture too small? Explain your reasoning.

4. What is your opinion of Al making this a successful venture? Explain your reasoning.

2. Sally Chin

Sally Chin had done much in the four years since leaving college. She had always had an interest in antiques and artifacts as well as a goal of managing her own business. That interest plus her years of experience in buying and selling antiques as a part of her job as an assistant curator in a large city museum, and the fact that the museum was cutting back on staffing and that she felt stifled, led her to think about going out on her own and becoming an antiques dealer. Scouting out locations in the antique district, she found a vacant store that was perfect. Now, she thinks, might be a good time to move ahead, but this would be an entirely new business and she has no idea about where to begin. At the least, she wants to do some financial planning.

1. Describe how Sally should start her financial planning. Where would she get basic information and how would she use this information to plan?

2. Where would Sally get funds to support her venture? Which sources might be the best? The worst? Explain your reasoning.

3. Do you think from the information given that Sally can be successful? Why or why not?

3. Max Vincent

Max Vincent went through high school in the shop course, specifically in automobile mechanics. After graduation, he worked in a service station's automobile repair business for six years. Max thinks that it's now time he went into business for himself. He believes he has a following of people who have come to know and trust him and provide a good base on which to begin. After looking around for the past two years, he located an auto repair business for sale. The owner was willing to provide past financial history.

1. How would Max draw up his financial plan? Be specific.

2. What would be Max's best source for funding? Explain your reasoning.

Max made up his mind to move ahead and bought the automobile repair business he had located. His first year's experience seemed to be successful. However, after examining his year-end figures, he was astounded to see that he had operated at a loss. It looked like he didn't make enough money to cover his expenses. As he was on a very limited budget, he was worried about making it through the next year.

3. Should Max have been surprised at these results? Why or why not? Explain your reasoning.

4. How can Max determine when he will be making a profit? If you know of a method that will help Max identify it, outline how Max can use it.

5. How should Max have planned his first three years? Explain the method Max could have used and how he could be solvent for the first three years.

Case

Kickstarter and Crowdfunding

Kickstarter and Crowdfunding are two terms new to the world of corporate fundraising. Kickstarter describes itself as allowing "creators to set a funding goal and deadline. If people like a project, they can pledge money to make it happen. Funding on Kickstarter is all-or-nothing—projects must reach their funding goals to receive any money. All-or-nothing funding might seem scary, but it's amazingly effective in creating momentum and rallying people around an idea. To date, an impressive 44% of projects have reached their funding goals."[68] Kickstarter is a home for everything from films, games, and music to art, design, and technology. Kickstarter is full of projects, big and small, that are brought to life through the direct support of people. Since launching in 2009, more than 4.4 million people have pledged over $688 million, funding more than 44,000 creative projects. Thousands of creative projects are raising funds on Kickstarter even as you read this case.

So far, Kickstarter raises funds but the investors cannot seek equity investment; they can only solicit donations or pre-sell their products.[69] Because of these restrictions, donors don't expect to make a return on their investment, and only hope to preorder a nifty gadget or fund a worthy project. This is a long-winded way of saying that Kickstarter does not, and is not legally allowed to, help companies issue securities (a financial instrument representing value).[70]

Steve Case, former CEO of AOL, believes crowdsourcing opportunities such as Kickstarter will help traditional venture capitalists to find valuable startups to invest their money. "My view is it will help entrepreneurs get going," he says. "Some of those companies, after they raise a few hundred thousand dollars through crowdfunding, might need a few million dollars and will turn to venture capitalists."[71]

Case does admit that if the trend towards Kickstarter keeps increasing it may put pressure on "some" venture capitalist firms. The top venture capitalist would still find good investments. But, the smaller venture capitalist might lose business opportunities to Kickstarter and other crowdsourcing opportunities.

Two of the most widely discussed successes of Kickstarter were Pebble watches and Zach Braff. Pebble raised over 10 million dollars for an innovative computer-based watch that was highly supported by the "crowd" of investors.

Pebble's website states "Pebble is the first watch built for the 21st century. It's infinitely customizable, with beautiful downloadable watch faces and useful internet-connected apps. Pebble connects to iPhone and Android smartphones using Bluetooth, alerting you with a silent vibration to incoming calls, emails and messages. While designing Pebble, we strove to create a minimalist yet fashionable product that seamlessly blends into everyday life."[72]

Kickstarter investors are receiving a watch in exchange for their support. Pebble has gone on to attract more money from traditional venture capitalists.

The comedy actor Zach Braff surpassed his Kickstarter goal of two million dollars for his next movie.[73] Although debate swirled that he could fund his own movie, he was eager to include the "crowd" of supporters who wanted to receive a copy of the movie or other such promotional items that will come out with the movie.[74]

At PAX East in Boston in 2013, many young entrepreneurs were looking for support for their video game ideas or their role-playing card games. Gamers, artists, photographers, bloggers, and 84,000 attendees visited the gaming conference. A Kickstarter presentation was very well attended with the "crowd" in the audience either looking for supporters of their own ideas or looking for other new ideas to support. Kickstarter's Cindy Au (Head of Community) and Luke Crane (Project Specialist for Games) moderated a discussion about what it's like to create, launch, and run a Kickstarter project.[75]

Crowdsourcing is also a global phenomenon. The online community VC4Africa (Venture Capital for Africa), which connects promising entrepreneurs in Africa with investors and startup resources, continues to gain momentum. VC4Africa welcomed its 10,000th member, and already 1,000 African enterprises are registered on the platform with many securing valuable partnerships to date.[76]

1. How is Kickstarter different than a traditional venture capitalist?

2. What is the meaning of the term "crowdfunding"?

Global Case—Kiva: Microfinance Loans That Changed the World

Can small entrepreneurs (micro-entrepreneurs) around the world benefit from loans as small as $25? This Nobel Prize-winning idea created the loans that are known as microfinance. Microfinance is a general term to describe financial services to low-income individuals or to those who do not have access to typical banking services. Microfinance is also the idea that low-income individuals are capable of lifting themselves out of poverty if given access to financial services.

A microloan is an essential first step in making a difference in the life of a micro-entrepreneur. Building good businesses often requires loan products that are well-adapted to borrower needs, alternative forms of collateral that make it easier for excluded people to qualify for loans, and business training or development services.

Kiva (www.kiva.org/about/socialperformance) aims to partner with organizations that offer entrepreneurial support to the people they serve. This support can come directly from the organization or in partnership with a separate, qualified agency. Borrowers, like Santa Isabel, are able to participate in classes to learn basic business skills like budgeting, allocation of profits, and market analysis.

Santa Isabel is from Ecuador; she is a Kiva borrower, a mother of two, and a hardworking corn, rice, and pea farmer. While she has long understood the mechanics of farming, Santa Isabel learned how to run her business with the help of Kiva's Field Partner (mentor) and the additional enterprise services it provided her.

In 2013, Kiva opened its Anglophone Africa Regional office in Nairobi, Kenya. Matt Flannery, co-founder and CEO, and Premal Shah, president, officially opened the Kiva regional office based at the Strathmore Business School at Madaraka. The Nairobi office is Kiva's first outside of the U.S.[77]

1. Does Kiva use debt or equity to help micro-entrepreneurs around the world?

2. Do funding sources promote social performance around the world?

Writing Your Business Plan

You (or in teams) can write a business plan during the semester. There are questions at the end of each chapter to help guide you through the thinking and analyzing process. Appendix B has a sample business plan you can use as a template for developing your own new venture business plan.

Since this is Chapter 11, the goal is to add information about the funding options available to finance the new business.

Highlighted Sections of the Business Plan (Chapters 1–11)

1. The Executive Summary is written last—but placed first in the business plan. You have to wait until you are finished with the business plan to properly write the executive summary.

2. Introduction:

   A. Background of the business: Includes a short review of its name, address (or addresses if there is more than one location), telephone number(s), email address, website address, hours of operation, and a brief history (if any). You want to state when the business was started or will be started.

   B. Management credentials and organization structure: It is common to list all the business's key managers and their duties and responsibilities, with their qualifications.

   C. Form of ownership: Will your business be a sole proprietorship, partnership, or corporation and how will any profits be distributed?

3. Strategy Formulation:

   A. Mission: What is the organization's purpose or reason for being (covered in Chapter 3)? The mission section of the business plan includes your business model (covered in Chapter 4), which can include a broad description of your present and future products and services to be offered. In the strategy section, it is not necessary to list all the products and services; they

are listed under the marketing section of the business plan and were discussed in Chapter 6.

   B. Objectives (prioritized): What does your organization wants to accomplish?

   C. Environmental analysis: It includes an analysis of the internal environment (which includes the mission and objectives) and its external environment resulting in a SWOT analysis.

4. The Marketing Function:

   A. The marketing plan: Your marketing plan must identify your target customers and product feasibility (Chapter 4) by using marketing research to better understand your industry and marketplace.

   B. The marketing mix: You need to include the 4 Ps of marketing in your marketing plan. What is your product? At what price point will you sell your product? Where (place) will you sell your product? And, how will you promote your product?

5. Location and Layout:

   A. Location: You want to consider such general location factors such as: (1) proximity to the market; (2) transportation facilities; (3) availability of raw materials; (4) labor supply; (5) community attitude; (6) water power; (7) land costs; (8) taxes; (9) specialized communities; (10) climatic conditions; (11) potential sister plants or warehouse; (12) the question of urban, suburban, or rural sites; and (13) how these factors affect specific site selection as either a home-based, Internet, or traditional manufacturing or retail location.

   B. Layout: Having committed to a location, you must then develop a layout. The layout is an arrangement of the physical facilities in the most efficient manner for specific business, for the interior in order to maximize profitability. You should draw a diagram of the layout you expect to utilize in your business.

6. **The Production/Operations Function:**
   A. **Production process:** What is your operational plan to transform inputs into outputs?
   B. **Quality:** What level of quality will you expect from your finished product?

7. **The Human Resources Function:**
   A. Who are the members of your new venture team (founder, investors, lenders, mentors, lawyer, accountant, banker, insurance agent, and any consultants)?
   B. How do you plan on using the human resources management process to attract, develop, and retain employees?
   C. What is your plan for management succession and an exit strategy?

8. **The Financing Function:**
   A. Who will be in charge of accounting? What processes will be put into place? What accounting software will be used to organize your accounting information?
   B. What sources of equity will you look to acquire? Which of the following sources will you try to use? Personal savings, seed capital, friends and family, partners, angel investors, venture capital and corporate venture capitalists, go public with an IPO, private placement, or crowdfunding?
   C. What will be your sources of debt financing? Loans, leasing, installment billing, trade credits, a bank loan, line of credit, insurance or retirement loans?
   D. Can you get financing from your vendors?
   E. Are other financing options available such as commercial finance companies, savings and loans, credit unions, or stock brokers?
   F. Can you use available government programs such as the Small Business Administration (SBA) loans and programs, Small Business Investment Companies (SBICs), federal, state, and local programs?
   G. Can you use bootstrap financing such as using, factoring, selling your personal belongings, choosing a home-based business, sharing, credit cards, college interns, and bartering?

9. **Controls**

10. **Appendix**

Chapter 12

Controls
How do You Keep the New Venture on Track?

This chapter recognizes that your firm's survival is dependent upon its profitability. Profits do not just happen; it takes careful planning and control to make certain that your company is operating in the best and most profitable manner. In order to run your business to make the greatest profit, you must use financial information that has been generated as a result of conducting business. Financial controls, utilizing the financial tools discussed in Chapter 10, make it possible to identify and keep track of your firm's financial position at any moment in time and as it changes over time. With this information you can determine your firm's financial health both internally and externally in comparison with other similar firms. Analysis of financial ratios will enable you to control your firm's operation for maximum profitability. The budgeting process is also presented as a tool to control the flow of funds spent inside the organization. The balanced scorecard is presented as a tool to evaluate your organization from four different perspectives. Risk management is introduced as well as various types of insurance a small business should consider purchasing to reduce its own risk as much as possible.

Learning Outcomes

After completing this chapter you should be able to:

1. Describe the steps in the control process;
2. List the guidelines for controlling quality and the guidelines for controlling cost;
3. Discuss the importance of quality and Total Quality Management (TQM) as part of the entrepreneurial process;
4. Discuss the role of budgets as part of the control process;
5. Identify different financial ratios to judge your firm's financial health compared with the other firms in your industry;
6. Identify the role of the balanced scorecard as part of the controlling process;
7. Describe how risk management can help an entrepreneur to control the growth of his or her own business;
8. Define the twenty-two key terms identified in this chapter.

Entrepreneur Profile—Jim Schell, CEO/Founder Opportunity Knocks

We begin each chapter with a short bio of an entrepreneur and provide a link so you can learn more about the person and his or her business venture. Short 3–5-minute videos of each entrepreneur can be found at the PBS Small Business School at: www.smallbusinessschool.org/. You can find more about Opportunity Knocks at: http://smallbusinessschool.org/video.cfm?clip=1141# and at: www.opp-knocks.org/.

Jim Schell's goal is to give employees key indicator responsibilities for two reasons. First, a key indicator, such as a target goal for gross margin or receivables, will make your management job easier. It allows you quick access to the important things in your business and it shows you the trend and the direction in which you are going. But an even more important use of the key indicator report is to engage your key employees in the management of the business. If you were handed a Profit & Loss Statement (P & L), balance sheet and cash flow statement, wouldn't you have trouble reading them? What do you expect of your employees?

For example, a bookkeeper has a key indicator report for the percentage of receivables over sixty days. If six months ago your percentage of receivables over sixty days was 10 percent and now it's 5 percent, then everybody in this meeting knows that your bookkeeper is improving at collecting your receivables.

Or, let's say you have a key indicator (goal) of 25 percent gross margin. This is your number one priority in this company. You should create a key indicator report and the top item should be gross margin. You should do everything you can do to focus on increasing that 25 percent to 30 percent, 35 percent, or whatever, in a reasonable timeframe.

Creating financial reports and tracking key indicators would be hard without software but now it's easy. We're able for the first time to get quality information back right now on where we are and what we're doing. We now know what our receivables are on a daily basis. We now know what our payables are. We now know that your accounting for payroll is going to be right.

When a business owner gets to the point where his or her favorite day is the day when the owner's financials come out, or, even better than that, his or her favorite day of the month is the day when the owner can push the button on his software and out will kick a preliminary P & L—when that's the favorite day of the month—then you know you've arrived at the point where financial statements are meaningful to you. That is when you know that you get it. That it's all about numbers.

Think it over.

1. Do you think a key indicator report should be used as a management tool?
2. Would you be willing to have a key indicator, such as net profit margins or gross revenues (sales), as a key indicator in your company?

The Interrelationship Between Control, Financial Analysis, and the Other Business Plan Components

Once you acquire the resources to start a business, you need to control them.[1] Controlling is the process of establishing methods and monitoring progress to ensure that the business objectives are achieved. The primary objective of a small-business owner or manager should be to provide a product of high quality at a minimum cost on time. In fulfilling that responsibility, the owner must make sure plans are carried out and that the firm's assets are protected. And that, as our definition implies, means controlling. The better your skills are at controlling, the greater are your chances of success in business.

Controlling is not a function; it is a method to ensure that plans in the functional areas of accounting and finance, marketing, production/operations, and human resources are successfully implemented. Business planning and control are inseparable. So, as you develop plans for each functional area, you should also develop controls for each functional area.

The controls established must also be coordinated as a system within the functional areas to ensure success. Control systems for production, sales, delivery, and accounting must be coordinated to ensure customer satisfaction. Producing more than the firm can sell, late deliveries, and bad debts cause problems.

Organizational Controls and Quality

Learning Outcome

1. Describe the steps in the control process.

The challenges are quite different when establishing a new venture than when the business is operating,[2] so you need controls to ensure success. In this section, we first explain the general control process and system, then controlling quality and costs, and the relationship between quality and costs.

The Control Process

The organizational control process includes setting objectives; establishing standards, methods, and times for measuring performance; measuring and comparing performance with standards; and reinforcing or correcting. See Exhibit 12-1 for an illustration of the steps in the control process.

Exhibit 12-1

Steps in the Control Process

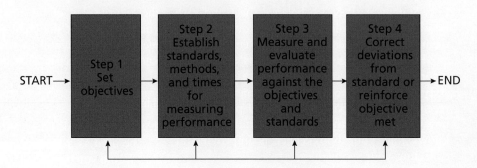

Step 1. Set objectives. The first step in the control process is also a part of planning. In Chapter 3 you learned about setting objectives.

Step 2. Establish standards, methods, and times for measuring performance. Complete standards *describe performance levels in the areas of quantity, quality, time, and cost.* Objectives are standards. However, additional standards are needed if objectives are to be achieved. In Chapter 10 and 11 you learned about setting accounting budgets and financial analysis ratios, which are standards. Budgets are commonly measured on a monthly basis.

Step 3. Measure and compare performance with standards. Once your budget is formulated it becomes the standard and at the end of the month you compare how much you planned to sell or spend with how much you actually did.

Step 4. Reinforce or correct. If you are selling or spending at standard you are achieving your objective, therefore you need take no action. However, if you are underselling or overspending there is a need for corrective action. You may have to go back to prior steps and change objectives or standards.

The Control System

Note that the control system is based on the parts of the transformation process to make the product or service, as discussed in Chapter 8. There are four types of controls in the control process:

1. **Preliminary/input controls** anticipate and prevent possible problems. One major difference between successful and unsuccessful entrepreneurs is their ability to anticipate and prevent problems, rather than solve problems after they occur. If preliminary controls work, you don't need to use concurrent, rework, or damage control to fix a problem.
2. **Concurrent/process controls** are actions taken during transformation that convert the inputs into outputs to ensure that standards are met. The key to success here is quality control. It is more efficient to reject faulty input than to rework output that does not function properly. Checking quality is also crucial during the transformation process and, of course, at the output stage.
3. **Rework/output controls** are actions taken to fix output. Rework is necessary when preliminary and concurrent controls fail. Most organizations inspect output before it is sold or sent as input to other departments in the organization. Sometimes rework is neither cost-effective nor possible, and outputs have to be accepted as is, discarded, or sold for salvage, all of which can be costly.
4. **Damage controls** are actions taken to minimize negative impacts on customers attributable to faulty products or services. You will have to refund the purchase price, fix the product, perform the service again, or replace the product with a new one. Handling customer complaints is a controlling technique.

As you can see, you should focus on preliminary and concurrent controls to avoid rework and damage controls. Budgets are actually three types of controls at different times. When the budget is developed it is a preliminary/input control designed to anticipate and prevent possible problems. As the months go by it becomes a concurrent/process control to measure and evaluate work in progress. At the end of the year the budget becomes a rework/output control; it's too late for corrective action, but the prior year's budget serves as the basis for the following year's budget. And you adjust the budget to avoid any damage control.

Controlling Quality and Cost

A quality product is an asset to the firm, and cost control is needed to make sure assets are not wasted. There are many examples of companies' efforts to increase quality and decrease cost. However, quality and cost must be balanced as a system.

Poor quality has a direct effect on costs and profits. Poor-quality products result in damage controls and loss of customers and lawsuits for damages caused by product injuries. The following are frequent causes of poor quality.

Managers tend to blame poor quality on employees. In most cases poor quality is out of the employees' control and is a result of some combination of the following causes.

1. **Lack of proper resources.** When management furnishes inferior tools, equipment, materials, or supplies, employees cannot do a quality job.
2. **Poor management.** Poor planning, unclear standards, and poor communication of expectations and instructions often result in poor quality. Managers frequently fail to enforce quality standards.
3. **Lack of training.** Employees cannot do a quality job unless they are properly taught to do so.
4. **Inefficient operations.** If the production/operations systems are inefficient, poor quality will result.

Total Quality Management and the Relationship Between Quality and Cost

In Chapter 8 we already discussed quality—Total Quality Management (TQM), benchmarking, statistical quality control, ISO 9000, Six Sigma, using technology, and manufacturing tips. Recall that TQM requires a continual commitment from everyone in the organization to continue to improve the process involved in creating the product or service sold. The two primary principles of TQM are (1) focusing on delivering customer value and (2) continually improving products or services and their processes. TQM also balances quality and cost.

Poor quality leads to damage control of lost customers and possible lawsuits. There is also corrective cost for poor quality, such as the cost of repairing a faulty product; handling and shipping faulty products; wasted parts, materials, and supplies; and hours of staff time to handle customer complaints. Corrective costs can represent anywhere from 2 to 10 percent of an organization's revenue.

There is a need to balance quality and cost. Poor quality is costly, but giving customers a higher level of quality than they want and are willing to pay for is also costly. As stated by the U.S. Small Business Administration (SBA) and the Partners for Small Business Excellence, "it is critical that entrepreneurs constantly review the way they do business, and keep costs as low as reasonably possible without compromising their operations."[3] The trick is to cut cost without compromising quality. Because quality and cost are directly related, managers should balance both as they focus on controlling both simultaneously.

Follow these six guidelines for what managers can do to control cost.

1. **Emphasize profits, not cost. Balance price, quality, service, and delivery.** When purchasing equipment, materials, or supplies don't simply buy the cheapest available. In the long run it may cost less to use higher-quality materials. Late delivery and poor-quality equipment that breaks down can result in idle employees for a time, with the need for overtime later to catch up. Advertising and salespeople are expenses, but if the result is increased sales they more than offset the cost.

2. **Set clear cost standards.** All employees should know production cost and expectations. Train employees in techniques that will minimize waste. To reduce cost, look for drains on financial resources through waste and duplication. Look for cost trends. Change the standards. Be sure to sell the employees on the benefits of cost savings to them and to the firm.

3. **Talk about and reward cost-consciousness.** Cost should not be a once-a-year subject when the budget is prepared. Part of TQM is talking about cost and quality on a regular basis. Cost control should be a part of employee evaluations. Reward employees for their successful reduction of cost. Many organizations give prizes or cash rewards.

4. **Enforce standards.** With TQM every employee is a quality control person who enforces the high standards. When quality standards are not met, the employee responsible should be informed. Whenever possible, that employee should be required to take corrective action. This employee should redo the job or apologize to the customer.[4]

5. **Use employee suggestions.** Employees often know or can develop ways to cut cost. Solicit employees' ideas and reward them for their success—it's part of TQM.

6. **Keep records and plan improvements.** Keep records and communicate results to employees. Combine quality and cost into one report, and plan for improvements in both areas together. Exhibit 12-2 summarizes what managers can do to control quality and cost.

Learning Outcome

2. List the guidelines for controlling quality and the guidelines for controlling cost.

Learning Outcome

3. Discuss the importance of quality and TQM as part of the entrepreneurial process.

Personal Application

1. Analyze the level of quality compared with the price you paid for a product or service, such as the smart phone or car you own. Does quality appear to be balanced with cost?

Exhibit 12-2

Controlling Quality
and Cost

1. Use quality resources and systems.	1. Emphasize profits, not costs.
2. Set clear quality standards.	2. Set clear cost standards.
3. Talk about and reward quality.	3. Talk about and reward cost-consciousness.
4. Enforce quality standards.	4. Enforce cost standards.
5. Use employee suggestions.	5. Use employee suggestions.
6. Keep records and plan improvements.	6. Keep records and plan improvements.

The Elevator Pitch

This skill-builder puts you in the venture capitalist position. You will watch an elevator pitch from the Internet and discuss if investors would or wouldn't invest in the new venture. The link for the elevator pitch for this chapter can be found at: www.nbcnews. com/video/your-business/31875791#31472949. Deborah Brenner pitches her business, *Women of the Vine Cellars,* as a female owner in the wine industry.

Think about it.

1. What score do you give the pitch?

Great product idea and pitch		Terrible product idea and pitch	
4	3	2	1

2. Would you fund a half million dollars for ownership into this business?

3. What does Deborah predict for a Return on Investment (ROI)?

Learning Outcome

4. Discuss the role of budgets as part of the control process.

Budgets

Internally, one of the most powerful and common control devices is the budget. While the budget appears to be identical with the historical balance sheets and income statement, it is not. Although the terms used are identical, the timeframe is different. A firm's annual financial statement is a historical summary of production and other costs that have actually been incurred. The budget is a preliminary written plan for future specific application whose purpose is to control future company activities. It becomes a master plan for the over-all coordination and control of the company as it moves toward achieving its objectives. Obviously there must be rational limits to the budget because it is primarily a statement of funds to be expended. These limits are provided by the estimated sales income because it is this income against which the expenses are drawn. Only in rare circumstances can expenses exceed income. A negative income or loss can exist for a short time and only if there are accumulated cash reserves from which to draw (see Chapter 11 on equity or debt financing).

It is not a coincidence that budgetary and cost accounting terminologies are similar. In fact, they are designed specifically so that the budget will present accounting details that are useful in controlling budget items. While the idea of budgeting is universally applicable, each budget is uniquely and individually drawn and tailored to a specific organization structure and objectives. It is necessary for your budget to conform to your specific business in order for it to be successfully used for planning and control.

Although it has not been explicitly mentioned previously, the budget is also a planning device. The very act of formulating expenditures requires some thought given to the source of cash and how it is to be expended. This activity is what is meant by planning. The outcome of the planning process, with its implications for forecasting and decision-making, is a formulated budget that is then used for control purposes to ensure that the organization is proceeding according to plan.

A most important caution should be kept in mind: budgets are still only a guide to measuring progress. The normal phenomenon of "change" will cause actual dollars to deviate from the plan. Documenting and understanding the changes from plan or budget will enable you to formulate better budgets and forecasts.

Keep in mind that the key to budgeting is not accounting skills but rather the ability to forecast sales revenue and to identify relevant expenses and how much they will cost. To be realistic, as a general guide, be conservative with sales and generous with expenses. Don't forget to put in your expected salary and/or percentage of the profit as an expense. Remember, if you are too optimistic with your profit projections, your plan may not be credible. On the other hand, if you are too pessimistic, your plan may not be accepted as worthy of starting.

Let us now look at how a budget might appear if, for example, Deburring Inc. is a firm that envisions sales during the next fiscal year of $800,000. Deburring Inc. removes burrs from a work piece.[5] In our case, we follow a small deburring company that we will use for this budget exercise. The entrepreneur has to shave (remove) the littlest particles on airplane parts so they will perform as expected each and every time.

The very act of determining the expense categories and the relative amount of money devoted to each category represents planning of the highest order. The $775,500 budget presented in Exhibit 12-3 for Deburring Inc. is a

Based on annual sales of $800,000 Consolidated budget, fiscal 2017	
Salaries	$400,000
Payroll taxes	$ 32,000
Insurance	10,000
Motor vehicle	10,000
Telephone	5,500
Rent	20,000
Repairs	5,000
Heat and light	2,500
Materials	175,000
Machinery	50,000
Advertising	35,000
Office	30,000
Total	**$775,000**

Exhibit 12-3
Deburring Inc.
Proposed Budget
2016

Salaries	$15,000
Payroll taxes	1,200
Insurance	200
Motor vehicle	400
Telephone	200
Rent	300
Repairs	500
Heat and light	500
Materials	5,000
Machinery	4,000
Advertising	1,000
Office	1,000
Total	**$29,300**

company-wide budget, representing a consolidation of many smaller department budgets. In a large business many individuals and/or departments have their own budgets, each of which is a part of the whole. Frequently, the yearly budget can be, and is, broken down into smaller time segments so that during each time segment the business owner can see if spending is conforming to the desired pattern. For example, the monthly budget of $29,300 for the milling department at Deburring Inc. might look like the one in Exhibit 12-4. Milling is a process where a milling cutter is spun about an axis while a work piece is advanced through it in such a way that the blades of the cutter are able to shave chips of material with each pass.[6] Deburring Inc. is shaving very small chips of material off of the airplane part.

Remember, the milling department is only one of many department budgets that are consolidated into the overall budget. For example, you cannot just divide the overall salary budget of $400,000 dollars by twelve months to equal $33,333 for the salaries for each month of the milling department. That would equal $400,000 dollars of salary for milling employees—and no money to pay the salaries of the employees in the other departments.

Variances in Budgets

The control function of the budgetary process becomes apparent when you examine your actual costs and compare the variance between the budgeted and the actual figures. Budget variance is a deviation from the established budgetary amount, as shown in Exhibit 12-5. Deburring Inc. shows it had a variance of –$1,266, which means the milling department actually underspent, spending $1,266 less than was actually budgeted for in the month of July.

	Budget	Actual Expenses	Variances
Salaries	$15,000	14,800	–200
Payroll taxes	1,200	1,184	–16
Insurance	200	200	n/c
Motor vehicle	400	350	–50
Telephone	200	250	+50
Rent	300	300	n/c
Repairs	500	650	+150
Heat and light	500	600	+100
Materials	5,000	4,500	–500
Machinery	4,000	3,900	–100
Advertising	1,000	500	–500
Office	1,000	800	–200
Total			**–$1,266**

Exhibit 12-5

Deburring Inc. Milling Department Monthly Budget Report, Month of July

The variance column makes it clear that the budgeted numbers for that period have either been exceeded or underspent. While overspending may not be desirable, it signifies that the department has failed to meet the plan and that corrective action is needed or that significant authorized growth has occurred.

It is important that each department budget be as simple as possible so any significant variation can be identified and corrected immediately. Each budget should also be flexible, allowing for changes in the environment. A flexible budget might show the allowable expenditure pattern, dependent upon estimated sales. This method of budgeting is also called variable budgeting.

Budget notes

1. Salaries. Represent 5 percent increase from previous for an across-the-board cost-of-living increase.
2. Payroll taxes. Computed at 8 percent of total wages.
3. Insurance includes property, vehicle, and workmen's compensation.
4. Motor vehicle. To cover replacement cost for sales reps' vehicles.
5. Repairs. Represents estimated costs for deferred building repairs.
6. Materials. Represents 4 percent increase from prior year required to fulfill contracts.
7. Advertising. Represents 2 percent decrease from prior year costs due to change in advertising strategy.
8. Office. Includes costs for additional computerized work station for accounting personnel.
9. The total amount is about $25,000 less than $500,000 to allow room for some adjustment.

Variable Budgeting

Personal Application

2. What experiences do you have with either a personal or a professional budget?

The concept of the variable budget is important because it transforms the simple budget from a passive tool to one that can respond to changes. A budget that can be used to plan and control in the light of many judgments about the future enables the manager to determine in advance the responses required to meet changing economic conditions, in order to develop plans detailing how to cope with the changing future.

Financial Ratio Controls and the Balanced Scorecard

Learning Outcome

5. Identify different financial ratios to judge your firm's financial health compared with the other firms in your industry.

Why do we use ratios? Possessing the ability to be creative will not ensure success. Your business must incorporate good management techniques and the ability to control adjustments by using the information generated by operations. All firms must have standards or guidelines against which they can measure their efforts. Controls are used to make sure the firm does what is planned.

A **ratio** *is the relationship between any two numbers derived from a firm's financial statements.* These relationships measure the firm's internal and external health. Analyzing the internal health of a firm requires answers to questions such as whether the firm has enough cash to cover its indebtedness or how the firm compares with other firms in the field, or to average ratios of all firms in the field. The purpose of ratios is to compare the firm with a typical healthy firm in the same type of industry, and to itself over time.

Personal Application

3. Apply your personal financial situation to the assets = liabilities + net worth equation.

To understand the use of ratios as control tools, it is necessary to describe the two major descriptive tools that a business must use if it is to function profitably. In fact, without a balance sheet and a profit and loss statement, the business can only conjecture, and poorly at that, how well it is doing.

As we discussed in Chapter 10, the balance sheet is a statement, at a point in time, of an organization's financial status. It shows

assets = liabilities + net worth

The Brown Corporation is a manufacturer of electrical equipment. The balance sheet for Brown on December 3, 2016 is shown in Exhibit 12-6. Although industry standards are used as measurement, unique characteristics of the Brown Corporation may give very plausible reasons not to measure equitably against these ratios.

The Income Statement

Because the primary function of any business is the creation of profit, without profit the organization cannot survive. The income statement is a flow concept. It shows the result of movement over time. A typical profit and loss statement for Brown Corporation is shown in Exhibit 12-7.

Assets			
Current Assets			
Cash		$450,000	
Marketable securities (at cost)		850,000	
Accounts receivable		2,000,000	
Inventory		2,700,000	
	Total current assets		$6,000,000
Fixed Assets			
Land		450,000	
Buildings		3,800,000	
Machinery		950,000	
Equipment		100,000	
		5,300,000	
	Less: depreciation	1,800,000	
	Net fixed assets		$3,500,000
Total assets			$9,500,000
Liabilities			
Current Liabilities			
Accounts payable		1,000,000	
Notes payable		600,000	
Wages payable		250,000	
Taxes payable		450,000	
	Total current liabilities	2,300,000	
Long-Term Liabilities			
Mortgages		3,000,000	
Total Liabilities		5,300,000	
Owner's equity			
Common stock ($1 par value)		500,000	
Accumulated retained earnings		3,700,000	
	Total equity	4,200,000	
Total Liabilities and Equity			$9,500,000

Exhibit 12-6

Brown Corporation
Balance Sheet,
31 December 2016

Exhibit 12-7

Brown Corporation
Income Statement
for the Period Ending
December 31, 2016

Net sales		$14,000,000
Cost of goods sold		
Materials	$4,000,000	
Labor	3,000,000	
Overhead	3,500,000	
Total cost of goods sold		$10,500,000
Gross profit		$3,500,000
Less expenses		
Selling and administrative	450,000	
Supplies	50,000	
Total expenses	500,000	
Profit from sales		$3,000,000
Provision for taxes		$1,500,000
Net Profit		$1,500,000

Ratios are the relationships of the firm's financial figures using balance sheet and income statement information that can be compared with industry averages and prior firm performance. These ratios are used as predictive or control devices.

The object of ratio control is to make certain that the organization's performance is in line with its goals and objectives. A deviation from prediction or normality signifies that further analysis and perhaps change must take place if the organization is to succeed. As the small business grows, the financial data can be compared over a two- or three-year time period. The goal would be to show improvement on each ratio from year to year.

The most common ratios are presented in Exhibit 12-8 and can be used to determine the financial condition of your business, the success of your marketing strategy, and the success of your human resource function.

Liquidity Ratios

The current and quick liquidity ratios represent the firm's ability to meet its short-term debt (current liabilities) with current assets or, stated another way, the ability of the firm to pay its debts.

In the current ratio, assets are divided into two categories: current assets and fixed assets. Those assets that can be converted into cash within one year are current assets. Current assets may be in the form of cash or other forms of negotiable instruments such as accounts receivable. Debts that will be due within one year are current liabilities. The relationship between current assets and current liabilities is the current ratio. Typically this ratio should be at least

Area	Ratio	Calculation	Information	
Finance				**Exhibit 12-8** **Financial Ratios**
Profitability	Gross profit margin	$\dfrac{\text{Sales–cost of goods sold}}{\text{Sales}}$	Shows efficiency of operations and product pricing.	
	Net profit margin	$\dfrac{\text{Net profit}}{\text{Sales}}$	Shows product profitability.	
	Return on investment	$\dfrac{\text{Net profit}}{\text{Total assets}}$	Shows return on total capital expenditures, or ability of assets to generate a profit.	
Liquidity	Current ratio	$\dfrac{\text{Current assets}}{\text{Current liabilities}}$	Shows ability to pay short-term debt.	
	Quick ratio	$\dfrac{\text{Current assets–inventory}}{\text{Current liabilities}}$	Shows stronger measure of bill-paying ability because inventory may be slow to sell for cash.	
Leverage	Debt to equity	$\dfrac{\text{Total liabilities}}{\text{Owner's equity}}$	Shows proportion of the assets owned by the organization.	
Operations	Inventory turnover	$\dfrac{\text{Cost of goods sold}}{\text{Average inventory}}$	Shows efficiency on controlling investment in inventory. The larger the number the better, because products are sold faster.	
Marketing	Market share	$\dfrac{\text{Company sales}}{\text{Total industry sales}}$	Shows the organization's competitive position. The larger the better, because it is outselling competitors.	
	Sales to presentation	$\dfrac{\text{Sales completed}}{\text{Sales presentations made}}$	Shows how many presentations it takes to make a sale.	
Human resources	Absenteeism	$\dfrac{\text{Number of absent employees}}{\text{Total number of employees}}$	Shows the ratio/percentage of employees that must be replaced for a given period, usually one year.	

(Continued)

Exhibit 12-8
(*Continued*)

Area	Ratio	Calculation	Information
	Turnover	$\dfrac{\text{Number of employees leaving}}{\text{Total number of employees}}$	Shows ratio/ percentage of employees that must be replaced for a given period, usually one year.
	Workforce composition	$\dfrac{\text{Number of a specific group}}{\text{Total number of employees}}$	Shows ratio/ percentage of women, Hispanics, African Americans, and so on.

2 to 1 for the firm to remain viable and indicates the money that is available to cover the firm's debts.[7] The current ratio for the Brown Corporation is:

current ratio = current assets/current liabilities
Brown = 6,000,000/2,700,000 = 2.6:1

Personal Application

4. Apply the current ratio to your own personal situation. What is your own current ratio? What do you have for current assets/current liabilities?

A firm is considered to be in a good position if the ratio of current assets to current liabilities is 2:1 or greater. Creditors would not be pleased if their coverage dips much below 2:1, but the investors would believe that coverage greater than 2:1 signified that too much money that could be put to other uses was being held out to pay bills. We are only talking about current assets and liabilities. The Brown Corporation above is therefore attractive to creditors and is competitive with the industry standards as it has a ratio of 2.6:1.

The *quick ratio or acid test ratio* shows the relationship between assets such as cash accounts, notes receivable, and market securities and current liabilities. The quick ratio should be at least 1 to 1 to show the firm's ability to immediately meet and pay its current debt load.

quick ratio = current assets – inventories/current liabilities
Brown: 6,000,000 – 2,700,000/2,300,000 = 1.4:1

This ratio is important because it shows how much cash, or near cash, is instantly available to pay bills. Other items such as inventory are also short-term assets, but if a slowdown occurs, it may be difficult or impossible to dispose of them at full market value leaving creditors with worthless paper and/or materials. The firm could be bankrupt in any kind of tight credit times. Brown is in a good situation with its quick ratio of 1.4:1.

Leveraging Ratios

Leverage ratios measure financing by a firm's owners against that supplied by creditors. A low-leverage debt to equity ratio means that the business owners supply less of the funds needed by the business and that creditors provide more of the firm's financing. Consequently, with less money invested by the owners, the firm will have more difficulty getting credit and is more vulnerable to going out of business—insolvency.

debt to equity ratio = total debt/total equity
Brown = 5,300,000/4,200,000 = 1.26:1

Most experts believe a company should have about 40–50 percent (although these figures fluctuate from industry to industry) of the company as debt and the other half as equity. As we can see, Brown owes more than it owns.

Operating Ratios

Operating ratios indicate how efficiently the firm is operating. The inventory turnover ratio measures the number of times inventory is turned over during the year.

inventory turnover ratio = sales/inventory
Brown = 14,000,000/2,700,000 = 5.2 times

The inventory turnover ratio indicates how long the inventory remains on your store shelf. An inventory turnover ratio of 5.2 times would mean each piece of inventory turned over a little more than five times in the last year. Brown does appears to be doing a good job turning over inventory considering the inventory turned over greater than the four seasons (winter, spring, summer, and fall). Like all ratios, inventory turnover should be evaluated each year to make sure the inventory is turning over properly. Also, like all ratios, the acceptability of a firm's ratio depends upon what is average and normal for the industry.

A firm does not want to keep its money tied up in inventory and cannot use it for other operating purposes if it is tied up in inventory. This has ramifications for pricing policy because the inventory must be stored and maintained and the cost of inventory varies with how long the firm must store it. Also, the longer merchandise sits on the shelves, the higher the price it must return in the market. Someone, usually the consumer, must pay.

Profitability Ratios

These ratios describe how profitable the firm is. They measure the bottom line and therefore they are a measure of success. In general, the higher the profit, the more efficiently and successfully you are managing your company. The following are three common ratios used to measure profitability.

The *gross profit margin* is a measurement of a company's manufacturing and distribution efficiency during the production process. The gross profit tells an investor the percentage of revenue/sales left after subtracting the cost of goods sold. A company that boasts a higher gross profit margin than its competitors and industry is more efficient.[8] Brown has a healthy gross profit margin of 25 percent. But, it is critical to compare the ratio against your industry competitors.

gross profit margin = (sales − cost of goods sold)/sales
Brown: (14,000,000 − 10,500,000)/14,000,000 = .25 = 25 percent

The *net profit margin* is a ratio of profitability calculated as net profits divided by sales. It measures how much out of every dollar of sales a company actually keeps in earnings. A higher profit margin indicates a more profitable company that has better control over its costs compared with its competitors.[9] Brown has a healthy 10.7 percent net profit margin. Many companies have lower than 5 percent. For example, supermarkets often have 1 percent or lower. Supermarkets work on a business model of high-volume sales at a lower price margin than most other industries.

net profit margin = net profit/sales
Brown: 1,500,000/14,000,000 = .107 = 10.7 percent

The calculation for return on investment (ROI) can be modified to suit the situation—it all depends on what you include as returns and costs. ROI attempts to measure the profitability of an investment and, as such, there is no one "right" calculation. In our case, we divided net profit by total assets. The higher the ratio, the more profit was made on the assets invested in the company. Under normal business conditions, a 15.8 percent return on investment is a healthy return on the assets held by the company.

ROI = net profit/total assets
Brown = 1,500,000/9,500,000 = .158 = 15.8 percent

Marketing Ratios

The role of marketing is to help create satisfied customers. The higher your company's market share, the higher the indication that your customers are happier with your products and services.

market share = company sales/total industry sales

Specifically geared to the sales portion of marketing, the sales to presentation ratio shows how many presentations it takes to make a sale. The goal is for a salesperson to complete as many presentations as possible to increase the company revenues and his or her own commissions.

sales to presentations = sales completed/sales presentations made

Overall, Brown measures quite well versus standard ratios across all industries. Using these ratios for internal control purposes will enable you to identify potential problems before they occur. Knowing the meaning of the ratios also points to the possible actions you can take to remedy problems. The Brown debt/equity ratio should improve with time as it pays off its debt and its net profits improve its owner equity. A few Web sites that help you to learn more about many ratios are listed below.

1. www.dnb.com/customer-service/understanding-financial-statements.html by Dun & Bradstreet.
2. www.investopedia.com/university/ratios/liquidity-measurement/ratio1.asp.
3. www.financeformulas.net/Corporate-Finance-Formulas.html, which includes a financial calculator for each ratio.
4. Risk Management Association (RMA), www.rmahq.org/file%20library/ tools%20and%20publications/statement%20studies/frb_definition_of_ ratios_201011.pdf.

As a small-business owner, you should strive to equal if not exceed industry averages. Keep in mind, though, that these ratios are averages and your deviation from them does not automatically mean that you have problems, but rather that you should consider why your results differ. Recognize that your ratios may differ from standards for perfectly valid reasons.

Balanced Scorecard

Robert Kaplan and David Norton realized that simply using financial measures to determine the effectiveness of a firm's management team tended to focus more on short-term tactical thinking and overlooked long-term strategic success.[10] They say the key to turning strategy into action is by using what they called a balanced scorecard. The scorecard monitors a company in four basic areas—instead of focusing only on financial performance. The balanced scorecard works equally well for small businesses as for large organizations. The following list outlines the four perspectives in a balanced scorecard.[11]

> **Learning Outcome**
>
> 6. Identify the role of the balanced scorecard as part of the controlling process.

1. **Financial perspective.** An entrepreneur needs to keep careful track of revenues and costs. Investors will evaluate the company's value based on the financial statements and ratios. Investors will expect the entrepreneur to reach the financial goals that were originally set.
2. **Customer perspective.** What measures should be in place to determine whether or not the customer's needs and expectations are being met? As a small business, what delivers value to your customers and how can their satisfaction be measured?
3. **Internal perspective.** This is a measure of the operations processes that run your company. Do customers receive the quality product or service they expect—at a reasonable cost? Is the product being delivered on time? Are the bills being paid properly and on a good payment schedule?

Personal Application

5. Complete a balanced scorecard for a small business in your community.

Learning Outcome

7. Describe how risk management can help an entrepreneur to control the growth of his or her own business.

4. **Learning and growth.** Does your company culture promote entrepreneurial thinking? Are your employees motivated to learn more about their jobs and improve the product they are producing?[12]

Risk Management

One big reason why businesses fail is poor risk management.[13] **Risk** *refers to a possible loss or other adverse event that has the potential to interfere with the financial stability of a business.* Risk management is the ability to address the risk in order to minimize its effect on your business. Once you assess those risks, you can begin taking steps to reduce them. Unfortunately, management of risk is often overlooked by entrepreneurs who wait until the risk occurs.

Risk Assessment

When you decide to start a new venture, you face uncertainty,[14] and you need to assess the risks you face.[15] To be proactive, you need to ensure that your own personal assets are protected as much as possible. As discussed in Chapter 5, it is important to make the correct choice of being a sole proprietor, corporation, or limited liability company or developing a strong partnership agreement.

Some risks can be avoided by obtaining insurance. However, there are a number of risks that cannot be avoided or minimized by insurance policies. These risks can include natural hazards, contracts and legal relationships, financial operations, misconduct by employees, acts or omissions of third parties, federal, provincial, and municipal laws or regulations, economic conditions, dependence on outside resources, property loss, use of technology, and workforce issues. Other risks such as economic conditions and the financial strength or weakness of the local community will also have a direct impact on the business.

Insurance

Insurance *is a contract (policy) in which an individual or entity receives financial protection or reimbursement against losses from an insurance company.* The insurance company pools clients' risks to make payments more affordable for the insured.[16] You have to pay a **premium,** *which is how much you want to spend monthly for the amount of insurance coverage desired.* There is normally a **deductible,** *which is the amount of money you have to pay before insurance pays on a claim.* Accepting a higher deductible will lower the monthly premium. In comparison, you can have a lower deductible amount, but you will have a higher premium.

Each person or business has to analyze each of the following types of insurance to calculate which type of insurance is required or needed for their type of business. **Farmers, Chubb, Travelers, Northwestern Mutual,** and many other great insurance companies provide insurance products and services to help manage the risks in your business. You can also have a local insurance agent that can draw from multiple insurance companies.

1. **Disability insurance.** What will you do if you, a business partner, or a key employee becomes disabled? Disability insurance coverage is designed to provide a benefit when the person is totally or partially disabled.[17]

2. **Key person(s) life insurance.** What happens to a small business when the owner, or any of the key employees, unexpectedly dies? The answer is the company can buy life insurance on its key employee(s), pays the premiums, and is the beneficiary of the policy. If that person unexpectedly dies, the company receives the insurance payoff. Hopefully, the money received from the policy can help the business to stay competitive during the transition to the new owner or employee.[18]

3. **Automobile insurance policies.** It is recommended that a company obtain a business automobile policy if employees use a company-owned vehicle, a leased company vehicle, or use their own personal vehicles for business purposes. An employee may not have enough personal liability coverage to adequately protect the business.[19]

4. **Liability insurance.** This is an insurance policy that protects an individual or business from the risk that they may be sued and held legally liable for something such as malpractice, injury, or negligence. Liability insurance policies cover both legal costs and any legal payouts for which the insured would be responsible if found legally liable.

5. **Business income insurance (business interruption coverage).** Business income coverage is protection against loss of income or profits, in which a business has suffered a property loss or damage from a covered peril, such as a fire, natural disaster, theft, or vandalism. This covers the time when the business is shut down until the property is repaired or replaced.[20] The tornadoes that touched down in places such as Moore, OK and Springfield, MA confirm that business interruption coverage is more important than ever.

6. **Workers' compensation insurance.** Worker's compensation is the system of laws meant to protect injured workers. The goal is to make sure that somebody who is injured at work receives appropriate medical care, lost wages relating to the on-the-job injury, and, if necessary, retraining and rehabilitation, so as to be able to return to the work force.[21]

7. **Machinery and equipment insurance.** What would cover your expensive production equipment or computer hardware should it become damaged? Equipment breakdown insurance provides coverage for the accidental breakdown of equipment.[22]

8. **Property and casualty insurance.** Property and casualty insurance is insurance on homes, cars, and businesses. Technically, property insurance protects a person or business with an interest in physical property against its loss or the loss of its income-producing abilities. Casualty insurance mainly protects a person or business against legal liability for losses caused by injury to other people or damage to the property of others.[23]

9. **Electronic data-processing insurance.** A newer form of insurance, electronic equipment can be insured for fire, theft, malicious damage, accidental damage, mechanical breakdown, or electrical breakdown. A separate electronic data-processing (EDP) policy can cover hardware as well as software.[24]

Other Options for Starting a New Venture, and Entrepreneurial Behavior

How do controls vary by type of entry into entrepreneurship?

Buying an Existing Business, Franchise, or Leasing Rights

Buying an Existing Business

The existing business should already have controls in place. However, has the current control system been producing the results that were expected? For example, how well has the budgeting process been used to help manage costs in the business you would be buying? Does the existing business use financial ratios to examine its financial situation compared to its competitors? Before buying a business, an accountant or you can calculate financial ratios to help you determine the value of the firm.

Buying a Franchise

If you buy a franchise, the franchisor will have control systems to use in its stores to maintain expected quality and financial levels. As a franchisee, you will need to adhere to the guidelines provided by the franchisor.

Buying Licensing Rights

If you buy a license, you are starting a new line of business and will have to report how your company performed in regards to sales to determine the royalty that you owe to the licensor. You will also be required to meet quality standards to maintain your licensing rights.

Starting a Corporate Venture

The company will most likely have control systems that you will need to follow, but, being a new venture, you will need to develop controls and maintain quality. The corporation will most likely have specific financial expectations and measures, and, if you don't meet goals, your venture may be closed.

Even though you are making money and believe you have the company's support, you can never be sure it will not sell, close down, or combine your operation. Your division could be spun off to get funds for other uses. Some or all of your resources can be allocated to other uses. Or, you could be absorbed back into the parent company or some other division.

Starting a Nonprofit

Nonprofits need to establish control features to make sure the money that is raised is properly spent. An important role of your board of directors is to help ensure that the nonprofit is controlling operations, quality, and finances. Nonprofits need to use the same tools as profits to make sure their control systems work properly. Thus, they should have income statements, balance sheets, calculate and analyze financial ratios, complete a cash flow analysis, and develop budgets for the different areas of their charitable operation.

Entrepreneurial Behavior

If you are not interested in starting a new venture, as an employee you can engage in entrepreneurial behavior by designing more effective control systems at your current workplace. Companies that develop true entrepreneurial cultures seek employee input to improve operations and profitability and reward employees for productivity improvements. They do not punish their employees for risk-taking and failure. In fact they thank them for trying and learning.

Take it to the Net

Visit www.routledge.com/cw/Lussier for the book's companion Web site, where you can:

- use learning aids, including taking a quiz;
- find links to resources in this chapter, as well as other links including videos;
- learn about and start the following activities: Continuing Integrated Case, Your Ninety-Second New Venture Pitch, the Paper Clip Entrepreneurship Challenge, College Entrepreneurial Spirit Award, and the Community Entrepreneurial Spirit Award.

Chapter Review and Summary

This summary lists the learning outcomes from the chapter and their answers.

1. Describe the steps in the control process

The control process includes setting objectives; establishing standards, methods, and times for measuring performance; measuring and comparing performance with standards; and reinforcing or correcting. Controlling is the process of establishing methods ensuring that the business objectives are achieved.

2. List the guidelines for controlling quality and the guidelines for controlling cost

The six guidelines for controlling quality are to use quality resources and systems, set clear quality standards, talk about and reward quality, enforce quality standards, use employee suggestions, and keep records and plan improvements.

The six guidelines for controlling costs are to emphasize profits, not costs, set clear cost standards, talk about and reward cost-consciousness, enforce cost standards, use employee suggestions, and keep records and plan for improvements.

3. Discuss the importance of quality and TQM as part of the entrepreneurial process

Quality is the most powerful weapon small businesses have over the large corporation. Quality is the predetermined standard that the product or service should meet. TQM requires everyone in the organization to continually improve products and services. The key to TQM is setting standards and continually striving to improve them.

4. Discuss the role of budgets as part of the control process

While you cannot control the fact that your business must pay taxes, it is incumbent on you to use the financial information your business generates to analyze and control your firm in order to maximize profitability. The development of pro forma statements or budgets cannot be accurate because it is impossible to predict the future. The budget is a preliminary written plan for future specific application whose purpose is to control future company activities. It is an indispensable tool. What you can do, however, is to compare what actually happens with your predictions and look for variances—deviations from the established budgetary amounts. This will enable you to determine how to change what you are doing in response to reality. As part of your management control, you evaluate the items that have the larger variances. You then take corrective action if necessary. You will know if corrective action is necessary as cost variances, the difference between actual costs and what they should have been, will become immediately evident.

5. Identify different financial ratios to judge your firm's financial health compared with the other firms in your industry

Financial ratios are the relationships of the firm's financial figures using balance sheet and income statement information that can be compared with industry averages. These ratios are used as predictive or control devices. The first groups of ratios used in the analysis of your business are the liquidity ratios, which tell if the business can meet its cash obligations as they become due. This ratio group consists of the current and quick ratios, where both show the relationship between current assets and current liabilities. Leveraging ratios measure financing by a firm's owners against that supplied by creditors. This group of ratios includes comparing the level of total debt to total assets. Operating ratios indicate how efficiently the firm is operating. They are extremely important and provide significant information. Inventory turnover ratio is an operating ratio that serves as an indication of how often merchandise is turning over.

6. **Identify the role of the balanced scorecard as part of the controlling process**

The balanced scorecard monitors a company in four basic areas—instead of focusing only on financial performance. These areas are a financial perspective, a customer perspective, an internal operations perspective, and an employee learning and growth perspective. The balanced scorecard works equally well for small businesses as for large organizations.

7. **Describe how risk management can help an entrepreneur to control the growth of his or her own business**

Risk management is the ability to address the risks involved in owning a business in order to minimize their effect on the business. Once you assess those risks, you can begin taking steps to reduce them. Potential risks that need to be assessed include natural hazards, contracts and legal relationships, financial operations, misconduct by employees, acts or omissions of third parties, federal, provincial, and municipal laws or regulations, economic conditions, dependence on outside resources, property loss, use of technology, and workforce issues. A small business should purchase insurance that fits the needs of its specific type of business.

8. **Define the twenty-two key terms in this chapter**

acid test (quick ratio)	leveraging ratios
	liquidity ratios
asset coverage ratio	operating ratios
balance sheets	premiums
budget	process
budget variances	profitability ratios
control	quality
controlling	ratio
cost variances	risk management
current ratio	standards
deductible	total quality management
insurance	

Review and Discussion Questions

1. Why is the control function and process so important to the small-business owner?

2. What is the role of standards in controlling quality?

3. Why is quality called a virtue of design?

4. What are some of the things managers can do to control quality and cost?

5. What is the chief difference between historical balance sheets and a firm's income statements and its budget?

6. How would you go about setting up a budget for your firm? What information would you need and how would you use it?

7. How would you use the budget as a control device?

8. What is the importance of a variance from the budget and what steps do you take when a variance occurs?

9. Define the term "operating ratio." How would you use ratios in your business for making decisions?

10. Define and explain the meaning of liquidity ratios.

11. Define and explain the meaning of leveraging.

12. Explain the current ratio. Would a ratio of 1:1 be considered a "good" current ratio? Why or why not?

13. What is the difference between the current ratio and the acid test ratio? If you were a supplier to the business, which ratio would you use and why?

14. What does the inventory turnover ratio tell you? What would be a satisfactory inventory ratio?

15. Define the proprietorship ratio. What is the standard usually accepted as being good for this ratio?

16. To quickly judge the overall health of a firm, which three ratios would you use and what would be considered good ratios?

Application Exercises

When doing these exercises, be sure to select a specific business where applicable, preferably one where you presently or previously work(ed) or a business you would like to own someday. If this is not possible, pick a specific organization to which you will refer. Be sure to identify the organization by name. Limit your answers to one or two pages per exercise.

1. Select a specific business you are familiar with and develop standard ratios that you would consider to be important for the business using sources such as the Risk Management Association (RMA) or Dun & Bradstreet.

2. Interview a local bank loan officer to find out what ratios are considered important and what values for these ratios are sought in judging business health.

3. Compare the information you located in question 1 and 2. Are the ratios being considered the same or are they different? Explain the differences or similarities.

4. Interview an established small-business person and obtain a copy of the firm's financial statements, current or past. Using this information:

   a. Compare the ratios used in this chapter;

   b. Using the RMA or Dun & Bradstreet, find the industry ratios for this type of business;

   c. Compare the information in questions (a) and (b) and make appropriate recommendations for the business.

Application Situations

1. Networth Company

Networth Company, founded by Peter Jurgen in 2010 after graduation from college, was a retail store specializing in selling expensive fabric to wealthy clientele. The first three years of the firm's existence saw an increase in sales by 50 percent, 75 percent, and 100 percent. In those years Peter was only able to show net profits of under 6 percent while the average profits for the industry were 14 percent. He attributed this to the unusually high startup costs and the expensive property he had leased on the most expensive street in the city. It would, he thought, take several years and everything would fall into place and he would be at least competitively profitable.

In 2014, however, there was a recession and Peter's sales dropped in two successive years by 25 percent in the first year and 30 percent during the following year. Profits became nonexistent. While not panicking, Peter decided to revise his credit policies. Previously he allowed thirty days net on his bills. Now he allowed forty-five days. Also recognizing that his customers might not have as much discretionary income as before, he relaxed enforcement. His average collection period ratio was now sixty days. Given enough time, he was sure that this strategy would turn the company around.

1. Does the fact that Peter's 6 percent profit fails to match industry standards signal a problem for the company? How would you measure profits? As a result of your findings, what would you recommend?

2. Are you comfortable with Peter's rented facilities? Support your position and indicate the effect that change of facilities might have on profits.

3. Is it too late for Peter's plan to save the company or is his timing wrong? Defend your opinion.

2. Jay's Antiques

Jay's Antiques, long a fixture in the antique district, managed to turn a respectable profit for fifty years. Jay, now reaching retirement age, began the process of transferring the business and responsibility for decision-making to his children, Sam and Beth. Both had been in the business for five years and, while they were happy, they disagreed with several of the policies Jay followed. For example, they were certain that Jay's approach to buying inventory was too conservative. Jay studied the market and bought only those items that were selling. She gave little consideration to future trends. Sam and Beth thought that the only inventory Jay acquired was already pre-sold because nothing Jay bought remained unsold for longer than thirty days. This approach often resulted in a sparse inventory, leaving clients with a small selection. Slowly, they began to buy more inventory so that buyers would have a wide range of choices. Sam, studying all the journals and economic predictions, bought inventory that, while not currently popular, would be good for future sales.

1. Based upon the above information, what ratios would be affected by the change in policy and how would these ratios change? Explain and be specific.

2. What does the term "respectable profit" tell you? If you were in the antique business, how would you measure success? Explain the measurements you would use and give several examples.

3. As a result of Beth and Sam's strategy, what do you think will happen to the business and why? Explain your position and, as a result of your conclusions, make some recommendations to Beth and Sam.

3. Zenotek

"Profit doesn't mean anything to me. As a measure of my success, it is lacking. All that matters is that I have enough cash to pay my bills." This statement was often made as Priscilla paid the bills incurred by her small manufacturing firm. Her company, Zenotek, manufactured high-capacity chips for use in many of today's appliances including computers and consumer durable goods such as washing machines, ovens, and even office machines. As technology is continually changing, Priscilla has to continue upgrading her facility with newer, more modern manufacturing equipment.

The future appeared bright and equipment manufacturers' terms were generous. If she wanted to, and often did, she could extend the payout on machinery to thirty or forty years. As a result of her firm's success, Priscilla bought a large building lot in a good suburb and erected a state-of-the-art

building. Her office and those of her administrative staff were spacious and expensively furnished.

1. Which of the ratios discussed in the text could be affected? How would these ratios be affected?

2. What recommendations would you make to Priscilla based on her belief or evidenced by her statements and the result of the ratios?

3. In your opinion, what is the likelihood of the firm's survival or is it too late? Explain your position.

Case

The Scuderi Engine Group Needs to Rev Up

The Scuderi Engine Group has competed against the largest engine and car manufacturers for over twenty years. They have experienced every facet of the entrepreneurship process as they have navigated through the different stages of growing their engine business.

Their story begins with their father, Carmen Scuderi. Before he passed away, he had the breakthrough idea of a new form of the combustion engine. After his death, his family raised $80 million dollars trying to bring his idea of a new engine to market.

The Scuderi family is quite large and each family member focused on one area within the business. The oldest sons were appointed president and vice-president and were actively involved in product design and patents. Younger family members were often involved in positions related to sales and marketing.

Their headquarters were a small building in West Springfield, MA. Interest in the community was very high about this new engine. The local newspaper often ran articles about the company and its progress with building a prototype engine. Studies conducted by its independent development partner, Southwest Research Institute, show significant increases in fuel efficiency and torque while emitting up to 80 percent less NOx than conventional "Otto Cycle" engines in use today.[25]

For many years the engine was associated with being useful for the automobile industry. However, because of the unique split-cycle design, the engine can be used in other applications outside of transportation, such as power generation and energy storage.

Making the actual engine would be extremely expensive. Thus, it was decided early on to build a prototype, have it tested at Southwest Research Institute, and then license the product.

Many local people, with little engineering or financial experience, bought shares of the company. It was very easy to go somewhere around the Western Massachusetts area and find investors in the company.

After nearly two decades, the engine was tested at Southwest and they concluded there would be increased efficiency if the engine was used in automobiles. The Scuderis have spent the last two decades hiring industry experts and trying to land a licensing agreement with a large automobile company such as General Motors or Honda. They established offices in many countries and often felt they had more success with their environmentally friendly engine outside the U.S.

Unfortunately, in 2013, the Securities and Exchange Commission (SEC) fined the company for various irregularities. The SEC said the Scuderi family spent $3.2 million of the $80 million it raised from investors on improper payments to Scuderi family members. The SEC also said that, "The Scuderi Group failed to register the stock offerings, which raised the $80 million, with the Commission. Further, the SEC said Scuderi, in order to exempt itself from such reporting, took too much money from investors with a relatively small net worth—investors who in theory, would be less able to absorb the loss if the company failed."[26]

The Scuderi Group agreed to pay the fine and is moving forward with the technology to bring the split cycle engine to the marketplace and reward its investors while saving energy to run engines in many different industries.

Think it over.

1. Draw a simple balanced scorecard to assess the current situation at the Scuderi Engine Group. In which of the four perspectives are they strongest? Which perspective is their weakest?

2. How should the Scuderi Group implement TQM?

3. Assess the economic and technological risk associated with trying to enter the transportation industry with a revolutionary engine that could increase efficiency, decrease our reliance on petroleum, and be better for the environment.

Global Case—Losing Control at Lululemon

Someone forgot to keep things under control at **Lululemon (www.lululemon.com)**. Lululemon is a popular Vancouver, British Columbia-based athletic apparel retailer. However, customers complained about the sheerness of the brand's popular black luon yoga pants. The company cited incomplete testing protocols that led to an "unacceptable level of sheerness" in 17 percent of the nylon/Lycra pants. In short, you could see through their yoga pants.

Investors have filed a class action lawsuit against Lululemon Athletica for allegedly making "false and misleading statements" to conceal the costs associated with its see-through yoga pants recall. The estimated recall cost the company between $12 million and $17 million. The stock has fallen 13 percent overall.[27]

How could this happen? What controls did Lululemon fail to use? Lululemon said the problem was caused by incomplete testing protocols and fabric that was on the lower end of its tolerance scale. How can you reduce the likelihood that this will happen again?

Lululemon needs to improve in regards to design aspects such as color, texture, and size. It is important to create new and exciting products. But, they should also meet ethical and industry standards. Lulu can also work closer with its suppliers to make sure they can provide the proper materials.

Lululemon has to improve its quality control. Its athletic wear has been popular and it was able to leave the startup stage of growth. However, with this growth, Lululemon might not have had the time or focus to improve its quality control procedures.[28]

The final story for Lululemon is not yet written. Will the scandal actually increase its company visibility? Some experts say that bad press is better than no press at all. Will fitness members actually want more Lululemon products that have an appropriate level of sheerness? Lululemon seems to be back to work. They recently sued fifty online sites for selling fake Lululemon apparel items.[29]

Think it over.

1. How can reviewing the budget process help to improve controls at Lululemon?

2. What needs to be in place for a TQM program at Lululemon to be successful?

3. Review the profitability ratios for Lululemon at Yahoo.com's Finance page. Make sure to search using its stock symbol, LULU, and then go its Key Statistics.

Writing Your Business Plan

You (or in teams) can write a business plan during the semester. There are questions at the end of each chapter to help guide you through the thinking and analyzing process. Appendix B has a sample business plan you can use as a template for developing your own new venture business plan.

Since this is Chapter 12, the goal is to control the product or service you provide to have the highest quality possible.

Highlighted Sections of the Business Plan (Chapters 1–12)

1. **The Executive Summary** is written last—but placed first in the business plan. You have to wait until you are finished with the business plan to properly write the executive summary.

2. **Introduction:**
   A. **Background of the business:** Includes a short review of its name, address (or addresses if there is more than one location), telephone number(s), email address, Web site address, hours of operation, and a brief history (if any). You want to state when the business was started or will be started.
   B. **Management credentials and organization structure:** It is common to list all the business's key managers and their duties and responsibilities, with their qualifications.
   C. **Form of ownership:** Will your business be a sole proprietorship, partnership, or corporation and how will any profits be distributed?

3. **Strategy Formulation:**
   A. **Mission:** What is the organization's purpose or reason for being (covered in Chapter 3)? The mission section of the business plan includes your business model (covered in Chapter 4), which can include a broad description of your present and future products and services to be offered. In the strategy section, it is not necessary to list all the products and services; they are listed under the marketing section of the business plan and were discussed in Chapter 6.

   B. **Objectives (prioritized):** What does your organization want to accomplish?
   C. **Environmental analysis:** It includes an analysis of the internal environment (which includes the mission and objectives) and its external environment resulting in a SWOT analysis.

4. **The Marketing Function:**
   A. **The marketing plan:** Your marketing plan must identify your target customers and product feasibility (Chapter 4) by using marketing research to better understand your industry and marketplace.
   B. **The marketing mix:** You need to include the 4 Ps of marketing in your marketing plan. What is your product? At what price point will you sell your product? Where (place) will you sell your product? And, how will you promote your product?

5. **Location and Layout:**
   A. **Location:** You want to consider such general location factors such as: (1) proximity to the market; (2) transportation facilities; (3) availability of raw materials; (4) labor supply; (5) community attitude; (6) water power; (7) land costs; (8) taxes; (9) specialized communities; (10) climatic conditions; (11) potential sister plants or warehouse; (12) the question of urban, suburban, or rural sites; and (13) how these factors affect specific site selection as either a home-based, Internet, or traditional manufacturing or retail location.
   B. **Layout:** Having committed to a location, you must then develop a layout. The layout is an arrangement of the physical facilities in the most efficient manner for specific business, for the interior in order to maximize profitability. You should draw a diagram of the layout you expect to utilize in your business.

6. **The Production/Operations Function:**
   A. **Production process:** What is your operational plan to transform inputs into outputs?
   B. **Quality:** What level of quality will you expect from your finished product?

7. **The Human Resources Function:**

   A. Who are the members of your new venture team (founder, investors, lenders, mentors, lawyer, accountant, banker, insurance agent, and any consultants)?

   B. How do you plan on using the human resources management process to attract, develop, and retain employees?

   C. What is your plan for management succession and an exit strategy?

8. **The Financing Function:**

   A. Who will be in charge of accounting? What processes will be put into place? What accounting software will be used to organize your accounting information?

   B. What sources of equity will you look to acquire? Which of the following sources will you try to use? Personal savings, seed capital, friends and family, partners, angel investors, venture capital and corporate venture capitalists, go public with an IPO, private placement, or crowdfunding?

   C. What will be your sources of debt financing? Loans, leasing, installment billing, trade credits, a bank loan, line of credit, insurance or retirement loans?

   D. Can you get financing from your vendors?

   E. Are other financing options available such as commercial banks, community banks, or credit unions?

   F. Can you use available government programs such as the Small Business Administration (SBA) loans and programs, Small Business Investment Companies (SBICs), or Small Business Lending Companies (SBLCs)? Can you qualify for a funding program at the Minority Business Development Agency (MBDA)? Can you find state and local programs that support small businesses?

   G. Can you use bootstrap financing such as selling valuable personable belongings? Set up your business as home-based? Share resources with a friend? Use college interns? Use credit cards wisely? Try to barter for goods and services?

9. **Controls:**

   A. What control systems and methods will you have in place in your new business?

   B. What are your expected levels of liquidity, leverage, and operating and profit margins for your new business?

   C. Develop a balanced scorecard for your new business.

   D. Conduct a risk assessment and determine what insurance is important for your business needs.

   E. At this point, it is a fairly simple task to change some of your assumptions in your business plan so that you may compare different scenarios. After doing so, choose the best projected results. You should always be comparing your actual results to the projections and constantly change your actions in accordance with actuality.

10. **Appendix**

Appendix A

Where Can You Get Help?
Sources of Domestic and Global Assistance

Domestic Entrepreneurship Resources

While writing this textbook we came across some great entrepreneurial organizations that offered resources online and at conferences that we attended. This first link is from the Extreme Entrepreneurship Tour (which motivates students to become entrepreneurs). Each organization's link is followed by a short paragraph from its organizational Web page.

www.extremetour.org/. The Extreme Entrepreneurship Tour brings the country's top young entrepreneurs to colleges, universities, work force boards and youth groups to help spread the entrepreneurial mindset during half-day, high-energy conference events all over the country.

The Extreme Entrepreneurship Tour is the only nationwide entrepreneurship tour. All of the entrepreneurs are under thirty and have created businesses that are changing the world or making over $1 million in revenue. We went to their STCC stop and watched them create great energy for entrepreneurship with 1000 high school students.

www.empact100.com. The Empact Showcase is a compilation of the top U.S. entrepreneurs age thirty-five and under with revenues over $100,000. Previously the companies were recognized by the White House.

www.c-e-o.org. Entrepreneurship as a field of study at colleges and universities across the U.S. and around the world has become a leading subject at the undergraduate and graduate level. With this increased attention, it is more important than ever to give students the opportunities to network not only with their student peers, but also with fellow entrepreneurs in the business world to promote entrepreneurship at all levels and in all environments. And, this is where the Collegiate Entrepreneurs' Organization (CEO) comes in.

http://enactus.org/. We also attended the Enactus national conference in Kansas City in May 2013. Enactus stands for Entrepreneurship, Action, and Us. Elms College had a student presentation that won "the Rookie of the Year" in 2013. We encourage your college or university to join Enactus. The organization used to be known as Students in Free Enterprise (SIFE). Its name was changed in 2013.

Enactus believes human progress depends on our ability to tap into the entrepreneurial spirit that lives within each of us and channel the unique talents, passions, and ideas we each possess toward creating good in the world.

www.valleyventurementors.org/. Valley Venture Mentors (VVM) was a great organization to learn about elevator pitches at their monthly meeting. Plus, they organized a trip to Boston, MA to learn more about Mass Challenge (www.masschallenge.org) and the i-lab at Harvard (http://ilab.harvard.edu/).

http://www.hgf.org/what-we-do/programs-and-resources/entrepreneurship. aspx. The Harold Grinspoon Entrepreneurship Initiative (EI) has been an extremely valuable organization that promotes entrepreneurship in twelve colleges. Many of the exercises such as the elevator pitch and Spirit Award Winners were adapted from projects that are coordinated by the EI.

www.sba.gov. The Small Business Administration (SBA) is a resource for everyone to learn about entrepreneurship and small-business management. Since its founding in 1953, the SBA has delivered millions of loans, loan guarantees, contracts, counseling sessions, and other forms of assistance to small businesses. As an example of one service, the SCORE Association (www.sba.gov/content/score) is a nonprofit association comprised of 13,000 volunteers throughout the U.S. SCORE members offer their services at no fee, as a community service.

Global Entrepreneurship Resources

www.kauffman.org/. Although the Kauffman Institute is based in the U.S., it has many resources for global entrepreneurship. The key to the site is to let yourself surf around and find all the global material such as the link (**www.unleashingideas.org/**) to the Global Entrepreneurship Week (GEW). During one week each November, GEW inspires people everywhere through local, national, and global activities designed to help them explore their potential as self-starters and innovators. These activities, from large-scale competitions and events to intimate networking gatherings, connect participants to potential collaborators, mentors and even investors—introducing them to new possibilities and exciting opportunities.

www.endeavor.org/. Endeavor is a great resource for global entrepreneurship. Founded in 1997 by Linda Rottenberg (current CEO) and Peter Kellner (current board member), Endeavor is the global nonprofit that pioneered the concept of High-Impact Entrepreneurship in emerging and growth markets. Headquartered in New York City, with seventeen offices across Latin America, the Middle East, Africa, Europe, and Southeast Asia, the organization transforms economies by identifying and supporting high-potential (or "high-impact") entrepreneurs. Practicing a tested "mentor capitalist" model, Endeavor affiliates help entrepreneurs overcome barriers to growth by providing the key ingredients to success: mentorship; networks; strategic advice; talent; skills; access to smart capital; and inspiration.

Appendix B

The Business Plan Example

21st Century Computer Training Centers
Business Plan for 2016
2121 Main St.
Hartford, CT 06101
Phone: 860-278-8765
Fax: 860-278-8173
E-mail: 21centuryCTC@gmail.com,
Web site: www.21centuryCTC.com

Business Plan Outline

1. **The Executive Summary**

2. **Introduction**

    A. *Background of the business*
    B. *Form of ownership*
    C. *Organization structure*

3. **Strategy Formulation**

    A. *Mission*
    B. *Business model*
    C. *Objectives*
    D. *Environmental analysis*

4. **The Marketing Function**

    A. *The marketing plan*
    B. *The marketing mix*

5. **Location and Layout**

    A. *Location*
    B. *Layout*

6. **The Production/Operations Function**

    A. *Production process*
    B. *Quality*

7. **The Human Resources Function**

    A. *New venture team*
    B. *Attract, develop, and retain employees*
    C. *Management succession and an exit strategy*

8. **The Financing Function**

    A. *Accounting information system—Peachtree accounting system*
    B. *Owner's sources of equity financing*
    C. *Sources of debt financing*
    D. *Venture capitalist*
    E. *Crowdfunding*
    F. *Government and Small Business Administration programs*
    G. *Capital expenses*
    H. *Pro forma profit and loss*

9. Controls

    A. Control systems

    B. Liquidity, leverage, operating, and profit margins

    C. Balanced scorecard

    D. Risk assessment

    E. Insurance

    F. Changing actions in accordance with actuality

10. Appendix

1. Executive Summary

21st Century Computer Training Center offers computer training to beginners, mid-level, and high-level users to be ready for computer jobs in the 21st century. We offer a relaxed atmosphere where students can learn individually and as part of a team. We offer courses to new computer students and to our most sophisticated computer users. 21st Century Computer Training Center is a retail- and online-level training center open for all users.

Our greatest competitive advantage is that we expect our students to learn the latest computer skills and are encouraged to look for internships and jobs as soon as they are finished with their first computer course. Students will be assisted with finding qualified positions in industries that need their newly developed computer skills.

The following table is a quick summary showing that a 25 percent classroom capacity will generate $1,456,800. As we increase capacity towards 100 percent we will generate over $5,000,000.

Each owner will be able to invest $50,000. While there is no intention of offering stock at this time, we would most likely consider offering stock after three training centers are established on the East Coast. A line of credit of an equal amount, $200,000, has been established with Newton Bank from Hartford, CT.

Classroom Capacity Used	Number of Student Seats Available per Session	Revenue Generated
100%	19,440	$5,832,000
90%	2,187	$5,248,800
75%	1,822	$4,372,800
50%	1,215	$2,916,000
25%	607	$1,456,800

Exhibit B-1

Summary of Classroom Capacity and Revenue

2. Introduction

A. *Background of the business.* 21st Century Computer Training Center is located in Hartford, CT at 2121 Main St., 06101, 860-278-8765; our email address is 21centuryCTC@gmail.com and our Web site address is www.21centuryCTC.com. The store training hours are 8:00 a.m to 8:00 p.m., Monday through Saturday. We are open for training online 24/7. Our courses are taped using Adobe Connect and students are able at any time to take a course online.

B. *Form of Ownership.* The four main owners of 21st Century Computer Training Center will have an equal partnership. All four partners have either taught computer courses or worked in the computer field for the last twenty years.

1. Dr David B. Brothers. Has spent over twenty years teaching Microsoft Office at the university and college level. Certified as an official Microsoft Office specialist. Specializes in social media applications.
2. Dr Robert Gregory. Has spent the last ten years teaching digital communications at the university and college level. Certified in Adobe Photoshop and other Adobe products. Course topics range from creating cell phone applications, designing new hardware, and three levels of graphic design.
3. Ivan Bundz. Has spent the last twenty years focused on programming. Works in the insurance industry coding high-level insurance products. A specialist in Java.
4. Christine Bay. Has been the CFO for two startup organizations. Previously, she spent ten years as an accountant with two different national accounting firms.

C. *Organization structure.*

1. David B. Brothers. Ph.D. Computer Systems, CEO.
2. Robert Gregory. Ph.D. Management Systems, COO.
3. Ivan Bundz. MBA Computer Science Engineering, CIO.
4. Christine Bay, CPA, CFO.

3. Strategy Formulation

A. *Mission.* The mission of 21st Century Computer Training Center is to be the premier training center for the latest advances in technology. Customers who attend a technology course will learn a skill that will allow them to apply for computer-related jobs.

B. *Business model.* Our business model is to offer technology courses from 8:00 a.m. to 8:00 p.m. Monday to Saturday. We will also offer technology courses online using the same blocks of times and course topics. Students can choose to either take the course online or in person. Each class period is seventy-five minutes and all courses meet twice a week for eight weeks.

C. *Objectives.* Our primary goal is to have thirty students enrolled in each course offered. However, we know we will have to recruit and build each course. Thus, our first-year objective is to have an average class size of at least ten to twenty students per class session.

D. *Environmental analysis:*

Strengths

1. Our greatest strength and most unique competitive advantage is that we teach our students the latest computer skills. Students are encouraged to apply for computer jobs as soon as they complete their first course.
2. Each partner teaches a different area of computer technology.
3. A central location on Main St., Hartford, CT places the training center at the heart of the insurance capital of the world. Insurance and national defense jobs are located in CT.

Weaknesses

1. Because 21st Century Computer Training Center is a startup, the organization is not well known in the Hartford area.
2. Although the business district of Hartford is strong, much of the city has suffered from the recession.

Opportunities

1. There will be an increasing need to train workers to use laptops, PCs, smart phone applications, and many other devices that consumers use to access the Internet.
2. The future of computer careers is expected to grow for many years.

Threats

1. There are competitors that recruit people to attend training schools. Most of these training schools appear to be a product of the 1980s. ITT Tech markets its school more frequently than any other training school in the New England region. ITT markets for students to take their bachelor degree with them at ITT.
2. The economy has been growing slowly for the past few years. Potential customers/students might find it prohibitive to take a course without some type of scholarship.

4. The Marketing Function

A. *The Marketing Plan*: Our primary target market is a male or female between the ages of 16–21, 22–31, and 32 and above. We expect to reach the younger population (below twenty), which has a tremendous desire to know everything about computers. The target market between 21–31 will most likely be people who are looking for a tangible skill that will be transferable to a computer-related job and career. Although we expect some demographic differences between people in the 32 years old and above category, we still believe that this segment is mostly composed of older workers who are ready to be retrained after being laid off, or who have taken an early retirement.

The following table shows that Hartford, CT is a city where the median age is 30.2 years old. We want a state, such as CT, that trends younger because we expect younger people to be interested in technology and the computer career training that we will provide.

Exhibit B-2

2010 Census Data for Hartford, CT

Population by Sex and Age		
Total 2010 Census Population for Hartford, CT	124,775	100.0%
Under 5 years	9,452	7.6%
5 to 9 years	8,460	6.8%
10 to 14 years	8,638	6.9%
15 to 19 years	11,593	9.3%
20 to 24 years	13,301	10.7%
25 to 29 years	10,580	8.5%
30 to 34 years	8,752	7.0%
35 to 39 years	7,752	6.2%
40 to 44 years	7,970	6.4%
45 to 49 years	8,141	6.5%
50 to 54 years	7,554	6.1%
55 to 59 years	6,223	5.0%
60 to 64 years	5,256	4.2%
65 to 69 years	3,646	2.9%
70 to 74 years	2,655	2.1%
75 to 79 years	1,983	1.6%
80 to 84 years	1,391	1.1%
85 years and over	1,428	1.1%
Median age (years)	30.2	(X)
16 years and over	96,368	77.2%
18 years and over	92,558	74.2%
21 years and over	83,403	66.8%
62 years and over	14,135	11.3%
65 years and over	11,103	8.9%

B. The Marketing Mix:

Product

We want our product to be a unique classroom experience. The classroom culture will be an informal atmosphere where ideas will be exchanged instead of a traditional lecture presentation. We believe our courses should be hands-on, where students are actively working and using computers to gain their new computer skills. We want to present our product as either a single computer course the customer wants to take, a series of courses the student wants to study, or a complete program of computer courses.

Price

We will price our courses to meet the community college rate of $400 a course. Reimbursement is 100 percent two weeks before the class, 90 percent one week before the class begins, and 80 percent during the first week.

Place

We will establish our brand in Hartford, CT. However, we expect to establish franchises in the Northeast as we become more established. As a startup organization, Hartford is a key geographic site because it is about two hours from either New York City or Boston. Springfield, MA and New Haven, CT are two other large cities that are less than an hour away from Hartford. We will be able to advertise in those cities and recruit more students.

Population	123,919
White population	39,871
Black population	51,022
Hispanic population	54,166
Asian population	4,055
Hawaiian population	446
Indian population	1,748
Other population	32,575
Male population	59,867
Female population	64,052
Avg house value	$196,100.00
Avg household income	$36,195.83
Avg persons per household	2.43
Median age	30.68
Median age (male)	29.70
Median age (female)	31.43

Exhibit B-3

Hartford, CT Demographic Information—Census Data 2010

Exhibit B-3, from the 2010 U.S. Census, contains demographic data that shows Hartford as a mix of white, black, and Hispanic population. 21st Century Computer Training Center is expected to reflect this diversity and train people of different racial backgrounds.

Average household income is quite high at $36,195 due to the high-paying jobs in the defense and insurance industries that are a large portion of the revenue and jobs in Connecticut. We expect to train students to enter these higher-paying industries.

The following is a list of large employers in the Hartford area where we will place our employees when they are either finished with a specialized course(s) or our entire course sequence.

- AARP Pharmacy.
- Aetna Insurance.
- Aetna Life.
- Allstate.
- Bank of America.
- Central CT Department of Motor Vehicles.
- CT Mutual Insurance Co.
- Hartford Insurance Group.
- Hartford National Bank.
- IRS Main Office.
- Lego Headquarters (Enfield area).
- Travelers Insurance.
- United Technologies (Carrier, Otis, UTC Aerospace, and Pratt & Whitney).[1]

Promotion

Promotion will initially be very important because we need to establish the 21st Century Computer Training Center brand. We expect to have a guerrilla marketing strategic approach where we use the following media to attract students.

Social media will be used to generate interest in specific courses as our prospective students should be already interested in using computers. We expect to be recruiting students for in-class and online courses twelve months a year. Our courses require having classrooms as full as possible. To reflect our own technology orientation, we will be using social media sites to recruit students. Facebook and LinkedIn will be used. However, lesser-known sites, such as CTJobs.com and MassLive.com, will be used because they are popular in the region.

We will also use traditional media to attract students. Hartford has an active bus system that is the primary mode of transportation beside automobiles. We will cover a few buses with advertising wrap to promote our training center at the ground level.

The four partners plan to rotate representing the company at local trade fairs and Chamber of Commerce meetings. We expect to have maximum exposure by attending events individually.

The following table outlines our marketing strategy and expected costs.

Marketing Medium	Example of Media Plan	Cost
Television—WFSB Hartford	*CBS Early Show* one-minute segments at $2,600 per ad, *WFSB Nightly News* at $3,800 per ad.	Gross Cost = $115,000 Agency commission = $17,000 Net amount due = $98,000[2]
Newspaper—local Hartford newspapers[3]	Advertising rate estimates are for a column inch of black and white advertising space.	Average rate is $11.00 per column inch. Daily ads of 2 × 2 and 3 × 3 = $30,000 budget.
Radio—WTIC-FM	Thirty-second spots.	The estimated rate for radio thirty-second spot ads is $279.00. One hundred ads = $27,900.
Direct mail—Allan Associates	Jumbo postcard to 5,000 people with mailing list is $2917.50;[4] direct-mail letter for 5,000 people with layout, design, and mailing list is $3,800.	A quarterly campaign to 20,000 people = $27,000.
Total marketing expenses		$183,000

Exhibit B-4

Marketing Strategy and Expected Costs

The *Hartford Courant* and other Hartford area newspapers will be used strategically weeks away from a new course session starting at our training center.

Direct mail will be used to reach each individual household. Direct-mail pieces will be designed, printed, sorted, and mailed from Allan Associates in West Hartford, CT. Allan also has access to the mailing lists where we can market to specific zip codes around Hartford.

Radio ads are inexpensive to run and can be produced at a reasonable cost. We need to establish a relationship with WTIC-FM, 96.5 in Hartford because it is the most respected and listened-to channel in the Hartford area.

Television ads could be expensive if done incorrectly. We would like to make our own ads using our computer skills. Once complete, WFSB in Hartford will then be used to carry our message throughout the Hartford area.

We plan on organizing a weekly guerrilla marketing campaign. These events will include cross-marketing with the local radio station, offering free courses for students who complete a survey at our Facebook site, and arranging office visits to local businesses to recruit new students.

A key guerrilla campaign will be to offer a weekly social hour to allow prospective students to visit our school. We have also planned for a series of student orientations where a student with his or her significant other or parent can visit our school.

5. Location and Layout

A. *Location.* The location on 2121 Main St. in Hartford has been rented for one year at $4,000 dollars a month. This street site is on the busiest street in Hartford and is close to the market that needs to receive computer training to enter the insurance and defense industries that are located in CT. Public transportation is provided by Peter Pan with buses that leave for either New York City, Boston, or Springfield, MA hourly. As part of a large city on the East Coast, we will have access to many business and computer professionals who we will ask to teach specialized courses.

B. Layout. The layout of our classrooms is critical to attract customers looking to learn about the latest in technology. We have to provide rooms where students can collaborate and work together to discuss computer-related material. The key is to create a lounge atmosphere (typically found in a coffee shop) where students and professors can interact during the class time.

We will be renting three classrooms and a common room for 15,000 sq. ft. at $11.00 a sq. ft. for a total cost of $165,000.

6. The Production/Operations Function

A. Production Process. The production process in our type of business is the actual schedule of courses to be taught. The following table includes nine (9) course meetings times per day between 8:00 a.m. and 8:00 p.m. Three courses are offered each meeting time. Thus, there are twenty-seven courses taught each day.

Each course has an average of thirty students. Thirty students times three courses a block equals ninety students per block of time. Ninety students per block times nine blocks per day equals 810 seats enrolled per day for each eight-week semester.

The same set of classes are held on Monday and Wednesday, Tuesday and Thursday, and Friday and Saturday. Thus, 810 seats are available on Monday and Wednesday, Tuesday and Thursday, and Friday and Saturday.

That means we have a potential of 810 times three times each course run in a session, which equals 2,430 seats per eight-week session. Students pay $400 a course to match the local community college course rate. The maximum potential revenue is

2,430 seats × $400 = $972,000 per eight-week session

$972,000 times six sessions per year equals a $5,832,000 maximum potential annual revenue per 21st Century Computer Training Center. However, our estimates are based on 25 percent classroom capacity, which equals a revenue projection of $1,456,800.

Exhibit B-5

Revenue Generated Based on Different Percentages of Classroom Capacity Used for One Session

Classroom Capacity Used	Number of Student Seats Available per Session	Revenue Generated
100%	2,430	$972,000
90%	2,187	$874,800
75%	1,822	$728,800
50%	1,215	$486,000
25%	607	$242,800

Classroom Capacity Used	Number of Student Seats Available per Session	Revenue Generated
100%	19,440	$5,832,000
90%	2,187	$5,248,800
75%	1,822	$4,372,800
50%	1,215	$2,916,000
25%	607	$1,456,800

Exhibit B-6

Eight (8) Sessions Total Revenue Generated Based on Different Percentages of Classroom Capacity Used

8:00–9:15	9:25–10:40	10:50–12:05	12:15–1:30	1:40–2:55	3:05–4:15
Intro. to Computers	Intro. to Programming 2	Operating Systems	Technology Through Film	2D Application	
Intro. to Programming	Advanced Computer Graphics	Database Design and Management	Assembly Language and Computer Organization	Java	Computer Internship 1, 2, & 3
Intro. To Computer Graphics	Software Engineer	Advanced Database	Mobile Application Development	Algorithms	
4:25–5:40	5:50–7:05	7:05–8:00			
Social and Technical Entrepreneurship 1, 2, & 3	Cyber Security 1, 2, & 3	Career Advising 1, 2, & 3			

Exhibit B-7

Class Schedule

Exhibit B-5 shows how much revenue will be generated based upon the different percentages of classroom usage.

Exhibit B-6 shows the revenue generated for the eight (8) sessions offered throughout the year.

Exhibit B-7 is the class schedule for three different computer courses each class period. The same class schedule is repeated on Monday/Wednesday, Tuesday/Thursday, and Friday/Saturday. Classes can also be taken as online courses.

Tuition

Students pay $400 per course. Each course lasts eight weeks. Students must pay for the course before the first week of classes.

Certification

A student who completes ten computer courses will receive a certificate of graduation. However, to support students in their search for jobs and careers, we will also give each student a certificate of completion for each course they finish.

B. Quality. We expect our students to be fully ready to enter an array of computer-related positions. As we will start in Hartford, CT, we expect to place students in the insurance and defense industries as often as possible.

7. The Human Resources Function

A. New Venture Team. Besides the four founding partners, many other professionals will support 21st Century Computer Training Center.

- Newton Bank agrees to be available with a line of credit in case extra short-term funding is required.
- New England Venture Mentors (NEVM) will be offering its entrepreneurship skills in helping our business to develop. NEVM will provide venture capitalists to help guide our technology school through the startup phase and into the growth stage.
- The law firm of Fisher, Bennett, and Brothers will be used to process all legal contracts.
- Our insurance agent suggested buying a life insurance policy from Farmer's Insurance.

B. Attract, develop, and retain employees. We expect to hire staff to support our classrooms. A technology specialist will work on an hourly rate, making sure the classroom technology such as the whiteboards, instructor computer, student computers, the Internet, and overhead projector are working properly for each course session.

We expect to hire faculty at the rate of $2,500 per eight-week course. Although all four partners expect to teach four courses each per semester, we will need to have about three to four courses per semester taught by an adjunct professor.

C. Management succession and an exit strategy. Our management succession plan involves our own children. All four owners have teenage children who are technology-savvy. Our exit strategy involves making one child from each of the four families a future owner of the business.

8. The Financing Function

A. Accounting information system. Dr Christine Bay will be in charge of accounting. She will be developing our accounting information system using the Peachtree accounting software.

B. Owner's sources of equity financing. As professionals in the technology industries, each owner will be able to invest $50,000. There is no intention of offering stock at this time. An offering of stock would most likely occur after three training centers are established on the East Coast.

C. Sources of debt financing. A line of credit of an equal amount, $200,000, has been established with Newton Bank from Hartford, CT.

D. Venture capitalist. We do not expect to need funding from a venture capitalist. However, our mentor, NEVM, will be guiding us along with their experiences from starting their own businesses.

E. Crowdfunding. Although crowdfunding sources, such as Kickstarter, were considered, we do not feel raising money in this fashion is appropriate for our business operations. We did consider setting a goal of $500,000, which we feel we would have raised. However, we feel the current setup of not rewarding Kickstarter investors with actual ownership is not appropriate for our business plan.

F. Government and Small Business Administration programs. As needed, we plan on using Small Business Administration (SBA) loans and programs, Small Business Investment Companies (SBICs), Small Business Lending Companies (SBLCs), and state and local programs that support small businesses. Finding local programs for retraining laid-off workers will be our primary area of effort when reviewing SBA and local training programs. Although we are not looking to acquire an SBA loan, we do want to keep updated with their efforts to help small businesses. SBA updates will be received by email at www. sba.gov/updates.

	FY 2016	%
Revenue		
Tuition	$1,456,800	
Total revenue	1,456,800	100%
Operating costs and expenses		
Cost of classroom equipment	160,000	10.98%
Rent	165,000	11.33%
Salary, wages, and benefits	345,000	23.68%
Professional membership fees	1,600	0.11%
Selling and marketing expenses	183,000	13%
General and administrative	135,000	9%
Telephone, Internet, and utilities	38,911	3%
Total operating expenses	1,028,511	70.60%
Income from operations	428,289	29.40%
Other income (expense)		
Interest income	0	
Interest expense	0	
Total other income (expense)	0	
Taxes incurred	119,921	28%
Net profit	$308,368	21%

Exhibit B-8

Pro Forma Profit and Loss Statement for the Period Ending December 31, 2016

Notes:

Tuition is based on 25 percent classroom utilization.

Selling and marketing expenses are $183,000, as outline in the marketing plan.

Overall taxes incurred are estimated at 28 percent.

G. Capital Expenses. Our largest capital expense will be purchasing the necessary computers and equipment to outfit our three classrooms. Exhibit B-11 in the Appendix shows a detailed proposal from Dell Inc. that indicates each classroom will need about $30,000 per classroom for a total of $90,000. Exhibit B-12 in the Appendix shows the furniture from School Outfitters would be about $7,300 for a total of $21,900 for three classrooms. Thus, furniture and equipment for each classroom would be approximately $38,000–$45,000. This range will allow us to purchase additional materials as needed. We expect a total capital expense of approximately $135,000.

H. Pro forma profit and loss. As 21st Century will be a startup business, we calculated tuition revenue at 25 percent classroom utilization. However, we expect that utilization rate to increase in each successive year.

I. Pro forma cash flow statement FY 2016. The pro forma cash flow statement is our view of how we will incur expenses. The statement will be used as a guideline to monitor all expenses.

9. Controls

A. Control Systems. Each course in our program will be evaluated by students each session. Evaluations will be in four areas: teacher effectiveness, relevancy of the course topic, updated course material, and overall cost/benefit of the course and program as of the time students complete the assessment tool.

B. Liquidity, leverage, operating, and profit margins. We expect to maintain liquidity by achieving a current ratio of at least 2:1. We do not expect high leverage because we do not foresee the need for a bank loan or other source of external funding. Although we have a line of credit, we expect to conduct operations with the owner's own equity and the cash flow from proceeding course sessions. We expect to achieve around a 20 percent profit margin as we build our business. To repeat, we will be quite profitable as long as we have a minimum of 25 percent of seats filled in our classroom.

C. Balanced Scorecard. Exhibit B-10 is a balanced scorecard developed for 21st Century Computer Training Center.[5]

D. Risk Assessment. We believe our financial risk will be minimal as long as we achieve a minimum of 25 percent occupancy in each course.

E. Insurance. We expect to consult with our insurance agent, Farmer's Insurance, to make sure we have at least life insurance on our four principal owners.

F. Changing actions in accordance with actuality. We are prepared to change this business plan as changes occur within and outside of our company and industry. For example, while writing this business plan, we saw an increase in ITT commercials recruiting more technology students in the Hartford, CT and Springfield, MA area.

Department	Areas
Finance	*Return on investment*. Will be evaluating the return on owner's investment of $200,000. *Cash flow*. Will be monitored closely due to startup cost of developing physical classrooms. Financial Results will be monitored yearly/quarterly/and by each session.
Internal business processes	*Classroom utilization*. We will be closely monitoring every session. Revenues are directly tied to the percentage of classroom seats filled. Duplicate activities between online and physical classes will be eliminated. For example, signup for either in-person or online courses will use the same application found at the company Web site. *Classroom process alignment*. We need to continually ask if the correct technology courses are being taught. *Process bottlenecks*. We need to determine if certain courses are overfilled and need to be offered more often. *Process automation*. We need to have training sessions for all students to learn how to use the learning management system (LMS) developed by the four investors in the company. Students need to use the LMS to do work online.
Learning and growth	*Expertise*. Is there the correct level of expertise for the job? *Employee turnover*. Is turnover higher or lower than expected? Why or why not? *Job satisfaction*. We need to conduct an annual job satisfaction online survey. *Training/learning opportunities*. Faculty and staff need to attend conferences within their field to support their own growth.
Student satisfaction	*Delivery performance*. Students/customers will evaluate the course during the third, sixth, and eighth course meeting. *Quality performance*. Student quality will be assessed at the end of each course to make sure students learn the material and how it can help them find a job and develop a career. *Student satisfaction rate*. Student success and satisfaction of the entire program will be conducted at the end of each eight-week session. *Student percentage of market*. Data will be gathered about key educational competitors (such as ITT Tech) to determine our regional and local success. PRIZM and the SBA will be monitored to keep track of competitors and the demographics of where they are located. *Student retention rate*. The rate at which students successfully complete each course will be gathered and closely monitored to ensure each course is a positive step in building a career in technology for each student.

10. Appendix

Dell Force10, S25P
SYSTEM COMPONENTS

Dell Force10, S25P	Qty	1
Force10, S25P, 24P 100FX/1GbE (SFP req) w/4 × 10/100/1000BASE-T ports, 2 mod slots, 2 × AC pwr supplies	Unit price	$6,696.00
Special offer		– $1,682.02
Catalog number:	4 BF10S25P	

Module	Description
S25	Force10, S25P, 24P 100FX/1GbE (SFP req) w/4 × 10/100/1000BASE-T ports, 2 mod slots, 2 × AC pwr supplies
Return policy	No returns allowed on Dell Force10 switches
Documentation	Force10, user documentation for S25N/V/P, DAO/BCC
Hardware support services	3 year ProSupport hardware warranty: NBD parts
Installation services	On-site installation declined
Remote consulting service	Declined remote consulting service
Power cords	Force10, power cord, 125V, 15A, 10 Feet, NEMA 5-15/C13, S-series
Power cords	Force10, power cord, 250V, 12A, 2 meters, C13/C14

TOTAL: $5,013.98

Dell 2335dn multifunction laser printer
SYSTEM COMPONENTS

Dell 2335dn multifunction laser printer	Qty	3
Dell 2335dn multifunction Laser printer	Unit price	$394.99
Limited time offer		– $135.00
Catalog number:	4 2335DNSAP	

Module	Description
2335DN multifunction laser printer 2335DN	Dell 2335dn multifunction laser printer
Hardware support services CS 2.0	1 year basic limited warranty and 1 year advanced exchange service

TOTAL: $1,049.97

Dell mobile projector (M900HD)

SYSTEM COMPONENTS

Dell mobile projector (M900HD)	Qty	3
Dell mobile projector (M900HD)	Unit price	$899.00
Limited Time Offer		– $300.00
Catalog number:	4 M900HD	

Module	Description	
Dell mobile projector (M900HD)	Dell mobile projector (M900HD)	
Hardware support services	1 year basic limited warranty and 1 year advanced Exchange service	

TOTAL: $2,397.00

PowerEdge T320

SYSTEM COMPONENTS

PowerEdge T320	Qty	3
PowerEdge T320	Unit Price	$1,204.00
Special offer		
Save 25% on select processor options		– $261.75
Save 25% on select memory options		– $153.00
Save 25% on select hard drive options		– $179.25
Save 25% on select operating system options		
Save $157 on select PowerEdge T320 Business PCs.		– $471.00
Special offer		
Catalog number:	4 BECT33D	

Module	Description	
PowerEdge T320	PowerEdge T320	
Warranty and service	3 yr basic hardware warranty repair: 5 × 10 HW-Only, 5 × 10 NBD onsite	
Installation services	No installation	
Proactive maintenance	Maintenance declined	
Remote consulting service	Declined remote consulting service	
Shipping	PowerEdge T320 shipping	
Add-in network adapter	On-board Broadcom 5720 dual port 1Gb LOM	
Embedded systems management	Basic management	

(Continued)

Chassis configuration	Chassis with up to 4, 3.5" cabled hard drives and embedded SATA
Bezel	No bezel
Power management BIOS settings	Power saving Dell Active power controller
RAID configuration	No RAID with embedded SATA (1–4 SATA HDDs) with cabled chassis
RAID controller	No controller
Processor	Intel® Xeon® E5-2403 1.80GHz, 10M cache, 6.4GT/s QPI, no turbo, 4C, 80W, max mem 1066MHz
Memory capacity	(2) 4GB RDIMM, 1333 MT/s, low volt, single rank, × 4 data width
Memory DIMM type and speed	1333 MHz RDIMMs
Memory configuration type	Performance optimized
Hard drives	500GB 7.2K RPM SATA 3Gbps 3.5in cabled hard drive
System documentation	Electronic system documentation and OpenManage DVD kit
Internal optical drive	No internal optical drive
Rack rails and casters	Tower chassis, no casters
Power supply	Single, cabled power supply, 350W
Power cords	NEMA 5-15P to C13 wall plug, 125 Volt, 15 AMP, 10 Feet (3m), power cord
Operating system	No operating system
OS Media Kits	No media required

TOTAL: $2,547.00

Dell E series E2313H 23" monitor with LED
SYSTEM COMPONENTS

Dell E series E2313H 23" monitor with LED	Qty	96
Dell E series E2313H 2" monitor	Unit price	$199.99
Limited time offer		– $250.00
Limited time offer		– $250.00
Catalog number:	4 E2313HSAP	
Module	Description	
Dell monitors	Dell E series E2313H 23" monitor	

ACCESSORIES

3 yr ltd warranty, 3 yr advanced exchange	Qty	96
Dell part# 983-2847	Unit price	$0.00
Manufacturer part# 00009		
Dell part# 983-2847		

TOTAL: $18,699.04

OptiPlex 3010 desktop
SYSTEM COMPONENTS

OptiPlex 3010 desktop	Qty	90
OptiPlex 3010 desktop for standard power supply, Windows 7 Home Premium, no media, 32-bit, English	Unit price	$673.00
Save 30% on select Optiplex 3010 business PCs Special Offer		– $1,009.50
Catalog number:	4 SPCTSBD1	

Module	Description
OptiPlex 3010 desktop	OptiPlex 3010 desktop for standard power supply
Operating system(s)	Windows 7 Home Premium, no media, 32-bit, English
Processors	Intel® Pentium® G2020 processor (3M cache, 2.90GHz w/HD graphics)
Memory	2GB, NON-ECC, 1600MHZ DDR3,1DIMM
Keyboard	Dell KB212-B USB 104 quiet key keyboard, English
Monitors	No monitor
Graphics cards	Intel® integrated graphics w/single HDMI/VGA
Boot hard drives	250GB 3.5" SATA 3Gb/s with 8MB DataBurst cache
Mouse	Dell MS111 USB optical mouse
Removable media storage device	16 × DVD-ROM SATA, data only
Thermals	Heat sink, mainstream, desktop
Speakers	Internal Dell business audio speaker
Power supplies	OptiPlex 3010 desktop w/ standard PSU
Documentation	Documentation English and French
Productivity software	Microsoft® Office trial, MUI
Energy efficiency options	No ESTAR settings
Resource DVD	No resource DVD
Warranty and service	3 year basic hardware service with 3 Year NBD onsite service after remote diagnosis
Security software	McAfee 12 month subscription
Security hardware	Chassis intrusion switch option
Low power mode	1 Watt ready low-power mode
Setup and features information tech sheet	No tech sheet
Ship packaging options	Shipping material for system, desktop
RSS label	Prebuilt system

TOTAL: $59,560.50

Exhibit B-12

School Outfitters' Furniture Cost for Each Classroom

Quantity	Description	Stock Keeping Unit (SKU)	Price	Total Price
1	600 designer series steel teacher desk—double pedestal (60" W × 30" D) Desk color combination: black base/maple top	SAN-DPR6030	$439.99	$439.99
30	Mesh back office chair w/ tilt control	OFM-E1001	$73.88	$2,216.40
15	Quattro Voltea computer table—24" W × 48" L Top and trim color: gray top/ gray base and quartz trim, 6-outlet power strip: no, CPU tower holder: no	BRE-QFT2448	$310.99	$4,664.85
			Total:	**$7,321.24**

Notes

Preface

1 S.D. Sarasvathy and S. Venkataraman, Entrepreneurship as method: Open questions for an entrepreneurial future. *Entrepreneurship Theory and Practice* 35 (1 2011): 113–135.

Chapter 1

1 Small Business School (www.smallbusinessschool. org/video.cfm?clip=1068). Retrieved September 21, 2012.

2 J. Tang and P.J. Murphy, Prior knowledge and new product and service introductions by entrepreneurial firms: The mediating role of technological innovation. *Journal of Small Business Management* 50 (1 2012): 41–62.

3 M. Griffiths, J. Kickul, S. Bacq, and S. Terjesen, A dialogue with William J. Baumol: Insights on entrepreneurship theory and education. *Entrepreneurship Theory and Practice* 36 (4 2012): 611–625.

4 K. Podoynitsya, H. Van der Bij, and M. Song, The role of mixed emotions in the risk perception of novice and serial entrepreneurs. *Entrepreneurship Theory and Practice* 36 (1 2012): 115–121.

5 U. Brixy, R. Sternberg, and H. Stuber, The selectiveness of the entrepreneurial process. *Journal of Small Business Management* 50 (1 2012): 105–131.

6 J.D. Werbel and S.M. Danes, Work family conflict in new business ventures: The moderating effects of spousal commitment to the new business venture. *Journal of Small Business Management* 48 (3 2010): 421–440.

7 B. Bird, L. Schojoedt, and J.R. Baum, Entrepreneurs' behavior: Elucidation and measurement. *Entrepreneurship Theory and Practice* 36 (5 2012): 889–913.

8 B. Bird, L. Schojoedt, and J.R. Baum, Entrepreneurs' behavior: Elucidation and measurement. *Entrepreneurship Theory and Practice* 36 (5 2012): 889–913.

9 M. Griffiths, J. Kickul, S. Bacq, and S. Terjesen, A dialogue with William J. Baumol: Insights on entrepreneurship theory and education. *Entrepreneurship Theory and Practice* 36 (4 2012): 611–625.

10 P.C. Patel and J.O. Fiet, Knowledge combination and the potential advantages of family firms searching for opportunities. *Entrepreneurship Theory and Practice* 35 (6 2011): 1179–1197.

11 R.N. Lussier and M.C. Sonfield, The effect of family size as firms grow: A USA–France comparison. *Journal of Small Business and Enterprise Development* 13 (3 2006): 314–325.

12 Wikipedia (www.wikipedia.org). Retrieved September 8, 2012.

13 Small Business Administration (SBA) (www.sba.gov). Retrieved September 8, 2012

14 U.S. Department of Labor (www.bls.gov). Retrieved October 3, 2012.

15 Small Business Administration (SBA) (www.sba.gov). Retrieved September 8, 2012.

16 Dell (www.dell.com). Retrieved September 8, 2012.

17 Wikipedia (www.wikipedia.org). Retrieved September 8, 2012.

18 E.S. Browning, S. Russolillo, and J.E. Vascellaro, Apple now biggest ever U.S. company. *The Wall Street Journal* (August 21, 2012): A1.

19 S.D. Sarasvathy and S. Venkataraman, Entrepreneurship as method: Open questions for an entrepreneurial future. *Entrepreneurship Theory and Practice* 35 (1 2011): 113–135.

20 M. Griffiths, J. Kickul, S. Bacq, and S. Terjesen, A dialogue with William J. Baumol: Insights on entrepreneurship theory and education. *Entrepreneurship Theory and Practice* 36 (4 2012): 611–625.

21 N. Classen, A. Van Gils, Y. Bammens, and M. Carree, Accessing resources from innovation partners: The search breadth of family SMEs. *Journal of Small Business Management* 50 (2 2012): 191–215.

22 T. Kontinen and A. Ojala, International opportunity recognition among small and medium-sized family firms. *Journal of Small Business Management* 49 (3 2011): 490–514.

23 M. Baum, C. Schwens, and R. Kabst, A typology of international new ventures: Empirical evidence from high-technology industries. *Journal of Small Business Management* 49 (3 2011): 305–330.

24 H. Lee, D. Kelly, J. Lee, and S. Lee, SME survival: The impact of internationalization, technology resources, and alliances. *Journal of Small Business Management* 50 (1 2012): 1–19.

25 B. Honig and M. Samuelsson, Planning and the entrepreneur: A longitudinal examination of nascent entrepreneurs in Sweden. *Journal of Small Business Management* 50 (3 2012): 365–388.

26 S.A. Zahra and M. Wright, Entrepreneurship's next act. *Academy of Management Perspectives* 25 (4 2011): 67–83.

27 R.N. Lussier and S. Pfeifer, A comparison of business success versus failure variables between the U.S. and Central Eastern Europe Croatian Entrepreneurs. *Entrepreneurship Theory and Practice* 24 (4 2000): 59–67.

28 Global Entrepreneurship Monitor (GEM) (www.gemconsortium.org). Retrieved September 10, 2012.

29 Based on D. Kelley, N. Bosma, and J.E. Amoros, *Global Entrepreneurship Monitor 2010 Global Report* (Babson College and Universidad del DeBartolo, 2011).

30 D. Sullivan and M. Marvel, How entrepreneurs' knowledge and network ties relate to the number of employees in new SMEs. *Journal of Small Business Management* 49 (2 2011): 185–206.

31 M.E. Davis and K.G. Shaver, Understanding gendered variations in business growth intentions across the life course. *Entrepreneurship Theory and Practice* 36 (3 2012): 495–522.

32 Small Business Administration (SBA) (www.sba.gov). Retrieved September 10, 2012.

33 N.D. Campbell, K.C. Heriot, A. Jauregui, and D.T. Mitchell, Which state policies lead to U.S. firm exits? Analysis with the Economic Freedom Index. *Journal of Small Business Management* 50 (1 2012): 87–104.

34 T. Kontinen and A. Ojala, International opportunity recognition among small and medium-sized family firms. *Journal of Small Business Management* 49 (3 2011): 490–514.

35 S. Reddy, Latinos fuel growth in decade. Based on census data. *The Wall Street Journal* (March 25, 2011): A2.

36 Kauffman Foundation, Taking the measure of entrepreneurs. *The Wall Street Journal* (November 12, 2012): R6.

37 K. Groves, C. Vance, and D. Choi, Examining entrepreneurial cognition: An occupational analysis of balanced linear and nonlinear thinking and entrepreneurship success. *Journal of Small Business Management* 49 (3 2011): 438–466.

38 D. Sullivan and M. Marvel, How entrepreneurs' knowledge and network ties relate to the number of employees in new SMEs. *Journal of Small Business Management* 49 (2 2011): 185–206.

39 D. Sardana and D.S. Kemmis, Who learns what?—A study based on entrepreneurs from biotechnology new ventures. *Journal of Small Business Management* 48 (3 2010): 441–468.

40 M. Presutti, C. Boari, and A. Majocchi, The importance of proximity for the start-ups' knowledge acquisition and exploitation. *Journal of Small Business Management* 49 (3 2011): 361–389.

41 S.D. Sarasvathy and S. Venkataraman, Entrepreneurship as method: Open questions for an entrepreneurial future. *Entrepreneurship Theory and Practice* 35 (1 2011): 113–135.

42 J. Tang and P.J. Murphy, Prior knowledge and new product and service introductions by entrepreneurial firms: The mediating role of technological innovation. *Journal of Small Business Management* 50 (1 2012): 41–62.

43 B.R. Barringer and R.D. Ireland, *Entrepreneurship* (Upper Saddle River, NJ: Prentice Hall, 2012).

44 B. Mycoskie, *Start Something That Matters* (New York: Spiegel & Grau, 2012).

45 B.R. Barringer and R.D. Ireland, *Entrepreneurship* (Upper Saddle River, NJ: Prentice Hall, 2012).

46 E. Spiegel, Faith in granola earned its makers millions, *New York Times* (January 27, 2008): 1, 6.

47 S. Cater, The rewards of entrepreneurship: Exploring the incomes, wealth, and economic well-being of entrepreneurial households. *Entrepreneurship Theory and Practice* 35 (1 2011): 39–55.

48 B.R. Barringer and R.D. Ireland, *Entrepreneurship* (Upper Saddle River, NJ: Prentice Hall, 2012).

49 K.B. Lamp, M. Lévesque, and C. Schade, Are entrepreneurs influenced by risk attitude, regulatory focus or both? An experiment on entrepreneurs' time allocation. *Journal of Business Venturing* 27 (4 2012): 456–476.

50 Justin Arrigo is married to one of the author's nieces.

51 A. Nadim and R.N. Lussier, Small business, community relations and sustainability: New approaches to success. *Journal of Small Business Strategy* 21 (2 2012): 79–95.

52 N.M. Scarborough, *Essentials of Entrepreneurship and Small Business* (Upper Saddle River, NJ: Prentice Hall, 2011).

53 B. Mycoskie, *Start Something That Matters* (New York: Spiegel & Grau, 2012): quote p. 193.

54 New Spirit (http://newspiritinc.org). Retrieved September 12, 2012.

55 S. Cater, The rewards of entrepreneurship: Exploring the incomes, wealth, and economic well-being of entrepreneurial households. *Entrepreneurship Theory and Practice* 35 (1 2011): 39–55.

56 U. Brixy, R. Sternberg, and H. Stuber, The selectiveness of the entrepreneurial process. *Journal of Small Business Management* 50 (1 2012): 105–131.

57 K.B. Lamp, M. Lévesque, and C. Schade, Are entrepreneurs influenced by risk attitude, regulatory focus or both? An experiment on entrepreneurs' time allocation. *Journal of Business Venturing* 27 (4 2012): 456–476.

58 M. Griffiths, J. Kickul, S. Bacq, and S. Terjesen, A dialogue with William J. Baumol: Insights on entrepreneurship theory and education. *Entrepreneurship Theory and Practice* 36 (4 2012): 611–625.

59 N.M. Scarborough, *Essentials of Entrepreneurship and Small Business* (Upper Saddle River, NJ: Prentice Hall, 2011).

60 B.R. Barringer and R.D. Ireland, *Entrepreneurship* (Upper Saddle River, NJ: Prentice Hall, 2012).

61 S.M. Farmer, The behavioral impact of entrepreneur identity aspiration and prior entrepreneurial experience. *Entrepreneurship Theory and Practice* 35 (2 2011): 245–273.

62 B. Honig and M. Samuelsson, Planning and the entrepreneur: A longitudinal examination of nascent entrepreneurs in Sweden. *Journal of Small Business Management* 50 (3 2012): 365–388.

63 R.A. Baron and J. Tang, The role of entrepreneurs in firm-level innovation: Joint effects of positive affect, creativity, and environmental dynamism. *Journal of Business Venturing* 26 (1 2011): 49–60.

64 R.N. Lussier and C.E. Halabi, A three-country comparison of the business success versus failure prediction model. *Journal of Small Business Management* 48 (3 2010): 360–377.

65 Small Business Administration (SBA) (www.sba.gov/sites/default/files/sbfaq.pdf). Retrieved September 17, 2012.

66 Small Business Administration (SBA) (www.sba.gov). Retrieved September 10, 2012.

67 S. Mariotti and C. Glackin, *Entrepreneurship and Small Business Management* (Upper Saddle River, NJ: Prentice Hall, 2012).

68 Small Business Administration (SBA) (www.sba.gov/sites/default/files/sbfaq.pdf). Retrieved September 17, 2012.

69 Lori Bonn Design (www.LoriBonn.com). Retrieved September 12, 2012. *And* K.R. Allen, *Launching New Ventures* (Mason, OH: Cengage, 2012).

70 J.B.D Garcia, A.I.R. Escudero, and N.M Cruz, Influence of affective traits on entrepreneur's goals and satisfaction. *Journal of Small Business Management* 50 (3 2012): 408–428.

71 D. Miller and I.L.B. Miller, Governance, social identity, and entrepreneurial orientation in closely held public companies. *Entrepreneurship Theory and Practice* 35 (5 2011): 1051–1076.

72 D. Eng, The king of travel and real estate. *Fortune* (January 14, 2013): 21–24.

73 J.M. Pollack, M.W. Rutherford, and B.G. Nagy, Preparedness and cognitive legitimacy as antecedents of new venture funding in televised business pitches. *Entrepreneurship Theory and Practice* 36 (5 2012): 915–939.

74 B.R. Barringer and R.D. Ireland, *Entrepreneurship* (Upper Saddle River, NJ: Prentice Hall, 2012).

75 V.C. Han, M. Frese, C. Binnewies, and A. Schmitt, Happy and proactive? The role of hedonic and eudaimonic well-being in business owners' personal initiative. *Entrepreneurship Theory and Practice* 36 (1 2012): 97–106.

76 J. Tang and P.J. Murphy, Prior knowledge and new product and service introductions by entrepreneurial firms: The mediating role of technological innovation. *Journal of Small Business Management* 50 (1 2012): 41–62.

77 C. Mitteness, R. Sudek, and M.S. Cardon, Angel investor characteristics that determine whether perceived passion leads to higher evaluations of funding potential. *Journal of Business Venturing* 27 (5 2012): 592–606.

78 M.M. Gielnik, M. Frese, J.M. Graf, and A. Kampschulte, Creativity in the opportunity identification process and the moderating effect of diversity of information. *Journal of Business Venturing* 27 (5 2012): 559–576.

79 M. Simon and R.C. Shrader, Entrepreneurial actions and optimistic overconfidence: The role of motivated reasoning in new product introductions. *Journal of Business Venturing* 27 (3 2012): 291–309. *And* J.C. Hayton and M. Cholakova, The role of affect in the creation and intentional pursuit of entrepreneurial ideas. *Entrepreneurship Theory and Practice* 36 (1 2012): 41–62.

80 B.R. Barringer and R.D. Ireland, *Entrepreneurship* (Upper Saddle River, NJ: Prentice Hall, 2012).

81 M. Simon, J. Kim, S.M. Houghton, and X. Deng, When it's right to be wrong: The effects of overconfidence and planning on product performance in a dynamic environment. *Journal of Small Business Strategy* 22 (1 2012): 21–46.

82 B.R. Barringer and R.D. Ireland, *Entrepreneurship* (Upper Saddle River, NJ: Prentice Hall, 2012).

83 R. Fini, R. Grimaldi, G.L. Marzocchi, and M. Sobrero, The determinants of corporate entrepreneurial intention within small and newly established firms. *Entrepreneurship Theory and Practice* 35 (2 2011): 245–273.

84 V.C. Han, M. Frese, C. Binnewies, and A. Schmitt, Happy and proactive? The role of hedonic and eudaimonic well-being in business owners' personal initiative. *Entrepreneurship Theory and Practice* 36 (1 2012): 97–106.

85 J.M. Haynie, D.A. Shepherd, and H. Patzelt, Cognitive adaptability and an entrepreneurial task: The role of metacognitive ability and feedback. *Entrepreneurship Theory and Practice* 36 (2 2012): 237–246.

86 K. Podoynitsyna, H. Van der Bij, and M. Song, The role of mixed emotions in the risk perception of novice and serial entrepreneurs. *Entrepreneurship Theory and Practice* 35 (2 2011): 245–273.

87 B.R. Barringer and R.D. Ireland, *Entrepreneurship* (Upper Saddle River, NJ: Prentice Hall, 2012).

88 S.M. Farmer, The behavioral impact of entrepreneur identity aspiration and prior entrepreneurial experience. *Entrepreneurship Theory and Practice* 35 (2 2011): 245–273.

89 N. Breugst, A. Domurath, H. Patzelt, and A. Klaukien, Perceptions of entrepreneurial passion and employees' commitment to entrepreneurial ventures. *Entrepreneurship Theory and Practice* 36 (1 2012): 171–188.

90 S.M. Farmer, The behavioral impact of entrepreneur identity aspiration and prior entrepreneurial experience. *Entrepreneurship Theory and Practice* 35 (2 2011): 245–273.

91 R.S. Shinnar, O. Giacomin, and F. Janssen, Entrepreneurial perceptions and intentions: The role of gender and culture. *Entrepreneurship Theory and Practice* 36 (3 2012): 465–484.

92 U. Brixy, R. Sternberg, and H. Stuber, The selectiveness of the entrepreneurial process. *Journal of Small Business Management* 50 (1 2012): 105–131.

93 M.E. Davis and K.G. Shaver, Understanding gendered variations in business growth intentions across the life course. *Entrepreneurship Theory and Practice* 36 (3 2012): 495–522.

94 R.S. Shinnar, O. Giacomin, and F. Janssen, Entrepreneurial perceptions and intentions: The role of gender and culture. *Entrepreneurship Theory and Practice* 36 (3 2012): 465–484.

95 S. Reddy, Latinos fuel growth in decade. Based on census data. *The Wall Street Journal* (March 25, 2011): A2.

96 W. Wales, E. Monsen, and A. McKelvie, The organizational pervasiveness of entrepreneurial orientation. *Entrepreneurship Theory and Practice* 35 (5 2011): 895–923.

97 J.G. Covin and G.T. Lumpkin, Entrepreneurial orientation theory and research: Reflections on a needed construct. *Entrepreneurship Theory and Practice* 35 (5 2011): 855–872.

98 D. Miller, Miller (1983) revisited: A reflection on EO research and some suggestions for the future. *Entrepreneurship Theory and Practice* 35 (5 2011): 873–894.

99 Y. Zhao, Y. Li, S.H. Lee, and L. Bo Chen, Entrepreneurial orientation, organizational learning, and performance: Evidence from China. *Entrepreneurship Theory and Practice* 35 (2 2011): 293–317.

100 J.G. Covin and W.J. Wales, The measurement of entrepreneurial orientation. *Entrepreneurship Theory and Practice* 36 (4 2012): 677–702.

101 Z. Su, E. Xie, and Y. Li, Entrepreneurial orientation and firm performance in new venture and established firms. *Journal of Small Business Management* 49 (4 2011): 558–577.

102 K. Wiklund and D.A. Shepherd, Where to from here? EO-as-experimentation, failure, and distribution of outcomes. *Entrepreneurship Theory and Practice* 35 (5 2011): 925–946.

103 R.C. Runyan, B. Ge, B. Dong, and J.L. Swinney, Entrepreneurial orientation in cross-cultural research: Assessing measurement invariance in the construct. *Entrepreneurship Theory and Practice* 36 (4 2012): 819–836.

104 J.D. Hansen, G.D. Deitz, M. Tokman, L.D. Marino, and K.M. Weaver, Cross-national invariance of the entrepreneurial orientation scale. *Journal of Business Venturing* 26 (1 2011): 61–78.

105 B.A. George and L. Marion, The epistemology of entrepreneurial orientation: Conceptual formation, modeling, and operationalization. *Entrepreneurship Theory and Practice* 35 (5 2011): 989–1024.

106 T. Kontinen and A. Ojala, International opportunity recognition among small and medium-sized family firms. *Journal of Small Business Management* 49 (3 2011): 490–514.

107 J.G. Covin and W.J. Wales, The measurement of entrepreneurial orientation. *Entrepreneurship Theory and Practice* 36 (4 2012): 677–702.

108 Based on G. Covin and W.J. Wales, The measurement of entrepreneurial orientation. *Entrepreneurship Theory and Practice* 36 (4 2012): 677–702. *And* B.A. George and L. Marion, The epistemology of entrepreneurial orientation: Conceptual formation, modeling, and operationalization. *Entrepreneurship Theory and Practice* 35 (5 2011): 989–1024.

109 J. Cook, Introducing the Elevator Pitch: Where entrepreneurs get 43 seconds to reach the top. *Geek Wire* (April 12, 2012).

110 U. Brixy, R. Sternberg, and H. Stuber, The selectiveness of the entrepreneurial process. *Journal of Small Business Management* 50 (1 2012): 105–131.

111 T. Kontinen and A. Ojala, International opportunity recognition among small and medium-sized family firms. *Journal of Small Business Management* 49 (3 2011): 490–514.

112 S.M. Farmer, The behavioral impact of entrepreneur identity aspiration and prior entrepreneurial experience. *Entrepreneurship Theory and Practice* 35 (2 2011): 245–273.

113 S.M. Farmer, The behavioral impact of entrepreneur identity aspiration and prior entrepreneurial experience. *Entrepreneurship Theory and Practice* 35 (2 2011): 245–273.

114 J.D. Werbel and S.M. Danes, Work family conflict in new business ventures: The moderating effects of spousal commitment to the new business venture. *Journal of Small Business Management* 48 (3 2010): 421–440.

115 U. Brixy, R. Sternberg, and H. Stuber, The selectiveness of the entrepreneurial process. *Journal of Small Business Management* 50 (1 2012): 105–131.

116 D. Sardana and D.S. Kemmis, Who learns what?—A study based on entrepreneurs from biotechnology new ventures. *Journal of Small Business Management* 48 (3 2010): 441–468.

117 A. Katre and P. Salipante, Start-up social ventures: Blending fine-grained behaviors from two institutions for entrepreneurial success. *Entrepreneurship Theory and Practice* 35 (5 2011): 967–994.

118 SCORE (www.score.org). Retrieved January 1, 2013.

119 A. Katre and P. Salipante, Start-up social ventures: Blending fine-grained behaviors from two institutions for entrepreneurial success. *Entrepreneurship Theory and Practice* 35 (5 2011): 967–994.

120 D. Sullivan and M. Marvel, How entrepreneurs' knowledge and network ties relate to the number of employees in new SMEs. *Journal of Small Business Management* 49 (2 2011): 185–206.

121 R. Schayek and D. Dvir, The impact of public assistance programs on small businesses: Strategic planning, entrepreneurship resources usage, and market orientation as mediating variables. *Journal of Small Business Strategy* 22 (1 2012): 67–98.

122 L. Miller, 5 Questions with . . . Livestream.com's Max Haot. *GigaOm* (April 10, 2010).

123 Retrieved from livestream.com on September 27, 2012.

124 A. Chowdhry, Live broadcast company, Mogulus raises $10 Million, *pulse2.com* (July 28, 2008).

125 A. Chowdhry, Mogulus turns into LiveStream.com, Paid $100,000 for the domain, *pulse2.com* (May 19, 2009).

126 *Inc.* (September 2012): 164.

127 Wikipedia (www.wikipedia.org). Retrieved September 27, 2012.

128 M. Naumov, Why young Russians live and breathe entrepreneurship. *Forbes* (March 11, 2013).

129 Associated Press, Trade a paper clip for a house? On the internet almost anything is possible. *msnbc.com* (April 16, 2006).

Chapter 2

1 www.wahoos.com/faq_franchise_info.php. Retrieved October 31, 2012.

2 http://smallbusinessschool.org/video.cfm?clip=1804. Retrieved October 31, 2012.

3 D.H.B. Welsh, A.E. Davis, D.E. Desplaces, and C.M. Falbe, A resource-based view of three forms of business in the startup phase: Implications for franchising. *Journal of Small Business Strategy* 22 (1 2012): 47–65.

4 S.C. Parker and C. Mirjam van Praag, The entrepreneur's mode of entry: Business takeover or new venture start? *Journal of Business Venturing* 27 (1 2012): 31–46.

5 Adapted based on a three-option approach from D.H.B. Welsh, A.E. Davis, D.E. Desplaces, and C.M. Falbe, A resource-based view of three forms of business in the startup phase: Implications for franchising. *Journal of Small Business Strategy* 22 (1 2012): 47–65.

6 M. Simon and R.C. Shrader, Entrepreneurial actions and optimistic overconfidence: The role of motivated reasoning in new product introductions. *Journal of Business Venturing* 27 (3 2012): 291–309. And J.C. Hayton and M. Cholakova, The role of affect in the creation and intentional pursuit of entrepreneurial ideas. *Entrepreneurship Theory and Practice* 36 (1 2012): 41–62.

7 B.R. Barringer and R.D. Ireland. *Entrepreneurship* (Upper Saddle River, NJ: Prentice Hall, 2012).

8 M. Simon, J. Kim, S.M. Houghton, and X. Deng, When it's right to be wrong: The effects of overconfidence and planning on product performance in a dynamic environment. *Journal of Small Business Strategy* 22 (1 2012): 21–46.

9 K. Podoynitsyna, H. Van der Bij, and M. Song, The role of mixed emotions in the risk perception of novice and serial entrepreneurs. *Entrepreneurship Theory and Practice* 35 (2 2011): 245–273.

10 J. Daley, Franchising is not for everyone. *Entrepreneur* (August 2012): 88–93.

11 S.M. Farmer, The behavioral impact of entrepreneur identity aspiration and prior entrepreneurial experience. *Entrepreneurship Theory and Practice* 35 (2 2011): 245–273.

12 N. Breugst, A. Domurath, H. Patzelt, and A. Klaukien, Perceptions of entrepreneurial passion and employees' commitment to entrepreneurial ventures. *Entrepreneurship Theory and Practice* 36 (1 2012): 171–188.

13 J.D. Werbel and S.M. Danes, Work family conflict in new business ventures: The moderating effects of spousal commitment to the new business venture. *Journal of Small Business Management* 48 (3 2010): 421–440.

14 V.C. Hahn, M. Frese, C. Binnewies, and A. Schmitt, Happy and proactive? The role of hedonic and eudaimonic well-being in business owners' personal initiative. *Entrepreneurship Theory and Practice* 36 (1 2012): 97–106.

15 U. Kaiser and N. Malchow-Møller. Is self-employment really a bad experience?: The effects of previous self-employment on subsequent wage-employment wages. *Journal of Business Venturing* 26 (5 2011): 572–588.

16 K.B. Lamp, M. Lévesque, and C. Schade, Are entrepreneurs influenced by risk attitude, regulatory focus or both? An experiment on entrepreneurs' time allocation. *Journal of Business Venturing* 27 (4 2012): 456–476.

17 Y. Zheng, Unlocking founding team prior shared experience: A transactive memory system perspective. *Journal of Business Venturing* 27 (5 2012): 577–591.

18 R.M Gemmell, R.J. Boland, and D.A. Kolb, The socio-cognitive dynamics of entrepreneurial ideation. *Entrepreneurship Theory and Practice* 36 (5 2012): 1053–1073.

19 Y. Zheng, Unlocking founding team prior shared experience: A transactive memory system perspective. *Journal of Business Venturing* 27 (5 2012): 577–591.

20 P.J. Murphy, A 2 X 2 conceptual foundation for entrepreneurial discovery theory. *Entrepreneurship Theory and Practice* 35 (2 2011): 359–374.

21 Wikipedia (www.wikipedia.org). Retrieved October 10, 2012.

22 Y. Zheng, Unlocking founding team prior shared experience: A transactive memory system perspective. *Journal of Business Venturing* 27 (5 2012): 577–591.

23 M. Griffiths, J. Kickul, S. Bacq, and S. Terjesen, A dialogue with William J. Baumol: Insights on entrepreneurship theory and education. *Entrepreneurship Theory and Practice* 36 (4 2012): 611–625.

24 McDonald's (www.mcdonalds.com). Retrieved October 10, 2012.

25 H. Meyer, Closing the deal. *Costco Connection* (August 2012): 22–24.

26 Adapted from the five steps of J. Martin, The time to sell is now! *FSB* (September 2006): 28–43.

27 Walgreens (www.walgreens.com). Retrieved October 10, 2012.

28 Ace Hardware (www.acehardware.com). Retrieved October 12, 2012.

29 Small Business Administration (SBA) (ww.sba.gov/content/buying-existing-business). Retrieved October 22, 2012.

30 International Business Brokers Association (www.ibba.org). Retrieved October 12, 2012.

31 BizBuySell (www.bizbuysell.com). Retrieved October 12, 2012.

32 Business for Sale (www.BusinessesForSale.com). Retrieved October 12, 2012.

33 Business Broker Net (www.businessbroker.net). Retrieved October 12, 2012.

34 Craigslist (www.craigslist.org). Retrieved October 12, 2012.

35 *The Wall Street Journal* (www.startupjournal.com). Retrieved October 12, 2012.

36 H. Meyer, Closing the deal. *Costco Connection* (August 2012): 22–24.

37 Small Business Administration (SBA) (www.sba.gov). Retrieved October 15, 2012.

38 M. Goodman, Trust funds. *Entrepreneur* (October 2012): 97.

39 M. Goodman, Trust funds. *Entrepreneur* (October 2012): 97.

40 H. Meyer, Closing the deal. *Costco Connection* (August 2012): 22–24.

41 N.M. Scarborough, *Essentials of Entrepreneurship and Small Business* (Upper Saddle River, NJ: Prentice Hall, 2011).

42 J. Barthélemy, Agency and institutional influences on franchising decisions. *Journal of Business Venturing* 26 (1 2011): 93–103.

43 J. Daley, Franchising is not for everyone. *Entrepreneur* (August 2012): 88–93.

44 W.R. Meek, B.D. Sramek, M.S. Baucus, and R.N. Germain, Commitment in franchising: The role of collaborative communication and a franchisee's propensity to leave. *Entrepreneurship Theory and Practice* 35 (3 2011): 559–581.

45 D. Grewal, G.R. Iyer, R.G. Javalgi, and L. Radulovich. Franchise partnership and international expansion: A conceptual framework and research propositions. *Entrepreneurship Theory and Practice* 35 (3 2011): 533–557.

46 W.E. Gillis, E. McEwan, T.R. Cook, and S.C. Michael, Using tournaments to reduce agency problems: The case of franchising. *Entrepreneurship Theory and Practice* 35 (3 2011): 427–447.

47 G.M. Kistruck, J.W. Webb, C.J. Sutter, and R.D. Ireland. Microfranchising in base-of-the-pyramid markets: Institutional challenges and adaptations to the franchise model. *Entrepreneurship Theory and Practice* 35 (3 2011): 503–531.

48 International Franchise Association (IFA) (www.franchise.org). Retrieved October 17, 2012.

49 J.G. Combs, D.J. Ketchen, and J.C. Short, Franchising research: Major milestones, and its future within entrepreneurship. *Entrepreneurship Theory and Practice* 35 (3 2011): 413–424.

50 D. Grewal, G.R. Iyer, R.G. Javalgi, and L. Radulovich. Franchise partnership and international expansion: A conceptual framework and research propositions. *Entrepreneurship Theory and Practice* 35 (3 2011): 533–557.

51 F. Chirico, R.D. Ireland, and D.G. Sirmon, Franchising and the family firm: Creating unique sources of advantages through familiness. *Entrepreneurship Theory and Practice* 35 (3 2011): 483–501.

52 N. Mumdziev and J. Windsperger, The structure of decision rights in franchising networks: A property

rights perspective. *Entrepreneurship Theory and Practice* 35 (3 2011): 449–465.

53 D.J. Ketchen, J.C. Short, and J.G. Combs, Is franchising entrepreneurship? Yes, no, maybe so. *Entrepreneurship Theory and Practice* 35 (3 2011): 583–593.

54 M.G. Diaz and V.S. Rodriguez, Why do entrepreneurs use franchising as a financial tool? An agency explanation. *Journal of Business Venturing* 27 (3 2012): 325–341.

55 Small Business Administration (SBA) (www.sba.gov). Retrieved October 22, 2012.

56 International Franchise Association (www.franchising.com). Retrieved October 17, 2012.

57 The American Association of Franchisees and Dealers (AAFD) (www.aafd.org). Retrieved October 19, 2012.

58 Franchising.com (www.franchising.com). Retrieved October 17, 2012.

59 *Entrepreneur* magazine (www.entrepreneur.com). Retrieved October 19, 2012.

60 *Entrepreneur* (January 2013).

61 Franchise Direct (www.franchisedirect.com). Retrieved October 19, 2012.

62 World Franchising (www.worldfranchising.com). Retrieved October 19, 2012.

63 Franchise Registry (www.Franchiseregistry.com). Retrieved October 19, 2012.

64 American Association of Franchisees and Dealers (AAFD) (www.aafd.org). Retrieved October 19, 2012.

65 American Association of Franchisees and Dealers (AAFD) (www.aafd.org). Retrieved October 19, 2012.

66 V.S. Rodriguez and M.G. Diaz, How to design franchise contracts: The role of contractual hazards and experience. *Journal of Small Business Management* 50 (4 2012): 652–677.

67 M.A.P. Davies, W. Lassar, C. Manolis, M. Prince, and R.D. Winsor, A model of trust and compliance in franchise relationships. *Journal of Business Venturing* 26 (3 2011): 321–340.

68 T. Stapp, World domination. *Entrepreneur* (October 2012): 121. Also available online at www.entrepreneur.com/franchises/topglobal/index.html.

69 Small Business Administration (SBA) (www.sba.gov). Retrieved October 15, 2012.

70 N.M. Scarborough, *Essentials of Entrepreneurship and Small Business* (Upper Saddle River, NJ: Prentice Hall, 2011).

71 G.M. Kistruck, J.W. Webb, C.J. Sutter, and R.D. Ireland. Microfranchising in base-of-the-pyramid markets: Institutional challenges and adaptations to the franchise model. *Entrepreneurship Theory and Practice* 35 (3 2011): 503–531.

72 Comment made by a franchise consultant, found in: G.M. Kistruck, J.W. Webb, C.J. Sutter, and R.D.

Ireland. Microfranchising in base-of-the-pyramid markets: Institutional challenges and adaptations to the franchise model. *Entrepreneurship Theory and Practice* 35 (3 2011): 503–531.

73 W.E. Gillis, E. McEwan, T.R. Cook, and S.C. Michael, Using tournaments to reduce agency problems: The case of franchising. *Entrepreneurship Theory and Practice* 35 (3 2011): 427–447.

74 H. Lee, D. Kelly, J. Lee, and S. Lee, SME survival: The impact of internationalization, technology resources, and alliances. *Journal of Small Business Management* 50 (1 2012): 1–19.

75 D.J. Ketchen, J.C. Short, and J.G. Combs, Is franchising entrepreneurship? Yes, no, maybe so. *Entrepreneurship Theory and Practice* 35 (3 2011): 583–593.

76 T. Stapp, World domination. *Entrepreneur* (October 2012): 121. Also available online at www.entrepreneur.com/franchises/topglobal/index.html.

77 Yum! Brands (http://yum.com/company/franchising.asp). Retrieved October 22, 2012.

78 Subway (www.subway.com/subwayroot/own_a_franchise/whychoosesubway.aspx). Retrieved October 22, 2012.

79 McDonald's (www.mcdonalds.com). Retrieved October 22, 2012.

80 Phone Halo (www.phonehalo.com). Retrieved October 8, 2012.

81 P.J. Murphy, The 2 x 2 conceptual foundation for entrepreneurial discovery theory. *Entrepreneurship Theory and Practice* 35 (2 2011): 359–374.

82 S.C. Parker, Intrapreneurship or entrepreneurship? *Journal of Business Venturing* 26 (1 2011): 19–34.

83 K.L. Johnson, The role of structural and planning autonomy in the performance of internal corporate ventures. *Journal of Small Business Management* 50 (3 2012): 469–497.

84 S.C. Parker, Intrapreneurship or entrepreneurship? *Journal of Business Venturing* 26 (1 2011): 19–34.

85 D.J. Ketchen, J.C. Short, and J.G. Combs, Is franchising entrepreneurship? Yes, no, maybe so. *Entrepreneurship Theory and Practice* 35 (3 2011): 583–593.

86 R. Lussier, author experience.

87 W. Wales, E. Monsen, and A. McKelvie, The organizational pervasiveness of entrepreneurial orientation. *Entrepreneurship Theory and Practice* 35 (5 2011): 895–923.

88 R. Fini, R. Grimaldi, G.L. Marzocchi, and M. Sobrero, The determinants of corporate entrepreneurial intention within small and newly established firms. *Entrepreneurship Theory and Practice* 35 (2 2011): 245–273.

89 K.R. Allen, *Launching New Ventures* (Mason, OH: Cengage, 2012).

90 K.L. Johnson, The role of structural and planning autonomy in the performance of internal corporate ventures. *Journal of Small Business Management* 50 (3 2012): 469–497.

91 K.R. Allen, *Launching New Ventures* (Mason, OH: Cengage, 2012).

92 M.H. Morris, J.W. Webb, and R.J. Franklin, Understanding the manifestation of entrepreneurial orientation in the nonprofit context. *Entrepreneurship Theory and Practice* 35 (5 2011): 947–971.

93 United Nations (UN) (www.un.org). Retrieved January 25, 2013.

94 A. Katre and P. Salipante, Start-up social ventures: Blending fine-grained behaviors from two institutions for entrepreneurial success. *Entrepreneurship Theory and Practice* 35 (5 2011): 967–994.

95 Silverbay YMCA (www.silverbay.org). Retrieved January 13, 2013

96 Mothers Against Drunk Driving (MADD) (www.madd.org). Retrieved October 29, 2012.

97 Boston Children's Hospital (www.childrenshospital.org) Retrieved January 16, 2013.

98 S.D. Sarasvathy and S. Venkataraman, Entrepreneurship as method: Open questions for an entrepreneurial future. *Entrepreneurship Theory and Practice* 35 (1 2011): 113–135.

99 D. Pallotta, Why can't we sell charity like we sell perfume? *The Wall Street Journal* (September 15–16, 2012): C1–C2.

100 M.H. Morris, J.W. Webb, and R.J. Franklin, Understanding the manifestation of entrepreneurial orientation in the nonprofit context. *Entrepreneurship Theory and Practice* 35 (5 2011): 947–971.

101 Boys & Girls Clubs (www.bgca.org/whoweare/Pages/Mission.aspx). Retrieved October 24, 2012.

102 World Alliance of YMCAs (www.ymca.int). Retrieved October 26, 2012.

103 New Spirit (http://newspiritinc.org). Retrieved October 26, 2012.

104 H.K Gibbs, Supplies on demand. *Costco Connection* (August 2012): 37. *And* www.donorschoose.org. Retrieved October 29, 2012.

105 Living Lands & Waters (www.livinglandsandwaters.org) Retrieved January 13, 2013. *And* C. Pregracke and J. Barrow, *From the Bottom up: One Man's Crusade to Clean America's Rivers* (Washington, DC: National Geographic Society, 2007).

106 Reading is Fundamental (RIF) (www.rif.org). Retrieved January 13, 2013.

107 Brookings Institute (www.brookings.edu). Retrieved January 13, 2013.

108 S. Forbes, Why philanthropy must have these 400-type entrepreneurs. *Forbes* (October 2012): 25–26.

109 S. Bertoni, International philanthropy: Going for broke. *Forbes* (October 2012): 99–100.

110 R. Lane, The Forbes 400. *Forbes* (October 2012): 42–56.

111 Bill & Melinda Gates Foundation (www.gatesfoundation.org). Retrieved October 26, 2012.

112 Wikipedia (www.wikipedia.org). Retrieved October 29, 2012.

113 D. Bornstein, *How to Change the World: Social Entrepreneurs and the Power of New Ideas* (New York: Oxford University Press, 2004).

114 Jewish Geriatric Services (www.jewishgeriatric.org). Retrieved January 15, 2013.

115 Wounded Warrior Project (www.support.woundedwarriorproject.org). Retrieved January 13, 2013.

116 Executive Service Corp (www.escus.org). Retrieved January 25, 2013.

117 J.C. Chrisman, J.H. Chua, and L.P. Steier, Resilience of family firms: An introduction. *Entrepreneurship Theory and Practice* 35 (6 2011): 1107–1119.

118 R.N. Lussier and M.C. Sonfield, A six-country study of first, second, and third-generation family businesses. *International Journal of Entrepreneurial Behaviour & Research* 16 (5 2010): 414–436.

119 T. Kontinen and A. Ojala, International opportunity recognition among small and medium-sized family firms. *Journal of Small Business Management* 49 (3 2011): 490–514.

120 R.N. Lussier and M.C. Sonfield, Founder influence in family firms: Analyzing combined data from six diverse countries. *Journal of Small Business Strategy* 20 (1 2009): 103–118.

121 M.C. Sonfield, R.N. Lussier, and R.J. Barbato, Generational stages in family firms: Expanding the database: Kosovo. *Southern Journal of Entrepreneurship* 4 (1 2011): 1–18.

122 T. Zellweger, P. Sieger, and F. Halter, Should I stay or should I go? Career choice intentions of students with family business background. *Journal of Business Venturing* 26 (5 2011): 521–536.

123 E. Mungai and S.R. Velamuri, Parental entrepreneurial role model influence on male offspring: Is it always positive and when does it occur? *Entrepreneurship Theory and Practice* 35 (2 2011): 337–357.

124 R. Lussier and C.E. Halabi, A three-country comparison of the business success versus failure prediction model. *Journal of Small Business Management* 48 (3 2010): 360–377.

125 P. Sharma and C. Salvato, Commentary: Exploiting and exploring new opportunities over life cycle stages of family firms. *Entrepreneurship Theory and Practice* 35 (6 2011): 1199–1205.

126 J.D. Werbel and S.M. Danes, Work family conflict in new business ventures: The moderating effects of spousal commitment to the new business venture. *Journal of Small Business Management* 48 (3 2010): 421–440.

127 F. Chirico, R.D. Ireland, and D.G. Sirmon, Franchising and the family firm: Creating unique sources of advantages through familiness. *Entrepreneurship Theory and Practice* 35 (3 2011): 483–501.

128 E.H. O'Boyle, J.M. Pollack, and M.W. Rutherford, Exploring the relation between family involvement and firms' financial performance: A meta-analysis of main and moderator effects. *Journal of Business Venturing* 27 (1 2012): 1–18.

129 G.T. Lumpkin and K.H. Brigham, Long-term orientation and intertemporal choice in family firms. *Entrepreneurship Theory and Practice* 35 (6 2011): 1149–1169.

130 P.C. Patel and J.O. Fiet, Knowledge combination and the potential advantages of family firms searching for opportunities. *Entrepreneurship Theory and Practice* 35 (6 2011): 1179–1197.

131 R.N. Lussier and M.C. Sonfield, Family businesses' succession planning: A seven-country comparison. *Journal of Small Business and Enterprise Development* 19 (1 2012): 7–19.

132 J. Shuffler, Keith Belling, Founder and CEO, Popchips. *San Francisco Business Times* (January 31, 2010).

133 S. Finz, Popchips doing healthy sales, expanding to Britain. *San Francisco Chronicle* (March 1, 2012).

134 L. Petrecca, Popchips CEO Keith Belling is "poptimist" on healthy snacks. *USA Today* (April 12, 2010).

135 S. Musafer, Family values help Greek shipping business go global. *BBC* (July 7, 2013).

136 S. Musafer, Family values help Greek shipping business go global. *BBC* (July 7, 2013).

137 www.pwc.com/gr/en/publications/family-business-survey-2012.jhtml. Retrieved October 3, 2013.

138 www.pwc.com/gr/en/publications/family-business-survey-2012.jhtml. Retrieved October 3, 2013.

Chapter 3

1 P.J. Murphy, A 2 X 2 conceptual foundation for entrepreneurial discovery theory. *Entrepreneurship Theory and Practice* 35 (2 2011): 359–374.

2 Statement by Ted Levitt, found in N.M. Scarborough, *Essentials of Entrepreneurship and Small Business* (Upper Saddle River, NJ: Prentice Hall, 2011): 33.

3 M.Z. Taylor and S. Wilson, Does culture still matter? The effects of individualism on national innovation rates. *Journal of Business Venturing* 27 (2 2012): 234–247.

4 N. Rosenbusch, J. Brinckmann, and A. Bausch. Is innovation always beneficial? A meta-analysis of the relationship between innovation and performance in SMEs. *Journal of Business Venturing* 26 (4 2011): 441–457.

5 S. Gronum, M.L. Verreynne, and T. Kastelle, The role of networks in small and medium-sized enterprise innovation and firm performance. *Journal of Small Business Management* 50 (2 2012): 257–282.

6 M.C. Withers, P.L Drnevich, and L. Marino, Doing more with less: The disordinal implications of firm age for leveraging capabilities for innovation activity. *Journal of Small Business Management* 49 (4 2011): 515–536.

7 L. Lee, P. Kam, W.M. Der Foo, and A. Leung, Entrepreneurial intentions: The influence of organizational and individual factors. *Journal of Business Venturing* 26 (1 2011): 124–136.

8 V. Parida, M. Westerberg, and J. Frishammar, Inbound open innovation activities in high-tech SMEs: The impact on innovation performance. *Journal of Small Business Management* 50 (2 2012): 283–309.

9 P.J. Murphy, A 2 X 2 conceptual foundation for entrepreneurial discovery theory. *Entrepreneurship Theory and Practice* 35 (2 2011): 359–374.

10 J.C. Hayton and M. Cholakova, The role of affect in the creation and intentional pursuit of entrepreneurial ideas. *Entrepreneurship Theory and Practice* 36 (1 2012): 41–60.

11 A.C. Cosper, Case in point. *Entrepreneur* (October 2012): 12.

12 M.M. Gielnik, M. Frese, J.M. Graf, and A. Kampschulte, Creativity in the opportunity identification process and the moderating effect of diversity of information. *Journal of Business Venturing* 27 (5 2012): 559–576.

13 M.C. Withers, P.L Drnevich, and L. Marino, Doing more with less: The disordinal implications of firm age for leveraging capabilities for innovation activity. *Journal of Small Business Management* 49 (4 2011): 515–536.

14 W. Wales, E. Monsen, and A. McKelvie, The organizational pervasiveness of entrepreneurial orientation. *Entrepreneurship Theory and Practice* 35 (5 2011): 895–923.

15 M.S. Cardon, M.D. Foo, D. Shepherd, and J. Wiklud, Exploring the heart: Entrepreneurial emotion is a hot topic. *Entrepreneurship Theory and Practice* 36 (1 2012): 1–21.

16 J.C. Hayton and M. Cholakova, The role of affect in the creation and intentional pursuit of entrepreneurial ideas. *Entrepreneurship Theory and Practice* 36 (1 2012): 41–60.

17 H. Reijonen, T. Laukkanewn, R. Komppula, and S. Tuominen, Are growing SMEs more market-oriented and brand-oriented? *Journal of Small Business Management* 50 (4 2012): 699–716.

18 P.C. Patel and J.O. Fiet, Knowledge combination and the potential advantages of family firms searching

for opportunities. *Entrepreneurship Theory and Practice* 35 (6 2011): 1179–1197.

19 J. Tang and P.J. Murphy, Prior knowledge and new product and service introductions by entrepreneurial firms: The mediating role of technological innovation. *Journal of Small Business Management* 50 (1 2012): 41–62.

20 J.P. Perry, G.N. Chandler, and G. Markova, Entrepreneurial effectuation: A review and suggestions for future research. *Entrepreneurship Theory and Practice* 36 (4 2012): 837–861.

21 M. Marvel, Knowledge acquisition asymmetries and innovation radicalness. *Journal of Small Business Management* 50 (3 2012): 447–468.

22 P.J. Murphy, A 2 X 2 conceptual foundation for entrepreneurial discovery theory. *Entrepreneurship Theory and Practice* 35 (2 2011): 359–374.

23 P.C. Patel and J.O. Fiet, Knowledge combination and the potential advantages of family firms searching for opportunities. *Entrepreneurship Theory and Practice* 35 (6 2011): 1179–1197.

24 P. Sharma and C. Salvato, Commentary: Exploiting and exploring new opportunities over life cycle stages of family firms. *Entrepreneurship Theory and Practice* 35 (6 2011): 1199–1205.

25 R.N. Lussier, *Management Fundamentals* (Mason, OH: Cengage, 2012).

26 R.N. Lussier, *Management Fundamentals* (Mason, OH: Cengage, 2012).

27 Staff, Google's quest. *The Wall Street Journal* (November 5, 2012): A1.

28 M.M. Gielnik, M. Frese, J.M. Graf, and A. Kampschulte, Creativity in the opportunity identification process and the moderating effect of diversity of information. *Journal of Business Venturing* 27 (5 2012): 559–576.

29 R.S. Rubin and E.C. Dierdorff, How relevant is the MBA? Assessing the alignment of required curricula and required managerial competencies. *Academy of Management Learning & Education* 8 (5 2009): 208–224.

30 N.M. Scarborough, *Essentials of Entrepreneurship and Small Business* (Upper Saddle River, NJ: Prentice Hall, 2011).

31 E. Napoletano, Some real kick-starters. *Entrepreneur* (October 2012): 27.

32 B.R. Barringer and R.D. Ireland, *Entrepreneurship* (Upper Saddle River, NJ: Prentice Hall, 2012).

33 R. Pearce, Development Editor, Routledge, personal contact, October 6, 2012.

34 T. Kontinen and A. Ojala, International opportunity recognition among small and medium-sized family firms. *Journal of Small Business Management* 49 (3 2011): 490–514.

35 S.M. Farmer, The behavioral impact of entrepreneur identity aspiration and prior entrepreneurial experience. *Entrepreneurship Theory and Practice* 35 (2 2011): 245–273.

36 J.C. Chrisman, J.H. Chua, and L.P. Steier, Resilience of family firms: An introduction. *Entrepreneurship Theory and Practice* 35 (6 2011): 1107–1119.

37 P. Sharma and C. Salvato, Commentary: Exploiting and exploring new opportunities over life cycle stages of family firms. *Entrepreneurship Theory and Practice* 35 (6 2011): 1199–1205.

38 B.R. Barringer and R.D. Ireland, *Entrepreneurship* (Upper Saddle River, NJ: Prentice Hall, 2012).

39 J.M. Haynie, D.A. Shepherd, and H. Patzelt, Cognitive adaptability and an entrepreneurial task: The role of metacognitive ability and feedback. *Entrepreneurship Theory and Practice* 36 (2 2012): 237–246.

40 N.M. Scarborough, *Essentials of Entrepreneurship and Small Business* (Upper Saddle River, NJ: Prentice Hall, 2011).

41 B. Haislip, If you want to beat 'em, learn from 'em first. *The Wall Street Journal* (November 12, 2012): R3.

42 S. Gronum, M.L. Verreynne, and T. Kastelle, The role of networks in small and medium-sized enterprise innovation and firm performance. *Journal of Small Business Management* 50 (2 2012): 257–282.

43 T. Semrau and A. Werner, The two sides of the story: Network investments and new venture creation. *Journal of Small Business Management* 50 (1 2012): 159–180.

44 N.M. Scarborough, *Essentials of Entrepreneurship and Small Business* (Upper Saddle River, NJ: Prentice Hall, 2011).

45 A. Tumasjan and R. Braun, In the eye of the beholder: How regulatory focus and self-efficacy interact in influencing opportunity recognition. *Journal of Business Venturing* 27 (6 2012): 622–636.

46 S.M. Farmer, The behavioral impact of entrepreneur identity aspiration and prior entrepreneurial experience. *Entrepreneurship Theory and Practice* 35 (2 2011): 245–273.

47 P.C. Patel and J.O. Fiet, Knowledge combination and the potential advantages of family firms searching for opportunities. *Entrepreneurship Theory and Practice* 35 (6 2011): 1179–1197.

48 B. Schoenfeld, *Entrepreneur* (October 2012): 23–24.

49 D. Eng, The king of travel and real estate. *Fortune* (January 14, 2013): 21–24.

50 P.F. Nunes, G. Godbey, and H.J. Wilson, Beat the clock. *The Wall Street Journal* (October 26, 2009): R6.

51 D. Eng, The king of travel and real estate. *Fortune* (January 14, 2013): 21–24.

52 B. Mycoskie, *Start Something That Matters* (New York: Spiegel &Grau, 2012).

53 N.M. Scarborough, *Essentials of Entrepreneurship and Small Business* (Upper Saddle River, NJ: Prentice Hall, 2011).

54 Groupon (www.groupon.com). Retrieved November 12, 2012.

55 GasBuddy Organization (www.gasbuddy.com). Retrieved November 12, 2012.

56 S.D. Sarasvathy and S. Venkataraman, Entrepreneurship as method: Open questions for an entrepreneurial future. *Entrepreneurship Theory and Practice* 35 (1 2011): 113–135.

57 Five Guys Burgers and Fries (www.fiveguys.com). Retrieved November 12, 2012.

58 N. Leiber, Caregiving: Elder care a click away. *Businessweek* (October 29–November 2, 2012): 60.

59 S.D. Sarasvathy and S. Venkataraman, Entrepreneurship as method: Open questions for an entrepreneurial future. *Entrepreneurship Theory and Practice* 35 (1 2011): 113–135.

60 D.A. Shepherd and H. Patzelt, The new field of sustainable entrepreneurship: Studying entrepreneurial action linking what is to be sustained with what is to be developed. *Entrepreneurship Theory and Practice* 35 (1 2011): 137–163.

61 Definition developed by the Brundtland Commission. Cited from Colvin interview of Linda Fisher, *Fortune* (November 23, 2009): 45–50.

62 A. Nadim and R.N. Lussier, Sustainability as a small business competitive strategy. *Journal of Small Strategy* 21 (2 2012): 79–95.

63 A.A. Marcus and A.R. Fremeth, Green management matters regardless. *Academy of Management Perspectives* 23 (3 2009): 17–26.

64 Advertisement, The value of sustainability. *Businessweek* (November 26–December 2, 2012): 2.

65 J.C. Hayton and M. Cholakova, The role of affect in the creation and intentional pursuit of entrepreneurial ideas. *Entrepreneurship Theory and Practice* 36 (1 2012): 41–60.

66 S.D. Sarasvathy and S. Venkataraman, Entrepreneurship as method: Open questions for an entrepreneurial future. *Entrepreneurship Theory and Practice* 35 (1 2011): 113–135.

67 C. Dibrell, J. Craig, and E. Hansen, Natural environment, market orientation, and firm innovativeness: An organizational life cycle perspective. *Journal of Small Business Management* 49 (3 2011): 467–489.

68 D. Brady, Innovator Julie Corbett: Bottles inspired by the iPhone. *Businessweek* (October 29–November 4, 2012): 45.

69 J. Tang and P.J. Murphy, Prior knowledge and new product and service introductions by entrepreneurial firms: The mediating role of technological innovation. *Journal of Small Business Management* 50 (1 2012): 41–62.

70 A. Chatterji, Why Washington has it wrong. *The Wall Street Journal* (November 12, 2012): R1–R2.

71 Staff, Robots: Rise of the iMowbot. *Businessweek* (October 29–November 2, 2012): 28–29.

72 X-1 (www.x-1.com).

73 O. Kharif, Mobile: The pirate-infested waters of App retailing. *Businessweek* (November 5–11, 2012): 44.

74 B.R. Barringer and R.D. Ireland. *Entrepreneurship* (Upper Saddle River, NJ: Prentice Hall, 2012).

75 C. Dibrell, J. Craig, and E. Hansen, Natural environment, market orientation, and firm innovativeness: An organizational life cycle perspective. *Journal of Small Business Management* 49 (3 2011): 467–489.

76 J.C. Hayton and M. Cholakova, The role of affect in the creation and intentional pursuit of entrepreneurial ideas. *Entrepreneurship Theory and Practice* 36 (1 2012): 41–60.

77 J.H. Pirouetting towards profits. *Entrepreneur* (October 2012): 98.

78 N. Karelaia, Predictably irrational: The hidden forces that shape our decisions. *Academy of Management Perspectives* 23 (1 2009): 86–88.

79 D. Dimov, Grappling with the unbearable elusiveness of entrepreneurial opportunities. *Entrepreneurship Theory and Practice* 35 (1 2011): 57–81.

80 Chegg (www.chegg.com). Retrieved November 21, 2012.

81 J. Espinoza, Filling up on bread. *The Wall Street Journal* (November 12, 2012): R3.

82 N. Karelaia, Predictably irrational: The hidden forces that shape our decisions. *Academy of Management Perspectives* 23 (1 2009): 86–88.

83 N. Canner, Ten new gurus you should know. *Fortune* (November 24, 2008): 158.

84 Smart Lid Systems (www.smartlids.com). Retrieved November 13, 2012. The information pertaining to Nick Bayss is taken from N.M. Scarborough, *Essentials of Entrepreneurship and Small Business* (Upper Saddle River, NJ: Prentice Hall, 2011).

85 G. Hirst, D. Van Knippenberg, and J. Zhou, A cross-level perspective on employee creativity: Goal orientation, team learning behavior, and individual creativity. *Academy of Management Journal* 52 (2 2009): 280–293.

86 L. Dragoni, P.E. Tesluk, J.E.A. Russell, and I. Oh, Understanding managerial development: Integrating developmental assignments, learning orientation, and access to developmental opportunities in predicting managerial competencies. *Academy of Management Journal* 52 (4 2009): 731–742.

87 S. Covy, Time management. *Fortune* (September 19, 2009): 28–29.

88 Smart Lid Systems (www.smartlids.com). Retrieved November 13, 2012.

89 G. George and A.J. Bock, The business model in practice and its implications for entrepreneurship research. *Entrepreneurship Theory and Practice* 35 (1 2011): 83–111.

90 J. Reingold, Still crazy after all these years. *Fortune* (January 14, 2012): 92–97.

91 D. Dimov, Grappling with the unbearable elusiveness of entrepreneurial opportunities. *Entrepreneurship Theory and Practice* 35 (1 2011): 57–81.

92 S. Mueller, T. Volery, and B. von Siemens, What do entrepreneurs actually do? An observational study of entrepreneurs' everyday behavior in the startup and growth stages. *Entrepreneurship Theory and Practice* 35 (5 2011): 995–1017.

93 J.H. Pirouetting towards profits. *Entrepreneur* (October 2012): 98.

94 J.P. Perry, G.N. Chandler, and G. Markova, Entrepreneurial effectuation: A review and suggestions for future research. *Entrepreneurship Theory and Practice* 36 (4 2012): 837–861.

95 M. Baum, C. Schwens, and R. Kabst, A typology of international new ventures: Empirical evidence from high-technology industries. *Journal of Small Business Management* 49 (3 2011): 305–330.

96 B. Larrañeta, S.A. Zahra, and J.L.G. González, Enriching strategic variety in new ventures through external knowledge. *Journal of Business Venturing* 27(4 2012): 401–413.

97 Papa John's (www.papajohns.com). Retrieved November 16, 2012.

98 Anthony's Pier 4 (www.pier4.com). Retrieved November 16, 2012.

99 Gap (www.gap.com). Retrieved November 16, 2012.

100 Whole Foods Market (www.wholefoodsmarkdet. com). Retrieved November 16, 2012.

101 FedEx (www.fedex.com). Retrieved November 16, 2012.

102 Domino's (www.dominos.com). Retrieved November 16, 2012.

103 Zoots (www.zoots.com). Retrieved November 16, 2012.

104 KFC (www.kfc.com). Retrieved November 16, 2012.

105 Andrea Lausier interview, November 16, 2012.

106 Wal-Mart (www.walmart.com). Retrieved November 16, 2012.

107 Jiff Lube (www.jiffylube.com). Retrieved November 16, 2012.

108 Google (www.google.com). Retrieved November 19, 2012.

109 McDonald's (www.mcdonalds.com). Retrieved November 21, 2012.

110 N.M. Scarborough, *Essentials of Entrepreneurship and Small Business* (Upper Saddle River, NJ: Prentice Hall, 2011).

111 Toyota (www.toyota.com). Retrieved November 19, 2012.

112 *The Wall Street Journal.*

113 D. Lavinsky, Master class. *Businessweek* (November 26–December 3, 2012): 103.

114 McDonald's (www.mcdonalds.com). Retrieved November 21, 2012.

115 FedEx (www.fedex.com). Retrieved November 21, 2012.

116 BigBelly Solar (www.BigBellySolar.com). Retrieved November 19, 2012.

117 Mariana's Supermarkets (www.marianasmarkets. com). Retrieved November 19, 2012.

118 Facebook (www.facebook.com). Retrieved November 19, 2012.

119 Google (www.google.com). Retrieved November 19, 2012.

120 S.E. Needleman and A. Loten, When freemium falls short. *The Wall Street Journal* (August 23, 2012): B1.

121 *The Wall Street Journal.*

122 Interview with Pete and Corby Clark, November 26, 2012.

123 J. Jargon, McDonald's replaces U.S. chief. *The Wall Street Journal* (November 15, 2012): B2.

124 P.C. Patel and B. Conklin, Perceived labor productivity in small firms—The effects of high-performance work systems and group culture through employee retention. *Entrepreneurship Theory and Practice* 36 (2 2012): 205–225.

125 Advertisement, 4 Ways Logistics can make your supply chain more sustainable. *Businessweek* (November 26–December 2, 2012): 64.

126 Land O'Lakes (www.landolakes.com). Retrieved November 21, 2012.

127 www.investorwords.com/1684/elevator_pitch.html# ixzz2EJuJ3gq0. Retrieved January 30, 2013.

128 J.M. Pollack, M.W. Rutherford, and B.G. Nagy, Preparedness and cognitive legitimacy as antecedents of new venture funding in televised business pitches. *Entrepreneurship Theory and Practice* 36 (5 2012): 915–939.

129 J.M. Pollack, M.W. Rutherford, and B.G. Nagy, Preparedness and cognitive legitimacy as antecedents of new venture funding in televised business pitches. *Entrepreneurship Theory and Practice* 36 (5 2012): 915–939.

130 www.businessdictionary.com/definition/elevator-pitch.html#ixzz2EJsWyZLZ.

131 B. Mycoskie, *Start Something That Matters* (New York: Spiegel & Grau, 2012): Chapter 2.

132 YMCA of Wabash (www.wabashcountyymca.org). Retrieved January 28, 2013.

133 S. Ponder, Power to the pita. *The Costco Connection* (December 2012): 26.

134 J. Hicks, The new French entrepreneur: The female millennial (*Forbes.com*, March 3, 2013). Retrieved September 27, 2013.

135 J. Hicks, French entrepreneurship is alive (even in August). *Forbes.com* (August 7, 2012).

Chapter 4

1 M.D. Foo, Emotions and entrepreneurial opportunity evaluation. *Entrepreneurship Theory and Practice* 35 (2 2011): 375–393.

2 K. Podoynitsya, H. Van der Bij, and M. Song, The role of mixed emotions in the risk perception of novice and serial entrepreneurs. *Entrepreneurship Theory and Practice* 36 (1 2012): 115–121.

3 J.C. Hayton and M. Cholakova, The role of affect in the creation and intentional pursuit of entrepreneurial ideas. *Entrepreneurship Theory and Practice* 36 (1 2012): 41–60.

4 G. Colvin, We're the intersection of media and technology. *Fortune* (December 24, 2012): 54–58.

5 B. Bird, L. Schojoedt, and J.R. Baum, Entrepreneurs' behavior: Elucidation and measurement. *Entrepreneurship Theory and Practice* 36 (5 2012): 889–913.

6 I.M. Welpe, M. Sporrle, D. Grichnik, T. Michl, and D.B. Audretsch, Emotions and opportunities: The interplay of opportunity evaluation, fear, job, and anger as antecedent of entrepreneurial exploitation. *Entrepreneurship Theory and Practice* 36 (1 2012): 69–87.

7 J.M. Haynie, D.A. Shepherd, and H. Patzelt, Cognitive adaptability and an entrepreneurial task: The role of metacognitive ability and feedback. *Entrepreneurship Theory and Practice* 36 (2 2012): 237–246.

8 K.R. Allen, *Launching New Ventures* (Mason, OH: Cengage, 2012).

9 M.S. Cardon, M.D Foo, D. Shepherd, and J. Wiklud, Exploring the heart: Entrepreneurial emotion is a hot topic. *Entrepreneurship Theory and Practice* 36 (1 2012): 1–21.

10 A. Chwolka and M.G. Raith, The value of business planning before start-up—A decision-theoretical perspective. *Journal of Business Venturing* 27 (3 2012): 385–399.

11 Based on B.R. Barringer and R.D. Ireland. *Entrepreneurship* (Upper Saddle River, NJ: Prentice Hall, 2012).

12 Isoldit (www.877isoldit.com). Retrieved November 30, 2012.

13 B. Bird, L. Schojoedt, and J.R. Baum, Entrepreneurs' behavior: Elucidation and measurement. *Entrepreneurship Theory and Practice* 36 (5 2012): 889–913.

14 H. Reijonen, T. Laukkanewn, R. Komppula, and S. Tuominen, Are growing SMEs more market-oriented and brand-oriented? *Journal of Small Business Management* 50 (4 2012): 699–716.

15 W. Tsai, K.H. Su, and M.J. Chen, Seeing through the eyes of a rival: Competitor acumen based on rival-centric perceptions. *Academy of Management Journal* 54 (4 2011): 761–778.

16 B Haislip, If you want to beat 'em, learn from 'em first. *The Wall Street Journal* (November 12, 2012): R3.

17 M.D. Foo, Emotions and entrepreneurial opportunity evaluation. *Entrepreneurship Theory and Practice* 35 (2 2011): 375–393.

18 All Web sites in Exhibit 4-3 where checked for accurate information on January 5, 2013.

19 Staff, SizeUp your business. *Costco Connection* (November 2012): 15.

20 Haislip, If you want to beat 'em, learn from 'em first. *The Wall Street Journal* (November 12, 2012): R3.

21 A. Handley, Keep it simple (but not stupid). *Entrepreneur* (January 2013): 60.

22 A. Katre and P. Salipante, Start-up social ventures: Blending fine-grained behaviors from two institutions for entrepreneurial success. *Entrepreneurship Theory and Practice* 35 (5 2011): 967–994.

23 J.T. Perry, G.N. Chandler, and G. Markova, Entrepreneurial effectuation: A review and suggestions for future research. *Entrepreneurship Theory and Practice* 36 (4 2012): 837–861.

24 D. Dimov, Grappling with the unbearable elusiveness of entrepreneurial opportunities. *Entrepreneurship Theory and Practice* 35 (1 2011): 57–81.

25 A. Handley, Keep it simple (but not stupid). *Entrepreneur* (January 2013): 60.

26 G. Fisher, Effectuation, causation, and bricolage: A behavioral comparison of emerging theories in entrepreneurship research. *Entrepreneurship Theory and Practice* 36 (5 2012): 1019–1051.

27 P.C. Patel and B. Conklin, Perceived labor productivity in small firms—The effects of high-performance work systems and group culture through employee retention. *Entrepreneurship Theory and Practice* 36 (2 2012): 205–224.

28 H. Reijonen, T. Laukkanewn, R. Komppula, and S. Tuominen, Are growing SMEs more market-oriented and brand-oriented? *Journal of Small Business Management* 50 (4 2012): 699–716.

29 S. Mueller, T. Volery, and B. von Siemens, What do entrepreneurs actually do? An observational study of entrepreneurs' everyday behavior in the startup and growth stages. *Entrepreneurship Theory and Practice* 35 (5 2011): 995–1017.

30 A. Katre and P. Salipante, Start-up social ventures: Blending fine-grained behaviors from two institutions for entrepreneurial success. *Entrepreneurship Theory and Practice* 35 (5 2011): 967–994.

31 B. Mycoskie, *Start Something That Matters* (New York: Spiegel & Grau, 2012).

32 E. Napoletano, Some real kick-starters. *Entrepreneur* (October 2012): 27.

33 S. Mueller, T. Volery, and B. von Siemens, What do entrepreneurs actually do? An observational study of entrepreneurs' everyday behavior in the startup and growth stages. *Entrepreneurship Theory and Practice* 35 (5 2011): 995–1017.

34 B. Mycoskie, *Start Something That Matters* (New York: Spiegel & Grau, 2012).

35 B. Mycoskie, *Start Something That Matters* (New York: Spiegel & Grau, 2012).

36 G. Colvin, We're the intersection of media and technology. *Fortune* (December 24, 2012): 54–58.

37 U.S. Census (www.census.gov/epcd/naics). Retrieved December 14, 2012.

38 U.S. Census (www.census.gov/epcd/naics). Retrieved December 14, 2012.

39 U.S. Census (http://factfinder2.census.gov/faces/nav/jsf/pages/index.xhtml#none). Retrieved December 21, 2012.

40 A. Katre and P. Salipante, Start-up social ventures: Blending fine-grained behaviors from two institutions for entrepreneurial success. *Entrepreneurship Theory and Practice* 35 (5 2011): 967–994.

41 Based on M. Porter, How competitive forces shape strategy. *Harvard Business Review* 57 (2, 1979): 137–145.

42 B. Mycoskie, *Start Something That Matters* (New York: Spiegel & Grau, 2012).

43 S. Mueller, T. Volery, and B. von Siemens, What do entrepreneurs actually do? An observational study of entrepreneurs' everyday behavior in the startup and growth stages. *Entrepreneurship Theory and Practice* 35 (5 2011): 995–1017.

44 A. Katre and P. Salipante, Start-up social ventures: Blending fine-grained behaviors from two institutions for entrepreneurial success. *Entrepreneurship Theory and Practice* 35 (5 2011): 967–994.

45 J.M. Haynie, D.A. Shepherd, and H. Patzelt, Cognitive adaptability and an entrepreneurial task: The role of metacognitive ability and feedback. *Entrepreneurship Theory and Practice* 36 (2 2012): 237–246.

46 B. Bird, L. Schojoedt, and J.R. Baum, Entrepreneurs' behavior: Elucidation and measurement. *Entrepreneurship Theory and Practice* 36 (5 2012): 889–913.

47 J.H. Pirouetting towards profits. *Entrepreneur* (October 2012): 98.

48 G. Colvin, We're the intersection of media and technology. *Fortune* (December 24, 2012): 54–58.

49 E. Napoletano, Some real kick-starters. *Entrepreneur* (October 2012): 27.

50 SCORE (www.score.org). Retrieved January 2, 2013.

51 M.S. Cardon, M.D Foo, D. Shepherd, and J. Wiklud, Exploring the heart: Entrepreneurial emotion is a hot topic. *Entrepreneurship Theory and Practice* 36 (1 2012): 1–21.

52 H. Reijonen, T. Laukkanewn, R. Komppula, and S. Tuominen, Are growing SMEs more market-oriented and brand-oriented? *Journal of Small Business Management* 50 (4 2012): 699–716.

53 B.G. Nagy, J.M. Pollack, M.W. Rutherford, and F.T. Lohrke, The influence of entrepreneurs' credentials and impression management behaviors on perceptions of new venture legitimacy. *Entrepreneurship Theory and Practice* 35 (5 2011): 941–965.

54 J.M. Pollack, M.W. Rutherford, and B.G. Nagy, Preparedness and cognitive legitimacy as antecedents of new venture funding in televised business pitches. *Entrepreneurship Theory and Practice* 36 (5 2012): 915–939.

55 B. Mycoskie, *Start Something That Matters* (New York: Spiegel & Grau, 2012).

56 G. Fisher, Effectuation, causation, and bricolage: A behavioral comparison of emerging theories in entrepreneurship research. *Entrepreneurship Theory and Practice* 36 (5 2012): 1019–1051.

57 J.T. Perry, G.N. Chandler, and G. Markova, Entrepreneurial effectuation: A review and suggestions for future research. *Entrepreneurship Theory and Practice* 36 (4 2012): 837–861.

58 P.C. Patel and B. Conklin, Perceived labor productivity in small firms—The effects of high-performance work systems and group culture through employee retention. *Entrepreneurship Theory and Practice* 36 (2 2012): 205–224.

59 V. Parida, M. Westerberg, and J. Frishammar, Inbound open innovation activities in high-tech SMEs: The impact on innovation performance. *Journal of Small Business Management* 50 (2 2012): 283–309.

60 G. Colvin, We're the intersection of media and technology. *Fortune* (December 24, 2012): 54–58.

61 I.M. Welpe, M. Sporrle, D. Grichnik, T. Michl, and D.B. Audretsch, Emotions and opportunities: The interplay of opportunity evaluation, fear, job, and anger as antecedent of entrepreneurial exploitation. *Entrepreneurship Theory and Practice* 36 (1 2012): 69–87.

62 J.T. Perry, G.N. Chandler, and G. Markova, Entrepreneurial effectuation: A review and suggestions for future research. *Entrepreneurship Theory and Practice* 36 (4 2012): 837–861.

63 B. Bird, L. Schojoedt, and J.R. Baum, Entrepreneurs' behavior: Elucidation and measurement. *Entrepreneurship Theory and Practice* 36 (5 2012): 889–913.

64 B. Mycoskie, *Start Something That Matters* (New York: Spiegel & Grau, 2012).

65 J.C. Hayton and M. Cholakova, The role of affect in the creation and intentional pursuit of entrepreneurial ideas. *Entrepreneurship Theory and Practice* 36 (1 2012): 41–60.

66 A.C. Cosper, Case in point. *Entrepreneur* (October 2012): 12.

67 A. Chwolka and M.G. Raith, The value of business planning before start-up—A decision-theoretical perspective. *Journal of Business Venturing* 27 (3 2012): 385–399.

68 J.M. Pollack, M.W. Rutherford, and B.G. Nagy, Preparedness and cognitive legitimacy as antecedents of new venture funding in televised business pitches. *Entrepreneurship Theory and Practice* 36 (5 2012): 915–939.

69 A.C. Cosper, Case in point. *Entrepreneur* (October 2012): 12.

70 R. Lussier and C.E. Halabi, A three-country comparison of the business success versus failure prediction model. *Journal of Small Business Management* 48 (3 2010): 360–377.

71 V. Parida, M. Westerberg, and J. Frishammar, Inbound open innovation activities in high-tech SMEs: The impact on innovation performance. *Journal of Small Business Management* 50 (2 2012): 283–309.

72 TOMS (www.toms.com). Retrieved January 2, 2013.

73 B. Mycoskie, *Start Something That Matters* (New York: Spiegel & Grau, 2012).

74 J.P. Mangalindan, Let the table war begin. *Fortune* (December 24, 2012): 34.

75 J.C. Hayton and M. Cholakova, The role of affect in the creation and intentional pursuit of entrepreneurial ideas. *Entrepreneurship Theory and Practice* 36 (1 2012): 41–60.

76 S.E. Needleman and A. Loten, When freemium falls short. *The Wall Street Journal* (August 23, 2012): B1.

77 H. Reijonen, T. Laukkanewn, R. Komppula, and S. Tuominen, Are growing SMEs more market-oriented and brand-oriented? *Journal of Small Business Management* 50 (4 2012): 699–716.

78 A.L. Maxwell, S.A. Jeffrey, and M. Lévesque, Business angel early stage decision making. *Journal of Business Venturing* 26 (2 2011): 212–225.

79 K. Podoynitsya, H. Van der Bij, and M. Song, The role of mixed emotions in the risk perception of novice and serial entrepreneurs. *Entrepreneurship Theory and Practice* 36 (1 2012): 115–121.

80 G. Fisher, Effectuation, causation, and bricolage: A behavioral comparison of emerging theories in entrepreneurship research. *Entrepreneurship Theory and Practice* 36 (5 2012): 1019–1051.

81 H. Reijonen, T. Laukkanewn, R. Komppula, and S. Tuominen, Are growing SMEs more market-oriented and brand-oriented? *Journal of Small Business Management* 50 (4 2012): 699–716.

82 All Web sites in Exhibit 4-5 were checked for accurate information on January 7, 2013.

83 D.K. Berman, Zipcar: Startup genius, public failure. *The Wall Street Journal* (January 3, 2013): B1.

84 R. Winkler, Avis puts some zip in its weekend. *The Wall Street Journal* (January 3, 2013): C10.

85 C. Tiger, Knock out the knockoffs. *Entrepreneur* (January 2013): 30–31.

86 A. Vance, Hiring a mercenary for the new patent war. *Businessweek* (August 13–26, 2012): 40–41.

87 A. Chatterji, Why Washington has it wrong. *The Wall Street Journal* (November 12, 2012): R1.

88 J. Jannarone, The return of Facebook's Winklevoss Twins. *The Wall Street Journal* (September 17, 2012): B1–B2.

89 V. Collewaert, Angel investors' and entrepreneurs' intentions to exit their ventures: A conflict perspective. *Entrepreneurship Theory and Practice* 36 (4 2012): 753–779.

90 J. Jannarone, The return of Facebook's Winklevoss Twins. *The Wall Street Journal* (September 17, 2012): B1–B2.

91 V. Harnish, How do you find a great accountant? Lawyer? Any kind of business specialist? *Fortune* (January 14, 2013): 27.

92 TOMS (www.toms.com). Retrieved January 10, 2013.

93 Recording Industry Association of America (www.riaa.org). Retrieved January 10, 2013.

94 A. Vance, Hiring a mercenary for the new patent war. *Businessweek* (August 13–26, 2012): 40–41.

95 B.R. Barringer and R.D. Ireland. *Entrepreneurship* (Upper Saddle River, NJ: Prentice Hall, 2012).

96 A. Chatterji, Why Washington has it wrong. *The Wall Street Journal* (November 12, 2012): R1.

97 B.R. Barringer and R.D. Ireland. *Entrepreneurship* (Upper Saddle River, NJ: Prentice Hall, 2012).

98 J. Jargon, Heinz sued over its Dip & Squeeze. *The Wall Street Journal* (August 17, 2012): B6.

99 C. Tiger, Knock out the knockoffs. *Entrepreneur* (January 2013): 30–31.

100 D. Mattioli and M. Spector, Kodak sets deal to sell patents for $525 million. *The Wall Street Journal* (December 20, 2012): B3.

101 O. Kharif, The pirate-infested waters of app retailing. *Businessweek* (November 5–11, 2012): 44.

102 M. Gibbs, A patent troll wants to charge you for emailing your scans! *Forbes* (January 5, 2013): 23.

103 A. Poltorak, On "patent trolls" and injunctive relief. *IP/Frontline.com* (May 12, 2006). Retrieved January 27, 2013.

104 K. Frieswick, The troll toll, *Inc.* (February 2013): 62.

105 S. Miller and J. Jargon, The father of chicken McNuggets. *The Wall Street Journal* (January 9, 2013): B7.

106 A. Payne, Ireland: A new European patent system is born. *Mondaq.com* (January 15, 2013).

107 D. Crouch, Coming soon: A European Unified Patent Court (UPC) and unified patents. *www.patentlyo.com* (December 12, 2012). Retrieved February 6, 2013.

108 www.epo.org/law-practice/unitary/patent-court.html. Retrieved February 6, 2013.

109 D. Crouch, Coming soon: A European Unified Patent Court (UPC) and unified patents. *www.patentlyo.com* (December 12, 2012). Retrieved February 6, 2013.

Chapter 5

1 www.smallbusinessschool.org/video.cfm?clip=1642#. Retrieved October 20, 2012.

2 B. Bird, L. Schojoedt, and J.R. Baum, Entrepreneurs' behavior: Elucidation and measurement. *Entrepreneurship Theory and Practice* 36 (5 2012): 889–913.

3 D. Miller and I.L.B. Miller, Governance, social identity, and entrepreneurial orientation in closely held public companies. *Entrepreneurship Theory and Practice* 35 (5 2011): 1051–1076.

4 G. George and A.J. Bock, The business model in practice and its implications for entrepreneurship research. *Entrepreneurship Theory and Practice* 35 (1 2011): 83–111.

5 Small Business Administration (SBA) (www.sba.gov/business-plan/1). Retrieved January 3, 2013.

6 B. Honig and M. Samuelsson, Planning and the entrepreneur: A longitudinal examination of nascent entrepreneurs in Sweden. *Journal of Small Business Management* 50 (3 2012): 365–388.

7 G. George and A.J. Bock, The business model in practice and its implications for entrepreneurship research. *Entrepreneurship Theory and Practice* 35 (1 2011): 83–111.

8 A. Chwolka and M.G. Raith, The value of business planning before start-up—A decision-theoretical perspective. *Journal of Business Venturing* 27(3 2012): 385–399.

9 Small Business Administration (SBA) (www.sba.gov/business-plan/1). Retrieved January 3, 2013.

10 B. Bird, L. Schojoedt, and J.R. Baum, Entrepreneurs' behavior: Elucidation and measurement. *Entrepreneurship Theory and Practice* 36 (5 2012): 889–913.

11 V. Parida, M. Westerberg, and J. Frishammar, Inbound open innovation activities in high-tech SMEs: The impact on innovation performance. *Journal of Small Business Management* 50 (2 2012): 283–309.

12 B. Honig and M. Samuelsson, Planning and the entrepreneur: A longitudinal examination of nascent entrepreneurs in Sweden. *Journal of Small Business Management* 50 (3 2012): 365–388.

13 M. Simon, J. Kim, S.M. Houghton, and X. Deng, When it's right to be wrong: The effects of overconfidence and planning on product performance in a dynamic environment. *Journal of Small Business Strategy* 22 (1 2012): 21–46.

14 T. Duggan, How to implement a global business plan. *Chron.com*, http://smallbusiness.chron.com/implement-global-business-plan-776.html.

15 Paloalto Software (www.businessplanpro.com). Retrieved January 3, 2013.

16 Small Business Administration (SBA) (www.sba.gov/business-plan/1). Retrieved January 3, 2013.

17 SCORE (www.score.com). Retrieved January 3, 2013.

18 G. George and A.J. Bock, The business model in practice and its implications for entrepreneurship research. *Entrepreneurship Theory and Practice* 35 (1 2011): 83–111.

19 P. Spiegelman, Deliver value to your employees— Your most important stakeholder. *Entrepreneur.com* (July 18, 2011).

20 J.H. Chua, J.J. Chrisman, F. Kellermanns, and Z. Wu, Family involvement and new venture debt financing. *Journal of Business Venturing* 26 (4 2011): 472–488.

21 www.pnc.com/webapp/unsec/ProductsAndService.do?siteArea=/PNC/Home/Small+Business/Financing+Your+Future/The+Five+Cs+of+Credit. Retrieved January 3, 2013.

22 www.pnc.com/webapp/unsec/ProductsAndService.do?siteArea=/PNC/Home/Small+Business/Financing+Your+Future/The+Five+Cs+of+Credit. Retrieved January 3, 2013.

23 www.strategicbusinessgroup.com/files/The%205%20Cs%20of%20Credit.pdf. Retrieved October 14, 2012.

24 B. Bird, L. Schojoedt, and J.R. Baum, Entrepreneurs' behavior: Elucidation and measurement. *Entrepreneurship Theory and Practice* 36 (5 2012): 889–913.

25 T. Duggan, How to implement a global business plan. *Chron.com*, http://smallbusiness.chron.com/implement-global-business-plan-776.html.

26 B. Sugars, What to consider before teaming up with a partner. *Entrepreneurship.com* (July 20, 2011).

27 www.uniformlaws.org/LegislativeFactSheet.aspx?title=Partnership%20Act. Retrieved January 4, 2013.

28 www.uniformlaws.org/shared/docs/partnership/upa_final_97.pdf. Retrieved October 21, 2012.

29   R.M Gemmell, R.J. Boland, and D.A. Kolb, The socio-cognitive dynamics of entrepreneurial ideation. *Entrepreneurship Theory and Practice* 36 (5 2012): 1053–1073.

30   B. Mycoskie, *Start Something That Matters* (New York: Spiegel & Grau, 2012).

31   www.investopedia.com/terms/c/c-corporation. asp#ixzz2F9QqB9zx. Retrieved December 15, 2012.

32   www.investopedia.com/terms/c/c-corporation. asp#ixzz2F9REOzpR. Retrieved December 5, 2012.

33   B. Mycoskie, *Start Something That Matters* (New York: Spiegel & Grau, 2012).

34   G. George and A.J. Bock, The business model in practice and its implications for entrepreneurship research. *Entrepreneurship Theory and Practice* 35 (1 2011): 83–111.

35   D. Miller and I.L.B. Miller, Governance, social identity, and entrepreneurial orientation in closely held public companies. *Entrepreneurship Theory and Practice* 35 (5 2011): 1051–1076.

36   A. Chwolka and M.G. Raith, The value of business planning before start-up—A decision-theoretical perspective. *Journal of Business Venturing* 27 (3 2012): 385–399.

37   H. Reijonen, T. Laukkanewn, R. Komppula, and S. Tuominen, Are growing SMEs more market-oriented and brand-oriented? *Journal of Small Business Management* 50 (4 2012): 699–716.

38   D. Ransom, Artsicle: On a mission to change the art world. *Entrepreneur.com* (June 26, 2012).

39   http://mediadevil.com/us/.

40   W. Wales, E. Monsen, and A. McKelvie, The organizational pervasiveness of entrepreneurial orientation. *Entrepreneurship Theory and Practice* 35 (5 2011): 895–923.

41   http://shop.holstee.com/pages/about. Retrieved October 10. 2012.

42   Dr. W. Edwards Deming 1988/1989 winner of the Dow Jones Award. *ESB* (Spring 1989): 3.

43   B. Larrañeta, S.A. Zahra, and J.L.G. González, Enriching strategic variety in new ventures through external knowledge. *Journal of Business Venturing* 27(4 2012): 401–413.

44   B. Bird, L. Schojoedt, and J.R. Baum, Entrepreneurs' behavior: Elucidation and measurement. *Entrepreneurship Theory and Practice* 36 (5 2012): 889–913.

45   V. Harnish, Five ways to get your strategy right. *Fortune* (April 11, 2011): 42.

46   W. Wales, E. Monsen, and A. McKelvie, The organizational pervasiveness of entrepreneurial orientation. *Entrepreneurship Theory and Practice* 35 (5 2011): 895–923.

47   G. Fisher, Effectuation, causation, and bricolage: A behavioral comparison of emerging theories in entrepreneurship research. *Entrepreneurship Theory and Practice* 36 (5 2012): 1019–1051.

48   P.C. Patel and B. Conklin, Perceived labor productivity in small firms—The effects of high-performance work systems and group culture through employee retention. *Entrepreneurship Theory and Practice* 36 (2 2012): 205–224. S. Ponder, Power to the pita. *The Costco Connection* (December 2012): 26.

49   J.H. Chua, J.J. Chrisman, F. Kellermanns, and Z. Wu, Family involvement and new venture debt financing. *Journal of Business Venturing* 26 (4 2011): 472–488.

50   P.C. Patel and B. Conklin, Perceived labor productivity in small firms—The effects of high-performance work systems and group culture through employee retention. *Entrepreneurship Theory and Practice* 36 (2 2012): 205–224.

51   B. Larrañeta, S.A. Zahra, and J.L.G. González, Enriching strategic variety in new ventures through external knowledge. *Journal of Business Venturing* 27(4 2012): 401–413.

52   H. Reijonen, T. Laukkanewn, R. Komppula, and S. Tuominen, Are growing SMEs more market-oriented and brand-oriented? *Journal of Small Business Management* 50 (4 2012): 699–716.

53   R.M.J. Wells, The product innovation process: Are managing information flows and cross-functional collaboration key? *Academy of Management Perspectives* 22 (1 2008): 58–60.

54   J. Skinner, A view from the top. *Fortune* (March 16, 2009): 110.

55   W. Tsai, K.H. Su, and M.J. Chen, Seeing through the eyes of a rival: Competitor acumen based on rival-centric perceptions. *Academy of Management Journal* 54 (4 2011): 761–778.

56   G.T. Payne, K.H. Kennedy, and J.L. Davis, Competitive dynamics among service SMEs. *Journal of Small Business Management* 47 (4 2009): 421–442.

57   M. Bustillo and T.W. Martin, Wal-Mart bets on reduction in prices. *The Wall Street Journal* (April 9, 2010): B1.

58   T. Yu, M. Subramaniam, and A.A. Cannella, Rivalry deterrence in international markets: Contingencies governing the mutual forbearance hypothesis. *Academy of Management Journal* 52 (1 2009): 127–147.

59   K.D. Dea Roglio and G. Light, Executive MBA programs: The development of the reflective executive. *Academy of Management Learning & Education* 8 (2 2009): 156–173.

60   J.W. Webb, L. Tihanyi, R.D. Ireland, and D.G. Sirmon, You say illegal, I say legitimate: Entrepreneurship in the informal economy. *Academy of Management Review* 34 (3 2009): 492–510.

61 P.M. Vaaler, How do MNCs vote in developing country elections? *Academy of Management Journal* 51 (1 2008): 21–43.

62 B. Larrañeta, S.A. Zahra, and J.L.G. González, Enriching strategic variety in new ventures through external knowledge. *Journal of Business Venturing* 27(4 2012): 401–413.

63 R.M Gemmell, R.J. Boland, and D.A. Kolb, The socio-cognitive dynamics of entrepreneurial ideation. *Entrepreneurship Theory and Practice* 36 (5 2012): 1053–1073.

64 M. Sonfield and R. Lussier, The entrepreneurial strategy matrix: A model for new and ongoing ventures. *Business Horizons*, 40 (3 1997): 73–77.

65 A. Chwolka and M.G. Raith, The value of business planning before start-up—A decision-theoretical perspective. *Journal of Business Venturing* 27(3 2012): 385–399.

66 www.dreamstudios.org. Retrieved January 12, 2013.

67 www.nba.com/celtics/community/heroes-december-06.html. Retrieved January 12, 2013.

68 J. Kenney, Western Massachusetts unemployment rate improves, but graduates expected to still face tough labor market. *The Republican* (April 24, 2012).

69 P. Goonan, Competing Springfield casino companies face deadline for final proposals. *The Republican* (January 1, 2013).

70 K. Zetter, Google to stop censoring search results in China after hack attack. *Wired* (January 12, 2010).

71 T. Duggan, How to implement a global business plan. *Chron.com*, http://smallbusiness.chron.com/implement-global-business-plan-776.html.

Chapter 6

1 A.I.P. Pena, D.M.F. Jamilena and M.A.R. Molina, Impact of market orientation and ICT on the performance of rural smaller service enterprises. *Journal of Small Business Management* 49 (3 2012): 331–360.

2 H. Reijonen, T. Laukkanewn, R. Komppula, and S. Tuominen, Are growing SMEs more market-oriented and brand-oriented? *Journal of Small Business Management* 50 (4 2012): 699–716.

3 S. Mueller, T. Volery, and B. von Siemens, What do entrepreneurs actually do? An observational study of entrepreneurs' everyday behavior in the startup and growth stages. *Entrepreneurship Theory and Practice* 35 (5 2011): 995–1017.

4 B. Evans, The entrepreneur's wheel. *Costco Connection* (February 2013): 11.

5 B.K. Brockman, M.A. Jones, and R.C. Becherer, Customer orientation and performance in small firms: Examining the moderating influence of risk-taking, innovativeness, and opportunity focus. *Journal of Small Business Management* 50 (3 2012): 429–446.

6 Z. Tang and C. Hull, An investigation of entrepreneurial orientation, perceived environmental hostility, and strategy application among Chinese SMEs. *Journal of Small Business Management* 50 (1 2012): 132–158.

7 M. Presutti, C. Boari, and A. Majocchi, The importance of proximity for the start-ups' knowledge acquisition and exploitation. *Journal of Small Business Management* 49 (3 2011): 361–389.

8 A. Handley, Keep it simple (but not stupid). *Entrepreneur* (January 2013): 60.

9 M. Baum, C. Schwens, and R. Kabst, A typology of international new ventures: Empirical evidence from high-technology industries. *Journal of Small Business Management* 49 (3 2011): 305–330.

10 G. Fisher, Effectuation, causation, and bricolage: A behavioral comparison of emerging theories in entrepreneurship research. *Entrepreneurship Theory and Practice* 36 (5 2012): 1019–1051.

11 M. Presutti, C. Boari, and A. Majocchi, The importance of proximity for the start-ups' knowledge acquisition and exploitation. *Journal of Small Business Management* 49 (3 2011): 361–389.

12 C. Subramanian, Survey: Fast food makes up 54% of restaurant sales in France. *Time* News Feed (May 5, 2013).

13 B. Evans, The entrepreneur's wheel. *Costco Connection* (February 2013): 11.

14 S. Kessler, Everyone has a tablet. Samsung launched a pen. *Fast Company.com* (August 15, 2012).

15 N. Wingate, R.I.P. Zune. *New York Time.com* (June 4, 2012).

16 B. Evans, The entrepreneur's wheel. *Costco Connection* (February 2013): 11.

17 H. Reijonen, T. Laukkanewn, R. Komppula, and S. Tuominen, Are growing SMEs more market-oriented and brand-oriented? *Journal of Small Business Management* 50 (4 2012): 699–716.

18 www.rankingthebrands.com/Brand-detail.aspx?brandID=34. Retrieved May 17, 2013.

19 M. Poh, 5 tips to better brand names. www.hongkiat.com/blog/better-brand-name-tips/. Retrieved December 30, 2012.

20 Steven M, So, who is the siren? www.starbucks.com/blog/so-who-is-the-siren. Retrieved January 5, 2011.

21 www.gs1us.org/resources/standards/ean-upc. Retrieved February 11, 2013.

22 Link to obtain a UPC barcode. www.gs1us.org/get-started/i-need-a-barcode.

23 J. Jargon, McDonald's replaces U.S. chief. *The Wall Street Journal* (November 15, 2012): B2.

24 M.B. Elmes, S. Jiusto, G. Whiteman, R. Hersh, and G.T. Guthery, Teaching entrepreneurship and innovation from the perspective of place and place making. *Academy of Management Learning & Education* 11 (4 2012): 533–554.

25 G. Fisher, Effectuation, causation, and bricolage: A behavioral comparison of emerging theories in entrepreneurship research. *Entrepreneurship Theory and Practice* 36 (5 2012): 1019–1051.

26 C. Hann, Get it out there. *Entrepreneur* (August 2012): 20.

27 B. Evans, The entrepreneur's wheel. *Costco Connection* (February 2013): 11.

28 D. Cole, The ideal elevator pitch. *Boston.com* (April 13, 2012).

29 A. Tumasjan and R. Braun, In the eye of the beholder: How regulatory focus and self-efficacy interact in influencing opportunity recognition. *Journal of Business Venturing* 27 (6 2012): 622–636.

30 S. Chowdhury, The moderating effects of customer driven complexity on the structure and growth relationship in young firms. *Journal of Business Venturing* 26 (3 2011): 306–320.

31 B.K. Brockman, M.A. Jones, and R.C. Becherer, Customer orientation and performance in small firms: Examining the moderating influence of risk-taking, innovativeness, and opportunity focus. *Journal of Small Business Management* 50 (3 2012): 429–446.

32 R. Abrams, How to make more money. *Costco Connection* (November 2012): 15.

33 D. Lavinsky, Master class. *Businessweek* (November 26–December 3, 2012): 103.

34 R. Abrams, How to make more money. *Costco Connection* (November 2012): 15.

35 www.destinationcrm.com/Articles/CRM-News/Daily-News/What-Is-CRM-46033.aspx. Retrieved January 15, 2013.

36 D. Prince, 5 reasons solo entrepreneurs need a CRM solution. www.futuresimple.com/blog/solo-entrepreneurs-crm-solution/ (March 14, 2012).

37 C. Davis, Big Y offers deal through Groupon. *wbjournal.com* (March 25, 2012).

38 B. Mycoskie, *Start Something That Matters* (New York: Spiegel & Grau, 2012): quote p. 193.

39 B. Schoenfeld, The expats. *Entrepreneur* (October 2012): 22–24.

40 J. Helmer, Pirouetting towards profits. *Entrepreneur* (October 2012): 98.

41 D. Birnbaum, Etc. hard choices, *BusinessWeek* (February 4–10, 2013): 80.

42 Staff, SizeUp your business. *Costco Connection* (November 2012): 15.

43 C. Rose, Charlie Rose talks to Sequoia's Nino Moritz, *BusinessWeek* (February 11–17, 2013): 34.

44 R. Abrams, How to make more money. *Costco Connection* (November 2012): 15.

45 R. Perrigot, M. Kacker, G. Basset, and G. Cliquet, Antecedents of early adoption and use of social media networks for stakeholder communications: Evidence from franchising. *Journal of Small Business Management* 50 (4 2012): 539–565.

46 www.gmarketing.com/articles/4-what-is-guerrilla-marketing. Retrieved January 15, 2013.

47 J. Conrad Levinson, *Guerrilla Marketing* (Boston: Houghton Mifflin, 1984).

48 H. Cohen, 30 social media definitions. http://heidicohen.com/social-media-definition/ (May 9, 2011).

49 A. Newman, Brands now direct their followers to social media. *New York Times* (August 4, 2011): B3.

50 N. Richardson, Blog to brand and grow your business. *Costco Connection* (November 2012): 15.

51 www.marketingterms.com/dictionary/viral_marketing/. Retrieved December 30, 2012.

52 www.brandchannel.com/home/post/2011/03/28/How-Coca-Colas-Happiness-Machine-Became-a-Viral-Smash-Success.aspx. Retrieved February 22, 2013.

53 http://mashable.com/category/e-commerce/. Retrieved January 15, 2013.

54 www.carrefour.com/content/multichannel-retail. Retrieved May 17, 2013.

55 Associated Press, Founder of e-commerce giant Alibaba, Jack Ma, stepping down as CEO, will stay on as chairman. *Washington Post* (January 15, 2013).

56 Central Intelligence Agency (CIA) (www.cia.gov). Retrieved February 22, 2013.

57 www.networksolutions.com/education/what-is-ecommerce/. Retrieved January 15, 2013.

58 http://websitehelpers.com/design/. Retrieved December 30, 2012.

59 http://mashable.com/2011/08/01/tips-better-website/. Retrieved December 30, 2012.

60 Z. Tang and C. Hull, An investigation of entrepreneurial orientation, perceived environmental hostility, and strategy application among Chinese SMEs. *Journal of Small Business Management* 50 (1 2012): 132–158.

61 D. Birnbaum, Etc. hard choices, *BusinessWeek* (February 4–10, 2013): 80.

62 Small Business Administration (SBA) (www.sba.gov/sizeup). Retrieved February 22, 2013.

63 Staff, SizeUp your business. *Costco Connection* (November 2012): 15.

64 K. Strauss, The new billionaire behind Twitter and Square: Jack Dorsey, *Forbes* (July 25, 2012).

65 S. Bennett, What do CEOs think of social media. www.mediabistro.com/alltwitter/social-media-ceos_b31999 (November 20, 2012).

66 R. Branson, Richard Branson on how to connect with your customers. www.entrepreneur.com/article/224362 (September 10, 2012).

67 B.P. Eha, Time to try the anti Facebook. www.entrepreneur.com/blog/225132 (December 1, 2012).

68 Women entrepreneurs making strides in Turkey. *SME Worldwide,* www.smeworld.org/story/top-stories/women-entrepreneurs-making-stride-turkey.php (August 2009).

69 G. Gul, B-fit Empowers Women Attracting Female Entrepreneurs. *Today's Zaman.com* (February 19, 2012).

70 J. Snow, Turkey's startup scene is still small, but women could be its secret weapon. *Quartz,* http://qz.com/10606/lady-turks-and-the-startup-scene/ (October 17, 2012).

Chapter 7

1 W. Li, R. Veltiyath, and J. Tan, Network characteristics and firm performance: An examination of the relationships in the context of a cluster. *Journal of Small Business Management* 51 (1 2013): 1–22.

2 www.globallocationstrategies.com/Slick/ClientFiles/PDF/KuwaitiPetroleumSuccessStory.pdf. Retrieved May 25, 2013.

3 J. Reilly, What a magical house! JK Rowling's eight-bedroom mansion where she wrote Harry Potter books goes up for sale for £2.25m. *Daily Mail* (November 26, 2012).

4 Failed IPO of the dot-com bubble. *Investopedia.com* (May 18, 2012).

5 D. Howell, How to setup a business on eBay. *TechRadar.com* (August 10, 2012).

6 eBay. www.ebay.com. Retrieved March 13, 2013.

7 eBay. http://pages.ebay.com/help/feedback/scores-reputation.html. Retrieved May 1, 2013.

8 http://services.amazon.com/content/case_studies.htm?ld=NSGoogleAS. Retrieved May 1, 2013.

9 Amazon. http://services.amazon.com/fulfillment-by-amazon/benefits.htm?ld=NSGoogleAS. Retrieved April 14, 2013.

10 S. Simpson, Webvan and other epic IPO failures. *Forbes.com* (December 13, 2010).

11 J. Hage, Wal-Mart welcomed to Princeton. *Princeton Union-Eagle* (February 6, 2013).

12 www.census.gov/cgi-bin/naics/index.cgi. Retrieved May 1, 2013.

13 E. Ailworth, New data center focuses on using less energy. *Boston Globe.com* (July 9, 2012).

14 M.J. Emmons, McDonald's historic preservation circa 1795 Georgian style burger joint. *historichouseblog.com* (May 5, 2012).

15 www.census.gov/econ/retail.html. Retrieved May 1, 2013.

16 D. Stevens. The future of the retail store. *Retail Customer Experience.com* (February 18, 2013).

17 Retail Customer Experience.com, Converse opens largest mall location in Jersey (May 7, 2012).

18 www.census.gov/cgi-bin/naics/index.cgi. Retrieved May 1, 2013.

19 www.thefrantzgroup.com/index.cfm/fuseaction/wholesale. Retrieved March 2, 2013.

20 www.bls.gov/iag/tgs/iag60.htm. Retrieved May 1, 2013.

21 www.sba.gov/content/buying-or-leasing-equipment. Retrieved April 16, 2013.

22 J. Fletcher, 6 Tips for creating an optimal retail store layout. *Intuit.com*. Retrieved January 2, 2013

23 R.M. Kanter, Values investing. *The Wall Street Journal* (January 25, 2010): p. R2

24 E. Byron and J.S. Lublin, Appointment of new P&G chief sends ripples through ranks. *The Wall Street Journal* (June 11, 2009): p. B3.

25 Urban geographers study consumer behavior when shopping and help stores make sales: The science of shopping. American Institute of Science (December 1, 2009).

26 E. Spangenberg. Study shows the right sounds and smells will make shoppers spend. *Retail Customer Experience.com* (December 19, 2012).

27 Walgreens celebrates 8,000 stores with opening of LA flagship. *Retail Customer Experience.com* (December 3, 2012).

28 T. Ryan, What does Apple get by trademarking its store design? *Retail Wire* (February 5, 2013).

29 www.costco.com/membership-information.html. Retrieved April 16, 2013.

30 D. Mall, Store size is more than the area; It's store psychology that matters. *Forbes India* (January 1, 2013).

31 www.sba.gov/content/buying-existing-business. Retrieved May 25, 2013.

32 www.sba.gov/content/franchise-businesses. Retrieved May 25, 2013.

33 R. Williams, The inventor's dilemma: Manufacturing vs. licensing. www.startupnation.com/business-articles/9459/1/manufacturing-licensing-dilemma.htm. Retrieved May 25, 2013.

34 www.mac-history.net/steve-jobs-discovers-the-macintosh-project. Retrieved May 15, 2013.

35 C. Chapman, Non profit website design: Examples and best practices. *Smashing Magazine* (May 14, 2009).

36 C. Tice. 7 layout secrets of the big retail chains. *Entrepreneur.com* (June 18, 2012).

37 S. Howard, 7 reasons opening a restaurant should scare you. *Chef's Blade,* Retrieved from Monster.com on March 22, 2013.

38 M. Nsehe, 30-under-30 Africa's best entrepreneurs. *Forbes* (February 23, 2013).

39 J. Karlende, 20-year-old paper bag entrepreneur, *Daily Monitor* (October 15, 2012).

Chapter 8

1 P.C. Patel and B. Conklin, Perceived labor productivity in small firms—The effects of high-performance work systems and group culture through employee retention. *Entrepreneurship Theory and Practice* 36 (2 2012): 205–224.

2 www.investopedia.com/terms/o/outsourcing.asp. Retrieved May 29, 2013.

3 G. Pisano and W, Shih, Restoring American competitiveness. *Harvard Business Review* (July–August 2009).

4 http://blogs.wsj.com/digits/2013/12/12/fla-says-foxconn-still-exceeds-working-hours/ (December 12, 2013). Retrieved January 2, 2014.

5 E. Lococo, Huawei says Apple's China experience teaches supply chain. *Bloomberg News* (May 29, 2013).

6 http://davitsioridze.blogspot.com/2011/02/nike-and-outsourcing.html.

7 http://www.investopedia.com/terms/w/warranty.asp.

8 IDC Manufacturing Insights, Few manufacturers consistently benchmark warranty operations. *Supply Chain Brain.com* (May 9, 2011).

9 J.H. Adams, F.M. Khoja, and R. Kauffman, An empirical study of buyer-supplier relationships within small business organizations. *Journal of Small Business Management* 50 (1 2012): 20–40.

10 www-01.ibm.com/software/commerce/supply-chain-management/.

11 A. Bodegraven and K. Ackerman, The new basics of supply chain management. *Supply Chain Management* (May 1, 2013).

12 www.umsl.edu/divisions/business/ms/.

13 C. Shu, Alibaba Group starts work on massive logistics network to provide 24-hour deliveries throughout China. *TechCrunch.com* (May 28, 2013).

14 M. Sowinski, Get down for the count. *Entrepreneur* (May 2013): 73.

15 www.deming.org/theman/overview. Retrieved May 31, 2013.

16 D. Hershberger and A. Hooper Pavlik, Eliminating waste in business processes. *The Greater Lansing Business Monthly* (September 12, 2012).

17 www.bain.com/publications/articles/management-tools-benchmarking.aspx.

18 www.iso.org/iso/home/about.htm. Retrieved May 30, 2013.

19 www.isixsigma.com/new-to-six-sigma/getting-started/what-six-sigma/. Retrieved May 30, 2013.

20 www.ge.com/en/company/companyinfo/quality/whatis.htm. Retrieved May 30, 2013.

21 www.amtonline.org/aboutamt/WhatisManufacturing Technology/. Retrieved May 30, 2013.

22 Adapted from World Bank. *Business Week* (April 22–28, 2013): 33.

23 J. Wang, How a small distillery is rethinking manufacturing. *Entrepreneur.com* (March 28, 2013).

24 L. Olmsted, A craft distillery worthy of the word "craft." *Forbes.com* (May 10, 2013).

25 J. Wang, How a small distillery is rethinking manufacturing. *Entrepreneur.com* (March 28, 2013).

26 M. Guarino, Japanese tsunami brought home hard lessons for automakers. *The Christian Science Monitor* (March 11, 2012).

27 M. Drukier, The practical entrepreneur: Purchasing and negotiations: Part VIII, *The Epoch Times* (June 30, 2010).

28 D. Fisher, Japanese disaster shakes up supply chain strategies. *Harvard Business School* (May 31, 2011).

Chapter 9

1 B. Roberts, Leadership Q&A. *Fortune* (December 24, 2012): 54–58.

2 D. Sardana and D.S. Kemmis, Who learns what?—A study based on entrepreneurs from biotechnology new ventures. *Journal of Small Business Management* 48 (3 2010): 441–468.

3 Y. Zheng, Unlocking founding team prior shared experience: A transactive memory system perspective. *Journal of Business Venturing* 27(5 2012): 577–591.

4 J. Brinckmann, S. Salomo, and H.G. Gemuenden, Financial management competence of founding teams and growth of new technology based firms. *Entrepreneurship Theory and Practice* 35 (2 2011): 217–243.

5 D.L. Brannon, J. Wiklund, and J.M. Haynie, The varying effects of family relationships in entrepreneurial teams. *Entrepreneurship Theory and Practice* 37 (1 2013): 107–132.

6 L. Schjoedt, E. Monsen, A. Person, T. Barnett, and J.J. Chrisman, New venture and family business teams: Understanding team formation, composition, behaviors, and performance. *Entrepreneurship Theory and Practice* 37 (1 2013): 1–15.

7 J.D. Werbel and S.M. Danes, Work family conflict in new business ventures: The moderating effects of spousal commitment to the new business venture. *Journal of Small Business Management* 48 (3 2010): 421–440.

8   www.google.com. Retrieved June 23, 2013.

9   www.investopedia.com/terms/b/boardofdirectors. asp. Retrieved June 13, 2013.

10 www.wisegeek.com/what-is-a-board-of-advisors. htm. Retrieved June 13, 2013.

11 V. Cheng, 3 ways to find your perfect board of advisors. *Entrepreneur.com* (May 3, 2013).

12 A.D. Cruz, C. Howorth, and E. Hamilton, Intrafamily entrepreneurship: Members of family entrepreneurial teams. *Entrepreneurship Theory and Practice* 37 (1 2013): 17–46.

13 www.score.org/.

14 www.sba.gov/content/small-business-development-centers-sbdcs.

15 www.sba.gov/local-assistance/wbc.

16 C. Ennico. How to hire an attorney. *Entrepreneur. com* (January 20, 2006).

17 www.entrepreneur.com/article/217784. Retrieved June 13, 2013.

18 M. Stettner, How can Entrepreneurs Impress Their Bank, *Chief Executive.com*, May 3, 2011.

19 www.entrepreneur.com/encyclopedia/insurance retrieved on June 13, 2013.

20 S. Allen, "Developing a Reputation," About.com.

21 D.S. Malewicki and C.A. Leitch, Female & male entrepreneurs' perceived value of formal networks: Are there differences? *Journal of Small Business Strategy* 22 (1 2012), 1–20.

22 Jens M. Unger, Andreas Rauch, Michael Frese and Nina Rosenbusch, Human capital and entrepreneurial success: A meta-analytical review. *Journal of Business Venturing* 26 (3 2011): 341–358.

23 B. G. Nagy, J.M. Pollack, M.W. Rutherford and F.T. Lohrke, The influence of entrepreneurs' credentials and impression management behaviors on perceptions of new venture legitimacy. *Entrepreneurship Theory and Practice* 35 (5 2011): 941–965.

24 A. Leung, M, Der Foo, and S. Chaturvedi, Imprinting effects of founding core teams or HR values in new ventures. *Entrepreneurship Theory and Practice* 37 (1 2013): 87–106.

25 L. Schjoedt, E. Monsen, A. Person, T. Barnett, and J.J. Chrisman, New venture and family business teams: Understanding team formation, composition, behaviors, and performance. *Entrepreneurship Theory and Practice* 37 (1 2013): 1–15.

26 www.sba.gov/content/writing-effective-job-descriptions.

27 J.D. Werbel and S.M. Danes, Work family conflict in new business ventures: The moderating effects of spousal commitment to the new business venture. *Journal of Small Business Management* 48 (3 2010): 421–440. www.google.com. Retrieved June 23, 2013.

28 M. Murphy, Massachusetts minimum wage would increase under a new bill on Beacon Hill. *Masslive. com* (February 20, 2013).

29 http://obamacarefacts.com/obamacare-facts.php. Retrieved July 15, 2013.

30 www.barackobama.com/health-care/access-and-affordability.

31 www.healthcare.gov/will-i-qualify-for-small-business-health-care-tax-credits/. Retrieved July 15, 2013.

32 N. Collamer, The perfect elevator pitch to land a job. *Forbes.com* (February 4, 2013).

33 www.sba.gov/content/independent-contractors-vs-employees. Retrieved June 25, 2013.

34 B. Roberts, Leadership Q&A. *Fortune* (December 24, 2012): 54–58.

35 N. Massenet, Follow your instincts. *Business Week* (April 11, 2013), online.

36 M.C. Bolino and W.H. Turnley, Going the extra mile: Cultivating and managing employee citizenship behavior. *Academy of Management Executive* 17 (3 2003): 60–71.

37 T. Gutner, Applicants' personalities put to the test. *The Wall Street Journal* (April 24, 2009): D4.

38 K. Pajo, A. Coetzer, and N. Guenole, Formal development opportunities and withdrawal behaviors by employees in small and medium-sized enterprises. *Journal of Small Business Management* 48 (3 2010): 281–301.

39 L. Lee, P. Kam, W.M. Der Foo, and A. Leung, Entrepreneurial intentions: The influence of organizational and individual factors. *Journal of Business Venturing* 26 (1 2011): 124–136.

40 www.investopedia.com/terms/e/exitstrategy.asp. Retrieved June 9, 2013.

41 T. Kontinen and A. Ojala, International opportunity recognition among small and medium-sized family firms. *Journal of Small Business Management* 49 (3 2011): 490–514.

42 http://buzzmg.com/.

43 A. Choi, When a family business should outsource human resources. *Entrepreneur.com* (May 7, 2013).

44 R. Branson, Richard Branson on taking the leap into entrepreneurship. *Entrepreneurship.com* (June 24, 2013).

45 R. Branson, Richard Branson: People power—The engine of any business. *Entrepreneur.com* (September 29, 2010).

Chapter 10

1   http://smallbusinessschool.org/video.cfm?clip = 1136.

2   www.irs.gov/Businesses/Small-Businesses-&-Self-Employed/S-Corporations.

3   K.B. Lamp, M. Lévesque, and C. Schade, Are entrepreneurs influenced by risk attitude, regulatory focus or both? An experiment on entrepreneurs'

time allocation. *Journal of Business Venturing* 27 (4 2012): 456–476.

4 A. Seghers, S. Manigart, and T. Vanacker, The impact of human and social capital on entrepreneurs' knowledge of financial alternatives. *Journal of Small Business Management* 50 (1 2012): 63–86.

5 J. Brinckmann, S. Salomo, and H.G. Gemuenden, Financial management competence of founding teams and growth of new technology based firms. *Entrepreneurship Theory and Practice* 35 (2 2011): 217–243.

6 S. Cater, The rewards of entrepreneurship: Exploring the incomes, wealth, and economic well-being of entrepreneurial households. *Entrepreneurship Theory and Practice* 35 (1 2011): 39–55.

7 J.M. Pollack, M.W. Rutherford, and B.G. Nagy, Preparedness and cognitive legitimacy as antecedents of new venture funding in televised business pitches. *Entrepreneurship Theory and Practice* 36 (5 2012): 915–939.

8 T. Semrau and A. Werner, The two sides of the story: Network investments and new venture creation. *Journal of Small Business Management* 50 (1 2012): 159–180.

9 S.M. Farmer, The behavioral impact of entrepreneur identity aspiration and prior entrepreneurial experience. *Entrepreneurship Theory and Practice* 35 (2 2011): 245–273.

10 V. Parida, M. Westerberg, and J. Frishammar, Inbound open innovation activities in high-tech SMEs: The impact on innovation performance. *Journal of Small Business Management* 50 (2 2012): 283–309.

11 Staff, How to handle past-due creditors. *Costco Connection* (September 2012): 9.

12 C. Mitteness, R. Sudek, and M.S. Cardon, Angel investor characteristics that determine whether perceived passion leads to higher evaluations of funding potential. *Journal of Business Venturing* 27 (5 2012): 592–606.

13 Z. Serrasqueiro and P.M. Nunes, Is age a determinant of SMEs' financing decisions? Empirical evidence using panel data models. *Entrepreneurship Theory and Practice* 36 (4 2012): 627–654.

14 J. Worth, Spend it wisely. *Entrepreneur* (October 2012): 90.

15 www.fasab.gov/pdffiles/jan06elementsrev.pdf.

16 J. Worth, Spend it wisely. *Entrepreneur* (October 2012): 90.

17 J.D. Werbel and S.M. Danes, Work family conflict in new business ventures: The moderating effects of spousal commitment to the new business venture. *Journal of Small Business Management* 48 (3 2010): 421–440.

18 www.irs.gov/Businesses/Small-Businesses-&-Self-Employed/Deducting-Business-Expenses.

19 http://ssa-custhelp.ssa.gov/app/answers/detail/a_id/430/related/1

20 www.irs.gov/publications/p583/ar02.html#en_US_2011_publink1000253194.

21 www.irs.gov/publications/p583/ar02.html#en_US_2011_publink1000253194.

22 www.irs.gov/taxtopics/tc453.html.

23 www.irs.gov/publications/p17/ch26.html.

24 C. De Aenlle, Entrepreneurs, climbing Mt. Paperwork. *New York Times.com* (February 11, 2012).

25 R. Creel, Easy steps to simplifying small business accounting.www.smead.com/hot-topics/small-business-accounting-1386.asp.

26 S. S. Amari. Paying taxes report 2013: Middle East remains least demanding tax framework. www.ameinfo.com/paying-taxes-report-2013-middle-east-320165 (June 6, 2013).

27 P. Gorondi, Oil up near $102 as concerns grow over Egypt. *The State Journal* (July 3, 2013).

28 B. Whitaker, Why taxes are low in the Middle East. *Guardian.co.uk* (August 4, 2010).

29 www.irs.gov/uac/Tax-Quotes.

Chapter 11

1 T. Semrau and A. Werner, The two sides of the story: Network investments and new venture creation. *Journal of Small Business Management* 50 (1 2012): 159–180.

2 S. Garg, Venture boards: Distinctive monitoring and implications for firm performance. *Academy of Management Review* 38 (1 2013), 90–108.

3 J. Brinckmann, S. Salomo, and H.G. Gemuenden, Financial management competence of founding teams and growth of new technology based firms. *Entrepreneurship Theory and Practice* 35 (2 2011): 217–243.

4 J.D. Werbel and S.M. Danes, Work family conflict in new business ventures: The moderating effects of spousal commitment to the new business venture. *Journal of Small Business Management* 48 (3 2010): 421–440.

5 A. Seghers, S. Manigart, and T. Vanacker, The impact of human and social capital on entrepreneurs' knowledge of financial alternatives. *Journal of Small Business Management* 50 (1 2012): 63–86.

6 Z. Serrasqueiro and P.M. Nunes, Is age a determinant of SMEs' financing decisions? Empirical evidence using panel data models. *Entrepreneurship Theory and Practice* 36 (4 2012): 627–654.

7 V. Parida, M. Westerberg, and J. Frishammar, Inbound open innovation activities in high-tech

SMEs: The impact on innovation performance. *Journal of Small Business Management* 50 (2 2012): 283–309.

8   A. Seghers, S. Manigart, and T. Vanacker, The impact of human and social capital on entrepreneurs' knowledge of financial alternatives. *Journal of Small Business Management* 50 (1 2012): 63–86.

9   J.M. Pollack, M.W. Rutherford, and B.G. Nagy, Preparedness and cognitive legitimacy as antecedents of new venture funding in televised business pitches. *Entrepreneurship Theory and Practice* 36 (5 2012): 915–939.

10 J.M. Pollack, M.W. Rutherford, and B.G. Nagy, Preparedness and cognitive legitimacy as antecedents of new venture funding in televised business pitches. *Entrepreneurship Theory and Practice* 36 (5 2012): 915–939.

11 Z. Serrasqueiro and P.M. Nunes, Is age a determinant of SMEs' financing decisions? Empirical evidence using panel data models. *Entrepreneurship Theory and Practice* 36 (4 2012): 627–654.

12 R.N. Lussier and C.E. Halabi.A three-country comparison of the business success versus failure prediction model. *Journal of Small Business Management*, 48(3 2010), 360–377.

13 V. Parida, M. Westerberg, and J. Frishammar, Inbound open innovation activities in high-tech SMEs: The impact on innovation performance. *Journal of Small Business Management* 50 (2 2012): 283–309.

14 V. Collewaert, Angel investors' and entrepreneurs' intentions to exit their ventures: A conflict perspective. *Entrepreneurship Theory and Practice* 36 (4 2012): 753–779.

15 M. Meuleman and M. Wright, Cross-border private equity syndication: Institutional context and learning. *Journal of Business Venturing* 26 (1 2011): 35–48.

16 J.M. Pollack, M.W. Rutherford, and B.G. Nagy, Preparedness and cognitive legitimacy as antecedents of new venture funding in televised business pitches. *Entrepreneurship Theory and Practice* 36 (5 2012): 915–939.

17 www.investopedia.com/terms/s/seedcapital.asp. Retrieved July 10, 2013.

18 Kauffman Foundation, By the numbers: Taking the measure of entrepreneurs. *The Wall Street Journal* (November 12, 2012): R6.

19 A.C. Cosper, Case in point. *Entrepreneur* (October 2012): 12.

20 A. Advani, Tapping your personal savings to fund your startup. *Entrepreneur.com* (June 5, 2006).

21 Y. Tan, H. Huang, and H. Lu, The effect of venture capital investment—Evidence from China's small

and medium-sized enterprises board. *Journal of Small Business Management* 51 (1 2013): 138–157.

22 A.L. Maxwell, S.A. Jeffrey, and M. Lévesque, Business angel early stage decision making. *Journal of Business Venturing* 26 (2 2011): 212–225.

23 How to get funding from angel investors (http://guides.wsj.com/small-business/funding/how-to-get-funding-from-angel-investors/).

24 M. Zwelling, Ten ways to attract angel funding. *Forbes* (October 27, 2009).

25 C. Mitteness, R. Sudek, and M.S. Cardon, Angel investor characteristics that determine whether perceived passion leads to higher evaluations of funding potential. *Journal of Business Venturing* 27(5 2012): 592–606.

26 R. Fairchild. An entrepreneur's choice of venture capitalist or angel-financing: A behavioral game-theoretic approach. *Journal of Business Venturing* 26 (3 2011): 359–374.

27 www.investopedia.com/terms/v/venturecapital.asp.

28 Y. Li and J.T. Mahoney, When are venture capital projects initiated? *Journal of Business Venturing* 26 (2 2011): 239–254.

29 M. Baucus, S. Human, T. Clark, and D. Rosenthal, P&G is selling Oxydol! *Entrepreneurship Theory and Practice* 35 (2 2011): 395–412.

30 J.S. Petty and M. Gruber, In pursuit of the real deal: A longitudinal study of VC decision making. *Journal of Business Venturing* 26 (2 2011): 172–188.

31 www.sba.gov/content/venture-capital. Retrieved July 10, 2013.

32 W. E. Jackson, T. Bates, and W.D. Bradford, Does venture capitalist activism improve investment performance? *Journal of Business Venturing* 27 (3 2012): 342–354.

33 A. Sherman, Corporate VC managers counter Fred Wilson's "patronizing"attack. *Bloomberg.com* (June 18, 2013).

34 www.investopedia.com/terms/p/privateplacement.asp.

35 J. Espinoza, Join the crowd. Sell some stock. *The Wall Street Journal* (November 12, 2012): R2.

36 J. Eaglesham, Crowdfunding efforts draw suspicion. *The Wall Street Journal* (January 8, 2013): C1, C2.

37 N. Leiber and J. Tozzi, A new grade of startup fuel. *BusinessWeek* (December 3–9, 2012): 55.

38 S.S. (no name), Should you buy in? *Costco Connection* (November 2012): 27.

39 www.kickstarter.com/help/guidelines.

40 M. Lev-Ram with K. Wagner, Game changer: Crowdfunding tries to grow up. *Fortune* (May 20, 2013): 40–43.

41 http://dailycrowdsource.com/crowdsourcing-basics/what-is-crowdsourcing. Retrieved July 11. 2013.

42 Clarity over JOBs Act could boost crowd funding in business sales. *Heraldonline.com* (July 11, 2013).

43 Staff, Extra credit. *Entrepreneur* (January 2013): 74–75.

44 C. Dougherty, Hungry for income, banks flirt with payday lending. *BusinessWeek* (November 5–11, 2012): 47–48.

45 www.sba.gov/community/blogs/who%E2%80%99s-lending-how-find-small-business-friendly-banks.

46 B. Kowitt, The sweetest pair. *Fortune* (April 29, 2013): 17.

47 www.investopedia.com/terms/l/lineofcredit.asp.

48 Staff, Extra credit. *Entrepreneur* (January 2013): 74–75.

49 N. Leiber, Matching for businesses and banks. *BusinessWeek* (October 29–November 4, 2012): 57–58.

50 www.iso.org. Retrieved July 17, 2013.

51 C. Hann, Space, the final frontier. *Entrepreneur* (October 2012): 28.

52 G. Moran, Go it alone. *Entrepreneur* (August 2012): 66–67.

53 www.entrepreneur.com/encyclopedia/bootstrapping.

54 G. Moran, Go it alone. *Entrepreneur* (August 2012): 66–67.

55 G. Moran, Go it alone. *Entrepreneur* (August 2012): 66–67.

56 G. Moran, Go it alone. *Entrepreneur* (August 2012): 66–67.

57 E. Pofeldt, Should you fund your startup business with a credit card? *Creditcards.com* (February 19, 2013).

58 J.D. Harrison, Bartering secrets: Entrepreneurs turn to age-old business strategy when money gets tight. *Washingtonpost.com* (March 6, 2013).

59 A. Advani, Tapping your personal savings to fund your startup. *Entrepreneur.com* (June 5, 2006).

60 www.sba.gov/community/blogs/who%E2%80%99s-lending-how-find-small-business-friendly-banks.

61 www.sba.gov/category/lender-navigation/sba-loan-programs/sbic-program-0.

62 www.sbia.org/?page=sbic_program_history.

63 www.sba.gov/content/sbic-program-0.

64 www.mbda.gov/pressroom/press-releases/mbda-2012-annual-performance-report-shows-record-breaking-year-job-creation.

65 www.mbda.gov/pressroom/press-releases/minority-business-development-agency-announces-66-million-investment-indian-country-create-jobs-and.

66 www.mb da.gov/businesscenters.

67 C. Steiner, States that truly bet on small business. *Forbes.com* (February 3, 2010).

68 www.kickstarter.com/hello?ref=footer.

69 J.J. Colao, Steve Case: Crowdfunding will augment—not replace—venture capital. *Forbes.com* (March 22, 2013).

70 J. J. Colao, Breaking down the JOBS Act: Inside the bill that would transform American business. *Forbes.com* (March 21, 2012).

71 J.J. Colao, Steve Case: Crowdfunding will augment—not replace—venture capital. *Forbes.com* (March 22, 2013).

72 http://getpebble.com/.

73 Z. Rivera, Zach Braff surpasses his $2 million Kickstarter campaign goal for new movie "Wish I Was Here." *New York Daily News* (April 20, 2012).

74 M. Eby, James Franco slams Zach Braff's Kickstarter campaign, *New York Daily News* (July 2, 2013).

75 http://east.paxsite.com/schedule/panel/the-official-kickstarter-panel. Retrieved July 15, 2013.

76 Crowdsourcing a startup movement across Africa (http://allafrica.com/stories/201303270028.html) (March 26, 2013).

77 D. Wasonga, Kiva opens office in Nairobi, Africa's hot spot for social innovation. *African Press International* (April 17, 2013).

Chapter 12

1 J.T. Perry, G.N. Chandler, and G. Markova, Entrepreneurial effectuation: A review and suggestions for future research. *Entrepreneurship Theory and Practice* 36 (4 2012): 837–861.

2 U. Brixy, R. Sternberg, and H. Stuber, The selectiveness of the entrepreneurial process. *Journal of Small Business Management* 50 (1 2012): 105–131.

3 www.agmrc.org/business_development/operating_a_business/finance/articles/spending-less-without-compromising-quality.

4 www.graniterock.com/news_events/press_releases/pr20020122.html.

5 www.thefreedictionary.com/deburring.

6 http://en.wikipedia.org/wiki/Milling_(machining).

7 www.rmahq.org/tools-publications/publications/annual-statement-studies/annual-statement-studies.

8 http://beginnersinvest.about.com/od/income statementanalysis/a/gross-profit-margin.htm.

9 www.investopedia.com/terms/p/profitmargin.asp.

10 R. Kaplan and D. Norton, *The Balanced Scorecard: Translating Strategy into Action* (Boston: Harvard Business School Press, 1996).

11 A. Gumbus and R. Lussier, Entrepreneurs use a balanced scorecard to translate strategy into performance measures. *Journal of Small Business Management* 44 (3 2006): 407–425.

12 www.outofthegarage.com/outofthegarage/2010/1/18/entrepreneurs-and-the-balanced-scorecard.html.

13 www.businessinsider.com/the-startup-entrepreneur-guide-to-risk-management-2009-6.

14 J.T. Perry, G.N. Chandler, and G. Markova, Entrepreneurial effectuation: A review and suggestions for future research. *Entrepreneurship Theory and Practice* 36 (4 2012): 837–861.

15 K. Podoynitsya, H. Van der Bij, and M. Song, The role of mixed emotions in the risk perception of novice and serial entrepreneurs. *Entrepreneurship Theory and Practice* 36 (1 2012): 115–121.

16 www.investopedia.com/terms/i/insurance.asp.

17 www.northwesternmutual.com/products-and-services/business/business-insurance/business-disability-insurance.aspx.

18 www.entrepreneur.com/encyclopedia/key-person-insurance.

19 www.investopedia.com/terms/b/business-automobile-policy-bap.asp.

20 www.icwgroup.com/agents/earthquake/documents/ICW-Group_Understand_Business_Income_and_Extra_Expense_Coverage.pdf.

21 A. Carson, Workmen's compensation: Know your rights. *Expertlaw.com* (2003).

22 www.park.ca/content/business/equipment.php.

23 www.iso.com/About-ISO/ISO-Services-for-Property-Casualty-Insurance/What-Is-Property/Casualty-Insurance.html.

24 www.entrepreneur.com/encyclopedia/special-coverage-insurance.

25 www.scuderigroup.com/about-us/.

26 J. Kenney, Scuderi Group cited, fined by Securities Exchange Commission; $3.2 million went to family members. *Masslive.com* (June 3, 2013).

27 A. Smith, Lululemon sued for see-through yoga pants. *CNN/Money.com* (July 3, 2013).

28 L. Lavine, How to avoid a product recall: Quality control essentials. *Entrepreneur.com* (April 24, 2013).

29 S. Maheshwari, Lululemon hit by elusive Chinese counterfeiters. *Buzzfeed.com* (July 15, 2013).

Appendix B

1 www.zip-codes.com/city/CT-HARTFORD.asp.

2 https://stations.fcc.gov/collect/files/53115/Political%20File/2012/Federal/US%20Senate/WFSB%20McMahon%20for%20Senate%20October%2030-November%206%202012-60s%20Invoice%20(13529934024826)_.pdf.

3 www.gaebler.com/Cost-of-Newspaper-Advertising-In-West+Hartford—CT.

4 www.mailingjet.com/direct-mail-costs/cost-to-mail-a-jumbo-postcard.

5 Adapted from www.businessballs.com/balanced_scorecard.htm.

Index